HUMAN BEHAVIOR IN THE SOCIAL ENVIRONMENT

HUMAN BEHAVIOR IN THE SOCIAL ENVIRONMENT

Second Edition

John F. Longres

University of Washington, Seattle

F. E. Peacock Publishers, Inc.
Itasca, Illinois

Cover and part openers:
Luncheon of the Boating Party by: Pierre Auguste Renoir./Phillips Collection, Washington, D.C./Superstock Inc.

Photo credits:

Page	
11	Wide World Photos
12	Elena Rooraid/PhotoEdit
38	Joseph Schuyler/Stock, Boston
56	Fredrik Bodin/Stock, Boston
61	Sidney/The Image Works
73	Michael Dwyer/Stock, Boston
84	Robert W. Ginn/PhotoEdit
117	HINE, Lewis H. *Italian Family Seeking Lost Baggage, Ellis Island.* 1905. Modern print made by The Photo League, 1942, from the original negatives in their possession. Gelatin-silver print, 5 ½ × 4 ¼". The Museum of Modern Art, New York. Purchase.
121	Cumberland County Historical Society, Carlisle, PA
124	Kathy McLaughlin/The Image Works
142	Chicago Historical Society
149	Reuters/ Bettmann Newsphotos
155	Elizabeth Hamlin/Stock, Boston
164	Wells/The Image Works
173	Bob Daemmrich/The Image Works
193	FPG International
209	Patrick James Watson/The Image Works
214	Katherine McGlynn/The Image Works
237	Lionel Delevingne/Stock, Boston
246	Elizabeth La Mar/NYT Pictures
258	Gale Zucker/Stock, Boston
267	Courtesy Liz Claiborne. Artist: Barbara Kruger
299	Jean-Claude Lejeune/Stock, Boston
323	UPI/Bettmann Newsphotos
341	Alan Carey/The Image Works
364	Ulli Steltzer
378	Wide World Photos
387	Michael Dwyer/Stock, Boston
401	Reuters/Bettmann Newsphotos
419	Michael Dwyer/Stock, Boston
428	Michael Weisbrot/Stock, Boston
440	Ulrike Welsch/PhotoEdit
460	Judy Canty/Stock, Boston
473	Rhoda Sidney/The Image Works
484	Elizabeth Crews/ Stock, Boston
490	Wide World Photos
524	Barbara Alper/Stock, Boston

Library of Congress Catalog Card No. 93-84980

ISBN 0-87581-379-8

Printed in the United States of America

Printing: 10 9 8 7 6 5 4 3

Year: 00 99 98 97 96

I dedicate this edition to my
three wonderful sisters
Betty
Elsa
Vikki

Contents

Preface

The second edition of *Human Behavior in the Social Environment* maintains the thrust of the original in that it continues to combine a critical perspective with a broad understanding of a systems framework. This is the strength of the book and a reason for its success.

A Critical Approach

I begin with a statement about the importance of social criticism for a practice profession. A critical approach emphasizes the search for social progress through evaluation of the effects of existing social structural arrangements on society and on individual well-being. The study of human behavior and development cannot stop at mere description but must proceed to prescription. When social service workers make policy, design and administer programs, and assess, analyze, and intervene in the lives of individuals and families, they cannot help but participate in the major debates taking place in society. The debates that we find ourselves in often focus directly or indirectly on those systems of inequality associated with class, race and ethnicity, gender, sexual orientation, physical ability, and age. As social workers, we must struggle with the ongoing conflict produced by inequality and with determining ways to alleviate and eradicate it. In our everyday practice with families; people of color; the homeless, unemployed, underemployed, and the poor; lesbians and gays; people with disabilities; the young and the elderly, we are at once hoping to strengthen their ability to function while helping to build a better world in which they may live. In this respect social workers are reformers operating as much from values as from knowledge.

A Systems Approach

Social service workers take on diverse roles in their practice. Most work directly with individuals, families, and groups. Some work with communities as organizers and planners. Others promote social policy, develop and administer programs, or supervise these programs. Increasingly, social workers are likely to be generalists, moving from one level of practice to another. Thus, this book is organized around levels of systems. The theme of social systems is introduced in Part One, followed by chapters on communities (Part Two), families (Part Three), large and small groups (Part Four), and individual development across the life span (Part Five).

Although I take a "systems approach," I do not rely exclusively on what many refer to as "systems theory." Systems theory is the application of a functionalist framework as developed in sociology, anthropology, and biology. A systems approach, on the other hand, aspires to be a content-free model for examining human behavior. At its core, it guides the social worker to look simultaneously at the environment of a system and at the system itself. My definition of a systems approach acknowledges that the behavior of any particular system—be it an individual, family, group, organization, or community—is always a function of the transactions between it and its environment. This definition allows me to introduce a number of functionalist and nonfunctionalist approaches to the study of systems, including such "conflict perspectives" as social exchange and Marxian theories, perspectives that many believe are more in keeping with critical thinking. I also incorporate ideas about systems into psychological theories and the study of the individual. In so doing, I get away from the idea that socialization takes place within a society marked by consensus, stability, and harmony.

What Is New?

One of the joys of having written the first edition is the contact it gave me with students, instructors, and educators from schools other than my own who sought me out and gave me feedback. This input from letters and telephone calls and encounters at conferences has been very important to me, and I always learn from it.

When I was a doctoral student, I once wrote a professor telling him I was using an article he had published and asking his advice on how to apply it to the research I was doing. He wrote back answering my questions but telling me how threatening it felt to be taken seriously, to actually influence other people. Like him, I have felt very humbled by the feedback I have been given. Those who have praised my work have obviously made me feel great, but it has also made me feel somewhat awkward to know I have influenced their own or their students' thinking. When the criticism has been negative I have been humbled, not antagonized nor humiliated, because I realize how seriously I have been taken and how much I still need to learn.

Three criticisms led to this revision. First, in the original edition, content on small and large groups was obscured by its inclusion in chapters on interpersonal relations. In this revision, a new chapter, "Social Interaction in Groups and Organizations," is added, and the chapters on theories of social interaction were rethought so as to highlight organizational and group issues. These three chapters make up Part Four, "Large and Small Groups."

Second, in the first edition the life span was treated in a single chapter, although the chapters on community and family life also contained material on life-span issues. Some have suggested that the book therefore failed to meet the curriculum policy standards of the Council on Social Work Education. There are those who claim that the Council requires courses on human behavior in the social environment to be organized around life-span development, but that is not my reading of the standards, nor is it the reading of most educators, accreditation commissioners, and site visitors to whom I have spoken. The standards indicate that life-span issues must be included along with content on various social systems. Courses organized around the life span tend to be weak in their handling of social systems, especially macro systems. Courses organized around systems often end up shortchanging the individual. Both styles of organizing human behavior in the social environment content have their strengths and weaknesses.

In this edition, much more attention is given to the individual. The two theory chapters in Part One are built around understanding the individual in the context of society, and Part Five incorporates four chapters on individual behavior and development. Three of these chapters are specifically devoted to the life span: prenatal influences and infancy; childhood and adolescence; and early, middle, and late adulthood.

The other parts of the book also carry information on the life span. Content on every phase can be found in the chapters on family life, and much of the discussion of community life and life in large and small groups is easily understood within the context of child and adult development. Community, especially the social class and ethnic and racial communities, forms a central context for understanding child and adult development. The historical and cultural background of children and adults bears directly on their ability to progress psychologically and socially throughout life. The experience of many populations as targets of continuing prejudice and discrimination must also be understood. The context of organizations and small groups is especially important in understanding adult development; Erik Erikson emphasizes that generativity—involvement in productive and creative activity—is a central issue. In industrial societies, the workplace and family life are the major factors in the "radius of significant relations" within which adults deal with the need for creativity and the fear of stagnation.

The third criticism has to do with a perceived weakness in the attention given to women's issues. In the first edition, there was no chapter, for instance, that specifically focused on women. The practice in the first edition of incorporating women's issues in the discussion of many topics has been carried over into this one. I take this approach because I do not see women as making up a unique level of social systems (a woman is or, in the case of organizations, increasingly can be a part of most systems in American society), and I believe that gender relations, rather than women's issues, is and should be the dominant concern in a book on human behavior. Nevertheless, in this edition I have incorporated more content on women's issues and have tried to make the content more visible.

Aims and Objectives

In spite of my own theoretical preferences and critical inclinations, I try hard to present both theory and substantive material as impartially as possible. I believe that the use of a systems and critical approach is enhanced by recognizing the contributions of a number of theories. I have been a social work practitioner and educator long enough to know that yesterday's passionate solution often becomes today's crushing problem. Since so many of the theories of social scientists have not been completely tested, it is premature for social workers to be committed to any particular viewpoint. Since so many well-intentioned reforms create their own, sometimes worse, problems, social workers must always turn their critical eye on their own thoughts and ideas.

Using a critical approach and trying to be balanced at the same time creates many dilemmas. I often find myself walking a tightrope and receiving criticism from both the right and the left. Some will find the ideas promoted in this book too radical, while others will complain that they are not radical enough. I would like instructors and students to keep their eyes on the two main objectives of this book: to create social workers with good critical thinking skills, and to promote the idea that social workers should be involved in progressive social reform. In my opinion, a good text is not one that you necessarily always agree with. There must be a rapport between a text and the aims of an instructor, but a good text is one that you talk to and even argue with, one that involves students and provokes debate.

I hope instructors who use this text will not be telling students "I am only presenting what Longres says." I do not know it all, nor do I pretend to. I am an educator who is trying to engage readers in material that I think is important. Instructors should try to engage students in the material and encourage them to put their own thoughts forward and articulate them as best they can. Students should selectively integrate the values, theories, and research they encounter into their own personal models of practice.

Style

Throughout the text I have tried to create a readable and lively style. I present theory and findings from studies and tackle controversial issues in ways that I hope will keep students interested. Each chapter begins with an introduction of the major themes discussed. Key concepts are highlighted and defined within context. New in this section are a glossary of important terms and an index that includes authors. To assure that human behavior content is bridged to practice, all chapters are introduced with a discussion of how they relate to social service work and end with a discussion of implications for practice. Each chapter also has study questions, not only to stimulate an identification with social work issues but also to help instructors organize class discussion and construct examinations. An instructor's manual to facilitate the development of tests is also available.

Acknowledgments

The task of rewriting this book has been helped along greatly by the comments received from students. They are indeed our hope for the future, and I thank them for making me be a better and more sensitive instructor. It has also been helped along by my colleagues at the University of Wisconsin, where I wrote the first edition, and at the University of Washington, where I finished the second edition. I have been blessed by the support of colleagues at both schools. I am also very grateful to my reviewers, Libby Zimmerman, Charles Cowger, Jack Findley, and Hugh Horan.

I have come to realize that books like this cannot become successful without a good editor and without the backing of a good publishing house. In this regard I have enjoyed more than I could have ever expected. This edition, as well as the first, is brought alive by the strong editorship of Gloria Reardon, the editor assigned to me by F. E. Peacock Publishers. She not only improves the mechanics of my writing but is wonderfully perceptive and instructive about content and its placement. The success of this book is attributable as much to her as to me. I reserve my special thanks for selecting her and for being so supportive of me as an individual author for Ted Peacock, my publisher. I feel that "I am in good hands" with Ted and his superlative staff.

A number of other people should be thanked for the direct support they have given me. Cynthia Springer, Yvone Smith, Doris Kogan, and Sheila Yacov helped me with the various chores of editing, correcting, and printing out the chapters. My professional colleagues with whom I teach or with whom I shared my thoughts and writing must also be recognized: Anne Minahan, Sheldon Rose, Aaron Brower, Alfred Kadushin, Diane Kravetz, Gary Seltzer, Marsha Seltzer, Pamela Spohn, Mary Gilfus, Mary Ann Test, Rosemarie Carbino, Dean Schneck, Beverly Flanagan, Irv Piliavin, and Jodi Schmitz. Some of my new colleagues at the University of Washington are already leaving their mark on me: Lorraine Gutierrez, Larry Icard, Henry Maier, Ted Teather, Roger Roffman, Nancy

Hooyman, Sue Sohng, Karen Frederickson, Mary Gilmore, Edwina Uehara, Noami Gottlieb, James Whittaker, Hy Resnick, Dick Weatherly, Margaret Spencer, James DeLong, Anthony Ishisaka, Paula Nurius, Judy Kopp, Cheryll Richey, and Lewayne Gilchrist. Professional colleagues continue to help me along: Gary Lloyd, Norm Wyers, Grant Farr, Palassana Balgopal, Aracelis Francis, Juan Paz, Don Beless, Michael Fromkin, and Ray Berger.

I give my thanks to Charles Whatley, my friend since the tenth grade, who is everything a childhood friend should be. I also give special thanks to my dear confidant and colleague Mona Wasow for making my time in Madison so warm and hospitable. My deepest respect and appreciation goes to Jim Nattinger, my special companion for the last 27 years, without whom no book could have been possible.

March 1994

John F. Longres
Longres@u.washington.edu

PART ONE

A Critical Perspective on Social Systems

A Critical Perspective

MAJOR THEMES DISCUSSED IN THIS CHAPTER

1. **A THEORY FOR PRACTICE.** The groundwork for a reform-oriented social service practice is laid by distinguishing among three kinds of theory: a theory for practice, a theory of practice, and a theory of caring.

2. **THE CRITICAL PERSPECTIVE.** A theory for practice and a theory of caring merge to form a critical perspective. In this perspective, social service workers participate in debates about social problems and take sides in building a better society.

3. **QUESTIONING THE CRITICAL PERSPECTIVE.** A critical perspective is not without detractors. As students begin social service practice, they must develop their own ideas about the strengths and limitations of a particular perspective.

4. **THE INTERACTION BETWEEN INDIVIDUAL AND SOCIETY.** Those who accept a critical perspective must recognize that social conditions, good or bad, are not the product of either individuals or society alone. Individuals influence society just as they are influenced by society, and the troubles individuals face in their own lives are as a rule inseparable from the problems society experiences as a whole. Social workers must try to understand the private troubles of individuals in terms of the social problems that are affecting them.

5. **CRITICAL THEORY AND SOCIAL CHANGE.** A critical theory of social service practice calls for action on the basis of study of the transactions taking place between the individual and the social environment. It can provide social workers with a comprehensive basis for resolving the difficulties of an individual in need by taking into account the individual's interactions with society.

THE IDEA THAT REAL SOCIAL PROGRESS is possible underlies social welfare institutions and social work practice. Social service policymakers and practitioners truly believe that if the right programs are developed and delivered effectively, clients, be they individuals or communities or whole societies, can progress from a relatively negative to a relatively positive condition.

A critical theory for social service practice is in keeping with such a social change philosophy. It is concerned less with what social service is than with what it might be and might accomplish. Unlike a theory *of* practice, which is derived from observations of social service workers' norms and roles, a theory *for* practice provides explanations to guide practice.

∽ A THEORY FOR PRACTICE

One way to formulate a theory of practice would be to observe social service workers as they go about their work and then codify what they are doing. From observations it should be possible to specify what social workers do and what results they get: How they conduct groups and handle conflict; how they assess problems in a particular client or family; how they identify harmony and conflict in organizational decision making, and so on. Theory building in this way is encumbered by the norms of the profession and the work organization as well as by the policy-derived roles of social service workers. A theory constructed from observations may describe present practices, but it has a limited ability to improve it or to bring about social change.

A **theory for practice**, in contrast, is a system of ideas or statements which explain social service practice. It provides for the development of practice models and principles out of which actual social service practice might evolve. Rather than being based in the norms and roles of social service, it is more likely to be indebted to the social and biological sciences. The proposed theory for practice which could be developed from the ideas and content in this book would incorporate knowledge from other disciplines, sociology and psychology in particular, and history, anthropology, economics, political science, and biology more generally. In addition, a theory for practice would draw from the clinical and empirical research of practitioners. From the point of view of client systems, research can examine needs and perceptions of problems and encourage seeking and accepting behavior. From the point of view of service providers, research can examine social delivery processes and outcomes of policies, programs, and interventions.

A theory for practice is a prerequisite for the development of a practice theory, which is undoubtedly the ultimate goal of those who try to formulate social service theory. Robert Vinter describes a **practice theory** as consisting of "a body of principles, more or less systematically developed and anchored in scientific knowledge, that seeks to guide and direct practitioner action." These principles are "directed not at understanding reality, but at achieving control over it."[1]

Since a theory for practice precedes practice theory, it can be understood as a system of statements intended to explain human behavior and make it comprehensible, toward the ultimate purpose of learning how to control human behavior. While such a theory may be used to explain all human behavior, in this book we primarily focus on explaining the problems and the needs, strengths, and weakness of clients. We seek to contribute to practice theory by developing a *metatheory* for practice, that is, "a synthesis of several theories of knowledge from a social systems perspective."[2]

Thinking about Social Service Work

A theory for practice would guide social service workers at all levels in thinking about the problems they encounter in their work. Consider the following case example:

Maria Santos came to the area from Texas some five years ago. She left high school when she became pregnant, and she is now the mother of a three-year-old asthmatic son. Though she is separated from the father, she still sees him on and off. He contributes very sporadically to their economic support. They recently quarreled about his jealous temper, and Maria says she isn't counting on seeing him again.

Maria Santos has never applied for public assistance, although her mother has received Aid to Families with Dependent Children (AFDC) payments since they have been in the city. For a while she managed by working at odd jobs, but during the past year she has not worked steadily because of a series of minor illnesses. She says she doesn't want to end up as "another Mexican failure."

She lives in a two-room apartment, is three months behind in her rent, and has received a notice of eviction. Her mother and younger sister live nearby. They babysit for her now and then, but she says they have their own problems to worry about and can't be worried about her.

During the interview she did not express a great deal of emotion, although she did say she was unhappy about her predicament. She stated a number of times that she didn't know what to do or where to turn and hoped that the services offered by the center could help her.[3]

The case of Maria Santos is hypothetical, but the problems presented in it are not unlike those confronted by social service workers in their everyday practice. Social workers, counselors, and other line workers work directly with people like Maria Santos, and they must determine ways to relieve or ameliorate the problems these people present. Supervisors must assist the line workers who bring them their questions about possibilities for helping people in situations like the ones in which Maria finds herself. Administrators, program developers, and social policy planners work indirectly with people having problems. These practitioners must see how a range of problems such as the one Maria presents is typical of a class of clients and develop and organize services accordingly.

How should social service workers think about the problems presented in a case like that of Maria Santos? Why does she find herself in her present predicament? What are her problems and needs? What are her strengths and limitations? What kinds of things can be done to help her? Thinking about the problems presented by clients and how to intervene in them is the subject of this book.

Control and Change in Social Service Work

Social scientists generally agree that the purpose or function served by the social services is to help people like Maria Santos out of their predicaments. In the process of doing this, it is hoped, a better society will be built.

Behind such vague, general statements, however, there lie many contradictions and complexities. Does social service help Maria and society by helping her adjust and cope with the realities and demands of the larger society? Or does it help her and society by championing her cause and insisting that society accommodate her needs? Those who would help her by asking that she learn to adjust and cope are acting in keeping with a social control philosophy. Those who support her rights and ask that society accommodate them and try to improve her situation are following a social change philosophy.

It is not always easy to distinguish between the social control and the social change philosophies. Most social service practice seems to be oriented somewhere in between. It follows what might be called a liberal philosophy, accepting a certain degree of conformity while working for a certain degree of within-system change.[4]

By tradition, most social service workers operate on the basis of a theory of caring. While theories of practice and for practice strive to be empirical and therefore free of values, a **theory of caring** is value-dominated.[5] Social service workers adopt the value that it is good to show care, and they support their practice with political and ideological values concerning the best ways to show care. This is both necessary and good, but practice cannot be based solely on values. **Values**, which are statements of worth, good or bad, that people either reject or accept and place their faith in, may inform practice and should infuse it. However, values cannot be substituted for practice theory. The issue of conformity versus change is a good value issue which is debated among professionals. Ultimately, it is an individual choice.

In this book we develop a perspective on practice which combines a theory for practice with a theory of caring, that is, with a particular set of underlying values. As we outline the systems approach and present theories of human behavior, therefore, we will evaluate them from a perspective that emphasizes the need to be concerned about social issues and social change.

THE CRITICAL PERSPECTIVE

The theory for social service practice that we are proposing combines a social systems approach with a critical perspective on society. From a **critical perspective**, it is not enough merely to observe and describe social conditions and interactions; they must be looked at critically and analytically, with a view to identifying problems and solving them. Some social scientists relate the critical perspective to the idea of social justice and the elimination or reduction of inequalities. Charles Anderson and Jeffry Gibson define a critical perspective as "the dual task of developing a critique of all forms of social oppression [and]…assist[ing] in the development of alternative social forms that uphold human dignity and provide the conditions for the positive cultivation of human mental and physical ability."[6]

Ernest Becker identifies two kinds of social science research with different methods and outcomes. In his terms, research that is *analytic descriptive* makes for placid descriptions. It merely reports observations and describes what is going on in human interactions. The other type of research, which is *evaluative critical* in nature, provides passionate prescriptions for the conditions it identifies. Rather than just describing a situation, it seeks to prescribe the means to improve it.[7]

Becker prefers research that provides such passionate prescriptions. By implication, he would say that a theory for social practice cannot be merely analytic descriptive. It ought also to be evaluative critical, acknowledging that scientists need to make judgments about society and the circumstances people find themselves in. We might say that a theory of caring ought to be infused into a theory for practice.

Thus, in thinking about social service work such as the problems of Maria Santos, the worker's aim is not merely to make a "placid description" of her life and experiences or of her present relationships and psychological functioning. The worker strives to make a "passionate prescription" for Maria; to help her, and thus to help society, meet the highest possible standards.

Critical Analysis in the Social Sciences

Critical perspectives have a long history in the social sciences and social service. Becker notes that in the nineteenth century the social sciences were not as divided as they are today.[8] Those who took up the profession did not think of themselves as psychologists or sociologists or economists or social workers, for instance, but as social scientists. They also seem to have been guided by a more clear-cut understanding of what questions needed to be answered. Unlike contemporary times, when there appear to be no identifiable central issues in social science, in the nineteenth century social scientists were collectively concerned with "the problem of the soul." They asked themselves: What is the happy life? What is the good society? And they didn't stop there. They also asked: How can the happy life and the good society be achieved? The central function of the social sciences, as they perceived it, was to provide ideas and prescriptions for building the best society possible.

Many contemporary scientists, however, are renewing the emphasis on critical evaluation or analysis of the human condition. Change is considered possible because the social sciences are not natural sciences. For example, as Anthony Giddens points out, the social processes studied in sociology are not governed by unalterable laws of nature:

> As human beings, we are not condemned to be swept along by forces that have the inevitability of laws of nature. But this means we must be conscious of the alternative futures that are potentially open to us....the task of sociology is contributing to *the critique of existing forms of society*.[9]

Social service work is inherently critical because it is oriented to social concern and social change. Edwin Thomas notes three ways in which practice theory differs from what he refers to as scientific theory: practice theory is "oriented to the objective of control rather than that of understanding alone, it tends to be value laden rather than value free, and it is prescriptive as well as descriptive."[10] The very process of assessing the case of Maria Santos, or of any other individual, group, family, or community, requires a value judgment about the well-being of the individuals and the functioning of society. The very process of planning an intervention requires a prescriptive judgment on what alternatives are most likely to produce personal happiness and the good society. In social work, values go hand in hand with skills.

◌ QUESTIONING THE CRITICAL PERSPECTIVE

Some social scientists do not believe the human condition can be improved through planned social change. One of these is Peter Berger, who describes himself as a "conservative humanist." In Berger's **conservative humanism**, values and ideologies that assume the human condition can be changed in any significant way are rejected. His preliminary definition of a conservative outlook is "fundamental hesitation regarding social change." Berger concludes, "The prototypical conservative maxim can be put as follows: 'Other things being equal, let society remain the way it is.' The prototypical maxim of the 'left,' be it liberal or radical in its particular coloration, can then be formulated: 'Other things being equal, let society change.'" He goes on to add, "A conservative accepts the messiness of history and is suspicious of the idea of progress."[11]

Unintended Consequences of Social Change

Berger makes another point which should not be overlooked: Changing society is no easy matter, and in the process people are likely to be hurt. The American War of

Independence and the French Revolution had noble aspirations to secure the blessings of liberty, equality, brotherhood, and the free pursuit of happiness for all the people; but the fact is that in the process of trying to achieve these goals, many lives were lost or socially and economically shattered. Social change always has costs as well as benefits. If the president or Congress tries to create a more just or fair system of taxation, for example, citizens who have become accustomed to loopholes, tax shelters, and the like are outraged when they are asked to start paying their share of the costs of government.

Similarly, if a social agency tries to get the father of Maria Santos's child to provide consistent child support, the father's personal liberties would be curtailed, and he would not be pleased at the social progress being made to assure that parents accept responsibility for their children. A liberal or radical humanist (as opposed to Berger's conservative humanist) may advocate change but must also be concerned with the difficulty of bringing it about and the possibility of creating harm as well as happiness.

Social reforms, however noble in their aspirations, do not always work perfectly. They may have a number of unintended negative consequences. A recent example is the effort to deinstitutionalize the care of individuals with mental health troubles or "problems in living."[12] In the 1960s, mental hospitals and institutions were judged to be harming patients rather than curing them, and the civil rights of the institutionalized were routinely violated. Social workers and others in the helping professions led the way in developing a national community-based mental health program that would have eventually closed down the institutions for the "mentally ill." Legislation was passed authorizing the construction and staffing of community mental health facilities, but many of them were never built and sufficient funds were not allotted to develop effective community-based programs. The movement toward deinstitutionalization therefore has had some adverse results.[13] Without community health centers to provide clinical services and counseling and without adequate means of support, many formerly institutionalized patients have been forced to cope with daily living on their own. Not only is their own situation often desperate, but they have congregated in cities and neighborhoods which do not welcome them and consider them a burden.

The Possibility of Human Progress

The belief in progress and human perfectibility through planned change which is inherent in the critical perspective expresses values that are essentially Western. People raised outside the Judeo-Christian tradition of **rationalism,** in which reason and experience are relied upon for the solution of problems, are likely to be skeptical of the critical perspective.

Russell Means, cofounder of the American Indian movement, is one of those who question European rationalism and its assumption that progress is possible through the use of technological inventions—including the technology of social welfare to overcome human suffering. He finds "Christians, capitalists, Marxists" to be all the same in that they represent European intellectual development: "They do what they do in order that European culture can continue to exist and develop according to its needs." Means endorses instead a Native American spiritual position which is concerned with what he calls the natural order: "Rationalism is a curse since it can cause humans to forget the natural order of things. A wolf never forgets his or her place in the natural order. Europeans do."[14]

Whether human progress is possible is something that only continual monitoring throughout history will demonstrate. In the meantime, social service workers ought to realize that progress through the use of rational planned change, an idea which reflects European intellectual tradition, is what the social services stand for. The social welfare movement in the United States and other Western countries has had a history of putting the concept of planned, rational social progress in motion.

Ralf Dahrendorf has reflected on the relationship between history and human progress. His point of view is one with which many in the social services are likely to agree:

> There may thus be a progress of liberty. There may be societies which give more space than others to the desire of men to reduce constraints; there may be more open and more developed societies in which life chances are enhanced and extended further. And since this is so, we must never rest in our quest for advancing the frontiers of freedom.[15]

∞ THE INTERACTION BETWEEN INDIVIDUAL AND SOCIETY

A critical theory for social service practice is based on the idea that social conditions, good or bad, are not the products of either individuals or society alone. Rather, they are derived from the transactions between the two. Thus, the problems individuals face in their own lives and the problems society recognizes and tries to solve in order to achieve human progress are interrelated.

Blame the Victim or Blame Society?

The term **blaming the victim** was coined by William Ryan as a way of advancing the cause of social change by defining society's reaction to people with problems as blaming them for their own troubles.[16] In Maria Santos, Ryan would see a victim of American society, a woman exploited by an economic system that cannot function to achieve its goals of producing profits without the presence of unemployment and social inequalities. In this view, Maria is discriminated against in a culture where Hispanic values, traditions, and physical appearance are looked down upon, and she is abused by a sexist society which keeps women vulnerable and dependent. Such victims should not be blamed for the predicaments they find themselves in, Ryan says.

Nevertheless, Ryan claimed that in the 1970s, when he was presenting this idea, social service systems were in fact blaming people like Maria Santos. He did not suggest that social service organizations and workers were being mean or nasty or that they were deliberately setting out to blame clients. Most people who enter the social service professions undoubtedly mean well and intend to demonstrate care and concern. Since Ryan's book came out, in fact, many social workers have taken pains to inform certain clients that they are not to blame for their situations. But they are missing the point; even as they tell clients of their blamelessness, they may participate in victim blaming.

Blaming the victim entails more than suggesting a client is at fault in a particular circumstance. Social service workers also blame the victim when they acknowledge the societal causes of problems but intervene only at the level of the individual. From line workers to administrators and policy formulators, social service practitioners often participate in this very contradiction. Ryan explains how:

The old-fashioned conservative could hold firmly to the belief that the oppressed and the victimized were born that way—"that way" being defective or inadequate in character or ability. The new ideology attributes defect and inadequacy to the malignant nature of poverty, injustice, slum life, and racial difficulties. The stigma that marks the victim and accounts for his victimization is an acquired stigma, a stigma of social, rather than genetic, origin. But the stigma, the defect, the fatal difference—though derived in the past from environmental forces—is still located within the victim, inside the skin. With such an elegant formulation, the humanitarian can have it both ways. He can, all at the same time, concentrate his charitable interests on the defects of the victim, condemn the vague social and environmental stresses that produced the defect (some time ago), and ignore the continuing effect of victimizing social forces (right now),....[17]

Ryan perceives a "terrifying sameness" in the programs that arise from this kind of analysis:

> All of this happens so smoothly that it seems downright rational. First, identify the social problem. Second, study those affected by the problem and discover in what ways they are different from the rest of us as a consequence of deprivation and injustice. Third, define the differences as the cause of the social problem itself. Finally, of course, assign a...bureaucrat to invent a humanitarian action program to correct the differences.[18]

In blaming Maria Santos for her predicament, a social service worker might focus on her psychological condition, her emotional or cognitive state (perhaps depression), or her personality makeup. The worker might explore Maria's inability to get along with her mother or try to determine what she had done (or not done) so that the father of her child was no longer around. Her need to learn work skills so she could be employed and parenting skills so she would not end up as she had would also be addressed. In short, the worker would focus on the things about Maria—her attitudes, beliefs, and behaviors—that are unique to her or, presumably, to others in her circumstances. These are the things that can be assumed to have produced her present crisis and that now require assistance.

Rather than blaming the victim in this way, Ryan would say, an assessment of Maria Santos should focus instead on the environmental stresses and the continuing effects of the social forces that are victimizing her. He would, in short, blame the society in order to change the society.

This, however, might very well be a trap. Blaming the victim would fit a theory of human behavior which suggests that people make their own destinies, for better or worse, and they are completely responsible for what happens to them. Blaming the society, on the other hand, would fit a theory of human behavior which suggests that people are completely shaped by environmental forces and are passive victims of social circumstances that cannot be controlled. It suggests that somehow society, "the system," is out there somewhere, some kind of vague, dark monster, working people over in ways that they are powerless to influence.

The Multicentered and Transactional Points of View

If we are to avoid victim blaming and society blaming, Jill Kagle and Charles Cowger suggest that we must begin to think of social work in both multicentered and transaction-centered terms.[19] The difficulties experienced by clients are described in *multicentered* terms when attention is called to the ways in which the environment and the individual both contribute to the problem. For example, a social worker might describe a child's school problems as "The child is misbehaving in the classroom, and the teacher does not know how to handle it." In a multicentered approach, the social worker needs to work independently with the child (and the child's family) to change the misbehavior and must also work independently with the teacher (and the school) to assure that teachers are trained to handle misbehavior in the classroom. Clients' difficulties are defined in *transaction-centered* terms when the focus is on the simultaneous interaction between the individual and the environment. For example, the social worker might describe the child's school behavior as "a breakdown in communication between child and teacher." In a transaction-centered approach, the social worker must bring the child and the teacher together to work on how they can communicate with each other better.

Following the lead of Kagle and Cowger, our point of view in this book acknowledges that both society and individuals contribute to problems. People are not completely responsible for what happens to them, but neither are they completely shaped by environmental forces. The individual and society are equally basic and primary; each influences and is influenced by the other, and they are inseparable. In taking this position, we will point out both the multicentered factors and the transactional processes that lead to the difficulties experienced by clients.

Private Troubles and Public Issues

The transactions between a society and the individuals who comprise it are diverse and varied in their scope and impact. The problems that arise for individuals and society in these transactions are likely to involve the **mirco environment** of individual beliefs, attitudes, and behaviors, as well as the **macro environment** of social institutions and processes. In the terms coined by C. Wright Mills, they may be either private troubles or public issues—or both.[20]

The term **private troubles** refers to the ways individuals experience problems. According to Mills, "*Troubles* occur within the character of the individual and within the range of his immediate relations with others; they have to do with his self and with those limited areas of social life of which he is directly and personally aware."[21]

Maria Santos feels miserable; she doesn't want to be a failure in life, she is worried about getting a job and paying the rent, she is concerned for her health and the health of her child, she is quarreling with her boyfriend and with her mother. These are her troubles, and she experiences them in a very personal or private way. They are her private troubles, not the troubles of other people.

The term **public issues** refers to the ways society experiences problems. According to Mills, "*Issues* have to do with matters that transcend these local environments of the individual and the range of his inner life." They have to do with the institutions of society as a whole, "the larger structure of social and historical life." Public issues also reflect contradictions and conflict in the ways society is organized:

> An issue is a public matter, some value cherished by publics is felt to be threatened. Often there is a debate about what the value really is and about what it is that really threatens it. This debate is often without focus if only because it is the very nature of an issue, unlike even widespread trouble, that it can not very well be defined in terms of the immediate and everyday environments of ordinary men.[22]

Public issues are not directly observable in the case of Maria Santos, but they can be sensed in the background. For one thing, there are many Maria Santos's who pass through

For women in the labor force, the need for affordable day-care services is often a private trouble. A Chinese-American garment worker in New York brings her child with her to work.

social service caseloads. Their shared troubles give evidence of the public issues, the debates about social problems that make up the political, social, and economic concerns of the nation. Why are divorce rates so high, and what should be done about them? Why aren't there enough good jobs, and how could they be provided? Should there be a public policy of national health insurance to give everyone access to a full range of medical services instead of just those who can afford them?

Mills gives several examples of how to tell when a private trouble reflects a public issue. One is unemployment:

> When, in a city of 100,000, only one man is unemployed, that is his personal trouble, and for its relief we properly look to the character of the man, his skills, and his immediate opportunities. But when in a nation of 50 million employees, 15 million men are unemployed, that is an issue, and we may not hope to find its solution with the range of opportunities open to any one individual.[23]

Another is marriage:

> Inside a marriage a man and a woman may experience personal troubles, but when the divorce rate during the first four years of marriage is 250 out of every 1,000 attempts, this is an

The need for day-care services can also be a public issue.
Chinese-American activists join to push for this social reform.

indication of a structural issue having to do with the institutions of marriage and the family and other institutions that bear upon them.[24]

Thus, while private troubles can be independent of public issues, often they are not. When there is a private trouble that is clearly unrelated to public issues, it would be reasonable to blame the person or persons experiencing the difficulty. Services that would try to overcome the personal limitations that apparently have caused the problem might be provided. When private troubles clearly reflect public issues, then it is unreasonable to blame the individuals for them or to see the troubles they are experiencing as a sign of their personal limitations. In such circumstances, there is a dual obligation to try to resolve both the trouble and the issue.

The Dual Nature of Social Service Practice

Practitioners have used different terms for the need for social services to attend to both the individual and the society: micro and macro, direct and indirect services, social work and social welfare. William Schwartz points out that the need to deal with both private troubles and public issues is responsible for the dual nature of social work practice or intervention.[25] Neil Gilbert and Harry Specht make a distinction between the direct-service worker, who provides assistance to those in need, and the social welfare specialist, who focuses on the institutional structure through which those in need are served.[26]

In this book we maintain that all social service workers must take into account the dual nature of social service practice. Social service line workers deal with individuals experiencing troubles, but they also need to have a vision of the issues that lie behind these troubles. They must find ways in which they can contribute, in however restrained a fashion, to the resolution of such issues: Social service administrators and planners deal with public issues and cannot translate them solely into the private troubles of individuals, but they must acknowledge these troubles. The goal of the social services, taken as a whole, is to try to resolve both private troubles and public issues simultaneously.

❧ CRITICAL THEORY AND SOCIAL CHANGE

The relation of public issues in society to private troubles in the individual's inner life and everyday experiences emphasizes the need for social service workers to take a broad, comprehensive viewpoint in their efforts to understand and alleviate human suffering. The micro-environmental troubles of an individual in need of help must be understood in terms of the larger environmental problems affecting that individual. The opposite is also true.

The idea that individual problems are usually social problems is a basic assumption of critical theory, according to Peter Findlay:

> Critical theory assumes that most individual problems are in fact social problems, caused by an inequitable social structure; that this social structure is fundamentally determined by the economic organization of society...; that social institutions...maintain this social structure even while trying to ameliorate its harmful social consequences; that many of the dominant cultural forms sustain this structure....[27]

The way to deal with this situation, Findlay says, is through analysis of socioeconomic structures and their configuration in society. In making this statement, Findlay expresses to a large extent the value position taken in this book. He also points out an important limitation to the usefulness of critical theory for social work, asserting that the problem critical theory poses is "the lack of middle-range guidelines for analysis and action."[28] Such guidelines would support change on neither the micro nor the macro level, in neither the individual nor the society. Rather, they would call for action on the basis of study of the transactions between the two.

The tendency for critical theory to channel attention to the need for large-scale, society-wide, even revolutionary social transformations reduces the effectiveness of its application to social service. Social workers caught up in searching for the big change often become impotent when face to face with clients like Maria Santos. The troubles she is experiencing might indeed reflect important public issues. These issues might be (probably are) related to inequitable and exploitative economic structures. However, the obligation of the direct-service worker face to face with Maria Santos, or the role of the program developer setting up services for her, is to help her deal with inequality and exploitation as she experiences and defines them in her everyday life. It does her little good for a worker to declare that she is a victim of social injustice, when only a major revolution could change that. Critical theory can only be of use by trying to develop strategies in the here and now which link individual and social change.

This is not a book about how to work with social service clients, though attention is given to practice methods and techniques. Rather, it is concerned with learning how to think about the problems presented by clients and determining how to intervene in these problems effectively. We examine the explanations offered in various theories of human behavior and consider how they might be applied to communities, families, large and small groups, and individuals in American society. In doing this, we begin to build a theory for social service practice which provides a specific rationale or way of thinking about such work—a critical theory which incorporates a social systems approach to human behavior. Our aim is to provide the background for a theory for practice in which the everyday services social workers provide for troubled clients could, by extension, bring about the changes necessary to improve the ability of social institutions to secure the common good.

DISCUSSION QUESTIONS AND CLASS PROJECTS

1. Identify and describe the following concepts:

   theory for practice
   theory of caring
   placid description
   passionate prescription
   conservative humanism
   rationalism
   the natural order of things
   blaming the victim
   blaming society
   public issues
   private troubles

2. A critical perspective requires that social workers evaluate the strengths and weaknesses of society and, through their practice, enter into the process of social change and reform. What does this task mean to you? In what ways do you feel comfortable with this task?

3. Describe two criticisms that have been leveled at the critical perspective. What do you think of these criticisms?

4. Do you believe that human progress is possible through social work practice?

5. In the case of Maria Santos, how would you explain the troubles she is experiencing without either blaming the victim or blaming society? How would you describe them in multi-centered terms? How would you describe them in transactional terms?

6. Identify the public issues that are evident in the case of Maria Santos.

NOTES

1. Robert D. Vinter, "Problems and Processes in Developing Social Work Practice Principles," in E. J. Thomas (editor), *Behavioral Science for Social Workers* (New York: Free Press, 1967), pp. 425–32.

2. Joseph Vigilante et al., "Searching for Theory: Following Hearn," paper presented at the 1981 Annual Program Meeting, Council on Social Work Education, Louisville, Kentucky.

3. John F. Longres, "Social Work Practice with Racial Minorities: A Study of Contemporary Norms and Their Ideological Implications," *California Sociologist*, vol. 4 (Winter 1981), pp. 55–56.

4. Ibid., pp. 54–71.

5. Vigilante et al., "Searching for Theory," p. 25.

6. Charles H. Anderson and Jeffry Royle Gibson, *Toward a New Sociology*, 3rd ed. (Homewood, IL: Dorsey Press, 1978), p. 17.

7. Ernest Becker, "The Rediscovery of the Science of Man," in J. M. Romanshyn (editor), *Social Science and Social Welfare* (New York: Council on Social Work Education, 1974), pp. 17–23.

8. Ibid., pp. 7–32.

9. Anthony Giddens, *Sociology: A Brief But Critical Introduction* (New York: Harcourt, Brace, Jovanovich, 1982), p. 26; italics in original.

10. Edwin J. Thomas, "Types of Contributions Behavioral Science Makes to Social Work," in E. J. Thomas (editor), *Behavioral Science for Social Workers* (New York: Free Press, 1967), p. 6.

11. Peter Berger, "On Conservative Humanism," in P. L. Berger and R. J. Neuhaus (editors),

Movement and Revolution (New York: Doubleday, 1970), pp. 20–30.

12. Thomas Szasz, *The Myth of Mental Illness* (New York: Harper & Row, 1961).

13. Mona Wasow, "Deinstitutionalization," *Practice Digest*, vol. 6 (Spring 1984), pp. 10–12.

14. Russell Means, "Fighting Words: On the Future of the Earth," *Mother Jones*, December 1980, pp. 24–28, 30, 31, 38.

15. Ralf Dahrendorf, *Life Chances* (Chicago: University of Chicago Press, 1979), p. 20.

16. William Ryan, *Blaming the Victim* (New York: Vintage Books, 1971).

17. Ibid., p. 7.

18. Ibid., p. 8.

19. Jill Doner Kagle and Charles D. Cowger, "Blaming the Client: Implicit Agenda in Practice Research?" *Social Work*, vol. 29 (July–August 1984), pp. 347–52.

20. C. Wright Mills, *The Sociological Imagination* (New York: Penguin Books, 1971).

21. Ibid., pp. 14–15; italics in original.

22. Ibid., p. 15.

23. Ibid., p. 15.

24 Ibid., p. 16.

25. William Schwartz, "Private Troubles and Public Issues: One Social Work Job or Two?" *The Social Welfare Forum* (New York: Columbia University Press, 1969), pp. 22–43.

26. Neil Gilbert and Harry Specht, "The Incomplete Profession," *Social Work*, vol. 19 (November 1974), pp. 655–74.

27. Peter C. Findlay, "Critical Theory and Social Work Practice," *Catalyst*, No. 3 (1978), p. 55.

28. Ibid., p. 59.

A Systems Approach to Human Behavior
The Individual as a System

MAJOR THEMES DISCUSSED IN THIS CHAPTER

1. **A SYSTEMS APPROACH.** In a systems approach to social service practice that follows from the critical perspective, human behavior is seen as the result of a multiplicity of factors, both internal and external, operating in transaction. A systems approach is an orienting framework rather than a specific theory of human behavior.

2. **HUMAN SYSTEMS.** The individual is the basic human system and the driving force of all social systems. Among the debates about the concept of human nature are the extent to which it is determined by biological or cultural factors, how it differs from animal nature and whether the biological differences between the sexes generate psychological differences.

3. **THE INDIVIDUAL AS A SYSTEM.** Individuals, like all other systems, are comprised of dynamic parts or states and processes which together make up subsystems or domains. Within the individual, the principal domains are the biophysical and the psychological, which has cognitive, motivational-affective, and behavioral subsystems. It is through the interdependence and continual interaction of these domains and subsystems that individuals change and develop.

4. **THE STUDY OF NORMALITY.** Social workers deal with issues of normal human behavior, yet no clear definition of normality exists. Four such definitions build on the ideas of normal as average, normal as health, normal as utopia, and normal as transactions. Normality can also be considered within the context of physical and developmental disabilities.

5. **IMPLICATIONS FOR PRACTICE.** In assessing the individual as a system, social workers can avoid blaming the victim by taking a multicentered or transactional approach. The strengths as well as the problems of individuals should be assessed.

THE CONCEPT OF SYSTEM has been a mainstay in social science literature for several decades, and a number of leading social service practice theory and human behavior texts have been organized around it.[1] As used by social workers, this concept originated in what sociologists refer to as functional theory.[2] At least two variants are presently popular in social work: the general systems model, introduced by Gordon Hearn, and the ecological model, introduced by Carol Germain and Alex Gitterman.[3] These models not only have produced important social work contributions, they also have reinforced the need to see clients "not as isolated, self-contained entities, but rather as interdependent systems interacting in complex larger systems, as persons-in-situation, persons-in-environment."[4]

A SYSTEMS APPROACH

The notion of system and the emphasis on person in environment are implicit not only in functional theory but in any number of social and psychological theories. For this reason, we will conceive of systems in the broadest way, one which acknowledges the contribution of functional thinking but is not limited to it. We will take what is referred to as a **systems approach**, "a loose cluster of theories, axioms, and hypotheses emerging from various disciplines."[5] In other words, in the systems approach to human behavior used here, we will attempt to be as free of concrete substantive knowledge and point of view as possible. Nevertheless, we will make two general substantive assumptions:

1. The state or condition of a system, at any one point in time, is a function of the interaction between it and the environment in which it operates.
2. Change and conflict are always evident in a system.

These assumptions follow from the discussion of critical theory presented in Chapter 1. Human behavior must be understood as the result of a multiplicity of factors, both internal and external, operating in transaction with one another. Individuals are not robots completely determined by their environment, nor are they independent actors operating solely on free will. Individuals both influence their environments and are influenced by them. Processes of mutual influence generate change and development.

A systems approach serves best as an orienting model or framework through which an analysis of human behavior can be made. It tells us everything and yet it tells us nothing at all. For the systems approach to come to life in social service practice, a whole range of concepts and perspectives must be incorporated into it. In this chapter we will lay out the approach, highlighting its major concepts. In the remainder of the book we will use these concepts selectively to examine communities, families, groups, and individuals as examples of systems.

HUMAN SYSTEMS

Ludwig von Bertalanffy defined a system as a "dynamic order of parts and processes standing in mutual interaction."[6] There are many kinds of systems in nature. A machine can be thought of as an inanimate system, for example, and a plant can be thought of as an organic system. However, these examples of systems usually do not interest social service workers. What is of interest to them are systems composed of human beings, or human systems. A **human system** is one in which one or more individuals are found. The individual, as a system, is the basic human system. A **social system**, considered only in regard to its basic characteristics, is simply a collection of interacting individuals. Friendships, small groups, families, communities, organizations, and nations are all social systems.

Human Nature: Biological and Cultural Determinants

Not only are individuals basic human systems in their own right, they also constitute the basic element and the driving force or energy of all social systems. Some discussion of the innate nature of human motives, needs, and drives therefore is inevitable in the systems approach. There is considerable debate, however, about human nature, even as to whether there is such a thing.

One debate centers on the relative importance of cultural (nurture) and biological (nature) determinants of human behavior. Those who argue for **cultural determinism** maintain that humans are born in a blank state or tabula rasa, with no human nature beyond obvious biological features such as a large brain, erect posture, opposable thumbs, and vocal abilities. These theorists maintain that human motives, needs, and drives are completely learned through social conditioning or cultural transmission.[7] At the other extreme are those who argue in favor of **biological determinism** and see individual and societal behavior as solely a function of genetic programming. This position is taken less often, but there has been a recent surge in interest in the biological origins of human behavior.[8] There is now good evidence to believe that a number of conditions once thought to be the result of environment, such as personality, psychopathology, and cognitive abilities, have significant genetic components.[9]

A related debate has to do with the extent to which human behavior differs from animal behavior, qualitatively or quantitatively. Many researchers maintain that humans are so unique that propositions based on the study of other animals do not hold for them and that humans can only be understood on their own terms. Ronald Fernandez, for instance, argues that "people are unique, different in kind from every other animal on Earth."[10] Others insist that the social sciences have not progressed to the status of a full science largely because they have ignored the comparative study of animals, including humans. On the basis of comparative study of mammals and other animal species, Pierre van den Berghe concluded that "the uniqueness of human behavior has been misunderstood." Human behavior, like the behavior of every other species, is unique in some respects, but it is not radically different from the behavior of other species.[11]

We will take the position that biological and cultural determinants of human behavior are equally important and that, while Homo sapiens have unique qualities, they are also similar to other animals in many ways. The behavior of human systems is a function of the transaction between biology and environment, so much so that it is impossible to separate the two. It is not that human behavior is composed of a certain discrete portion of biology and another discrete portion of environment, as if the two components could simply be added together. The parts are completely interwoven and interdependent. For instance, sex is often believed to be a purely biological drive, yet studies indicate that environmental factors not only can block the development of sexual maturity but also can shape sexual expression in profound ways. Harvey Gochros suggests, therefore, that "sexual behavior must be viewed...within the social context in which it exists."[12]

A Theory of Human Nature

Although it is clear that human nature is guided by the continually evolving interplay between biological and cultural factors, it is difficult to pin down its exact properties. Milton Gordon advances a theory of human nature which cogently summarizes the generally accepted view.[13]

Gordon suggests that at least five elements make up human nature. First, there are physiological needs, such as hunger, thirst, and sexual desire. Second, there is the capacity for basic emotional or affective expressions, such as feeling anger, fear, anxiety, attachment, and dependence. Somewhat after birth, and only partly as a result of learning, the capacities to feel shame and pride also become apparent. Third, there are cognitive capacities, the ability to conceptualize, to apprehend, to evaluate, and to rationalize ourselves and others. Fourth, there are overarching drive motivations which represent the implacable tendencies of the total organism and are not traceable to any specific neurological mechanisms or sources. Presumably these drives are products of evolutionary development which can be attributed to self-preservation tendencies in the lower animals but must be conceptualized and described in much more complex terms for humans. These include the search for pleasure and avoidance of pain, the need to defend the self from disapproval and denigration, and the desire for immortality. The fifth element in human nature is derived behavioral patterns, the most important of which, Gordon believes, are cooperation and aggression. Both are presumed to be elicited by environmental and cultural factors acting on the biological organism.

Male and Female Differences

One question about human nature is whether there is only one or there are in fact two, a male human nature and a female human nature. The anatomical, biological differences between physiologically normal men and women are obvious. Generally, men are larger and stronger than women, and while only men can impregnate, only women can menstruate, gestate, and lactate.[14] The question is whether these biological differences generate clear-cut cognitive, emotional, and behavioral differences between the sexes.

Some say the answer to this question is decidedly yes. Men, they argue, are by nature active, aggressive, rational, mathematical, and concerned with autonomy; women are by nature passive, nurturant, emotional, verbal, and concerned with relationships. Others say the answer is just as decidedly no. Human nature, they assert, is not sex-bound. The differences that may exist between the sexes are generated by cultural norms and instilled through socialization processes.

Even **feminists,** those women and men who are committed to improving the status of women in society, differ in their beliefs about human nature.[15] Liberal and socialist feminists believe that men and women are basically the same, and the differences that do occur are likely the product of social norms and institutions. Radical feminists, in contrast, believe in the existence of basic differences between women and men; in their view, women are loving, caring, and spiritual, while men are individualistic, competitive, and pragmatic. This controversy is an important issue in the study of changing gender roles.

The research literature demonstrates the existence of any number of statistically significant male-female differences. Some of Eleanor Maccoby and Carol Jacklin's findings in their exhaustive literature review support the contentions of those who believe that there are differences in the nature of males and females, but most of them do not. For instance, a good deal of the research concurs that, especially after age 11, girls surpass boys in verbal ability and that, after age 13, boys outperform girls on mathematical tests. Boys also seem to be better able to manipulate three-dimensional objects and to perceive differences between a figure and its surroundings. Males seem to be more active as infants and more aggressive throughout life.[16]

The search for deepseated, irreconcilable gender differences picked up momentum with studies by feminists such as Carol Gilligan, although her work has since been used as

---

Why They Just Don't Understand One Another

In *They Just Don't Understand*, Deborah Tannen summarizes her study of differences in the approach taken by men and women in conversation. She calls communication a continual balancing act in which people juggle the conflicting needs for intimacy and independence. Women's conversations typically are negotiations for intimacy in which they seek to establish or maintain connections with others. For men, the negotiations are likely to be for independence, and the goal is to maintain status and position in a hierarchical social order.

Status and connection can be used by either gender "as a means to get things done by talking." (p. 36) But the focus in men's conversations is on status; the focus in women's is on connection. Tannen gives the example of a conversation that led to the end of a long-term relationship. The couple had agreed each was free to see others, but they would not hurt one another. When he began to sleep with other women she protested, and her protest made him angry. Their conversation was along these lines:

She: How can you do this when you know it's hurting me?
He: How can you try to limit my freedom?
She: But it makes me feel awful.
He: You are trying to manipulate me. (p. 40)

The key issue for the man was his independence to do what he wanted; for the woman, it was her interdependence and how his action affected her feelings.

Source: Deborah Tannen, *You Just Don't Understand: Women and Men in Conversation* (New York: William Morrow, 1990).

---

an argument for maintaining women's subordinate position (see Chapter 15). Gilligan suggests that moral development is distinguished by inherently different female and male "voices." Men are more concerned with personal autonomy and independence, while women are more concerned with social welfare and relationships.[17] Deborah Tannen echoes Gilligan with her assertion that women and men have distinct conversational styles. She argues that women use conversation to enhance intimacy and explore cooperative solutions to common problems, while men use conversation competitively to protect their independence and demonstrate their mastery and control over a situation.[18]

Close inspection of the research literature which has uncovered these male-female differences has failed to confirm whether the results reflect biological or cultural differences. Many of the samples in these studies are small, much of the methodology is flawed, and few of the differences seem to hold up across the board. When statistically significant differences are consistently found, they often are so small as to be virtually meaningless.[19] Thus science has yet to determine if the anatomical and biological differences between men and women lead to innate cognitive, emotional, or behavioral differences.

In this controversy, therefore, it is best to reject determinist theories, which assume there is a single, all-encompassing cause of human behavior, either biophysical or sociocultural. Biological determinism, according to Ruth Bleier, has always been a voice of oppression. She argues that

> We may indeed value the characteristics that in our Western societies are associated with femaleness...but we need not justify them as natural, biological, or innate....The chance for liberating ideas lies not with trying to turn traditional or misogynist or racist ideologies 180

degrees around and in our favor, but in turning them under completely, destroying their roots. We cannot replace one false illusion with another.[20]

Instead, Bleier would have us remember that human behavior is the product of biological, psychological, and social factors in continuous interaction and that as male and female humans we have an enormous capacity for change and development.[21]

✆ THE INDIVIDUAL AS A SYSTEM

Individuals, like all other systems, are comprised of dynamic parts or processes that together make up a subsystem or larger domain (see "The Individual as a System"). Two such domains are usually described in the literature, the biophysical and the psychological.

The Biophysical Domain

Because biological capacities most directly determine human nature, the **biophysical domain** is the basic building block or infrastructure of the individual as a system. In addition to inborn capacities, this domain includes all those elements necessary for the functioning of the organism, such as the skeletal, sensorimotor, respiratory, endocrine, circulatory, waste elimination, sexual-reproductive, digestive, and nervous systems. The biophysical domain is affected by genetic endowments as well as by disease, illness, and accident; and because it is associated with the processes of maturation and aging, its normal functioning differs across the life span.

Biophysical processes have significant effects on human behavior. In looking for explanations of clients' behaviors, social service workers tend to emphasize social and psychological processes and to underestimate the importance of biology. Knowledge of the biophysical domain, however, can be vital to the use of accurate and appropriate interventions (see "The Biophysical Domain and Social Work Practice").

Biology's fundamental importance to individual functioning has a number of dimensions. For one thing, biophysical states and processes that are unique to the human species provide the outer limit of behavior and development. Although medical advances have improved the likelihood that increasing numbers of people will live to a ripe old age, for example, there is little indication that members of the species are able to live for much more than 110–120 years. This seems to be an outer limit related to biology or human nature.

Individual genetic inheritance also affects human behavior[22] (see Chapter 16). Julia Rauch defines *human genetics* as dealing with those qualities that distinguish human beings from other species or that differentiate among individuals, families, and human populations. Through the study of genetic processes, Rauch says, it is possible to examine "the causes of hereditary similarities and differences among humans, the ways in which they are transmitted from generation to generation, and those factors, both internal and external, that affect gene action and outcome."[23]

Although there is considerable debate surrounding the relative importance of genetics to individual behavior, there is little doubt that it is significant. Individual intelligence, personality, abilities, health, and disease all have genetic components. Mental health experts, for instance, are becoming increasingly aware of the significance of genetic background to such illnesses as schizophrenia and severe depression.[24]

The Individual as a System

Individuals are composed of dynamically related biophysical and psychological domains. The biophysical domain is made up of genetic endowments and functional elements such as the nervous system. In the psychological domain are subsystems consisting of cognitive, behavioral, and motivational-affective (emotional) states and processes.

Biophysical
domain

Biogenetic states and processes

Psychological
domain

Cognitive
subsystem

Psychological
states and processes

Motivational-
affective
subsystem

Behavioral
subsystem

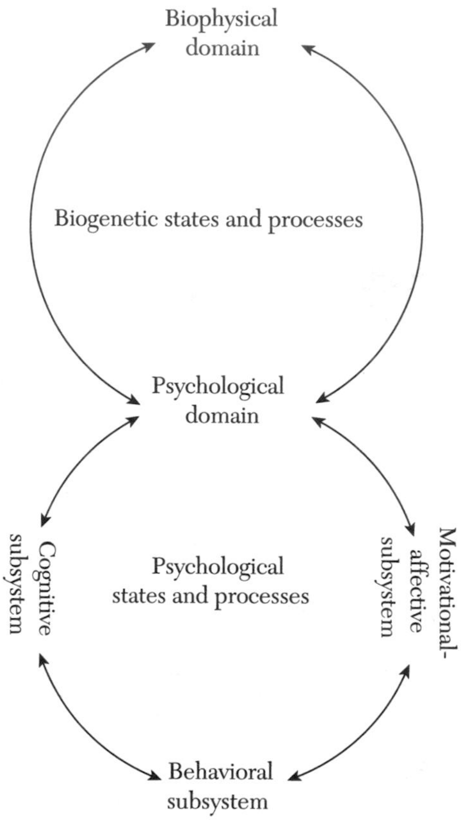

Biology also affects individual functioning because changes in physical condition due to illness, injury, or disability or to physical growth or decline may lead to alterations in cognitive, affective, or behavioral performance. People who are ill experience changes in mood, in perceptions, and in their ability to perform everyday tasks; if the condition can be reversed, their alterations may be temporary. Physical growth provokes psychological change and provides possibilities for development. Physical decline also produces changes, but in this process a good deal of compensatory development may occur.

The Psychological Domain

The **psychological domain** may be thought of as a group of interrelated subsystems made up of cognitive, motivational-affective, and behavioral states and processes. It is

---

The Biophysical Domain and Social Work Practice

Social workers often find that knowledge of the biophysical domain is helpful in their practice. The following three case vignettes from academic colleagues demonstrate different aspects of the application of knowledge of the biophysical domain to social work practice situations.

Case Vignette 1

Mona Wasow of the University of Wisconsin provides an example of how knowledge of specific illnesses and their symptoms can help social workers assure more effective services for their clients. A social worker in a mental health hospital was working with a young athlete who had been diagnosed as schizophrenic because he was hallucinating. The worker noted that the man was having coordination problems; he was not steady in his walk, bumped into things, and often tripped. Because she knew that poor coordination is not usually associated with schizophrenia, she informed the doctor. Further medical examination of the patient uncovered a benign brain tumor, which, once removed, eliminated both the hallucinations and the poor coordination.

Case Vignette 2

An example by Joan Burns, also of the University of Wisconsin, shows that sometimes social workers fail to take into account sufficiently the possibility of biological factors in their assessment of client problems. A teacher reported to a school social worker that a pupil with a number of visible bruises appeared to have been physically abused.

The social worker spoke to the girl, but she did not indicate in any way that she had been harmed by her parents. A few weeks later, however, the child again appeared bruised, so the social worker spoke to the parents and informed them that under mandatory reporting laws, they would have to be reported to the authorities. The parents insisted that they had never harmed their child. They said they also had noticed the bruises but could not understand how they occurred. The social worker then suggested a medical examination for the girl, and the results indicated Menke's disease, a lethal disorder in which a child easily bruises and breaks bones.

Case Vignette 3

Sometimes biophysical explanations are given when in fact they are wrong. Julio Morales of the University of Connecticut tells of a school social worker who was working with a newly immigrated Puerto Rican boy. Since the boy did not speak English, the social worker asked an older, bilingual Puerto Rican child to translate what the boy was saying. When the translator reported that the boy had said, "They're eating my brains," the social worker concluded that the immigrant was hallucinating and referred him to a mental health clinic. Further investigation uncovered that the Spanish expression "eating one's brains" means "being brainwashed." The boy was really saying that his teacher was brainwashing him. This wasn't hallucinatory behavior but an expression of an interpersonal problem between the boy and his teacher.

---

of central importance in social service work because many of the assessment and intervention tasks performed by workers have to do with promoting healthy psychological functioning.

The Cognitive Subsystem

The **cognitive subsystem** in the psychological domain is composed of cognitive states and processes, including perception, sensation, memory, imagination, judgment, and language, as well as intelligence and other aspects of intellectual functioning such as knowledge, beliefs, and opinions. Through these processes, the individual assigns and attributes meaning and understanding to the world. The meanings attached to places, objects, and situations, to society and other human beings, and, above all, to the self are involved. Of primary interest to social service workers are the meanings attributed to the cause of behaviors.

The attribution of causation   **Attribution theory** is a major area of cognitive study which deals with how people gather, combine, and use information to arrive at causal explanations for their own behavior and the behavior of others.[25] Much of what transpires between social workers and the individuals and families they serve is the exchange of meaning about the nature and origin of personal troubles.[26] Even in their first contacts with social workers, clients often have some basic understanding about the troubles they are having. In assessing clients' needs and formulating intervention plans, workers also reach conclusions about the reasons for these troubles. One way of thinking about clinical intervention, therefore, is as a process whereby social workers and clients exchange understandings about the causes and resolutions of problems and, when they do not concur, attempt to alter those understandings.

The work of Fritz Heider provides the background for contemporary studies of attributional processes. The basis for his work is the belief that people have a need to anticipate and control what happens to them and others and that this need is best met by understanding the causes of behavior. For Heider, a naive, commonsense psychology underlies inferences of causation; that is, we observe others and thereby reach conclusions about why behaviors occur. The conclusions we reach are a function of both the persons being observed (their behavior and the contexts in which it is enacted) and the person doing the perceiving (the manner in which the perceiver experiences the behavior and the characteristics and preconceptions of the perceiver). A key issue in the inference of causation is whether behavior will be perceived as being caused by the person doing the act or by the situation the actor is in.[27]

Heider's ideas led to a vast amount of research about the rules people use in making attributions about causation. Most of these rules are quite primitive, and children learn them by the age of three. A common rule is: Things that occur closely in time and space with a behavior (the effect) are likely to be seen as the cause of the behavior.[28] Adults using more sophisticated principles of reasoning may recognize that causation can be distal or delayed, that is, located in a place or time very distant from the event.

But people generally rely on elementary principles of reasoning, so it is not surprising that they are often wrong in the causal attributions they make. A number of attributional errors and biases have been identified by Susan Fiske and Shelley Taylor:

1. The *fundamental attributional error* is the tendency to attribute the behaviors of others to dispositional causes such as personality, attitudes, and values and to minimize and not take into account situational causes such as contextual, background, or status/role conditions.

2. The *actor-observer effect* is the tendency to infer dispositional causes to the behavior of others but situational causes to one's own behavior.

3. The *false or self-based consensus effect* is the tendency to assume that one's own judgment is the same as that of others. People assume their way of thinking is typical of group norms and others would see things exactly the same way they do.

4. The *self-serving attributional bias* is the tendency to take credit for success and deny responsibility for failure.

5. The *self-centered bias* is the tendency to take more responsibility for a joint outcome than is one's due. Whether the outcome is positive or negative, people tend to see themselves as more responsible than others for achieving it.[29]

The tendencies to make such attributional errors should give social workers pause. Do they misperceive the origins of client problems? Do they tend to blame the victim and make self-serving judgments about clients? The research suggests that such may be the case, but with proper training and careful observation, they should be able to avoid such biases. Attributional biases are not universal phenomena but seem to be learned within the context of particular cultures. The finding that children do no think about others in dispositional terms until late childhood suggests this is a learned bias, and cross-cultural studies have shown that the fundamental attributional error is more common in Western than in other societies.[30]

Biases in attributional processes may be reduced through strategies such as being aware of bias, using self-monitoring techniques, and adopting a systems perspective which takes into account multiple internal and external factors. Communication with others to share ideas and opinions can also be helpful, as long as we make sure we don't just talk to people who always agree with us.

The Motivational-Affective Subsystem

The motivational-affective subsystem in the psychological domain includes states and processes usually concerned with the internal, emotional life of individuals—their motives, needs, drives, feelings, sentiments, and interests. This subsystem also involves the crises individuals may be experiencing and their conscious and unconscious adaptations to them. Motives have a forward reference in time. They are concerned with the purpose and the anticipated consequences of acts.

The psychology of motivation   The study of motives has been a central topic in many schools of psychology. Early psychologists developed lists of biologically rooted instincts that were believed to form the basic motives, including mating, parenting, curiosity, repulsion, escape, and self-assertion. In the middle of the twentieth century, emphasis shifted to learned motives such as the need for achievement, the need for affection, and the need for power. More recently, motivational theory has focused on the **locus of control**, that is, whether people are motivated by *intrinsic* motives or incentives, which propel them forward from the inside, or *extrinsic* motives or incentives, which pull them forward from the outside.[31] People who experience intrinsic motives believe they have control over their fate, whereas those who experience extrinsic motives believe they are controlled by others or by chance or fate.

The existence of internal, intrinsic motives is stressed in most of the psychodynamic theories used by social service workers, including Freudian theory and its contemporary offshoots ego psychology and self-psychology (see Chapter 15). Freud posited the existence of two basic drives: the search for erotic or sensual pleasure and the fulfillment of aggressive needs. In the evolution of this theoretical framework, other drives, such as social and attachment needs, and the needs for individuation and separation and for mastery or competence, have been proposed.

Humanist psychology, based on the philosophy of **humanism,** which asserts the dignity and worth of individuals and their capacity for self-actualization through reason, has also placed a great deal of emphasis on the concept of internal motives. Abraham Maslow, for example, introduced a theory of human behavior based on a particular *hierarchy of needs*[32] (see "Maslow's Hierarchy of Needs"). First to be addressed are basic human needs that enable survival, such as the needs for food, clothing, shelter, and safety. Maslow refers to these as *physiological needs* and *safety needs*; until they are satisfied, the individual will strive for nothing more. Next the *need for belongingness and love* can be addressed. Behavior is motivated by the need for friendship and the intimacy and love of family members and lovers.

As these needs are met, *esteem needs* can be addressed. These needs are expressed in terms of self-esteem, "the desire for strength, for achievement, for adequacy, for mastery and competence, for confidence in the face of the world, and for independence and freedom," and in terms of the esteem of others, "the desire for reputation and prestige…, status, dominance, recognition, attention, importance, or appreciation." Finally, individuals who have achieved self-esteem can turn their attention to the *need for self-actualization,* or self-fulfillment, "the desire to become more and more what one is, to become everything that one is capable of becoming."[33] Thus realizing one's potential is the ultimate human need. The important point, according to Maslow, is that only when the basic survival needs have been met will individuals begin to sense and be able to satisfy the higher-level needs for esteem and self-actualization.

The Behavioral Subsystem

The states and processes in the **behavioral subsystem** are concerned with the ways individuals express themselves in action. Behaviors differ from cognitive and affective processes in that they always involve the actual things people say and do. Mannerisms, habits, and interpersonal and communications skills are all behaviors. Nevertheless, learning theories often recognize the effects of cognitive or motivational states on behavior. Social learning theory, for instance, takes into account a number of cognitive processes associated with learning, and operant conditioning theory builds on extrinsic rewards as the motivator of human behavior (see Chapter 15).

Learning or behavioral theories have become increasingly important in social service work. Bruce Theyer suggests that social work practice with both individuals and larger social systems can be organized around the behavioral concept of "contingencies," or operant conditioning.[34] He posits three behavioral propositions:

1. Individuals, families, groups, communities, and entire societies engage in behavior.
2. All behavior is followed by consequences, positive consequences such as monetary rewards, affection, stability, and safety, as well as negative consequences such as punishment, dislike, quarreling, and injury.
3. The consequences of a given behavior, to a very large extent, influence the future occurrence of that behavior. In general, positive consequences reinforce a behavior, while negative consequences discourage a behavior.

Theyer also posits a fourth proposition that may best be thought of as the implications of operant conditioning for social work practice:

4. Empirical analysis of the contingencies of which behavior is a function provides an effective intervention tool. By working with clients to examine the consequences of

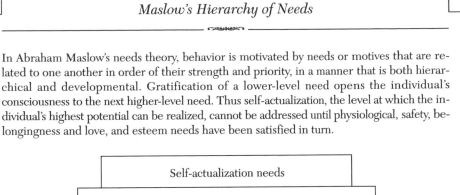

Maslow's Hierarchy of Needs

In Abraham Maslow's needs theory, behavior is motivated by needs or motives that are related to one another in order of their strength and priority, in a manner that is both hierarchical and developmental. Gratification of a lower-level need opens the individual's consciousness to the next higher-level need. Thus self-actualization, the level at which the individual's highest potential can be realized, cannot be addressed until physiological, safety, belongingness and love, and esteem needs have been satisfied in turn.

> Self-actualization needs
>
> Esteem needs: Self-esteem and the esteem of others
>
> Belongingness and love needs
>
> Personal safety needs
>
> Basic physiological needs

Source: Abraham H. Maslow, *Motivation and Personality* (New York: Harper & Row, 1954), and "Synergy in the Society and in the Individual," *Journal of Individual Psychology,* vol. 20 (1968), pp. 153–64.

their behavior, social workers can help clients eliminate unwanted behaviors and stimulate desired behaviors.

Level of Systems within Individuals

The domains and subsystems described in this section exist at the micro or most elementary level of states and processes that comprise the individual as a system. Within them, more complex states or processes may be differentiated. Thus it is possible to visualize the individual as an intricate pattern with increasingly comprehensive levels of systems (see "Levels of Systems within Individuals").

The genetic and biological states and processes of the biophysical domain, as we have noted, provide the infrastructure for the existence of the psychological domain. The states and processes of the psychological subsystems arise from the interaction of the biological (nature) and cultural or environmental (nurture) transactions, but the psychological domain exists independently of its origins. It is not completely reducible to either the biological or the environmental. The cognitive, motivational-affective, and behavioral subsystems in the psychological domain themselves combine to form more complex systems within the individual. For instance, an attitude is a combination of beliefs (cognition), feelings (emotions), and behaviors. Single attitudes combine to form the individual's attitude system, value system, and belief system, and these in turn combine to form the individual's character, personality, self, and identity. These last four concepts,

---

Levels of Systems within Individuals

It is possible to abstract many levels of systems and subsystems within the individual as a system. At the most elementary (micro) level are the biophysical domain and the cognitive, motivational or affective, and behavioral states and processes in the psychological domain. The intermediate (meso) level consists of attitudes and belief and value systems, and at the highest (macro) level are the structures of character, personality, the self, and personal identity.

Macro level   ↑   Character, personality, self, and identity

Meso level   ↑   Attitudes, values, and beliefs
                     Attitude, value, and belief systems

                  Psychological domain
                     Cognitive, motivational-affective, and behavioral states and processes

Micro level   ↑   Biophysical domain
                     Biogenetic states and processes

---

taken together, summarize the entire cognitive, affective, and behavioral makeup of the individual. Those who study personality and self are concerned with how these structures emerge and change and are reflected in private and social behavior.

✿ DYNAMICS OF THE INDIVIDUAL AS A SYSTEM

All systems are marked by dynamic interaction among their component parts. Not only are the parts often inseparable from one another, but they are in a state of continual interaction and interdependence. The domains and subsystems comprising the individual are therefore dynamically interrelated, as are the various levels of systems. The differences among the cognitive, motivational-affective, and behavioral subsystems often blur, as do the differences among the micro, meso, and macro structures. By the same token, the processes taking place in each of the subsystems and at the various levels influence all the others.

At the micro level, there is a mutual influence between the biological and the psychological. We feel differently about ourselves, depending on our age and our physical health and abilities. A man might be 50 years old, for instance, but if he is in good health and has kept his body in condition, he could have a sense of being young. Similarly, cognition, emotion, and behavior mutually influence one another in the psychological domain. If we believe something is not good, we are likely to act (or not to act) in accordance with our belief, and then we feel that we have done something good. For instance, regardless of how important an exam may be and how little prepared a woman is for it, if cheating goes against her moral principles, she may choose to fail rather than cheat.

Although these domains and subsystems mutually influence one another, it should not be assumed that one necessarily follows directly from another. In the study of attitudes, for example, it has been found that our beliefs are often in contradiction with our actual behaviors. We may think and feel in one way and yet do something quite different.

Behavior and Development

In studying the individual as a system, we must distinguish between human behavior and human development. With regard to individuals, **human behavior** is a generic term used to describe cognitions and emotions as well as actual behaviors. In terms of dynamics, the focus is on how behavior is acquired, maintained, and changed, at any point in time, as a function of past and present biological, psychological, and social influences. The study of human behavior incorporates all the various theories generated by social and behavioral scientists: theories of cognition, motivation, and learning; theories of social interaction; theories of groups and families; and theories of community, organizational, and social life.

Human development is a special, more limited way of understanding human behavior. Development has to do with how behavior is acquired, maintained, and changed as a function of the biological processes of aging—birth, growth, maturation, decline, and dying. Psychological and social factors are believed to influence development, but only as they are triggered by biological processes. The focus of inquiry is usually on the development and functioning of the self or personality across the life span (see Chapters 16, 17, and 18).

The concepts of behavior and development are not limited to the study of individuals. In addition to the individual, in various parts of the book we will focus on the behavior of communities, families, groups, and organizations. Similarly, we will apply the concept of development to the study of societies, organizations, groups, and families, as well as to individuals.

Change and Development

We must also distinguish between the concepts of change and development as they are related to human behavior. *Change* refers to any alteration, positive or negative, backward or forward, in human behavior; *development* refers to positive and forward change. The notion of inevitable progress is built into many developmental perspectives, but it is not altogether clear that, over the short or long run, the continual changes taking place in individuals and other social systems automatically lead to progress. In fact, research indicates that individual change across the life span is nonsequential, multidirectional, and at times even reversible.[35] Development, therefore, may be more a utopian concept than an accurate description of personality change across the life span. It defines the possible rather than the actual. Nevertheless, development is one of the major goals of a critical perspective on social service practice, and it is an important social work value. A central task of the social service worker is to promote development and prevent negative or backward change.

Achieving the Steady State

In early systems theory, it was suggested that systems are self-regulating entities which exist in a state of balance or equilibrium known as **homeostasis**.[36] In this view, balance is achieved as each element in a system successively serves as input, throughput, and output, generating the feedback which enables the elements to adapt to one another constantly. Survival of the system is thus assured. More recent thinking on systems has pointed out limitations to the concepts of homeostasis and feedback. Ludwig von Bertalanffy argues that homeostasis makes sense when referring to inanimate, mechanical systems but not when referring to complex, changing, dynamic systems like living organisms. He posits instead the concept of steady state.[37]

Living systems are in the process of continuous generation, decay, and regeneration. This process takes place for one of two reasons: because tensions existing inside a system demand readjustment, or because disturbances in the environment force readjustment. **Steady state** is the self-regulation and readjustment which take place to enable the organism to be maintained in a relatively consistent condition. The steady state ensures that organisms do change, but slowly, and in no particular direction. From one point to the next organisms are not the same, but they are similar.

The steady state also ensures that there is no one way by which an organism goes from one state to the next. Although feedback helps to regulate systems, it should not be regarded as the only way by which living systems maintain themselves. In systems theory, the **principle of equifinality** is that different systems will arrive at similar states if they receive similar inputs.[38] How a system achieves steady state is largely indeterminate and involves a great deal of flexibility and creativity.

A system in a steady state, according to Ralph Anderson and Irl Carter, "is maintaining a viable relationship with its environment and its components, and its functions are being performed in such fashion as to ensure its continued existence.[39] Yet it would be misleading to say that all living systems always achieve steady state. Individuals may aim to and they may hope to do this, but they do not always succeed. Often when clients seek social services it is because the tensions within them and the disturbances coming from their environment have destroyed any semblance of balance; their very survival may be in jeopardy. The worker must help them figure out the flexible and creative solutions that could restore a steady state.

The steady states that people do achieve need not be functional to their development. For instance, Gail Kadison Golden describes the dependence on abusers often felt by women and children. They become so attached that separation from the abuser is experienced as worse than the abuse itself.[40] In such a case, social service workers may have to focus not on reinforcing an existing steady state but on severing it and promoting an alternative one.

System Boundaries

All systems have boundaries, in the sense that the elements making them up are distinguishable from the elements making up their environment. The boundaries of a system are not easily determined, however, and they do no exist as a legal demarcation, as the boundaries of a nation do. The boundaries of a system are always dynamic and changing, and they are more or less evident from time to time. To some extent, therefore, they are one and the same with their environment.

Take, for instance, the boundary of an ethnic community. We might say that the Asian community is made up of all Asians living in the United States. Well and good, but just who is and isn't included in this community? Are we referring only to those who have American citizenship, those whose parents are both Asian, those who live in a particular neighborhood or geographic area, or those who identify with being Asian?

The boundary of an individual is also dynamic and not clearly demarcated. It is clearest at the physical level; the skin, hair, and other visible features certainly form a boundary. But what of the psychological boundary of the individual? Much of the personality is learned, and much of the information about the self comes from the various groups and individuals with whom the individual interacts in everyday life. The "I" and the "me" are intimately connected to the "they" and the "them." As we develop we gain a sense of our own uniqueness, our own separate ways of feeling, thinking, and behaving. We become self-conscious and take on an identity, and this subjective understanding of ourselves becomes our boundary.

The tightness of the boundary of a system is important because it affects the degree to which a system (the "I" and "me") will be influenced by its environment (the "they" and "them"). Because human systems are interdependent, they are **open systems.** To the extent that individuals close themselves off from others, they are **closed systems,** and they have no means of surviving. Humans are innately social animals dependent on others for the fulfillment of basic and higher-level needs like hunger, shelter, protection, love, belonging, and personal fulfillment. Human systems therefore must respond to their environment and can never be completely self-sufficient.

Nevertheless, individuals differ in the degree to which they open themselves up to others, and this can have important implications for their well-being. Some mental health theorists believe that too much openness or too little openness can create difficulties. Family practitioners, for instance, postulate that the individuals composing a family need to maintain some degree of openness to other family members if they are to contribute to the family and meet their own needs. In *enmeshed families,* the members have opened themselves up so much that their own individuality has been lost. In *disengaged families,* the members are closed off to one another, and there is no give and take in their interaction. Both extremes are considered indications of poor interpersonal relationships.[41]

Working at the boundary between systems is often seen as a primary task in social work, and various intervention tasks derived from boundary considerations have been identified. The foremost task is to bring about mutual adjustments: coping and adaptation on the part of the client system, and alteration and change on the part of environmental systems.[42]

∽ THE STUDY OF NORMALITY

A primary concern of social service workers is normal or abnormal human behavior. In many fields of social work practice—child welfare, mental health, family practice—the central question is, What is a normal individual? Social work services are usually provided under the assumption that clients are not operating at a level that might be considered normal, and the services provided are designed to help clients achieve some level of normal functioning. From the point of view of clients who may be concerned about whether they (or their loved ones) are thinking, feeling, or behaving in a normal way, social workers are looked to for either some assurance of normality or some help in achieving it.

In studying normality and trying to find answers to this question, it becomes apparent that knowledge of normality is still in its infancy and that no simple definitions can be stated. The complexity of the concept and the difficulty of developing some understanding of what it means to be psychologically normal must be appreciated. It is essential, therefore, for social service workers to exercise a good deal of caution in applying ideas about normality to their clients.

At least four different definitions of normality have been advanced, each with very different implications about individual functioning. Daniel Offer and Melvin Sabshin have described these as normality as average, normality as health, normality as utopia, and normality as transaction or transactional systems.[43] In our discussion, transactions are considered not so much as a type of normally but as the source of all normality.

Normality as Average

The concept of normality often is stated in terms of a statistical principle. On a bell-shaped or normal curve, normality is depicted as the center of the bulge at the top of the curve or some range around that center. The center can be described as the mean, an average score or standing; as the median, the point where 50 percent of the scores fall above and 50 percent fall below; or as the mode, the most common score or standing. The range around the center is often described in terms of scores around or standard deviations from the mean. For instance, normal intelligence is usually defined as an IQ score somewhere between 100 and 130. Individuals who score somewhat below 100 are said to have low, although normal, intelligence; and those who score below 70 are considered to be "retarded." Individuals who score somewhat above 130 are seen as "precocious" and those who score above 160 as "geniuses." Individuals at either extreme are suspect, since they are not like most everybody else but are either too dull-witted or too intelligent and therefore not normal.

The idea of **normal as average** pervades much of the research literature on human behavior and development. People feel emotionally stable when they are neither seriously depressed nor seriously hyper or manic. People who are of average height and weight will often come to feel normal, not too tall, not too short, not too fat, not too skinny. Teenagers with names like Steve and Brad and Cindi and Lori may feel normal because they do not stand out in American society, while those with names like Rosario, Rafael, Eiko, and Kenji may be made to feel quite abnormal. Social workers often comfort clients by telling them that the kinds of difficulties they experience are common for people in their circumstances.

Normality defined as an average is a useful concept in making assessments of individual functioning. Humans, being social animals, can take comfort in the knowledge that they are "just like everybody else," and averages can serve as relatively objective standards for evaluating growth and maturation. But normality as average can have connotations of conformity and intolerance. Whatever is not average is not normal and, therefore, is considered bad or deviant. Thus girls who do not like to play with dolls, or boys who are left-handed, or teenagers who like classical music, or unmarried single adults, or grandmothers who are interested in sex are made to feel out of step, presumably not like everybody else. Normality as average is the basis for social norms under which difference is scorned and neutrality or conformity is championed.

Normality as Health

The term *normality* often is used in a medical or psychiatric context to signify a positive level of individual functioning which usually is described as adequate, or as the absence of pathology or illness. Offer and Sabshin call it a "*reasonable* rather than an *optimal* state of functioning."[44] The *Diagnostic and Statistical Manual of Mental Disorders* developed by the American Psychiatric Association (see Chapter 3), which is used frequently in mental health services, is an application of the idea of **normal as health**, or the absence of pathology.

The concept of normality as health is often used as the basis of studies of social indicators of personal satisfaction and happiness, as well as epidemiological studies of the incidence and distribution of problems or disorders in mental health.[45] Perhaps the most famous epidemiological study using this technique was the work of Emile Durkheim on suicide in Europe in the nineteenth century.[46] In the first part of the twentieth century, Chicago sociologists used epidemiological techniques to trace the relationship between place of residence in a city and the distribution of first admissions to mental hospitals.[47]

More recently, sophisticated survey techniques have been introduced to examine the incidence of mental illness among the noninstitutionalized population. The National Institute of Mental Health released results in 1988 of a survey of 18,000 adults in five cities, conducted over several years to provide information on the prevalence of specific mental disorders in the population, as well as estimates of the number of people in need of mental health services[48] (see Chapter 18).

Normality as health is the most common approach to normalcy used by social service practitioners. It acknowledges the debilitating potential of stressful life events and the relatively high proportion of the population that does not have psychiatric symptoms. It is a pragmatic approach that provides for the use of reasoned, specific criteria in making diagnoses.

There are some difficulties, however, with the concept. When measuring physical health, some adequate level of functioning is relatively easy to determine. Health is the absence of a fever or virus or some other incapacitating condition. In mental health, adequate functioning involves any number of biological, psychological, and social considerations. Some psychological disturbances such as schizophrenia may indeed be biological in origin and therefore lend themselves to notions of health and illness. Other disturbances seem far more social or psychological in their origins, and it is only the meanings attached to the behaviors that cause some to be designated as health and others as illness. Some social scientists have suggested that the language of health and illness ought to be replaced by the idea of **problems in living,** which can be addressed in the political, social, and economic environments.[49] In this view, the labels *health* and *illness* are applied by more powerful people to less powerful people when they cause more discomfort than the powerful are willing to endure.

Normality as health also is related to the idea of psychological survival. The literature on social work often focuses on developing clients' skills at coping and adaptation, to help them survive difficult situations, endure stress, and deal with the problems of contemporary life. Indeed, many people regard themselves as doing well if they are just surviving. The emphasis on survival, however, may imply that people cannot and should not be expected to be in control of social circumstances and their own lives, and the emphasis on coping and adapting can be taken to mean that social reality must always be accepted, and societal conditions and situations can never be changed.[50] Perhaps the best example of this kind of thinking is the reality therapy developed by William Glasser. He asserts that normality is best thought of as responsible behavior, and this requires an acceptance of reality and a willingness to meet personal needs within the constraints of that reality. According to Glasser:

> …our basic job as therapists is to become involved with the patient and then get him to face reality. When confronted with reality…he is forced again and again to decide whether or not he wishes to take the responsible path. Reality may be painful, it may be harsh, it may be dangerous, but it changes slowly. All any man can hope to do is to struggle within it in a responsible way by doing right and enjoying the pleasure or suffering the pain that may follow.[51]

The concept of **adaptation**, which derives from the European psychoanalytic literature, became a central concept in the United States when ego psychology was imported by psychoanalysts escaping Nazi Germany. It has nevertheless been characterized as a very American concept, in which the goal of psychotherapy is seen as "a reflection of the culturally encouraged virtue of fitting in by getting the patient to adapt to the environment."[52] Thus normality, defined as health or adequate functioning and the absence of pathology, may not always be an acceptable criterion for judging psychological well-being.

In many ways the concept of normality as health is not too different from the concept of normality as average. By focusing on the absence of illness rather than some optimal level of functioning, researchers are obviously using some notion of average. The World Health Organization and other commissions attempting to define health have been opposed to definitions that are built around reasonable and adequate functioning. These groups would prefer to define health in more positive terms, as the enhancement of a state of health or as "a state of complete physical, mental and social well-being."[53]

Normality as Utopia

The idea of **normal as utopia** is an attempt to state a maximum level of human functioning. It goes beyond averages and adequate functioning to envision realization of the full psychological potential of human beings. Thus it may be seen as unworkable, of interest to dreamers but not to researchers, clinicians, and other serious students of human development and behavior.[54] In many ways the difference between normality as health and normality as utopia is one of degree. Those with utopian visions of normality call for the development of more than the ability to cope and adapt to social reality. They espouse development of the ability to create new and more positive realities.

Much of the literature on human behavior fits this definition of normality. For instance, social service practice theory has begun to emphasize the notion of individual competence, which derives from the work of Robert W. White and other ego psychologists.[55] **Competence** sets a higher standard for assessing the individuals' coping and adaptation strategies because they are expected to go beyond survival toward mastery of social reality. Competence is defined in both objective and subjective ways. Objectively, it is the capacity, based on cumulative experiences, to interact effectively with the environment. Subjectively, it is the perception that the individual has accumulated the strengths and abilities required to control his or her own destiny.

Another concept that fits a utopian vision of normalcy is that of **empowerment:** The individual must confront social situations that are oppressive or that distort psychological well-being and gain power or control over them. Elaine Pinderhughes defines the term *power* as the "capacity to influence the forces which affect one's life space for one's own benefit." She believes that the ultimate goal of social workers ought to be to help clients exert power in a way that enables them to obtain the necessary resources to meet their needs. Social work treatment should give people "the ability and capacity to cope constructively with the forces that undermine and hinder coping, the achievement of some reasonable control over their destiny."[56]

Radical theorists go even further, introducing the notions of freedom and liberation. Eric Fromm, for instance, wrote about the oppressiveness of free-market, industrial societies, arguing that they are dehumanizing and inculcate authoritarian needs, destructiveness, and conformity. In such societies individuals are unable to liberate themselves; they have a fear of freedom from which they cannot escape. Rather than defining normality in terms of ability to fulfill social roles in a society, Fromm sees normalcy "as the optimum of growth and happiness of the individual."[57] In his view, individuals should aspire to achieve liberation from the demands of oppressive social circumstances.

Two utopian visions of normality have already been presented in this chapter. The humanist emphasis on self-actualization, which Maslow identified as the highest need motivating human behavior, is a utopian vision, as is the idea from evolutionary theory that the life course is marked by unending progress or development. Neither self-actualization nor development is a fact of life, in that they do not automatically occur, but they both represent ways to achieve the optimum human potential.

The concept of normality as utopia has all kinds of problems. Pragmatists note that the visions are dreamlike; researchers say that visions are vague and difficult to make sufficiently concrete for study and are not easily stated in terms that can be measured. Sociologists note that there is no consensus among the visions; rather, they represent the interests of particular theorists and particular ideologies.[58]

Yet this vision of normality as utopia is noble. It suits a critical social service practice because it rejects the status quo of reality and encourages striving for the best possible world and the best possible place in it for humans. Although the concept is vague and means too many things to too many people, this can be seen as a strength, not a shortcoming. Encouraging people to empower themselves, to be competent, liberated, self-actualized, developing individuals, encourages them to aspire to human perfectibility. Utopian visions represent the human spirit in its highest form of creativity.

Normality as Transactional Systems

The three definitions of normality considered so far stress particular characteristics or traits of individuals: the average individual; the adapting individual; the competent, empowered, or liberated individual. The idea of **normal as transactions** starts with the premise that humans are social systems embedded in social contexts. Normality therefore is not a characteristic of an individual but a characteristic of the interaction between individuals and their environments.

The transactional point of view combines some of the notions of the other definitions of normality yet arrives at a unique understanding of individual functioning by recognizing its intrinsic limits. A person is a social animal who cannot exist without other people, but other people have needs as well. Therefore, people's needs often are in conflict. A built-in tension exists in all human interaction, a tension between the quest for one's own well-being and the quest for the collective well-being. Rather than being an egocentric, or personal, vision of well-being, normality as transaction proposes that individual normality requires a collective search for the common good.

The idea of normality as transaction also suggests that the social environment must be normal. In this respect it is much like the utopian vision. It suggests that it is not always necessary for individuals to conform to other systems making up a social environment and that these systems have certain responsibilities for meeting the needs of those who must deal with them. Besides making demands on people, environments ought to supply opportunities for normal functioning.

The conflict among the needs and interests of individuals and their environments is real and can be seen daily in social work practice. A father comes in to ask the social worker to make his son, Bruiser, obey, that is, to get the son to do what the father thinks is important. The social worker talks with Bruiser and finds that he has some legitimate gripes about his father and would like to enlist her support in getting his father to be a "better man." Or the police bring in Ophelia and expect the worker to keep her from a life of prostitution; that is, to get her to conform to the accepted image of a woman. After talking with Ophelia, the worker realizes that women with little education and very limited legitimate economic opportunities do not think they are in need of change. Or John and Mary seek help because they cannot deal with the pressure they are getting from their parents; they want support for their decision to live together without a marriage license.

As these examples suggest, there are differences between conformity to others and the conformity of others. In numerous cases, social service workers earnestly believe that people should conform, for their own well-being and that of the society. None would justify murder as a way of liberation from the antimurder norms of society. Most would insist that employers and landlords conform to laws and regulations prohibiting discrimination against women and minorities. There are also many cases where social service workers earnestly believe that society should conform to individuals' expectations about rights and opportunities. Most believe that it ought to be possible for women to share the occupational status and pay men can achieve. Most also would not insist on respect for traditional expectations about the roles of husband and wife; they would not expect all women to stay home, mind the children, and care for their working husbands.

When conflicts exist in the needs and interests of individuals, mediation in the form of negotiation and compromise is often required. In this process the concern is for the goodness of fit, or the fit between the person and the environment. The role of the social service worker is to negotiate the boundary, that is, the line between individuals and the expectations of others.

Toward an Integrated Approach to Normality

Normality as average, as health, and as utopia are three independent yet not completely distinct types of normality. Each can have its uses in the assessment of individual functioning, and the types may be combined in an eclectic approach. But the notion of normality as transaction refers not so much to a type of normality as to a source of normality. Individuals come to be considered normal or to have achieved normality as a function of the transactions that take place between them and their social environments. Transactions between individuals and environments, in fact, generate all three types of normality. As a result of transactions with others, an individual may turn out to be normal, or, like most others, to be surviving without any serious disorders, or to be near perfect (see "Normality: Source, Domains, and Types").

The Transactional Context of Psychological Normality

Normality is a social construction of reality. What is average, what is healthy adaptation, and what is utopian are all defined by individuals in their interaction with other individuals in the context of groups, families, communities, and organizations. David Karp and William Yoels point out

> The sociological study of everyday interactions analyzes how persons through their communication with others socially construct and use the meanings which they then confer on things. The existence of shared meaning structures, that is to say, common definitions of social reality, must be assumed, but not all social groups construct identical versions of reality.[59]

Normality: Source, Domains, and Types

Definitions of the concept of normality involve both characteristics of individuals and transactions between individuals and their social environments. Because both the biophysical and psychological domains affect individual psychological functioning, they influence the extent to which the individual achieves normality by any definition.

		Types of Normality		
Source of Normality	Domains of Normality	As Average	As Health	As Utopia
Transactions in the social environment	Biophysical Psychological Cognitive Motivational-Affective Behavioral	Like most others	Without disorder	Near perfect

---

A focus on the transactions between individuals and their social environment demonstrates the variability of many aspects of normality, which can differ according to cultural traditions and historical periods, interpersonal expectations, and, indeed, particular persons. Psychological normality, whether defined as average, health, or utopia, is a social construction of reality which changes from culture to culture, from one historical moment to the next, from one specific interpersonal situation to another, and from one person's thoughts and beliefs to another's. As such, there are no behaviors, emotions, or beliefs, in and of themselves, that are inherently normal or, for that matter, abnormal.

Normality and Disability

The normality of the disabled seems to be a contradiction in terms. A physically, cognitively, or emotionally disabled person, by definition, would appear to be deficient in health and to vary from statistical averages. Yet because of interpersonal transactions currently taking place in groups, families, communities, and organizations, a new social construction of reality is taking form which is reshaping American culture (see "A Disabled Child's Mother Speaks Out"). The belief that normality must be redefined to include people with disabilities was embodied in public policy with passage of the federal Americans with Disabilities Act of 1990. Implementation of the act, which bans discrimination on the basis of physical or mental disability in employment, public accommodations, transportation, or telecommunications services, is reinforcing this construction of social reality in American society.

The term *disability* is itself a social construction of reality; just what is and is not a disability is an issue that is being openly debated. Two overlapping types of the disabled have been identified. A **physical disability** is any kind of physical impairment brought about in any way. Medical definitions consider as physically disabled those who have

Supporters cheer a young woman as she competes in a Special
Olympics event. Changing public attitudes have promoted the idea of
mainstreaming people with physical and developmental disabilities
into activities others take for granted.

experienced "chronic disease leading to various courses of treatment" and those who suffer from postpolio complications, cerebral palsy, epilepsy, and so on.[60] The physically disabled also can include people who have suffered from accidents and are not able to complete certain physical functions connected with work and everyday living or people who
have experienced an illness or a birth-related defect which has left them chronically impaired. A **developmental disability** is a severe or chronic disability which is attributable
to mental or physical impairment, manifested before the person attains 22 years of age,
and likely to continue indefinitely.[61] Developmental disabilities may include severe, moderate, and mild forms, but usually only the more serious handicaps require intervention.
Nevertheless, developmental and physical disabilities both can limit individuals' abilities
in the areas of self-care, receptive and expressive language, learning, mobility, self-direction, capacity for independent living, and economic self-sufficiency.

People with disabilities used to be essentially cut off from society. Labels such as *in-
valid* or *crippled* were applied as a way of indicating their status as abnormal. In definitions today, the more likely argument is that people with disabilities are a minority or
disadvantaged group that has experienced systematic prejudice and discrimination. As
William Roth observes:

In the psychosocial model, disability is related to society. It is not taken for granted that medical illness, economic definition, or functional limitation by themselves say what is significant

---

A Disabled Child's Mother Speaks Out

Rosemary Alexander, the mother of a developmentally disabled child, has been an advocate for families with disabled children. As a way of improving the relationship between social service workers and these parents, she wrote (with Patricia Tompkins-McGill) the following plea to workers to treat her son as much as possible as a human being with normal potential:

See my child in more than one dimension. Each specialist tends to evaluate a patient in terms of that specialty alone. A developmental specialist looks for signs of abnormal development....That is what I need you to do and what I pay you to do. However, also remember that my child is a person whom I love. I see his or her endearing traits as well as the problems. You evaluate along one scale, but I cherish things that are on no scale. Treat my child as a many-faceted human being, not just a one-dimensional problem with a single label. . . .

Judge my child in terms of his or her own progress. Your job is to judge my child against your set of norms. Problems are measured in contrast to a norm, and you must tell me how my child is not "normal," but also remember to view my child in terms of what progress he or she has made.

For example, my child is a year behind in most areas of development; by comparison with the norms he is "developmentally delayed." We can live with this problem more easily, however, if we also judge how much more self-sufficient he is now than he was a year ago. On this first birthday, he was struggling to learn to sit up. This year, on his second birthday, he sits up as if this action had never been a problem. Now he struggles with walking. Realizing that progress gives me great hope, a commodity that I need every day.

Source: Rosemary Alexander and Patricia Tompkins-McGill, "Notes to the Experts from the Parent of a Handicapped Child," *Social Work*, July–August, 1987, p. 361.

---

about disability. Rather, what is significant can be revealed only by the ecological framework in which the disabled person exists, by the interactions through which society engages a disability, by the attitudes that others hold, and by the architecture, means of transportation, and social organization constructed by the able-bodied.[62]

As a consequence of changing social definitions and the legal prohibition of discrimination against people with disabilities, progress is being made toward mainstreaming them or including them with people of normal capabilities in the mainstream of society. Instead of being segregated in a protective environment, they are being viewed as capable of performing within the range of normalcy in classrooms, workplaces, and living arrangements.[63]

∽ IMPLICATIONS FOR PRACTICE

Social service practice theory is concerned with prevention or amelioration and the use of logical, problem-solving process to give help to clients. In their practice, social workers try to help people achieve some state of normalcy in their lives. This may mean achieving some kind of average state or the ability to function adequately or even maximally; for the disabled, it may mean normalizing behavior or achieving the ability to participate in society.

The problem-solving process applied in the social services has been described in diverse terms such as "the basic helping approach" or "practice skill areas," but the underlying process is the same.[64] The first step in problem solving is assessment, that is, making an accurate determination of the problems and needs and the strengths and resources of clients. The second step is determining the objectives of the intervention and formulating a plan for reaching them. The third step is putting into practice intervention strategies designed to resolve the problem and meet the need. And the last step is evaluating the intervention to determine if its objectives have been met.

The use of terms such as *steps* to describe the problem-solving process is itself a heuristic or problem-solving mechanism. In actual practice the steps blend, merge, and overlap and problem solving is more a circular process than a linear one. It is not unusual to reach one step and find that it is necessary to go back over the whole process again. For example, determining the exact problems or needs of clients and constituencies sometimes requires three or four reviews. A social worker, for instance, may think she understands a presenting problem, but as she tries to put a plan for resolving it into operation she comes to see that her understanding is off target.

The Assessment Phase of Problem Solving

Assessment, the process by which social workers come to identify and understand the problems and needs presented by clients, may be thought of as the first step in the helping process. When the client is an individual, assessment therefore necessarily takes that individual into account. But an individual is a system, and a systems approach specifies that the state or condition of a system, at any point in time, is a function of the interaction between it and the environment in which it operates. Put another way, the needs and problems of individual clients are always a function of things about these individuals and things about the environment in which they live.

Yet, from a critical perspective, assessing the individual raises the specter of blaming the victim. Does trying to determine the things about an individual that may be creating needs and problems mean taking a "person-centered" approach? Certainly not. A **person-centered approach** blames the victim when it only looks for deficiencies and weaknesses in clients and ignores examining the way in which the environment also creates needs and problems.

Social workers can avoid blaming the victim in assessing clients by adopting a multicentered approach or a transactional approach. Another way to avoid blaming the victim is by emphasizing the client's own strengths and resources.

A Multicentered Approach

A **multicentered approach** examines the ways person and environment contribute independently to the presenting problem. Such an assessment might determine that both factors are equal contributors or that one is primary and the other is secondary. A lot depends on the situation being analyzed.

For instance, in assessing a situation of wife abuse and child abuse by a husband and father, it is likely that the primary contributor is the abuser, his personality, his early life socialization into the male role, the stress he is under at work, an illness or disability he may have, or his own low self-esteem and need for power. But the child or the wife might also be contributing to the situation, due to their innocence, trust in the abuser, lack of knowledge about alternatives, or dependence on the abuser for financial and emotional support.

A similar situation might prevail in assessing unemployment among minority individuals. In the case of Maria Santos described in Chapter 1, we might conclude that problems of racism or problems in the economy and in the health-care system are primarily responsible for the condition in which she finds herself. But we might also note that her lack of knowledge of resources and lack of education are making her easy prey of a system looking for victims.

Nevertheless, there are many problems in which the contributions of the person and the environment are pretty much equal. The adage "It takes two to tangle" is probably not too far off the mark when we think about most cases of domestic conflict, conflict between parents and children, and conflict between friends.

A Transactional Approach

Whereas the multicentered approach examines the independent contributions of person and environment, a **transactional approach** looks at **person in environment**, or person and environment simultaneously. A transactional approach requires all the parties in the transaction to be together so that the worker can observe the transactions between them. A social worker analyzing the problem a son is having with his mother, a wife with her husband, a student with his teacher, or a worker with her boss would have to make some direct observations of the transactions in order to assess them properly. The transactional approach is particularly well suited to analyzing interpersonal or small-group communication problems.

A Strengths Approach

Assessments can take into account the strengths as well as the problems of individuals. The multicentered and transactional approaches do this by balancing the assessment of deficits with an assessment of strengths. Another possibility is to use a **strengths approach** and consider clients' situations entirely in terms of their own strengths and resources.

Ann Weick and her associates challenge the need to examine deficits at all, advocating instead what they refer to as "a strengths perspective."[65] In their view, any focus on deficits encourages a person-centered assessment which ensnares social workers in a strategy of working only on the deficits. There is a bias toward identifying and analyzing deficits that makes it difficult to imagine a practice in which only the strengths and resources of clients are examined. Nevertheless, these authors propose that it can be accomplished by focusing exclusively on clients' physical, behavioral, cognitive, and motivational capacities. The question social workers should be asking, therefore, is "not what kind of a life one has had, but what kind of a life one wants, and then bringing to bear all the personal and social resources available to accomplish this goal."[66]

Assessing the Person in Environment

Regardless of whether social workers examine only strengths or also examine deficits, their assessments must be made in terms of fundamental domains making up the individual as a system. Assessment focuses on biophysical states and processes as well as those in the cognitive, motivational-affective, and behavioral domain. It may combine these factors in examining attitudes and values or in looking at the entire personality, the self, or the identity of the person.

In any assessment, individuals cannot be divorced from the environments in which they live out their lives. To focus only on the individual is likely to lead to victim blaming. This is clear with regard to examining deficits, but it is equally true in examining strengths. To the extent that only the strengths in individual clients are considered, they may inadvertently be led to believe that they have all the power within themselves to do anything they wish. They may conclude that there are no socially induced obstacles they need worry about and that the real world outside is of no consequence. This is tantamount to advancing the concept of rugged individualism, based on the idea that people stand or fall solely on the basis of their personal capacities. Examining strengths and deficits of individuals, therefore, means examining them within the context of specific transactions or specific environments.

An examination of the subjective environment, however, is not the same as an examination of the objective environment. The study of subjective environments is, in the end, person-centered, for they only tell us about the environment from the point of view of the client. While this is certainly necessary, it does not eliminate the need to examine the environment in a more objective way: from observation of the other individuals, groups, and organizations that comprise it, or from observation of the functioning of society, its norms, institutions, social arrangements, and the status and roles people take in them. These topics are the focus or the next chapter.

⌘ DISCUSSION QUESTIONS AND CLASS PROJECTS

1. In reviewing Gordon's theory of human nature, notice that he says nothing about a "spiritual nature." To what extent do you believe that humans are spiritual by nature? To what extent do you believe that humans are spiritual because of learning?

2. Define what is meant by the term *a system*. Give at least four specific examples of human systems.

3. What does the research literature say about innate differences between men and women?

4. Systems are made up of parts or elements. List and describe the internal components of the individual as a system discussed in this chapter.

5. Do growth and change in human systems always follow a progressive path?

6. Describe and give examples of the following concepts: homeostasis, feedback, steady state, equifinality.

7. Why is the study of biophysical processes important to the study of human behavior?

8. List and describe the common attributional errors, effects, and biases. To what extent do you think they are common in your own thinking? How might you help others overcome such biases?

9. Describe the four meanings of normality described in this chapter. Give examples of each.

10. What do you see as the strengths and weaknesses of each type of normality?

11. Distinguish between type of normality and source of normality.

12. How would you explain the table in "Normality: Source, Domains, and Types"? How might it be useful in helping you think about assessing individual functioning?

13. Distinguish among the multicentered, transactional, and strengths approaches to assessment.

∞ NOTES

1. Some of the more popular texts have been Allen Pincus and Anne Minahan, *Social Work Practice: Model and Method* (Itasca, IL: F.E. Peacock Publishers, 1973); Carol Germain and Alex Gitterman, *The Life Model of Social Work Practice* (New York: Columbia University Press, 1980); and Ralph E. Anderson and Irl Carter, *Human Behavior in the Social Environment: A Social Systems Approach*, 4th ed. (Hawthorne, NY: Aldine de Gruyter, 1990).

2. Jonathan Turner, *The Structure of Sociological Theory*, rev. ed. (Homewood, IL: Dorsey Press, 1978).

3. Gordon Hearn, *Theory Building in Social Work* (Toronto, Ontario: University of Toronto Press, 1958), pp. 38–51; Germain and Gitterman, *Life Model of Social Work Practice*.

4. Genevieve De Hoyos and Claigh Jensen, "The System Approach in American Social Work," *Social Casework*, Vol. 66 (October 1985), pp. 490–96.

5. Anderson and Carter, *Human Behavior in Social Environment*, p. 1.

6. Ludwig von Bertalanffy, *General Systems Theory*, rev. ed. (New York: George Braziller, 1968), p. 208.

7. Burrhas F. Skinner, *Beyond Freedom and Dignity* (New York: Alfred A. Knopf, 1971); Ruth Benedict, *Patterns of Culture*, 2nd ed. (Boston: Houghton Mifflin, 1959).

8. For readings in sociobiology, see Edward O. Wilson, *On Human Nature* (Cambridge, MA: Harvard University Press, 1978), and T. H. Clutton-Brock and Paul H. Harvey (editors), *Readings in Sociobiology* (San Francisco: W. H. Freeman, 1978).

9. Robert Plomin, "The Role of Inheritance in Behavior," *Science*, Vol. 248 (April 1990), pp. 183–88.

10. Ronald Fernandez, *The I, The Me, and You: An Introduction to Social Psychology* (New York: Frederick A. Praeger, 1977), p. 20.

11. Pierre L. van den Berghe, *Man in Society: A Biosocial View*, 2nd ed. (New York: Elsevier, 1978), p. 34.

12. Harvey L. Gochros, "Sexuality," in *Encyclopedia of Social Work*, 18th ed. (Silver Spring, MD: National Association of Social Workers, 1987), Vol. 2, p. 581.

13. Milton M. Gordon, *Human Nature, Class, and Ethnicity* (New York: Oxford University Press, 1978), pp. 48–64.

14. John Money and Patricia Tucker, *Sexual Signatures: On Being a Man or a Woman* (Boston: Little, Brown, 1975), p. 38.

15. Janet A. Nex and Peter Iadicola, "Toward a Definition of Feminist Social Work: A Comparison of Liberal, Radical, and Socialist Models," *Social Work*, Vol. 34 (January 1989), p. 13.

16. Eleanor Maccoby and Carol Jacklin, *The Psychology of Sex Differences* (Stanford, CA: Stanford University Press, 1974).

17. Carol Gilligan, *In a Different Voice: Psychological Theory and Women's Development* (Cambridge, MA: Harvard University Press, 1982).

18. Deborah Tannen, *That's Not What I Meant!: How Conversational Style Makes or Breaks Your Relations with Others* (New York: William Morrow, 1986), and Tannen, *You Just Don't Understand: Women and Men in Conversation* (New York: William Morrow, 1990).

19. Marie Richmond-Abbott, *Masculine and Feminine: Sex Roles over the Life Cycle* (New York: Newberry Award Records, 1983), pp. 41-81.

20. Ruth Bleier, *Science and Gender: A Critique of Biology and Its Theories on Women* (New York: Pergamon Press, 1984), p. 12.

21. Ibid., p. 52.

22. Julia B. Rauch, "Social Work and the Genetics Revolution: Genetic Services," *Social Work*, Vol. 33 (September–October 1988), pp. 389–91.

23. Ibid., p. 389.

24. Edward H. Taylor, "The Biological Basis of Schizophrenia," *Social Work*, Vol. 32 (March–April 1987), pp. 115–21.

25. Susan T. Fiske and Shelley E. Taylor, *Social Cognition*, 2nd ed. (New York: McGraw-Hill, 1990).

26. Stanley L. Witkin, "Cognitive Processes in Clinical Practice," *Social Work*, Vol. 27 (September 1982), pp. 389–95.

27. Fritz Heider, *The Psychology of Interpersonal Relations* (New York: John Wiley and Sons, 1958).

28. S. M. Kassin and John B. Pryor, "The Development of Attribution Processes," in J. B. Pryor and J. Day (editors), *The Development of Social Cognition* (New York: Springer-Verlag, 1985), pp. 3–34.

29. Fiske and Taylor, *Social Cognition*, pp. 66–95.

30. Ibid., p. 68.

31. Nora Gold, "Motivation: The Crucial But Unexplored Component of Social Work Practice," *Social Work*, Vol. 35 (January 1990), pp. 49–53.

32. Abraham H. Maslow, *Motivation and Personality* (New York: Harper & Row, 1954), pp. 80–92.

33. Ibid., pp. 90, 92.

34. Bruce A. Theyer, "Contingency Analysis: Toward a Unified Theory for Social Work Practice," *Social Work*, Vol. 32 (March–April 1987), pp. 151–57.

35. Paul B. Baltes, "Life-Span Developmental Psychology: Some Converging Observations on History and Theory," in P. B. Baltes and O. G. Brim

(editors), *Life Span Development and Behavior*, Vol. 2 (New York: Academic Press, 1979), p. 263.

36. See the discussion of the work of W. B. Cannon in Ludwig von Bertalanffy, *General System Theory*, rev. ed. (New York: George Braziller, 1968), pp. 160–63.

37. Von Bertalanffy, *General Systems Theory*, pp. 156–60.

38. Anderson and Carter, *Human Behavior in Social Environment*, pp. 56, 263.

39. Ibid., p. 26.

40. Gail Kadison Golden, "Attachment—Not Dependence," *Social Work*, Vol. 35 (March 1990), p. 101.

41. Salvador Minuchin et al., *Families of the Slums: An Exploration of Their Structure and Treatment* (New York: Basic Books, 1967).

42. Gordon Hearn, "General Systems Theory and Social Work," in F. J. Turner (editor), *Social Work Treatment: Interlocking Theoretical Approaches*, 2nd ed. (New York: Free Press, 1979), pp. 333–59.

43. Daniel Offer and Melvin Sabshin (editors), *Normality and the Life Cycle: A Critical Integration* (New York: Basic Books, 1984), pp. xii–xiii.

44. Ibid., p. xii; italics in original.

45. See Gerald L. Klerman and Myrna M. Weissman, "An Epidemiologic View of Mental Illness, Mental Health, and Normality," in Offer and Sabshin (editors), *Normality and the Life Cycle*, p. 341.

46. Emile Durkheim, *Suicide* (New York: Free Press, 1951).

47. Robert E. L. Faris and H. Warren Dunham, *Mental Health Disorders in Urban Areas: An Ecological Study of Schizophrenia and Other Psychoses* (Chicago: University of Chicago Press, 1967).

48. Klerman and Weissman, "Epidemiologic View of Mental Illness," pp. 328, 331, 333.

49. Thomas Szasz, *The Myth of Mental Illness* (New York: Harper & Row, 1961).

50. Christopher Lasch, *The Minimal Self: Psychic Survival in Troubled Times* (New York: W. W. Norton, 1984).

51. William Glasser, *Reality Therapy* (New York: Harper & Row, 1965), p. 41.

52. Daniel Offer and Melvin Sabshin, "Patterns of Normal Development," in Offer and Sabshin (editors), *Normality and the Life Cycle*, p. 412.

53. Daniel Offer and Melvin Sabshin, "Implications and New Directions," in Offer and Sabshin (editors), *Normality and the Life Cycle*, p. 428.

54. This idea is expressed in Bennett L. Leventhal and Kenneth Dawson, "Middle Childhood: Normality as Integration and Interaction," in Offer and Sabshin (editors), *Normality and the Life Cycle*, p. 31.

55. Anthony N. Maluccio, *Promoting Competence in Clients: A New/Old Approach to Social Work Practice* (New York: Free Press, 1981). The writings of Robert W. White include "Motivation Reconsidered: The Concept of Competence," *Psychological Review*, Vol. 66 (September 1959), pp. 297–333, and "Competence and the Psychosexual Stages of Development," in M. Jones (editor), *Nebraska Symposium on Motivation* (Lincoln: University of Nebraska Press, 1960), pp. 97–141.

56. Elaine B. Pinderhughes, "Empowerment for Our Clients and for Ourselves," *Social Casework*, Vol. 64 (June 1983), pp. 331–38.

57. Eric Fromm, *Escape from Freedom* (New York: Avon Books, 1965), p. 159.

58. See Robert N. Emde and James F. Scorce, "Infancy: Perspectives on Normality," in Offer and Sabshin (editors), *Normality and the Life Cycle*, p. 4.

59. David A. Karp and William C. Yoels, *Sociology in Everyday Life*, 2nd ed. (Itasca, IL: F. E. Peacock Publishers, 1993), p. 38.

60. William Roth, "Disabilities: Physical," in *Encyclopedia of Social Work*, Vol. 1, pp. 434–48.

61. Lynn McDonald-Wickler, "Disabilities: Developmental," in *Encyclopedia of Social Work*, Vol. 1, pp. 422–34.

62. Roth, "Disabilities: Physical," p. 434.

63. Emde and Scorce, "Infancy," p. 21.

64. Max Siporin, *Introduction to Social Work Practice* (New York: Macmillan, 1975), pp. 17–36; Pincus and Minahan, *Social Work Practice*.

65. Ann Weick, Charles Rapp, W. Patrick Sullivan, and Walter Kisthardt, "A Strengths Perspective for Social Work Practice," *Social Work*, Vol. 34 (July 1989), pp. 350–54.

66. Ibid., p. 353.

Person in Environment

Social Systems and Social Roles

MAJOR THEMES DISCUSSED IN THIS CHAPTER

1. **PHYSICAL AND SOCIAL ENVIRONMENTS.** Individuals' lives are interdependent with their environments, both the physical environment (the geographical and spatial context in which people live) and the social environment (the other individuals, groups, organizations, communities, and institutions in which they live). Social service workers deal primarily with the social environment which functions for individuals as a source of strength as well as a source of trouble.

2. **SOCIAL SYSTEMS.** Social systems, the basic elements in a social environment, are composed of individuals who share a common identity, who are held together by social norms and institutions, and who are organized in terms of roles and statuses. The competing forces of stability and conflict in social systems are always present in both primary and secondary groups.

3. **NORMS AND INSTITUTIONS.** Social norms, or shared agreements, hold a system together, regulate it, and give it order and purpose. Norms are experienced by individuals as expectations, both of themselves and others, for proper behavior, and they are constantly being revised as individuals define them in their interactions. Some norms, known as social institutions, represent standardized, authorized ways of meeting people's needs and dealing with their problems. Other types of norms, known as institutional arrangements, reflect agreements that characterize all social institutions. They include symbols, cultures, and status divisions.

4. **ROLES: PERSON MEETS ENVIRONMENT.** Individuals are tied to social systems through their roles and statuses, that is, the social positions they occupy. Roles can be defined from the point of view of others in the system (the prescribed role), the individual (the perceived role), or the behaviors of people in the roles (the enacted role). There are everyday roles in family, group, and work life, and master roles and statuses which connect individuals to the institutional structures of society. The basic transactions between the individual and the social environment are recruitment, socialization, interaction, innovation, and control.

5. **IMPLICATIONS FOR PRACTICE.** To meet the need for a diagnostic tool that fully takes the social environment into account, social workers have been developing *The Person in Environment Manual* to use instead of or together with the *Diagnostic and Statistical Manual* of the American Psychiatric Association. But both of these approaches are problem-focused and tend to overlook the strengths in clients' social environments, which can be determined with the social network assessment strategy.

This sculpture on the campus of Portland State University in Oregon is
a conceptualization of the holon, which expresses the idea that every
social system is simultaneously a whole and a part of a whole. It is
dedicated to Gordon Hearn, the founding dean of the School of Social
Work there, who was largely responsible for introducing the systems
perspective into social work.

IN STUDYING SYSTEMS, perhaps the most important fact is that every system is a **holon**; it
is a whole—a unit unto itself—and a part of a whole, both at the same time. Human systems, therefore, do not exist in isolation. The idea that an individual comes to have a
self-conscious identity clearly acknowledges the presence of an environment. There can
be no "I" without an "it," "you," "he," "she," and "they." The same can be said of social systems. Families, for instance, are systems, and they do not live in isolation. They have a social boundary (as indicated by the "we" and the "they"), and they must interact with those
other systems—extended kin, schools, places of work and business, churches, government agencies—that lie outside their boundary and make up their environment. In this
chapter we examine social systems as units and as contexts for understanding the individual as a system.

✆ PHYSICAL AND SOCIAL ENVIRONMENTS

As human systems, individuals can only be understood within the context of their physical and social environments. The **physical environment** of a system is the geographically or spatially structured context in which it exists, and the **social environment** of a system is its location within a socially and historically determined context. Social service workers are usually, although certainly not always, concerned with social environments—the interactions among individuals and groups of individuals. The emphasis in this book is on the social context of system behavior, but the physical environment cannot be ignored.

The Physical Environment

For individuals and social systems, the physical environment refers to a whole range of conditions having to do with the material structure and organization surrounding them. It can refer to the geography and climate in which people live or to dimensions of their residence or location in cities, suburbs, or rural areas. It can describe the housing in which people live: private homes, condominiums, privately owned or rented apartments, subsidized public housing, hotels and other residences, or even on the streets with no permanent residence. The condition known as homelessness is one of the most difficult social problems demanding solutions in American society today.

Homelessness as Private Trouble and Public Issue

Most people take for granted that they will live in a stable household in comfortable surroundings, with a roof over their heads and their own kitchens, baths, and beds. Yet for many in the United States, this is not the case; they are, in fact, homeless. The size of the homeless population is unknown, but in 1990 it was estimated that anywhere from 300,000 to 3 million Americans were living without homes or shelter. The homeless are a diverse group. In most cities the majority are single men, but in some they are families with children. There are also sizable numbers of women alone and young people. Because homeless people usually reflect the ethnic and racial composition of the cities and regions where they take refuge, white people, people of color, and rural and urban populations are all found among the homeless.[1]

Research has determined that for individuals and families, the physical circumstances of being homeless wreak havoc on their ability to function or well-being.[2] Most homeless people are unemployed and have little or no income or resources. They are likely to suffer from health problems, both physical and mental, and to exhibit problem behaviors associated with alcohol and drug addiction. For women, the effects of homelessness are likely to be nervousness, low energy, anger, and loneliness.[3] For children, a possible link has been found between homelessness and cognitive development and performance.[4]

In social work policy and practice, homelessness is often treated as a private trouble, on the assumption that its principal cause is the individual's own condition—most often, unemployment, substance abuse, or illness, particularly mental illness. Direct services are offered to individuals in the hope of overcoming these conditions. But there is a public-issue dimension to homelessness that is often ignored in the development of services. A major reason for homelessness is deinstitutionalization, the movement that promised to remove the mentally ill from institutions and treat them in community-based centers.

The number of residents in state mental health facilities dropped from 552,000 in 1955 to 119,000 in 1990, but enough community clinics and halfway houses were never set up to provide the needed care for those released and programs are nonexistent or underfunded. Up to 30 percent of the homeless in the United States are believed to suffer from serious mental disorders.[5] Another major reason for the rise in homelessness in the 1980s was the decline in availability of low-cost housing. Rents rose twice as fast as the average income, and housing subsidies were cut by 75 percent.[6] The national economy, which in recent years has meant unemployment, underemployment, or lower wages for many workers, is another cause of homelessness.

Homelessness is a feminist issue, due to the relation between its causes and the roles of women and men in society. In a study of male and female users of a social service, Jan Hagen found that the most common reasons for homelessness among both genders were unemployment and interpersonal relations. But she also noted some important differences. Because of their traditional economic and social dependence on men, women were more likely to be homeless as a result of eviction or domestic abuse. Men were likely to be living on the streets as a result of alcohol abuse or jail release.[7]

The Social Environment

The social environment consists of the personal and impersonal relations surrounding individuals and social systems. It includes the individual as a system and the social systems—the other persons and the groups, families, communities, organizations, societies, and nations—with which the individual interacts and which directly or indirectly influence the individual's behavior and development.

Private troubles often arise from conditions in the social environment, not only in the more immediate environment of friends and families but in the larger environment of communities, organizations, and societies as well. Children's self-confidence and sense of well-being, for instance, are influenced by how much they are loved and how well they are treated by their parents, which in turn are influenced by the parents' access to economic and social resources. Similarly, the troubles of members of a racial or ethnic minority or other disadvantaged group may be connected to the prejudice and discrimination against it operating in a society.

Environmental Problems and Strengths

Six major groupings of environmental problems that may be the focus of social work intervention have been identified for the *Person in Environment* diagnostic manual being developed by a task force of the National Association of Social Workers (NASW).[8] These types of problems are:

1. *Economic problems and problems of basic needs*. The troubles experienced by individuals often derive from differences in the ways resources, goods, and services, such as wealth, employment, food and shelter, or transportation are allocated within the economy. Economic problems are implicated in many of the difficulties experienced by older people, people of color, women, and other groups that are the object of institutionalized prejudice and discrimination.

2. *Problems in educational training and attainment*. Schools and other educational resources are manifestly concerned with developing the intellect, encouraging social

The Pros and Cons of Social Support

The support group, based on the principles of self-help and mutuality, is the principal vehicle for providing social support, and it is a potentially powerful form of intervention for clients who share a variety of human troubles. Its use has been recommended for adult female survivors of child sexual abuse and for family members of persons with AIDS, for example.

Such uses stress the positive functions of social support, such as the ability of support groups to reduce a sense of isolation, to instill optimism regarding the future, and to facilitate the development of closer friendships among individuals experiencing similar problems. Groups ideally allow individuals to discuss their deepest fears and anxieties in an atmosphere of trust and respect, and they provide role models for use of the adaptive strategies needed to overcome troubles. Members may profit from experiencing a sense of altruism and reciprocity, of being helped while at the same time helping others. When they leave support groups, it may be with higher self-esteem and confidence and a heightened sense of purpose and belonging.

There are also disadvantages to social support, however, and Robert Schilling believes they have not been given adequate attention. A major issue is that social support systems are not necessarily supportive. Peer group, community, and family support groups may not be helpful because relations in such areas of the social environment are not inherently supportive; in fact, peer pressure, illegitimate neighborhood opportunities, and poor or coercive parenting can create serious problems for those who are caught up in them. Moreover, support systems are generally homogeneous groupings, composed of people from the same socioeconomic class, race, ethnicity, age, gender, or physical or emotional condition, so they do not always offer a wide range of opinions and points of view and may limit rather than expand clients' choices. Support systems can occasionally even be harmful, especially if they underestimate clients' needs and attempt to force them to "face reality" too quickly.

> Every individual does not want to participate in support groups, and some will not benefit from them. Much of the literature on social support groups and networks suggests that everyone requires and needs social support, but many attitudinal and personality factors have to be taken into account. There is some evidence, for instance, that people who are relatively more self-reliant will benefit less from support groups than people who are more other-reliant.

> The use of social support systems therefore cannot be considered a universal solution to the problems with which people must deal.

Sources: Robert F. Schilling II, "Limitation of Social Support," *Social Service Review*, vol. 61 (March 1987), pp. 19–31; Carolyn Knight, "Use of Support Groups with Adult Female Survivors of Child Sexual Abuse," *Social Work*, vol. 35 (May 1990), pp. 202–09; James Kelly and Pamela Sykes, "'Helping the Helpers': A Support Group for Family Members of Persons with AIDS," *Social Work*, vol. 34 (May 1989), pp. 239–42.

skills, and fostering optimal achievement. Troubles arise when educational resources are lacking or when discrimination in the larger society reduces the availability of educational opportunities.

3. *Problems in the judicial and legal system.* People experience troubles when the justice system fails to protect them, or lower-class status, race, gender, age, and other forms of discrimination reduce protections against crime and injury.

4. *Problems in the health-care and social service systems.* People's troubles may be

increased if their access to physical or mental health care or other social services is limited by financial means, regulatory barriers, or the absence or unavailability of services.

5.   *Problems in voluntary associations*. When associations such as religious, community, and other groups that provide for participation in social events and leisure activities are not open to all members of a society, or they are inaccessible, people who are left out experience exclusion, isolation, and loneliness.

6.   *Problems in primary-group relations*. Profound troubles will be experienced by individuals whose primary-group relations—those with families, extended kin, lovers, friends, acquaintances, and coworkers—fail to give support.

But environments also supply the strengths and resources by which troubles may be overcome or at least ameliorated. A family suffering from economic troubles might find strength in the financial support of relatives and the help of friends and neighbors in finding work, or an ethnic community may devise ways to impart courage and a sense of worth to members demoralized by prejudice or discrimination. Thus while social environments can cause trouble, they also can give strength.

Social service workers have pioneered the use of informal systems of social support and social networks to help people who are experiencing troubles. **Social support** has been defined as "the comfort, assistance, and/or information one receives through formal or informal contacts with individuals or groups." **Social networks** involve "the entirety of social links between persons in a finite community of relationships."[9] They are sometimes referred to as *natural helping networks*.[10]

The effectiveness of using the social environment to provide social support, however, is open to question (see "The Pros and Cons of Social Support"). Social service workers need to weigh carefully the possible advantages and disadvantages.

∞ SOCIAL SYSTEMS

The primary element in the social environment is the social system. The smallest social system is the **dyad**, a system composed of only two individuals. Successively larger and more complex systems are the triad, the small group, the family, the community, the bureaucracy or organization, the nation, and the international community. Regardless of size, social systems, like individuals, are dynamic orders of parts and processes standing in mutual interaction.

At their core, social systems are simply collections of individuals, but they are much more than this. The individuals in a social system share a common identity, a "we" and "us" which separates them from outsiders; that is, they have a boundary which is larger than the boundary of any individual in the system. The individuals also are organized in terms of roles and statuses and, especially in complex systems, divided into units or departments, each of which has separate functions. The roles and units making up the system are often organized vertically and horizontally to show authority and power, as in an organizational chart. They are also held together by working agreements, norms, and traditions which give the system its unique culture or way of operating. All the parts of a system are in dynamic interaction with one another, so change and development are constantly taking place.

Social systems are the vehicle through which **transactions** between the individual and society take place. These transactions may be conducted at the interactional or sociocultural level, depending on whether the system is a primary or secondary group.[11]

Interactional-level transactions involve face-to-face contact and relatively deep personal commitments and attachments. The social systems that generate such transactions are usually referred to as **primary groups**, those that are believed to be basic to an individual's identity and personality (see Chapter 12). Examples of primary groups are friends, peers, and family, kin, and other intimate relationships. Communities based on common identities such as nationality, religion, or race and ethnicity may also serve as primary groups.

Sociocultural-level transactions are more impersonal and usually take place within the larger, more complex social systems and institutions making up the environment. Social systems typified by impersonal transactions are referred to as **secondary groups**. The assumption is that, because these groups are less immediately personal, they are less central to the identity and personality of an individual. The needs met by secondary systems are more utilitarian, such as the needs for income and physical comfort. Secondary groups include work organizations, schools, political parties, religions, and other associations in which individuals assume such roles as citizen, producer, consumer, or client.

Stability and Conflict in Social Systems

Social theorists continually debate questions about how much stability or consensus and how much conflict or change can be expected in social systems and what their normal state is. Should social relations be expected to be orderly and harmonious, or could conflict-ridden and chaotic relations be considered normal? Different answers are offered by two sociological perspectives on social systems, functionalism and conflict theory (see "Conflict or Consensus").

In **functional theory**, social systems are said to exist in a relatively continuous state of harmony. Each element making up the system serves a function which assures the maintenance, that is, the survival, of the system, and the functions are coordinated so that the system emerges as a well-integrated whole. Social systems are held together through a consensus of shared norms and values; everyone agrees on the goals and purposes of the system and works hard to achieve them. As a result, conflict and change are looked upon as dysfunctional, a threat to the survival of the system, and conformity is championed as being necessary.[12]

Conflict theory promotes an alternative picture of social systems. Instead of a shared consensus, the elements of a system are said to operate from competitive, self-interested motives. Systems are poorly integrated and riddled with dissension. Interest-group politics predominate, so that change and conflict are the normal state of a system. People in a system are always trying to get others to do what they want so they can shape the system in their own image. Every element contributes to the disintegration rather than the maintenance of the system. Conflict theorists look upon stability and harmony as suspect, a sign of coercion and forced compliance, and an indication of underlying tensions.[13]

In fact, social systems are at the same time riddled with conflict and bathed in the harmony that comes from a consensus on values. The two theories are two sides of the same coin. Depending on which side you look at, social systems can seem to be harmonious and stable or conflict-ridden and chaotic. If you ask yourselves why you are reading this book, for example, you might say, "Because I'm interested in the subject matter and think it will help me become a good social worker." Or you might say, "Because if I don't, I won't pass the exam, and then where will I be?" The first response reflects the functional vision of the world: People do things because they want to do them; they believe in the

Conflict or Consensus: A Comparison of
Functional and Conflict Theories

Assumptions of Functional Theory

1. The working agreements in a system derive from a consensus of shared values
   among the members and units.

2. Every system has a well-integrated social
   organization; each of its elements serves a
   function by contributing to its maintenance.

3. Harmony and stability are the natural
   state or condition of a system.

4. Conflict and change are normal but only
   when they contribute to the ultimate survival of the system and they occur within
   a range of acceptable behaviors.

Assumptions of Conflict Theory

1. The working agreements in a system derive from the ability of some elements to
   make other elements agree with them.

2. Every system is a poorly integrated social
   organization; each element serves a function by contributing to its disintegration.

3. Conflict and change are the natural state
   or condition of a system.

4. Harmony and stability are good only
   when they reflect equity and equality in
   opportunities and outcomes among the
   elements.

Source: Adapted from Ralf Dahrendorf, *Class and Class Conflict in Industrial Society* (Palo Alto, CA: Stanford University Press, 1959), pp. 161–62.

norms and values of the system (in this example, education), and therefore they willingly do what is expected of them. The second response reflects the conflict vision of the
world: People do things because they have to do them; they don't particularly believe in
the system and the way it is organized, but they comply because they don't really see any
alternative. If they could have their way, they would completely alter the system.

In recognition of the need for a synthesis between the two sociological theories on social systems, there has been some merging of the conflict and functional viewpoints.
Functional thinking, in particular, has evolved so that conflict, change, and nonconformity
are not always seen as dysfunctional. Lewis Coser has proposed that conflict serves positive functions. It may draw a group together against a common enemy and thereby promote solidarity, or it may promote innovation and creativity. Conflict also may help the system confront realistic sources of tension; it may help release tensions; or it may encourage
those in positions of power to acknowledge that problems must be confronted.[14]

Functional and conflict theories, however, continue to have different meanings for social service workers. Functional theory forces them to make an assessment of whether
conflict is functional or dysfunctional. They must always be concerned about the survival
of the system they are working with. Conflict theory puts no such constraints on workers,
since it asserts that all conflict, regardless of whether it leads to the survival or the disintegration of a social system, is positive.

Conflict and the Critical Perspective

The argument for the positive functions of conflict is inherent in a critical approach to
practice. Certainly social service workers ought to be concerned about the survival of social systems. Conflict and change create a great deal of havoc for people, and numerous

unintended negative consequences are possible. Yet every social system, and the norms, roles, and institutions within it, is not worth maintaining. Many workers are committed to ending racism and sexism and the classism that supports a free-market economy. They believe these systems are not worthy of saving in some steady state and should be totally transformed.

Recognition of the importance of system-disintegrating as well as system-maintaining functions goes right to the heart of a critical approach to social service practice. To the extent that workers concern themselves only with the survival needs of social systems, they inadvertently limit change and reinforce the status quo. Jeffry Galper's definition of social work as "conservative politics" focuses on precisely this issue. He argues that too much of the attention of social workers is directed to assuring the maintenance and survival of existing systems and too little is directed to system change and disintegration.[15]

✎ NORMS AND INSTITUTIONS

Social systems are collections of individuals who are held together by norms and values regarding human behavior and social interaction. Some of these norms become institutionalized within the system as standardized, authorized ways of meeting people's needs and dealing with their problems. Norms and institutions, together with roles and statuses (discussed in the next section), are the principal characteristics of social systems.

Social Norms

The most important attributes of a social system are the norms that hold it together. **Social norms** consist of all the agreements, formal or informal, explicit or implicit, which regulate and give order and purpose to a system, be it a primary or secondary group. Examples include goals and objectives; values and ideologies; traditions, lifestyles, and folkways or mores; dogmas, laws, policies, and procedures; and rules, regulations, obligations, and duties. Social norms are experienced by individuals as expectations, the expectations of other people as well as the expectations that emerge from the self as a function of participation with other people. A person entering the social work profession, for instance, is expected to abide by a set of professional ethics which have been collectively agreed to (see "Social Work Professional Ethics").

An example of social norms on a larger organizational scale is the Bill of Rights, the first ten amendments to the United States Constitution, passed by Congress in September 1789 and ratified in December 1791. For about 200 years, these amendments, setting forth the rules by which the power of government is to be limited and the rights of citizens are to be protected, have guided the political organization of the United States. The first amendment, for instance, is:

> Congress shall make no law respecting an establishment of religion, or prohibiting the free exercise thereof; or abridging the freedom of speech, or of the press; or the right of the people peaceably to assemble, and to petition the Government for a redress of grievances.

Norms evolve through democratic as well as nondemocratic processes. People sometimes earnestly believe in the agreements that regulate their transactions, but other times they experience them as coercive. Norms give stability and a sense of unity to social sys-

Social Work Professional Ethics: An Example of Social Norms

Code of Ethics adopted by the 1979 Delegate Assemble of the National Association of Social Workers

Preamble

This code is intended to serve as a guide to the everyday conduct of members of the social work profession and as a basis for the adjudication of issues in ethics when the conduct of social workers is alleged to deviate from the standards expressed or implied in this code....

Summary of Major Principles

I.   The Social Worker's Conduct and Comportment as a Social Worker

    A.   Propriety. The social worker should maintain high standards of personal conduct in the capacity or identity as social worker.

    B.   Competence and Professional Development. The social worker should strive to become and remain proficient in professional practice and the performance of professional functions.

    C.   Service. The social worker should regard as primary the service obligation of the social work profession.

    D.   Integrity. The social worker should act in accordance with the highest standards of professional integrity.

    E.   Scholarship and Research. The social worker engaged in study and research should be guided by the conventions of scholarly inquiry.

II. The Social Worker's Ethical Responsibility to Clients.

    F.   Primacy of Clients' Interests. The social worker's primary responsibility is to clients.

    G.   Rights and Prerogatives of Clients. The social worker should make every effort to foster maximum self-determination on the part of clients.

    H.   Confidentiality and Privacy. The social worker should respect the privacy of clients and hold in confidence all information obtained in the course of professional service.

    I.   Fees. When setting fees, the social worker should ensure that they are fair, reasonable, considerate, and

tems but are also a major source of conflict in them. For this reason, all norms are best thought of as working agreements which are continually being invented, worked out, debated, and negotiated.

Social Institutions

In large industrial societies such as the United States, there are certain kinds of norms known as **social institutions** which include clusters or orders of social systems sharing similar functions. Gerhard and Jean Lenski note that institutions develop in the following way: "Because human societies have so many needs, and because these needs persist over long periods of time, every society develops more or less standardized and traditional ways of dealing with them. These 'continuing answers' to 'continuing problems' are known as institutions and institutional systems."[16]

But social institutions are not just standardized and traditional ways of dealing with problems. As Hans Gerth and C. Wright Mills point out, social institutions are the orga-

commensurate with the service performed and with due regard for the clients' ability to pay.

III. The Social Worker's Ethical Responsibility to Colleagues

J.   Respect, Fairness, and Courtesy. The social worker should treat colleagues with respect, courtesy, fairness, and good faith.

K.   Dealing with Colleagues' Clients. The social worker has the responsibility to relate to the clients of colleagues with full professional consideration.

IV. The Social Worker's Ethical Responsibility to Employers and Employing Organizations.

L.   Commitments to Employing Organizations. The social worker should adhere to commitments made to the employing organizations.

V.   The Social Worker's Ethical Responsibility to the Social Work Profession

M.   Maintaining the Integrity of the Profession. The social worker should uphold and advance the values, ethics, knowledge, and mission of the profession.

N.   Community Service. The social worker should assist the profession in making social services available to the general public.

O.   Development of Knowledge. The social worker should take responsibility for identifying, developing, and fully utilizing knowledge for professional practice.

VI. The Social Worker's Ethical Responsibility to Society

P.   Promoting the General Welfare. The social worker should promote the general welfare of society.

Source: Adapted from Appendix 1, "Code of Ethics of the National Association of Social Workers," in *Encyclopedia of Social Work*, 18th ed. (Silver Spring, MD: National Association of Social Workers, 1987), pp. 951–56.

nization of roles and systems that are "guaranteed by authority."[17] Institutions are considered the correct way to deal with problems, and those who choose not to follow them or who wish to alter them can expect that social control will be applied to ensure that the organization remains intact.

Social institutions are usually discussed in terms of the common, manifest functions they serve for society as a whole. Gerth and Mills describe five major institutional orders in industrial societies:

1. The *political order*, which regulates the distribution of power and authority.

2. The economy or *economic order*, which regulates the production and distribution of goods and resources.

3. The *military order*, which regulates the legitimate use of violence.

4. The *kinship order*, or marriage and the family, which regulates sexual behavior, procreation, and the rearing of children.

5. The *religious order*, which regulates the worship of God or other deities.[18]

No place in the United States, not even in front of the
White House, is entirely free of the vexing problem of
homeless people. Their presence is a constant reminder of
the limitations of our economic and political institutions.

Other institutional orders could be added to this list. The welfare order, for instance,
might express the traditional and authoritative ways developed by the society to deal with
problems of individual functioning.

Because social institutions are experienced by individuals through their participation in specific primary and secondary groups, they influence individuals profoundly.
Being norms, they come into individuals' cognitive and emotional systems as expectations for proper behavior. The United States is a representative democracy, with a profit-making, achievement-oriented, free-market or capitalist economy and a Judeo-Christian religious tradition. It is a society with a kinship order that is oriented to the nuclear
family and heterosexual coupling and is somewhat patriarchal in its authority structure.
Young people are instructed in the "correct ways" of participating in American society and
are expected to conform to them. Those who do not or cannot succeed in meeting the expectations generated by social institutions are likely to experience difficulties in their
personal lives. Social service workers often are involved in helping people cope with the
expectations of social institutions.

Institutionalized Social Arrangements

There are other kinds of social norms which pervade society but do not necessarily reflect an ordering of functions. Rather, they reflect agreements that crosscut and therefore characterize all social institutions. Like institutions, however, they are guaranteed by authority and represent continuing solutions to continuing problems. These norms are referred to as institutionalized social arrangements, or **institutional arrangements**.

Symbols and cultural backgrounds are major examples of such arrangements. In the United States, for instance, American English, derived from a northern European cultural heritage, is the valued and sanctioned way for people to express themselves verbally and in writing. Although the United States has no "official" language, it is very hard for a person who is not fluent in English to function adequately in the United States. All laws are written in English, business transactions take place in English, English is the language of most educational instruction and the mass media, religious services are largely conducted in English, and social services are primarily delivered in English.

Other institutional arrangements are status hierarchies in society which represent working agreements about the distribution of wealth, power, and prestige. In many societies, hierarchies are institutionalized around socioeconomic opportunities and the prestige and privilege associated with race, ethnicity, gender, age, or sexual orientation.

Institutional arrangements, like social norms more generally, create stability in a society, but they also generate a good deal of conflict and change. Newcomers such as immigrants and refugees coming into a society often have problems because they are unfamiliar with the symbols and culture that are taken for granted by those already there. Certain institutionalized inequities are particularly important to social service workers because of the troubles they create for clients. The United States has a class society based on differential access to education, employment, and, ultimately, wealth. It is a society in which racial and ethnic groups are stratified in terms of prestige, wealth, and power, and where discrimination also occurs on the basis of gender, age, sexual orientation, and physical ability.

Terms such as *classism, racism, sexism,* and *ageism,* used to describe these inequities, underscore both how they harm people and how they need to be changed. More important, these terms refer to the incorporation of inequities in the structure and organization of social life. Discrimination therefore is not solely dependent on the attitudes and behaviors of individuals. Sexism, for instance, may be defined as those norms and expectations existing in law, in religious dogma, or in kinship relations that assign women a subordinate place with regard to men. Once they are the norm and thus imbued with value and authority, these expectations, as much as the attitudes of individuals, can be said to be the reason for the existence of sexist inequities. A father may thoroughly love his daughter and reject any limitations on her personal happiness or achievement, for example, and yet feel compelled to encourage her to comply with traditional expectations about womanhood.

∞ ROLES: PERSON MEETS ENVIRONMENT

Individuals are connected to social systems through the roles they occupy in them. Roles are at the same time an element of the individual and an element of a social system. They represent the joint boundary between the two, the point at which person meets environment.

The Concept of Role

The concept of role has been borrowed from the theater. Most of what it conveys in the theatrical sense it also conveys in the social scientific sense. For instance, the role of Hamlet was written by Shakespeare in the seventeenth century. Over the years numerous actors have taken the part, each giving their own interpretations, but the role of Hamlet continues, regardless of who is playing it. In the same way, the roles we play in life or the positions we occupy are a part of the social systems to which we belong, and they somehow exist separate from ourselves. Husbands and sons, wives and daughters, students and teachers, social workers and clients exist as parts in the theater of everyday life. People enter these social roles and leave them, but the system and the roles that comprise them usually continue.

Role refers to the more dynamic aspects of a status or position in a social system. It is concerned with specifying the attitudes and behaviors expected of people in particular positions. **Status** differs from role in that it locates individuals in terms of their **social positions**. It is a description of where they fit within a chain of command or in an authority or power structure. A direct-service social worker, for instance, can be located between the client, to whom service is given, and the supervisor, who assures that agency policies and professional principles are followed.

Definitions of Role

Role is not an easy concept to define, partly because of the tension which usually exists between roles and the individuals who take them. In the theatrical imagery, the role of Hamlet exists as a series of lines to be spoken by an actor. The actor has to speak them if he is to play the role, and so the role constrains the actor. In real life, roles also constrain individuals. Mothers, students, and clients are expected to behave in certain ways. But roles in real life rarely constrain us in the same way roles in the theater do. There are no exact lines that must be declaimed. Life is a living drama in which the individual actors often become authors who rewrite the drama.

The rewriting of roles in everyday life creates tensions. On the one hand, all the other members of the system have their ideas of how the role should be performed. On the other hand, the person in the role has his or her own idea about the role. How the role is eventually performed is a function of the negotiations taking place among the actors.

It is not surprising, then, that a person's role is usually defined in not one but three ways, as Morton Deutsch and Robert Krauss have done (see "Definitions of Role"). In one way, often identified with sociology, role is defined from the point of view of the other actors, that is, in terms of "the expectations which exist in the social world surrounding the status." This is defined as the expected or **prescribed role**. In another way, more identified with psychology, role is defined from the point of view of the actor in the role, that is, "those specific expectations the occupant of a position perceives as applicable to his own behavior when he interacts with the occupants of some other position." This is defined as the subjective or **perceived role**. And role is also defined in terms of the actual outcome of the interaction between the actor and the other actors, that is, "the specific overt behaviors of the occupant of a position when he interacts with the occupants of some other position." This is referred to as the **enacted role**.[19]

In the role of social worker, all three of these definitions of role apply. The role is at once defined by the expectations of the administrator, the supervisor, and the client about what the worker is to do, the expectations of the worker about what is to be done, and the actual behaviors of the worker.

Definitions of Role

A person's role in any situation is defined in three ways: from the perspective of the expectations of others for people in that role (the prescribed role), the expectations of the person taking the role (the perceived role), and that person's actual behaviors (the enacted role).

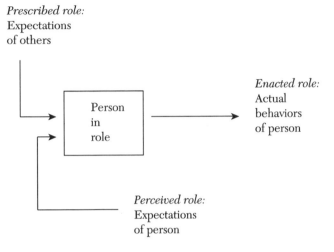

Prescribed role:
Expectations
of others

Person
in
role

Enacted role:
Actual
behaviors
of person

Perceived role:
Expectations
of person

Source: Based on Morton Deutsch and Robert M. Krauss, *Social Psychology* (New York: Basic Books, 1965), pp. 175–77.

Roles in Everyday Life

The roles and positions people occupy in everyday life determine the expectations of themselves and others for their ordinary social transactions. The NASW Person in Environment task force has identified four types of these roles which have to do with the family, interpersonal relations, work, and special life situations.[20] Each of these roles is associated with fairly specific expectations about proper, or normal, human behavior.

Family roles are carried out in the context of a family setting in which individuals are linked by blood, law, or informal arrangement. They include roles as parent, spouse or partner, child, sibling, parent-in-law, grandparent, and "significant other," such as family friend. Conflict in family roles is described in Chapter 11.

Interpersonal roles are played out in close relationships with others who are not family members but who, because of proximity or common interest, interact regularly with one another. These can range from roles as sexual intimates or lovers who do not live with each other to friends, neighbors, associates, group or club members, and acquaintances.

Occupational roles are performed in the paid or unpaid economy or in schools. They include the role of the paid worker, the unpaid worker in the home, the volunteer worker, and the student.

Special life-situation roles are defined as time-limited, situation-specific roles which may be taken on voluntarily or involuntarily. Formal, written expectations often govern these roles. They include the role of consumer or customer or role situations in which money for goods and services is exchanged. They also include the voluntary patient or client role, and the involuntary probationer, parolee, or prisoner role. The immigrant role—legal, undocumented, or refugee—is another example of special life-situation roles.

Master Roles and Statuses

Roles in everyday life are derived from another series of roles and statuses within the larger, institutionalized structure of society. These have been referred to as **master roles and statuses**: "A status that is so important that it serves to define individuals both for themselves and for the larger society."[21] Master roles and statuses are not only central to people's experiences and opportunities, they are also central to the individual's character and personality. These are not temporary roles but may engulf people throughout their entire lives, or at least for a considerable period. They include social class roles as affluent, middle class, working class, poor, or underclass. They also include roles as majority or minority group member; male or female gender; heterosexual or homosexual; and able-bodied or disabled. Age may also be thought of as a master status. Everyone ages, but being in the role of child, adolescent, adult, or elderly significantly shapes the kinds of experiences a person can expect.

Transactions Between Individuals and Social Systems

Roles are acquired, maintained, and changed through a series of transactions between individuals and social systems. George McCall and J. L. Simmons identify five overlapping basic social processes which are transactional in nature. These processes are related to the tasks through which a social system attempts to maintain or alter itself: recruitment, socialization, interaction, innovation, and control.[22] They form the basis for the discussion of group theory and the political economy in Chapter 12 and are also referred to in relation to social interaction in Chapter 14.

Recruitment refers to the processes by which the individual's participation in a social system is initiated. In recruitment, criteria for membership in particular statuses and roles are decided, and individuals who meet these criteria are selected for participation. The basis for recruitment may be ascriptive, determined by birth; conscriptive, determined by law; or achieved, determined by merit. Recruitment through **ascription** is found in many social systems; certain roles and statuses may be set aside for individuals with certain characteristics of sex, race and ethnicity, social class, or age. **Conscription** is the basis for recruitment in military drafts and other laws and regulations that require participation by certain types of people. Recruitment processes based on **achievement** involve the setting of cognitive, behavioral, or motivational-affective standards that allow membership only to those who are capable of meeting the standards.

Socialization refers to the processes through which individual participation is defined and refined as individuals learn to function as system members. Included are the processes by which people become aware of the expectations of others and learn the attitudes, knowledge, and abilities necessary to comply with those expectations. While socialization is often thought of in terms of infants and children, it is a broader phenomenon which takes place throughout the life cycle whenever an individual participates in a social system. And, rather than being a one-way process whereby established members simply pass on expectations that new recruits are compelled to accept, socialization in most systems is a negotiation between old and new in which new expectations constantly evolve.

Interaction refers to the processes through which individual participation in the system is implemented. Through the continual, overarching process of interaction, members influence one another, and social systems are shaped and refined. Interaction takes place through formal and informal channels, through face-to-face contact, or through more impersonal means such as letters and phone calls. The size of the social system has a lot to do with this; in general, the smaller the social system, the more likely it is that interaction will be informal and direct. However, even large, complex systems have informal, face-to-face processes as well as formal, impersonal processes.

Innovation refers to the processes through which individual participation in a system is altered or changed. Innovations may be externally imposed, as when changes in the physical environment force system members to rethink the ways they relate to their environment, or internally planned, as when conditions within a society force the enactment of new laws. Much of the time, however, innovation comes about through improvisation, especially at the level of statuses and roles. Individuals' personalities or particular abilities may lead them to begin to change the expectations connected with a role or status.

Social control refers to the processes through which individual participation in a system is limited or constrained. Social control may be implemented through positive or negative means. Often systems of reward are devised to assure compliance with group ex-

This social worker and client in a counseling session at a community house for urban youth are enacting the roles they occupy in a social system. How social workers enact their roles in the social services is influenced by the norms of the profession, the policies of the agency, the expectations of clients, and the cultural and personal attributes of the individual social worker.

pectations. If you go to school, get an education, and apply yourself, you are more likely to be rewarded with a good job and less likely to confront the inequities in the society's economic opportunities. But social control also includes various punishments or sanctions. Rewards may be taken away, restrictions may be forcefully placed on behavior, a person may be ignored or ostracized or even physically punished.

The Person-in-Role-in-Environment Relationship

The relationship between person and environment can be depicted in such a way as to bring together most of the concepts discussed in this chapter (see "Person in Role in Environment"). The individual, a dynamic ordering of biophysical and psychological states and processes, is a part of and in transaction with the social environment, a dynamic ordering of primary and secondary social systems, norms, institutions, institutional arrangements, and roles and statuses. Individuals and environment are joined together by roles. In the transactions taking place—recruitment, socialization, interaction, innovation, or control—the expectations of the person are always juxtaposed with the expectations of the social environment. Through the negotiation of roles, specific behaviors are enacted which have the effect of maintaining or altering the individual or the society.

Social service workers must take into account the roles and statuses that make up the social systems of the clients with whom they work. Humans are never just individuals trying to meet their own needs; they are social in nature, and their years are lived out in the context of social systems and the roles they hold in them. The meeting of individual needs is intimately caught up in the dynamics of the system as a whole. For both clients and workers, the expectations of others are always impinging on the expectations of self. The task of the worker often is to clarify the various expectations and negotiate the working agreements that lead to revision of the roles and systems. In this way, social service workers contribute to individual and social change and renewal.

∞ IMPLICATIONS FOR PRACTICE

The concept of person in environment distinguishes the focus of social workers from others in the helping professions. This can be seen in comparing the *Diagnostic and Statistical Manual* of the American Psychiatric Association, commonly used by mental health professionals, and the *Person in Environment Manual* being developed by social workers.

The Diagnostic and Statistical Manual

A widely used tool for assessing the mental health or normality of individuals is the *Diagnostic and Statistical Manual of Mental Disorders* published by the American Psychiatric Association and based on an international system for the categorization of diseases developed by the World Health Organization. Early editions were not very successful, but the third edition, informally known as *DSM–III*, has achieved widespread use in the United States. A revised edition, *DSM–III–R*, was published in 1987.[23]

This manual describes mental disorders and other symptoms which may not be disorders but for which psychiatric treatment may be sought. Fourteen major diagnostic

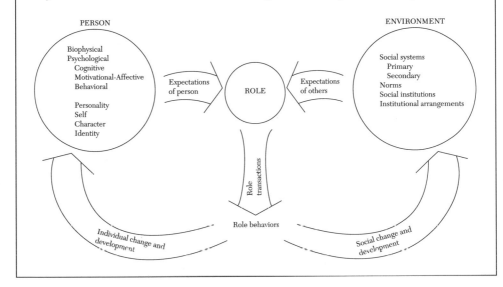

Person in Role in Environment

The interactions between the person and the environment are conducted through role transactions, which are mediated by the expectations of the person and of others in the social environment. As a result of role transactions, role behaviors, which may contribute to individual or social change and development, emerge.

categories of disorders are identified in *DSM–III–R*, and information on each one includes the essential features, prevalence, likely age of onset, sex ratio, the familial pattern, predisposing factors, likely course of the disorder, and any physical impairments or other complications that may be associated with it. This helps in identifying individuals who are characterized by behavioral or psychosocial functioning which conforms to an identified disorder. Thus the *DSM* offers relatively specific criteria for helping practitioners identify various problems in psychological well-being.

DSM–III calls for a complex assessment of mental and physical disorders and other aspects of **psychosocial functioning**. Using a multiaxial system, diagnosticians make five assessments or diagnosis, one for each of the following axes:

Axis I.   The mental disorder or condition that is the focus of treatment.

Axis II.   Any personality disorders or specific developmental disorders that may exist along with the mental disorder.

Axis III.   Any physical disorders and conditions that may be present.

Axis IV.   The severity of the psychosocial stressors being experienced.

Axis V.   The highest level of adaptive functioning at the present and during the previous year (a global assessment).

By requiring attention to a variety of conditions and circumstances, the multiaxial system supplies a more holistic picture of people seeking treatment. And, because *DSM–III* is a medical manual, it promotes the ideal that the organic basis of a problem in living must be ruled out before psychological and psychosocial causes can be considered.

Evaluation of the *DSM–III*

The *Diagnostic and Statistical Manual* is valuable to mental health professionals; it contributes to better communication among them, provides for comprehensive assessments and effective treatments, and is a useful educational tool.[24] It lists relatively clear, concise, and standardized categories of the disorders, something that few other approaches to the study of individual behavior, not even a systems approach, are capable of doing.

Social service workers, however, are divided in their opinions on the use of the manual. Francis Turner criticizes it as a tool for negative labeling.[25] Florence Lieberman charges that many of the childhood disorders listed in *DSM–III* are not based on extensive research and are not appropriately treated by psychiatry.[26] Herb Kutchins and Stuart Kirk argue that social workers who are forced to use it in order to be reimbursed by insurance programs may adopt unethical practices such as assigning arbitrary diagnostic codes and run the risk of being the target of investigations or malpractice suits.[27] They also believe that the reputed reliability of the manual—major reason for its success—is suspect.[28]

For social workers, the most relevant shortcoming of *DSM–III* may be that it does not take a person-in-environment perspective. Of its five diagnostic axes, only one includes the possibility of assessing the environment of a client; Axis IV calls for the assessment of "psychosocial stressors," a concept which is only superficially defined when compared to the richness of its descriptions and definitions of mental, personality, and physical disorders.

The *Person in Environment Manual*

An assessment instrument that does take a person-in-environment perspective is the system being developed by the NASW task force described in the section on environmental problems and strengths. The project is sponsored by the National Association of Social Workers, with the encouragement of the National Institute of Mental Health. The *Person in Environment (PIE) Manual* has undergone several revisions; the ninth revision (1989) is discussed here.[29]

The project coordinators for this manual, James Karls and K. E. Wandrei, have taken a stand on the focus of social work practice by asserting that social workers are experts on problems of *social functioning*, that is, social role performance as influenced by the environment. In their words, "Social work intervention is sought or is appropriate when role performance becomes a problem either to the individual or to others. It is also sought or is appropriate when environmental problems limit social functioning."[30]

Like the *DSM–III*, the *PIE* manual is a multiaxial diagnostic system that leads to a rich assessment. The system consists of four idexes and four factors, identified as follows:

Factor 1.   Social role problems—type, severity, duration, and individual's coping ability.

Factor 2.   Environmental problems—type, severity, duration.

Factor 3.   Mental and personality disorders.

Factor 4.   Physical disorders.

In keeping with a person-in-environment perspective, the manual identifies two primary areas for social work assessment in factors 1 and 2: social role problems and environmental problems. First the social worker must identify the family, interpersonal, occupational, and special situational roles (and, by implication, the master roles and statuses) occupied by the client. The next steps are to determine the kinds of problems the client is having with respect to each role, assess their severity and duration, and determine the client's ability to cope or deal with these problems. The problems in the social environment to be identified and assessed, which have already been described, may be derived from the economy and basic needs fulfillment, the educational system, the judicial and legal systems, the health and social service systems, voluntary associations, and primary-group affiliations.

Only after role problems and environmental problems have been assessed is the social worker expected to make assessments of mental, personality, and physical disorders. The *PIE* manual thus does not disassociate itself completely from *DSM* but refocuses in accordance with the special expertise of social workers.

The *PIE* manual is still in its infancy. Although its framers caution that social workers need to examine the strengths of clients, the manual only focuses on problems. A categorization scheme for role problems and for environmental problems has been developed, however, and its ability to produce reliable assessments is being tested. The manual does hold the promise of giving social workers a clear place in the mental health professions and merits consideration. To prepare for its use, social work students should focus on the study of roles and problems that emerge from the environments in which individuals and families live.

Social Support Resources

Both *DSM* and the *PIE* manuals are problem-oriented; they do not alert social service workers to the strengths as well as the problems of client or how these strengths can be used to build positive interventions. An assessment of a social environment, like an assessment of the psychological dimensions of a person, needs to examine the social supports that exist.

Elizabeth Tracy and James Whittaker have developed a social network assessment strategy that is useful in helping practitioners think about the social support resources available to individuals and families.[31] In this study, 45 families receiving child welfare services were asked to identify the individuals, families, groups, and organizations they could turn to for support. The family service workers doing the interviews collected information on the type of support provided, as well as the network size and composition, frequency of contact with the support system, the perceived availability of the support, and whether the support process was considered reciprocal. Recognizing that social networks are not always supportive, they also asked if members of their support systems were critical of the clients.

The social networks of the families were divided into seven types of systems: friends, neighbors, family members, nonfamily household members, people at work or school, professional people, and formal organizations. These systems provided emotional and informational support and concrete assistance with tasks and chores.

On average, a family support network included 18.9 people or organizations, more than half of which had been known for over five years. The families were in contact with 70 percent of their support networks at least once a week, and 41 percent of those in the network were perceived to be "almost always" available. In over half the cases the supportive relationship was considered reciprocal, and when the supportive person was another family member, the likelihood of a reciprocal helping relationship was even higher. Twenty-nine of the families could identify someone in their systems who was critical of them, and some 12 percent of their networks represented people who were almost always critical of them. In spite of this, the families tended to be in daily contact with critical persons or organizations.

Practitioners can use the same strategy to assess the strengths in the social environment of their clients. By asking questions about the composition, type of support, and quality of clients' networks, they are likely to find that few clients are without any strengths. Recognizing their own strengths helps clients to feel good about themselves and to know that they are neither isolated nor helpless.

∞ DISCUSSION QUESTIONS AND CLASS PROJECTS

1. What is meant by the term *holon*? Would you ever describe yourself as a holon?

2. Why is the study of the social environment important to human behavior? Is the use of social support groups and networks always a good thing?

3. Describe and discuss the differences between the interactional and sociocultural levels of social systems.

4. Compare the visions of social systems found in functional and conflict theories. In what ways do their views about conflict differ? Do you think the functional approach or the conflict approach to the study of systems is better for social work?

5. What are the differences among social norms, social institutions, and institutional arrangements?

6. The concept of role has been defined in three ways. Describe and give examples of each.

7. Distinguish between master and everyday roles and statuses. Identify the roles you occupy and indicate how they could be sources of support or sources of troubles for you.

8. Describe five major forms of transactions that take place between individuals and social systems and give examples of each.

9. The figure in "Person in Role in Environment" pulls together the concepts discussed in this chapter. Can you use it to describe an individual client with whom you have worked or are working?

10. Describe the multiaxial systems around which practitioners' diagnoses of clients are structured, using the *Diagnostic and Statistical Manual* and the *Person in Environment Manual*.

11. What do social workers regard as the contributions and limitations of the *Diagnostic and Statistical Manual*?

12. Identify professional social workers in your area who are working in a mental health setting. Interview them about their experiences in using *DSM*. Ask them what they think about its uses and limitations.

13. Locate copies of the *DSM* and the *PIE* manuals if possible. Compare what you know about them. Which do you believe is more useful to social workers?

14. Describe how you might go about assessing the sources of positive social support for an individual or family.

∽ NOTES

1. Nancy Gibbs, "Answers at Last," *Time*, December 17, 1990, p. 45; Crystal Mills and Hiro Ota, "Homeless Women with Minor Children in the Detroit Metropolitan Area," *Social Work*, vol. 34 (November 1989), pp. 485–89. Also see Sarah Connell, "Homelessness," in *Encyclopedia of Social Work*, 18th ed. (Silver Spring, MD: National Association of Social Workers, 1987), Vol. 1, pp. 789–93.

2. R. J. First, D. Roth, and B. D. Arewa, "Homelessness: Understanding the Dimensions of the Problem for Minorities," *Social Work*, vol. 33 (March–April 1988), p. 123.

3. J. L. Hagen and A. M. Ivanoff, "Homeless Women: A High Risk Population," *Affilia: Journal of Women and Social Work*, vol. 3, pp. 19–33.

4. Barbara Y. Whitman, Pasquale Accardo, Mary Boyert, and Rita Kendagor, "Homelessness and Cognitive Performance in Children: A Possible Link," *Social Work*, vol. 35 (November 1990), pp. 516–21.

5. Anastasia Toufexis, "From Asylum to Anarchy," *Time*, October 22, 1990, p. 58. Also see Steven P. Segal, "Deinstitutionalization," in *Encyclopedia of Social Work*, 18th ed. (Silver Spring, MD: National Association of Social Workers, 1987), Vol. 1, p. 381.

6. Ann Hartman, "Homelessness: Public Issue and Private Trouble," *Social Work*, vol. 34 (November 1989), p. 483; Gibbs, "Answers at Last," p. 45.

7. Jan L. Hagen, "Gender and Homelessness," *Social Work*, vol. 32 (July–August 1987), pp. 312–16.

8. James Karls and K. E. Wandrei, project coordinators, "Person in Environment: A System for Describing, Classifying, and Coding Problems of Social Functioning," conceptualized and developed by a task force of members of the National Association of Social Workers, Revision 9, October 1989.

9. Robert F. Schilling II. "Limitation of Social Support," *Social Service Review*, vol. 61 (March 1987), p. 19.

10. See Diane L. Pancoast and Alice Collins, "Natural Helping Networks," in *Encyclopedia of Social Work*, 18th ed. (Silver Spring, MD: National Association of Social Workers, 1987), Vol. 2, pp. 171–81.

11. See the discussion by Genevieve De Hoyos, Arturo De Hoyos, and Christian B. Anderson, "Sociocultural Dislocation: Beyond the Dual Perspective," *Social Work*, vol. 21 (January–February 1986), pp. 61–67.

12. Ralph Lehninger, "Systems Theory," *Journal of Sociology and Social Welfare*, vol. 5 (July 1978), pp. 481–98.

13. Ralf Dahrendorf, *Class and Class Conflict in Industrial Society* (Palo Alto, CA: Stanford University Press, 1959).

14. Lewis A. Coser, *The Functions of Social Conflict* (New York: Free Press, 1956).

15. Jeffry H. Galper, *The Politics of Social Services* (Englewood Cliffs, NJ: Prentice-Hall, 1975), pp. 88–110.

16. Gerhard Lenski and Jean Lenski, *Human Societies* (New York: McGraw-Hill, 1982), p. 54.

17. Hans Gerth and C. Wright Mills, *Character and Social Structure: The Psychology of Social Institutions* (New York: Harbinger Books, 1964), p. 23.

18. Ibid., p. 26.

19. Morton Deutsch and Robert M. Krauss, *Social Psychology* (New York: Basic Books, 1965), pp. 175–77.

20. Karls and Wandrei, "Person-in-Environment."

21. G. Ritzer, K. C. W. Kammeyer, and N. Yetman, *Sociology: Experiencing a Changing Society*, 3rd ed. (Boston: Allyn and Bacon, 1987), p. 111.

22. George J. McCall and J. L. Simmons, *Social Psychology: A Sociological Approach* (New York: Free Press, 1982).

23. American Psychiatric Association, *Diagnostic and Statistical Manual of Mental Disorders*, 3rd ed. (Washington, DC, 1980), and 3rd ed., rev. (Washington, DC, 1987).

24. See Janet B. W. Williams, "Diagnostic and Statistical Manual," in *Encyclopedia of Social Work*, 18th ed. (Silver Spring, MD: National Association of Social Workers, 1987), Vol. 1, pp. 389–93.

25. Francis J. Turner, "Mental Disorders in Social Work Practice," in F. J. Turner (editor), *Adult Psychopathology: A Social Work Perspective* (New York: Free Press, 1984), pp. 1–5.

26. Florence Lieberman, "Mental Health and Illness in Children," in *Encyclopedia of Social Work*, 18th ed. (Silver Spring, MD: National Association of Social Workers, 1987), Vol. 2, p. 114.

27. Herb Kutchins and Stuart A. Kirk, "DSM–III and Social Work Malpractice," *Social Work*, vol. 32 (May–June 1987), pp. 205–11.

28. Herb Kutchins and Stuart A. Kirk, "The Reliability of DSM–III: A Critical Review," *Social Work Research and Abstracts*, vol. 22 (Winter 1986), pp. 3–13.

29. "NASW's PIE Manual: Problem-coding System Gets Boost from NIMH," *NASW News*, November 1989, p. 14.

30. Karls and Wandrie, "Person in Environment," p. 4.

31. Elizabeth M. Tracy and James Whittaker, "Identifying Social Support Resources of At-Risk Families," *Social Work*, vol. 35 (May 1990), pp. 141, 252–57.

PART TWO

Communities in Society

CHAPTER 4

Diversity in Community Life

MAJOR THEMES DISCUSSED IN THIS CHAPTER

1. **COMMUNITIES AS SOCIAL SYSTEMS.** Three types of communities are locational, based on common residence; identificational, based on common identity; and interest, based on common goals and objectives. Our focus is on identificational communities.

2. **LIFE IN IDENTIFICATIONAL COMMUNITIES.** Three identificational communities, based on a shared identity of social class, religion, and sexual orientation, are presented as examples. Social class position is primarily determined by income, occupation, and education, but the majority of Americans consider themselves part of the middle class. In communities based on religion, over half of Americans prefer Protestant faiths and 25 percent are Catholics, with social attitudes ranging from conservative to liberal. The emergence of a community of gay men and lesbians is a relatively recent development arising out of a movement for civil rights.

3. **RACIAL AND ETHNIC COMMUNITIES.** Pervasive influences on the formation and maintenance of communities in American society are racial and ethnic heritage. Ethnic groups are communities within a nation which are based on collections of families with a sense of common ancestry.

4. **MAJORITY AND MINORITY.** In multigroup societies some communities come to be defined as minority and others as majority. Minority groups are usually small in number, negatively valued, and treated with hostility in a society. Majority groups create or enforce the negative valuation and have the power to discriminate against minorities. The hostility in relationships among these types of groups derives from the conflicting desires of the majority to maintain its position and of the minority to better its position.

5. **IMPLICATIONS FOR PRACTICE.** Communities form a major social context in which people live out their everyday lives. Individuals' attitudes and values, needs and problems, strengths and resources are all associated with community life. The cultural uniqueness of communities and their status in a society must be taken into account when working with clients, especially clients in communities which diverge from majority communities.

THE STUDY OF COMMUNITY LIFE PROVIDES essential knowledge for social service workers. Some of the major social roles in American society derive from people's membership in various communities; they may have such roles as urban dweller or rural dweller; African American, Latino, or Asian; unemployed, professional, or executive; Protestant, Catholic, Jewish, or Islamic; and heterosexual or homosexual, among others. Connected to these roles are statuses: majority or minority; upper class, middle class, or lower class; deviant or "normal." The communities in which people live and with which they identify also form a major social context for human behavior and development. Many of our attitudes and values derive directly from the continual transactions in which we engage through our participation in community life. And communities supply many of the resources and social supports that are essential for individuals' social and psychological well-being. The organizations, associations, families, kin, and friendship groups which comprise communities all can contribute to healthy human behavior and development.

There is also a darker side to community life. Because many of the needs of people must be satisfied in a community context, the everyday transactions among individuals in communities can create problems. Perhaps even more important from a critical perspective is the conflict that may arise from the transactions in community life that link individuals and the society as a whole. A complex industrial society, such as contemporary American society, is composed of many communities, often in competition or conflict with one another. The relationships among communities, as well as the status of each community within a society, have important implications for the social and psychological functioning of community members. To the extent that individuals are connected to communities which are powerful and valued and have a wealth of resources, they will experience advantages over those who are connected to communities which are less powerful and less valued and have more limited resources. This does not mean that there is a one-to-one relationship between community and individual. The influence of other social systems, in particular the family, and the adaptive capacities of individuals also have a lot to do with how they experience and resolve their needs and problems.

∞ COMMUNITIES AS SOCIAL SYSTEMS

A **community** is a type of social system which is distinguished by the personal or affective nature of the ties that hold its members together. It is a group of people who sense a common identity, bond with one another, and become attached to or affiliated with one another through regular interaction. Sociologists often describe this type of community as a *gemeinshaft*, that is, a societal group characterized by "a high degree of personal intimacy, emotional depth, moral commitment, social cohesion, and continuity in time."[1]

Communities are very similar to other groups such as the society and the family. All three types of groups are based on common identity and interpersonal bonding; if we go back far enough in history, there probably were no differences among them. The national society, in which large, centrally regulated states supersede regional communal ties, is a relatively new phenomenon. Similarly, in many cultures and historical eras, communities have incorporated numerous attributes which are associated with families today.

Probably the greatest differences among the community, the family, and the society have to do with size and the degree to which intimacy is possible. At least in contemporary industrial societies, families are typically quite small, and membership is expressed in intimate personal attachments. National societies are usually quite large, and personal attachments most often are expressed through patriotic rituals mediated through impersonal bureaucracies such as government and business. Many national societies are *pluralist*, that is, composed of many subcultures or community groups. Communities lie somewhere between family and society in these respects. They are relatively homogeneous, or uniform in composition, neither very small nor very large, and not very intimate but not very bureaucratic, either.

Types of Communities

Sociologists have identified three principal types of communities: locational, identificational, and interest.[2] **Locational communities**, which are based on a common residence or territory, are believed to have developed with the evolution of agriculture, as nomadic hunters and gatherers began to settle in one place. Thus, in part, the bonding and attachment that take place in a community are to the place as much as to the people. Perhaps the most pertinent example of communities based on location is the neighborhood. Neighborhoods vary a great deal; some offer evidence of the strong interpersonal attachments and closeness of the gemeinshaft, but others do not. Many observers today believe that neighborhoods in American society are losing the sense of community which typified them in the past. Since sociologists first turned their attention to urban living, inner-city neighborhoods have been described as disorganized, conflict-ridden, impersonal, and with little sense of attachment among the residents.[3] Even contemporary suburban neighborhoods may lack a sense of community. Philip Slater describes American suburban communities as being in "pursuit of loneliness": families living in individual houses, glorying in their privacy, fencing or hedging themselves in, and limiting their contacts with neighbors.[4]

Identificational communities are based on a common identity. Jessie Bernard uses the term *the community* to refer to locational communities and the term *community* to refer to identificational communities.[5] In identificational communities, residence is of less consequence than ties based on affection and common identity. Examples include social class, racial and ethnic, and religious communities, and, more recently, communities based on sexual orientation. African Americans, Italians, and Catholics are good examples. Their sense of commonality and affection derives from the historical experiences they have in common and carry around within themselves, regardless of where they may live.

The third type of community is based on a shared interest, with common goals and objectives. Although locational and identificational communities also are held together by common interests, their interests are likely to be more general and inclusive. In **interest communities**, the affection and attachment derive from a much more narrowly focused concern. They include professional or occupational associations; science, for instance, has been described as the work of communities of scientists. Social workers and other groups within the helping professions commonly think of themselves as a community.[6]

Attributes of Identificational Communities

The focus of this chapter is on identificational communities. However, there is a considerable overlap between locational and identificational communities. In many societies, identificational communities occupy particular territories. The United Kingdom of Great Britain and Northern Ireland is composed of Scottish, Welsh, Irish, and English populations, each primarily occupying a particular region. An ethnic, cultural, or religious identification may be stronger than the ties to a larger national identity, as in the persistent attempts of Irish Catholics in Northern Ireland to rejoin it to the Republic of Ireland. The conflict among Serbs, Croats, and Muslims that has destroyed the nation of Yugoslavia, with roots in disputes dating back to the thirteenth century, and the dissolution in 1993 of Czechoslovakia into Czech and Slovak republics are examples of the forces of identificational and territorial ties formerly held in check by national governments.

The United States is a cohesive union of 50 states, but American society includes a number of identificational communities that exist to some extent in physical segregation.

Urban, working-class Italian Americans celebrate a Catholic festival in the North End neighborhood of Boston. To a greater or lesser extent, community cohesion, spirit, and identity characterize different types of neighborhoods in the United States.

The most obvious basis for such segregation is race and ethnicity. African Americans, Puerto Ricans on the continent, and Mexican Americans are likely to live in segregated communities, often in decaying inner-city areas. Because of social policies dating back to the nineteenth century, many Native Americans (Indians) still live on segregated reservations. Segregation also is evident on the basis of social class; American neighborhoods are shaped by the residents' income or wealth. Some religious communities are more-or-less segregated, though often, as in the case of Catholics and Jewish people, the basis for separation may be more a matter of ethnicity than of religion. Recently, neighborhoods composed of lesbians and gay men have become apparent in some cities.

Because of such patterns of segregation in American society, identificational communities are also likely to be locational communities. Indeed, when social service workers become involved with community work, they are likely to do so through the neighborhoods served by their agencies. But identificational communities go beyond locational communities in two respects. They incorporate the issues of the larger group, rather than being limited to the needs and problems of a particular area, and they include communities that are important to individuals and families but may not exist as clearly demarcated neighborhoods. A focus on identificational communities makes it possible to incorporate the study of neighborhoods with the study of larger groupings of people who consider themselves communities.

There are two other attributes which distinguish identificational communities: Each community develops a culture, and each is accorded a certain status. The concept of group culture is usually associated with ethnic groups, but it is equally relevant to other communities. **Culture** is not an easy concept to define, but it generally incorporates all the symbolic meanings—the beliefs, values, norms, and traditions—that are shared in a community and govern social interactions among community members or between members and outsiders. The values and norms of the various social classes, of religious denominations, of gays and lesbians, and of ethnic and racial groups constitute their cultures. Such communities also vary in terms of their status in the society. Racial and ethnic minorities and minority individuals, who are devalued and experience hostility as a result of their group membership, have low social status; racial and ethnic majorities and majority individuals enjoy a higher status. Differences in status are explicit in the notion of social classes, and religious denominations, which often are linked to social class and race and ethnicity, also may differ in terms of status.

∞ LIFE IN IDENTIFICATIONAL COMMUNITIES

In examining community life, we will first consider examples of several different kinds of identificational communities: social class communities, religious denominations, and the gay and lesbian community. A more pervasive type of identificational community in American society is based on race and ethnicity or on minority or majority status. These topics, which are introduced in the next two sections of this chapter, are the focus of discussion in Part Two. The other three chapters in this part describe the history and present conditions of racial and ethnic groups and minority-majority relations in the United States.

Social Classes as Communities

Social classes are not communities in the sense of being based on a shared location, identification, or interest. Nevertheless, they can give rise to communal action, that is, the development of common neighborhoods, a common identity, and common interests.[7] The term **social class** has a distinctly economic meaning. It is used to describe people in terms of the economic opportunities available to them, the economic goods and resources they command, and the occupations or positions they hold in the economy.

Two Approaches to the Study of Social Class

Sociologists approach the study of social class in two basic ways, by regarding it as a descriptive tool or as an analytic tool (see "Social Stratification and Social Classes"). Most regard it as a tool for describing **social stratification**; that is, society is described as a ladder composed of a series of rungs or prestige rankings, each a step higher than the preceding one. Individuals in the society are located on this vertical ladder according to such standards as the amount of money they earn, the level of education they have completed, the prestige of their occupation, or the prestige conferred on them by others in the community. Then the ladder is divided in some logical but nevertheless arbitrary way. For instance, those whose education, income, and job status get them only up the first two or three rungs are said to be lower class. Those whose education, salary, and job status get them all the way to the top are said to be upper class. Those located at the middle rungs are the middle class.[8] In this way, sociologists have designated various social classes. W. Lloyd Warner, for instance, proposed a schema with six classes: upper-upper, lower-upper, upper-middle, lower-middle, and lower-lower.[9]

Marxian-influenced sociologists use classes as an analytic tool. Social classes are defined in a structure of associations or social roles in the economy and in the workplace. The work organization in a free-market or capitalist economy is divided into a number of roles, each with a set of responsibilities, privileges, duties, and obligations. *Owners* put up the capital for the business or service, define what the product or service will be, and decide how the work will be done. They are the ultimate authority on who will be hired, how much will be paid in wages, and who will be fired. *Managers* follow the direction of the owners and put the plans for service and production into operation; they are likely to do the actual hiring and firing. Thus owners and managers often are regarded as two different strata within the same social class. *Workers* offer their mental and physical skills to the managers and owners in return for wages. Workers also may be considered as different strata in the same class, such as white-collar workers, skilled workers, and semiskilled workers.[10]

According to this definition, class is a position a person occupies within a hierarchy or authority structure. The essential element has to do with domination and subordination. In this sense social class is more than a description of prestige rankings and can be used as a tool for analyzing social relationships. With the concept of social class, we can look at the potential for role conflict, or, in the Marxian terminology, **class conflict**. We can understand the circumstances that will make a worker content and evaluate whether workers are being underpaid or overworked; whether workers are allowed to be autonomous or creative and whether owners and managers are authoritarian or exploitative (see Chapter 13).

In contemporary industrial societies, social class distinctions are very complex. The simple designations of owner, manager, and worker are replaced with far more complicated patterns. Traditionally the two principal categories of workers have been blue collar or white collar, ordinarily determined on the basis of whether they work more with their hands (construction workers) or with their minds (bookkeepers). There are also the categories of unskilled workers (janitors, waiters), skilled workers (computer technicians

---

Social Stratification and Social Classes

Some sociologists define social classes descriptively, as a series of prestige rankings, while others define them analytically, in terms of the role a person occupies in the economy.

Descriptive Approach	Analytic Approach
Classes as prestige rankings	Classes as social roles in production and service
Upper-upper class Upper class	Owner
Lower-upper class Upper-middle class	Manager
Middle class Lower-middle class	White-collar worker
Upper-lower class Lower class Lower-lower class	Blue-collar worker

---

and programmers), and professional workers (lawyers, urban developers). Managers may include supervisors, department heads, and executives. Owners are those who own small- and medium-size businesses, as well as those who have controlling interests in large companies and corporations. The American class structure, based on roles and statuses within roles in a free-market economy, is an example of such a complex hierarchy.[11]

Social Class Position

Although the two ways of approaching the study of social class are quite different, there are overlapping areas between them. Owners of businesses, especially large businesses, are likely to be educated and to have a great deal of income and a fair amount of occupational prestige. Managers and professionals similarly are likely to have high educational, prestige, and income rankings. Both groups, therefore, are likely to be found among the upper classes. White-collar workers are likely to have middle-level incomes, education, and occupational prestige; and blue-collar workers, especially nonunionized, unskilled workers, are most likely to be in the lower-middle to lower classes. In poverty-class families (see Chapter 9), the head of the household is chronically unemployed, underemployed, or dependent on welfare, or at best working for a subsistence wage.

Social class position, therefore, is primarily determined by occupation, income, and education. Since the founding of the United States, Americans have rejected inherited class distinctions and considered themselves free to advance upwardly; ideally, American society is classless. This perception is borne out when Americans are asked what social class they consider themselves in. The General Study Surveys conducted by the National Opinion Research Center (NORC) ask this question, given the four categories of lower, working, middle, and upper class. Results changed only slightly in the 19 surveys conducted between 1972 and 1993. Less than 10 percent put themselves in either the lower class or the upper class; about 45 percent said they were in the working class and another 45 percent in the middle class. If the working class is considered to be part of the middle class (and the line between these classes can be indistinct), 90 percent of the people believe they are middle-class members.[12]

Although most Americans believe they are part of a large middle class and free to advance, the objective reality of social class may be quite different. As important as the issue of mobility is, there is remarkably little empirical evidence on it. Most studies are marred by measurement error, unrepresentative samples, a failure to study the very rich, or a preoccupation with men. Early studies suggested that although there was a good deal of intergenerational social mobility, most of it involved short upward movement; in general, white-collar fathers have sons who also work in white-collar occupations, and blue-collar fathers have sons who also work in blue-collar jobs. These studies also found that mobility rates among black men were substantially lower than those among white men.[13] Two recent longitudinal studies point to even less mobility than the earlier studies did. Gary Solon, using the Panel Study of Income Dynamics, found little difference in the incomes earned by fathers and sons; and David Zimmerman, examining the National Longitudinal Survey, found little difference in the occupational status of fathers and sons.[14]

Regardless of how social class position is defined, it is highly correlated with many variables of human behavior. Compared to people in lower socioeconomic positions, those in higher positions gain more wealth and income, experience greater social prestige, and command greater power (see "Life Conditions and Social Classes").

Social class position has a lot to do with neighborhood formation. American neighborhoods are segregated by class, that is, they tend to be inhabited by people holding similar economic positions in the society, with similar incomes and occupational and educational backgrounds. A walk through most American cities readily indicates where the rich, the middle classes, and the poor live. This was not always the case, however; there used to be much more social class mixing in neighborhoods. For instance, middle- and lower-class African Americans formerly tended to be grouped in "black neighborhoods." Today, such inner-city neighborhoods are described as being inhabited by an underclass, which essentially consists of unemployed or marginally employed unskilled workers (see Chapter 7). Upper- and middle-class blacks are not identified with these neighborhoods.[15]

Class Consciousness

Class position forms a basis for the development of community spirit. In the United States, this type of spirit has emerged periodically in various communities, but it has never persisted. For instance, no labor party has taken hold in the United States in the same way such political organizations have developed in European nations.

The great majority of Americans who think of themselves as being middle class do not identify strongly with a particular social class; and very few of those who are members of the upper class, according to financial standards, acknowledge that status. Thus Americans do not have a great deal of class consciousness; the failure of middle-class prestige and incomes to keep pace with changing economic conditions in the 1980s and 1990s, for example, has led to a perception that the upper and middle classes are merging (see "Is the Middle Class Vanishing?").

In some situations, however, communities of interest based on class position have emerged in the United States. The labor movement, that is, the development of trade unions and other workers' organizations, grew out of the common interests of skilled and

Life Conditions and Social Classes

An interesting portrait of social classes in contemporary American society is drawn by Leonard Beeghley, who describes four classes in terms of approximate share of the population, range of family incomes, occupational categories, source of income, and relative political power. These class categories—the rich or upper class, middle class, working class, and the poor—are not always mutually exclusive. For instance, income levels and occupational categories overlap and there always are individual exceptions, so earning a certain income is not correlated with specific occupations. Nevertheless, the stratification system in the United States is fairly orderly and allows for predictions about life circumstances in various classes. Beeghley believes these classes are inherent in the structure of a free-market economy, and he sees little chance that they will change, given present political and economic realities.

The rich or upper class constitutes about 5 percent of the population, but as an aggregate they control about 29 percent of the wealth of the country. In 1985, they were likely to earn an annual taxable family income in excess of $80,000 and to be employed in upper-level, white-collar executive and professional occupations that carry a good deal of prestige and allow for creativity and autonomy. Since 1985, their share of income has increased steadily, while those of the other classes have tended to stagnate. Their income is bolstered by assets such as property and investments. The super rich, those with incomes and assets approaching seven figures, are likely to have gained their wealth through inheritance or windfall profits, a sudden, extraordinary return on an investment. The rich have influence over government decisions and policy because they are likely to be well informed and to associate with other powerful people. Their voting participation is high and they are likely to contribute to and work for political candidates with whom they identify.

The middle class constitutes about 50 percent of the population, though their numbers seem to be declining due to recent changes in the structure of the economy. In 1985 they were likely to earn an annual taxable family income somewhere between $20,000 and $80,000. Most have white-collar occupations with secure health and other fringe benefits such as pension plans, sick leave, and paid time off. At the upper levels they are likely to be professionals and managers with expense accounts, use of company cars, membership in private clubs, and stock options. Although most middle-class families generally depend on their salaries to meet everyday needs, many have assets that derive from home ownership. Although not as involved as the rich, middle-class people have high rates of political participation and

unskilled blue-collar workers. Most of the welfare programs developed during the Great Depression of the 1930s and the War on Poverty of the 1960s were instituted because lower- and middle-income workers joined together and pushed for them.[16]

To protect them from economic troubles over which they had no control, these workers saw the need for a strong "safety net" in the form of such government programs as social security, unemployment insurance, Aid to Families with Dependent Children, community mental health, and support for education. Indeed, the inability of the Reagan and Bush administrations to completely dismantle the welfare state, as such programs are collectively referred to, is testimony that at least some basic level of class consciousness among lower- and middle-income groups still exists in the United States.

Irving Krauss suggests that if community is to emerge from class, five conditions must be met:

make their voice heard in the political process.

The working class comprises about 35 percent of the population. Since 1900 their numbers have steadily declined due to increased industrialization, the eclipse of manufacturing jobs, and the growth of service industries. Blue-collar work settings may be unpleasant and dangerous, marked by the close supervision, petty work rules, and intense production pressures. Although the common perception is that blue-collar workers earn incomes equivalent to the middle class, such is not the case. In 1985, their annual taxable family incomes ranged from approximately $12,000 to $30,000 mostly from hourly wages, and they have tended to remain the same since. Working-class people have little job security, and unemployment rates are consistently higher in blue-collar than in white-collar occupational categories. They are also less likely than the upper or middle classes to have savings and other assets to see them through difficult times, so they often experience lower levels of self-esteem and higher levels of family disruption. Most working-class families have lifestyles that are very different from those of middle-class families. For instance, they are less like to own their homes, and they spend a higher proportion of their incomes on housing which is smaller and has fewer amenities such as air conditioning and extra bathrooms.

The poor constitute about 10 percent of the population, and about 30 percent of this class is persistently poor. Thus only a small percentage of the poor may be characterized as a relatively stable, self-perpetuating underclass. The number of families in poverty declined in the 1960s, remained stable in the 1970s, and rose somewhat in the 1980s. Although most poor people are white, African Americans and Latinos are disproportionately found among the poor. Female-headed families are more likely to be poor than two-parent families or single-parent families headed by men. They are also less likely to have completed high school or college than those in the higher classes. The annual family income of the poor is likely to be less than $15,000, earned through hourly wages in low-paying, low-skill, dead-end jobs with few if any benefits or received through public welfare programs such as Aid to Families with Dependent Children and Supplemental Security Income. Because of their low earnings, the income of the poor often is at or below a level necessary for basic subsistence. They are generally the least informed among the electorate and have the lowest rates of organizational, political, and electoral participation.

Source: Leonard Beeghley, *The Structure of Social Stratification in the United States* (Boston, MA: Allyn and Bacon, 1989).

1. There must be a common associational context; that is, people must see that their roles in the workplace and the things that are happening to them as a result of those roles are pretty much the same.

2. There must be a high degree of similarity in background and in life chances. People's incomes and educations have to be similar.

3. There must be a shared awareness of undesirable conditions.

4. People must agree that others in the association (owners, managers, or other categories of workers) are the cause of the undesirable conditions.

5. Some kind of organized attempts to bring about change must take place. In this process, leaders must emerge to direct the energies of the class.[17]

Is the Middle Class Vanishing?

Are the middle classes—that great majority of Americans who are neither rich nor poor—declining in number? Many economists believe that since the mid-1980s this is indeed the case. Some even predict that the middle class will disappear altogether, leaving a country divided between rich and poor.

From the end of World War II until the early 1970s, real income (income adjusted for changes in consumer prices) rose rapidly. The increase was spread fairly evenly across the national income distribution, so income and wealth positions changed very little. Between 1970 and 1990 real income growth faltered, and the gains that did occur were among families and households at the upper end of the distribution. The result was greater inequality and a decline in the income and wealth of those in the middle. Between 1947 and 1984, the middle 60 percent of Americans received approximately 52.5 percent of family income. Between 1984 and 1989, that share fell to 49 percent. The share held by the bottom 20 percent of Americans remained stable, and the top 20 percent reaped the benefits of the middle-class decline.

Although these changes are significant, the lack of good long-term data and the relatively small changes in income distribution warrant caution in using terms like the "vanishing" or "disappearing" middle class. It is not unusual for distributions in the share of income and wealth to fluctuate. Nevertheless, at least four interrelated factors appear to be contributing to the present decline in the income and wealth of the middle class:

1. The changing family composition, particularly the rise in single-parent, female-headed families.

2. The loss of higher-paying jobs in industry and the growth of lower-paying jobs in service occupations.

3. The relocation of industry from the more unionized Northeast and Midwest to the less unionized South and West sections of the country and the loss of industrial jobs to foreign nations.

4. The increased prevalence of part-time jobs, particularly among those who prefer full-time work but must accept part-time work.

While the middle-class decline may be temporary, it is real enough for those experiencing it. Barbara Ehrenreich proposes that the decline is creating a "fear of falling" and fostering a shift to social and economic conservatism among middle-class Americans, especially those in professional and middle-management occupations. Confronted by stagnant wages, a decline in real income and wealth, and occupational insecurity, the middle classes have come to see the poor, who have not gained by their decline, as their enemy, and the rich, who have gained by it, as their friend.

Sources: Charles M. Beach, "The 'Vanishing' Middle Class? Evidence and Explanations," Madison, WI: Institute for Research on Poverty, Discussion Paper #864–88. July 1988; M. L. Oliver and T. M. Shapiro, "Wealth of a Nation: A Reassessment of Asset Inequality in America Shows at Least One Third of Households Are Asset-Poor," *American Journal of Economics and Sociology*, vol. 49 (April 1990), pp. 129–52; and Barbara Ehrenreich, *Fear of Falling: The Inner Life of the Middle Class*, (New York: Pantheon Books, 1989).

Social Classes and Racial and Ethnic Stratification

The differences in class status and in racial and ethnic status in the United States overlap considerably. Large percentages of people of color—African Americans, Puerto Ricans, Mexican Americans, and Native Americans, in particular—are found in the lower social class. Researchers have coined the term *ethclass* to describe the relation between social class and minority status. Especially where minorities of color are involved, social class as well as subcultural factors must be taken into account. As Wynetta Devore and Elfriede Schlesinger note, "this intersect of ethnicity and social class generates identifiable dispositions and behaviors."[18]

It would be inaccurate, however, to maintain that only ethnic and racial minorities have lower-class status in the United States. White ethnics—part of the majority white group—may be mired in lower-class status, fearful of unemployment and living on low incomes, even in poverty. The problems of the "white poor" in the South and in Appalachia have been the subject of many studies,[19] as have the white, working-class ethnic neighborhoods in such sections of the country as the Northeast and the Midwest. The delivery of effective social services to these groups depends on recognition and understanding of their unique characteristics.

Michael Novak describes white southern and eastern European ethnic groups affectionately as "PIGS" (Polish, Italians, Greeks, and Slavs), because they tended to be identified with factions opposing the civil rights movement in the 1960s and 1970s. He insists, however, that their attitudes were not racist (in the sense that they believed that blacks are inherently inferior) but rather were rooted in their own ethnic and class-based interests. Novak eloquently described the history of these largely Catholic and Jewish groups in the United States, the kinds of struggles they encountered and the adaptations they had to make in a society dominated by whites, Anglo-Saxons, and Protestants. They had to become more individualistic and competitive and less oriented to family and community. They also had to redefine the way they understood their sexuality. Protestantism, Catholicism, and Judaism all constrain sexual activity and preach that sex outside of marriage is sinful. But in Protestantism, sex is not only sinful, it is also dirty. For Catholics and Jews from southern and eastern Europe, sex may have been sinful, but it also was "delicious."[20]

In a like manner, Richard Sennett and Jonathan Cobb have described the life of white ethnics and the "hidden injuries of class" they suffer. Not having "made it" economically, they come to believe that their relatively low status is their own fault, and they live for the possibility that their children will not repeat what they believe were their own mistakes.[21]

Religious Denominations as Communities

Religion is another factor around which community life is organized. In the United States, unlike other nations, there is no official religion. Nevertheless, a strong Protestant Christian tradition has shaped this nation's heritage.

Today the United States is a mosaic of religions, Protestant, Catholic, Jewish, and others. According to surveys on religious preference conducted by the Gallup Organization, in 1990 56 percent of Americans said they were Protestants, 25 percent Catholics, and 2 percent Jews. Six percent had some other religious preference, and 11 percent had none.[22] Within religions, especially among Protestants, Jews, and "others," there is considerable variation. Protestants, for instance, may be Episcopalian, Baptist, Lutheran, or any number of other denominations. Jews may be Sephardic, Orthodox, Conservative, and so on. Other religions practiced by Americans include Muslim, Buddhist, and Hindu. Each religion or denomination unites people not only in terms of religious doctrine but also in terms of social and cultural values.

Religion is difficult to define in community terms because, like social class and, to some extent, ethnicity, the degree to which an individual or family identifies with a religion can vary a great deal. To say that a person is a Protestant does not describe the degree to which that person believes in the principles of a Protestant faith, nor does it describe the person's level of participation in a church and its activities. Religious attachment seems to differ among denominations. In one survey, Protestant fundamentalist denominations appeared to have created the greatest sense of attachment: 51 percent said they attend weekly services, and 58 percent rated their faith strong. Catholicism also seemed to be promoting a strong identity: just over 40 percent of Catholics rated their participation and their faith strong. The Episcopalians were less closely affiliated; 18 percent said they attend weekly services and 31 percent rated their faith strong.[23] However, a recent survey casts doubt on these findings. At the 1993 annual meeting of the American Sociological Association, Kirk Hadaway, Penny Long Marler, and Mark Chaves reported that approximately 20 percent of Protestants and 28 percent of Catholics attended church in any given week. They suggest that when Americans are asked to rate their own attendance, they are inclined to give a socially desirable response and thus overestimate their actual participation.[24]

Religious Affiliation and Social Attitudes

The NORC has been documenting the relation between religious affiliation and social attitudes since 1972. One of their findings is that certain Protestant denominations can be grouped together along a liberal-conservative continuum. At the liberal end of the Protestant scale are Episcopalians, Unitarians, Presbyterians, and Congregationalists; moderates include Methodists and Lutherans; and at the other, conservative end of the scale are a number of fundamentalist groups, as well as Baptists and Southern Baptists. Sectarian differences among Jews (Reformed, Orthodox, Conservative, etc.) are not documented in these studies, but in general they are seen as quite liberal. Such distinctions are useful in analyzing social and cultural attitudes.[25]

Protestant fundamentalists and Baptists evidence the most conservative attitudes. According to the NORC criteria, they are "often unwilling to allow an atheist the basic civil liberties—to make a speech, teach in a college, or have a book in a public library." Only about 20 percent in this group support all three of these rights. The percentage of support is much higher in other religious groups: 40 percent among Catholics, 54 percent in liberal Protestant denominations, and 61 percent among Jews.

Similar differences are apparent with regard to attitudes about sex, marriage, and child rearing. Fundamentalists and Baptists express the most conservative attitudes (see "Social Services for Fundamentalist Christian Families"). They condemn homosexual behavior, premarital sex, abortion, birth control information for teens, divorce, and new roles for women. Catholic attitudes resemble those of fundamentalists but are somewhat more lenient toward homosexual behavior. Protestant liberal denominations and Jews are the most progressive on all of these issues, and moderate Protestant denominations are somewhere in the middle. Fundamentalists and Baptists also put great emphasis on the obedience of children to parents; 45 percent see it as among the top three most important child-rearing values, compared to around 30 percent of Lutherans, Methodists, and Catholics. Only around 18 percent of Jews and Episcopalians consider obedience that important.

Despite these differences on sex, marriage, and child rearing, religious groups hardly differ with respect to their level of marital satisfaction reported in the NORC studies. About 45 percent of the people in each religion and denomination have reported "a very great deal of satisfaction" with their family life.

Social Services for Fundamentalist Christian Families

Religious fundamentalism among Christians is a social and historical movement directed against the liberalization of mainstream Protestant denominations. Although fundamentalism has been associated with rural Americans, this is less the case today than in the past. Fundamentalists tend to have in common a belief in the Bible as the authoritative, literal word of God. They assert the authority of the church over the family and the authority of the family over the individual. Their patriarchal orientation affirms the dominance of men over women, prohibits divorce, and places the sanctity of fetal life ahead of women's choice to control their bodies.

Families and individuals who belong to fundamentalist Christian religions, including charismatics, evangelicals, and Pentecostals, are seen by social service practitioners in a variety of settings, including family services, child welfare, services to youth, and mental health services.

Social workers who are not fundamentalist Christians, themselves often confront ethical dilemmas in working with such families. A basic conflict is whether to attempt to change clients' religious beliefs in order to change their behaviors. For some, doing so would violate the principle of client self-determination. For others, particularly if these beliefs promote violence against women and children, it is absolutely necessary.

Conflicts also arise when the worker has derogatory attitudes and opinions about religion or holds it responsible for the problems clients are experiencing. Other conflicts emerge when the worker is deeply religious and encourages clients to adopt a belief or join a church or religious group.

Roy Denton suggests certain practice strategies in working with fundamentalist Christian families. Workers should maintain a focus on the importance of religion to the client rather than on the validity of the client's religious beliefs or image of God. They need to show respect for the beliefs of clients and be willing to learn from them. They must strive for neutrality and refrain from judging clients' beliefs. They should try to locate the strengths in religious fundamentalism and value the helpful aspects of the religious experience for resolution of clients' problems. A social worker who is unable to do this should responsibly withdraw from the case.

Source: Roy T. Denton, "The Religiously Fundamentalist Family: Training for Assessment and Treatment," *Journal of Social Work Education*, vol. 26 (Winter 1990), pp. 6–14

The Gay and Lesbian Community

The relatively recent emergence of a community of gay men and lesbians provides an excellent example of how communities develop in a society. There is a question, however, as to whether gays and lesbians represent one "homosexual" community or two distinct communities. Although lesbians and gay men share a number of common experiences, they also have had different kinds of experiences. For instance, Philip Blumstein and Pepper Schwartz find that gay men share a common male socialization experience with "straight" men which makes them more similar in thought and action to other men than to lesbian women. The same is true the other way around; lesbians generally have more commonalties with heterosexual women than they do with gay men.[26] Frances Fitzgerald observes that gay men and lesbians also differ in their relationships to one another and in the way they have developed community life. While acknowledging the many healthy strengths in these communities, she points out that gay men tend to form atomistic and

Americans of different class, ethnic, racial, and religious backgrounds march in Washington, D.C., in 1993 in support of the homosexual community. Lesbians, gay men, bisexuals, and civil rights supporters have pushed for a change in perceptions of the community as a minority rather than a deviant group.

impersonal communities and to be very business-oriented, rationalistic, and hierarchical. Lesbians tend to be far more communal; even their business groups are likely to include encounter groups and other structures which encourage open communication and cooperation. She also notes that lesbians tend to become involved in close and emotionally intense friendships, "private and intimate to the point of suffocation."[27]

Two characteristics distinguish the lesbian and gay community or communities from heterosexual communities. First, gays and lesbians are not socialized into the homosexual community as children; that is, they do not learn the roles, values, and expectations of the community in the normal process of growing up. They learn the ways of the homosexual community after they have "come out," that is, after they have made a more-or-less conscious choice to become a part of that community. Second, because of the severe stigmatization they experience, lesbians and gays tend to be enveloped in a certain amount of protective secrecy, and relations with heterosexuals are often guarded.[28]

Deviant Group or Minority Group?

Everyone would not agree that gays and lesbians ought to be seen as a community or communities. Sociologists have defined them as deviants and therefore distinguishable from minorities, and homosexual conduct has been studied in courses on abnormal psychology and social deviance rather than normal growth and development. William Newman sees a good deal of commonality in **deviant groups** and minority groups, in that both are devalued, experience hostility, and have little social power. But deviants, he believes, "explicitly reject and violate legal norms" and would not be recognized as having a legitimate claim to power.[29] He also notes that distinguishing between minority groups and deviant groups raises other questions. When blacks rejected and violated Jim Crow laws which forced them to sit in the back of the bus or to drink from a segregated water fountain, were they acting as deviants rather than as minorities who were calling attention to unjust laws? Similarly, are homosexuals who reject and violate legal norms about homosexual behavior being deviant or are they clamoring against injustice?

In American society, deviant and minority groups represent opposite ends of a continuum of group status. But social movements can change perceptions about the status of groups in a society; when enough members of a society recognize a just cause and struggle to achieve it, deviant status may be overcome. The gay and lesbian rights movement of the past 25 years appears to be such a social movement. The basic right lesbians and gays have claimed is that they should be seen as minority communities, not as deviants. As Donald Webster Cory, one of the earliest defenders of homosexual rights, observes:

> ...our minority status is similar, in a variety of respects, to that of national, religious, and other ethnic groups: in the denial of civil liberties; in the legal, extra-legal, and quasi-legal discrimination; in the assignment of an inferior social position; in the exclusion from the mainstreams of life and culture; in the development of the protection and security of intra-group association; in the development of a special language and literature and a set of moral tenets within our group.[30]

In many countries, including the United States, it is legal to discriminate against lesbians and gays. Meredith Gould maintains that statutory (legal) oppression and **homophobia**, or irrational fear of homosexuals, characterize all American social institutions.[31] Our laws and attitudes in respect to homosexual behavior are deeply embedded in history. Sexual behavior not intended for procreation was condemned as unnatural after Constantine proclaimed Christianity the official religion of the Roman Empire, early in the fourth century A.D. For centuries, under church law, men and women suspected of homosexual behavior were tortured, mutilated, or burned at the stake. After a return to secular law in the twelfth century, antihomosexual attitudes became a cultural value supported by the developing science of medicine. Beginning in the nineteenth century, psychiatry also gave credence to antihomosexual values.[32]

The civil rights movement among gays and lesbians, supported by sympathetic heterosexuals, has challenged this history of discrimination and encouraged public acknowledgment of this community as a part of American society. The American Psychiatric Association no longer considers homosexual behavior a mental disorder. States (Wisconsin was the first) and cities have passed laws forbidding discrimination based on sexual orientation. In Colorado, the state supreme court agreed in July 1993 with a lower court that an amendment to the state constitution banning state and local laws prohibiting discrimination based on sexual orientation, which had been passed by 53 percent of the state's voters, should not be put into effect. The ruling was on the grounds that "to a reasonable

---

Diversity in Homosexual Lifestyles

In their study titled *Homosexualities: A Study of Diversity among Men and Women,* Alan Bell and Martin Weinberg identify five types of homosexuals.

Closed couples are gays or lesbians in long-term relationships in which the partners are deeply involved and rely on each other for sexual and interpersonal satisfaction. They are the most well adjusted psychologically and the least likely couples to regret being homosexual. Closed-coupled males represented 13.8 percent of the study sample and closed-couple females constituted 38.4 percent.

Open couples are lesbians or gays who live with sexual partners in long-term relationships but find them unsatisfying. Individuals in open relationships tend to have other sexual affairs. They are as psychologically well-adjusted as the average homosexual. Open couples represented 24.7 percent of the male sample and 24.1 percent of the female sample for the study.

Functionals are homosexuals who come close to the idea of swinging singles, organizing their lives around sexual activities. They are the least likely singles to regret being homosexual and are involved in the lesbian and gay community. Their good psychological profiles may be attributed to their personalities; they are energetic, self-reliant, cheerful, and optimistic. They do not score quite as high as closed couples in psychological adjustment. Functionals represented 21 percent of the male sample and 14.2 percent of the female sample.

Dysfunctionals are homosexuals who most resemble the negative stereotype of gay or lesbian. They are the most unhappy homosexuals and tend to regret having this status. They are likely to have a fair amount of sex but feel inadequate about finding and keeping a partner; generally, they think of themselves as sexually unappealing. They often have had negative experiences associated with being homosexual, such as robbery, assault, extortion, and job difficulties. Dysfunctionals represented 17.7 percent of the men and 7.6 percent of the women in the sample.

Asexuals are gay men and lesbians who have little social and sexual involvement with others. The men tend to be unhappy, and the women are likely to give up on finding professional help with sexual issues. Asexuals have the highest incidence of suicidal thought. They are the least likely to think of themselves as exclusively homosexual, and the men, especially, have few homosexual friends. Asexuals constituted 22.7 percent of the males and 15.6 percent of the females in the sample.

Source: Adapted from Alan P. Bell and Martin S. Weinberg, *Homosexualities: A Study of Diversity among Men and Women* (New York: Simon and Schuster, 1978), pp. 217–28.

---

probability," the amendment violates the Fourteenth Amendment to the U.S. Constitution, which forbids states from denying equal protection under the law to anyone. In cities, antidiscriminatory laws have been easier to pass if, as in Chicago in 1988, they are named "human rights" rather than "gay rights" ordinances and extend protection not only to homosexuals but to anyone whose marital or parental status, military discharge status, or source of income, as well as race, color, sex, age, or religion, might be a source of discrimination.

By 1993, at least 16 cities, from New York to San Francisco, were also recognizing unmarried partners in one or more of three areas: benefits such as sick leave, bereavement leave, and health insurance for unmarried employees' domestic partners; tax credits for private companies that offer such benefits for nontraditional couples; and legal registration of domestic partnerships similar to marriage licenses. Although such ordinances are usually perceived as a gay rights issue, in cities that have adopted domestic partner legislation, such as Berkeley, California, and Madison, Wisconsin, the experience has been that at least half of those who register as domestic partners are of the opposite sex.[33]

Acceptance of the community of gays and lesbians does not mean that Americans' attitudes toward homosexuality have completely changed, and they are now universally accepted as a minority rather than a deviant group. The civil rights of lesbians and gays may be officially recognized—including, to some extent, the right to serve in the armed forces—but not even sympathy for the victims of AIDS has been able to eradicate the feelings of hostility, hatred, or contempt that some Americans direct to members of this community (see "AIDS and the gay and Lesbian Community" in Chapter 9). They tend to overlook the fact that the culture that has emerged in it is rich and diverse; gays and lesbians are not homogenous groups that can be easily identified by the behaviors and lifestyles of some members[34] (see "Diversity in Homosexual Lifestyles").

Emergence of the Community

The emergence of a gay and lesbian community appears to be a unique historical phenomenon. While homosexuality has been practiced in almost every society and in every historical period, a common homosexual identity, with an emphasis on coupling and the development of community, appears to be related to advanced industrial, free-market societies. Barry Adam hypothesizes that the same forces which shaped changes in heterosexual family life with the development of capitalism also promoted the modern homosexual community. As a feudal, agricultural society changed to an industrial, free-market society, the dominant heterosexual kinship was weakened. When exclusive homosexuality became possible, so did autonomous, self-aware homosexual communities.[35]

Gay and lesbian voluntary associations have existed in the United States throughout most of the twentieth century.[36] Vigorous organizing activities in the community followed the "Stonewall riots" in 1969, when New York City police met with resistance as they tried to shut down the Stonewall Inn, a bar frequented by "counterculture" gays. A "gay liberation front" emerged, accompanied by a number of gay and lesbian civil rights organizations, social clubs, business organizations, newspapers and magazines, and social service associations. As a result, a strong community spirit developed both within neighborhoods and across the country.

The lesbian and gay community is largely identificational, made up of people who share a common identity and who have developed unique subcultural lifestyles. In certain large cities, however, it also has become a locational community based in certain neighborhoods. This is particularly true for gay men. Such areas as West Los Angeles, the Castro in San Francisco, and Christopher Street in New York are largely gay neighborhoods. In smaller cities, the tendency is for gays to live near one another. The lesbian neighborhood is not as common; lesbian communities generally have been regarded as being comprised of individuals loosely joined by history, jargon, and significant activities. Deborah Goleman Wolf notes that the term *lesbian community* is "used by the women themselves to refer to the continuing social networks of lesbians who are committed to the lesbian-feminist lifestyle, who participate in various community activities and projects, and who congregate socially."[37] She concludes that there is a sociopsychological unity which holds lesbians together. Fitzgerald observes that in San Francisco there are small, loose enclaves of lesbians, but they are not nearly as clearly defined as those in which gay men live.[38]

Lesbians and gay men are found in all racial and ethnic groups, in all social classes, and undoubtedly in all religions. The experience of being homosexual and being part of another community or class may add to the difficulties they face. Some religions, for example, are extremely intolerant of homosexuals. Ethnic and racial communities vary in terms of their acceptance of homosexual conduct and identity.[39] Latinos are often assumed to be particularly repressive, and Native Americans, who often accorded social approval and dignity to homosexual behavior before they were conquered and displaced by Europeans, appear to have adopted more hostile attitudes toward it.

Recognition of the gay and lesbian community has improved and expanded the social services provided to members. Until recently, according to Betty Sancier, "the only 'help' that homosexuals could expect from the human service professions was in the direction of being made over to become 'normal' heterosexuals."[40] Now the community is one focus of social work intervention, including support services for parents of gays and lesbians, work with teenagers, counseling for couples, services for the elderly, and help for people with sexually transmitted diseases such as acquired immune deficiency syndrome (AIDS).[41]

∞ RACIAL AND ETHNIC COMMUNITIES

The most common bases for identificational communities in the United States are race and ethnicity. In this and the following section, we examine these concepts as the basis for the diversity in American society that both gives it strength and presents it with problems. For the social service worker, these concepts focus on different ways to develop an understanding of the individual strengths and problems that may become evident among members of various groups, an understanding that is essential in planning and providing them with social services.

The Meaning of Race

Race refers to biological differences among groups of people. Although we use the term frequently in everyday language, it is relatively new, originating in the enlightenment period of eighteenth-century Europe.[42] Naturalists, who used scientific methods to study human variation, began to classify people according to their visible differences. The use of classification systems, sometimes referred to as *typologies* or *taxonomies*, is one of the oldest and most respected methods in science.

Attempts at Racial Classification

In a work on the unity of man and nature which was published in 1735, Carolus Linnaeus, a Swedish botanist, identified the human species and classified humans into four color groups. He saw these as fixed subgroups within the species but acknowledged that the division was arbitrary. He did not, however, refer to these four groups as races.

George Louis LeClerc was the first to use the term *race*. He distinguished six races but saw them not as fixed subgroups but as existing in a continual, flexible, ever-changing process. Johann Blumenbach, the father of physical anthropology, later proposed a typology of five races based on differences in human skull measurements. He created the "science" of phrenology but, like Linnaeus, maintained that his division into five races was arbitrary and that human differences are so complex that they defy the creation of a reliable classification system.

It was nineteenth-century scholars and political officials who developed the ideas of race and racism. Whereas eighteenth-century naturalists studied differences, nineteenth-century thinkers looked for *invidious differences* of an objectionable nature which could cause envy, discontent, or resentment. Arthur de Gobineau, a French aristocrat, argued in 1854 that the French nobility had descended directly from a noble Aryan race and thus was superior to the peasants and city dwellers who had promoted the French Revolution. Some 50 years later, in Britain, Henry Stewart Chamberlain argued for a connection between race and culture, maintaining that because Aryans were of a superior race, their culture also was superior and they were deserving of the empires they had built. Francis Galton, a British anthropologist who developed the science of eugenics, went even further with his dictum that only superior people should populate the world. Influenced by these ideas, Adolf Hitler would argue in the twentieth century for the superiority of Aryans and would attempt to eliminate the "inferior" Jewish race.[43]

The ideas of thinkers such as these came to be regarded as "common knowledge" and "common sense" about race. According to these early ideas, a small, fixed number of pure races or racial types exists. These races consist of a series of highly interrelated physical attributes (skin color, blood, hair type, etc.) which are passed down in their entirety from one generation to another. Thus races are immutable differences which can be traced back to the dawn of creation. External physical attributes are passed on as a package, and the mixing of people from two different races leads to a fairly predictable blending of the races. These externally visible racial characteristics determine culture and individual behavior. When races are placed on an evolutionary scale, certain races can be shown to be superior, as evidenced by their culture and behavior.

At the same time this kind of thinking was pervading everyday life—and to some extent it still may be—evidence was being gathered to disprove it. Though his work was virtually ignored for years, Gregor Mendel, a nineteenth-century Austrian botanist, patiently studied the genetics of inheritance and mapped out the *law of segregation*, which maintains that inheritance rests "not on blends of parental qualities, but on combinations of parental genes, units that preserve their own particular nature unchanged through the generations. Every individual is a new combination of existing genes."[44] In short, Mendel taught that **phenotype**, or external physical characteristics, could not indicate anything about **genotype**, or internal characteristics. Knowing what a group of people look like today is no indication of what they might have looked like in some distant past.

While Mendel's work was being ignored, scientists were continually trying to classify humans into discrete or separate races. No two scientists, it would appear, were ever able to agree on the number of races. Some said there were 4, others said there were 34.[45] In popular culture in the United States, the idea of three pure races—Caucasoid, Mongoloid, and Negroid—was adopted.

All attempts to classify humans into discrete races are inevitably doomed to failure, since most differences that exist among peoples are continuous, not qualitative. Classification systems based on continuous differences, such as height, skin color, or skull shape, are necessarily arbitrary. Height, for instance, is measured in inches (or centimeters): each person can be rated as relatively tall or short, but one person may be 5 feet 10 inches and another 5 feet 11 or 9 inches. Where can the lines possibly be drawn to divide the world's populations into short, tall, and medium heights? Another example is skin tone, which is determined by the relative mix of three hormones possessed by all humans: melanin, hemoglobin, and carotene. From the North Pole to the equator, skin tones show less hemoglobin and more melanin, but there is no clear dividing line between people who are dark and those who are light. There are, however, some differences among people that are qualitative. Blood is the best example; blood types may be A, B, AB, or O. But blood types cannot be used successfully to divide the races. There is no such thing as "black blood" or "white blood." All groups have all blood types, to a lesser or greater extent.

Contemporary Ideas on Race

Today, theorists generally either reject the concept of race altogether or define it in such terms as **gene pools** or *breeding populations*.[46] This idea of race, based on the Mendelian law of segregation, suggests that races essentially are formed by groups of people living in geographical or social isolation. Peoples who live and procreate among themselves inevitably develop a pool of genes out of which similarities in physical appearance emerge. The most physically and socially distant are the most likely to be noticeably different in appearance. This view acknowledges, however, that races are not discrete, distinct groups but simply "local limitations in the total variation in man."[47] Those who reject the idea of race altogether argue that since any designation of race is essentially arbitrary in nature and since the concept has caused so much harm, it should be dismissed from scientific discourse.

Regardless of whether or not the concept of race should be rejected, its political and social natures cannot be ignored. Race may or may not be a biological fact, but it is certainly a social fact. In the political sense, race can be understood as a social construction of reality, something created by peoples and used for political purposes as a way of justifying enslavement, colonial conquest, or genocide. To understand the politics of this social construction we need only compare how race is defined in the United States with how it is defined in other societies.

In American society, traditional definitions of the "Negro" race, for instance, stipulate that a person is black or African American to the extent that he or she has any identifiable features which indicate African ancestry. In some states, court decisions have produced legal definitions. In Louisiana, "colored persons" were legally defined in *Lee v. New Orleans Great Northern RR Co.* (1910). "Colored persons," the decision read, were "all persons with any appreciable mixture of Negro blood."

If it were possible to stand back from the "common sense" of American culture, we could ask why members of the white race are not defined as people "with any appreciable mixture of white blood" or "any person who has in his or her veins any Caucasian blood whatsoever." In the United States, to be white is to be "pure," and to be black is to be tainted. A child born of a white father and a black mother might just as easily be considered white as black. Puerto Rico is a society which traditionally has taken this approach. Until very recently, Puerto Ricans measured their whiteness; to be considered black (*prieto*), a person had to be virtually of pure African ancestry. Puerto Ricans used a host of terms, such as *mulatto, trigueño*, and *moreno*, to describe people who are white but might have some African ancestry. The word *negro* (black) was used not to designate a race but simply to designate the color black, or it was used as a term of endearment between spouses, lovers, and friends. It carried no connotation of skin color until recently, when, as an unfortunate consequence of colonialization in Puerto Rico, *negro* began to mean color of skin.

Defining a person as nonwhite proves just as difficult. Native Americans and Asians are designated as nonwhite in the U.S. Census. Native Americans are defined by law; to be on the roll of most tribes, a person must be at least 25 percent American Indian.

Definitions of Asian are more difficult; there is no standard for how many generations of Asian ancestry are required for this designation. Latinos are designated as white unless a particular Latino person says she or he is not white. This is the case even though most Mexican Americans are *mestizo*, that is, of mixed Spanish and Indian heritage.[48]

Ethnic Communities and Ethnicity

The difficulties of defining race are one reason we have referred to racial *and* ethnic communities rather than racial *or* ethnic communities. We consider the concepts of ethnicity and race to be equally inclusive. Races can include peoples of many ethnic groups. Ethnic groups can include people of any color.

An **ethnic group** has been defined by Richard Burkey as "a community group based upon the ascribed status of a diffuse ancestry that is maintained by similarities of culture, language, and/or phenotype"[49] and by Richard Shermerhorn as "a collectivity within a larger society having a real or putative common ancestry."[50] These definitions take into account four important features of ethnic groups.

First, ethnic groups generally are subcommunities within a larger national state. Thus, where everyone might be American, individuals might also be European Americans, African Americans, Jewish Americans, or Irish Americans. The former citizens of the Soviet Union have become known separately as Russians, Ukrainians, Uzbeks, Byelorussians, Lithuanians, Estonians, Jews, Georgians, Armenians, Latvians, and members of other ethnic groups.

Second, ethnic groups are based on a sense of common ancestry. That is, the subjective reality, the perception of members that they are as one and are perceived by others in the same way, is more important than the objective reality, actually being of a common ancestry. Many peoples who became part of the ethnic mix of the United States did not arrive with a sense of common ancestry but only developed such a sense once they were here. The people we think of as Italian Americans in actuality came to the United States as Sicilians, Calabrians, and a myriad of other identities. While often these identities still are important in individual families, they tend to get lost in the identity of Italian American. When blacks were forced to come to the United States, they were brought from different parts of Africa and from different tribes within Africa. Their identity as a group in the United States emerged only as a result of their being forced together by whites.

The sense of common ancestry emerges in the course of history as new experiences with other nations and communities are encountered. It comes about because other communities define a people as of similar ancestry, and they come to accept that definition and start to act as a separate, distinct community. It follows, of course, that ethnic groups also decompose. In this respect there are two opposing views of American social development. The idea of the society as a melting pot implies that ethnic identities should eventually disappear and only a single American identity should remain (see Chapter 5). The idea of a multicultural society implies that ethnic identities should not be amalgamated and that American society should remain a mosaic of separate, diverse, and equally proud identities.

The third feature of ethnic groups is that they are, at their root, collections of families with a common ancestry. Ancestry implies marriage, procreation, birth, and socialization of the young. Ethnic groups thus are pools of possible partners for mating, and new members enter primarily through birth or adoption. Selection for membership is on an ascriptive basis, determined by characteristics present at birth (see Chapter 3), and members of ethnic groups hold an ascribed status. An achieved status, in contrast, results when selection is on an achievement basis. Members join these groups more or less because they want to. In sum, ethnic groups are those that people are born into and are reared to cherish.

Fourth, the sense of shared ancestry is reflected in the development of an ethnic identity, or *ethnicity*. Ethnic groups are held together for a number of reasons, including coercive experiences from outside or within the particular group. However, the most important ingredient holding an ethnic group together usually is its ethnicity. Ethnicity can be thought of as the psychological or attitudinal core of the group. It reflects all those things the members believe they share in common.[51]

Factors Associated with Ethnicity

Burkey identifies three factors commonly associated with ethnicity: language, culture, and physical type.[52]

Language   The boundaries between ethnic groups are most often structured around language and styles of speech. Ethnic group members maintain and, in many cases, develop their own language and socialize each other to speak it properly. Outgroup members become "foreigners." This phenomenon is apparent even when ethnic groups share the same language as the host society. Members develop subtle styles and inflections and unique words and phrases, and in this way they set themselves apart. African Americans are believed to have developed a special way of speaking English which is based in part on African influences and in part on their need to celebrate their uniqueness.[53]

Culture   The term *culture*, as we have noted, generally refers to symbolic meanings that are shared among members of a society; that is, all the beliefs, values, norms, and traditions that govern social interaction among members or between members and outsiders. But, although shared symbolic meanings form the attitudinal core out of which actual behaviors emerge, behaviors are not always a good indication of beliefs, values, and norms. It is not uncommon for situations, especially those that are cross-cultural in nature, to demand a behavior which is not in keeping with the culture. Similarly, as James Green aptly points out, culture and ethnicity should not be thought of as some fixed set of traits which define a group and make for easy categorization of it. Social workers who presume that members of particular ethnic groups can be pigeonholed into categories will unwisely stereotype their clients.[54] They must recognize that ethnic culture is dynamic and constantly emerging and changing.

Physical type   The practice of continual intermarriage in ethnic communities leads to the development of certain kinds of physical features which distinguish members from other groups. There is considerable debate about the reality of race, as we have seen, and there is no such thing as a pure race. Races are formed essentially through the social, environmental, and biological processes surrounding birth and mate selection. Thus, ethnic communities (Italians, Mexican Americans, Swedes, etc.) acquire certain physically distinguishing characteristics, not because they originated from some pure race which existed in antiquity but simply because, as they have come to see themselves as one, they have increasingly intermarried and procreated. Of course, there is considerable variation in physical appearance within these groups. Many members do not look at all as they might be expected to look. Moreover, sometimes what appears different about people's appearance is not so much what they look like but how they act. Two first cousins, both of Polish ancestry, looked like they could have been twins. But one was born in Argentina and the other in the United States, and one had an obviously Latino demeanor while the other was just as obviously American. Anyone seeing them separately would not mistake their ethnic origin, but seeing them together was startling.

Ethnic Community Relations

As ethnic communities emerge, they celebrate their sense of common ancestry by developing organizations or associations which serve to hold the group together as well as to help the group meet its goals and obtain needed resources. Ethnic associations include churches, lodges, clubs, businesses, political parties, banks, and interest groups or lobbies. It is not uncommon for social services to be provided by ethnic groups. These associations often represent the "natural helping systems" within the community.

Those who understand multigroup societies in terms of ethnic groups and ethnicity generally emphasize that the source of problems between groups has to do with cultural differences and the difficulty of bridging the cultural gap between groups. Problems between Latinos and Anglos (whites), for instance, are believed to relate to the fact that Latinos have developed language and cultural values and norms which are very different from those developed by Anglos. When members of these groups get together, communication often breaks down and expectations get confused. Similarly, when the problems that are assumed to exist between whites and blacks are seen in terms of ethnicity, the focus is on differences in communication styles.[55] When a social worker of one ethnic group meets a client of another ethnic group, for instance, the worker must become aware of the ethnically distinct origins of her own behavior, while respecting and trying to tune into the ethnically distinct origins of her client.

∽ MINORITY AND MAJORITY

Another way multigroup societies can be understood is through the concepts of minority and majority. These terms refer to a status hierarchy which operates in terms of numbers, differences, prestige, and power. For instance, in contemporary American society, European Americans, including all those with origins in northern and western Europe, are ethnic groups, but they are not minority groups. African Americans, Puerto Ricans, Mexican Americans, and Native Americans are ethnic groups which are also minority groups.

In everyday usage, *minority* and *majority* are terms which refer to the size of a group; minorities are groups that are believed to be relatively small in size, whereas majorities are believed to be relatively large. But this everyday usage somehow falls short in the case of specific examples. For instance, the white community of apartheid South Africa was seldom referred to as a minority group, even though whites represented less than 10 percent of the population. In the United States, it is not unusual for women to be referred to as a minority group, although they constitute slightly more than half of the population. Size may be a consideration in determining minority status, but size per se is not the distinguishing characteristic of minority and majority groups.

When sociologists use the term *minority group* they usually mean a group that is negatively valued and treated with hostility within a society. Perhaps the most frequently quoted definition was written by Louis Wirth. He describes a minority group as "a group of people who, because of their physical or cultural characteristics, are singled out from others in the society in which they live for differential and unequal treatment and who therefore regard themselves as objects of collective discrimination."[56] Other definitions generally focus on the same issues. According to John R. Howard, "the fundamental fact of ethnic stratification is domination of one group by another. Members of minority groups experience stigma on categorical grounds."[57] Edward Sagarin notes that "it is when the social differentiation takes place followed by the social inequality,...resulting in collective and irrelevant discrimination, that the minority emerges."[58]

While definitions of minorities abound, definitions of majorities are seldom found. As a result, the concept of *majority group* is less well understood, and this in turn produces a less-than-full understanding of minority groups.

Newman uses the criteria of relative group size, social differences, and power to distinguish minority from majority:

> Minority groups may be defined as groups that vary from the social norms or archetypes in some manner, are subordinate with regard to the distribution of social power, and rarely constitute more than one-half of the population of the society in which they are found....In contrast to minority groups, majority groups may be defined as those groups that create or enforce the social norms or exemplify the social archetypes (trait characteristics of groups that are the most highly desired or rewarded), are superordinate with regard to the distribution of power, and are neither extremely large nor extremely small.[59]

Aside from the issue of group size, the two key features of Newman's definition are that majorities "create or enforce the social norms" and are "superordinate with regard to the distribution of power." If words like *stigmatized, victimized, discriminated against, oppressed,* and *disadvantaged* are associated with ethnic minorities and minority individuals, then words like *advantaged* and *powerful* are associated with ethnic majorities and majority individuals. Majority groups create the stigmas attached to minorities and are powerful enough to victimize, discriminate against, and take advantage of them.

Minority Groups and Minority Individuals

Minority status is generally an ascribed status in that the people making up the minority group have been born into the status or at least are believed to have had little choice in the matter. Therefore, the term is most often used to refer to ethnic and other groups that are at their core collections of families and pass on their status and heritage from one generation to the next. Examples include African Americans, Chinese Americans, the Amish, and Jehovah's Witnesses. Their stigmas and disadvantages are suffered collectively in family life, and their children must learn to deal with a hostile environment.[60] The whole family confronts hostility and devaluation by the larger society.

In contemporary usage, however, the concept of minority is not always applied in this way. Women, the aged, sexual minorities, and the disabled often are referred to as minorities and are believed to suffer common devaluation and hostility, but they are not at their core collections of families that pass on a common ancestry. Membership in such groups is ascribed on the basis of people's characteristics as individuals, not as family members. To distinguish members of these groups from ethnic minorities, we refer to them as *minority individuals*. The positions of women, children, and the elderly in society are examined in Chapter 8 in the section on family politics. The position of the disabled as a minority group capable of being mainstreamed in society is discussed in Chapter 2 in the section on normality and the disabled.

Types of Minorities

Minority groups and individuals are singled out on the basis of particular traits that members are believed to have in common. Not only are they perceived to be different from the majority in the particular trait, but the difference is considered undesirable. Minorities differ in various ways. Some differences are accorded high value and assure people of supportive experiences, while others are accorded low value and result in hostile experiences. Having a British accent or eating French food are differences that often are considered favorably in American society. Having a Mexican accent or eating soul food have not been so valued, at least until recently.

Newman postulates that minority status—both ethnic-minority and minority-individual status—evolves around physical, cognitive, or behavioral characteristics.[61] While these categories are not mutually exclusive, they are useful in thinking about various kinds of minority groups.

Physical minorities are those who look different from the majority of people. Perhaps the most important example is race. African Americans have been singled out for differential treatment largely on the basis of their skin color. To be dark-skinned and have tightly curled hair in a society which equates beauty with fair skin and blondness is to suffer minority status. Other physical differences, however, can can be used as a basis for singling out minorities. According to Newman, to the extent that people with disabilities and the aged are considered minority groups or minority individuals, they also are physical minorities.

Cognitive minorities are those whose low status has evolved around the beliefs and values they hold. Ethnic and religious groups are the most obvious examples; they believe and follow their own cultural and religious traditions. Minority status also can evolve around political beliefs. The Libertarian Party in the United States can be considered a minority, distinguishable from the Democratic-Republican majority.

Behavioral minorities are those who do not so much look or think differently from the majority but behave in ways the majority believes are undesirable. Perhaps the most obvious example, according to Newman, is gays and lesbians. They do not necessarily think differently from the heterosexual majority, and they do not necessarily look different. It is their behavior, their attempt to fulfill themselves sexually, that is not valued in society and produces their minority status.

Women as a Minority

Women constitute a very slight gender majority in the population of the United States; in 1991, there were 95.2 males for every 100 females.[62] Nevertheless, women usually are included in discussions of minority groups. Certainly, as the chapters on family life in Part III will discuss more fully, women are the object of economic and other forms of discrimination. Women's wages still were just 74 percent of men's in 1991; median weekly earnings for men employed full-time were $497, while for women they were $368. Single mothers heading families are the most disadvantaged; in 1990 when the median money income for all families was $35,353, it was just $13,092 for family households headed by

The Three Faces of Feminism

Feminist consciousness is evident among women in some racial and ethnic communities, but it is most apparent among affluent white women of European background who have mainstream Jewish or Christian beliefs. Feminist consciousness takes different forms, however. Janet A. Nes and Peter Iadicola identify three strains within feminism which differ on a number of dimensions, including their understanding of human nature, inequality and the factors perpetuating it, and the good society and how it is to be achieved.

Liberal feminists believe that men and women do not differ in their human nature; inequality becomes a problem only when there is too much of it or it results from discrimination. They also maintain that through gender-role socialization, women are taught to deny discrimination exists. They believe that a better society can be achieved by working within the system to bring about equal opportunity.

Radical feminists believe that women are different from men; women are more caring, loving, and spiritual and less competitive and individualistic. Inequality is not natural to humans but stems from patriarchy, that is, from sex-gender oppression by men.

Sexual inequality is perpetuated largely because men benefit from it and work in their own self-interest. The good radical society is one in which women's values become dominant, and it can only come about through self-help, separatism, consciousness raising, and the promotion of androgyny (attitudes, beliefs, and behaviors that are not specific to one gender).

Socialist feminists believe that women and men have different values due to the structure of sex and gender roles in society. Inequality is rooted in social class as well as in patriarchy, and it is maintained not only because men benefit but also because capitalist interests benefit; a sex-segregated labor force and unpaid labor in the home (housework) assure greater profit. The good socialist society is one in which all forms of oppression are eradicated, including those based on social class and sex or gender. This society can only be achieved by organizing all oppressed groups and building coalitions among them.

Source: Janet A. Nes and Peter Iadicola, "Toward a Definition of Feminist Social Work: A Comparison of Liberal, Radical and Socialist Models," *Social Work*, vol. 34 (January 1989), pp. 12–22.

women.[63] Women also continue to have a subordinate social status. While the religious and secular laws that gave men authority over women in the family and in society have largely been discarded, women's social position still is subordinated. Women may be regarded as somehow deviant, treated as sexual objects, spoken to rather than listened to, excluded from occupational and political leadership, segregated into female-oriented occupations, or expected to function largely within the realm of family life.[64]

Nevertheless, despite such evidence of discriminatory treatment, it is not clear that the term *minority group* pertains to women. As we have noted, minority groups have traditionally been understood as collections of ethnic or racial families. By themselves, heterosexual women do not form families or communities, though homosexual women may do so. The status of all women, therefore, cannot be adequately understood by defining them as a separate community or as a group independent of the communities of which they are a part. The nature and extent of subordination women experience are largely determined by the ways in which they are tied to various social class, religious, and ethnic and racial communities. Their status also differs across time and space; as Johnnetta Cole notes, all women are not discriminated against in the same ways.[65]

Newman does not consider women in general to be a minority group because, he says, the norms of heterosexual women do not differ from the norms of society. In 1973, when Newman wrote, societal expectations were that women would be heterosexual and function largely within family and social life, and he could define women involved in the women's movement as a cognitive minority group.[66]

But categorizing women as those who are a minority and those who are not is unwarranted. The position we take is that all women in contemporary society are subordinated, but their status is best understood in terms of the class, religious, and racial and ethnic communities of which they are a part. The question is not whether women are subordinate to men, but why it is that some women perceive themselves to be subordinate members of their communities and other women do not. The issues are very similar to those about social class consciousness raised earlier in this chapter. For feminist consciousness to emerge, a number of social and psychological preconditions are necessary: There must be a common associational context, a high degree of similarity in background, a shared awareness of undesirable status, an agreement as to the cause of this status, and some kind of organized attempt at change. There must also be opportunities within the communities for a feminist view to take hold (see "The Three Faces of Feminism"). There are many communities in American society in which these conditions are not met, and it should not be surprising that women of different communities have very different understandings of their status.

Minority-Majority Relations

Minority groups and individuals exist in a social relationship with majority groups and individuals, and they must be understood in those terms. Newman's differentiation between minority and majority groups on the basis of the social power of the majority to stigmatize and discriminate against the minority (discussed above) is useful in developing such an understanding.

Competition and Conflict

The relationship between minority and majority essentially is one of hostility; competition and conflict are inherent in the distinctions between the two groups. This hostility is generated not only because the groups may have developed different languages and cultures, so their communication is hampered, but because they have very different interests. Majorities are interested in maintaining their advantage; they want to continue to create and enforce the social norms and to hold their superordinate position. Minorities are interested in reducing or overcoming their stigma and disadvantage. They want a hand in creating and enforcing the norms, and they want to be able to experience some degree of autonomy and power.

Just what is it that minorities and majorities are fighting over? The nature of the hostility obviously will vary, depending on the type of minority group involved. In the broadest sense the struggle is about dominance and control, and since the struggle of minority and majority takes place within a national society, the prize they are seeking is dominance and control of the state. Burkey makes the point abundantly clear: "A dominant ethnic group or race exists when the majority of the major positions of the state are occupied by the members of one ethnic group or race."[67] The struggle, however, often is played out around more specific issues. With respect to ethnic and racial minority groups, at least two areas of competition and conflict can be identified. One is economic, and the other involves national character or cultural ascendancy.

In part, the hostility between minority and majority groups is economic and is demonstrated in social class relationships. As workers, minorities and majorities often are part of the same class, and the conflict is about which group will get the good jobs, the seniority, the security, and the good paycheck. Economic issues such as jobs and housing are believed to be at the root of much of the conflict between minorities of color and dominant whites in the United States today.[68]

Minorities and majorities also are engaged in conflict over the national character. This struggle can be defined in two ways. In the first, the struggle is over whose cultural characteristics are to typify the nation; whose language will be official, whose heroes will be honored, whose traditions and holidays will be observed. This struggle is most often associated with ethnic and religious differences, but it is also in the background of other differences. In Canada, for example, the people of Quebec have made several attempts to separate the province from the rest of the nation, in order to preserve their French language and customs. In the second, the struggle is over whose physical and behavioral characteristics are to typify the national image. In the United States, this involves decisions about what physical features are to be taken as the standard in identifying beauty and personifying the typical American. What does Uncle Sam look like? Who will be chosen as Miss America, the typical all-American boy, or the girl next door?

Limitations to Hostility

Although the relationships between majority and minority is by definition hostile, the hostility need not always be open, nor must it necessarily be intense. It is not unusual for a semblance of harmony to appear in the relations between minorities and majorities. At one time there may be civil strife, while at another the relationship may actually appear amicable. During the latter periods, majority-group members may assume there is no problem, and minority-group members may be happy. It is also quite possible for the stigma and disadvantage to operate in subtle ways rather than being evident. In some periods hostility may take the form of warfare or genocide, while in others it takes the form of social snobbery or failure to extend friendship.

Moreover, even though hostility typifies minority-majority relations, minority and majority persons are not always aware of it. Hostility is often obscured by "the way things are." Where we live and whom we make friends with are often shaped by the hostility that pervades minority-majority relationships, but few in the majority group would assume that they are acting in a hostile manner when they make friends and choose a place to live. They perceive their behavior as normal and natural, merely a matter of finding a good place to live and making compatible friendships. Nevertheless, minority-group members are likely to feel the hostility which is perhaps inadvertently generated by the majority-group members in making such decisions.

∞ IMPLICATIONS FOR PRACTICE

This chapter has explored the nature of community life in the United States, giving special attention to communities based on identification: those communities that are held together by affection, historical circumstances, and a sense of common destiny.

Identificational communities are important to social service workers for at least three reasons. First, many of the attitudes and values of individuals derive from their everyday experiences in communities. Second, many of the social and psychological troubles experienced by individuals and families have their origin in the public issues connected to the communities in which they live. Third, communities support their members, and thus they build strengths and resources to help individuals and families cope and adapt. Social service workers, therefore, need to orient themselves to the community context of client behavior.

Building a Helping Relationship

There are many ways to incorporate the notion of identificational community into social service practice with individuals and families. We will synthesize the discussion of community life by focusing on how direct-service social workers build helping relationships with clients whose communities differ from their own. To build such relationships, the worker must generate accurate empathy and rapport with clients and thus come to understand their needs and problems from their own point of view. Building good helping relationships is a vital first step in effective practice.

Throughout this chapter two attributes of identificational communities have been stressed: Each community develops a unique culture, and each carries with it a certain status. In order to empathize and build rapport accurately, social workers must become sensitive to both of these attributes of communities.

When things go wrong in the relationship between a client and a social worker, the source of the difficulty may very well be in the cultural gap that exists between them. An African American social worker, raised in his own community, may make assumptions about the society which are foreign to his white, Latino, or Hmong clients. A social worker with an affluent, Episcopalian background is likely to hold values and norms that are very different from those of a poverty-class client who is a Southern Baptist. Experiences in different communities can generate breakdowns in communication and lack of clarity in expectations on the part of both workers and clients. When they come from different communities, they usually have been socialized to think and feel in particular ways and may fail to understand one another. Client "resistance" may then be evidenced in lower service utilization rates, higher rates of dropping out of service or missing appointments, and difficulties in reaching agreement as to the nature of a presenting problem and an appropriate intervention plan.

In establishing a helping relationship, social workers also must take into account how communities vary in terms of their status in a society. The important point for social work practice is that differences in interest are inherent in status differences. This has been brought out in the discussions in this chapter of majorities and minorities, social classes, and the lesbian and gay community. Lower-status groups are interested in improving their status, while higher-status groups are interested in maintaining theirs. The two goals may very well conflict, especially in a society of limited opportunities and resources. As a result, a special kind of dynamic may be present in relationships between clients from lower-status communities and social workers from higher-status communities.

Lower-status clients are not likely to accept the notion that higher-status social workers have their best interests in mind. They are more likely to perceive workers as members of "the system" who are not really interested in helping them. Gay men and lesbians are likely to distrust heterosexual social workers; ethnic-minority and lower-class clients are likely to distrust ethnic-majority and affluent, more educated social workers. Much of the resistance of lower-status clients, therefore, may originate in the status differences they perceive between themselves and social workers. If social workers are to establish a good helping relationship, they usually must attempt to see the problem from the perspective of clients who are of lower status than they themselves are. They must appreciate their clients' struggle to get ahead in spite of the devaluation and hostility they experience in the larger society. And they must demonstrate, through their attitudes and behaviors, that they are working in the best interests of their clients.

In summary, the study of community life helps social workers to anticipate potential difficulties in helping clients. Building a helping relationship requires getting beyond differences in culture and status and avoiding a breakdown in communication between social workers and clients. They may fail to communicate because they hold different attitudes, values, norms, and traditions or because clients do not trust workers to have their best interests at heart.

∞ DISCUSSION QUESTIONS AND CLASS PROJECTS

1. Discuss the three reasons why social service workers should study community life that are identified in this chapter. Give any other reasons you can think of why the study of communities is useful.

2. Define what is meant by locational, identificational, and interest communities. Using these concepts, identify the communities to which you belong.

3. Describe the differences between the two approaches sociologists have used in the study of social classes.

4. Do you think the United States is a class society? How would you define social classes? How many classes do you think there are in American society? To what class do you belong? Do you think it is important for people to have a strong identification with or consciousness of their social class?

5. Are you a member of a religious denomination? How active are you in it? Can you identify the values and attitudes you hold which are associated with this denomination? Do you think it is important for people to

have a strong identification with or consciousness of their religion?

6. Do you consider gay men and lesbians a deviant group or a minority group? What do you know about the gay and lesbian community in your area?

7. What is race? How many races are there? Are African Americans a race?

8. Define and distinguish among the following:

   ethnic group
   ethnicity
   minority group
   majority group
   minority individuals
   genotype
   phenotype
   racial group

9. Select a community from your area (social class, religious denomination, gay and lesbian, ethnic and racial, majority or minority). With respect to this community, gather information on the following: culture (attitudes, values, norms, and traditions), status, strengths and resources, and problems and needs.

∞ NOTES

1. Robert B. Nisbett, *The Sociological Tradition* (New York: Basic Books, 1967), p. 47. The term *gemeinschaft* was coined by Ferdinand Tönnies in the nineteenth century to define a primary or folk community as one of two types of society. The other type, a *gesellschaft*, is an association with a common purpose which members join voluntarily.

2. These categories were identified by Jessie Bernard, *The Sociology of Community* (Glenview, IL: Scott, Foresman, 1973), pp. 3–5.

3. An example of such descriptions of urban life is Robert E. Park, Ernest W. Burgess, and Roderick D. McKenzie, *The City* (Chicago: University of Chicago Press, 1967).

4. Philip E. Slater, *The Pursuit of Loneliness* (Boston: Beacon Press, 1970).

5. Bernard, *Sociology of Community*, pp. 3–4.

6. Ibid., p. 5. The idea of social work as a community underlies Gary A. Lloyd's *The Culture and Politics of Social Work* (San Jose, CA: San Jose State University, School of Social Work, 1978).

7. Max Weber, "Class, Status, Party," in V. Jeffries and H. E. Ransford (editors), *Social Stratification: A Multiple Hierarchy Approach* (Boston: Allyn and Bacon, 1980), pp. 89–98.

8. See Irving Krauss, *Stratification, Class, and Conflict* (New York: Free Press, 1976), pp. 12–17.

9. W. Lloyd Warner and Paul S. Lunt, *The Social Life of a Modern Community* (New Haven, CT: Yale University Press, 1941).

10. For a Marxist description of social classes, see K. Charles Loren, *Classes in the United States* (Davis, CA: Cardinal, 1977).

11. Erik Olin Wright, Cynthia Costello, David Hachen, and Joey Sprague, "The American Class Structure," *American Sociological Review*, vol. 47 (December 1982), pp. 709–26.

12. Charles Leroux, "The American Middle Class Is…," *Chicago Tribune*, March 7, 1993, Section 4, p. 1.

13. Leonard Beeghley, *The Structure of Social Stratification in the United States* (Boston, MA: Allyn and Bacon, 1989), pp. 57–79.

14. Gary Solon, "Intergenerational Income Mobility in the United States," *American Economic Review*, vol. 82, no. 3 (1992), pp. 393–400, and David Zimmerman, "Regression toward Mediocrity in Stature," in the same issue, pp. 409–29.

15. William Julius Wilson, *The Declining Significance of Race* (Chicago: University of Chicago Press, 1980).

16. The writings of Frances Fox Piven and Richard A. Cloward stress this point. See especially *Poor People's Movements: Why They Succeed, How They Fail* (New York: Pantheon, 1977).

17. Krauss, *Stratification, Class, and Conflict*, pp. 23–27.

18. Wynetta Devore and Elfriede G. Schlesinger, *Ethnic-Sensitive Social Work*, 2nd ed. (St. Louis, MO: C. V. Mosby, 1981), pp. 4–6.

19. Mark Pilisuk and Phyllis Pilisuk (editors), *Poor Americans: How the White Poor Live* (New Brunswick, NJ: Transaction Books, 1970).

20. Michael Novak, *The Rise of the Unmeltable Ethnics* (New York: Macmillan, 1973).

21. Richard Sennett and Jonathan Cobb, *The Hidden Injuries of Class* (New York: Vintage Books, 1972).

22. U.S. Bureau of the Census, *Statistical Abstract of the United States: 1992*, 112th ed. (Washington, DC, 1992), Table 75.

23. Tom W. Smith, "America's Religious Mosaic," *American Demographics*, vol. 6 (June 1984), pp. 19–23.

24. Tom Roberts, "New Study Claims Past Polls Inflated Church Attendance," *The Oregonian*, September 4, 1993, p. C6.

25. Smith, "America's Religious Mosaic." Other data in this section are also from this source.

26. Philip Blumstein and Pepper Schwartz, *American Couples: Money, Work, Sex* (New York: William Morrow, 1983), pp. 324–30.

27. Frances Fitzgerald, "A Reporter at Large (The Castro, I)," *The New Yorker*, July 21, 1986, pp. 59–60.

28. Carol A. B. Warren, *Identity and Community in the Gay World* (New York. John Wiley and Sons, 1974), p. 4.

29. William M. Newman, *American Pluralism: A Study of Minority Groups and Social Theory* (New York: Harper & Row, 1973), p. 21.

30. Donald Webster Cory, *The Homosexual in America* (New York, Paperback Library, 1963), p. 24.

31. Meredith Gould, "Statutory Oppression: An Overview of Legalized Homophobia," in M. P. Levine (editor), *Gay Men: The Sociology of Male Homosexuality* (New York: Harper Colophon, 1979), pp. 51–67. Also see Jeannine Gramick, "Homophobia: A New Challenge," *Social Work*, vol. 28 (March–April 1983), pp. 137–41.

32. Gould, "Statutory Oppression," pp. 51–52.

33. Kathleen Furore, "Unmarried Couples Beginning to Gain Cities' Recognition," *Chicago Tribune*, May 30, 1993, sect. 6, pp. 1, 9.

34. Alan P. Bell and Martin S. Weinberg, *Homosexualities: A Study of Diversity among Men and Women* (New York: Simon and Schuster, 1978).

35. Barry D. Adam, "Structural Foundations of the Gay World," *Comparative Studies in Society and History*, vol. 27 (October 1985), pp. 658–70.

36. Toby Marotta, *The Politics of Homosexuality* (Boston: Houghton Mifflin, 1981), pp. 3–21.

37. Deborah Goleman Wolf, *The Lesbian Community* (Berkeley: University of California Press, 1979), p. 73.

38. Fitzgerald, "A Reporter at Large."

39. For an interesting set of readings on black gays, see Joseph Beam, *In the Life: A Black Gay Anthology* (Boston: Alyson, 1986). Also see Essex Hemphill (editor), *Brother to Brother: New Writings by Black Gay Men* (Boston: Alyson, 1991).

40. Betty Sancier, "A Challenge to the Profession," *Practice Digest*, vol. 7 (Summer 1984), p. 3.

41. See the issue of *Practice Digest* titled "Working with Gay and Lesbian Clients," vol. 7 (Summer 1984).

42. Michael Banton and Jonathan Harwood, *The Race Concept* (New York: Frederick A. Praeger, 1975).

43. Newman, *American Pluralism*, pp. 252–61. Also see Banton and Harwood, *Race Concept*, pp. 35–42, 61–90.

44. William W. Howells, "The Meaning of Race," in R. H. Osborne (editor), *The Biological and Social Meaning of Race* (San Francisco: W. H. Freeman, 1971), p. 3.

45. James W. Vander Zanden, *American Minority Relations*, 4th ed. (New York: Alfred A. Knopf, 1983), pp. 32–60.

46. Ibid., pp. 36–37. Also see Banton and Harwood, *Race Concept*, pp. 47–60.

47. Howells, "Meaning of Race," pp. 3–10.

48. Carlos E. Cortes, "Mexicans," in S. Thernstrom (ed.), *Harvard Encyclopedia of American Ethnic Groups* (Cambridge, MA: Belknap Press, 1980), p. 699.

49. Richard M. Burkey, *Ethnic and Racial Groups* (Menlo Park, CA: Cummings, 1978), p. 12.

50. Quoted in ibid., p. 5.

51. James W. Green, *Cultural Awareness in the Human Services* (Englewood Cliffs, NJ: Prentice-Hall, 1982), pp. 9–13.

52. Burkey, *Ethnic and Racial Groups*, pp. 9–12.

53. David Dalby, "Black through White: Patterns of Communication in Africa and the New World," in W. Wolfram and N. Clarke (editors), *Black-White Speech Relationships* (Washington, DC: Center for Applied Linguistics, 1971), pp. 99–138.

54. Green, *Cultural Awareness in the Human Services*, p. 9.

55. R. L. McNeely and Mary Kenny Badami, "Interracial Communication in School Social Work," *Social Work*, vol. 29 (January–February 1984), pp. 17–28.

56. Louis Wirth, "The Problem of Minority Groups," in R. Linton (editor), *The Science of Man in the World Crisis* (New York: Columbia University Press, 1945), p. 347.

57. John R. Howard (editor), *Awakening Minorities* (New Brunswick, NJ: Transaction Books, 1970), p. 3.

58. Edward Sagarin (editor), *The Other Minorities* (Waltham, MA: Xerox College Publishing, 1971), p. 17.

59. Newman, *American Pluralism*, pp. 33–41.

60. See Leon W. Chestang, "The Black Family and Black Culture: A Study in Coping," in M. Sotomayor (editor), *Cross Cultural Perspectives in Social Work Practice and Education* (Houston, TX: Graduate School of Social Work, University of Houston, 1976). Also see Harriette Pipes McAdoo (editor), *Black Families* (Beverly Hills, CA: Sage, 1981).

61. Newman, *American Pluralism*, pp. 20–21.

62. U.S. Bureau of the Census, *Statistical Abstract of the United States: 1992*, Table 20.

63. Ibid., Tables 654, 706.

64. Virginia Sapiro, *Woman in American Society* (Palo Alto, CA: Mayfield Publishing, 1986), pp. 169–91, 221–336. Also see Edwin M. Schur, *Labeling Women Deviant* (New York: Random House, 1984).

65. Johnnetta B. Cole, "Commonalities and Differences," in J. B. Cole (editor), *All American Women: Lines That Divide, Ties That Bind* (New York: Free Press, 1986), pp. 1–30.

66. Newman, *American Pluralism*, pp. 135–37.

67. Burkey, *Ethnic and Racial Groups*, pp. 20–21.

68. Ronald F. Walters, "Race, Resources, Conflict," *Social Work*, vol. 27 (January 1982), pp. 24–30.

CHAPTER 5

A Social History of Ethnic Communities in the United States

MAJOR THEMES DISCUSSED IN THIS CHAPTER

1. **SOCIOECONOMIC ACHIEVEMENT AND ETHNIC COMMUNITIES.** In American society, socioeconomic achievement is related to ethnic and racial status. Four ethnic minorities continue to lag well behind the white majority: African Americans, Mexican Americans, Puerto Ricans, and Native Americans and Alaskan Natives. In addition, Chinese, Japanese, Filipino, and other Asian Americans may find their success blocked at the top of the achievement ladder.

2. **UNDERSTANDING RACIAL AND ETHNIC RELATIONS.** When racial and ethnic communities come together, a stratification system is likely to develop in which some groups become dominant and others become subordinate. The processes that lead to the development and maintenance of ethnic stratification systems are ethnocentrism, competition, and differential power. Different theories of minority-majority relations are based on a cycle of relations, from contact to assimilation, or on a persistent state of competition and conflict.

3. **U.S. IMMIGRATION POLICIES.** Over the years, the immigration policies of the United States have determined the extent to which people of various nationalities, races, and ethnic backgrounds have been welcomed and, once here, have been able to participate in the American dream. The open-door policy of the young Republic, by which virtually everyone who wanted to could enter, was replaced by regulations. The entry of Asians was severely restricted, and quotas were set to limit the immigration of eastern and southern Europeans. The Immigration Act of 1965, which set up a more equitable system for allotting visas, began to correct this imbalance.

4. **HISTORICAL FACTORS IN SOCIOECONOMIC SUCCESS.** The histories of how northern and western Europeans, southern and eastern Europeans, and people of color became a part of American society is related to their socioeconomic achievement. The achievement of each group has had to do with the manner in which it was recruited into the United States, the economic opportunities it was offered, and the amount of hostility it received from dominant ethnics. The values held by a group, its willingness to be cohesive and help its members, and its preparation for entering the United States also are important in understanding its achievements.

5. **IMPLICATIONS FOR PRACTICE.** Social service workers must recognize that the socioeconomic well-being of individuals is related to the status of the ethnic and racial

groups to which they belong. Workers' attempts to help ethnic minorities are improved if they acknowledge historical processes of group conflict and competition.

THE COMMUNITIES PEOPLE BELONG TO have a good deal to do with the needs they have and the problems they experience. Nowhere is this more true than in the connection between socioeconomic achievement and racial and ethnic communities. The data on a group's **socioeconomic well-being**—that is, the data on the levels of education, occupation, and income achieved by members—reveal vast disparities based on racial and ethnic differences.

Five racial and ethnic communities in the United States have been officially designated as minorities: African Americans, Native Americans and Alaskan Natives, Asian Americans, Mexican Americans, and Puerto Ricans. They have been identified as **ethnic minorities** because of the prejudice and discrimination they have faced in American society, as a result of which they are likely to live in poverty or to be denied full participation in the economic resources generated by the society. The other ethnic groups making up American society, mostly white and of European origin, are considered **ethnic majorities.**

As an outcome of the civil rights legislation in the 1960s and 1970s, a policy of **affirmative action** was developed to provide more equal access to educational and occupational opportunities for members of ethnic minorities. Under this policy, employers and governments must show good faith and have positive plans for remedial actions to ameliorate the effects of past racial (or sexual) discrimination that has placed ethnic minorities (or women) at a socioeconomic disadvantage. The policy was repeatedly challenged in the 1980s by administrative actions and legal rulings, but it has been upheld in principle, particularly in regard to employment, and some sectors of some ethnic minorities have made progress in achieving socioeconomic success comparable to that of the white majority (see Chapter 7).

ᘇ SOCIOECONOMIC ACHIEVEMENT AND ETHNIC COMMUNITIES

Socioeconomic achievement is studied through *social indicators*, quantitative measures which have been mapped out over extended periods of time so that trends can be traced. Social indicators attempt to measure well-being, that is, whether attainment by a particular group in a particular socioeconomic index can be considered to have been good or not so good. By looking at trends it is possible to evaluate not only whether a situation is good or bad but whether it is getting better or worse or staying the same.[1] In this section we will consider a number of social indicators: income, occupation, education, and satisfaction with one's economic condition.

Some social indicators are based on *subjective measures* such as people's perceptions of how satisfied they are with their economic condition. This is what researchers call the "sense of well-being" or "direct perceptions of well-being."[2] Angus Campbell and his associates at the University of Michigan have done an important series of studies on the sense of well-being of Americans in a number of "domains" or areas of life. These include areas associated with economic well-being, such as satisfaction with income, jobs, and place of residence.[3] While it would be helpful to have good comparisons between ethnic majorities and minorities on such indicators, most studies do not systematically make such comparisons. Usually the comparison is between whites and blacks. For instance, Campbell summarized a number of findings comparing these two groups between 1970 and 1978:

> The situation of low-income black people is unique; they suffer both from being poor and from being black. Poor white people also have relatively low feelings of well-being, but they are clearly more positive than those of black people in the same low-income category. Black people of all income levels describe their lives less positively than white people do.
>
> A high income raises a black person's sense of well-being, but not to the level of a white person of that income. Black people lack what income alone will not give them, equal social and political status. Their sense of inequity is sharply expressed in the large proportion of black people who feel they have had less than their share of the happiness a person can reasonably expect in life—over twice the proportion found among white people.[4]

Other social indicators are based on *objective measures* rooted in inferences about well-being which are externally based. Usually, these measures are derived from statistics provided by government agencies and departments such as the U.S. Census Bureau. Although objective measures and subjective measures are significantly correlated, the correlation is less strong than might be imagined. Campbell demonstrated that while the objective economic well-being of Americans rose dramatically in the 1950s and 1960s, their psychological well-being did not change and actually seemed to decrease.

Socioeconomic Well-Being from 1960 to 1990

An excellent survey of socioeconomic well-being during the civil rights era (1960–1976) is a publication of the U.S. Civil Rights Commission, *Social Indicators of Equality for Minorities and Women*.[5] This report, which is based on objective measures, is the only one to compare systematically the five designated minority groups with one another and with the majority white population. Equal attention is given to minorities and women, and the commission concludes that sexual inequality is at least as important as racial and ethnic inequality, if not more important.

During the period 1960–1976, the educational, economic, and occupational achievements of most Americans were improving dramatically. Yet the achievement of four minority groups—African Americans, Native Americans and Alaskan Natives, Mexican Americans, and Puerto Ricans—continued to lag behind, and there was no indication that they were catching up. These groups were likely to have lower rates of college completion, jobs in lower-prestige occupations, higher rates of unemployment for both teenagers and adults, lower per capita household incomes, and higher rates of poverty. In addition, the commission found that differences in income between these four minority groups and the white majority continued to be evident even when age, occupational prestige, number of weeks worked, hours worked during the previous week, and average income in the state of residence were taken into account.

The fifth minority group examined by the commission, Asian Americans, included Japanese, Chinese, and Filipinos. These three fared much better than the other four minorities and sometimes even better than the white majority. For instance, the rates of college completion and the prestige ranking of occupations were comparable for the three Asian groups and whites. Japanese families, on average, earned significantly more income than white families, but Asians did not always do as well as the white majority. In particular, they had significantly higher rates of college overqualification than whites. This means that Filipino, Japanese, and Chinese people tended to be employed in occupations for which they were overqualified and in which they could not use the education and skills they had acquired. Overqualification also showed up in income levels. College-educated male Asians tended to earn less income than college-educated male whites. However, no differences were apparent between white and Asian college-educated women.

The report of the commission on Civil Rights for 1960–1976 represents a standard of excellence that has not been equaled since. More recent data systematically comparing groups are not readily available; most information comes from reports and studies by various government agencies or organizations comparing whites and blacks and, occasionally, Hispanics, or Latinos. In U.S. Census Bureau reports, the category of blacks often includes "other races not shown separately" and Latinos are described as Hispanics, who "may be of any race."

Economic data and social indicators both suggest that the disadvantages apparent in 1976 have been maintained if not increased. The data indicate that 1977 was a high point for equality in the United States; between the depression years of the 1930s and 1977, economic inequality generally shrank. During the Reagan administration in the 1980s, however, as Barbara Ehrenreich puts it, "the combination of spending cuts for the poor and tax cuts for the rich produced a massive, government-induced upward redistribution of wealth."[6] Even among the white majority, the rich got richer and the poor got poorer, and middle-class incomes failed to grow. By the end of the eighties, Ehrenreich observes:

> ...[T]he gap between the haves and the have-nots—not only between the rich and poor but between the middle class and the working class—is wider than it has been at any time since World War II, so that America's income distribution is now almost as perilously skewed as that of India.... We simply care less, or we find the have-nots less worthy of our concern.[7]

It is not surprising, therefore, that the economic situations of African Americans and Latinos, disproportionately located, on average, among the have-nots at the lower end of the scale, have not shown significant improvement in recent years. For instance, the median money income of all American families (in constant 1990 dollars) increased from $33,238 to $35,353 between 1970 and 1990. But while it increased from $34,481 to $36,915 for whites, it grew only from $21,151 to $21,423 for blacks in the same period. Between 1975 and 1990, the median income of Hispanic families increased from $23,203 to $23,431. Thus the relative differences in family income among these groups has barely changed. Compared to white families, African-American and Latino families are generally in no better position than they were in 1970.[8]

There have been some changes, of course. Conservative blacks, particularly, have pointed to certain improvements: a growing black middle class, more black-owned industrial enterprises, and increases in the number of blacks who have moved from deteriorated inner-city neighborhoods to the suburbs.[9] However, these changes may not have meant improvement for the African-American community as a whole. In 1990, for example, families in the lowest fifth of the population as a whole, by money income, received 5.2 percent of all income distributed that year, and those in the highest fifth received 41.5 percent. For black families, the discrepancy between rich and poor was even greater; those in the lowest fifth received 3.3 percent of all income distributed to black families, and those in the highest fifth received 47.3 percent of it.[10]

Inequalities among Ethnic Communities

Based on the available reports, we can conclude that two groupings of ethnic minorities have developed in the United States. One, composed of blacks, Native Americans, Mexican Americans, and Puerto Ricans, includes a large number of people who are seriously disadvantaged in meeting the basic human needs of everyday life. The other, composed of Chinese, Japanese, Filipinos, and other Asians, includes large numbers who are largely able to meet their basic human needs but find themselves blocked at the upper levels of American society. Edna Bonacich calls these **middleman minorities**.[11] They have the skills and education required to reach the top but tend to be overqualified for the jobs they hold, and their earnings seldom are comparable to those of their white counterparts. In the competition for socioeconomic success in American society, both of these ethnic-minority groupings must vie with the predominant white, European-based ethnic majority.

What accounts for the socioeconomic differences among racial and ethnic groups? Following a systems approach, we can conclude that socioeconomic success or failure is a function of the historical and contemporary transactions taking place between minority and majority ethnic groups. It results from the things minorities do to propel themselves forward and the things majorities do to facilitate or hinder the advance of minorities. Although well-being is a function of such transactions, this does not necessarily mean that minorities and majorities contribute equally. Sometimes minorities achieve success in spite of all obstacles thrown at them; sometimes failure comes about in spite of superhuman efforts to avoid it. Sometimes majorities help minorities along, and sometimes they make every effort to keep them down. In this chapter we will look at one facet of the transactions between minorities and majorities, those that took place as ethnic groups were being recruited and socialized into the United States, primarily in the nineteenth and early twentieth centuries.

∞ UNDERSTANDING RACIAL AND ETHNIC RELATIONS

When ethnic groups come in contact with one another, the transactions between them are likely to result in the formation of a stratification system in which one becomes dominant and the other remains subordinate. According to Donald Noel, three conditions are necessary for stratification to occur: ethnocentrism, competition, and differential power.[12]

Ethnocentrism has been described as the view that one's own group is central or the best, and all other groups or individuals are evaluated in reference to it (see Chapter 7). Ethnocentrism, in other words, is the glorification of one's own group over all others. *Competition* has to do with the interaction between two or more groups striving to achieve or acquire the same scarce goal or resource, such as wealth, land, or prestige. *Power* is usually described as the ability to get one's way. A group is powerful to the extent that it has the technical, military, or legal capacity to exploit other groups. Power may be exercised through force but also through the control of rewards.

Noel demonstrates that these three conditions were evident in the relationships between early American colonists and blacks and that they led to the enslavement of blacks. It would not be difficult to prove that in early American society, ethnocentrism, the emphasis on competition, and differences in powers and abilities to exploit led to minority-group status for a number of groups entering the society.

Nevertheless, many groups have evolved from minority status to inclusion in the majority in American society. The major examples are the European immigrants who came to the United States during the nineteenth and twentieth centuries. Many of them arrived in poverty and were greeted with hostility, but they eventually became participants in the American dream. Thus conditions that encourage advancement and allow the elimination of minority status also exist in American society.

Theories of Minority-Majority Relations

With the experience of southern and eastern Europeans in mind, Robert Park developed a theory of group relations based on a cycle of race relations.[13] Park assumes that racial and ethnic relations proceed in a specific, inevitable manner. He postulates that as groups come into *contact* through exploration, migration, or some other process, *competition* among them naturally emerges for land, natural resources, and various scarce goods and services. This competition may erupt into violent *conflict* or remain relatively peaceful, but as an outcome of the competition one group establishes dominance. The period of competition and the establishment of dominance is followed by a process of *accommodation* through which there is a "progressive merging" of the subordinated group into the dominant group. Eventually, **assimilation** takes place, and all distinguishing signs of group differences disappear.

In rethinking Park's cycle of race relations, Milton Gordon makes the point that assimilation is better conceived of as a collection of subprocesses rather than a single process. He distinguishes among a number of forms of assimilation: cultural, structural, marital, identificational, and civic. These subprocesses of assimilation are not stages of development in the usual sense, since one does not lead automatically to the others and each may occur to a greater or lesser extent. *Cultural assimilation*, referred to as **acculturation**, is often the first to take place. It involves changing one's cultural patterns and language to those of the dominant or "host" society. *Structural assimilation* involves large-scale entrance and participation in cliques, clubs, and institutions of the dominant society as well as the development of primary-group friendship ties. *Marital assimilation* is apparent when large-scale intermarriage occurs. *Identificational assimilation* occurs when the subordinate group develops a sense of peoplehood based exclusively on the dominant society. *Civic assimilation* is present when there is an absence of value and power conflict.[14]

According to Gordon, in the United States the process of assimilation has produced not a single melting pot, in which the various racial and ethnic groups lose their separate identities and are melded into a uniquely American culture, but various melting pots[15] (see "Where 'The Melting Pot' Came From"). Three of these involve religious groups; Protestants, Catholics, and Jews generally have erased their ethnic subdivisions. Another has to do with race. An example of how racial assimilation occurs can be seen in the example of contemporary Haitian immigrants.[16] In the United States, any person with an African ancestry is labeled as black. This is a uniquely American definition of race. New groups coming into the country often are confronted with the necessity to "assimilate" into

---

Where "The Melting Pot" Came From

The term *the melting pot* is accredited to an author, Israel Zangwill, who used it in a play which opened in this country in 1908. With this term, he dramatically described the assimilationist doctrine of the times:

> America is God's crucible, the great Melting Pot where all the races of Europe are melting and re-forming! Here you stand, good folk, think I, when I see them at Ellis Island, here you stand in your fifty groups, with your fifty languages and histories, and your fifty blood hatreds and ri-

valries. But you won't be long like that, brothers, for these are the fires of God you've come to—these are the fires of God. A fig for your feuds and vendettas! Germans and Frenchmen, Irishmen and Englishmen, Jews and Russians—into the crucible with you all! God is making the American.

Source: Quoted in Milton M. Gordon, *Assimilation in American Life: The Role of Race, Religion, and National Origin* (New York: Oxford University Press, 1964), p. 120.

---

one of the existing American racial categories. Thus within two generations after coming to the United States from Haiti, the Haitian identity begins to fade and the black identity emerges. Regardless of the "pot" into which new arrivals "melt," Gordon, as well as Park, acknowledges that the change is always toward accepting the ways of the dominant group.

The theory of a cycle of race relations, with its emphasis on assimilation into the ways of the dominant group, has been criticized for its assumption that the experiences of European immigrants represent a natural law of assimilation. A second way of looking at minority-majority group relations is conflict theory, which rejects the idea that these relations ultimately lead to accommodation and assimilation. William Newman, for instance, maintains that minority and majority group status and conflict are inevitable, unalterable features of society. Through conflict, however, majorities may become minorities, minorities may become majorities, and minorities and majorities may coalesce and create new minorities. Thus Newman sees society as in a state of continual conflict among groups which leads to the constant realignment and redefinition of status.[17]

These two approaches to the study of minority-majority group relations, the cycle of race relations proposed by Park and Gordon and the conflict theory suggested by Newman, are essential to an understanding of the relations between racial and ethnic groups (see "Outcomes of Minority-Majority Group Relations"). However, the thinking of Park and Gordon captures a certain reality in the outcomes of race relations in American society. Most groups have assimilated in some basic ways to the dominant Anglo culture. We think of ourselves as African Americans, Irish Americans, Mexican Americans, Italian Americans, and so on. At the same time, minority-majority status differentiations have not disappeared, and realignments have taken place. In the course of the twentieth century, southern and eastern Europeans have blended into the northern and western European majority in American society. Blacks, Latinos, and other people of color remain as new minorities aligned against this changed majority. What realignments the future might bring are unclear, but it is important to understand how people of color have come to be the minority groups in the latter half of the twentieth century.

Outcomes of Minority-Majority Group Relations

Some sociologists, such as Robert Park and Milton Gordon, believe that relationships between minority and majority groups and individuals follow a cycle that inevitably leads to harmonious assimilation. Others, like William Newman, believe that conflict always marks group relations, although new alignments may take place. The outcomes of these two prominent theories of minority-majority group relations are graphically presented here:

The Cycle of Race Relations

Contact → Competition/Conflict → Accommodation → Assimilation

          a. Cultural

          b. Structural

          c. Marital

          d. Identificational

          e. Civic

The Conflict Theory of Majority-Minority Relations

Contact → Competition/Conflict → Majority/Minority Status →

Competition/Conflict → Realignment of Status →

Competition/Conflict → Realignment of Status

Source: Robert E. Park, *Race and Culture* (New York: Free Press, 1964); Milton M. Gordon, *Assimilation in American Life* (New York: Oxford University Press, 1964); William Newman, *American Pluralism: A Study of Minority Groups and Social Theory* (New York: Harper & Row, 1973).

The Immigrant and Colonialist Analogies

It is generally believed that the United States is basically a land of immigrants, but this is not entirely the case. **Immigrants** take up stakes, more or less voluntarily, in one national society and migrate to another land, where they become part of a new national society. Many groups in the United States were indeed immigrants, but some were not. In terms of minority-majority group relations, whether or not a person is an immigrant has a lot to do with that person's likelihood of success. Southern and eastern European immigrant groups chose to come to the United States, and in making that choice they were aware of the need to accommodate to American society. The dominant white Anglo-Saxon Protestant community, while not completely receptive to these largely Catholic and Jewish immigrants, nevertheless offered them basic opportunities for accommodation and ultimate socioeconomic success. Because of this dynamic, immigrant groups could expect to succeed eventually in the United States. But for significant numbers of Americans who unwillingly became immersed in the American melting pot, such an **immigrant analogy** did not apply.

Robert Blauner uses the **colonialist analogy** to describe the experiences of those who were forced to become part of American society and who, as a result of this forced inclusion, never were given the opportunities for success and assimilation that European immigrants enjoyed. Blauner refers to these as *colonized groups*, principally African Americans or Native Americans and Alaskan Natives. Blauner suggests that other groups such as Mexican Americans might also be thought of as colonized groups (see the introduction to the section on people of color).[18]

In using a colonialist analogy, Blauner distinguishes between classical colonialism and internal colonialism. In **classical colonialism**, as in the British Empire at the turn of the twentieth century, the colonized natives usually constitute the majority of the population. Accordingly their culture pervades the land and continues to develop, although they are accorded less prestige than the colonizers. While the colonized do not have the rights of citizens of the empire, they generally are free to continue their cultural traditions. The colonizers are more interested in taking out and using up the wealth and resources of the colony than in shaping its culture. In **internal colonialism**, many aspects of classical colonialism prevail. The wealth and resources of internally colonized groups are removed from their communities, to the benefit of the dominant group. However, the native peoples are less dominant, the colonized groups are generally smaller, and their culture is not as evident. Those who have come to colonize the country take it over, and their culture prevails.

The immigrant and colonialist analogies describe underlying motivations in the relationships between dominant and subordinate ethnic communities. Both immigrants, who are basically motivated to participate in the economy and to strive for achievement, and colonized groups, who are basically motivated to escape their confinement and to seek autonomy, may be considered subordinated groups. Nevertheless, the dominant groups, who are motivated to remain in control, lend a helping hand to immigrants but put obstacles in the way of colonized groups.

In the United States, the differences between the experiences of immigrants and internally colonized groups are best described by reference to three differing circumstances: the manner in which they become part of American society, the opportunities they are given for participation in American economic institutions, and the degree of cultural oppression they experience at the hands of the American majority (see "Differences between Immigrant and Colonized Groups").

The Minority Response to Subordination

Some theorists argue that all groups coming into the United States have experienced hostility from the dominant groups. To a great extent this is true, although the degree of hostility experienced varies considerable. In any event, these theorists have focused on the ways new groups respond to the obstacles that have been put in their way.

Thomas Sowell describes at least three dimensions of the response of new groups to obstacles to socioeconomic success: the preparedness, cohesiveness, and value system of the group. Whether immigrant groups do well in competition with other groups depends to some extent on whether they are prepared by their occupational experiences in the home country for similar experiences in the adopted country. Immigrants from rural, agricultural communities in the homeland who are offered only urban, industrial jobs in the new country will not adapt readily to their new environment. Success in the new country also depends on how well immigrants pull together to help each other; a cohesive immigrant group has a better chance of overcoming the obstacles imposed by the dominant group. Since many immigrant groups come in waves, the cohesion between the various waves is as important as the cohesion within any one wave. Perhaps of greatest importance is the value system of the group. Certain kinds of values are more important than others; values of thrift, hard work, and orientation to future rather than immediate fulfillment facilitate socioeconomic success, regardless of the obstacles confronted.[19]

Differences between Immigrant and Colonized Groups

Ethnic and racial groups have entered American society in different ways, some as immigrants and some as colonized peoples. As a result they have had different experiences in the economy and in social relationships with the majority.

This table lists the differences between immigrant and colonized groups in American society as ideal types. Ideal types are not intended to portray a specific reality but rather to describe characteristics along particular dimensions, thus making it possible to compare the experiences of actual groups.

Circumstance	Immigrant Groups	Colonized Groups
Entry into society	Voluntary	Forced
Participation in labor market	Mainstreamed	Secondary labor market
Cultural oppression	Minimal	Total

Source: Adapted from Robert Blauner, *Racial Oppression in America* (New York: Harper & Row, 1972).

☞ U.S. IMMIGRATION POLICIES

The success of ethic communities in the United States is closely related to the governmental policies connected with their immigration. Official views on whether a racial or ethnic group is to be welcomed or their immigration is to be limited vary as social and economic conditions dictate. Immigration policies have both reflected and helped shape the environment confronted by various immigrant groups as they have attempted to enter and to achieve success in a new land.

William Bernard traces four periods of immigration to the United States. The first period, 1776–1881, was the **open-door period**; virtually anyone who wanted to immigrate to the United States could do so. The second period, 1882–1916, was the era of regulation; for the first time, immigration was controlled. The first laws excluded categories of people such as convicts, lunatics, idiots, illiterates, incapacitated persons who might become public charges, mental defectives and persons involved in crimes of moral turpitude, anarchists, paupers and beggars, and the like. In this period, also, laws were passed to exclude Chinese immigrants, and steps were taken to control immigration from Japan. In the period 1917–1964, the *era of restriction*, laws were passed setting up quotas based on national origin and race. This is the period that will most concern us in this chapter. In the present period, the *era of liberalization*, quotas based on national origin and race have been eliminated.[20] Since 1965, numerical limits have been set and preference is given to family members of citizens, professionals and workers with needed skills, and special categories of immigrants such as ministers and foreign medical graduates.

The "open door" began to close in 1882, when the Chinese Exclusion Act passed by Congress in 1880 took effect. The act forbid the immigration of Chinese laborers for ten years and barred all foreign-born Chinese then in the United States from acquiring citizenship. The legal precedent was the Naturalization Act of 1790, under which citizenship was limited to "free white persons." The Chinese Exclusion Act was strengthened and renewed several times (see "A Timeline of Chinese Exclusion" in the section on Chinese immigration).

Beginning in 1882, also, patterns of European immigration into the United States began to change. Until then, approximately 87 percent of Europeans who immigrated were from northern and western European nations such as Great Britain, Germany, Holland, France, and the Scandinavian countries. After 1882, the bulk of the immigrants were from southern and eastern European nations such as Italy, Greece, and Russia, and Slavic and Polish-speaking peoples. Several million immigrants arrived between 1890 and 1914 alone. The flood was abated only by periodic economic problems in the United States.

In the eyes of many "native Americans," the term used in that era to refer to Europeans born in the United States, the peoples from southern and eastern Europe were decidedly undesirable. It was believed that something should be done to keep them from entering the country. From the point of view of economic elites, they represented a class of people who would adopt socialist ideas and were willing to participate in labor organizations. From the point of view of working people, they represented cheap labor which could be used as "scabs" to undercut wages and break strikes. To Americans in general, they represented inferior "races" who would mongrelize the nation and dilute the prized Aryan stock.[21]

The Setting of Quotas

As a result of this kind of sentiment, the U.S. Congress passed an act in 1921 setting **immigration quotas**. The unabashed purpose of this legislation was to limit the influx of immigrants from southern and eastern Europe. In addition to putting a ceiling on the number of immigrants who could enter, the act set annual quotas for immigrants from each nation, based on 3 percent of the number from that nation who had entered the United States, according to the 1910 census. This law was considered ineffective and was amended by the Immigration Act of 1924, which set national quotas based on 2 percent of the number from each nation residing in the United States in 1890. The law then gave 84 percent of the quotas to northern and western European nations and 14 percent to southern and eastern European nations. It not only reaffirmed the Chinese Exclusion Act of 1882 but also barred many groups from the Asian-Pacific triangle, who had been declared racially ineligible for citizenship by a 1922 Supreme Court decision. For these groups, including the Japanese, no quotas at all were set.

As a consequence of this legislation, immigration was considerably reshaped to realize the racist and ethnocentric goals of its framers. The law drastically changed the "complexion" of those who immigrated; in effect, it provided affirmative action in favor of white, Anglo-Saxon Protestants. After the 1924 act, the annual quota for immigrants from countries in northern and western Europe was 140,999; for countries in southern and eastern Europe, it was 20,847.

Five years later, the "permanent" quotas for each country went into effect, based on the national origins of the U.S. population in 1920. This system was abolished by the Hart-Cellar Immigration Act of 1965, under which the Eastern Hemisphere (Europe, Africa, and Asia) was given a quota of 170,000 a year and the Western Hemisphere (Canada and Latin America) was given an annual quota of 120,000, with a maximum of 20,000 from any one country. No national quotas were imposed, but preference in obtaining

visas was given to people with family members in the United States and those with needed skills or professional occupations. Under the Immigration Act of 1990, the total number of numerically limited immigrants allowed to enter the United States annually in
1992–1994 was raised to 700,000. The inscription on the Statue of Liberty, "Give me
your tired, your poor, your huddled masses yearning to breathe free" no longer reflects
government policy, nor does it describe who now immigrates to the United States (see
Chapter 6).

∞ SOCIOECONOMIC SUCCESS OF EUROPEAN IMMIGRANTS

To explain why different ethnic groups met with varying degrees of success in trying to
"make it" in American society, we will present in this and the following section brief historical sketches of the conditions confronting them as they entered the country and became a part of it. In this analysis we argue that immigrant groups—those that more or less
chose to come to the United States and were more or less positively received by Americans—had an easier time than groups that were colonized or forced into the country.
The underlying motivation for entry and receptivity of the dominant group weigh heavily in determining the eventual success of an incoming group, but they do not explain
everything about it. In Sowell's terms (discussed earlier), the preparedness of the group,
its cohesiveness, and its value system also must be taken into account, especially when the
social context of the new society is particularly hostile.

This section considers factors affecting the ability of the two groups of European
immigrants—from northern and western Europe and from southern and eastern Europe—to achieve socioeconomic success. The next section describes how people of color
in the United States, a broad category which includes Native Americans and Alaskan natives, African Americans, Mexican Americans, Puerto Ricans, and Asian Americans, have
struggled to achieve similar socioeconomic success, despite their position as ethnic
minorities.

Northern and Western European Immigrants

Peoples from northern and western Europe, in general, found it easiest to realize the
American dream. The hard part was getting here. Many aspiring immigrants met death or
disease while crossing the ocean in steerage, crowded into the hulls of small, filthy cargo
vessels; one estimate was the 2,000 Germans died at sea on voyages to Philadelphia in
1749. Once in this country, it was common for northern and western European immigrants to put in a period of indentured servitude before they were free to hold jobs. Most
of them, however, arrived during the colonial era or in the early days of the Republic,
when there were few immigration laws and land was readily available for settlement.

The early American economy was based on agriculture, and the new arrivals became
landowners and farmers, participating in the mainstream of that economic system. Colonial governments eagerly sought immigrants from northern and western Europe and not
only provided information about the colonies and transportation to them but also subsidized the purchase of lands and tools for new settlers.[22] The early national government of
the United States, however, did little to promote immigration, leaving it up to market
conditions to set the demand and to state and territorial governments to see to it that

workers were supplied. Some states had publicity agents who sent out brochures written in the European languages, extolling the virtues of settling in their states. As an inducement, public lands could be purchased for as little as $1.25 an acre. Northern and western Europeans were certainly welcomed.

As these immigrants settled in the new country, regional and communal segregation patterns developed. Germans settled in Pennsylvania, the Ohio Valley, and the Midwest; the Scotch-Irish in Appalachia; Scandinavians in the upper Mississippi area; the Dutch in upstate New York. This allowed the new arrivals to maintain their languages and traditions for some time. The Germans even toyed with the idea of creating a separate state. A public school system was barely evident, so there was no incentive to learn to read and speak English. Many groups maintained their own newspapers and schools. Although there are recorded incidents of violence and hostility toward these ethnic groups, it is difficult to say that they were ever considered minorities in the United States. The history of such groups as Germans and Norwegians makes this clear.[23]

The Irish Catholics in the United States

One exception among the northern and western European immigrant groups was the Irish, who have been described as the first major immigrant minority group in the United States.[24] Irish immigration took place throughout the colonial era but began to increase significantly around 1820 and represented the first major wave of immigration to the United States. The hostile experiences the Irish faced were as difficult as those encountered by an immigrant group before or since. Not until the beginning of the twentieth century did the Irish begin to show evidence of "making it" in American society.[25] In comparison, most European immigrants could do so in about two generations.[26]

Why was entry into American society so difficult for the Irish? They had a number of advantages that ought to have made it easier for them.[27] They spoke English, regarded by many immigrant peoples as necessary to success. They had a respected literature, which helped Americans to understand and appreciate the Irish cultural heritage. They were also familiar with the Anglo-Saxon legal system, which was not shared with most other European groups. Furthermore, although Ireland was a devastatingly poor country and Irish immigrants were poor by American standards, they seldom came from among the very poorest of the Irish.[28] But in spite of these apparent advantages, other conditions were operating which indeed put them at a disadvantage.

In many ways the Irish did not really immigrate at all. Immigration always involves a certain amount of push and pull—people's feelings that they have to leave and at the same time want to leave. For the Irish, the push away from Ireland was far stronger than the pull to the United States. Potato-harvest failures in the nineteenth century deprived the Irish poor of their principal food source and made the choice either to immigrate or to die. According to Oscar Handlin, "Irishmen fled with no hope in their hearts—degraded, humiliated, mourning reluctantly-abandoned and dearly-loved homes."[29]

The decision to come to the United States was not that much of a choice, in any case. Ireland was not a free country but a colony of the British. The Irish were a classically colonized group, making their way from one sector of the British Empire to a recently liberated but nevertheless culturally enmeshed ex-colony. While Irish immigrated to many parts of the world, by far the greatest number came to the United States. This had a lot to do with the limitations imposed by the available means of travel; a person traveled by trading ship and went where the ships went. Since Irish immigrants left from British ports, they mostly ended up in Boston and other ports on the northeastern coast. Relatively few went to the South or to the frontier, although by the nineteenth century, significant numbers had made their way to San Francisco and other parts of the West.

Once in the United States, the Irish were forced to live in squalor. The men could find work only as manual laborers in the dirtiest, hardest, and most unstable jobs, and the women became servants to fashionable New Englanders. The worst slum areas of the cities became home for the Irish. They were crowded into "shanty towns" where indoor plumbing was unheard of and disease and death were everyday occurrences. Crime rates were high, and alcoholism and family dissolution were common. Prejudice and discrimination hounded them; they were seen as dirty, thriftless, boisterous, and worthless, and "Irish need not apply" signs rebuffed them when they searched for work. They were a prime target of the American political party whose members were called "Know-Nothings" because they refused to discuss their program: a pledge to vote only for native Americans, demands for a 21-year naturalization period, and vigorous opposition to Catholicism.

Thus the Irish found themselves a despised minority in the United States not only because they were a colonized people but because they were Catholic. At one time, religious hostilities were dominant factors in ethnic relations. Europeans fought wars over religion; England endured a civil war when the state separated from the Catholic Church, and Anglo-Saxon Protestants were alienated from Anglo-Saxon Catholics. The intense, violent conflict in Northern Ireland today should give a sense of the extreme hostility faced by the Catholic Irish in coming to the United States, an English-speaking country.

The Irish-Catholic immigrants were despised even by Protestants of their own nationality. In the colonial era the term *Irish* referred to any people from Ireland, but much of the early immigration was from the Protestant North. The immigration that took place during the third and fourth decades of the nineteenth century was from the Catholic South. The Protestant Irish established in the new country rejected the Catholic Irish and coined the term *Scotch-Irish* to distinguish themselves from the later arrivals. Sowell notes that no helping hands were extended, and the Catholics and Protestants certainly did not become a cohesive Irish group and pull together.[30]

The Irish response to obstacles to their socioeconomic success also was lacking in the other two dimensions identified by Sowell.[31] In these respects, they were less well equipped to succeed than other northern and western European groups who arrived at about the same time. The Irish became urban dwellers, though they had been agricultural and small-town people back home. Unable to reproduce their lifestyle in the United States, they did not join the economic mainstream but became day laborers and servants. Sowell points out that efforts were made to encourage the Irish to disperse from the cities to the farmlands, but they resisted. One reason was that the kind of land on which they had grown potatoes in Ireland was very different from the kind of land available in the United States. Another was that, due to their cultural nature, they did not enjoy living on isolated farms; they were too gregarious for American rural living, with its vast open spaces.

This gregariousness and similar values also hindered their progress. They were an expressive people, given to enjoying the moment, convivial and loquacious. These qualities made the Irish very creative and likable, and they became excellent political organizers. Eventually they exerted considerable control over politics in the cities they inhabited. With such a value system, however, they failed to acknowledge the need to delay immediate gratification or to put their energies into building an economic base in their communities.

Southern and Eastern European Immigrants

The immigrant experiences of southern and eastern Europeans—peoples from such nations as Italy, Greece, Poland, and Russia—were quite a bit different from those of most peoples from northern and western Europe. In the struggle for socioeconomic success, they were more like the Irish.

Southern and eastern Europeans began to immigrate to the United States after the Civil War, and their immigration reached a peak during the latter part of the nineteenth and early part of the twentieth century. However, all of them did not plan to stay permanently in this country. With transatlantic passenger ships running regular routes, new arrivals knew they could return if they chose. Many Italians came as **sojourners**, intending to stay only until they had amassed enough money so they could go home and live more comfortably. It was not unusual for sojourners to go back and forth several times before deciding to stay in the United States.[32] Others came with the hope of starting a new life away from the hardships they were experiencing in their native lands. Russian Jews, for instance, were being subjected to pogroms, or governmental-sanctioned violence against them, and to discriminatory laws which controlled where they could live, where they could go, and the occupations to which they could aspire. The pull of the United States

Italian mother and children on arrival at Ellis Island, New York, in 1905. The search for economic opportunity led many impoverished southern and eastern European peasant families to immigrate to the United States at the turn of the twentieth century. (HINE, Lewis H. *Italian Family Seeking Lost Baggage*, Ellis Island. 1905.)

was also strong for these groups, The Statue of Liberty being placed in New York harbor symbolized the promise of a better life and greater opportunities.

The economy found by these newcomers to the United States was different from the agricultural system that had been encountered by earlier immigrants from northern and western Europe. As the United States underwent industrialization, southern and eastern Europeans were actually recruited and encouraged to immigrate to become workers in the factories and mines and to help build the bridges, railroads, and cities. They came as free laborers, able to move about the country in search of the best industrial employment or other opportunities they could find. For many who had been serfs and urban dwellers in Europe, in a society which was still quite medieval and controlled by landed aristocrats, this was an enormously liberating experience. While the best jobs were not available to them, their work could lead to self-improvement and advancement, if not for themselves, at least for their children. Moreover, opportunities as free laborers in a free-market economy allowed them to aspire to majority status in the United States. Fundamentally, these immigrants were programmed for success; the opportunities were there.

Nevertheless, for many southern and eastern European immigrants, the way was not easy. They did hold minority status in the United States and were confronted with ethnocentrism, prejudice, and even racism, as we have noted. Racist fears led to the development of the first federal immigration laws, aimed specifically at controlling the flow of these immigrants. All those who were not Aryan or Anglo-Saxon were seen as being not only of different nationalities but of different races.

It probably is incorrect to state that peoples from southern and eastern Europe are still minorities in the United States. Yet their status as ethnic-majority groups is not entirely secure, either. In general, Italians, Poles, and other such groups have done well economically, but there are pockets of poverty among them. Moreover, groups such as Jewish Americans, who have been very successful, seldom have been accepted at the top of the socioeconomic status hierarchy. No Jewish person has become president of the United States or has been appointed to a directorate in certain major business sectors, such as banking. Jewish success has generally come in such areas as radio, television, and publishing.[33] And prejudice against southern and eastern Europeans lingers in American public opinion. "Polish jokes" swept the nation in the late 1970s, for instance; Italian criminal stereotypes are still apparent; and anti-Semitism is not unusual. Thus, while southern and eastern Europeans generally have achieved socioeconomic success, they still are not completely free of minority status.

Italian Americans

The experience of Italians was fairly typical for southern and eastern European immigrants. Early immigration tended to be from the richer northern states of Italy, but by the turn of the century it came primarily from the rural, impoverished South. Immigrating Italians were generally peasants from rural and small-town backgrounds. In the United States, they crowded into "little Italy" sectors in the slums of eastern cities. The men worked at the manual-labor jobs that were being vacated by the Irish. Often they were at the mercy of unscrupulous *padrinos* who helped them find jobs but milked them of their earnings.[34]

The Italian immigrants became alienated from the Catholic Church, which was largely controlled in the United States by the Irish. The Italians brought no tradition of education, and problems with the public school systems, dominated by Anglo-Saxons, were common. Protestant social workers attempting to Americanize the Italians often made them feel inferior in the process. It was not unusual for violence to be directed at them, especially in the South; in some areas, Italian children were required to attend segregated schools.[35] Despite these problems, the Italians accepted the economic opportunities available to them and coalesced to gain community strength. Together, they began to achieve socioeconomic success by the third generation.

Russian Jews in the United States

An atypical experience among southern and eastern European immigrants was that of the Russian Jews. They were one of the most impoverished groups to come to the United States, and they faced severe religious prejudice and discrimination. Nevertheless, within one generation members of this ethnic group were already showing signs of significant success.[36]

The three factors affecting the struggle of immigrant groups to overcome the obstacles facing them in American society cited by Sowell—cohesiveness, preparedness, and values—help explain the rapid success of Russian Jews.[37] Considerable credit has to be given to the ability of Russian Jews and German Jews to coalesce in an ethnic community. The differences between the religious orientations of Russian Jews and German Jews, who had come to the United States earlier in the nineteenth century, were at least as pronounced as the differences between Catholic and Protestant Irish. The two Jewish groups did not necessarily like each other, but the Germans did not turn their backs on the Russians when they arrived. Instead, they helped set up social services which laid the groundwork for the success of the Russian Jews in the United States.

Another factor in their success was preparedness to enter the American economy. Though they were impoverished, they brought with them industrial and urban skills which proved as good as, if not better than, money. In Russia (indeed, in many parts of Europe), Jews could not own land and were forced into urban occupations. By some twist of fate, this form of oppression turned out to have beneficial effects in the United States. Rather than taking manual-labor jobs, as the Italians were forced to do, they became factory workers, tailors, or merchants, creating an ethnic economy which often served to provide jobs for newcomers. It is estimated that 64 percent of the gainfully employed Russian Jews were skilled workers.

The values Russian Jews brought with them also facilitated their success. They had a profound respect for education and eagerly took advantage of the opportunities available through the public school systems. They also had a strong commitment to economic success and pursued it by using their ethnic economy as a springboard to the mainstream economy. They were willing to delay immediate gratification for long-term economic goals.

ᏟᏅ SOCIOECONOMIC SUCCESS AND PEOPLE OF COLOR

People of color is a term used loosely to refer to Americans from countries that formerly were included in European colonial empires—racial and ethnic groups from Africa, Asia, and South America—as well as to indigenous Native Americans and Alaskan Natives. Following U.S. Census Bureau designations, not all of these are considered racial groups; Hispanics, in particular, are officially designated "white" unless they indicate otherwise. Not everyone to whom this term may be applied necessarily accepts it, and social workers are advised to use it cautiously. In social work and much of the social science literature, however, the term *people of color* is increasingly being used.[38]

According to Blauner, these groups are best seen not through the immigrant analogy but through the colonialist analogy.[39] It seems especially appropriate to describe the experiences of African Americans and Native Americans in these terms. Puerto Ricans also fit the analogy fairly well, but the evidence for including Mexican Americans and Chinese and Japanese immigrants to the United States is not so clear-cut. In each case, at any rate, the hostilities experienced by these groups and the opportunities they were offered severely constrained their ability to achieve socioeconomic success in American society. The cultural and family lifestyles of these peoples of color, or racial and ethnic minorities, are described in Chapter 9.

Native Americans and Alaskan Natives

The designation *Indian* is a fiction imposed on the indigenous or native peoples who inhabited the Western Hemisphere at the time European explorers and settlers first arrived. Upward of 200 different tribes, or nations, as the Europeans called them, existed at that time, and there still are numerous groups, each with its own culture and language.[40] The 1990 census of the U.S. population, which included the first count of tribal membership, indicated that there were 1.9 million American Indians, Eskimos, and Aleuts in the United States. Most of the 542 American Indian tribes counted had fewer than 1,000 members; only four—the Cherokee, Navajo, Chippewa, and Sioux—had more than 100,000.[41] The appropriate terms to use with respect to this extremely heterogeneous group are still debated. Generally, we prefer the designation *Native American* to the term *American Indian*. For indigenous people from Alaska—Inuits (formerly referred to as Eskimos) and Aleuts—we use the term *Alaskan Natives*.

The new settlers, with some exceptions (notably the Quakers and some German immigrants), treated the Native Americans harshly. The hostility probably had relatively little to do with the race of the original population and quite a bit to do with their religion; they were considered barbarians and heathens because they did not acknowledge Christianity.[42] But race did play a part, especially under government policies with regard to the native populations.

Native Americans did not choose to become part of the United States; they are a conquered people. During much of U.S. history, Native Americans did not have rights to land, to jobs, or even to citizenship. They were not incorporated into the economy as free workers, as European immigrants were. The initial policy of the federal government was to remove the native populations from the land coveted by the settlers. Starting in the 1820s, "voluntary removal" was undertaken at government expense all along the frontier, from Canada to the Gulf of Mexico, and one by one Indian tribes were escorted to lands west of the Mississippi. In Alaska, the Indians as well as Alaskan Natives were not so much conquered as "purchased." Neither the United States nor Russia, from which Alaska was purchased in 1867, asked the indigenous population whether they wanted to be purchased. Aleuts, who were fairly well acculturated into Russia civilization, and Inuits are referred to as Alaskan Natives because they were not considered part of the "uncivilized tribes" living outside the Russian settlements.[43]

Forced Resettlement

At first neither the Native American population nor the invading colonists wanted to accommodate one another. Some Indians did accommodate the American culture in the Southeast. The "five civilized tribes"—Cherokee, Choctaw, Chickasaw, Seminole, and Creek—settled into a relatively American way of life, owning their homes, living as farmers,

School portrait of Chiricahua Apache children in uniform four months
after being sent away to Carlisle Indian School in Pennsylvania in 1886.
In order to "civilize" them, Native American children were routinely
taken from their families and sent to distant boarding schools.

developing a written script and becoming literate, and joining in a loosely federated republic with a bicameral legislature and an appellate judiciary. But they were not to be
given a place in American society. In 1828 and 1829, the state of Georgia annexed their
lands, and the native populations sued. The Supreme Court, in *Cherokee Nation* v. *Georgia* (1831), set what has become national policy ever since. Chief Justice John Marshall argued that the Cherokees were not a foreign nation; in his written opinion he noted that
"tribes which reside within the acknowledged boundaries of the United States…may more
correctly, perhaps, be denominated domestic dependent nations." In *Worcester* v. *Georgia*
(1832), however, Marshall did assert that "the Cherokee Nation is a distinct community, occupying its own territory…in which the laws of Georgia can have no force."[44]

Regardless of these rulings, President Andrew Jackson adopted a policy of forced
resettlement. Under the Indian Removal Act of 1830, the tribes were coerced to abandon
their lands. The 900-mile march from Georgia to what is now Oklahoma is often referred
to as the "Trail of Tears." The U.S. Army forcibly removed some 100,000 native people
from the southern states, costing the lives of thousands and shattering any trust they
might have placed in their European dominators.

As the white settlers moved on to the lands west of the Mississippi and began to
covet Indian lands there, a new government policy was adopted. Indian wars were

declared, and the adage "The only good Indian is a dead Indian" expressed the attitude of the government and the white settlers. The effect was near genocide. Native Americans who were not killed by bullets were starved to death as soldiers and settlers slaughtered the buffalo, the principal food for those who lived on the central plains.

Reservations and Cultural Suppression

Under the system of reservations, the natives were required to live on lands that usually were unsuited to either agriculture or industry. Edward Spicer refers to this system as operating on a policy of *coercive assimilation*, whereby whites aimed to "replace Indian ways with their own ways and to help [Indians] become self-sufficient farmers and artisans, under conditions dictated by whites."[45] This policy was embodied in the Dawes Act of 1887, which was promoted by Christian religious and political leaders as a solution to the Indian wars. Thus, as the United States was being industrialized, Native Americans were being trained to the ways of Christian family life on farms that could not support it. Furthermore, the policy was instituted at a time when the rural American society was in decline and being drained to feed the growing urban and industrial populations of the Northeast and the West.[46]

Moreover, efforts were made to destroy the cultures of American Indian tribes. In many instances, their religious traditions and ceremonies were outlawed. Christian missionaries were in fact extremely successful, so much that by 1930 the majority of Native Americans professed a Christian affiliation. Systematic attempts also were made to extinguish the various Native American languages and dialects. Children often were required to leave the reservations and attend boarding schools hundreds of miles away, where they could be Americanized. The Dawes Act called for breaking up the tribal lands, with 160 acres to be allotted to each family. Titles were to be held in trust by the government for 25 years, and "surplus" land was to be sold to the United States. Tribes that would not agree to these provisions had their tribal governments dissolved under an act of Congress.

The first federal statute granting citizenship to an entire tribe (the Brothertons) was passed in 1839, but the effect of the law was to dissolve the tribe. The Winnebagos were offered the option of becoming citizens in 1870, provided they could prove that they were sufficiently intelligent and prudent, that they had adopted habits of "civilized life," and that they had supported themselves and their families for the preceding five years. It was not until 1924 that citizenship was granted unconditionally to all Native Americans. Because of confusion over their wardship status in Arizona and New Mexico, however, the right to vote was not extended in these states until 1948.[47]

Reorganization and Termination

The Indian Reorganization Act, which reversed much of the previous policy, was passed in 1934. This act recognized the cultural distinctiveness of the tribes and stipulated that no efforts were to be made to alter them further. Nevertheless, the tribes were encouraged to adopt governing structures modeled after state and federal governments. Under these more humane policies, intertribal organizations emerged, the educational level of Native Americans rose, and the Native American population began to increase.

In 1953, the federal government instituted a policy of termination, whereby protection and assistance for Native American tribal communities were to be withdrawn. A number of small tribes and two large ones, the Menominee of Wisconsin and the Klamath of Oregon, lost their tribal status. (The Menominee regained their status in 1973 under the direction of Ada Deer, an activist member of the tribe who was confirmed as the first woman to be head of the Bureau of Indian Affairs in 1993.) In some ways the policy of termination made sense, since Native Americans had been made prisoners on reservations where only limited economic development was possible. Yet the policy proved to be disastrous for them, because it deprived them of their land and whatever economic potential it had. Some tribes began to fight back, filing suit to reclaim the lands that had been taken from them almost 200 years ago. In 1970, the Oneida Nation of Wisconsin challenged the legality of a 1795 purchase by New York State because it had been made without the authority of the federal government, which had exclusive jurisdiction to deal with the Indians under the Constitution and the Indian Trade and Intercourse Act of 1793. A Supreme Court ruling on this suit in 1985 established that a tribe holds a common-law right to recover land wrongfully taken from it after the effective date of the Constitution. This principle is being used by the Oneida and other nations to press claims to additional land.

American Blacks and African Americans

The ancestry of many ethnic groups in the United States can be traced to Africa. Included are American blacks, whose forefathers were largely brought to the United States as slaves, as well as other African-origin groups such as those from the West Indies—Jamaicans, Haitians, and Virgin Islanders—and some from Central and South America. Also included are recent immigrants directly from African nations. Many, though not all, individuals among these groups prefer the ethnic designation *African American* to the racial designation *black* or *black American*. We will use both terms, depending on the context.

Slavery in American Society

American blacks were forced to migrate to the United States. They came not as people with rights to land and participation in a free-market economy but as indentured servants. Many European whites also were indentured, but after a brief, fixed period they became free workers. Blacks were relegated to slave status, which was perpetual and cross-generational, handed down from parent to child. To be a slave meant being owned by slaveholders or masters and having no rights to seek opportunities to improve one's own lot or that of one's family. In fact, family life was deliberately undermined to make it easier for slave owners to buy and sell humans according to their need for labor and profit. American whites have never been subjected to such degradation (see "An Abolitionist's View of American Slavery").

The place of blacks in the United States has always presented a problem for whites. The framers of the Constitution did not know what to do about slaves. They "conceived the nation in liberty," as Abraham Lincoln would later declare, and stated that all men were created equal, but still they allowed slavery. This contradiction continues to this day; American values hold that all men are created equal, yet American blacks and the dominant white ethnic groups are not treated equally. Gunner Myrdal refers to this contradiction as "an American dilemma."[48]

In no other society did slavery exist quite the way it did in the United States.[49] It was situated within a decentralized democracy, in which the doctrine of "states rights" worked to put slavery under local control, out of the jurisdiction of the federal government. It was

African Americans participating in a Kwanzaa celebration in Poughkeepsie,
New York, enact a play depicting how African slaves were forcibly brought
to the Americas.

largely a southern rural phenomenon, flourishing in a mild climate where slaves could
work the fields year-round so they would not be a drain on the financial resources of the
slaveholders. Some northern "free states," such as Oregon, prohibited slavery not because of moral outrage but simply because their climate was too harsh and would not
allow for year-round work.[50] The rural plantation setting also allowed slaveholders to retain considerable control over their slaves and made escape difficult. Plantation slaves had
nothing they could call their own and were completely dependent on the owner. In the
cities, it was easier for slaves to learn to read and write and to escape or seek their freedom. Throughout the slavery period there were some free blacks in the United States, but
severe restrictions were placed on their ability to participate in government or many economic enterprises.[51]

Freedom and Segregation

The United States is the only nation in which a civil war was necessary to free the slaves.
This conflict occurred just about the time industrialization was beginning to redefine the
American economy. After the war, blacks could have been used as free workers in the bur-
geoning industries that European peasant immigrants were being invited to enter; but instead, after a postwar period of considerable freedom, blacks were subjected to **Jim**

An Abolitionist's View of American Slavery

In *American Slavery as It Is: Testimony of a Thousand Witnesses*, published by the American Anti-Slavery Society in May 1839, Theodore Weld exposed the inhumanity of the American slave system. He reproduced observations on the cruelties being inflicted on slaves and answered the arguments of the slaveholders one by one. In his Introduction, Weld compared the conditions of free workers and slaves:

> Two million seven hundred thousand persons in these States are in this condition [slavery]. They were made slaves and are held such by force, and by being put in fear, and this for no crime! Reader, what have you to say of such treatment? It is right, just, benevolent? Suppose I should seize you, rob you of your liberty, drive you into the field, and make you work without pay as long as you live, would that be justice and kindness, or monstrous injustice and cruelty? Now, everybody knows that the slaveholders do these things to the slaves every day, and yet it is stoutly affirmed that they treat them well and kindly, and that their tender regard for their slaves restrains the masters from inflicting cruelties upon them. We shall go into no metaphysics to show the absurdity of this pretence. The man who robs you every day, is forsooth, quite too tenderhearted ever to cuff or kick you! True, he can empty your pockets with qualms, but if your stomach is empty, it cuts him to the quick. He can make you work a life time without pay, but loves you too well to let you go hun-

> gry. He fleeces you of your rights with a relish, but is shocked if you work bareheaded in summer, or in winter without warm stockings. He can make you go without your liberty, but never without a shirt. He can crush, in you, all hope of bettering your condition, by vowing that you shall die his slave, but though he can coolly torture your feelings, he is too compassionate to lacerate your back—he can break your heart, but he is very tender of your skin. He can strip you of all protection and thus expose you to all outrages, but if you are exposed to the weather, half clad and half sheltered, how yearn his tender bowels! What! Slaveholders talk of treating men well, and yet not only rob them of all they get, and as fast as they get it, but rob them of themselves, also; their very hands and feet, all their muscles, and limbs, and senses, their bodies and minds, their time and liberty and earnings, their free speech and rights of conscience, and their right to acquire knowledge, and property, and reputation;—and yet they, who plunder them of all these, would fain make us believe that their soft hearts ooze out so lovingly toward their slaves that they always keep them well housed and well clad, never push them too hard in the field, never make their dear backs smart, not let their dear stomachs get hungry.

Source: Richard O. Curry and Joanna Dunlap Cowded, *Slavery in America: Theodore Weld's American Slavery as It Is* (Itasca, IL: F. E. Peacock Publishers, 1973), pp. 4–5.

Crow laws, which restricted their physical movement and social position. These laws regulated relations between races in such aspects of daily living as travel and transportation, eating and sleeping, friendship and sexual fulfillment, and ability to vote in elections. The laws were incorporated into a **separate but equal doctrine** instituted by the Supreme Court under which the separation of blacks and whites was allowed on the premise that equal public accommodations would be provided. As a result, many blacks were reduced to the status of sharecroppers, working the land for a landowner in return for a share of the crop, minus expenses. This was little better than slave status, since it was tied to the land and the authority and economic domination of the landowners. Thomas Holt describes this post–Civil War period as "the failure of freedom."[52]

Cultural oppression against blacks was as total as it was against the Native American populations. In the slave trade, peoples of different tribes and languages were mixed together. Since blacks were not able to talk to one another freely, they developed a dialect which still retains many traces of African languages. They were unable to practice their religions, and the slave owners' total control made family life extremely difficult for blacks. That they survived centuries of misery is testimony to their strength. Their contributions to the political and cultural dimensions of American society have been enormous.[53]

Not until the twentieth century did blacks begin to migrate from the rural South to the industrial North and West. They were recruited as cheap labor by industrialists to break strikes and the organizing efforts of labor unions. Not incidentally, they were greeted by hostile white workers who were fearful of losing their jobs and favored continued oppression of blacks. The competition for jobs between two newcomers, European immigrants and southern blacks, helped provoke "race riots" in which bodily harm was inflicted on blacks by whites, even the police. The situation for blacks did not improve appreciably until after World War II and the civil rights legislation of the 1960s (see Chapter 7).

Mexican Americans

The term *Mexican American* correctly refers to all groups in the United States with an ancestral origin in Mexico or what was once Mexican territory. But there is no satisfactory term to describe this large and diverse group of people. They may refer to themselves as Hispanics or Latinos, designations for all Spanish-heritage groups in the United States, and during the 1960s the term *Chicano* became popular, especially among those committed to the civil rights movement. The roots and meaning of such terms as *Hispanic* and *Chicano* are unclear, however, and because of their political connotations there are Americans of Mexican descent who do not feel comfortable with them. Generally, they refer to themselves as Mexican American, but when they see themselves as part of the larger group of Spanish-surnamed or Spanish-speaking Americans, they tend to prefer *Latino* or *Hispanic*.

Almost all of the southwestern part of the United States was obtained as a result of territorial conflict with Mexico. Northern Mexico had four major provinces: Texas, New Mexico, Arizona, and California. The boundaries of these settlements stretched as far north as the present states of Nevada, Colorado, and Wyoming. New Mexico had the largest population and an extensively developed cultural life centered in Santa Fe. California was also fairly well developed, with missions, towns, and ranches up and down the coast. Texas, with its center in San Antonio, and Arizona, with its center in Tucson, were less densely settled.

In Texas, American settlers, invited to immigrate into the territory, quickly outnumbered the Mexican population and rebelled against the Mexican government. In spite of their loss at the Alamo, they were eventually victorious and created the Lone Star Republic. Texas became a state in 1845, and the following year the United States became embroiled with Mexico over disputed boundaries and offered to purchase areas in the Southwest. When the Mexican government refused to part with them, the U.S. Army attacked, marching through New Mexico and toward California, which already was in the process of separating from Mexico. Though little blood was shed, eventually there was armed retaliation by Mexican citizens. After U.S. forces captured Mexico City in 1848, the war was ended with the signing of the Treaty of Guadalupe Hidalgo. Article VIII gave Mexicans the right to remain where they were or to withdraw to Mexico within two years. Those who stayed in the United States were given the option of becoming American citizens or retaining Mexican citizenship. All rights to property belonging to Mexicans in the territory were to be guaranteed and protected by law.

Little by little, however, the Mexicans who stayed behind lost their lands to Americans who laid claim to them. Instead of automatically accepting all land titles, in the spirit in which the treaty had been written, American officials put the burden of proof of ownership on the Mexican landholders. Americans were allowed to take over the land, and Mexicans soon found themselves with the status of second-class citizens. Often they resisted, and, as late as 1915, they periodically resorted to arms in attempts to right such injustices. By the end of the nineteenth century, Mexicans were the numerical minority in all states that had previously been part of Mexican provinces, with the exception of New Mexico. This area was a special case because of its cultural center and leadership by an economic and social elite. New Mexico entered the Union as an officially bilingual state. As elsewhere in the Southwest, Mexicans lost land and Anglo governors were appointed, but only recently have Anglos begun to outnumber Mexicans and take political control in New Mexico.

It is clear that conquest played an important role in the history of the Southwest, but whether Mexican Americans can be considered a conquered group is open to debate. Joan Moore points out that at the time of conquest, relatively few Mexicans were living in that vast area. She estimates that the largest population of Mexicans, some 60,000, were in New Mexico, and there were about 7,500 in California, 5,000 in Texas, and 1,000 in Arizona.[54] Most Mexican Americans do not trace their background to the period of conquest and annexation. Mexicans began to immigrate to the United States in large numbers about 1912, pushed by civil strife and poverty in Mexico. The extent to which these Mexicans regarded themselves as immigrating to the United States is questionable, however. Blauner points out that until the 1940s, Mexican schoolchildren were taught that the Southwest was Mexican territory under the control of the American government. He argues that many early immigrants believed they were going from one part of Mexico to another, and thus they were not immigrating so much as going to their rightful place.[55]

Mexicans continue to cross the U.S. border today in large numbers, both as documented immigrants or visitors and as undocumented aliens (see Chapter 6). In March 1991 the Current Population Survey of the U.S. Census Bureau counted 13,400,000 Americans of Mexican descent in the United States, by far the largest population of Spanish origin.[56] The number of such residents who are not counted is impossible to estimate.

It has been suggested that the slow assimilation of Mexicans in American society is related to the proximity of the United States to Mexico, which encourages them to retain their national identity and loyalty. The hostility encountered by many Mexicans in the United States undoubtedly contributes to this loyalty. The experiences of Mexicans in the American labor market provide evidence of their subordinate status. While Mexicans were neither enslaved nor forced onto reservations, their opportunities for work have been as constrained as those of blacks and Native Americans. Historically, Mexican Americans were used as farm labor, which formerly was not subject to minimum-wage restrictions or social security contributions. They also were employed in unskilled jobs on ranches and in mining, food processing, construction, and the railroads, even though many of them had the skills and experience necessary for supervisory positions.

Mexican Americans also have experienced harsh cultural oppression. Although their language and religion were not outlawed, they were subjected to segregation laws. In Texas, where southern whites made up the bulk of those who migrated there, and in California, the law effectively segregated Mexicans from the mainstream populations, restricting them to certain schools, recreational facilities, restaurants, and theaters. During the 1930s the U.S. government adopted a repatriation program through which 500,000 Mexicans were forced to leave the country, though many of them were American citizens. It is estimated that the Mexican-American population of Texas declined by 40 percent as a result. Even in New Mexico, some 9,000 Latinos lost their small farms and ranches because of their inability to pay taxes. Again, during the period 1953–1955, 2.2 million Mexicans in the United States were rounded up and sent back over the border; some were deported more than once.[57]

Puerto Ricans

In many ways Puerto Ricans who have come to the U.S. mainland from the island appear to have immigrated. If only this movement is considered, this is probably the case. However, to ignore the social relationship between the island of Puerto Rico and the government of the United States is a serious error. Moreover, independence from the United States has been a continuing desire for many Puerto Ricans.

Puerto Rico was annexed by the United States as a result of the Treaty of Paris (1898), which settled the Spanish American War. American armed forces had invaded Puerto Rico and marched across the island, proclaiming it American territory. Although there was no insurrection by Puerto Ricans against the American soldiers and even a certain amount of support for them, there also was no referendum to allow Puerto Ricans to choose their destiny. Many who supported the U.S. invasion believed that Puerto Rican independence would follow. This was not to be the case.[58]

Since prior to the conquest the United States had never owned overseas territories, it was necessary to clarify the use of the term *territory* with respect to Puerto Rico. Previously, a territory within the continental United States had rights to statehood; when the territory had been incorporated and a provisional government had been set up, it could acquire the status of a state. However, in a 1905 Supreme Court case, *Downes* v. *Bidwell*, Puerto Rico and similar territories were declared unincorporated and therefore not eligible for statehood. The rationale for this decision was in keeping with the racism prevalent at the turn of the century. Puerto Rico could not become a state because it was a racially mixed society.[59]

After the conquest Puerto Ricans were removed from power, English became the language of public school instruction, and Protestant missionaries came in large numbers. The Foraker Act of 1900 took political power away from Puerto Ricans and placed it in the hands of Americans. U.S. officials appointed the governor and the eleven-member Executive Council, only five of whom had to be Puerto Rican; citizens were allowed to elect only representatives to the lower house of their legislature. The country could not set trade tariffs or negotiate commercial treaties with foreign countries. The election of Louis Muñoz Marín as the first freely elected governor in 1948 marked a turning point. He instituted a program for economic development called Operation Bootstrap, under which manufacturing was encouraged and the tourist trade was developed by provisions for selective tax exemption, low-interest loans, and other incentives. Gradually, Puerto Rican culture was allowed to reassert itself. In 1991, Spanish became by law the nation's only official language, ending 89 years in which Spanish and English were the joint official languages.[60]

Puerto Ricans were granted U.S. citizenship in 1917, and in 1952 they adopted a new constitution under which the country has the status of a commonwealth of the United States. Residents have all the rights of U.S. citizens except the right to vote in federal elections. They are represented in Congress by an elected resident commissioner who can speak in the House of Representatives but cannot vote. Puerto Ricans need not go through any naturalization procedure and may travel freely in the states in search of employment. While commonwealth status is believed to be equal to statehood, the meaning of the term is quite unclear.[61] Sizable numbers of Puerto Ricans of all political persuasions believe that *commonwealth* in reality means little more than *territory*, but the population on the island remains divided on the issue. The election of a pro-statehood governor seemed to indicate that this sentiment was growing in popularity, but in a nonbinding plebiscite in which 73.6 percent of the eligible voters participated in 1993, a slim majority voted in favor of maintaining commonwealth status. The results were 48.4 percent for the commonwealth and 46.2 percent for statehood. Just 4.4 percent voted for independence from the United States.[62]

Puerto Ricans coming to live in the United States do so more-or-less willingly, and, within the limitations of their skills, they can seek employment in a free-market economy. Discrimination has been cited as a reason for their continued poverty, unemployment, and underemployment. The hostility Puerto Ricans have experienced from Americans on the continent is probably not very different from that experienced by southern and eastern European immigrants. Their Catholic religion has not been challenged, and there has been no overt attempt to break up family life. However, since the Puerto Rican ethnic mix is essentially a blend of European (Spanish) and African, with traces of Native American, many Puerto Rican immigrants have endured the same kinds of racial prejudice in the United States as African Americans have.

Asian Americans

Historically, the two largest Asian groups in the United States have been the Japanese and the Chinese. Only recently has a wider range of Asian groups begun to enter in large numbers. The Chinese replaced the Japanese as the largest Asian group in 1980. In 1990, *Time* called the Pacific Coast of the United States "a twentieth-century Asia Minor," inhabited by Cambodians, Thais, Filipinos, Koreans, Japanese, Asian Indians, Vietnamese, Indochinese hill people, and Chinese from the People's Republic, Taiwan, and Southeast Asia.[63]

The Chinese and Japanese, like most Asian groups, are generally considered immigrant groups. No conquest or forced entry marked their arrival in the United States. The decision to immigrate was largely voluntary, with push-and-pull factors that were not too different from those for European immigrants: economic and political difficulties at home, coupled with perceived opportunities in the United States. Like the Italians, many Chinese and Japanese came as sojourners expecting to return to the homeland after making their fortune in the United States. Most of the early immigrants were men, which hindered the development of family life.

There are elements of the Japanese and Chinese experience, however, which suggest that their entry and their quest for well-being in the United States also resembled those of groups that were forced in. For instance, their immigration has to be seen as part of the social upheavals caused by the forced opening of China and Japan to American and European markets. Moreover, the beliefs of European Americans in the racial inferiority of Asians provoked intense hostility toward them. The opportunities of Asians in the U.S. labor market were severely constrained, to a degree not experienced by most Europeans.[64]

The Chinese Immigrant Experience

As a result of the public hostility to Chinese immigration to the United States in the nineteenth century, the U.S. government began to rethink its commitment to the open-door policy. After England opened isolationist China to European exploitation, the Chinese economy, already in decline, worsened, thus setting the stage for emigration. An estimated 322,000 Chinese entered the United States between 1850 and 1852; the movement accelerated after signing of the Burlingame Treaty in 1868, under which Chinese nationals were allowed free and unrestricted immigration into the country. Large numbers also went to the independent kingdom of Hawaii, where they constituted the main labor force on the sugar plantations.[65]

In both Hawaii and the United States, the Chinese met with hostility and discrimination. They did the hard work on the railroads and in the mines and canneries, as well as farm labor, but they began to gravitate to small industries such as shoe and garment factories and to develop farms of their own. The industry of the Chinese inspired a conviction among Americans that Chinese labor was undermining the standards of American labor. This sentiment, spearheaded by labor unions and supported by small entrepreneurs and farms, led to a campaign of organized violence against Chinese communities in California and Oregon. In some towns, Chinese communities were evicted; in San Francisco, a city ordinance restricted their use of the streets. The Chinese were also subjected to segregated schools and theaters. In Hawaii, attempts were made to limit intermarriage with Chinese.

As anti-Chinese sentiment spread in the United States, China agreed to restrict emigration voluntarily, and finally provisions of the Burlingame Treaty were revised to allow Congress to suspend the immigration of Chinese nationals. The Chinese Exclusion Act of 1880, to take effect in 1882, was passed and signed by the president. As the result of a series of similar measures, immigration by Asians and Pacific Islanders became effectively cut off until 1943[66] (see "A Timeline of Chinese Exclusion").

The Japanese Immigrant Experience

As the number of Chinese immigrants declined, business interests needing a cheap labor supply began to encourage Japanese immigration. Between 1891 and 1924, about 300,000 Japanese entered the United States legally, and equally large numbers had already entered the kingdom of Hawaii. The kinds of immigrants leaving Japan were quite different from the kinds leaving China or most of those leaving Europe. When Japanese immigration first started, vagrants were recruited off the streets of Tokyo. Trouble in Hawaii over these "first-year men" soon led Japanese officials to be more selective about whom they allowed to immigrate. In order to avoid the difficulties confronted earlier by the Chinese, the Japanese sent workers who were suited to contract labor. The result was a more capable, more middle-class type of Japanese immigrant.[67]

The Japanese worked in many of the same areas as the Chinese, but they found the best possibilities for advancement in agriculture. A Japanese immigrant might begin as an ordinary laborer; progress to contract farming, share tenancy, and cash leasing; and finally

A Timeline of Chinese Exclusion

The Chinese Exclusion Act was not a single law which took effect in 1882 but a series of acts designed to severely limit or prohibit the immigration of Chinese nationals and other Asians. The timeline below shows how the discriminatory exclusion was gradually strengthened and extended until it was finally eliminated from American immigration policy.

1882 Chinese Exclusion Act, passed by Congress in 1880, takes effect. Chinese laborers are barred from entering the country for a period of ten years.

1884 Second Chinese Exclusion Act is passed, tightening the provisions of the 1882 act.

1888 New Chinese Exclusion Act forbids Chinese workers who have left the United States from returning.

1892 Geary Chinese Exclusion Act extends provisions of the first act for another ten years. All Chinese residents of the United States are required to register within a year or face deportation.

1898 the U.S. Supreme Court rules that a child born of Chinese parents in the United States is a citizen and cannot be denied entrance by the exclusion laws of 1882 and 1892.

1902 The Chinese Exclusion Act of 1882 is revised to prohibit the immigration of Asians from U.S. island territories such as Hawaii and the Philippines. Exclusion is made permanent.

1917 Immigration law is passed requiring immigrants to pass a literacy test in any language. Immigrants from most of Asia and the Pacific Islands are excluded.

1943 President Franklin D. Roosevelt signs the "Chinese Act," which repeals the exclusion acts of 1882 and 1902. Chinese residents of the United States are made eligible for citizenship, and an annual quota of 105 Chinese is established.

1965 President Lyndon Johnson signs a new immigration law which abolishes the national quota system. Entry is permitted, within limits, for any alien who meets the qualifications of education and skill, provided no job held by an American is jeopardized.

Source: Based on information in James Trager, *The People's Chronology* (New York: Henry Holt, 1992).

achieve truck farm ownership. Their success soon inspired anti-Japanese sentiment, and legal support for discrimination against them was found in the laws stipulating that Asians are aliens and ineligible for citizenship. First-generation Japanese (*Issei*) were not only refused citizenship but could be blocked from owning or leasing agricultural lands. Attempts were made to block them from passing on previously owned lands to their second-generation, American-born children (*Nisei*), but these were not successful.

The Japanese government took an active role in the relations between Japanese immigrants and the U.S. government. In 1907, the two governments signed a gentlemen's agreement whereby Japan set self-imposed quotas to limit the immigration of Japanese nationals to the United States. Regardless, when U.S. immigration quotas were set in the 1920s, Japan, like other Asian countries, was denied a quota. The Japanese government considered this a complete repudiation of the gentlemen's agreement, and there is no doubt that the new immigration laws played a part in provoking Japanese hostilities in World War II.

When strong governments become enemies, enemy nationals can expect to suffer. German Americans, for instance, endured a great deal of hostility during World War I. The Japanese, an "undesirable race" from an undesirable country, were subjected to even more. After the bombing of Pearl Harbor, a move to "relocate" Japanese Americans took hold in California. Curfews and other restrictions were imposed on Japanese neighborhoods. In 1942, President Franklin D. Roosevelt signed an executive order which forced the evacuation of Japanese Americans to internment camps. In the process, Japanese community and family life was seriously disrupted, and many of them were economically ruined. Although the Japanese in Hawaii also were faced with some restrictions, the size of the Japanese population there, coupled with more liberal racial attitudes, precluded evacuation and internment.

In 1944, the U.S. Supreme Court determined that the relocation of the Japanese, whose loyalty to the United States was not at issue, had been unconstitutional. After the war many Japanese relocated to states other than California. The situation for them, as for all Asian groups, improved enormously. While many had lost their livelihood and their land, some compensation was given, and the Japanese community was able to draw together again.

Since the war the Japanese have done well, both economically and politically, especially in Hawaii but also on the mainland. Yet there is the possibility that the typical Japanese immigrant, like the Chinese, Filipino, and more recent Asian immigrants, could be blocked from reaching more than middleman minority status, barred by prejudice and discrimination from the upper levels of socioeconomic success. As Harry Kitano notes, "Japanese progress, if measured by their movement upward, is impressive, but if progress is measured by their distribution at the top, it is less so. Few are in the highest leadership positions and many are overqualified for the jobs they hold."[68]

∽ IMPLICATIONS FOR PRACTICE

This chapter emphasizes two points for social service workers. It demonstrates that the socioeconomic well-being of Americans is very much related to the status of their ethnic or racial groups. It also demonstrates that as workers attempt to help members of racial or ethnic minorities, they necessarily are involved in a larger historical process of group conflict and competition.

Human Needs

According to Abraham Maslow's hierarchy of human needs, which was introduced in Chapter 2, higher-level needs such as belongingness, self-esteem, and self-actualization cannot be satisfied until lower-level, survival needs such as food and water and safety have been met. Taking Maslow's lead, we should expect African-American, Puerto Rican, and Mexican-American clients to be caught up in the struggle to meet basic human needs. This does not imply that all clients in these groups have the same basic needs or that clients in the white majority never have such needs. In general, however, these ethnic minorities are more likely than others to be struggling to survive. Asian Americans, at least the Chinese and Japanese discussed in this chapter, are likely to evidence needs that are more akin to those of white Americans. Their self-actualization, however, may be blocked at the top. High education levels and hard work do not always pay off for them as significantly as they do for whites.

One of the dilemmas of social work as a profession is that it is increasingly being divorced from the struggles of poor people.[69] Professional social workers today are less likely to be working with the poor and the unemployed in the income-maintenance programs of public agencies. More likely, they are working for private, not-for-profit or profit-making organizations or in private practice, offering services geared to meet the more-advanced human needs. Some social workers who do encounter ethnic minorities and the poor become insensitive to the necessity of meeting basic human needs. They have good intentions and sincerely wish to serve such people, but the nature of the organizations for which they work and the services they have been trained to provide are not the kinds required by individuals and families in these groups. To be of help to them, social workers must become as adept at assessing and intervening in basic human needs as they are in meeting advanced needs.

Intergroup Conflict and Competition

Helping minorities and the poor involves historical processes of competition and conflict. Thus a social worker dealing with the private troubles of a minority individual or family also must try to resolve larger public issues of group competition and conflict.

The social histories of racial and ethnic groups presented in this chapter supply a background for understanding the larger issues. In the same way social workers take a case history of an individual or family, this chapter has taken case histories of ethnic and racial groups. These histories demonstrate that the needs and problems of individuals and families are very much related to events and conditions that occurred in their ethnic and racial communities in the past and over which they had no control. By accident of birth, the chances for meeting even basic human needs are diminished for people of color and enhanced for white ethnics.

Knowing the social histories of these groups makes it possible for social workers to go a step further in establishing accurate empathy and rapport with ethnic-minority clients. Rather than blaming a client as an individual for the troubles being experienced, the worker should be able to see the connection between the individual's problems and the problems of the community as a whole. This makes it easier to recognize when the distrust a client expresses has its basis in the reality of past group conflict and to appreciate the strengths of clients who, for example, continue to prevail despite a history of abuse. By taking a critical perspective, the worker may recognize that helping to solve the problems of ethnic-minority clients requires a personal and professional involvement in the eradication of group conflict and competition in the society.

Knowing the social histories of racial and ethnic groups also gives social workers a sense of hope. European and Asian ethnics have done fairly well as communities in the United States, and there is every reason to believe that the system is open enough to allow for the eventual advance of many African Americans, Native Americans, Alaskan Natives, Mexican Americans, and Puerto Ricans. Social workers who are willing to work with and on behalf of ethnic minorities can help to speed up the process by which these communities become part of the majority.

∞ DISCUSSION QUESTIONS AND CLASS PROJECTS

1. Search in your library for data on the social and economic achievements of a racial or ethnic group of your choice. Determine for yourself the educational, income, and occupational needs of the group, and compare it with at least one other such group.

2. Describe and compare the approaches of the cycle of race relations and conflict theory to the study of ethnic and racial stratification. Which approach do you think describes more accurately what has happened and can take place in the United States?

3. Describe what is meant by the following concepts:

   social indicators
   ethnocentrism
   cultural assimilation
   structural assimilation
   marital assimilation
   identificational assimilation
   civic assimilation
   immigrant and colonialist analogies

4. Is the United States a land of immigrants?

5. Compare and contrast the history of one or more European ethnic groups and one or more people of color in the United States.

6. Identify your ethnic community or communities of origin. Read up on the history of your community and talk to your parents, grandparents, or other relatives to see how the history of your family fits with the history of the community.

7. Identify the significance of:

   the Trail of Tears
   coercive assimilation
   policy of termination
   an American dilemma
   the Naturalization Act of 1790
   the Treaty of Guadalupe Hidalgo
   Operation Bootstrap
   the Foraker Act
   the Chinese Exclusion Act of 1882
   the gentlemen's agreement
   middleman minorities

∞ NOTES

1. Howard E. Freeman and Eleanor Bernert Sheldon, "Social Indicators," *Encyclopedia of Social Work*, 17th ed., Vol. 2 (New York: National Association of Social Workers, 1977), pp. 1350–55.

2. Arthur G. Neal, *Social Psychology: A Social Perspective* (Reading, MA: Addison-Wesley, 1983), pp. 477–94; Frank M. Andrews and Stephen B. Withey, *Social Indicators of Well-Being: Americans' Perceptions of Life Quality* (New York: Plenum Press, 1976), p. 23.

3. Angus Campbell, *The Sense of Well-Being in America: Recent Patterns and Trends* (New York: McGraw-Hill, 1981).

4. Ibid., pp. 232–33.

5. U.S. Commission on Civil Rights, *Social Indicators of Equality for Minorities and Women* (Washington, DC, August 1978).

6. Barbara Ehrenreich, *Fear of Falling: The Inner Life of the Middle Class* (New York: Pantheon Books, 1989), p. 202, and Ehrenreich, "Is the Middle Class Doomed?" *The New York Times Magazine*, September 7, 1986, pp. 44, 50, 54, 62, 64.

7. Ehrenreich, *Fear of Falling*, p. 8.

8. U.S. Bureau of the Census, *Statistical Abstract of the United States: 1992*, 112th edition (Washington, DC, 1992), Table 702.

9. Reverend E. V. Hill, Glenn Loury, G. A. Parker, Joseph Perkins, Clarence Thomas, and Robert Woodson, "Black America under the Reagan Administration: A Symposium of Black Conservatives," *Policy Review*, no. 34 (Fall 1985), pp. 27–41.

10. U.S. Bureau of the Census, *Statistical Abstract of the United States: 1992*, Table 704.

11. Edna Bonacich, "A Theory of Middlemen Minorities," *American Sociological Review*, vol. 38 (October 1973), pp. 583–94.

12. Donald L. Noel, "A Theory of the Origin of Ethnic Stratification," in N. R. Yetman and C. H. Steele (editors), *Minority and Majority* (Boston, MA: Allyn and Bacon, 1971), pp. 109–20.

13. Robert E. Park, *Race and Culture* (New York: Free Press, 1964).

14. Milton M. Gordon, *Assimilation in American Life* (New York: Oxford University Press, 1964).

15. Ibid., pp. 60–83, 115–31.

16. Tekle Wodemikael, "Becoming Black Americans: The Case of Haitian Immigrants," paper presented at the 78th annual meeting of the American Sociological Association, August–September 1983, Detroit, Michigan.

17. William Newman, *American Pluralism: A Study of Minority Groups and Social Theory* (New York: Harper & Row, 1973), pp. 97–190.

18. Robert Blauner, *Racial Oppression in America* (New York: Harper & Row, 1972) pp. 51–75.

19. Thomas Sowell, *Race and Economics* (New York: David McKay, 1975).

20. William S. Bernard, "Immigration: History of U.S. Policy," in S. Thernstrom (editor), *Harvard Encyclopedia of American Ethnic Groups* (Cambridge, MA: Belknap Press, 1980), pp. 486–95.

21. Richard M. Burkey, *Ethnic and Racial Groups* (Menlo Park, CA: Cummings, 1978), pp. 246–51.

22. Bernard, "Immigration," p. 487.

23. See Kathleen Neils Conzen, "Germans," and Peter A. Munch, "Norwegians," in *Harvard Encyclopedia of American Ethnic Groups*, pp. 406, 750–61; also see Dietmar Rothermund, "The German Problem of Colonial Pennsylvania," and Carl Wittke, "Ohio's Germans, 1840–75," in L. Dinnerstein and F. C. Jaher (editors), *Uncertain Americans: Readings in Ethnic History* (New York: Oxford University Press, 1977), pp. 48–57, 114–23.

24. Thomas Sowell, *Ethnic America* (New York: Basic Books, 1981), pp. 17–42.

25. Patrick J. Blessing, "Irish," in *Harvard Encyclopedia of American Ethnic Groups*, pp. 539–40.

26. Sowell, *Race and Economics*, pp. 71–80.

27. Michael Novak, *The Rise of the Unmeltable Ethnics* (New York: Macmillan, 1971), pp. 85–136.

28. Sowell, *Ethnic America*, pp. 17–42.

29. Oscar Handlin, *Boston's Immigrants, 1790–1865: A Study in Acculturation*, rev. ed. (Cambridge, MA: Harvard University Press, 1941), p. 129.

30. Sowell, *Race and Economics*, pp. 76–78.

31. Ibid., pp. 142–48.

32. Humbert S. Nelli, "Italians," in *Harvard Encyclopedia of American Ethnic Groups*, pp. 547–49.

33. Joe R. Feagin, *Racial and Ethnic Relations* (Englewood Cliffs, NJ: Prentice-Hall, 1984), pp. 153–58.

34. See Sowell, *Race and Economics*, pp. 80–90. Also see Nelli, "Italians," pp. 545–60.

35. Feagin, *Racial and Ethnic Relations*, pp. 129, 116.

36. Arthur A. Goren, "Jews," in *Harvard Encyclopedia of American Ethnic Groups*, pp. 579–88.

37. Sowell, *Race and Economics*, pp. 665–71, 115–57.

38. Doman Lum, *Social Work Practice and People of Color* (Monterey, CA: Brooks/Cole, 1986).

39. Blauner, *Racial Oppression in America*, pp. 10–14, 51–75.

40. Edward H. Spicer, "American Indians," in *Harvard Encyclopedia of American Ethnic Groups*, p. 58.

41. U.S. Bureau of the Census, *Statistical Abstract of the United States: 1992*, Table 43, and news report, November 18, 1992.

42. Newman, *American Pluralism* (New York: Harper & Row, 1973), pp. 35–36.

43. Dorothy M. Jones, "Aleuts," and Arthur E. Hippler, "Eskimos," in *Harvard Encyclopedia of American Ethnic Groups*, pp. 28–29, 336–39.

44. C. Dale McLemore, *Racial and Ethnic Relations in America*, 2nd ed. (Boston, MA: Allyn and Bacon, 1983), p. 334.

45. Edward H. Spicer, "American Indians: Federal Policy Toward," in *Harvard Encyclopedia of American Ethnic Groups*, p. 114.

46. Joseph G. Jorgensen, "Indians and the Metropolis," in J. O. Waddel and O. M. Watson (editors), *The American Indian in Urban Society* (Boston, MA: Little, Brown, 1971), pp. 67–113.

47. James E. Officer, "The American Indian and Federal Policy," in Waddel and Watson (editors), *American Indian in Urban Society*, pp. 9–65.

48. Gunnar Myrdal, *An American Dilemma: The Negro Problem and Modern Democracy* (New York: Harper and Brothers, 1944).

49. Sowell, *Race and Economics*, pp. 3–33.

50. Daniel G. Hill, Jr., *The Negro in Oregon: A Survey*, unpublished master's thesis, University of Oregon, Eugene, June 1932.

51. Sowell, *Race and Economics*, pp. 11–18.

52. Thomas C. Holt, "Afro-Americans," in *Harvard Encyclopedia of American Ethnic Groups*, p. 13.

53. See, for instance, Holt's description of their contributions to literature, ibid., pp. 16–17.

54. Joan Moore, "Colonialism: The Case of the Mexican Americans," *Social Problems*, vol. 17 (Spring 1970), pp. 463–72.

55. Blauner, *Racial Oppression in America*, pp. 53–70.

56. U.S. Bureau of the Census, *Statistical Abstract of the United States: 1992*, Table 44.

57. Carlos E. Cortes, "Mexicans," in *Harvard Encyclopedia of American Ethnic Groups*, pp. 707, 711; Otto Friedrich, "The Changing Face of America," *Time*, July 8, 1985, p. 28.

58. Manual Maldonado-Denis, *Puerto Rico: A Socio-Historic Interpretation* (New York: Vintage Books, 1972), pp. 52–62, 65–129. Also see Juan Angel Selin, *We the Puerto Rican People: A Story of*

Oppression and Resistance (New York: Monthly Review Press, 1971), pp. 60–66.

59. Diana Christopulos, "Puerto Rico in the Twentieth Century," in A. Lopez and J. Petras (editors), *Puerto Rico and Puerto Ricans* (New York: John Wiley and Sons, 1974), pp. 126–27. Also see Maldonado-Denis, *Puerto Rico*, pp. 83–129.

60. "Commonwealth of Puerto Rico," in Mark S. Hoffman (editor), *The World Almanac and Book of Facts: 1993* (New York: Pharos Books, 1993), pp. 647–48.

61. See, for instance, Henry Wells, "Puerto Rico's Commonwealth Status and Its Relevance to the U.S. Virgin Islands: An Outline," in J. A. Bough and R. C. Macridis (editors), *Virgin Islands: America's Caribbean Outpost* (Wakefield, MA: W. F. Williams, 1970), pp. 174–80.

62. Larry Rohter, "Choosing Status Quo," *The New York Times*, November 16, 1993, p. 8A.

63. Howard G. Chua-Egan, "Strangers in Paradise," *Time*, April 9, 1990, p. 32.

64. See Harry H. L. Kitano, "Japanese," and H. M. Lai, "Chinese," in *Harvard Encyclopedia of American Ethnic Groups*, pp. 560–71 and 217–34.

65. Lai, "Chinese," pp. 218, 231; James Trager, *The People's Chronology* (New York: Henry Holt, 1992), p. 512.

66. See John F. Kennedy, "Immigration Policy," in *A Nation of Immigrants* (New York: Harper & Row, 1964).

67. Kitano, "Japanese," pp. 570–71; McLemore, *Racial and Ethnic Relations in America*, pp. 163–65.

68. Kitano, "Japanese," pp. 570–71.

69. See Norman L. Wyers, "Income Maintenance and Social Work: A Broken Tie," *Social Work*, vol. 28 (July–August 1983), pp. 261–68, and "Whatever Happened to the Income Maintenance Line Worker?" *Social Work*, vol. 25 (July 1980), pp. 259–63. Also see Linda Cherrey Reeser and Irwin Epstein, "Social Workers' Attitudes toward Poverty and Social Action: 1968–84," *Social Service Review*, vol. 61 (December 1987), pp. 610–11.

The New Arrivals

MAJOR THEMES DISCUSSED IN THIS CHAPTER

1. **THE NEW AMERICANS.** New ethnic and racial groups continue to enter the United States, adding to the cultural mosaic and becoming incorporated into the status hierarchies of dominant and subordinate groups. Some of the new groups are immigrants, others are refugees or seeking asylum, and still others enter as undocumented aliens. None have been colonized by the United States.

2. **THE NEW IMMIGRANTS.** Immigrants now entering the United States are least likely to come from Europe and most likely to come from Latin America or Asia. Because of U.S. immigration laws, most immigrants must have occupational skills that are needed in this country. Therefore they can succeed more quickly than many immigrants of the past could.

3. **REFUGEES AND ASYLUM SEEKERS.** Many new arrivals have come to the United States as refugees or seekers of asylum. The numbers of refugees forced out of countries under communist regimes have declined, and many today are seeking asylum for various political or human-rights reasons. The president decides each year the number of aliens to be admitted.

4. **UNDOCUMENTED ALIENS.** This population is largely unskilled, uneducated, and rural in character. It has the closest resemblance to the "teeming masses" that came from Europe at the turn of the century.

5. **IMPLICATIONS FOR PRACTICE.** Social service workers can help assure that new arrivals to the United States do not take on the status of minority groups. They must not only respect and help sustain cultural values and traditions of these groups but facilitate their socialization into American society.

IN THE SOCIAL HISTORY OF ETHNIC communities in the United States presented in Chapter 5, we described the generally low socioeconomic status of various groups as they sought to make a place for themselves in American society. Some of these groups overcame the difficulties with relative ease, but for others socioeconomic well-being has remained out of reach.

In general, European groups and certain racial groups have greatly improved their socioeconomic position. The European groups immigrated to the United States more-or-less willingly and were offered opportunities as free workers in a market economy; others, such as the Japanese, had unique skills and sets of values which enabled them to overcome extremely hostile early experiences. The ethnic and racial minority groups that have not done well in the United States did not immigrate, or their immigration was restricted. They were systematically excluded from the competitive labor market and experienced severe prejudice and discrimination and cultural oppression in American society.

This chapter turns from the social history of immigrant and colonized groups to consider arrivals in the contemporary era. New ethnic and racial groups entering the United States are adding their own distinctive traditions, norms, and values to the cultural mosaic. Of the over 1.5 million legal immigrants entering the United States in 1990, only 112,000 came from Europe, more than 60 percent of them from the former Soviet Union, Poland, the United Kingdom, and Ireland. By far the largest number came from North America, including Mexico, Central America, and the Caribbean nations. The number of immigrants from Asia, including the Philippines, was increasing rapidly, as was the number from Africa, which nevertheless sent far fewer immigrants than any other continent.[1]

⌘ THE NEW AMERICANS

The waves of new arrivals who have washed up on the shores of the United States since the mid-1960s have made the study of ethnic and racial minority communities in the United States increasingly complex. They represent a variety of ethnic and racial groups previously unknown in the United States, and many of them have not entered as immigrants.

According to definitions of the U.S. Immigration and Naturalization Service (INS), immigrants are aliens admitted to the United States for legal permanent residence. They are sponsored by an individual, family, or organization and are lawfully granted the right to employment. The category of immigrant also includes those who enter the country as non-immigrant aliens or refugees and then change their status to permanent resident. Within the numerical limits set by the Immigration Act of 1990, 700,000 immigrants were to be allowed to enter the United States annually in fiscal years 1992–1994. **Refugees**, defined as persons outside their country of national origin who are unable or unwilling to return because of persecution or a well-founded fear of it, are not included in the numerical limits. An additional number of such persons can be admitted to avoid persecution on account of race, religion, nationality, membership in a social group, or political opinion.[2] The proportions of immigrants or refugees from various nations or parts of the world admitted into the United States in a specific period thus are related to national political policy.

The kinds of immigrants admitted within the numerical limits are also determined by law. By far the largest number of visas to be distributed under the Immigration Reform and Control Act of 1990 are to go to **family-based immigrants:** immediate relatives (sons and daughters or brothers and sisters) of U.S. citizens, or spouses and children of lawful permanent residents (immigrants). The other significant category is **employment-**

based immigrants: 28.6 percent of the visas in this category go to **priority workers**, those with extraordinary ability and acclaim in the sciences, arts, education, business, and athletics; senior-level professors and researchers with national or international recognition; and executives and managers of multinational corporations. Second preference (another 28.6 percent) is for professionals with advanced degrees and aliens of exceptional ability; and third is for skilled workers, professionals, and "other," or unskilled, workers (no more than 10,000 visas a year). Beginning in fiscal year 1995, at minimum 675,000 visas are to be distributed, including 480,000 for family-based immigrants, 140,000 for employment-based immigrants, and 55,000 for "diversity immigrants."[3]

Most of the new arrivals are neither white nor European (see "New Arrivals by Continent of Birth"). In 1985 a special issue of *Time* on immigration included portraits of new arrivals at New York's Kennedy airport from India, Rumania, Kampuchea, Afghanistan, the Philippines, Ethiopia, Laos, the former Soviet Union, Ghana, South Korea, Cuba, and Ireland.[4]

The reasons for the entry of these groups vary widely. None was conquered or forced to enter by the U.S. government. Some have immigrated, but under immigration laws that are quite a bit different from those of the late nineteenth and early twentieth centuries. Others have come as refugees or seeking political asylum, fleeing from oppressive regimes in their native countries. Still others have come as undocumented or illegal immigrants, pushed primarily by economic forces and eager to enter but unwillingly accepted socially or politically. The new immigrants and refugees enter with the status of free workers; that is, they can join the labor force directly or try to obtain the education necessary to advance themselves. Undocumented aliens can expect severe restrictions in the labor market; often they have no choice but to work for below-minimum wage, without social security and other fringe benefits and under constant threat of being discovered and deported. Those who have to repay the smugglers who contrive to get immigrants without visas into the country ("coyotes" charge Mexicans and Dominicans $50 to $1,000 and "snakeheads" charge Chinese $20,000 or $30,000 each) must live and labor under deplorable conditions, virtually as indentured servants.[5]

The new arrivals are clearly ethnic groups, but it is not clear that all are minority groups. Minority groups, as described in Chapter 4, are oppressed groups within a society; the oppression must be widespread both in time and place. The new immigrant and refugee groups are too new to be automatically considered minority groups in the United States. They have entered a society that has embraced the values of cultural pluralism and that has, since 1965, enacted immigration laws that tend to favor highly educated professionals or skilled workers. While some new arrivals, particularly Asians, have met with hostility, it has not been as detrimental as that experienced by enslaved African Americans, conquered Native Americans, or immigrating Catholic Irish. It is probably even less than the hostility directed to southern and eastern Europeans at the turn of the twentieth century. For many of the newest arrivals, minority status in the United States may never materialize. The provision of social services to all immigrants and refugees can help avoid this outcome for any of them.

Undocumented aliens are another matter. Those who are Haitian or from a Spanish-speaking nation (e.g., Mexican or Central American) have a very strong likelihood of either being incorporated into existing African-American or Latino minorities or becoming new minority groups. A new wave of undocumented aliens are Chinese from Taiwan, Hong Kong, and the People's Republic, who quickly disappear into Chinese communities in the United States. In the following sections we consider the experiences of new immigrants, refugees, and undocumented aliens entering the United States in recent years.

New Arrivals by Continent of Birth, 1961–1990

Patterns of immigration to the United States have changed dramatically since the 1960s. In the three decades between 1961 and 1990, the number of legal entrants from Europe declined significantly, but the decline was slowed by newly allowed emigration from the former Soviet Union and Poland. Immigration to the United States from other parts of the world continually increased during the same period. The number coming from Asia increased almost sixfold, and the number from Africa, while small, increased almost fivefold. The data from South America and from North America, which includes Mexico, Central America, and the Caribbean as well as Canada, also showed huge gains. One reason is that the data for 1989 and 1990 include undocumented aliens who registered to become legal residents under the provisions of the Immigration Reform and Control Act of 1986. The data below, from the U.S. Immigration and Naturalization Service, do not include estimates of other undocumented workers.

	Number of Immigrants (by decade)		
Continent of Origin	1961–70	1971–80	1981–90
Europe	1,238,600	801,300	705,600
Asia	445,300	1,633,800	2,817,400
North America	1,351,100	1,645,000	3,125,000
Canada	286,700	114,800	119,200
Mexico	443,300	637,200	1,653,300
Caribbean	519,500	759,800	892,700
Central America	97,700	132,400	458,700
South America	228,300	284,400	455,900
Africa	39,300	91,500	192,300

Source: U.S. Bureau of the Census, *Statistical Abstract of the United States: 1992*, 112th edition (Washington, DC, 1992), Table 8.

∞ THE NEW IMMIGRANTS

Immigrants move more-or-less voluntarily from their country of national origin to a different nation. They tend to become part of the new national society and often seek nationalized citizenship. To some extent, the immigrants arriving today differ from those who came to the United States from the early days of the Republic, up to the middle of the twentieth century. As we noted in Chapter 5, the Hart-Cellar Act passed in 1965 significantly altered immigration patterns. The law, which went into effect in 1968, abolished quotas based on national origin and abandoned use of the designation *Asian-Pacific Triangle*, an area from which immigration had been severely restricted. A limit on the total annual immigration to the United States was set at 290,000 immigrants with no more than 20,000 from any one nation. While the law did not assign preferences by national origin, in practice people from the Eastern Hemisphere with family members in the United States and with occupational training and skills which were in demand were more likely to be admitted.[6] The Immigration Reform Act of 1990 boosted legal immigration levels by 40 percent, to 685,000 beginning in 1995. Preference is again given to immediate family members or citizens, but the allowance for employment-based immigrants heavily favors professional priority workers.

The new immigration laws thus changed the types of persons likely to be admitted into the United States. Immigrants still come from Europe; in the late 1980s, for instance, large numbers of Jews were allowed to leave the former Soviet Union under that nation's policy of *glasnost*, or openness. With the collapse of the Soviet Union and other communist countries, increased emigration from eastern Europe could be expected. The largest numbers are arriving from Latin America and Asia, however, and recently there has been an increase in immigration from Africa.

The changes in immigration policy have increased the chances for socioeconomic success of the new immigrants. Because immigration policy today gives preference to family members, especially those in the nuclear family, many immigrants arrive with an informal support system in place. Because the policy favors well-educated people, they are better prepared for life in the United States. Preference is also given to aliens "with extraordinary ability" or "investors" or entrepreneurs who bring at least $1 million to invest in urban areas (or a lesser amount for investment in rural or high-unemployment areas).[7] Most immigrants still face problems—leaving one's homeland and giving up one's culture is not easy. But immigrants arriving today are very unlike those impoverished and illiterate southern and eastern Europeans who came almost a century ago.

Asian-Indian Immigrants

Between 1820 and 1965, fewer than 17,000 Asian Indians (sometimes called East Indians) had entered the United States; prior to 1965, India was included in the Pacific-Asian Triangle.[8] In 1990 alone, 31,000 legal immigrants entered the United States from India, and the 1990 U.S. Census found that 463,000 people had been born there.[9] Many Asian Indians have settled in the New York area, California, and Illinois.

Asian Indians are a heterogeneous group. India is a large country divided into 30 territories and states, with a wide range of diverse racial, religious, and linguistic groups. The Indian government recognizes 15 national languages, among them English, which most emigrants speak fluently. Hinduism is the dominant religion in India, and Hindus make up the largest group of East Indian immigrants to the United States.

It might have been predicted that these immigrants would have a difficult time adjusting to life in American society, considering the attitudes that Americans had demonstrated toward them in the past. In 1926, when Emory Borgardus first reported **social distance** scores, designed to measure a person's willingness to work with, live in the same neighborhood with, befriend, and marry members of various ethnic and racial communities, Asian Indians were ranked lowest on the list of 30 groups studied, lower than all the racial minorities we have been discussing. As recently as 1966, they were still seen as the least desirable group for neighborhoods, for friendship, and for marriage.[10] Asian Indians also experience considerable prejudice and discrimination in Great Britain and South Africa, where they are considered "colored."

The transition to American life appears to have been relatively easy for recent immigrants from India, however; their average personal income in 1990, considering both legal and illegal immigrants, was $13,578, the highest among the ten largest immigrant groups.[11] There are exceptions, but most are well educated and arrive with their families. Between 1965 and 1975 alone, about 46,000 Asian-Indian engineers, physicians, scientists,

Fabrics are displayed by an Asian-Indian shopkeeper at the Taj Sari
Palace in Chicago. He is one of the many Asians and Pacific Islanders
immigrating to the United States since the changes in immigration law
enacted in 1965 to permit their entry.

professors, teachers, and business people entered the United States, along with almost
47,000 of their wives and children.[12] According to the 1980 census, 50 percent of Asian Indians in the United States were in management or professional positions. This percentage
was higher than that for any other Asian group and considerably higher than that for
white Americans, only 25 percent of whom held such positions. Similarly, 52 percent of
Asian Indians 25 years of age and older in the United States were college graduates in
1980, compared to 17 percent of whites.[13]

Undoubtedly their relatively high level of training and their ability to speak English
have made the transition into American society relatively smooth for Asian Indians. However, becoming an American has not been free of difficulty for all of them. Some have experienced occupational discrimination, especially as they have attempted to move into administrative and top-level management positions. Medical graduates from India, for
example, find it hard to get residency positions in hospitals and must sometimes settle for
jobs as lab technicians or hospital orderlies.[14] They also face racial discrimination because of their generally dark complexions.

Family difficulties arise as Asian Indians try to adapt to life in the United States. Although their extensive families provide close-knit, supportive relationships, in the context
of American culture their family patterns generate difficulties. The Asian-Indian family
has traditionally been hierarchical, male-dominated, authoritarian, and strict in child
rearing. The emphasis is on conformity and the denial of individual autonomy. These
traditions are disrupted as the women join the labor force and the children are exposed to
American youth culture. The parents are likely to behave in traditional ways—controlling

their children, forbidding dating, arranging marriages, and communicating in an author-itarian manner. The children are likely to rebel openly, become passive-aggressive, or otherwise challenge parental authority.[15] In hopes of maintaining their heritage and re-sisting assimilation, Asian-Indian immigrants often join voluntary associations to promote cultural programs, and community schools are provided to teach children regional lan-guages, music, and dance. Nevertheless, the gender and intergenerational conflict creat-ed by immigration is forcing these families to adapt their traditions to fit the customs of American society.

☞ REFUGEES AND ASYLUM SEEKERS

Refugees differ from immigrants in that they do not voluntarily leave their native coun-try to come to another; they are forced out. Refugees also differ from colonized groups; they have not been forced into another society by a colonizing or conquering state.

The first laws covering the entrance of refugees to the United States referred to them as *displaced persons*. Their history is tied to international politics, particularly U.S. relations with communist nations. After World War II, there were many displaced persons in the eastern European, Baltic nations that were then coming under Soviet domination. The first Displaced Persons Act, passed in 1948, allowed 220,000 Baltic-nation refugees to enter the United States under "mortgaged" immigration quotas; that is, they could borrow against future quota allowances. In 1953 the law was changed to allow displaced persons to enter as "nonquota immigrants," and annual quotas for this category were ended in 1956. While special provisions of the Refugee Act of 1980 allow the president to designate a limited number of applicants to enter the country because they fear perse-cution or oppression, the definition of who qualifies under these rules is a controversial issue (see "In U.S. Policy, Not All Refugees Are Equal").

Although humanitarian motives were involved in the displaced-persons acts, their prin-cipal use was as a weapon in Cold War politics; they favored opponents of communist regimes, including Hungary in 1956, Dutch Indonesia in 1957, and Cuba and China in 1960. More recently, refugees from Cuba and communist-controlled Southeast Asia have been allowed to enter under these acts. At the same time, people fleeing persecution in non-communist countries such as El Salvador and Haiti have been denied legal entry as refugees.

Most of the 130,000 refugees allowed to resettle in the United States in 1993 still came from Vietnam and the former Soviet Union. Another recent refugee policy has been to settle refugee groups in safe havens in their own countries, as was done for the Kurds in Iraq after the Gulf War or as attempted in Haiti and Bosnia by international agencies. The United States also must deal with new arrivals who circumvent the official refugee system by entering the United States illegally and requesting asylum once they are in the country (see "Chinese Asylum Seekers"). Because the INS has neither the officers nor the detention space to hold all such **asylum seekers** until they can prove they qual-ify as refugees, they are released until their cases come to court, and many never show up for the hearings. As word spread of the inability of the INS to control the flow of asylum seekers, the number of applicants rose fivefold between the mid-1980s and 1993.[16]

Refugees now entering the United States tend to be more like the new immigrants than those of the late nineteenth and early twentieth centuries. While there is wide vari-ation among refugees and asylum seekers, they generally are educated and skilled, and they can benefit from government programs aimed at helping them make a smooth tran-sition to life in the United States. In no way should the suffering these refugees endured

In U.S. Policy, Not All Refugees Are Equal

The roots of U.S. policy regarding the entry of refugees are in the conflict between the United States and the communist regimes of eastern Europe and other parts of the world. Refugees fearing persecution under communism have found it easier to enter the country than refugees fearing persecution under other authoritarian or oppressive governments or political circumstances.

Since the reversals of communism in Eastern Europe, the U.S. State Department has supported the growth of democracy and free-market economies in the new national states. At the same time, however, political conflict has erupted in noncommunist nations; in Africa alone, some 6 million people have been uprooted by civil war, tribal massacres, anarchy, drought, or famine. Several hundred thousands have been forced out by political upheavals in Southeast Asia and parts of the Middle East, including Burma, Buhtan, and the Republic of Tajikistan. The horrors lived through by Bosnian and Muslim victims of the civil wars and ethnic cleansing in the former Yugoslavia and the plight of Haitians desperately trying to reach American shores have been recorded by the media.

American refugee policy appears to be still caught up in the old realities, however. Although the Cold War has ended, people wanting to leave eastern European nations still receive special consideration. Under President Bill Clinton's refugee allocations for 1994, 120,000 refugees are to be given asylum. Of the total permits, 45,000 will be allotted to residents of the former Soviet Union and another 45,000 to Vietnamese, Cambodians, and Laotians living under or threatened by communist regimes. Bosnians will receive 10,000 permits (one third of the remainder). Only 4,000 will be allotted to Latin American and Caribbean nations, including Haiti, and 7,000 are reserved for people from African nations.

Source: Christopher Hanson, "Not All Refugees Equal: U.S. Policy Based on Cold War While Needy Are Shut Out," *Seattle Post-Intelligencer*, October 25, 1993, pp. AI, A8.

in leaving their homelands and building a new life for themselves be minimized. But, simply put, on the whole refugee groups entering legally have not been oppressed in the United States and probably should not be thought of as subordinated minority groups.

Indochinese Refugees

The term *Indochinese* includes the many Southeast Asian peoples under French colonial rule in the nineteenth century. Of these, the Vietnamese, the Cambodians, and the Laotians are the three major groups that have come to the United States. Each is a linguistically and culturally distinct group.

After the French were defeated in their attempt to regain control of Vietnam after World War II, the country was partitioned into the Democratic Republic of Vietnam (the communists) in the North and the Republic of Vietnam (the nationalists) in the South. A civil war broke out between the North and South Vietnamese, and the U.S. military forces became heavily involved. In April 1975 the South Vietnamese government collapsed, the U.S. forces withdrew, and the communists took control.

Relatively few Indochinese were living in the United States prior to 1975, and there are no data on the Cambodians and Laotians then in this country. The Vietnamese who

Chinese Asylum Seekers

Ever since the California gold rush and throughout the years when the legal immigration of Asians to the United States was prohibited, Chinese gangs or crime syndicates have been smuggling Chinese workers into this country. The same system used then is the mechanism used today to get illegal Chinese aliens in.

The usual procedure for a person who wants to leave China for America is to locate a snakehead (a smuggler), make a down payment on the price of passage, and pay off the balance once the person begins earning money in the United States. The fare varies; it was from $15,000 to $35,000 apiece for the voyage of the Golden Venture, a tramp steamer loaded with 300 illegal Chinese aliens that ran aground off New York City in 1993. Many Chinese nationals thus enter the country deeply indebted to violent gangs and are forced to work off the balance of their passage with long hours of hard labor at low pay.

Illegal aliens from China who enter the country undetected, usually at remote points, simply disappear into nearby Chinese enclaves. Those who are apprehended and do see an immigration officer almost always claim asylum under the terms of an executive order signed by President George Bush in 1989. This order provided that anyone who left China to escape the strict family-planning policies of their government, under which a family is allowed to have only one child, was to be granted asylum.

About 85 percent of the Chinese who have asked for asylum under the terms of the Bush order have gotten it. Moreover, Chinese nationals have virtually never been deported in this period. Immigration officials estimated in 1993 that up to 100,000 Chinese enter the country outside the limits of lawful immigration every year, more than nearly any other ethnic minority.

Source: Brian Duffy, "Coming to America," *U.S. News & World Report*, June 21, 1993, pp. 26–31; Paul Glastris, "Immigration Crackdown," *U.S. News & World Report*, June 21, 1993, pp. 34–39.

had immigrated generally were wives or children of American servicemen. But within five months of the collapse of the South Vietnamese government, almost 190,000 Vietnamese, Laotians, and Cambodians arrived. This first wave of refugees did not represent a cross section of the Indochinese people; by and large, they were from the urban, affluent, better-educated sectors. Most were young (82 percent were under 35) and male. Forty percent were Catholic, though only 10 percent of the Vietnamese population was Catholic.[17]

Temporary refugee camps were set up, and funds for services to help settle and integrate the refugees were allotted under the Indochinese Migration and Refugee Assistance Act of 1975. In the camps, the refugees received educational and medical services: schooling for children, language and vocational training for adults, and lessons in such skills as shopping, applying for jobs, and renting apartments. The services also attempted to locate sponsors, American citizens who would assume responsibility for helping refugee individuals and families enter American society.

Between 1980 and 1985, 250,000 more Vietnamese entered the United States. Some 100,000 remained in refugee camps in Asia, many of whom had expressed a preference for entering the United States. These refugees were not so educated or skilled as the first wave. According to the 1980 U.S. Census, only 13 percent of the Vietnamese in the United States held managerial or professional positions, and their median family income was $13,000. On both these indexes they were below not only white Americans but all other Asian-American groups.[18] They also did not have the access to government benefits or sponsors that was available to the first wave, but they were generally known as being willing to start at the bottom and accept hardship.[19]

According to INS data, in 1990 48,800 legal immigrants entered the United States from Vietnam and 5,200 entered from Cambodia. The 1990 U.S. Census found that 4 percent of the total population had been born in Vietnam and 0.1 percent were Cambodians by birth.

In general, the Vietnamese have found a comfortable, successful place in American society. By 1990, for instance, more than 80,000 of them had settled in an area called Little Saigon on Orange County, California, one of the largest Vietnamese communities outside Indochina. Here they can satisfy their native preferences at 800 stores and restaurants and attend Buddhist ceremonies. Many have achieved socioeconomic success, and they often are assimilated into American society within a generation. For the 40,000 Cambodians who have settled in Long Beach, California, the prospects are not so good. With few marketable skills, they enter the labor force at the lowest levels. Like many Asians, they are the victims of discrimination, not only from the white majority but from Latinos, African Americans, and even other Asians.[20]

∽ UNDOCUMENTED ALIENS

Over the years changes in immigration laws that have attempted to control access to the United States have resulted in a patchwork of regulations that often have unintended consequences. For instance, as a result of the changes in laws favoring immigrants with work skills and professional expertise in demand in the United States, the "illegal" immigration of unskilled workers has increased considerably.

The Immigration Reform and Control Act (IRCA) of 1986 was a complex, detailed plan to reduce the number of aliens entering illegally by legalizing the status of up to 3 million alien residents who could prove they had entered the United States before January 1, 1982. There was also a special amnesty program to allow up to 1 million temporary agricultural workers to seek U.S. residency status. The law tried to prevent any further illegal immigration by denying residency status to aliens entering illegally later, imposing sanctions on employers who hire workers without proper documentation, and expanding patrols along the U.S.–Mexico border. Employers also were forbidden to discriminate against people who might just appear to be of foreign birth but are legal residents or citizens. None of these efforts, however, has been successful in reducing the number of aliens entering the United States illegally (see "The Failure of an Immigration Law").

The actual number of such *undocumented aliens* (or *illegal aliens*, as they are also known) in the United States can only be estimated; the number has been put as high as 8 million. The number of aliens expelled provides a measure of the strength of the enforcement of immigration law. The peak since 1970 was 1,808,000 deportations in 1986, the year of passage of IRCA; thereafter it declined during 1987–1989 and then rose to 1,045,000 in 1990 and 1,091,000 in 1991.[21] Because undocumented aliens are largely unskilled, uneducated, and rural, they are more like the "teeming masses" that once came from southern and eastern Europe than like the other new arrivals.

Alejandro Portes notes that illegal immigration is caused not only by push factors in the country of origin but by pull factors in the country of destination—U.S. businesses and agricultural interests encourage the illegal immigration of low-wage workers to maximize profit. Portes regards the flow of illegal aliens as a movement of people who are looking not for a welfare handout but for honest work to fulfill basic human needs. Moreover,

The Failure of an Immigration Law

There are many reasons why the Immigration Reform and Control Act of 1986 failed to have the expected effect of limiting if not eliminating the entry of undocumented aliens into the United States. For one thing, many fewer than the 3.9 million illegal residents who were expected to apply to legalize their status as immigrants did so. Applicants were granted temporary-resident status for 18 months and could earn permanent-resident status if they had a minimal knowledge of spoken English and civics. After five more years, they were to become U.S. citizens. The Immigration and Naturalization Service opened special offices to process applications; social service agencies participated in the program; and private groups encouraged aliens to put aside their fear and distrust of the government and register. Nevertheless, the number of applicants under this program was only slightly more than 1.5 million, 70 percent of whom lived in Texas or California. The major reasons given for not applying were confusion about the program, fear that family members would be separated, and inability to meet the cost of filling out applications. By 1990, just 1,369,186 undocumented aliens had been converted to legal residents.

By contrast, the number of applicants in the program for temporary agricultural workers was far more than the 600,000 expected. To qualify, these workers only had to show that they had come to the United States to pick crops or work on farms for 90 days between May 1, 1985, and May 1, 1986. This program had a later deadline than the legalization program, and by the time it ended in December 1988, some 1.2 million applications had been received. Many who could not qualify under the stricter residency requirements of the legalization program may have sought to stay by representing themselves as farm workers.

Under the employer sanctions section of the legislation, penalties are to be imposed on employers who knowingly hire, recruit, or refer aliens who are not authorized to work in the United States. But employers are required only to examine any 2 of 17 proofs of citizenship before hiring workers, and some of these can easily be forged. The law sets fines and jail terms for employers who are not in compliance, but it has no teeth; in 1990 the average penalty was $850, and no employer had been sent to jail. The law was also supposed to increase the number of Border Patrol officers in the INS to as many as 6,000, but Congress never voted the funding. The ranks of INS agents remain far too thin to police all the possible entry points or to staff detention facilities. In 1991, 4,968 Border Patrol agents were authorized, and 4,312 were on duty.

The antidiscrimination sections were put in place because Asian Americans and Latinos feared that in order to avoid hiring undocumented aliens, employers would discriminate against legal residents and citizens who merely looked or sounded like foreigners. A General Accounting Office survey found "no consistent pattern of unfair hiring practices," but by 1990, 774 discrimination charges had been filed with the special counsel for immigration-related unfair employment practices. Critics maintain that adequate funding of this program would encourage the filing of more complaints and a better likelihood of findings favorable to employees.

The primary goal of the Immigration Reform and Control Act of 1986 was to reduce the number of undocumented aliens entering the country. The law was also expected to alter the economics of migrant labor by forcing employers to compete for a shrinking supply of legal workers by improving wages and working conditions. When it first went into effect there was indeed a sizable drop in the number of people illegally crossing the Mexico–United States border. In spite of increased patrols and arrests, however, within two years illegal immigration was fast approaching its level before the law was enacted and the remedies were tried. In 1991,

continued

continued

1,152,700 deportable aliens or U.S. citizens engaged in smuggling or other INS violations were apprehended, compared to 1,272,400 in 1985. The numbers not apprehended are of course unknown.

Sources: W. A. Finch, "The Immigration Reform and Control Act of 1986: A Preliminary Assessment," *Social Service Review*, vol. 64 (June 1990), pp. 224–60; Dicken Kirshten, "Immigration: 'Citizen-Only' Hiring," *National Journal*, vol. 22 (January 27, 1990), pp. 191–95; Peter T. Kilborn, "Tide of Migrant Labor Tells of a Law's Failure," *The New York Times*, November 4, 1992, p. A24; Richard Behar, "The Price of Freedom," *Time*, May 14, 1990, pp. 70–71; U.S. Bureau of the Census, *Statistical Abstract of the United States: 1992*, 112th edition (Washington, DC, 1992), Table 308.

illegal immigration is not always permanent but often is a cyclical process in which people move back and forth between nations according to the opportunities available to them.[22]

The majority of immigrants entering the country without visas come from Mexico, but by no means are all undocumented aliens in the United States Mexican. Others come from Haiti, the Dominican Republic, Guatemala, Honduras, El Salvador, and even Canada. As economic conditions throughout the world worsened and the enforcement effects of the IRCA law were felt, tens of thousands of aliens from such diverse places as Turkey, Korea, West Africa, and India began to enter illegally through the U.S.–Mexico border. They could take advantage of the well-established system under which Mexican smugglers, or coyotes, charge a fee to guide undocumented aliens across the border. As *The New York Times* observed, "an illicit trade that was once loosely organized and local in character is rapidly becoming a lucrative, professional international industry."[23]

Most Mexican Americans are legal citizens of the United States who either have been in this country since before the American takeover of the Southwest or have immigrated legally. Mexicans who enter illegally come largely from the rural, northern parts of Mexico, pushed by poverty and unemployment and pulled by business interests in the United States which welcome them as a source of willing, cheap labor. Undocumented Mexicans also contribute to the American economy as consumers and by paying federal income and social security taxes. They are not a burden on public welfare; few receive public assistance.

State and local funds are strained where there are large populations of undocumented aliens, however. In California, Governor Pete Wilson estimated in August 1993 that "illegal immigrants" (primarily Mexicans and Asians) represent about 2 million of the state's nearly 12 million residents. He claimed that the state spends $1 billion a year to educate members of these groups and $750 million for their emergency health care, as mandated by the federal government, as well as $500 million to incarcerate those who break the law.[24] In an economically stressed society, such pressures can inspire public attitudes that increase the likelihood that undocumented aliens will be relegated to minority-group status.

Haitians

Haitians have been identified as another ethnic group with large numbers of undocumented aliens in the United States, though there have been Haitians in this country since colonial times. A troop of 800 "men of color" from Haiti fought on behalf of American

Haitian boat people en route to Florida who were taken into custody
by the U.S. Coast Guard are returned to Port-au-Prince, Haiti, in 1986.
U.S. immigration policy on Haitians has gone through several changes,
but very few have been allowed to enter the United States as asylum
seekers or refugees in recent years.

independence, and the first permanent settler and founder of the city of Chicago was
Haitian.[25] Recent Haitian immigration began in 1957 with the totalitarian regime of
François "Papa Doc" Duvalier, who was elected president and subsequently named himself President for Life. It intensified in the turmoil which precipitated the exile of Duvalier's successor, his son "Baby Doc," and the appointment of a military-civilian council in
1986. Under a new constitution approved by the voters the following year, five presi-
dents had been elected and subsequently overthrown by military coups by 1993.

Most Haitians who came to the United States as immigrants prior to 1970 represented the middle class of this impoverished island. In the early 1960s, about 50 percent
of gainfully employed Haitian immigrants were professional or white-collar workers.[26]
Since then the occupational and educational profile of Haitian immigrants has changed.
Included in recent waves have been "boat people" who leave the island on their own,
using small boats to make the dangerous crossing to Florida. They are mostly rural peasants fleeing poverty and political repression, but instead of being accepted into this country as refugees they have been considered illegal immigrants. Those who are apprehended are held for deportation, even if return to Haiti means certain death.

The change in administration that followed the 1992 presidential election did little to
change the desperate situation of Haitian boat people; they are still being pushed by intolerable conditions at home and repelled by immigration policy in the United States.
They continue to leave Haiti in hopes of reaching America, though few succeed. Many

end up in detention centers, often sent from one to another for several years until their requests for asylum can be heard. They exist in a legal limbo, dependent on a society that is unable to reach a clear consensus on their status.[27]

∞ IMPLICATIONS FOR PRACTICE

Social service workers have at least two goals in working with new arrivals. One is to assure that none of the new groups becomes a minority group. The other is to assure that socialization into American society takes place, while respecting and helping to sustain the cultural values and traditions of the new arrivals.

The new arrivals today are not colonized groups, forced into the United States and therefore subjected to minority status. Both the immigrants and some of the refugees are more likely to succeed than either immigrants or colonized peoples in the past. Because of their educational background and occupational skills, they are better prepared to achieve socioeconomic success. Moreover, social services often are available to help them move quickly into the American mainstream. Undocumented aliens present another problem. Although they come to the United States voluntarily, looking for work, they live under the threat of being expelled. Often they are associated with ethnic groups such as Mexican Americans and African Americans who already hold minority status in the United States.

The task of the social service worker in working with new arrivals is the same as it was with earlier arrivals, however. Leaving one country and taking up residence in another always involves social and economic hardships. The crucial objective of workers is to help new arrivals make their transitions into American society without experiencing the severe hostility that produces minority status for a group. This can be done through advocacy efforts on behalf on immigrants, refugees, asylum seekers, and undocumented aliens, as well as by developing social and economic opportunities, providing appropriate services, and making referrals to other needed services.

In working with new arrivals, social service workers become involved in their clients' socialization into the attitudes and values, norms and traditions of American society. In the past, the task of socialization was often accomplished at the expense of the new arrivals' own cultures. Workers advocated assimilation into the society and often acted as if the old ways were of no value. Today, they are more likely to espouse cultural pluralism, the value that the United States should be culturally diverse and everyone should not be forced into a single mold (see Chapter 7). Tied to this value is the idea that new arrivals should become bicultural, that is, able to function competently within the norms, traditions, and values of their own culture, as well as in the culture of the United States.

A theory of bicultural socialization proposed by Diane de Anda is relevant to social service work with new arrivals.[28] She maintains that social and personal well-being requires being adequately socialized within both one's own culture and the dominant culture. While new arrivals may understand what is expected if they are to be successful within their own communities, they lack knowledge of what is expected in order to be successful in the majority community.

The factors facilitating successful **bicultural socialization** are described in the next chapter. Two of them offer ideas about how social workers can help new arrivals become bicultural. One is the use of translators and models from the same ethnic group as clients, to help them develop an understanding of the values of the majority community and learn the behavior patterns expected in it, while maintaining their own values and behavior patterns. Workers also can use mediators from the dominant group to serve as guides for ethnic minorities. The second factor is the provision of corrective feedback. Social service workers themselves can serve as translators, models, and mediators and can offer feedback. A worker who is of the same ethnic group as the client can serve as a translator or model; a worker who is not can serve as a mediator and give feedback.

∾ DISCUSSION QUESTIONS AND CLASS PROJECTS

1. Distinguish among immigrants, asylum seekers, and undocumented aliens. Give examples of each and describe their experiences in coming to the United States.

2. Select an immigrant or refugee group that is settling in your area and collect information on them by searching your library or conducting interviews with people knowledgeable about them. See what you can learn about their cultural values and traditions, their strengths and resources, and their needs and problems.

3. From your experience, would you say that any new immigrant or refugee group is likely to become a minority group in the United States? Why or why not?

4. In what ways can social workers be helpful to new arrivals?

∾ NOTES

1. U.S. Bureau of the Census, *Statistical Abstract of the United States: 1992*, 112th edition (Washington, DC, 1992), Table 8.

2. Ibid., pp. 2–3; also see Diane Drachman and Angela Shen-Ryan, "Immigrants and Refugees," in A. Gitterman (editor), *Handbook of Social Work Practice with Vulnerable Populations* (New York: Columbia University Press, 1991), p. 620.

3. Immigration Act of 1990, Pub. L. No. 101–649, 104 Stat. 4978–5088 (1990); also see "U.S. Immigration Law," in Mark S. Hoffman (editor), *World Almanac and Book of Facts 1993* (New York: Pharos Books, 1992), p. 821.

4. The special issue of *Time* on immigration, July 8, 1985, provides an interesting, well-illustrated account of the diverse new racial and ethnic groups that are "rapidly and permanently changing the face of America."

5. Brian Duffy, "Coming to America," *U.S. News & World Report*, June 21, 1993, pp. 26–31; John Greenwald, "The Price of Freedom," *Time*, May 14, 1990, pp. 70–71.

6. William S. Bernard, "Immigration: History of U.S. Policy," in S. Thernstrom (editor), *Harvard Encyclopedia of American Ethnic Groups* (Cambridge, MA: Belknap Press, 1980), pp. 486–96.

7. Mark Dowie, "Bring Us Your Huddled Millionaires: A New U.S. Immigration Policy Opens Doors for the World's Wealthiest," *Harper's*, November 1991, pp. 58–59.

8. Joan M. Jensen, "East Indians," in *Harvard Encyclopedia of American Ethnic Groups*, pp. 296–301.

9. U.S. Bureau of the Census, *Statistical Abstract of the United States: 1992*, Tables 8 and 46.

10. Emory S. Bogardus, "Comparing Racial Distance in Ethiopia, South Africa, and the United States," *Sociology and Social Research*, vol. 52 (January 1968), p. 162.

11. Paul Glastris, "Immigration Crackdown," *U.S. News & World Report*, June 21, 1993, p. 38.

12. Jensen, "East Indians," p. 299.

13. Leon F. Bouvier and Anthony J. Agresta, "The Fastest Growing Minority," *American Demographics*, vol. 7 (May 1985), pp. 31–33.

14. Scott Brown, "Strangers in Paradise," *Time*, April 9, 1990, p. 34.

15. U. A. Segal, "Cultural Variables in Asian Indian Families," *Families in Society*, vol. 72 (April 1991), pp. 233–42.

16. Glastris, "Immigration Crackdown," pp. 34, 38.

17. Mary Bowen Wright, "Indochinese," in *Harvard Encyclopedia of American Ethnic Groups*, pp. 508–13.

18. Bouvier and Agresta, "Fastest Growing Minority."

19. Bowen Wright, "Indochinese," pp. 512–13.

20. Brown, "Strangers in Paradise," pp. 33–34.

21.   U.S. Bureau of the Census, *Statistical Abstract of the United States: 1992*, Table 307.

22.   Alejandro Portes, "Illegal Immigration and the International System, Lessons from Recent Legal Mexican Immigrants to the United States," *Social Problems*, vol. 26 (April 1979), pp. 425–27.

23.   Larry Rohter, "Soft Underbelly: Sneaking Mexicans (and Others) into U.S. Is Big Business," *The New York Times*, June 20, 1989, p. A8.

24.   George de Lama, "Hostility to Immigrants Increasing," *Chicago Tribune*, August 15, 1993, sect. 1, pp. 19, 24.

25.   Michel S. Laguerre, "Haitians," in *Harvard Encyclopedia of American Ethnic Groups*, p. 446.

26.   Ibid., p. 447.

27.   Diane Drachman, "A Stage of Migration Framework for Service to Immigrant Populations," *Social Work*, vol. 37 (January 1992), p. 70.

28.   Diane de Anda, "Bicultural Socialization: Factors Affecting the Minority Experience," *Social Work*, vol. 29 (March–April 1984), pp. 101–07.

CHAPTER 7

Ethnic Community Relations
in American Society

MAJOR THEMES DISCUSSED IN THIS CHAPTER

1. THE SOCIAL CONTEXT OF MINORITY-MAJORITY RELATIONS. In contemporary American society, Native Americans, Mexican Americans, and Puerto Ricans continue to encounter poverty, unemployment, and other problems in numbers disproportionate to their representation in the population as a whole. To what extent is their situation a product of racism and ethnocentrism? Do prejudice and discrimination still operate to make American society racist?

2. INSTITUTIONAL RACISM. Racism can exist independent of the attitudes and beliefs of individuals. When it is built into the norms, traditions, laws, and policies of a society, so that even those who have nonracist beliefs are compelled to act otherwise, racism is said to be institutionalized.

3. BIOLOGICAL AND CULTURAL ATTRIBUTES OF ETHNIC-MINORITY COMMUNITIES. A systems approach not only examines the social context of ethnic-minority communities but assesses factors in systems which may contribute to their needs and problems. The issue of the influence of biological or genetic factors on one hand and cultural attributes on the other is highly controversial.

4. PROSPECTS FOR PROGRESS IN MINORITY-MAJORITY RELATIONS. Successful outcomes for ethnic relations, in the form of assimilation or cultural pluralism, are possible but not guaranteed. Historically, as a result of ethnic and racial conflict and competition, some minority groups have been exterminated or expelled and some have seceded or violently rebelled against the majority.

5. IMPLICATIONS FOR PRACTICE. Social workers must strive to alter the conditions that limit success in the larger society and in minority groups. The problems of individuals and families in minority groups can never be divorced from the problems of the communities in which they live. Social service workers must be able to assess the effects of continuing prejudice and discrimination on the well-being of their clients.

THE PRESENT STATE OF RACIAL- AND ethnic-minority communities (in particular the established minorities in American society—African Americans, Native Americans and

Alaskan Natives, Mexican Americans, and Puerto Ricans) is the topic of this chapter. Many members of these groups continue to be mired in adverse socioeconomic conditions precipitated by unemployment, underemployment, or poverty. Historical circumstances have shaped their situations, but contemporary socioeconomic conditions are of even greater consequence. It is in the present that minorities must struggle to achieve social, economic, and political success and that society must initiate the social changes necessary to secure a better future for these groups. We will establish the background necessary to understand the contemporary economic and social environments of the ethnic-minority communities and the factors within these communities that are acting to hinder or facilitate their achievement of socioeconomic success.

∞ THE SOCIAL CONTEXT OF MINORITY-MAJORITY RELATIONS

Minority-majority relations in American society are carried out within the context of the ethnic-minority and ethnic-majority communities in the society and the individuals who comprise them. Underlying these relations are in the social norms and roles and the institutions and institutional arrangements which are generated through social interactions within the society (see Chapter 3). The question to be considered in this section is whether the social context confronted by ethnic-minority communities is a hostile one which acts to block their progress to secure socioeconomic well-being. If the answer is yes, we can go a long way toward understanding the disadvantages still being experienced by minorities.

Racism and Ethnocentrism

Does the United States have a racist society? **Racism** is most often defined as a set of beliefs which attributes inferiority to others because of their presumed physical characteristics: their skin color, "blood," or some other aspect of their physical or genetic makeup. A racist society would be one that promotes such beliefs.

Historians and political observers are quick to point out that this traditional definition of racism needs to be updated in the light of present circumstances. Social scientists have documented that relativity few Americans now believe in the doctrine of the innate inferiority of racial groups. John McConahay and Joseph Hough argue that symbolic racism is now more characteristic of the thinking of the white majority, especially affluent suburban whites. They define *symbolic racism* as rejecting doctrines of racial inferiority and segregation and focusing instead on three affective elements:

1. Beliefs that minorities are pushing too much and demanding too much in an attempt to get more than they merit.
2. Beliefs that minorities are not playing by "the rules of the game" and want success but do not want to work hard or delay gratification to get it.
3. Negative attitudes about welfare, urban riots, crime in the streets, affirmative action, and quota systems, all of which are associated with minority groups.[1]

National Socialist White People's Party members arrive in Boston to participate in a demonstration opposing busing to integrate schools. The activities of such groups are evidence that racism, ethnocentrism, and other forms of intolerance are far from being eradicated in the United States.

The question might equally well be: Does the United States have an ethnocentric society? William Graham Sumner defines *ethnocentrism* as "this view of things in which one's own group is the center of everything, and all others are scaled and rated with reference to it."[2] James Vander Zanden describes it as:

> ...the tendency of group members to appraise peoples of other cultures by the standards of judgment prevailing in their own culture. Individuals assume that in the nature of things other people should be organized according to the same assumptions as prevail within their own group. Ethnocentrism entails strong positive feelings toward an in-group, even in-group glorification.[3]

In the past it was clear that American society was both racist and ethnocentric. There is evidence that residents of the United States used to be more open about their prejudices, more flagrant in their discrimination, and more demanding that new arrivals assimilate to American ways. Moreover, laws and government policies which formerly gave official sanction to discrimination no longer exist. Whereas 30 states had laws prohibiting interracial marriage in 1950, for instance, there are no such laws presently.[4]

The evidence for the existence of outright ethnocentrism and racism in American society has been harder to find since the civil rights legislation of the 1960s and 1970s. Observers, even those from minority communities themselves, are divided about the relative importance of racism in holding back minorities today. Some, such as William J. Wilson, believe that while racism still is evident, it is no longer of consequence for economic success.[5] Others, such as Ronald Walters, see the struggle for economic resources as a continuing factor in prejudice and discrimination.[6] Before considering this debate, we must clarify the concepts of prejudice and discrimination.

Prejudice and Discrimination

Racism and ethnocentrism are forms of prejudice in that they have to do with people's beliefs and attitudes. Sociologically, the term **prejudice** is used in a specific way. William Newman defines prejudice as "any set of ideas and beliefs that negatively prejudge groups or individuals as members of groups on the basis of real or alleged group traits or characteristics."[7] Four components make up this definition.

First, prejudice is a state of mind in that it refers to thoughts, feelings, and intentions but does not refer to actions or behaviors. It is studied by asking people what they think, feel, or intend to do.

Second, prejudice is group-based and thus a social phenomenon. For social scientists, prejudice is not the study of individual biases or personal likes and dislikes but the study of how the attitudes of individuals reflect their group membership. It is the study of how "I" as a member of one group dislike "you" as a member of another group.

Third, prejudice is a prejudgement and exists regardless of the experiences an individual might have with members of another group. People who never have had contacts with outgroup members still can form stereotypes and expectations about what such people are like.

Fourth, prejudice represents negative beliefs and attitudes about others. While favorable prejudices certainly might be held, social scientists have been more concerned with documenting negative, group-based prejudices.

Newman defines discrimination as "any act of differential treatment toward a group or an individual perceived as a member of a group." Moreover, he notes, "the intent and/or effect of differential treatment is to create a disadvantage of some sort."[8] Thus discrimination differs from prejudice primarily in that one defines an attitude and the other defines a behavior. Both reflect group processes whereby **in-group** members express negative attitudes or behaviors toward **out-group** members. To study discrimination we would have to observe the actual behaviors of people and organizations.

Discrimination is extremely difficult to measure. In studying prejudice people can be asked what they feel, think, and intend to do, but studying discrimination requires observation in some fairly direct ways of what people actually do. Because of the difficulty of studying discrimination, social scientists have largely focused on prejudices, on the assumption that there is at least a reasonable link between what people believe, feel, and think they will do and what they actually *do*. As we shall see, however, this may not be altogether a good assumption.

In a 1958 study of whether prejudice and discrimination go hand in hand, Melvin DeFleur and Frank Westie wrote to motel owners asking them if they would accept Chinese patrons.[9] The majority who wrote back indicated that they would not, but when the researchers actually brought Chinese patrons to these motels, their business was rarely turned away. Depending on personality and situation factors, prejudicial attitudes may not lead to discriminatory behavior and discrimination may come about even when prejudice is not apparent.

Robert Merton distinguishes between prejudice and discrimination by referring to four possible types of adaptation[10] (see "Prejudice and Discrimination Typology"). The term **bigot** usually refers to someone who is both filled with prejudice and consistently discriminates. Old-style southern political leaders come readily to mind. The term *liberal,* in this sense, applies to a person who is consistent in attitude and behavior in that he or she neither is prejudiced nor discriminates. Most people in the social services tend to think of themselves as liberals in terms of this definition.

Prejudice and Discrimination Typology

Prejudice and discrimination do not always go hand in hand. The situations people find themselves in can alter such attitudes and behaviors. In Robert Merton's typology, a bigot is both prejudiced and discriminates, but a timid bigot, while prejudiced, does not discriminate. A liberal is not prejudiced and does not discriminate, but a fair-weather liberal does.

Person is \ Person	Discriminates	Does not discriminate
Prejudiced	Bigot	Timid bigot
Not prejudiced	Fair-weather liberal	Liberal

Source: Based on Robert Merton, "Discrimination and the American Creed," in R. MacIver (editor), *Discrimination and National Welfare* (New York: Harper & Row, 1949).

There are, however, prejudiced people who, because of particular constraints, do not act on their prejudices. An example is the university bureaucrat or the agency administrator who would rather not follow affirmative action guidelines in recruiting students or workers but nevertheless does obey the letter of the law. Merton refers to such people as *timid bigots*. There also are many people who sincerely do not believe they are prejudiced but who nevertheless might discriminate in particular situations. This is the *fair-weather liberal*. One example is the worker or manager who sees discrimination going on in the workplace but does nothing about it. Another is the unprejudiced person who would not move into an integrated neighborhood or might even block neighborhood integration efforts, not because of personal opinions deriding racial and ethnic minorities but because of a desire to avoid creating problems in the neighborhood.

The Principle of Nondiscrimination

If American society is to be defined as racist, then there would have to be, at a minimum, fairly widespread prejudice and fairly open discrimination by individuals. On the whole, Americans would have to believe in principle that discrimination is a good thing. The attitudes and actions of a handful of bigots are not sufficient evidence that the United States has a racist society. It is necessary to consider what kinds of attitudes about ethnic-minority group members are expressed by the white ethnic-majority community.

On the surface there is less evidence of bigotry in the United States now than in the past. Researchers have noted that during the most active period of the civil rights movement in the 1960s, whites' attitudes toward blacks (the focus of the bulk of these studies) and toward most other minority groups changed appreciably in a positive direction.

Stereotypes: Negative and Positive

Stereotypes are rigid opinions in which characteristics are uncritically attributed to all members of a particular group. Stereotypes may be negative or positive; negative stereotypes are applied to members of out-groups by members of in-groups, who may view the same characteristics in others as positive stereotypes. Robert Merton cites as an example Abraham Lincoln's habit of working far into the night, which is regarded as evidence that he was "industrious, resolute, perseverant, and eager to realize his capacities to the full." But if out-groups such as Jews or Japanese work equally hard, this is likely to be considered evidence of "their sweatshop mentality, their ruthless undercutting of American standards, their unfair competitive practices."

The concept of stereotyping was explored in a series of studies in which Princeton University students were asked in 1933, 1951, and 1967 to characterize various ethnic and racial groups. A large percentage of the students in 1933 easily agreed that Negroes were superstitious, lazy, happy-go-lucky, and ignorant; that the Chinese were superstitious, sly, and conservative; that Italians were artistic, impulsive, and passionate; and that the English were sportsmanlike, intelligent, and conventional. By 1951, student willingness to make such stereotypical generalizations had declined significantly, and many expressed irritation at being asked to do so. As a result, a "fading effect" was predicted for such stereotypes. Princeton students in 1967 also expressed indignation at being asked to come up with stereotypes and

regarded the task as an insult to their intelligence.

The 1967 students who undertook the task of stereotyping nevertheless produced several important results. Their stereotypes were more uniform; that is, the students could agree on what the stereotypical traits of each group were. There was also a fair amount of consistency between the stereotypes noted in 1933 and those noted in 1967. However, the content of the stereotypes did change. In general, the negative stereotypes declined and were replaced by more positive stereotypes. For instance, only 14 percent of the students in 1967 stereotyped blacks as superstitious, down from 84 percent in 1933; and 47 percent described blacks as musical, up from 26 percent in 1933. Similarly, 6 percent of the students in 1967 described the Chinese as sly, down from 29 percent in 1933; and 50 percent described them as "loyal to family ties," up from 22 percent in 1933.

Sources: Robert Merton, *Social Theory and Social Structure*, 2nd ed. (New York: Free Press, 1968); Daniel Katz and Kenneth W. Braly, "Racial Stereotypes of One Hundred College Students," *Journal of Abnormal and Social Psychology*, vol. 28 (October–December 1933), pp. 280–90; Richard Centers, "An Effective Classroom Demonstration of Stereotypes," *Journal of Social Psychology*, vol. 34, 1st half (August 1951), pp. 41–46; Marvin Karlins, Thomas L. Coffman, and Gary Walters, "On the Fading of Social Stereotypes: Studies in Three Generations of College Students," *Journal of Personality and Social Psychology*, vol. 13 (September 1969), pp. 1–16.

Examining public opinion and other surveys of racial attitudes dating back to 1942, Howard Schuman, Charlotte Steeh, and Lawrence Bobo showed that prior to World War II, the population of the United States generally supported the principle of segregation of minorities and discrimination against them. After the civil rights movement, this principle lost popular support and Americans generally embraced the **principle of nondiscrimination**.[11]

In 1942, for instance, 42 percent of Americans surveyed said they believed that "Negroes have the same intelligence as white people, given the same education and training."

By 1963 the proportion who agreed with this statement had jumped to 78 percent. Similarly, support for Jim Crow segregation laws seems to have declined a great deal. In 1942, 44 percent believed "there should not be separate sections for Negroes in streetcars and buses," compared to 79 percent in 1963 and 88 percent in 1970. Even in terms of neighborhood integration, prejudicial attitudes seemed to decline. In 1942, 35 percent of American whites believed that "if a Negro with just as much income and education as you had moved into your block, it would not make any difference." By 1963, 64 percent of white Americans said they believed this; by 1972, 81 percent agreed.[12] There is also evidence that by 1967 Americans had become increasingly uncomfortable with negative **stereotypes** of the group characteristics of racial and ethnic minorities (see "Stereotypes: Negative and Positive").

At the same time, white Americans were becoming more willing to associate openly with members of ethnic and racial minority groups. In his studies on social distance, Emory Bogardus attempted to measure racial distance by asking whites how willing they were to welcome members of such groups to "employment in my occupation," "my street as neighbors," "my club as personal chums," and "close kinship by marriage." These studies were completed in 1926, 1946, 1956, and 1966, and throughout this period the relative rankings of the groups remained fairly constant. In general, ethnic groups from northern and western Europe were seen as more desirable that groups from eastern and southern Europe, who were in turn seen as more desirable than minorities of color. Nevertheless, significant changes were apparent over the years. The distance white Americans felt obligated to maintain in 1926 had shrunk a good deal by 1966. Whereas they drew the line against minorities of color at neighborhood integration in 1926, in 1966 they drew it at the level of friendships.[13]

The degree to which there has been a broad change toward less racism and ethnocentrism, as expressed in attitudes, depends on the particular issue or sphere of life being examined. By 1972 virtually all Americans said they believed that discrimination in employment is wrong and that equal economic opportunity should exist for all Americans, but 25 percent also said they would not vote for a black president. Intermarriage is another area in which the principle of nondiscrimination seems to fall short. By 1983 only about 35 percent of white Americans approved of interracial marriages—about the same level of approval that integrated transportation had achieved in the 1940s.[14]

Taking data such as these into account, Schuman, Steeh, and Bobo concluded that "this overall picture of change points to a broad cultural shift in the norms that influence white attitudes toward the treatment of blacks in America."[15] White Americans, they argue, are by and large not bigots; they believe, in principle at least, in equal treatment and opportunity for all. While these researchers focused on attitudes toward blacks, it can be generalized that their findings are applicable to other ethnic and racial communities as well. In support of their findings, they reject the possibility that there are many "timid bigots" among Americans who say things they do not really mean when they are confronted by interviewers: "Outright lying is probably rare in these data; there is compelling evidence that most people assume that others—in this case white interviewers—agree with their own views."[16]

The Economy-Bigotry Connection

It can be said that present-day Americans generally believe that, regardless of race and ethnicity, there should be equal job opportunities, that everyone should be able to live where they wish, that all students should attend the same schools, that means of transportation should not be segregated, and that interracial marriages should not be prohibited. In other words, they believe in the principle of nondiscrimination. Yet there has been evidence in recent years that progress in rejecting racism and ethnocentrism has slowed and that considerable bigotry does exist in American society. The early 1970s, in fact, seem to have been the high point in achieving more tolerant racial attitudes among white Americans. Little change in attitudes about intermarriage, for instance, has been documented since that time. Schuman, Steeh, and Bobo, in fact, found "even a partial reversal of trend" on a broad question they asked survey respondents about the desirability of desegregation in general.[17]

The abatement in the movement toward greater equality is most often attributed to a faltering economy. As Thomas Byrne Edsall observes:

> Just as the civil-rights movement reached its height, high-paying union jobs and big-city patronage—which had served to foster upward mobility for each succeeding immigrant generation—began to dry up. Many blacks lost even a toehold on the ladder, while whites slipped down, sometimes just a rung, sometimes all the way to the bottom.[18]

The polarization of the interests of white working and lower-middle classes with those of poor blacks and other ethnic-minority groups has focused new attention on Americans' racial attitudes. In a *New York Times*/CBS News poll conducted in March 1993, more than half of both blacks and whites interviewed rated the nation's race relations as generally bad rather than good—55 percent of whites and 66 percent of blacks. On the 25th anniversary of the death of Martin Luther King, both blacks and whites agreed that significant progress had been made toward his dream of equality—64 percent of whites and 62 percent of blacks. But they differed in comparing race relations to those of 25 years ago. Among white respondents, 54 percent said race relations were better, 16 percent said they were worse, and 26 percent said they were the same. About the same percentage of blacks thought relations were worse, but only 45 percent thought they were better, and 37 percent thought they were the same. The largest area of disagreement in this poll was affirmative action, or preferential hiring and promotion of minorities. When asked "Do you believe that where there has been job discrimination in the past, preference in hiring or promotion should be given to blacks today?" 28 percent of whites said it should be given and 58 percent said it should not. Blacks had the opposite reaction: 66 percent favored the policy and 24 percent opposed it.[19]

In follow-up interviews for the *Times*/CBS News poll, many blacks said they believed the promise of the civil rights legislation had not been translated into lasting social or economic gains, and both blacks and whites believed that the gains they had observed in their lifetimes were being threatened by economic pressures and competition between racial and ethnic groups for jobs. In keeping with this, a white social worker from Somerset, Massachusetts, was quoted as saying, "When there's economic tension, when there are a lot of people out of work, when people are competing against each other for few jobs and the jobs that do exist don't seem to pay enough to make ends meet, then the old prejudices and hatreds resurface."[20]

Moreover, the late 1960s and 1970s were a period of liberalism in the United States and the 1980s were a period of political conservatism in which "race, rights, and taxes" became key forces.[21] Therefore, we should expect the "timid bigots" to feel freer to express their views. Nevertheless, research supports the possibility that when societal attitudes reject the expression of prejudice or outright discriminatory behavior, even openly prejudiced persons may experience societal constraints to avoid them.[22]

Implementing the Principle of Nondiscrimination

While documenting an attitudinal shift to the principle of nondiscrimination, Schuman, Steeh, and Bobo also found considerable disagreement among whites and blacks as to the ways in which that principle should be implemented. It is one thing to accept the belief that nondiscrimination is good and another to agree on specific ways to implement it. For instance, should court orders mandating changes such as busing and magnet schools be used to achieve racial integration of schools? Should there be affirmative action programs to ensure the hiring or promotion of racial minorities? Should there be bilingual programs to help nonnative speakers learn standard American English? Should neighborhoods actively attempt residential integration? These are not easy questions, and Americans are much more divided on them than they are on the principle of nondiscrimination. White Americans, for example, showed much lower support for government intervention on behalf of nondiscrimination than for the principle of nondiscrimination itself. In only rare instances did support for particular policies to implement equal treatment surpass 50 percent. For instance, very few whites said they would resist the presence of one or a few blacks in a neighborhood or school, but such resistance was more likely if larger numbers of blacks were proposed. In some cases attitudes among blacks were no different from attitudes among whites. Both groups reported less support for busing than for any other implementation issue, although blacks were generally more supportive of busing than whites.[23]

Is it racist to oppose a particular approach to achieving the principle of nondiscrimination? Is everyone who opposes affirmative action programs, for example, prejudiced? As long as the principle of nondiscrimination is valued, we can accept honest disagreements over the best ways to achieve nondiscrimination as being constructive debate or conflict that may have positive outcomes. However, when such attitudes mask underlying disrespect for the principle, we can brand them as unfair.

∞ INSTITUTIONAL RACISM

The study of attitudes and behaviors of individuals goes only part of the way in developing an understanding of what is meant by a racist society. To determine whether or not contemporary American society should be considered racist, we must also study what has been called institutional racism and its corollary, institutional discrimination. It may very well be that while most Americans sincerely believe in the principle of nondiscrimination, they nevertheless support racism because in their everyday lives they live up to norms and traditions that are racist.

Social institutions and institutional arrangements, which were introduced in Chapter 3, may be seen as systems of norms that, by instructing people as to what constitutes "good behavior," contribute to social stability and provide continuing answers to continuing problems.[24] They are guaranteed by authority, since failure to act according to social norms elicits punishment.[25] The systems of norms in social institutions represent an ordering of the major functions of a society, such as the political system, the economy, and religion. In institutional arrangements, the systems of norms represent agreements such as status hierarchies and cultural backgrounds that apply to all institutions.

These institutions and arrangements are experienced by people through norms that are expressed as laws, policies, and standard operating procedures by secondary groups or formal organizations such as social service agencies and schools. They are also experienced through norms that are adopted in primary groups or in informal social relationships such as neighborhoods, friendship cliques, and personal interactions; examples are family traditions, interpersonal expectations and behaviors, and neighborhood and social club values. At the informal level, the system of norms is often not written down or explicitly stated but exists on an implicit, between-the-lines basis.

Racism as an Institutional Arrangement

In order to answer the question of whether the United States has a racist society, it is necessary to examine the institutional arrangements that regulate everyday social interaction. To what extent do the norms that govern economic, political, religious, and family life reward prejudice and discrimination on the basis of race or ethnicity? To what extent do the norms of formal and informal groups lead respected members of a society to adopt racism?

Like other institutional arrangements, racism takes a variety of forms which represent different combinations of formal or informal and intentional or inadvertent characteristics (see "Institutional Racism Typology"). There is disagreement as to whether deliberation and intent must be present before **institutional racism** or **institutional discrimination** can be said to exist in a society. Some norms intend to discriminate; there are rules and regulations that specifically aim to punish one group in favor of another. The traditional apartheid system of South Africa is an excellent example. Other rules and regulations do not intend to discriminate but nevertheless do so, as in the use of intelligence tests and some forms of merit testing. Although such tests aim to distinguish on the basis of intellectual, attitudinal, or behavioral merit, due to unintentional biases in the test instruments they often distinguish on the basis of race and ethnicity.

Louis Knowles and Kenneth Prewitt argue that regardless of intent, rules and regulations that discriminate on this basis are racist. Using the example of University of Mississippi admission policies in the late 1960s, they observe:

> A university admissions policy which provides for entrance only to students who score high on tests designed primarily for white suburban high schools necessarily excludes black ghetto-educated students. Unlike the legal policies of Mississippi in the past, the university admission criteria are not intended to be racist, but the university is pursuing a course which perpetuates institutional racism.[26]

Knowles and Prewitt conclude that "Both the individual act of racism and the racist institutional policy may occur without the presence of conscious bigotry, and both may be masked intentionally or innocently." Richard Burkey disagrees, arguing that the term *institutional discrimination* should only be used to mean intentional discrimination: "Discrimination is a form of conflict and therefore is intentional. It is to be distinguished from other social conditions and policies that may perpetuate inequality but that are not intentional."[27]

Whether or not discrimination is intentional, it is harmful. In social service work, one question is the proper terminology to be used in trying to deal with discrimination. An organization should be labeled as *racist* if its policies and procedures deliberately discriminate. But when this is not the case, workers schooled in interpersonal skills might do better to refer to "inadvertent racism" or the "discriminatory effects" of particular procedures. Implying intention when none is present can only cause confusion and offense, and this may work against the achievement of common goals.

Institutional Racism Typology

One reason racism can pervade a society is that it takes many forms, ranging from formal policy and written legislation to individual attitudes. The results may be intentional outcomes or inadvertent consequences.

Results / Form	Formal	Informal
Intentional	Written laws, such as the immigration quota act of 1921 and Jim Crow laws	Unwritten laws, such as friendship norms and norms of mate selection
Inadvertent	Merit and other procedures with nonracist criteria which nevertheless place members of certain groups at a disadvantage	Being willing to help friends get jobs, but having no friends who are members of other groups, so effect is discrimination

Institutional Racism in Contemporary American Society

Important social changes have altered the nature of racism in the United States today. *Formal intentional racism*, which formerly limited access to educational and occupational opportunities, has given way to *informal intentional racism*, which effectively excludes racial minorities from the self-help, support networks people often use to locate opportunities, further their achievement, or gain economic advancement.

Informal Intentional Racism: Interpersonal Relationships

At the level of *informal intentional racism*, it is easy to document the racist character of the society of the United States. Neighborhood segregation, which is apparent in almost every American city, stands as a bastion of racism in spite of laws that prohibit discrimination in selling or leasing property. Similarly, the usual interpersonal friendships and marital partners chosen by people demonstrate the racist character of intimate relationships. While laws prohibiting interracial marriage or association no longer exist, intimate relationships rarely cross ethnic and racial boundaries. From an early age, Americans know who they are supposed to live next to, become friends with, and make love to. These patterns exist over and above the attitudes of individuals, because social life is organized in such a way that they become inevitable. Individuals have to go out of their way to avoid maintaining racism; and when they do not maintain it, society often reacts with negative sanctions. Americans therefore maintain racism simply by where they buy or

Participants in a multicultural workshop discuss ways to deal with instances of discrimination, intolerance, and misunderstanding in their work and daily lives.

rent housing and whom they choose as friends and marriage partners. Thus informal racist norms govern ordinary, everyday behavior.

In his studies of social distance, Bogardus demonstrates the existence of normative racist patterns controlling neighborhood, friendship, and marital patterns.[28] Such studies have shown that these informal laws operate not only in the white community but in minority communities as well.[29] People learn to have racist expectations in a number of ways. Sometimes they are reminded of them intentionally by parents and friends. Harry Kitano has demonstrated that the roots of prejudice and discrimination can be found in family life; children learn these attitudes as they are taught by their parents to be good family members.[30] They are also learned casually through the media, in motion pictures, on television, and in advertising and periodicals. Sometimes such learning occurs in ways that are not very obvious. Since community life is structured so that groups are separated, the absence of contact socializes individuals into believing that such attitudes and behaviors are of no concern. Informal racism is so normal and natural that often people do not even recognize its presence. At this level, the pervasiveness of racism is astonishing. We maintain a racist system through the ordinary activities of our everyday lives.

Informal racism is related to some forms of personal success and well-being: being part of the "in crowd," living in the "right" neighborhood, marrying the most "socially valued" person. But the question we have been addressing in Part Two is more concerned with whether racism is important to socioeconomic well-being: educational, occupational, and financial success. To answer this question we need to look at more formal forms of institutional racism.

Formal Intentional Racism: Government Laws and Policies

The racist character of the society of the United States formerly was clear. As we saw in Chapter 5, federal laws and policies worked to promote the well-being of immigrants from northern and western Europe at the expense of those from southern and eastern Europe, and they worked even more stringently to the disadvantage of non-Europeans. This disparity was evident in immigration laws, voting regulations, and legal access to employment opportunities, housing, transportation, public accommodations, and education, among other areas of daily living. Native Americans, African Americans, and Asians were excluded from citizenship at various times, and a "separate but equal" philosophy justified discrimination against minorities. This was **formal intentional racism**.

In the past three decades, however, American society has changed a good deal. Some scholars contend that it has entered a new era in which the effects of racism on the lives of people of color have been much diminished. With regard to blacks, William J. Wilson maintains that

> ...race relations in the United States have undergone fundamental changes in recent years, so much so that now the life chances of individual blacks have more to do with their economic class position than with their day-to-day encounters with whites....
>
> In the pre–Civil War period, and in the latter half of the nineteenth through the first half of the twentieth century, the continuous and explicit efforts of whites to construct racial barriers profoundly affected the lives of black Americans.[31]

Wilson traces three periods of race relations with respect to blacks in the United States. The first two follow the social history of the African-American community discussed in Chapter 4. After the American Revolution, race relations in the preindustrial South were institutionalized in the form of slavery or a caste system of oppression, with a small landed aristocracy in control of the plantation economy. After the Civil War, blacks became citizens, protected under the Constitution, but a series of Jim Crow laws restricted them to a life of sharecropping and little mobility. Legally, blacks were "separate but equal," but the laws were worked out to assure the separate rather than the equal aspects of this relationship. These laws no longer reflected the power and needs of the landed aristocracy. Rather, they developed out of the potential competition between white and nonwhite workers.

With the end of World War II, first federal and then state and local laws began to change. The civil rights movement forced governments to make a major shift—from supporting whites against nonwhites to supporting the equal rights of all groups. Civil rights laws replaced the Jim Crow laws. Affirmative action laws were developed to allow minorities to "catch up" after the systematic discrimination of the past. All government agencies and firms doing business with the federal government were required to safeguard the rights of racial and ethnic minorities. Discrimination on the basis of race, religion, or national origin was not permitted.

Because of these important changes, Wilson believes that racism no longer is a deterrent to the socioeconomic success of blacks and other racial minorities in the United States. Affirmative action policies helped to make upward mobility possible for a relatively small number of better-off blacks, whose daily lives are comparable to those of upper-middle-class whites. But government policy did not help the bulk of the blacks, who emerged as part of an urban underclass, living in poverty with little hope for advancement. This underclass is held back, not by individual or institutional discrimination, but by the operation of an advanced industrial, capitalist economy. As Wilson observes, "class is clearly more important than race in predetermining job placement and occupational mobility."[32]

Class conflict, however, has little role in Wilson's thinking. He believes poverty for blacks results not because management needs cheap labor or because workers compete for a limited number of jobs, but because the inner cities have decayed and economic opportunities have moved to the suburbs. Blacks are poor because they are isolated from the mainstream economy. The theme of black isolation rather than racism has been promoted by other leading black scholars as well.[33]

Yet Wilson does not maintain that racism is of no contemporary consequence whatever. He cites the racial division of labor which has been created by centuries of discrimination and prejudice. This division is reinforced, he says, "because those in the low-wage sector of the economy are more adversely affected by impersonal economic shifts in advanced industrial society."[34]

The Continuing Influence of Informal Intentional Racism

Though intentional racism and discrimination have been prohibited by government laws and policies, they still operate in contemporary American society to limit the socioeconomic success of blacks and, by extension, other minority groups. Charles Willie contends that economic well-being must be seen as a complex structure which includes social and personal conditions as well as government laws and policies. Thus he argues that patterns of neighborhood, social, and friendship segregation which are still very evident today are intimately connected with economic well-being. Put another way, informal institutional racism still impedes the progress of blacks. Willie cites evidence from other studies which demonstrates an association between economic opportunity, educational opportunity, and residential location. Furthermore, he argues that Wilson's class perspective "tends to mask the presence of opportunities that are institutionally based such as attending the 'right' school, seeking employment in the 'right' company or firm, and being of the 'right' race."[35]

Willie also believes that successful blacks are not free of racism, as Wilson would have us imagine. Blacks and other minorities who have achieved success with the help of affirmative action policies are often treated as if they could not have made it any other way, as if they were really unqualified and merely symbols or tokens. Self-doubt and the constant need to establish their worth have created major socially induced stress for blacks. On the basis of his case studies of black families who have moved into racially integrated neighborhoods and work situations, Willie concludes that "race for some of these pioneers is a consuming experience. They seldom can get away from it. When special opportunities are created...the minorities who take advantage of them must constantly prove themselves."[36]

Willie suggests that the struggle against racism should be shifted to neighborhood integration and friendship development. His thesis supports the view that informal residential, friendship, and kinship patterns mediate social achievement. It might be suggested that acquaintance processes, or social affiliations a step below friendship, also are influenced by racism and mediate achievement. Acquaintances made in clubs, civic service groups, and other voluntary associations often can provide information about economic and educational opportunities. Minorities who are routinely denied these opportunities cannot profit from what Mark Granovetter calls "the strength of weak ties."[37]

☞ BIOLOGICAL ATTRIBUTES OF MINORITY COMMUNITIES

In addition to the obstacles to the socioeconomic well-being of racial and ethnic minorities which are inherent in the social context of minority-majority relations, there are factors within these minorities that can limit their quest for the American dream.

Researchers have had particular interest in the relative importance of the biological and cultural attributes of various minorities. Both of these types of attributes are believed to be related to socioeconomic achievement, though these beliefs have inspired considerable controversy and debate. Intelligence is a biological attribute which is discussed in this section. The following section considers such cultural determinants as the culture of poverty and cultural values and traditions.

The biological foundations for the concept of race were discussed in Chapter 4. While specific attempts to classify humans into discrete races on a biological basis have been unsuccessful, some credence is being given to the definition of race in terms of gene pools or breeding populations. Considerable research also has examined the belief that differences in socioeconomic well-being can be attributed to genetically based deficiencies in the intellectual capacities of minorities. The hypothesis is that significant differences in intelligence exist between races, in particular between whites and blacks, and that these differences have an effect on socioeconomic well-being.

Differences in Intelligence-Test Scores

Intelligence tests have been used by educational psychologists to measure intelligence for almost a century, and the results have documented significant differences among ethnic groups, as well as differences between rural and urban groups. Early tests found evidence to support the superiority of people from northern and western Europe over those from southern and eastern Europe.[38] In Great Britain, significant differences favoring the English over the Irish continue to be reported.[39] Such findings have provoked controversy in the past and continue to be controversial.

The current controversy centers on the differences in intelligence-test scores of American blacks and whites in general. The studies have focused on these two groups, so whites have not been compared with a "pure" black race. In a review of research on intelligence tests for the *Harvard Educational Review* published in 1969, Arthur Jensen found, on average, a 15-point difference in IQ scores favoring whites over blacks.[40] There has been no dispute over this finding; the dispute lies in how to interpret it. **Hereditarians** attribute the difference to biological or genetic variables, and **environmentalists** attribute it to the effects of social class and racism. Neither side in the debate has been able to prove its point conclusively, but the environmentalists seem to have the upper hand.

The Hereditarian Position

Along with Hans Eysenck, another outspoken hereditarian,[41] Jensen attributes the black-white difference in IQ scores to inborn genetic traits. Hereditarians note that in studies which take into account differences in family environment, including socioeconomic status, these IQ differences are reduced but remain significant. Even in studies that use culture-fair tests, the differences are present and, in some cases, are more pronounced. This is taken as evidence that cognitive ability is largely determined genetically.

Jensen estimates that genetic inheritance, or **heritability**, accounts for some 60 percent of the scores on intelligence tests. Genetic inheritance is measured through heritability estimates, which express "the proportion of variation in intelligence in a population which is attributable to genetic variation within the population."[42] Heritability does not measure individual genetic endowment; it is a group estimate. It also is a within-group not between-group estimate, so the intelligence of blacks and whites is considered separately. To measure heritability, Jensen used studies of twins reared apart in which the subjects were mostly white twins of American, British, and Danish nationality. The proportion of variation in his heritability estimate for whites then was used as the basis for a heritability estimate for blacks.

In evaluating arguments for genetic inheritance, it is important to consider some of the things Jensen is not saying. He is not saying that all whites are superior in intelligence to all blacks. Rather, he is making a generalization, while noting that there are many instances in which blacks score as well as or higher than whites. Indeed, in a more recent study, Jensen found that on certain dimensions of intelligence, blacks in general do better than whites in general.[43] He did not regard his earlier findings as definitive but acknowledged the need for further confirmation. He recognized the possibility of an environmental explanation of the differences, but he concluded in a book on the merits and validity of intelligence tests published in 1979 that IQ tests showing blacks scoring lower than whites are fair and accurate and that the results are not skewed by culture.[44]

The Environmentalist Position

Environmentalists reject the hereditarian position on the genetic determination of intelligence. Some question the value of IQ tests, arguing that only in a racist society would there be attempts to measure differences in IQ across racial and ethnic groups. They also question the relevance of IQ tests as a measure of intelligence. Intelligence is multidimensional, and forms of intelligence other than knowledge of vocabulary and mathematics would have to be measured. Thus they maintain that test scores predict not success in life but success in school.[45] People whose school-age IQ scores were not high can become very successful, both socially and financially. Other environmentalists accept testing but point out the need for more sophisticated studies of family background. Without analysis of differences in such things as parenting styles and parental values, gross measures of occupation and education are insufficient explanations of family background.

Environmentalists also have taken a hard look at biases in the testing situation. Irwin Katz, for instance, has done a series of studies demonstrating that the anxiety provoked by testing is so great among blacks that their performance is inhibited. When black students are told they are being compared to students at predominantly white colleges, their performance is significantly lower than when they are told they are being compared to other black students.[46] In a somewhat different approach, Carl Milofsky compared testing procedures in schools with high and low percentages of black students. He found that though such testing or "child study" requires a good deal of time and care, much less time is spent on it in schools with a high percentage of blacks. In such schools child studies on average took 3.9 hours, compared to 6.3 hours in schools with a low percentage of blacks.[47]

Perhaps the most devastating critique of the hereditarian position has been done by Leon Kamin. By closely examining the studies used to develop heritability estimates, he was able to show that the results had been flagrantly falsified. Most of the studies done on heritability were conducted by Cyril Burt, a prominent English psychologist. Kamin noticed consistent errors in the reporting of correlation coefficients in these studies. The proof of falsification, however, came in an independent biography of Burt by an admirer and supporter who was forced to conclude that the figures had been falsified.[48]

More recent studies of twins reared apart have been able to eliminate some of the methodological problems of earlier studies and have demonstrated that the influence of the parent rearing the child is more important than the natural parent or the genetic background of the child. In correlating intelligence scores in adoptive parents who also had biological children, studies in Texas and Minnesota found that adopted and biological children reared by the same parents had pretty much the same IQ scores.[49]

∽ CULTURAL ATTRIBUTES OF MINORITY COMMUNITIES

The term *culture*, as we noted in Chapter 4, refers to the beliefs, attitudes, values, norms, and traditions that are shared in a society or community and govern interactions among the members. The study of culture develops an understanding of the plasticity of human nature: Different groupings of individuals produce different shared meanings and behavior patterns. A number of social scientists have found a relationship between the culture of a group and its social and economic achievements.

This does not mean that the culture of a community is necessarily at fault when its members do not do as well as those of other communities. There are many strengths in ethnic-minority communities, but there also may be limitations and weaknesses. From a systems perspective, social service workers look at the attributes of the focal system in the context of the social environment. To avoid blaming the victim (see Chapter 1), they must not lose sight of the social context as they examine a particular focal system. With this caution in mind, we will consider some theories which attempt to explain how group culture affects the socioeconomic status of ethnic-minority communities.

The Culture of Poverty

Oscar Lewis coined the term **culture of poverty** as an expression of his belief that the cultural adaptations of poor people to poverty make it extremely difficult for them to escape from that condition.[50] Lewis primarily studied Mexicans and Puerto Ricans,[51] but he concluded that the culture of poverty transcends regional, rural-urban, and national differences. Thus the term is not a description of a particular ethnic community but concerns many kinds of communities living in poverty.

A culture of poverty is regarded as both a cause and an effect of socioeconomic distress. It is said to come about as an adaptation to poverty, that is, as an effect of living under poverty conditions. Yet everyone who experiences poverty does not develop a culture of poverty. Many college students experience economic hardship as they struggle to get through school, but college students as a community do not develop a culture of poverty. Similarly, a culture of poverty would not be expected to emerge in a community of highly educated or skilled refugees or immigrants, who may experience enormous but temporary economic hardship in coming to the United States.

Lewis contends that a culture of poverty develops in communities with certain living conditions which are prevalent in Western industrial or industrializing nations. The societies in which the culture might be found have the following characteristics:

1. A cash economy, labor for wages, and production for profit.
2. Persistently high rates of unemployment and underemployment.
3. Low wage scales.
4. Failure to provide social, political, and economic organization, on either a voluntary or government-sponsored basis.

Culture of Poverty, Culture of Resistance

The concept of the culture of poverty is built on the premise that self-defeating traits are culturally transmitted to members of poor and minority communities. What it fails to acknowledge is that these communities also struggle against the exploitative environments in which they exist.

The Appalachian region of the United States has been an area of poverty and limited economic opportunities and growth for decades, providing an early impetus for the War on Poverty. Since 1970, economic crisis and decline have been greater in two-thirds of the counties in the region than in the rest of the nation. Thousands of jobs have been lost. West Virginia was especially hard hit, with a 27 percent decline in manufacturing jobs between 1980 and 1987. Employment in the coal mines, which has been the lifeblood of the region, has declined as much as 83 percent.

The concept of the culture of poverty has been applied in attempts to understand the depressed circumstances of the families and individuals, regardless of race, who live in Appalachia. David Cattell-Gordon describes the region as an environment of trauma and suggests that the large numbers of people there who report experiencing depression, anxiety, hypochondria, apathy, or insomnia are suffering from a culturally transmitted post-traumatic stress syndrome. Like Oscar Lewis, he clearly recognizes the effects of oppression in a class-stratified capitalist economy, but his primary attention is to the way this has led to internalized, self-defeating behaviors and attitudes.

Karen Tice and Dwight Billings argue that this interpretation is faulty because it casts those who live in Appalachia as helpless victims who are powerless to influence their environments. In their view Appalachians must be understood not only in terms of how they are influenced by the nation's economic and political environments but also in terms of how they attempt to influence those environments. If the strong resistive forces among Appalachians are recognized, their culture of poverty might be better understood as a culture of resistance.

Appalachians, like others who live for a long period in or near poverty, have participated in a complex relationship of resistance and complicity in regard to capitalist development. Although there have been times when they have responded to oppression with a sense of powerlessness and quiescence, their history is dotted with instances of opposition. During the 1920s and 1930s, coal miners in the region were among the most militant and class-conscious workers in the United States. Again in the late 1960s, miners in Appalachia challenged industrial power, medical and legal knowledge, and government apathy to win recognition of black lung disease. More recently they have fought to defend their jobs from the effects of corporate restructuring, strip-mining, and environmental issues. Their history has been marked by the adaptability and resilience of Appalachian families and the impressive results of grassroots organizing.

The ideas of Tice and Billings suggest that use of the culture of poverty in efforts to understand poor or minority communities presents a one-sided view of what life is like among the poor. The culture of a community should be seen not as a fixed set of traits passed on from one generation to the next but as a dynamic discourse through which people constantly make and remake their worlds and in which resistance to oppression is as important a process as acquiescence to it.

Sources: David Cattell-Gordon, "The Appalachian Inheritance: A Culturally Transmitted Traumatic Stress Syndrome," *Journal of Progressive Human Services*, vol. 1, no. 1 (1990), pp. 41–57; Karen Tice and Dwight Billings, "Appalachian Culture and Resistance," *Journal of Progressive Human Services*, vol. 2, no. 2 (1991), pp. 1–18.

5. A bilateral kinship system in which descent is determined by both the paternal and maternal lines and the nuclear family is the ideal.

6. Values in the dominant class which stress the accumulation of wealth and property.[52]

A group's development of a culture of poverty, Lewis says, should not be seen as just a negative or dysfunctional reaction to economic deprivation. The culture of poverty develops as a positive or functional adaptation; it demonstrates the ability of people to cope and survive under the most debilitating circumstances. But it is both a reaction and an adaptation of the poor to their marginal position in society—an effort to cope with hopelessness and despair which develop from the realization of the improbability of achieving success (see "Culture of Poverty, Culture of Resistance"). Once this way of life comes into existence, it tends to perpetuate itself from generation to generation, through child-socialization processes. By the time children in a culture of poverty are 6 or 7 years old, they have usually absorbed the basic values and attitudes of their subculture. They are not psychologically geared to take full advantage of changing conditions or increased opportunities which may be presented in their lifetimes, and they may not be able to take advantage of the social services that are provided on their behalf. In this respect, the culture of poverty becomes a cause of continued poverty.

Lewis defines the culture of poverty itself in terms of the following traits which are said to be characteristic of members:

1. A lack of effective participation and integration into the major institutions and the economic, political, and religious systems of the larger society.

2. Severely thwarted family life, typified by such factors as an absence of childhood; early initiation into sex, free unions, and consensual marriages; a tendency toward female-headed households; much greater knowledge of maternal relatives; a strong predisposition to authoritarianism; a lack of privacy; and a verbal emphasis on family solidarity, which is only rarely achieved in actuality.

3. A minimum of social organization beyond the level of family, so that while there may be a certain sense of commonality, there is very little ability to organize around community interests.

4. Individual attitudes of marginality, helplessness, dependence, and inferiority.[53]

Lewis's theory was criticized harshly, and in some respects the criticism was unfair. Lewis did attribute the development of the culture of poverty to the oppressive economic conditions the poor were forced to endure. However, this part of his theory tends to get lost in his description of the traits that become internalized by individuals and families and maintain them in poverty. Furthermore, the programs and policies derived by social service professionals from the work of Lewis emphasized the need to alter the culture, rather than the need to alter the harsh economic conditions that had created it.

While the theory of the culture of poverty is no longer widely cited, many of its "victim-blaming" particulars have resurfaced in descriptions of the predominantly minority urban **underclass**[54] (see "Explaining the Underclass"). The lifestyle characteristics of Latinos and African Americans living in poverty-stricken inner-city neighborhoods have been described in ways that emphasize lack of integration into the major social institutions, disorganized family life, inability to provide effective self-help, and feelings of marginality and helplessness. By the same token, conservative ideas, taken out of the context of the culture of poverty and the literature on the underclass, have been used to describe white, lower-class behavior. Charles Murray, in assessing teenage pregnancy rates, for

---

Explaining the Underclass

The culture of poverty is one of two explanations for the continued presence of an economic underclass in an otherwise prosperous society. In this view, the underclass is
attributed to the dominance of norms and
values in its own culture which do not prepare members to take advantage of economic opportunities that present themselves. Ill
health, unemployment, and crime are perpetuated, and the underclass is sustained by
the existence of a welfare state.

The other explanation sees the underclass
of the effect of discrimination against racial
and ethnic groups as well as against the poor.
In this view the underclass, primarily composed of minorities, is a product of institutional racism operating in education, the job
market, housing, and the criminal justice system.

Joan Moore believes that both the cul-
ture-of-poverty and racism approaches are
oversimplified. Both also focus on categories

of individuals rather than communities. The
explanation for the existence of the underclass, she maintains, must be found in the
dynamics of the social process at work within the minority community. The focus should
be on differentiation within such communities, as in her study of Chicano youth gangs
in East Los Angeles. Within that community,
she found social processes at work which
both were creating and could be used to
eliminate the treatment of families as members of the underclass.

Sources: Vincent N. Parrillo, "Minorities," in J.
Stimson and A. Stimson (editors), *Sociology: Con-
temporary Readings*, 2nd ed. (Itasca, IL: F. E.
Peacock Publishers, 1987), p. 218; Joan W. Moore,
"Isolation and Stigmatization in the Development
of an Underclass: The Case of Chicano Gangs Is
East Los Angeles," *Social Problems*, vol. 23 (1985),
pp. 1–12; reprinted in Stimson and Stimson,
Sociology, pp. 224–32.

---

instance, describes poor whites as "white trash," in line with what he believes is an internalized culture of poverty.[55]

Cultural Values and Traits Needed for Success

A different perspective on socioeconomic success is taken by Thomas Sowell, whose
ideas are based on a comparison of the advances made by the various racial and ethnic
groups in American society. He contends that new groups achieve success, as measured
by economic parity with white, Anglo-Saxon Protestants, in about two generations. Some
groups succeed more quickly—the Japanese, Russian Jews, and Asian Indians, for instance—and others succeed more slowly—the Irish in the nineteenth century, African
Americans, Puerto Ricans, and Mexican Americans. Sowell believes that cultural differences explain these varying rates of success.[56]

Sowell maintains that racism and "other causes of poverty" do not greatly affect such
community progress. He argues that "low income origins, overcrowded and substandard
housing, prejudice and discrimination, inadequate educational opportunities, and a general failure of public service—such as the police, schools, and garbage collection" are
not unique to contemporary minority groups; rather, "all those things impeded the
progress of all American minorities."[57] He also argues that color or race, per se, does not
preclude success. While the record is "not unequivocal," it "provides at least some basis
for believing that color acceptance is not impossible in the United States."[58]

Similarly, Sowell cites evidence that political power is of little importance facilitating

Mexican Americans in traditional dress celebrate their cultural heritage
and pride on a float in a San Antonio parade commemorating the
coming of spring.

socioeconomic success. Groups such as the Jews and Japanese, on entering the United States, had little power to influence local, state, or federal elections and policies, but they generally succeeded. The Irish and, more recently, African Americans have excelled at political organizing, but this has not necessarily helped them do well economically.

Thus Sowell takes a far more conservative stance than Lewis does. Where Lewis argues that a debilitating social environment can create a culture of poverty, Sowell maintains that all racial and ethnic groups in American society have confronted a similarly harsh environment, but some have been able to deal with it better than others. He acknowledges, however, that the functioning of the economic system in the late twentieth century makes success more difficult now than in the past. Labor unions have not been responsive to the needs of minorities. The standardization of jobs, wages, and promotions through objective criteria such as tests and formal credentials, which minorities must deal with in the labor market today, did not confront immigrants in the past. Whereas the problems of European immigrants were low wages and difficult working conditions, contemporary minorities face the possibility of becoming mired in the underclass, where unemployment, underemployment, and public assistance prevail.

In order for groups to overcome their harsh environments, Sowell believes they must possess certain cultural traits such as group cohesiveness and family stability. Group cohesiveness, or a sense of common identity, is important because communities that stick together, encourage mutual aid, and overcome inevitable internal conflicts are likely to do well. Moreover, the style in which group identity is expressed is important. He suggests that Jews and Japanese were quiet about their identity, while blacks and Irish loudly proclaimed theirs. Since Jews and Japanese have been singularly successful, he proposes that blacks should be quieter in their expressions of solidarity.

While groups that have done well in American society have all evidenced stable family life, Sowell contends that family stability alone is insufficient to produce success. Some immigrant groups, such as Italians, that did have high family stability nevertheless did not succeed quickly. Family stability must be coupled with the teaching of particular values to children. When these values are taught within stable environments, success is more likely.

Sowell maintains that the cultural trait that seems to predict economic success best is a **future orientation**, that is, "a belief in a pattern of behavior that sacrifices present comforts and enjoyments while preparing for future success."[59] The cultural traits which appear to predict slow economic progress and which characterize the less successful minorities are "a high value on immediate fun, 'excitement' and emotionalism." Thus, Sowell says, if an ethnic-minority community is to advance, parents should be encouraged to stabilize their family life and teach their children to delay gratification.

In proposing his point of view, Sowell says he does not want to cast blame: "There is no place for praise or blame…here." Nor does he suggest that cultural traits reflect "superior insight by one's ancestors." He maintains that culture develops as a response to historically specific demands, and developments at one point in time may or may not be helpful at other times. As we noted in Chapter 5, because Jews were not allowed to own land and were forced into urban occupations in Russia, they valued education and developed skills which turned out to be useful in the emerging industrial economy of the United States. The Irish and Italians, who were largely peasants from rural areas, developed cultural traditions which were appropriate in their native lands but proved to be a hindrance to their success in this country.

While Sowell's ideas are interesting, some of his analysis is questionable. For instance, although it is true that the Japanese did not have the numbers to become a politically potent force within the United States, they did have the strong backing of the Japanese government. As an example, when the Japanese were being forced to attend segregated schools in the United States and laws were being considered which would exclude them from immigration, Japanese government officials protested.[60] Similarly, Sowell tends to overplay the importance of cultural traits while underplaying some of the important differences in the environmental conditions confronted by minorities. Thus he does not acknowledge the difference between colonized and immigrant groups or the role of formal intentional discrimination in blocking the success of African Americans and Native Americans.

∽ PROSPECTS FOR PROGRESS IN MINORITY-MAJORITY RELATIONS

As the chapters on community life in Part Two have demonstrated, socioeconomic success is possible in the United States, although it is rarely achieved without great effort, Immigrant minorities from Europe have done well for the most part, especially in socioeconomic terms. There is evidence that minorities of color are also "making it" in the United States. Many Asian Americans, in particular, have achieved social and economic success. Affluent and middle-class American blacks, Latinos, and Native Americans are

---

American Diversity as a Myth

Many believe that the United States is a multicultural society, one in which several sets of often-competing cultural values and traditions exist side by side. Furthermore, increased immigration from Africa, Asia, and Latin America is promoting the belief that American society is becoming even more racially and culturally diversified.

Louis Menand represents a different point of view: "The belief that the United States is becoming more racially and culturally diversified, more like a mosaic and less like a can of mixed paint, is not supported by any statistics that I am aware of." In support of his argument he notes the following:

1. A much smaller percentage of the population is foreign-born than was the case six or seven decades ago.

2. The rate of interracial marriage has increased dramatically.

3. The Census Bureau projects that the country will remain about 80 percent white and 90 percent Christian well into the next century, according to Menand.

Menand also argues that people in the United States, regardless of how ethnically conscious they may be, as always want to be considered American. Assimilation is taking place not because people are being forced or oppressed into it but because by accepting diversity we actually mainstream it. People who celebrate their ethnic or racial background, their religion, their gender, or even their sexual orientation are actually being very American. They are not "a separate and rival realm of value but a different flavor in the same dish." Echoing Tocqueville, Menand says that "the United States is a country in which people, permitted to say whatever they like, all somehow end up saying the same thing."

For Menand, the real change that has occurred in the past decade has been economic. Inequality in the shares of national income held by the affluent and the poor has widened; and since people of color and new immigrants and refugees are more likely to be poor, we have confused "economic ghettoization" with "diversity." The growing inequality in the United States, he contends, is the result of bad public policy and has little to do with any presumed cultural differences between European and non-European Americans.

Sources: U.S. Department of Labor, *Opportunity 2000: Creative Affirmative Action Strategies for A Changing Workforce* (Washington, DC, 1988); Louis Menand, "The Myth of American Diversity," *Harper's Magazine*, March 1993, pp. 26–29.

---

increasingly evident. They are achieving success through their own efforts and because the legal obstacles that prevented it in the past have been for the most part eliminated. The principle of equal opportunity, in the form of affirmative action and civil rights legislation, has brought hope to racial and ethnic minorities in the United States.

But American society is still involved in a debate concerning ethnic community relations. Some champion the traditional desire for assimilation, and others champion the cause of cultural pluralism. These philosophies are quite different, and in some cases they conflict (see "American Diversity as a Myth"). For instance, in the cultural pluralist view, English is regarded as a second language for native speakers of another tongue. Advocates of the assimilation view see English as the only official language of the United States, and by 1988 this position had been adopted in 17 states. Assimilationists also are challenging multilingual provisions of the federal Voting Rights Act, seeking to limit bilingual education programs, and recommending the tightening of English-language proficiency standards for citizenship.[61]

Happy Endings: Assimilation and Cultural Pluralism

Assimilation has historically been championed by members of the dominant group as the eventual outcome of intercommunity relations. According to assimilation philosophy (see Chapter 5), all groups were expected to become "American," that is, white, Anglo-Saxon, and Protestant, leaving behind their own cultural traditions and values. When the philosophy was first espoused, nonwhite groups were seen as unassimilable and were excluded from the United States through immigration laws. Nonwhite groups already in the country were to be kept in a "separate but equal" status.

Cultural pluralism was envisioned as the outcome of immigration by minorities from southern and eastern Europe, and it continues to be the dream of many contemporary minority groups.[62] According to the philosophy of **cultural pluralism**, each group is to retain allegiance to its own traditions and values, and all groups in the society are to learn to respect these differences and allow them to flourish. Cultural pluralism always involves a bicultural perspective. The implicit assumption is that, rather then everyone becoming American, there will be Irish Americans, Japanese Americans, African Americans, and so on (see "Mutliculturalism in the 1990s"). Each group is to retain its own traditions, but it is also to accept a certain degree of Americanization.

Assimilation and cultural pluralism have one thing in common: They are happy endings. Assimilation is the ending envisioned by many in the dominant group: "They will all become like us." Cultural pluralism is the ending envisioned by minorities: "We will retain our own ways but adopt their ways as well." Both are happy endings in the sense that they will see some ultimate good conclusion to cultural and ethnic conflict. These philosophies provide positive goals to aim for. They keep attention focused on the need for solutions that advance the common good.

Unhappy Endings: From Extermination to Secession

Minority-majority relations do not always have happy endings, of course, and neither assimilation nor cultural pluralism takes into account some harsh realities. Progress in intercommunity relations is neither linear nor automatic. There are no natural laws of social relationships to assure that societies will evolve or develop in positive ways.

Historical evidence affirms the rise and fall of groups within a society. For instance, the history of Jews has been marked by success as well as oppression. Who would have predicted at the turn of the twentieth century that Jews in Germany, a group that was socioeconomically successful and even admired and respected, would within a few short years be systematically stripped of their possessions and subjected to the incredible humiliation and devastation of the World War II death camps? In the United States, negative turnarounds in the destiny of groups are also evident. With the end of the Civil War, a great liberal era was ushered in with the promise that the recently freed slaves would soon join the mainstream society. Yet by the end of the nineteenth century, Jim Crow laws were in place to assure their segregation.[63]

Richard Burkey describes a number of possible unhappy endings to minority-majority relations.[64] Extermination and expulsion are two ways that majority groups try to deal with the real or imagined threat of minority groups. *Extermination* occurs when the dominant group in a society attempts to annihilate a particular minority group. The Germans under Hitler attempted to annihilate Jews, and American military policy in the mid-nineteenth century was to exterminate Native Americans on the western plains. *Expulsion*, or

---

Multiculturalism in the 1990s

The coexistence of different racial and ethnic groups within the same national borders is a source of destructive conflict in many nations today. Within American society, it is dividing minority groups from one another and from the white, Euro-American majority. Multiculturalism is the center of controversy between those whose principal objective is to preserve the distinctive characteristics of minority groups and those who seek primarily to integrate all diverse cultures into a single national identity.

Clarence Page, a black syndicated columnist, provides a good example of the latter approach in a letter he received from a reader:

> I can readily see how you, as an African-American, can be upset by the treatment of Asian-Americans in California. I can readily understand that for personal reasons.
>
> I am a Scotch-Irish American. My wife is an English-Welsh-American. Our kids are Scotch-Irish-English-Welsh-American.
>
> My daughter married a German-Polish-American. Her kids are Scotch Irish-English-Welsh-Polish-German-Americans. Her son is going with an African-American. If they get married their kids will be Scotch-Irish-English-Welsh-German-Polish-African-Americans.

The reader goes on to warn of an imminent "Balkanization of the United States" and to suggest that Arthur Schlesinger Jr.'s *The Disuniting of America* is an excellent book on the subject. Page points out, however, that the subtitle, *Reflections on a Multicultural Society*, is a better indication of its perspective. Schlesinger, a renowned historian, criticizes only multiculturalists who are extreme in their ethnocentrism, those who have rejected cultural pluralism and embraced "a cult of ethnicity...to denounce the idea of a melting pot, to challenge the concept of 'one people,' and to protect, promote, and perpetuate separate ethnic and racial communities." (p. 15)

Schlesinger also cautions the integrationists that...the burden to unify the country does not fall exclusively on the minorities. Assimilation and integration constitute a two-way street. Those who want to join America must be received and welcomed by those who already think they own America. ...Not only must *they* want assimilation and integration; *we* must want it too. The burden to make this a unified country lies as much with the complacent majority as with the sullen and resentful minorities. (p. 19)

Page ends this column by noting that if the reader's grandson should get serious with his African-American girlfriend, most Americans would not call their children by any hyphenated name. They would simply call the children black.

Sources: Clarence Page, syndicated column, "The De-hyphenization of America," *Chicago Tribune*, April 19, 1992, sect. 4, p. 4; Arthur M. Schlesinger, Jr., *The Disuniting of America: Reflections on a Multicultural Society* (New York: W. W. Norton, 1992).

---

forced removal of a minority group by a majority group, is another adverse outcome. Jews were expelled from Spain when the Catholic monarchs Ferdinand and Isabella ascended to the throne, and in the Great Depression Mexican Americans were rounded up and deported from the United States. A more recent example is the attempted expulsion of Muslims from Bosnia by both Croats and Serbs, while they were fighting one another for territory.

There are also ways by which minorities can attempt to overcome their oppressors. *Revolution* is the use of armed forces by subordinated groups to throw off the shackles of domination. Thus Native Americans rebelled against the onslaught of white settlers attempting to appropriate their lands on the frontier, and today armed rebellion is pitting not only blacks against whites but whites against newly empowered blacks as South Africa attempts to form a new government without apartheid laws and regulations. *Secession* is an attempt by subordinated groups to leave the territory controlled by their dominators and relocate elsewhere. It can also be seen in attempts by minorities to carve out an independent territory within the area controlled by the dominant group and claim it as their own. Both types of succession movements have been seen in American history. Marcus Garvey led a back-to-Africa movement at the turn of the twentieth century, and Reis Lopez Tijerina tried to reclaim Mexican lands in New Mexico during the 1960s.[65] More recently, Puerto Rican islanders have debated the issue of secession to secure independence from the United States.[66]

Conflict between minorities and majorities is serious business. It should not be minimized as simply a misunderstanding or a breakdown in communication in an otherwise harmonious world. The stakes are often high—control over a government as well as control of the lion's share of a nation's wealth. With the stakes so high, anything can happen.

The Dual Perspective and Progress in Minority-Majority Relations

Social workers have developed a dual, bicultural perspective on the acculturation of minorities which acknowledges the strengths of ethnic-minority communities. According to Dolores Norton, the concept of the dual perspective "grew out of the idea that every individual is a part of two systems: the larger system of mainstream society, and the smaller system of the client's immediate physical and social environment."[67] The dual perspective is offered as a means for creating a stronger society.

The dual perspective proceeds from a philosophy about racial and ethnic diversity under which social workers are expected to recognize the cultural roots of both their own and their clients' attitudes and behaviors and to develop an "empathic appreciation of both the majority societal system and the minority client system."[68] It rejects the idea that minority members must fully assimilate into the mainstream society in order to attain socioeconomic well-being. Rather, it espouses cultural pluralism and the view that a society should allow for and appreciate diversity. **Biculturalsim** is presented as a social good for minority individuals; similarly, **multiculturalism** has emerged as a social philosophy to challenge the assimilationist ideas of the white majority in American society.

Those who work within the dual perspective acknowledge the strengths of the ethnic minority communities. Leon Chestang, for instance, describes the ways in which the black community nurtures its members but sees no such strengths in the majority community which would help minorities. Rather, he argues that the majority community is not supportive of blacks, which makes the development of healthy personalities difficult for them.[69]

Strengths have also been located in Latino communities, which are often believed to lack cohesiveness or the ability to organize in their own behalf. Salvador Alvarez disproves this by describing a wide range of formal voluntary associations, including labor unions, which have been developed by Mexican Americans.[70] Others have described the natural support systems often found in Puerto Rican communities. Melvin Delgado and Denise Humm-Delgado see such systems as "an inherent source of strength for individuals that can be explored as resources in the development of culture-specific counseling or in the development of service plans, programs, and policies."[71]

Bicultural Socialization

The concept of the dual perspective also provides an explanation for why members of ethnic-minority groups may not succeed. Diane de Anda's construction of a theory of success or failure in American society based on the concept of bicultural socialization was introduce in Chapter 6. She believes social and personal well-being for ethnic minorities requires them to be adequately socialized within both the minority and the majority cultures. Minority-group members must know both what is expected of them if they are to be successful within their own community and what is expected of them if they are to be successful in the majority community. Success in the larger society is jeopardized when minority individuals do not understand how it operates.[72]

De Anda hypothesizes that six factors are necessary for successful bicultural socialization. First, it is facilitated when there is a great deal of cultural overlap between ethnic groups. Failure is more likely when there are large differences between the minority and majority cultures. The values and attitudes of a minority group and the ways members think about the world may be so different from those of majority groups that they cannot operate successfully in both systems. De Anda claims that the bicultural socialization of African Americans, Latinos, and Asians is more difficult in American society because of the vast dissimilarities between their cultural backgrounds and that of European Americans.

Second, bicultural socialization is facilitated when people are available to act as translators, mediators, and models. *Translators* are successful bicultural minority-group members who are "able to share their own experiences, provide information that facilitates understanding of the values and perceptions of the majority culture, and convey ways to meet the behavioral demands made on minority members of the society without compromising ethnic values and norms." *Mediators* are majority-group members "who serve as providers of information and guides for ethnic minority persons." A *model* is a minority-group member "whose behavior serves as a pattern to emulate in order to develop a behavioral repertoire consistent with the norms of the majority and minority culture."[73]

Third, bicultural socialization can be achieved through corrective feedback, or positive reinforcements by minority and majority socializing agents. With patience, these agents can point out the positive aspects in a minority person's behavior, be specific in pointing out errors, and give concrete suggestions about how to correct errors.

Fourth, bicultural socialization is more likely when the individual being socialized has problem-solving skills, that is, a cognitive style or "a repertoire of modes of perceiving and interpreting one's interpersonal and material environment." If minorities are to operate within the dominant system, according to de Anda, they must have a cognitive analytic style. To the extent that they are embedded in their own cultures and unable to develop such a style, they will not achieve adequate socialization.

Fifth, the degree of bilingual ability in a minority group also plays a part in successful bicultural socialization. Ethnic and racial groups with competence in both languages are most able to learn the norms of the majority culture.

Sixth, to the extent that the physical appearances of minority- and majority-group members are similar, bicultural socialization is more likely. De Anda notes that minority individuals with the ability "to pass," that is, to go undetected among the majority, are better able to learn the majority culture. Not only are they directly exposed to that culture, but they also become aware of negative opinions about members of their community. Thus they learn not only what to do but also, and perhaps more important, what not to do.

De Anda's perspective on dual socialization has the merit of fostering a culturally plural society. It also gives social workers some concrete ideas about how they can help minorities achieve success within the dominant society. But her perspective does have shortcomings. For one thing, new arrivals may have values and attitudes which are vastly different from those of the majority culture, but it is unlikely that the values and attitudes of the "old minorities"—African Americans, Native Americans, Japanese, Chinese, Mexican Americans, and Puerto Ricans—whose families go back generations, are to any extent similarly different. De Anda does not specify what these vast differences in values are. For the old minorities it seems, therefore, that more has to be taken into consideration than a lack of knowledge of expectations. Her perspective ignores an understanding of the processes of conflict and competition and the ideologies of racism and ethnocentrism which are in operation among communities. The role of the majority community in preventing success for minorities is not considered in depth, although she does ask majority-group members to serve as mediators and calls on social workers to help majorities understand the values of minorities. Success also seems to mean conformity to the ways of the larger society. Thus, according to de Anda, minorities must learn to work within the dominant culture, adding a second level to their abilities, and should not aim to change the dominant culture.

☙ IMPLICATIONS FOR PRACTICE

In the past, social service work often was identified with the goal of assimilation for racial and ethnic minorities. Social workers, representing the dominant society, worked to control the aspirations of African Americans, Native Americans, Asians, and Latinos in the United States. But social service work has changed. Today social workers, whether they are members of the majority group or of a minority group, generally support the goal of cultural pluralism. While this is undoubtedly a worthy goal, the meaning of the term in social service work is not clear. In actual practice, the concept often resembles assimilation more than cultural pluralism. Nevertheless, at the attitudinal level, at least, and in their conscious intentions, most social workers accept the ideal of cultural pluralism and the happy endings it promises for minority-majority relations.

Social service workers can get caught up in the unhappy endings, however. When Mexican Americans were deported during the Great Depression, for instance, it was often social service workers who identified those to be returned to Mexico. In the late 1970s, public social service workers in the state of Oregon were instructed to tell their Southeast Asian clients to leave the state, because no welfare funds were available to support them. The questions for social workers are difficult: How do they respond to such injunctions? Do they do what agency and department administrators tell them to do, or do they take a professional stance and advocate against such injustices? Social service workers need to work hard to secure a happy ending for minorities, while they steel themselves against the possibility of not being able to achieve this.

The problems of minority individuals and families should never be divorced from the problems of their communities. Prejudice and discrimination have declined since the early 1960s, both in individual attitudes and informal social norms and in discriminatory practices. But they are still evident in the United States; in fact, there has been evidence of a reversal of the trend to support the principle of nondiscrimination. At the informal institutional level, the persistence of racism is clearly evident in segregated neighborhoods and friendship patterns. At the formal institutional level, the civil rights legislation of the 1960s and early 1970s mandated equal opportunities for all racial and ethnic groups and prohibited discrimination in many areas of social life. But the mechanisms for enforcing provisions of the legislation were weakened in the 1980s and early 1990s by the policies, personnel appointments, and regulatory decisions of the Ronald Reagan and George Bush administrations.

Social service workers, therefore, must continue to be concerned with prejudice and discrimination. Direct-service social workers must become adept at assessing the ways that prejudice and discrimination continue to hinder the progress of their clients. To avoid blaming the victim, they must understand that the context of the social environment can have a negative influence on individuals and families. They must also, through advocacy and the development of social policies and programs, work to change the social context in which their clients are involved.

Change in the social context is likely to go hand in hand with change in individuals and families. To the extent that ethnic minorities have internalized values and attitudes which make social economic success less likely for them, social workers must strive to alter these values and attitudes. In these efforts the use of models, mediators, and translators, as de Anda suggests, can be of value. So can the use of corrective feedback and the teaching of problem-solving skills. But in the process of helping minorities achieve, social service workers must continue to evaluate the goals of the larger society from a critical perspective.

∽ DISCUSSION QUESTIONS AND CLASS PROJECTS

1. Define prejudice and discrimination. Do the two necessarily go together?

2. How would you define racism? Does the United States still have a racist society? What reasons can you give for your opinion?

3. Interview representative individuals from an ethnic-minority group in your area. Determine if they believe that prejudice and discrimination limit the achievement of their group members. Ask them if they have ever been discriminated against.

4. What do you see as the problems of implementing the principle of nondiscrimination? Is someone who doesn't believe in such things as court orders to achieve integrated schools, affirmative action, or bilingual education programs racist?

5. Do you think social workers who work face to face with individuals and families should concern themselves about the possibility of discrimination? How should they try to deter-

mine if discrimination affects the lives of their clients?

6. Interview professional social workers to determine how they attempt to assess discrimination and intervene to resolve it when working with ethnic- and racial-minority individuals and families.

7. Describe the debate regarding intelligence testing. Would you say you are a hereditarian or an environmentalist on this issue? Do you favor such testing, or are you against it?

8. Do you think the attitudes and values of a community have anything to do with the social and economic success of their members? What kinds of values, attitudes, and community norms have been said to favor success or to limit achievement?

9. Make a list of the attitudes and values you believe are important for social and economic success. Try to determine the extent to which they are present in an ethnic-minority

population in your area by interviewing representative individuals from that community.

10. Define the following concepts:

symbolic racism
institutional racism

principle of nondiscrimination
culture of poverty
underclass
the dual perspective
bicultural socialization

∞ NOTES

1. John B. McConahay and Joseph C. Hough, Jr., "Symbolic Racism," *Journal of Social Issues*, vol. 32 (Spring 1976), pp. 23–45.

2. Quoted in James W. Vander Zanden, *American Minority Relations*, 4th ed. (New York: Alfred A. Knopf, 1983), p. 68.

3. Ibid., p. 68; italics in original.

4. David M. Heer, "Intermarriage," in S. Thernstrom (editor), *Harvard Encyclopedia of American Ethnic Groups* (Cambridge, M.A.: Belknap Press, 1980), p. 514.

5. William Julius Wilson, *The Declining Significance of Race* (Chicago: University of Chicago Press, 1980).

6. Ronald Walters, "Race, Resources, Conflict," *Social Work*, vol. 27 (January 1982), pp. 24–31.

7. William M. Newman, *American Pluralism: A Study of Minority Groups and Social Theory* (New York: Harper & Row, 1973), pp. 196–99.

8. Ibid., pp. 199–201.

9. Melvin L. DeFleur and Frank R. Westie, "Verbal Attitudes and Overt Acts: An Experiment on the Salience of Attitudes," *American Sociological Review*, vol. 23 (December 1958), pp. 667–73.

10. Robert K. Merton, "Discrimination and the American Creed," in R. MacIver (editor), *Discrimination and National Welfare* (New York: Harper & Row, 1949), pp. 99–126.

11. Howard Schuman, Charlotte Steeh, and Lawrence Bobo, *Racial Attitudes in America: Trends and Interpretations* (Cambridge, MA: Harvard University Press, 1986).

12. Survey cited in Richard T. Schaefer, *Racial and Ethnic Groups* (Boston, MA: Little, Brown, 1979), p. 67.

13. Emory S. Bogardus, "Comparing Racial Distance in Ethiopia, South Africa, and the United States," *Sociology and Social Research*, vol. 52 (January 1968), pp. 149–56, and Bogardus, *A Forty-Year Racial Distance Study* (Los Angeles: University of Southern California, 1967).

14. Schuman, Steeh, and Bobo, *Racial Attitudes in America*, p. 195.

15. Ibid., p. 194.

16. Ibid., p. 203.

17. Ibid., p. 195.

18. Thomas Byrne Edsall with Mary Edsall, "Race," *The Atlantic Monthly*, May 1991, p. 69.

19. Peter Applebome, "Still a Dream 25 Years after King's Assassination," *The New York Times*, April 4, 1993, p. 16L.

20. Ibid.

21. Edsall with Edsall, "Race," p. 54.

22. Lyle G. Warner and Melvin L. DeFleur, "Attitude as an Interactional Concept: Social Constraint and Social Distance as Intervening Variables between Attitudes and Action," *American Sociological Review*, vol. 34 (April 1969), pp. 153–69.

23. Schuman, Steeh, and Bobo, *Racial Attitudes in America*, pp. 86–162.

24. Gerhard Lenski and Jean Lenski, *Human Societies*, 4th ed. (New York: McGraw-Hill, 1982), p. 54.

25. Hans H. Gerth and C. Wright Mills, *Character and Social Structure: The Psychology of Social Institutions* (New York: Harbinger Books, 1964), p. 23.

26. Louis Knowles and Kenneth Prewitt, *Institutional Racism in America* (Englewood Cliffs, NJ: Prentice-Hall, 1969), p. 5.

27. Richard M. Burkey, *Ethnic and Racial Groups: The Dynamics of Dominance* (Menlo Park, CA: Cummings, 1978), p. 81.

28. Emory S. Bogardus, *Social Distance* (Yellow Springs, OH: Antioch Press, 1959).

29. See Vander Zanden, *American Minority Relations*, pp. 96–97.

30. Harry H. L. Kitano, "Passive Discrimination: The Normal Person," *Journal of Social Psychology*, vol. 70 (October 1966), pp. 23–31.

31. William Julius Wilson, "The Declining Significance of Race," in N. R. Yetman with C. H. Steele, *Minority and Majority*, 3rd ed. (Boston, MA: Allyn and Bacon, 1982), p. 385.

32. Ibid., p. 390.

33. See Kenneth B. Clark and John Hope Franklin, *A Policy Framework for Racial Justice* (Washington, DC: Joint Center for Political Studies, 1983), pp. 9–13.

34. W. Julius Wilson, "Cycles of Deprivation

and the Underclass Debate," *Social Service Review*, vol. 59 (December 1985), p. 550.

35. Charles V. Willie, "The Inclining Significance of Race," in Yetman and Steele, *Minority and Majority*, pp. 393–94.

36. Ibid., p. 398.

37. Mark S. Granovetter, "The Strength of Weak Ties," *American Journal of Sociology*, vol. 78 (May 1973), pp. 1360–80.

38. Hans J. Eysenck vs. Leon Kamin, *The Intelligence Controversy* (New York: John Wiley and Sons, 1981), pp. 90–95.

39. Ibid., pp. 77–79. Also see Michael Banton and Jonathan Harwood, *The Race Concept* (New York: Frederick A. Praeger, 1975), pp. 91–115.

40. Arthur R. Jensen, "How Much Can We Boost IQ and Scholastic Achievement?" *Harvard Educational Review*, vol. 39 (Winter 1969), pp. 1–123.

41. Eysenck vs. Kamin, *Intelligence Controversy*, pp. 1–90, 157–72.

42. Banton and Harwood, *Race Concept*, p. 96.

43. Cecil R. Reynolds and Arthur R. Jensen, "Wisc-R Subscale Patterns of Abilities of Black and Whites Matched on Full Scale IQ," *Journal of Educational Psychology*, vol. 75 (April 1983), pp. 207–14.

44. Arthur Jensen, *Bias in Mental Testing* (New York: Free Press, 1980).

45. See Banton and Harwood, *Race Concept*, pp. 105–15.

46. Irwin Katz, "The Socialization of Academic Motivation in Minority Group Children," in D. Levine (editor), *Nebraska Symposium on Motivation* (Lincoln: University of Nebraska, 1967), pp. 133–91.

47. Carl Milofsky, "Intelligence Testing and Race in the Public Schools," paper presented at the American Sociological Association meeting, Detroit, Michigan, August–September 1983.

48. Eysenck vs. Kamin, *Intelligence Controversy*, pp. 98–105.

49. Ibid., pp. 114–25.

50. Oscar Lewis, "The Culture of Poverty," in M. Pilisuk and P. Pilisuk (editors), *Poor Americans: How the White Poor Live* (New Brunswick, NJ: Transaction Books, 1971), pp. 20–26.

51. See Oscar Lewis, *The Children of Sanchez* (New York: Random House, 1961); *Five Families* (New York: Science Editions, 1962); *La Vida* (New York: Vintage Division of Random House, 1968).

52. Lewis, "The Culture of Poverty," in *La Vida*, pp. xlii–xliii.

53. Ibid., pp. xlv–xlviii.

54. Ken Auletta, *The Underclass* (New York: Random House, 1982). For an excellent critique of the concept of the underclass, see Michael W. Sherraden, "Working over the 'Underclass,'" *Social Work*, vol. 29 (July–August 1984), pp. 391–92.

55. Charles Murray, "White Welfare, White Families, White Trash," *National Review*, vol. 38 (March 25, 1986), pp. 30–34.

56. Thomas Sowell, *Race and Economics* (New York: David McKay, 1975).

57. Ibid., p. 143.

58. Ibid., p. 142.

59. Ibid., p. 144.

60. Harry H. L. Kitano, "Japanese," in *Harvard Encyclopedia of American Ethnic Groups*, pp. 561–71.

61. Margaret Carlson, "Only English Spoken Here," *Time*, December 5, 1988, p. 29.

62. Newman, *American Pluralism*, pp. 67–68.

63. For an interesting book on the transition from post–Civil War Reconstruction to segregation, see C. Vann Woodward, *The Strange Career of Jim Crow*, 2nd ed. (New York: Oxford University Press, 1966).

64. Burkey, *Ethnic and Racial Groups*.

65. See the discussion on Garvey in Burkey, *Ethnic and Racial Groups*, pp. 270–71. For a discussion on Tijernia, see F. Christ Garcia and Rudolp O. de la Garza, *The Chicano Political Experience: Three Perspectives* (North Scituate, MA: Duxbury, 1977), pp. 128, 155, 158.

66. For insights into the various positions on Puerto Rican Independence see Manuel Maldonado-Denis, *Puerto Rico: A Socio-Historical Interpretation* (New York: Vintage Books, 1972); Adalberto Lopez and James Petras (editors), *Puerto Rico and Puerto Ricans* (New York: John Wiley and Sons, 1974).

67. Dolores Norton, with Eddie Frank Brown, Edwin Garth Brown, E. Arecelis Francis, Kenji Murase, and Ramon Valle, *The Dual Perspective: Inclusion of Ethnic Minority Content in the Social Work Curriculum* (New York: Council on Social Work Education, 1978), p. 3.

68. Ibid.

69. Leon Chestang, "Environmental Influences on Social Functioning: The Black Experience," in P. Cafferty and L. Chestang (editors), *The Diverse Society: Implications for Social Policy* (Washington, DC: National Association of Social Workers, 1976), pp. 59–74.

70. Salvador Alvarez, "Mexican American Community Organizations," in O. Romano, V (editor), *Voices: Readings from El Grito* (Berkeley, CA: Quinto Sol, 1971), pp. 91–100.

71. Melvin Delgado and Denise Humm-Delgado, "Natural Support Systems: Source of Strength in Hispanic Communities," *Social Work*, vol. 27 (January 1982), p. 83.

72. Diane de Anda, "Bicultural Socialization: Factors Affecting the Minority Experience," *Social Work*, vol. 29 (March–April 1984), pp. 101–07.

73. Ibid., p. 104.

PART THREE

Family Life

CHAPTER 8

The Family as a Social Institution

MAJOR THEMES DISCUSSED IN THIS CHAPTER

1. **THE FAMILY AS AN INSTITUTION: AN ANTISEXIST APPROACH.** Study of the family as a social institution involves examining what society believes is the good and correct way to create and maintain family life. In looking at the family we examine trends and definitions and reflect on the traditions behind the organization of American families. The position we take in studying the family stems from antisexist and feminist values.

2. **FUNCTIONS OF THE FAMILY.** The family is the primary institution for the procreation and socialization of children, a means for providing affection and emotional stability, and a vehicle for economic production and consumption. It also has latent functions, such as sustaining racism and sexism.

3. **VARIATIONS IN THE STRUCTURE OF FAMILY LIFE.** Family life is taking on a number of forms in contemporary society. Serial monogamy is increasing; the married-couple, two-parent family form is declining as single-parent families and stepfamilies increase. Also increasing are cohabitation among unmarried heterosexual and gay and lesbian couples and single people living alone or sharing households in nonsexual relationships.

4. **FAMILY POLITICS IN AMERICAN SOCIETY.** Family politics—the struggle for equality among family members—is producing changes in the family as an institution. The present positions of women, children, and the elderly reflect improvements in the traditional patriarchal society, but they are still disadvantaged in some respects.

5. **CHANGES IN ROLE EXPECTATIONS.** Expectations for the various roles in the family began to change from those of the traditional male-dominated family with the industrialization of Western societies. Gender-role and parent-child relations are becoming increasingly egalitarian and democratic. The classical extended-kin family is now rare, but relationships with the elderly are being maintained by adult children.

6. **IMPLICATIONS FOR PRACTICE.** The perception that the family is breaking down, which suggests that the institution is a fixed, closed system, forces social service workers to try to maintain the past. But problems in the traditional family have generated a need for change, and intervention in the lives of families can help reshape the American family as an institution.

THE STATE OF THE AMERICAN FAMILY, which has become a social and political issue, is also a major factor in the critical perspective. Most people live out their lives within the family, and it is perhaps the most important human system in terms of individual change and development. There is ample evidence that family forms and functions are changing, but whether these changes are contributing to the breakdown of the institution of the American family or are merely evidence of ongoing modifications in family life is open to question.

☙ THE FAMILY: AN INSTITUTION OR AN ORGANIZATION

At the heart of the controversy over changing family structures and functions are the competing goals of preserving the institution of the family or enhancing the well-being of family members. The ideal form of the American family has been changing from the traditional family, in which the roles of husband and wife are clearly separate and the husband monopolizes power and makes the major family decisions, to a more egalitarian, democratic family in which husband and wife work together to meet the family's needs, make the decisions, and care for the children. In the new concept of the American family, each member's desire for self-identity and equality, even the children's, is taken into account.

This challenge to the traditional family form can be considered by viewing the family as both a social institution and an organization (see "The Family as Social Institution and Organization"). As an institution, the family is concerned with societal ideals and contradictions and involves public issues. As a social organization it is concerned with how these ideals and contradictions are handled in the family and involves private troubles. Together, however, the family as an institution and an organization forms a single entity in which the private troubles of family life are intrinsically related to the public issues concerning public life. Institutional norms—especially the contradictions found in them, the debates over them, and the obstacles to either changing or achieving them—create the problems that lead family members, voluntarily or involuntarily, to seek out social services. Moreover, the family members' perceptions of the ways their lives are organized may not seem to fit their image of what family life ought to be. In working with clients on the organization of their everyday lives in families, therefore, social service workers must take into account the opposing forces of social control and innovation, and the ways they handle the helping situation can affect the maintenance or change of existing institutions.

In this chapter we look at the family as an institution; in the remaining chapters in Part Three it is considered more as an organization. Chapter 8 discusses variations in the characteristics of family life in communities differentiated by social class or race and ethnicity, as well as the family lifestyles developed in the gay and lesbian community. Chapters 9 and 10 identify and analyze well-being in the family as a social organization.

☙ THE FAMILY AS AN INSTITUTION: AN ANTISEXIST APPROACH

The study of social institutions focuses on the ways people endow collective behavior with value and authority: value in the sense that certain behaviors are seen as preferred, and authority in the sense that failure to conform provokes sanctions and other forms of

The Family as Social Institution and Organization

The public issues concerning family life, as expressed in the ideals and contradictions of the family as a social institution, cannot be separated from the private troubles of family life which derive from the handling of these ideals and contradictions within the family. Together they form a single entity.

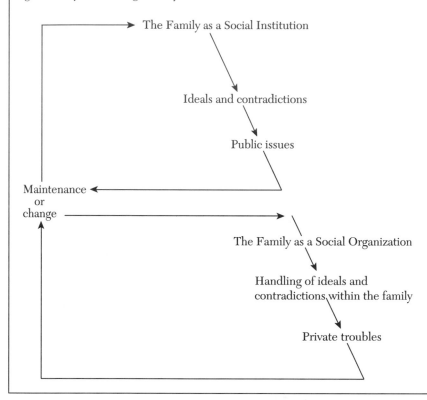

The Family as a Social Institution

Ideals and contradictions

Public issues

Maintenance or change

The Family as a Social Organization

Handling of ideals and contradictions within the family

Private troubles

social control. Social institutions are often formalized in laws and regulations, but just as often they are distilled into the unwritten but binding traditions of a society. Study of the family as a social institution, therefore, examines what members of a society believe to be good and correct ways of creating and maintaining family life. It looks at the traditions underlying family life and the societal expectations that guide the formation of families and the assumption of family roles, and it examines how these preferred ways change over time.

It is difficult to maintain objectivity in studying the family. Family roles and relationships are very intense and shape our emotions and thoughts in basic ways. Our individual and collective positions in the public debate on the family also make it difficult to be objective. Is a family ideally a mother and a father with two little children living in a private house in the suburbs? Can a family be an unmarried heterosexual couple with no desire to have children, or a lesbian couple rearing a child? Is the only proper goal of sexual relations to procreate, or is giving and receiving sensual pleasure an acceptable goal in itself? Is abortion the murder of innocent babies or the right of women to control their own bodies? Should mothers of young children work outside the home? Should fathers willingly do housework and care for the children? Should divorce be avoided at all costs?

These are examples of the intense public debates surrounding family life in contemporary society. At the heart of these debates are concerns about the role of women and the function of sexuality in society. A whole range of opinions on these matters can be found, but for simplification, people either favor supporting past traditions concerning women and sexuality, or they favor change. This and the following chapters on the family are not written from a value-neutral position. The theory of caring on which they are based stems from feminist and antisexist values.

Looking at the family from an antisexist point of view does not mean that objectivity must be abandoned, however. As noted in Chapter 4, feminism is not a single phenomenon but includes differing liberal, radical, and socialist ideas. Furthermore, no easy prescriptions for good family life can be found. There are only difficult questions and limited, complex answers. The traditional family in Western society is a sexist institution because it subordinates the interests of women to those of men. It is also sexist in that social mores, or moral attitudes, restrain sexuality to the procreative function, thus condemning both heterosexual and homosexual sex for pleasure. As issues are raised about definitions of the family, family functions, family lifestyles, family problems, and theories about the family, we will strive for objectivity. Nevertheless, we will be concerned with encouraging social service workers to think critically about family life and from an antisexist viewpoint.

Trends in Family Life

In considering how the American family is changing, the starting point is the traditional family, a form which has developed over time on the basis of a number of assumptions. It is assumed that the family is a heterosexual institution, with prescriptions about how a man and a women ought to be joined together and live together. The proper family form is assumed to be the nuclear family, that is, a family composed of a married man and woman and their children. It is assumed that the husband is the head of the family, with ultimate authority over wife and children, and that in their clearly separated roles the husband is the income-earner and the wife is the homemaker and provider of child care. It is also assumed that the family lives by itself in its own house or residence.

There are data, such as those supplied by the U.S. Bureau of the Census, to document the changes taking place in this traditional American family form. While the interpretation of these data as indicators of social trends varies, certain changes have been identified as taking place in contemporary American society. Andrew Cherlin, a sociologist who is a noted authority on marriage and divorce, has identified the following trends:

1. More men and women are living together before getting married.

2. First marriages are taking place at a later age.

3. Married couples are having fewer children.

4. The number of births to unmarried women is increasing.

5. Wives, even mothers of small children, are increasingly employed in the labor force.

6. More marriages are ending with divorce.

7. Single-parent families are more prevalent.

8. Remarriage is likely to follow divorce rather than widowhood.

9. Remarriage rates are declining, especially for women.[1]

Some of these trends are clearer than others. Data on family life in the United States have been kept for about a century. "Good" data have been kept for a much shorter time, and much of the available data are very primitive. For instance, there can be no reliable data on the incidence of cohabitation, that is, the number of unmarried men and women living together in a sexual liaison. Similarly, there is insufficient data on out-of-wedlock births and the work experiences of mothers. For the most part, it can only be said that in general and in the recent past (say since the 1950s), the prevalence of cohabitation, out-of-wedlock births, and working mothers has increased.

Some trends, viewed in a long-range historical context, appear not to be trends at all. The age at which men and women normally marry is the same now as it was 100 years ago, though it has fluctuated; a short-range increase in the 1940s and 1950s due to widespread postponement of marriage in wartime made it appear that a change had occurred. Other trends appear to be following established patterns rather than representing a sharp break with tradition. Divorce rates have been increasing and families have been having fewer children for well over a century. Single-parent families and stepfamilies were very common in the past, although the reason for them was different. Many marriages formerly were dissolved and followed by remarriage because of the death of a parent or partner. Today single parenthood and remarriage are more likely to be a response to divorce.

Some social scientists see in these changes the breakdown of the family, to the detriment of the society. We take the position that family institutions and systems, like all human systems, are open, take many forms, and are constantly changing. In considering the family as an institution, therefore, we will describe the forms the family has taken and the ways it appears to be changing. As Harold Robbow and Candace Clark point out, "even as institutional changes [in patterns of family organization] take place, they do not represent radical departures from the previous values and norms, but rather adaptations that preserve a great deal from the past."[2]

Defining Family Life

The concept of the family is difficult to define. Part of the difficulty is that in everyday language, the term *family* is used to describe a number of relationships. These range from the biological, nuclear family of mother, father, and child and siblings; to the more extended family which includes several generations of blood relatives or relatives through marriage; to close and intimate friends; even to humankind, or the "family of man." As popularly used, *family* has connotations about the quality or nature of the relationship: meaningful sexual relationships, loving parent-child relationships, permanent or long-lasting relationships, intimate relationships, faithful and loyal relationships. The term is also used to apply to the activities, tasks, or functions of the family: procreative activities, socializing activities, nursing and protective activities, materially helpful activities, or consumption activities.

Formal Definitions

The wide variation in everyday usage is less apparent in formal definitions, but even here there is a lack of consensus. Formal definitions do not always fit generally recognized definitions. The U.S. Bureau of the Census, which collects information used by social scientists, defines **family** as "a group of two or more persons related by blood, marriage, or adoption and residing together in a household." The bureau defines a **household** as comprised of "all persons who occupy a 'housing unit,' that is, a house, an apartment, or other group of rooms, or a single room that constitutes 'separate living quarters.'"[3] These definitions consider the family in terms of only its structure and legal status, not the qualities of the relationship or its functions or activities. The Census Bureau thus would accept as a family two legally related people who hated each other and were just living together for their mutual economic advantage. Their definition also includes sexual and nonsexual relations; married women and men living together in sexual unions are families, but so are brothers and sisters living together in nonsexual unions. In terms of family structure, the Census Bureau definition is quite inclusive. Nevertheless, it considers cohabitating unmarried couples as households, not families, though a parent-child dyad in such a household would be considered a family. Any others in the household are referred to as *unrelated individuals*.

Anthropologists and sociologists have offered quite different definitions. George Murdock's is perhaps the most commonly quoted. After examining descriptions of 250 representative societies, he concludes that "the family is a social group characterized by common residence, economic cooperation, and reproduction. It includes adults of both sexes, at least two of whom maintain a socially approved sexual relationship, and one or more children, own or adopted, of the sexually cohabiting adults."[4] This definition excludes all nonsexual relationships and all sexual relationships without the intention of procreation and child rearing. It would also appear to exclude those that allow for the rearing of children but not reproduction, such as a grandmother taking responsibility for the care of a daughter's child.

In Murdock's definition, study of the family would be limited to procreative, heterosexual marriages. But family life persists throughout the entire life cycle, not just the period in which husbands and wives are having and caring for children. Recognizing this, social scientists often distinguish between the family of origin and the family of procreation. Most of us are simultaneously members of two families: the **family of origin**, into which we are born and of which we are always considered a member, even if we leave it, and the **family of procreation**, which we join as adults for the purposes of procreation and rearing children.[5] Some social scientists also distinguish marriage from family and see the two as independent of one another. They argue that the family can exist regardless of whether the couple are married. Christopher Harris sees marriage as a public ceremony which joins together two kinship groups and in so doing lays out some important rights over children, domestic authority, and sexual matters.[6] Marriage is also the ritual through which children are made legitimate in the eyes of the parents and the society. Marriage therefore is a social ceremony, whereas family need not be.

Alternative Explanations

In terms of family functions, most social scientists, like Murdock, consider the family as a means of procreation and socialization of children, as well as the development of interpersonal ties in carrying out these functions. Some definitions, however, would extend the use of the term *family* to social groups and activities that involve neither procreation nor socialization. In this direction, Ann Hartman and Joan Laird say that a family is created "when two or more people construct an intimate environment that they define as a family, an environment in which they generally will share a living space, commitment, and a variety of the roles and functions usually considered part of family life." Their definition implies that any two or more people can call themselves family as long as they are acting like family members. It is interesting because it measures the quality rather than the structure of the relationship, and it has deliberate, progressive social policy implications. Hartman and Laird believe family practice should be based on an "inclusive, self-determining, or phenomenological definition of the family."[7]

Karen Lindsey also explicitly includes other relationships in the family. In *Friends as Family*, she argues that ultimate choice should prevail in family development and processes. The concept of family should apply to "people who have shared history, who have loved each other and lived through major parts of each other's lives together." She notes that "friends, neighbors, co-workers have often lived through as many experiences together as husbands and wives—have created, perhaps unconsciously, equally strong bonds."[8] To Lindsey, the idea of family embodies not sexual relationships or even kin relationships, but strong emotional attachments.

Rayna Rapp follows the U.S. Census Bureau definitions in making a distinction between family and household. *Family* implies only a procreation and socialization function and suggests a separation of family from the rest of society, in particular from economic institutions. *Household*, in addition to often being a procreative unit, is also an economic unit, since it is through households—the people we live with—that money and other goods and resources are transferred into and out of the economy through consumption. Family and household are connected in social norms that stress the proper way for households to be set up is through nuclear families and that consider other kinds of households to be variations or deviant. Rapp suggests abandoning the concept of family and substituting the concept of household.[9]

The majority of social scientists and other observers accept the definition of the family as a socially approved, heterosexually oriented grouping of a male, a female, and their children through which the biologically based activities of procreation and socialization take place (in the family of procreation) and the lifelong bonds or kin relations initiated by these activities are nurtured (in the family of origin). Nevertheless, there is significant support for a rationale in which the family is seen as relationships that are not restricted to heterosexuality, marriage, procreation, socialization, and kinship activities.

The Nuclear Family and Other Institutionalized Forms

Some sort of family life exists in all societies. Anthropologists have uncovered three major types of families which have been institutionalized in societies: the nuclear family, the extended-kin family, and the plural marriage or family. The **nuclear family** has been defined as "two adults of opposite sex, living together in a socially approved sexual relationship, and their own or adopted children."[10] In this form and the extended-kin family, marriage is **monogamous**; that is, to only one person at a time. In the **extended-kin family**, the parent-child relationship is broadened to include several generations. The key characteristic of the extended family, according to Harris, is that "adult children continue to be members of, and subject to the authority of, the group in which they were born."[11] The head of the family is always the oldest parent figure. In a **plural marriage**, the husband-wife relationship is extended to include multiple spouses living together. Plural marriages may either be **polygamous**, one husband with multiple wives, or **polyandrous**, one wife with multiple husbands. The polygamous form is far more common.

Although the nuclear family has been institutionalized in Western, industrial societies, it is not the most common type of family. In examining 192 societies for which there was documentation, Murdock found that the extended-kin and plural-marriage family types

In this idealized image of the traditional family, father the breadwinner kisses mother the homemaker (complete with apron) good-bye as he leaves their suburban home for a hard day's work at the office, and the happy child keeps her place in the background.

were more common, especially among preindustrial societies, but he regards extended-kin families and plural marriages as mere offshoots of the nuclear family.[12]

In analyzing the idea of the nuclear family as a universal form, social scientists have found, for instance, that the concept of a nuclear family is not found in every society. Indeed, as Clyde Kluckholm notes, the vocabularies of some nonliterate people do not include words that correspond with a procreative or biological family unit.[13] In preindustrial societies, *family* denoted only households, lineage, and kinship.[14] Harris concludes that usage of the term *nuclear family* and the patterns of behavior to which it refers are distinctive aspects of Western, industrialized societies. The term cannot be applied to other cultures without further definition.[15]

The most substantial evidence for the universality of the nuclear family comes from Western anthropologists who have identified it in other societies, even though the term, or its equivalent, is never used by their people. Murdock, for instance, argues that he could identify a nuclear unit in all societies regardless of how the people in those societies thought about themselves. Following the same line, Norman Bell and Ezra Vogel conclude that

> ...if the nuclear family is a unit found in all societies, it is a stable point of reference for systematic analysis. Despite arguments to the contrary we maintain [it] is such a universal unit.

The nuclear family may not be the normal household unit…*but we contend that it is always identifiable as a unit.*[16]

Murdock's assertion that the nuclear unit of mother, father, and child is the atom around which all forms of family life take shape has also been reevaluated. In considering the question "Is the family universal?" Kathleen Gough studied the history of the Nayars, a primitive tribe in southern India. There was no concept of biological fatherhood in this culture. A Nayar woman might have as many as eight husbands, none of whom lived with her. The husband visited a wife after supper and left before breakfast the next morning, and he had no responsibility for maintaining the wife or their children. This responsibility fell to the mother's male kin or relatives. Nayar children used the term *lord* or *leader* to refer to all their mother's lovers, without any connotation of paternity. In this culture, family was defined as "a relationship established between a woman and one or more other persons, which provides that a child born to the woman under circumstances not prohibited by the rules of the relationship, is accorded full birth status rights common to normal members of his society or social stratum."[17]

Harris concludes from such findings that the nuclear family unit is not the basis of family life. He emphasizes that the nuclear family unit is mother and children, not mother, father, and child, as Murdock proposes. Indeed, the atoms around which family life is organized may very well be mother and child.[18]

∞ FUNCTIONS OF THE FAMILY

The family, like other evolving social institutions, is undergoing increased specialization. It has been relieved of the need to fulfill many arduous, basic functions, those that were "calculated to ensure the survival of members of the group, to secure their existence and to counter the threats of nature."[19] Families in the past were responsible for religion, government, raising armies and fighting wars, and providing basic medical care. They had to produce their own food, shelter, and materials for earning a living. Families today do not perform these functions in the same way or to the same degree that they did in the past. By the early twentieth century, at least six of the functions served by the American family in preindustrial times had been lost or had undergone significant change: the economic, protective, religious, recreational, educational, and status-conferring functions.[20] The contemporary American family serves a narrower range of functions, some that are manifest and some that are latent.

As we have shown, most definitions of the family explicitly include two *manifest functions*, or readily perceived activities: procreation and the socialization of children. The family is still the major institution through which procreative sexual behavior is organized and children are reared, especially in their early years. In contemporary society, day care and schools are agents of socialization, but the family continues to have the major responsibility for child rearing. In addition, the family has manifest productive, consumptive, and affective functions.

In most discussions of family, the emphasis is on those manifest functions that are believed to foster family system maintenance and adaptation to the environment. In this regard, discussions of socialization usually center on the ways that societal values such as individuality, achievement and hard work, and the ability to delay gratification are passed on from one generation to the next. But socialization also can perform certain *latent functions*, which are unintended, often unrecognized, and can have negative consequences.[21]

Latent Functions

Through the socialization of children and the ways in which the cognitions, emotions, and behaviors of family members, both adults and children, are controlled, the family contributes to institutional arrangements such as racism and sexism. The latent functions of the contemporary family can act to promote and sustain such attitudes in a society.

The Family and Ethnocentrism and Racism

Children are not born with prejudicial attitudes, and they do not automatically discriminate among racial and ethnic groups. Racism becomes institutionalized within a society when the social mores support status, power, and privilege differences along racial and ethnic lines. The antagonisms thus created can be supported only to the extent that they exert influence over how families are formed and children are socialized.

A number of authors have studied the ways by which the young are socialized into taking on the prejudicial attitudes of their families and communities. Mary Ellen Goodman describes a three-step process. First there is simple awareness; children learn that people differ according to color. Then an incipient racial orientation develops, and negative feelings are attached to color differences. The final stage is the development of full-fledged negative attitudes.[22] Phyllis Katz has developed an eight-stage model which, like Goodman's, begins with learning to distinguish racial cues and culminates with the crystallization of prejudicial attitudes. In between these two end points, she postulates a series of cognitive and perceptual elaborations aimed at showing how such attitudes are learned.[23]

Harry Kitano has shown that in the course of socialization, children normally learn the prejudices and discriminatory tendencies of their parents. This study is particularly interesting because it focuses on the Japanese community, which has itself been subjected to harsh prejudice and discrimination in the United States. Thus it demonstrates that regardless of a family's ethnic status, its children may be taught prejudice against other groups.[24]

The Family and Sexism

Socialization techniques have a lot to do with the ways in which gender-role status, privilege, and power are distributed in a society. Adults bring with them into the parent role societal expectations about appropriate behaviors for girls and boys. From the birth of their children, parents attribute to them the stereotypes associated with traditional masculine and feminine roles.[25] John Scanzoni points out that many studies have demonstrated how, from their earliest years, "males in our society are socialized to adopt aggressive, active, forceful behaviors. Females, conversely, are socialized to accept passivity, conformity, and 'goodness of conduct.'"[26]

Parents still generally treat girls and boys differently throughout childhood, though to varying degrees they may adopt gender-free standards. Adults engage in roughhouse play with boys and provide them with toys, sports equipment, and clothing considered appropriate to the masculine role; they tell them "Big boys don't cry" and discourage them from showing their emotions. Girls imitate their mothers in play and may request toys and clothing appropriate to the feminine role. Teaching the feminine role may not be apparent to either the parent or the child, however. In a study of children and mothers, Robert Sears found that the mothers reacted very differently to acts of aggression by girls than to such acts by boys. Girls were much more restricted in showing aggressive behavior toward neighborhood children or parents. They were not encouraged to fight back, though boys were expected to do so. Mothers usually disciplined the girls, using withdrawal of love, a psychological punishment. Boys were more likely to receive physical punishments, administered by their fathers.[27]

By the age of five boys and girls have become acquainted with the gender roles expected of them, and they project the same expectations on infants. In one study, kindergarten children were allowed to play with a four-month-old baby. Some saw the baby dressed as a boy and were told the baby's name was John. Others saw the baby dressed as a girl and were told the name was Laura. When the children were asked to describe the baby after playing with it, those who had played with John described the baby as big and tough, while those who had played with Laura described the same baby as little and gentle.[28]

Manifest Functions

The manifest functions of the family, in addition to the recognized ones of procreation and socialization, include production, consumption, and emotional support. The family's affective function is of special importance for the social service worker, for it is in the family setting that "the individual can freely express personality needs and expect to receive understanding, consideration, and love."[29]

The Family as Producer and Consumer

Families today no longer are required to produce the goods necessary to sustain their members; generally, they do not grow their food, build their houses, make their furniture, sew their clothes, or fashion their means of transportation. But the family is still a unit of economic production; it may not be a goods-producing unit, but it is certainly a service-producing unit. Ruth Schwartz Cowan demonstrates that the family, particularly the woman in the family, has in fact been assuming productive functions related to transportation and water, gas, electricity, and other utilities.[30] She notes that technology, instead of making household production chores easier, has made many of them more difficult. Merchants used to bring products to the home. Milk was delivered to the doorstep each morning; the Fuller brush man and other peddlers made their rounds; Sears Roebuck and Montgomery Ward made household products available through catalogs and mail orders; and purchases made at local stores were delivered. Public transportation proliferated with bus, train, and trolley systems. Today, the wife is both the shopper and provider of transportation. She is engaged in the production of services which are time-consuming, and she provides them free of charge.

As a unit of consumption for the goods and services created in the economy, the family or household is the organization through which the food, housing, furniture, clothes, and automobiles necessary for preparation in society are purchased. Members must seek employment outside the home to earn wages so they can purchase the necessities of life. Thus the economy depends on the family to consume, and the family depends on the economy to produce.

As part of its consumptive functions, the family also has cultural functions. It has assumed responsibility for many activities through which members participate in the community and fill their leisure time.[31]

Emotional Climate in the Working-Class Family: From Peasants to Middle Class

To demonstrate how the emotional climate of families changed with the rise of capitalism and industrialization, Mark Poster compares peasant farmers of feudal Europe with American lower-class families at the turn of the century and into the 1950s. By extension his work can be used to understand both the affective function of the traditional middle-class family and the challenges to it that are being met in the more egalitarian family at the end of the twentieth century.

Feudal Peasant Families

Most peasant families of feudal times lived in villages, the all-important social unit around which family life was structured. Kin and friends lived close by and households intruded on one another. Village norms and traditions were to be upheld, and the village held authority over families. Marriage took place through collective forms of courtship; the village had a strong role in mate selection.

Men and women had separate functions, with women generally subordinate. However, social authority was not vested in men, and women's work was vital to the survival of the family and the village. The attachments of married couples came less from love than from trying to sustain the household in a difficult agricultural economy.

Children were needed for economic survival; a basic indifference to them was in part due to their high mortality rate. Infants were swaddled and fed by the mother but were often undernourished. Older children often were sent away from home to be apprenticed in a trade. The responsibility for rearing children was vested in the village, and failure to heed its will could lead to severe punishments and sanctions. As in the aristocratic family, children had a low sense of personal identity and an extremely high sense of social hierarchy and social order. Poster concludes:

> The child was not trained to defer its gratifications, to accustom itself to a clocklike

schedule of rewards, to face the world alone and be prepared to make autonomous decisions, to regulate emotional energy for a competitive struggle against others. Life for peasants had a fixed pattern, governed by innumerable traditions which were not to be questioned by individuals. (p. 188)

Twentieth-Century Working-Class Families

The origin of the lower-middle-class or working-class family was in the peasant family of feudal times. As peasants were recruited into the industrial working class, they tended to hold on to the patterns that had been instilled through village authority. While children in urban neighborhoods often worked, they were reared by the community in the street and by other workers in the factory. Since wives and husbands both had to work outside the home to provide the family income and working-class urban communities were not the self-contained islands of the rural villages, the norms regulating marriage and sexual relations failed to apply. There was considerable sexual promiscuity.

Concern for the perceived immorality of the working class was an impetus for the growth of social welfare policy and services. Middle-class women took on the role of "friendly visitors," who sought to protect and provide for working-class women and children. The charity organization societies helped secure child-labor and compulsory-education laws and family welfare legislation and services, and working-class people came to accept the family and sexual values of the middle class. Changes in the composition of the labor force, the development of skilled labor, and the family wage for the male head of the household also helped change the ideals of working-class family life.

Wives were discouraged from participating in the labor force, and children were

continued

---

continued

---

excluded from it. The mother presided in her private house, devoting her life to her children and to the emotional or sensual needs of her husband. When urban neighborhoods were replaced by the suburbs starting in the 1950s, the identification of the working-class family with middle-class norms was complete.

Source: Mark Poster, *Critical Theory of the Family* (New York: Seabury Press, 1978).

The Family as a Means of Emotional Support

The contemporary family has become a private world in which members are expected to give the emotional support necessary to help members endure the harsh realities of an increasingly impersonal society. In Christopher Lasch's terms, the family is a "haven in a heartless world."[32] The affective function of the family is sometimes seen as its most distinguishing feature. Indeed, most social service practice with families takes the affective function as the point of departure. The focus is on ways to maintain and improve emotional support, nurturance, and bonding among family members.

The idea that family life is the seat of emotional support and deep personal commitment has been firmly established. In distinguishing family life from economic life, for instance, Talcott Parsons maintains that family life is personal and members are accepted for what they are, whereas economic life is impersonal and people are accepted for their talents and abilities.[33] Social historians point out, however, that this distinction between a public, impersonal economic world and a private, personal family world is relatively recent (see "Emotional Climate in the Working-Class Family"). The family of today may be largely concerned with subjectivity and emotional support, but this was not always the case.[34] In upper-middle-class, bourgeois families at the turn of the twentieth century, for instance, romantic love was the motive for marriage, but love and sex, like business, had a symbolic meaning. The threat of withdrawal of love was the dominant means of disciplining children, and they had to trade off satisfaction of their own needs for the affection of their parents.[35]

∞ VARIATIONS IN THE STRUCTURE OF FAMILY LIFE

Along with changing functions, American family life is taking different forms. **Serial monogamy,** or repeated marriages to one person at a time after divorce or widowhood, is increasingly evident. A married-couple, two-parent family may be followed by a single-parent family or stepfamily. Cohabitation among unmarried couples and single people living alone is also more prevalent (see "American Households, 1980–1991").

Two-Parent and Married-Couple Families

The traditional nuclear family form is declining among households in the United States. In 1991, 55 percent of all households were classified as married-couple families by the U.S. Census Bureau, down from 61 percent in 1980. The percentage classified as married-couple families with children under 18 also declined, from 31 percent in 1980 to 26 per-

American Households, 1980–1991

The total number of households in the United States in the period 1980–1991 grew from 80,776,000 to 94,312,000, an increase of 17 percent. All types of households increased with the exception of married-couple families with children under 18, which declined by 2 percent. The highest increase (92 percent) was in the number of male householders with no spouse present and children under 18; nevertheless, this type represented only 1 percent of all households in both 1980 and 1991. The number of female householders with no spouse present and children under 18 increased by 25 percent, but this type represented 7 percent of all households both years. Family households represented 74 percent of all households in 1981 and 70 percent in 1991.

Type of Household and Presence of Children	Percentage Distribution of All Households	
	1980	1991
Family Households	74%	70%
With own children under 18	38	34
Without own children under 18	35	36
Married-Couple family	61	55
With own children under 18	31	26
Without own children under 18	30	29
Male householder, no spouse present	2	3
With own children under 18	1	1
Without own children under 18	1	2
Female householder, no spouse present	11	12
With own children under 18	7	7
Without own children under 18	4	5
Nonfamily Households	26%	30%
Living alone	23	25
Male householder	11	13
Living alone	9	10
Female householder	15	17
Living alone	14	15

Source: U.S. Bureau of the Census, *Statistical Abstract of the United States: 1992*, 112th edition (Washington, DC, 1992), Table 62.

cent in 1991, but this family form still represented 76 percent of all family households with children in 1991.[36] Nevertheless, it has been estimated that the family with a father in the labor force, an at-home mother, and their own or adopted children—the nuclear family—represents only 15 percent of all families in the 1990s.

Perhaps the biggest change among two-parent families is the growing number of mothers in the labor force. Especially among families of limited means, the working mother has been a reality for some time. In certain periods, as during World War II, large numbers of women from all social classes, married and unmarried and with and without children, participated in the labor force necessarily or as a patriotic duty. In the recent past, however, there has been an extraordinary increase in the participation rate of married women in the labor force, going from 30.5 percent in 1960 to 58.5 percent in 1991. The increase is notable among married women with children under age six, going from 18.6 percent in 1960 to 59.9 percent in 1991.[37] The most dramatic increase in labor force participation has been among middle-class, well-educated women who formerly would have dropped out of the labor force during their child-rearing years.[38]

Racial and ethnic differences in the percentage of married mothers who participate in the labor force are narrowing somewhat. In 1975, 44 percent of white married mothers with children under age 18 were working, compared to 58 percent of black married mothers; in 1991, this proportion was 66 percent of whites and 77 percent of blacks.[39] The percentage of Hispanic married mothers working outside the home is lower than that for either whites or blacks.[40]

Changes in the labor force participation rates of married women have necessarily brought changes in the roles taken by men and women in the family. It has been estimated, for instance, that employed men with working wives spend about 2.7 hours more per week on household duties than men with wives at home. This is a small concession, however. According to Philip Blumstein and Pepper Schwartz, who studied thousands of American couples:

> Working wives do less housework than homemakers, but they still do the vast bulk of what needs to be done. Husbands of women who work help out more than husbands of homemakers, but their contribution is not impressive. Even if a husband is unemployed, he does much less housework than a wife who puts in a forty-hour week.[41]

In a study of working parents and the "revolution at home," Arlie Hochschild reported finding a "leisure gap" between men and women in the home that matched the wage gap between them in the workplace. She concluded that "Most women work one shift at the office or factory and a 'second shift' at home."[42] The men and women she interviewed differed about such issues as how right it is for mothers of young children to work a full-time job and how much a father should be responsible for at home. Underneath the statistics, she discovered "a set of deeply emotional issues":

> What should a man and woman contribute to the family? How appreciated does each feel? How does each respond to subtle changes in the balance of marital power? How does each develop an unconscious "gender strategy" for coping with the work at home, with the marriage, and indeed, with life itself?[43]

Working husbands and wives need to redefine their expectations for each other, and this process can be quite painful. People raised in traditional ways do not easily change. Lillian Rubin makes it clear that as women change they may experience enormous guilt and that as men change they may be frustrated and come to think of themselves as less of a man.[44] Even men and women who are sincere about their desire for change are likely to have these feelings. The theoretical and historical backgrounds for changing gender roles in the family is discussed in the next two sections.

The One-Parent Family

The number of one-parent families in the United States went from 3.2 million in 1970 to 8 million in 1991. These family households constituted 25 percent of all families with children under 18 in 1991, and by far the majority were headed by the mother. Only 4 percent of all families were single-parent families headed by the father alone.[45]

Although single-parent families are found in all social classes and in all ethnic groups, the likelihood of living in a single-parent family is greater among blacks and Hispanics than among whites. In 1991, 54 percent of black children and 27 percent of Hispanic children under age 18 were living with their mothers only, compared to 17 percent of white children. Only 4 percent of black children and 3 percent of Hispanic children were living with their fathers only.[46]

There have always been single-parent families, but they are being formed in a different way. In the past, these families usually resulted from the death of a parent; now they are likely to result from divorce or unwed pregnancy (see Chapter 10).

A number of special problems confront single-parent families headed by females, but the major problem is economic survival.[47] Households in which women live alone with their children constitute a major poverty group in the United States; in 1990, 13 percent of family households headed by females with the husband absent had an income of under $5,000, about one-sixth the median money income of all households that year ($29,943).[48] Not only are the incomes women can earn considerably lower than those obtainable by men, but the need to support the family while providing adequate child care presents a dilemma to many single-parent families. A large share of single mothers are employed at least part-time. In 1984, for 69 percent of children between the ages of 6 and 17 and 50 percent of younger children with single mothers, the mothers worked outside the home.[49]

Stepfamilies or Reconstituted Families

Despite the decline in the number of two-parent families and the rise in the number of single-parent families, by far the majority of children in American society are reared by two parents. Increasingly, however, one of the parents is not a biological or adoptive parent but has married into the family.[50] Parent-child and sibling relationships within reconstituted or blended families can be especially difficult, and some children must cope with being simultaneously members of two such families. Andrew Cherlin, who has studied remarriages, notes that the emerging norms governing such relationships

> …seem to be moving in the direction of expanding the concept of the family to include step-relationships and other quasi-kin ties. Indeed, family ties after remarriage often extend across two or three households. The result is that our commonsense equation of "family" with "household" often breaks down. The basic question of what constitutes a family and what its boundaries are becomes less clear.[51]

Cohabiting Couples

Cohabitation, or two unrelated adults of the opposite sex living together outside of marriage, is a comparatively recent development; prior to 1970, the practice was uncommon.[52] According to the National Survey of Family Growth, about 58 million unmarried women 15–44 years old were living with a partner or boyfriend in 1988, and 47 million of them were white. In 1991, the U.S. Census Bureau estimated that just 6 percent of all persons 15 years of age and older (both heterosexuals and homosexuals) were unmarried and living with nonrelatives.[53]

While cohabitation is not a major pattern among American households, its increase since the 1970s has been dramatic, according to Blumstein and Schwartz, who included cohabiting couples in the samples for their study of American couples. The 1.8 million unmarried couples of the opposite sex living together in March 1981 represented an increase of 14 percent over 1980 and a threefold increase since 1970. They attribute this to a change of attitude toward the practice; cohabiting couples are less reluctant to admit to it, and public opinion is much more accepting of it. But cohabitation is not a lifetime commitment; most couples either get married or end their relationships in a short time. Couples who want to have children together usually become married first.[54]

As a stage of life, cohabitation commonly precedes marriage for young adults, though elderly households also take this form for financial or family reasons. Eleanor Macklin's typology of cohabitating arrangements indicates the wide differences in reasons why heterosexual couples decide to live together outside of marriage. Couples may see cohabitation as a matter of:

1.   Temporary, casual convenience. These couples share living quarters because it is convenient and cost-effective.

2.   Affectionate dating or going together. These couples stay together as long as the partners enjoy being with one another.

3.   Trial marriage. These couples are engaged to be engaged or are consciously testing the relationship before making a permanent commitment.

4.   A temporary alternative to marriage. The partners are committed to staying together but are waiting for the right time to marry.

5.   A permanent alternative to marriage. The partners live together in a long-term, committed relationship similar to marriage, but without the traditional religious or legal ties.[55]

Cherlin differentiates between the kinds of couples who regard cohabitation as an alternative and those who see it as a prelude to married life. Young, college-educated, middle-class couples who cohabitate for a period and then either break up or are married generally consider it a test of compatibility prior to marriage. Other cohabiting couples, which usually involve at least one divorced or separated member, regard the practice as an alternative to marriage.[56]

Gay and Lesbian Couples

Most traditional definitions of the family specifically exclude the use of the terms *marriage* and *family* for cohabiting homosexual couples. Scanzoni points out, however, that some definitions of marriage allow for a much wider range of relationships than a heterosexual couple living together in a socially approved manner for purposes of procreation and child rearing. To make the point that marriages must provide for both economic and expressive relations, he cites the following statement by Murdock, whom we have recognized as the author of the conventional definition of family: "Sexual unions without economic cooperation are common, and there are relationships between men and women involving a division of labor without sexual gratification…but marriage exists only when the economic and the sexual are united into one relationship, and this combination occurs only in marriage."[57] Scanzoni adopts this definition in his work on the politics of power in the American marriage because, he says:

It is exceedingly parsimonious and flexible in that the form or structure of the economic and sexual (or expressive) relations could theoretically take any conceivable shape whatsoever, including polygynous or group marriage. It is also broad enough to subsume communal arrangements, as well as homosexual or lesbian relationships. All that is required is that the persons (whatever their number) in the marriage maintain both types of interdependencies.[58]

The desire of lesbians and gay men to form long-term relationships has not been well explored, as Blumstein and Schwartz point out in their study of American couples which included samples of lesbian and gay male couples. They cite a study done at the Kinsey Institute in the late 1960s that found 71 percent of the sample of gay men between the ages of 36 and 45 were living with a partner.[59] In a study of lesbians, Alan Bell and Martin Weinberg found that 82 percent of the women they talked to were living with someone and that for one-fourth of the women, being in a permanent arrangement was "the most important thing in life."[60]

There has been some recent research on gay and lesbian couples, however, and social service agencies and social workers in private practice have been using marital counseling and family therapy techniques with such couples.[61] We will not apply the terms *family* and *marriage* to gays and lesbians, even though many such couples do think of themselves as married or as families, because this would imply that they ought to be judged by heterosexual norms.[62] In Chapter 9, we refer to gay and lesbian couples as having a family lifestyle.

Single Persons

Over 90 percent of the U.S. population marries at least once in a lifetime. While it appears that the number of people not marrying has increased recently, a closer examination of the data reveals that the number of marriages in the 1950s and 1960s, following World War II, was unusually high. By comparison with what it has been in the past, the proportion of never-married persons now in the population is not out of line.[63]

Nevertheless, according to the U.S. Census Bureau, the proportion of single (never married) persons age 18 and over in the population increased from 19 percent of males and 14 percent of females in 1970 to 26 percent of males and 19 percent of females in 1991. Both men and women are staying single longer; the median age at first marriage increased from 22.5 years for males and 20.6 years for females in 1970 to 25.5 years for males and 23.7 years for females in 1988.[64]

Single persons are a diverse group, since individuals live alone for a number of reasons. In addition to the never-married singles there are many who have been divorced or widowed. Peter Stein's typology of single persons distinguishes among four types, varying according to personal circumstances or preferences:

1. Voluntary singlehood. Individuals who have never married or were formerly married but now choose to be single. They may not like the idea of marriage, or their religious convictions may prevent it.

2. Voluntary but temporary singlehood. Individuals who have postponed marriage but are not opposed to it.

3. Involuntary but temporary singlehood. Individuals who would like to marry but have not yet found an appropriate partner.

4. Involuntary singlehood. Individuals who may have never married or were previously married and would like to marry but have not found a partner. They are more-or-less resigned to living as single persons.[65]

Studies of single, heterosexual individuals have not examined the ways in which bachelors and single women build their own households and connect with friends and family. Studies in the 1970s did find that singles were often treated with suspicion and considered somehow deviant. Particularly for women, staying single was often attributed to lack of sex appeal, psychological problems, unwillingness to commit to a relationship, or homosexuality.[66] Economic independence, social support from like-minded people, and increased autonomy have helped solve these problems for single women. Though the lives of single persons may be troubled by loneliness and insecurity, so are the lives of some married couples. Many singles, women as well as men, have chosen this way of life.

∞ FAMILY POLITICS IN AMERICAN SOCIETY: WOMEN, CHILDREN, THE ELDERLY

Changes in the structure and functions of family life have been accompanied by changes in relationships among members of the family and in societal expectations for the roles each is to perform, a field of study known as *family politics*. The traditional American family is a *patriarchy*, a system in which power and authority are arbitrarily vested in the male head of the household. This position is being challenged by other members of the family, particularly the female partner but also the children and the elderly. In order to understand their roles in the family, it is necessary to consider their position as subordinate individuals in the family as an institution.

Women in Society

The success of the women's movement of the second half of the twentieth century can be measured in terms of expanding the choices for women in the society and the family. At the founding of the National Organization for Women (NOW) in 1966, it adopted a statement of purpose calling for attacks on discrimination in the legal system, employment, and education that had limited women's ability to control their own lives. In regard to women's role in the family, the statement declared: "We believe that a true partnership between the sexes demands a different concept of marriage, an equitable sharing of the responsibilities of home and children and of the economic burdens of their support."[67]

While the condition of women in contemporary society has improved, a status in society and in the family which is fully equal to men's has not been achieved.[68] Despite the successes of women in securing legislation forbidding discrimination, *sexism*, beliefs and attitudes or norms and values which promote or justify the subordination of one sex to the other, persists in institutionalized forms, both formal and informal and both intentional and inadvertent. Women are by far most often the target of sexism in American society, and they continue to have unequal power and status in it.

Thomas Kando identifies four kinds of oppression which have kept women in a disadvantaged position. Because of *structural discrimination*, women are less likely than men to be emotionally fulfilled and to achieve sexual satisfaction. Their ability to control conception and birth is threatened or restricted, and real equality of opportunity in education and access to meaningful jobs and careers is yet to be achieved. Because of *cultural discrimination*, the inferiority of women is embedded into the norms and beliefs of the society by means of language, socialization processes, and cultural stereotyping. Because of the *role strain* created by marriage and motherhood in the procreative family, women have suffered legal, economic, social, and psychological harm. And because of **sexual exploitation**, both inside and outside the family, women are still threatened by the double standard in sex favoring men, sexual harassment and intimidation, and violence in the form of abuse and rape.[69]

Women continue to be most disadvantaged by their lack of money, however. As Cynthia Harrison notes, "The women's movement has been able to do little to change the fact that by and large women who are not attached to men are poorer than single men and also poorer than married women."[70] In 1990, the median money income for all families was $35,353. For married-couple families it was $39,895; for families with male householders and no wife present, $29,046; and for those with female householders and no husband present, the median money income was just $19,632. For unrelated individuals, the median money income in 1990 was $17,927 for males and $12,450 for females.[71]

Even the fact that growing numbers of women are participating in the labor force has done little to improve their financial situation. In 1991, women's wages, on average, were still just 70 percent of men's, down from 72 percent in 1990, according to a survey for *Working Women* magazine drawn from U.S. Bureau of Labor statistics and interviews with economists and women's studies experts.[72] The bureau's statistics alone were more optimistic; based on median weekly earnings of $497 for men and $368 for women, the wage gap in 1991 was 74 percent (from 71 percent in 1990).[73] In any case, the gap between pay for men's work and women's work, on average, was more than 25 percent. Many women's choices are confined to low-paying, little-future, service-oriented jobs (see "Comparable Worth" in Chapter 13). Despite some gains in women's accessibility to traditionally male work roles, in many occupations sex segregation is continuing or even increasing; the population of female social workers, for instance, increased from 61 to 68 percent between 1975 and 1991 (see "Women's Occupations and Men's Occupations").

The growing number of single women supporting children is a principal reason that poverty affects women and children more than men. The number of persons in families with a female householder and no husband present living below the poverty level increased from 13.5 million in 1979 to 17.2 million in 1990. When the poverty rate for the population as a whole was 13.5 percent in 1990, it was 19.9 percent for children under 18 in all families and 54.6 percent for children in families headed by the mother alone.[74]

In both married-couple and single-parent families with children, the principal drawback for women in their attempts to achieve equality in political or economic terms is the fact that their primary responsibility continues to be the care of the family, particularly the children. While many men as well as women have accepted the idea of sharing this responsibility, it remains primarily vested in the mother. Because she cannot match the father's dedication to work or public life, she is at a disadvantage.

Deborah Swiss and Judith Walker say professional women hit a "maternal wall" that penalizes them if they have children or take advantage of provisions for flexible schedules or part-time work in order to fulfill family obligations. From their survey of 902 female graduates of the schools of law, medicine, and business at Harvard University, they concluded that graduates who are welcomed to the workplace face an increasingly hostile environment once they begin to have children. While 85 percent of the Harvard professionals who responded to the survey said they had been "successful" at combining career and family, 53 percent said they had changed their jobs or specialties as a result of their family obligations, and 39 percent said that balancing work and family matters had slowed career advancement for them. One-fourth of those with MBS degrees had left the workplace completely; many said they felt forced out of their positions when they became mothers. The authors observe that the anger and frustration about the problems of being

Women's Occupations and Men's Occupations

While women's overall position in the labor force has improved in terms of compensation and job satisfaction, a deep chasm persists between the occupations traditionally open to men and those open to women. Women's representation in a number of "male" occupations substantially improved in the period 1975–1991, going from 7 to 19 percent of all lawyers and judges, 9 to 28 percent of all mail carriers, and 13 to 46 percent of all economists. But they still represented 98 percent of dental assistants but only 10 percent of dentists, 86 percent of elementary school teachers but 41 percent of college teachers, and 66 percent of computer operators but 34 percent of computer programmers.

Occupation	Women as Percent of Total Employment	
	1975	1991
Airline pilots and navigators	—	3.4
Architects	4.3	17.1
Child-care workers	98.4	96.0
Computer systems analysts	14.8	33.7
Dentists	1.8	10.1
Dental assistants	100.0	98.2
Economists	13.1	45.7
Elementary school teachers	85.4	85.9
College/university teachers	31.1	40.8
Lawyers and judges	7.1	18.9
Librarians	81.1	83.0
Mail carriers	8.7	27.8
Physicians	13.0	20.1
Registered nurses	97.0	94.8
Social workers	60.8	68.0

Sources: 1975 data, Sara E. Rix (editor), *The American Woman 1988-89: A Status Report* (New York: W. W. Norton, 1988), Table 18, p. 382; 1991 data, U.S. Bureau of the Census, *Statistical Abstract: 1992* (Washington, DC, 1992), Table 629.

a working mother reported by these women is likely to be much greater for those who do not have the advantages of a Harvard education or a professional career.[75]

Nevertheless, the women's movement has brought them gains in education, employment, law, and government. Legal discrimination has ended, sexual harassment in the workplace has been officially barred, and educational and occupational opportunities have been enlarged. There are as many women voters as men, and slightly more in presidential elections. More women are holding public office; in the 1992 national election the number of women in the U.S. House was doubled from 24 to 48, and the number in the U.S. Senate was increased from 2 to 6. Women have been elected to offices at all levels in local and state governments. In many areas of daily living, women have more choices in shaping their lives now than they have ever had.

Children in Society

Some social scientists believe childhood has never been better. According to Lloyd De-Mause, for instance, as parent-child relations have evolved, children have been granted total care and appreciation by their parents.[76] Others argue that children are the individuals with the least power in American society, with no vote and no voice even in matters which directly concern them, such as school referendums. There is no general agreement, however, that in socializing children, parents have the right as well as the duty to maintain discipline by setting rules and seeing to it that they are obeyed.

Letty Cottin Pogrebin maintains that "America is a nation fundamentally ambivalent about its children, often afraid of its children, and frequently punitive toward its children."[77] This attitude underlies the political failure to provide adequate funds for public education at all levels, child health programs, or child-care facilities, and the reluctance to prosecute parents as child abusers or to remove abused or neglected children from their family of origin. The attitude also can be detected in public opinions and policies which keep one-fifth of all children under 18 in families living in poverty; in 1990, 15 percent of white children, 44 percent of black children, and 39 percent of Hispanic children were in families with incomes below poverty level ($12,292 for a family of four).[78] Some do not have a roof over their heads; Jonathan Kozol estimates that there are about 500,000 homeless children in the United States, mostly unseen because they are scattered in a thousand cities. In his study of the homeless, which focuses on the women and children in "welfare hotels" in New York City, he notes that Americans throughout the country seem to fear homeless children: "Our treatment of these children reaffirms the distancing that now has taken place. They are not of us. They are 'the Other.' "[79]

A consensus has been forming that children are the most neglected sector in American society. While the rate of poverty for children increased from 15 percent in 1970 to 20 percent in 1990, for persons 65 years old and over it declined in the same two decades, from 25 percent to 12 percent.[80] By the mid-1990s, the redistribution of resources to families with children (or children without families) was becoming a public issue. Despite masses of words and data in numerous reports, however, very little had been done to act on the recommendations (see "Putting Children First").

The Elderly in Society

In the past, relatively few people lived to old age; most deaths, in fact, occurred at birth or in early childhood. The twentieth century, however, has been a period of steadily increasing life expectancy for Americans. In 1920, both females and males at birth could expect to live 54 years. By 1950, life expectancy was 66 years for males and 71 years for females, and by 1990, it was 72 for males and 79 for females. In 1990, 12.5 percent of the total population, or 31 million persons, were 65 years old and over; about 18 million were 65 to 74, 10 million were 75 to 84, and slightly more than 3 million were 85 or older. Because of their longer life expectancy, women represent a larger share of the elderly population; in 1991 there were just 67.5 males to each 100 females 65 years of age or older.[81] Better nutrition, medical advances, and less strenuous lifestyles are among the reasons the life expectancy of Americans continues to increase.

In the social history of aging, there is evidence that the elderly have experienced many disadvantages in industrial societies. American society values youth, and prejudiced attitudes and discriminatory acts against old people have been documented. As

Putting Children First

The concern for the health and welfare of children in the 1990s is an international issue. Leaders from more than 70 nations came together at United Nations headquarters in October 1990 to devise a ten-year plan to reduce mortality rates and poverty among children and to improve access to immunizations and education.

In the United States, a bipartisan federal advisory panel, the National Commission on Children, followed in 1991 with recommendations for various measures representing "a huge investment in children." Most of them were never adopted by Congress, including a federal tax credit of $1,000 for each child in the United States and universal health insurance for children and pregnant women. But debate on these and other measures—to improve the collection of child support payments, to provide prenatal care for pregnant women, to give parents a wider choice of schools, and to expand Head Start for preschoolers—aroused public consciousness of the problems. Calls for making children "the No. 1 priority" began to be heard.

Two years later, however, when a series of reports on American teenagers was published in *The New York Times*, a bleak picture was drawn with the portraits of poor adolescents living in the nation's cities:

> They are the children of the shadows: the impoverished youth who live in the tumbledown neighborhoods of the American inner city; the children of often desperate and broken families...; the young people who daily face the lures of drugs, sex, fast money and guns; the unnoticed youths who operate in a maddening universe where things always seem to go wrong.

The statistics presented in this report were an indication of the severe problems adolescents were facing:

1. In 1990, for every 100,000 youths age 10 to 17, there were 431 arrests for violent crimes (murder, rape, robbery, and aggravated assault).

2. In 1991, there were 2,702 murder victims 15 to 19 years old, 86 percent of them boys and 14 percent girls, and 59 percent of them blacks and 38 percent whites.

3. In 1990 the high school dropout rate among people 16 to 24 years old was 12 percent for whites, 13 percent for blacks, and 32 percent for Hispanics.

4. In 1992 20 percent of youths from 16 to 19 years old were in the work force (available for work) but unemployed.

5. Through 1992, 946 teenagers had been infected with the HIV infection which results in AIDS, 71 percent of them boys.

Three years after the 1990 UN summit, *The Progress of Nations,* a report published by the UN Children's Fund (UNICEF) in September 1993, included the shocking statistic that 90 percent of youth homicides in the industrial world were occurring in the United States. The 20 percent of children living in poverty in the United States was the largest percentage of any industrial nation; only Canada, Australia, and Great Britain, each with about 10 percent of children living below the poverty line, came close. This report concluded that rich nations (the United States and Great Britain were singled out) were not doing as much for the health and welfare of children and young people in proportion to their resources as were many poor nations, such as Sri Lanka and Vietnam. According to Richard Jolly, a UNICEF official, "the single most important lesson of the report is that income and wealth is no guarantee of success....It really depends on what priority a country gives to its children."

Sources: News reports, June 4, 1991 and September 26, 1993; "The Children of the Shadows," *The New York Times*, April 4, 1993, page L21.

These members of the frail elderly—those over 85, the fastest growing segment of the U.S. population—require institutional care, which at its best stimulates them to interact with others and participate in activities.

early as the age of 50, job discrimination makes work hard to find, and corporate mergers and downsizing have multiplied the numbers of workers forced into unemployment or retirement even though they have the health, energy, and motivation to continue to produce. The elderly still make up a significant portion of the poor, particularly among women and ethnic minorities, and some elderly persons must cope with isolation, loneliness, ill health, abuse, and abandonment.

Such disadvantages have led some observers to conclude that **ageism** permeates American society. They believe there is an institutionalized age stratification system that generates inequality and conflict between younger adults and older persons and, because the elderly are systematically deprived of opportunities for participation in society, that they should be thought of as a minority group or minority individuals. One of the first to advance this argument was Robert Butler, whose book published in 1975, *Why Survive? Being Old in America*, describes a "deep and profound prejudice against the elderly." According to Butler:

> In America, childhood is romanticized, youth is idolized, middle age does the work, wields the power and pays the bills, and old age, its days empty of purpose, gets little or nothing for what it has already done. The old are in the way, an ironic example of public-health progress and medical technology creating a huge group of people for whom survival is possible but satisfaction in living elusive.[82]

Butler later modified this view. Noting that "The desire for the extension of a robust, vigorous, healthy life is a powerful human urge," he forecast an increase in vigor and health for the elderly, not just an extension of life.[83] A poll by the *Los Angeles Times* of 3,500 adult Americans in 1989 found that nearly two-thirds of the respondents over age 65 said they were satisfied with their personal lives, compared to only about half of those between 18 and 49 years old.[84]

How satisfied the elderly are with their position in American society is related to their financial position. Couples with substantial incomes from pensions, investments, and social security benefits cannot be considered disadvantaged related to other groups. But whether or not the elderly as a group can be considered a disadvantaged minority depends on the particular roles or activities being considered. P. K. Ragan and J. B. Wales point out that in terms of the differential distribution of the resources of a society according to age, "in certain respects (work roles, income, and prestige) the aged are systematically disadvantaged, while in other respects (political power, discretionary time, categorical benefits, and obligations) the aged are not disadvantaged."[85]

According to Vern Bengtson, conclusions that in modern societies favorable evaluations of aging have declined or relationships between young and old are marked by a severe generational gap are unwarranted. While there are differences in values depending on generation, there are also many similarities. Members of three-generation families—child, parent, and grandparent—showed similar rankings on the relative importance of respect, "loyalty to your own," and friendship as well as on the relative lack of importance of possessions and appearance.[86] Evidence that adult children in industrial societies show a great deal of care and affection for their elderly parents also has challenged the idea that most elderly need fear being abandoned or alienated from their children.[87]

Social security, Medicare, and other benefits have greatly improved the economic position of the elderly. But while the poverty rate for persons 65 years old and over was 12.2 percent in 1990, a little less than the 13.5 poverty rate for the population as a whole, for blacks 65 and over the rate was 33.8 percent, and for Hispanics, 22.5 percent.[88] The poverty rate was also higher for older women, largely because they are more likely to be living alone and supporting their own households, due to the shorter life expectancies of men. In 1990 about 82 percent of the men aged 65 and over were living with their spouses or other relatives, compared to 58 percent of the women that age. Women over 65 also are less likely than men to have access to pensions and social security income in their own names.

As a group, the elderly have had an advantage in the ratio of taxes paid to benefits received. In 1986, for example, elderly households paid $61 billion in taxes, representing 10 percent of all income and payroll taxes paid; they received $204 billion in government benefits, including Medicare and social security payments from the retirement insurance trust fund, representing 68 percent of all benefits paid to individuals that year.[89] Such comparisons have led to calls for limits on "entitlements" for the elderly as a means of controlling the federal deficit. Beginning in 1994, social security recipients with higher incomes from pensions, investments, or employment must pay income taxes on up to 85 percent of their benefits, and those between 65 and 69 years of age who continue to work after registering for social security lose $1 for every $3 they earn over about $11,000. Numerous social services, such as meals programs, senior centers, transportation services, and activity programs, have been developed, but their ability to assure that all the elderly can live out their lives actively and with dignity is limited by shrinking funds for the programs.

∞ CHANGES IN ROLE EXPECTATIONS AMONG FAMILY MEMBERS

Changes in expectations about the roles to be taken by various members of American families underlie many of the changes that have affected them in contemporary society. Within the family of procreation, changes in the relationships between spouses and between minor children and parents have accelerated in recent years. With regard to kin, relationships between elderly parents and their adult children are increasingly at issue as the population ages.

Changing Gender Roles in Family Life

In the traditional family of Western societies, the division of rights and duties in the family was strictly along biological, male and female lines. The "man of the house" was expected to fulfill the duties and obligations of the head of the family and to receive in return certain rights and privileges. His duties included taking the role of breadwinner, being committed to the world of work for pay, and providing for the material comfort of wife and children. The privileges he received for fulfilling these socioeconomic or *instrumental roles* included the respect and obedience of the wife and children. The "woman of the house" was accorded the socioemotional or *expressive roles*—the homemaker who maintained the livability of the hearth, nurtured the children, and comforted the husband. To her was given the responsibility for reducing tensions and assuring the equilibrium of family life. In return, her ways of rearing the children were to be supported by the husband, and her husband and children were to show her love, respect, and devotion.

Certain other qualities were expected to infuse the roles of husband and wife in the traditional family. Husbands were to be assertive, competitive, rational, and achievement-oriented; wives were to be passive, emotional, sensitive, and nurturing. The sexual relationship between husband and wife was to be monogamous, but it was recognized that the male had greater sexual urges and required more frequent satisfaction. Sons and daughters were expected to follow in the gender roles of their fathers and mothers, respectively.

As family functions have changed and variations in the structure of American families have emerged, gender roles in traditional families have been challenged by changes in role expectations for the various members of the family. These roles, in fact, have become a political issue, with conservatives espousing "family values," a return to the divided responsibilities and male authority of the traditional family, and liberals promoting "family issues," including the passage of the Family and Medical Leave Act of 1993 and the development of programs such as child care and flextime to accommodate the needs of families with self-actualizing, working wives and mothers.

As noted in Chapter 2, the roles men and women assume in the family are not tied to any biological or "natural" order. Rather, there is overwhelming anthropological evidence that sociocultural factors have a lot to do with the assignment of family roles and statuses.[90] Given tensions in the traditional family, it is not surprising that gender roles are changing.

The Historical Background of Changing Gender Roles

Changes in the roles of women and men in the family have been engendered by recent social movements, but they have a much longer social history. The dominant role of the male in the patriarchy began to be challenged with the advent of industrialization and capitalism and the growth of the nuclear family form.[91] While Western societies are still governed in general by patriarchal norms, the absolute authority of the husband over the wife and children has been considerably diminished.

In hunting and gathering societies, the most primitive form of economy, male and female gender roles were relatively egalitarian. Male dominance became the norm with the development of agricultural economies. Since greater strength was needed for plowing and irrigation, men did the heavy agricultural labor. From control over the economy it was an easy step to control over the polity, the military, and religion. Patriarchy infused the social structure, and institutionalized sexism, based on formal and informal laws, norms, and policies, prevailed.

Early in the move to industrialization, male dominance was reinforced by religious teachings and men's continued hold on politics and the economy. Social structural arrangements favored men, and the socialization of children reinforced the institutionalized discrimination. But it soon became apparent that success in an industrialized society is less dependent on physical strength than on personality and intelligence, in which the abilities of men are not superior to those of women. Men became less powerful in the society and lost authority in the family as they became less vital to the family's survival. Increasing industrialization reduced the husband's control of the family's productive function, and the availability of labor for wages reduced the importance of inheritance. By the twentieth century, the husband's role of patriarch had become more that of a companionate provider.[92]

Throughout the industrial era, conflict regarding gender roles and gender expectations has been growing. As a result of these conflicts between females and males, opportunities have opened up for relations between spouses to become more egalitarian. Thus, the traditional American family is being challenged by the equal-partner marriage (see "From Wife as Property to Wife as Equal Partner").

Hochschild differentiates among three types of ideology of marital roles in contemporary families: traditional, transitional, and egalitarian. The "pure" traditional wife wants to identify with her activities at home and wants her husband to identify with work; she wants less power than he has. The husband wants the same arrangement. The "pure" egalitarian wife wants to identify with the same sphere as her husband and wants an equal amount of power in the marriage. Between these two "pure" types is a variety of transitional types blending the two. A transitional wife wants to identify with her role at work as well as at home, but she believes her husband should base his identity more on work than she does. A transitional husband wants his wife to work but expects her to take the main responsibility at home. Hochschild found that most of the couples she talked to were transitional types, but she also found differences between what they said they believed about the marital roles and how they felt about these roles.[93]

Gender Roles and the Women's Movement

The direct challenges to the traditional gender roles in the family have come from two related developments in the latter half of the twentieth century—the increasing number of women in the labor force and the women's movement. In 1963 Betty Friedan, recognized as one of the founders of the movement, defined the cultural view of women as "the feminine mystique": "The image of women completely fulfilled in her role as husband's wife, children's mother, server of physical needs of husband, children, home." Women's need to be recognized as individuals in their own right was the impetus behind the efforts to help them fulfill their own personhood, to find their own identity as separate from

From Wife as Property to Wife as Equal Partner

John Scanzoni coined the term *equal-partner marriage,* using it in the 1972 first edition of *Sexual Bargaining: Power Politics in the American Marriage* to describe the ultimate goal of a process of ongoing change in relations between husbands and wives. He traces these changes to the beginning of the feminist movement in the early nineteenth century and places the wife's position on a continuum which ranges from property to complement, to junior partner, to equal partner.

In 1972, Scanzoni would place most married women at or near the complement position, where the needs and interests of the husband and his work, as well as those of the children, are more important than the wife's, although she does have more authority than in the property position. A minority of wives, including most who work outside the home, would be placed around the junior partner position. Only a "minute percentage" would be found at or near the equal partner position. He concludes that "the actual social position possessed by women, both out of the family, and in it, remains subordinate to that of men."

Scanzoni does not change his evaluation of the position of women in the second edi-tion, published ten years later. He notes in the Preface to this edition that changes in family patterns have been occurring for almost 200 years and will continue in evolutionary fashion for the foreseeable future. The catalyst for these changes continues to be women's desire for equality—"for greater rewards and fewer costs relative to men's"—both in the family and in the world of work.

While women have a way to go before approaching parity with men, there has been a good deal of discussion about a greater preference among both men and women for equal rights and duties in marriage. Scanzoni points out that there is a difference between what people say they prefer and how they actually behave. Nevertheless, he perceives a trend in favor of the equal-partner marriage, in which there would be reciprocity between husband and wife in the essential instrumental or socioeconomic and expressive roles of marriage, and the provider role would be interchangeable.

Source: John Scanzoni, *Sexual Bargaining: Power Politics in the American Marriage,* first edition (Englewood Cliffs, NJ: Prentice-Hall, 1972) and second edition (Chicago: University of Chicago Press, 1982).

men, marriage, and child rearing, and to demand equal opportunity with men and power of their own. But in what Friedan describes as "the second wave" of the movement, she calls the family the "new feminist frontier." She warns that women cannot live the personhood they have achieved "as if this somehow excludes all those emotions, capacities, needs that have to do with having babies, mothering children, making a home, loving and being loved, dependence and independence, softness and hardness, strength and weakness, in the family."[94]

To second-generation feminists like Susan Faludi, such talk represents a backlash against the movement's modest social, economic, and political gains which serves the purposes of the champions of male domination and the traditional family. She identifies two "demographic trends" that have both encouraged women's advancement and produced the backlash against it—a woman's claim to her own paycheck and a woman's control over her own fertility. It is on these fronts that the 1970s women's movement made its greatest progress, and "now, once again, as the backlash crests and breaks, it crashes hardest on these two shores." The loss of a collective spirit that has resulted from the backlash, producing a new generation of "postfeminists," is perhaps its most debilitating effect.[95]

Gloria Steinem, who has maintained her position as an activist in the women's movement, has broadened her interest in empowerment to include men as well as women. In a review of her book *Revolution from Within*, she notes that "the full self necessary for self-esteem has been denied more to women—but also to men." She promotes self-actualization for both genders, saying that "Self-esteem is a way of saying to men that equality will help you become whole too."[96]

Gender Roles and the Men's Movement

The changes in the roles of men in the family have not been as fundamental as the changes in the roles of women. For men, the principal role is still related to earning a living in the world of work. Nevertheless, the dialogue calling for a more equal sharing of the instrumental, or socioeconomic, and expressive, or socioemotional, roles in marriage has opened up the range of choices for men as well as women. Men, too, have been questioning their traditional gender roles, and some observers have identified a men's movement which is basically comparable to the women's movement.[97]

While husbands now are more likely to share household chores and the duties of child care,[98] the principal change is in men's gender-role expectations. It is clear that the traditional male role gives men an advantage in power, prestige, and privilege, in both the

A divorced single parent oversees the morning routine of making sure his children eat a good breakfast before going to school. While this gender role is uncommon for men (in 1991 only 4 percent of single-parent families were headed by males), their acceptance of child-care and household responsibilities is growing.

society and the family, but that role is also a source of great strain.[99] It limits and constrains men, especially with regard to intimacy. Men typically reveal less personal information about themselves, have a tendency to have secrets, do not like being known by others, show a good deal of tension, often view others as threatening, and fear a sense of vulnerability and dependence. Because they tend to ignore their feelings, men also are less sensitive to signs of trouble in interpersonal relations. Difficulty with intimacy affects not only male-female relations but friendships with other men, and accusations of homosexuality may be a threat.

Barbara Ehrenreich maintains that, from the emphasis on organizational norms in the "gray flannel suit" period of the 1950s through the beginnings of the men's movement in the late 1960s, men were rebelling against the traditional male role which puts economic success and responsibility ahead of interpersonal success and responsibility. Men, like women, now are more likely to value an androgynous gender identity, with both masculine and feminine characteristics.[100] As Philip Lichtenberg notes, "Men will strive to be masculine based on unique traits and abilities:...some men will have preferences that were once identified as feminine and others will have traditional masculine tendencies; but all will be able to utilize various characteristics that are relevant to many new circumstances."[101]

The Feminization of Sexuality

One aspect of spousal relations in which significant change has taken place is the rights and obligations of consenting partners in the sexual act. Traditional norms surrounding sexual behavior allowed only one function, procreation. Yet there was a double standard; sexual satisfaction was considered to be the exclusive right of men. In addition to participating in procreation, men could take pleasure, both in marriage and outside it, in sexual intercourse. Women supposedly did not desire such satisfaction. They were expected to be monogamous and submissive, to satisfy the sexual needs of their husbands, and to bear children.

In popular opinion, recent changes in these norms are so far-reaching that a sexual revolution is said to have taken place. The effects of the revolution are most apparent in the behaviors of women who claim equal rights with men to sexual satisfaction.[102] Increasingly, women are likely to insist that sexual relations need not be limited to procreation, and a man has an obligation to satisfy the woman's sexual needs as well as his own. Having learned to participate more fully in the "joy of sex," women are exploring diverse forms of sexual activity. Even marital sex manuals published by conservatives have endorsed new freedom for women and new obligations for men in the sex act.[103] The nature of intimate relations between men and women has changed a great deal.

Changes in Parent-Child Relationships

Parent-child relations have also been changing. DeMause has documented a series of changes in the authority relations between parents and children in Western cultures since industrialization. He asserts that psychogenetic factors, which he relates to the biological evolution of the species, are more important than cultural and historic factors. In the history of parent-child relations, the power of parents over children has evolved from brutality to a commitment to the welfare of the child.[104]

Up to the fourth century of the Christian era, the infanticide mode of parent-child relations predominated. Social norms gave complete and absolute authority to parents to do with children as they wished. Their anxieties about the desirability or worth of children justified routine killing. In the feudal era, from the fourth to the thirteenth centuries, the abandonment mode prevailed. The idea that the child has a soul made killing unacceptable, so parental anxieties about children were relieved by abandonment or severe control. With the beginning of the Renaissance and up to the seventeenth century, parent-child relations were in an ambivalent mode. Parents of this era had more concern for their children, who were seen as soft wax to be molded by a caring but forceful hand. Parents attributed original sin to children, and anxieties about molding them correctly led to whipping or beating as a way to maintain control. The eighteenth century brought the intrusive mode, in which parents no longer visited their anxieties on their children but sought to conquer them and win them over. Parents prayed with children but did not play with them, and hitting was permissible but whipping was not. From the nineteenth to the mid-twentieth century, in the socialization mode, the object of parents was to train children and guide them into proper pursuits. Child labor was prohibited, and it became proper for children to spend their days at play.

DeMause refers to contemporary parent-child relations as the helping mode, the high point in their history. In this mode, children know better than their parents what their own needs are. Parents are not expected to discipline children or to encourage the formation of good habits, and striking children is no longer proper. Parents see themselves as the servants of children, tolerating their regressions, responding to their needs, and most of all helping them discover their own needs and ways of meeting them.

This view of the current state of childhood is controversial, however. Phillipe Aries describes the contemporary family as a "prison of love" in which the emotions are so intense that the relationship is destructive.[105] Valerie Suransky, in a more reasoned analysis, suggests that as adults have come to love and protect children, they have also attempted to structure, contain, and reduce their autonomy. Childhood, she says, has been eroded:

> We now separate children from the world of work; we dichotomize play from work; we deny the significance of the child's contribution to the cultural forms of everyday life. We infantilize children's perceptions and "school" their minds through the domestication of their critical curiosity and consciousness.[106]

We can conclude that for most children in American society, family experiences include a great deal of love and nurturance which at times may be stifling and constraining. It is clear, however, that parental treatment of children is moving away from authoritarian to more democratic patterns, with the primary goal of assisting children to determine and help satisfy their own needs and desires.

Family Relationships with the Elderly

Regardless of the structure of the family—married couple, single parent, reconstituted, cohabiting, or single person—most families in contemporary American society live apart from their kin. There are few *matrilocal* or *patrilocal families*, that is, kinfolk living in the household or under the authority of the eldest female or male. The usual form is *neolocal families*, in which a married couple or partners set up their own household apart from either set of parents. The existence of neolocal patterns, however, does not detract from ties to kin and elderly parents.[107] Although the classic extended-kin family form is rare, there are complexes of viable, supportive kin relationships which M. B. Sussman refers to as the "modified-kin family."[108]

Kin relationships continue to be very important to contemporary families. Grandparents often take on nurturant and affective roles in the neolocal family, as well as contributing financial support in various ways, from providing housing and paying tuition to buying shoes for the children. Grandchildren often give grandparents valued love, companionship, and physical assistance. But no kin relationship is more important than that between parents and their adult children.

The attachments that form between parents and children continue to develop as both mature. Even with the rise in social services for the elderly, their major source of emotional support often comes from their own families, particularly their adult children. It has been estimated that 78 to 90 percent of older people with living children visit with their children and are in contact with them by telephone at least once a week.[109] Although in part this contact derives from a sense of duty or obligation, affections seems to be the basic reason for it. One study found that about 90 percent of adult children felt "close" or "very close" to their elderly parents, and only 2 percent or less said their relationship was "not close at all." Most of the relationships are quite smooth, with only about 5 percent of adult children saying they were in frequent conflict with their parents.[110]

Considerable mutual help is exchanged between adult children and the elderly, both instrumental, as with transportation and housekeeping, and expressive, such as companionship and sympathy. Early in life parents overwhelmingly give more help to children than children give to parents. Help from parents may continue for young adults whose education, early work experience, or troubles with jobs or in marriage keep them in a dependent position. This situation evens out when both generations are active and healthy adults, and eventually it is the adult child who gives most help.

Adult children appear to monitor the needs of their aging parents and are disposed to give help as required. Stress and conflict are clearly evident in the relationship when parents become very dependent on their adult children, who may come to feel physically and emotionally exhausted, frustrated by a seeming lack of appreciation, helpless, guilty, financially strapped, tied down, or caught between the needs of their parents, their own family members, and their personal lives. Since it is often the adult daughter who assumes most responsibility for care of elderly family members, women are particularly affected by the stress of providing such care. With people 80 years old and over the fastest growing segment of the 65-and-over population, as Ken Dychtwald observes, "The average American woman can expect to spend more years caring for her parents than she did caring for her children."[111]

∞ IMPLICATIONS FOR PRACTICE

The history of social services is very much concerned with family life and well-being; indeed, no other profession may be so involved with family issues. Many of these services are explicitly dedicated to family well-being; and even where the individual is the principal client, the family represents the major social context for assessing needs and problems and for providing support.

This chapter has reviewed the family as a changing social institution. No agreement exists among social scientists as to the meaning of the term *family*, but most use it to mean a socially approved, heterosexually oriented grouping of a male, a female, and their children through which the biologically based activities of procreation and socialization take place and the lifelong bonds or kin relations initiated by these activities are nurtured.

Although all societies devise ways to raise and care for children, there is no clear evidence of a universal nuclear family resembling the traditional family in American society. Family relations have taken any number of forms across time and place, and such values as heterosexuality, a male head, sexual fidelity, monogamy, nurturance, and emotionally laden interpersonal relationships have not always been found to be part of family life. The family in American society is best seen as a social invention, constructed out of a history of competing interests, which is continually provoking conflict and, through it, change.

While the family is a changing social institution, it is not breaking down. That is a conservative image in which the family is seen as a closed, fixed, and unchanging system. Rather, like all human systems, the family is an open system in which change is the natural state. The idea of the demise of the family would force social service workers into the role of guardians of tradition. There are many good things about the traditional nuclear family but many problems in it as well. These problems have generated the need for change.

Social service workers cannot help but participate in these changes in the family that are taking place. Through the social policies and programs they help to develop, they make statements about how family life ought to be. Through their everyday practice with families in need they reinforce or help dissolve the norms and traditions of society. To intervene in the lives of families is to help reshape the family as an institution. Social service workers can work to sustain clients in traditional nuclear family relations when the clients so desire it, but they also can help clients generate new and better interpersonal relationships.

Certain functions that exist in contemporary families have to be maintained. Workers can help clients form families in which procreation and child rearing can be carried out without producing the emotional problems they generated in nuclear families of the past. They can help clients find better ways to meet their needs for affection, productivity, and consumption. They can help rid the family of the latent functions of maintaining sexism and racism.

As social service workers help clients they must also take into account family ideals that seem to be worth striving to achieve. For many people, the ideal family would be egalitarian and less constrained by rigid gender roles. Parent-child relations would be more democratic, and parents would serve as expediters, allowing children to develop according to their own needs and desires. This kind of family would attempt to maintain strong kin ties across generations. Social service workers can help today's families work toward these kinds of ideals and thereby influence how the institution of the family functions in American society.

∞ DISCUSSION QUESTIONS AND CLASS PROJECTS

1. Identify at least three different definitions of the family used in the literature and evaluate their merits and limitations. How would you define *family*?

2. Define the following terms:

   traditional family

   nuclear family
   extended-kin family
   feminization of sexuality
   household
   family of origin
   family of procreation
   plural marriage
   institutionalized sexism

equal-partner marriage

antisexist approach to study of the family

3. Describe the three major institutionalized family forms identified by anthropologists.

4. Would you agree that the nuclear family—mother, father, child—is universal? On what sources do you base your opinion?

5. List and describe at least five manifest functions often associated with family life. Would you agree that the family also serves latent functions? If so, describe these latent functions.

6. Do you believe the family is a racist and sexist institution? Why or why not?

7. A lot of different forms of families can be seen in contemporary society. Describe the following types: single-parent families, stepparent families, cohabitating couples, single people, and married-couple, two-parent families. With others in the class, identify people who can be interviewed about these types of families and interview them to determine what needs and problems, as well as strengths and resources, are available in them.

8. Describe the four ways in which Kando says women are oppressed in contemporary society. Would you agree?

9. Do you agree that men's gender roles are changing? Make a list of traditional male activities and chores in the family. Make a list of the ways you believe males should be behaving in the family. Conduct a survey of husbands and young sons to determine if these changes are coming about.

10. Describe the changes that DeMause believes have taken place in parent-child relations since industrialization. Do you believe that parents today are more likely to want to help children discover their own needs and desires?

11. What is meant by the term *ageism*? Do you believe that ageism permeates American society, including family life? In what ways are the aged advantaged and disadvantaged in our society?

✺ NOTES

1. Andrew J. Cherlin, *Marriage, Divorce, Remarriage* (Cambridge, MA: Harvard University Press, 1981).

2. Howard Robboy and Candace Clark, *Social Interaction: Readings in Sociology*, 2nd ed. (New York: St. Martin's Press, 1983), p. 391.

3. U.S. Bureau of the Census, *Statistical Abstract of the United States: 1992*, 112th edition (Washington, DC, 1992), p. 6.

4. George Peter Murdock, "The Universality of the Nuclear Family," in N. W. Bell and E. F. Vogel (editors), *The Family* (Glencoe, IL: Free Press, 1960), p. 37.

5. Christopher C. Harris, *The Family and Industrial Society* (London, England: George Allen and Unwin, 1983), pp. 34–39.

6. Ibid., pp. 16–30.

7. Ann Hartman and Joan Laird, "Family Practice," in *Encyclopedia of Social Work*, 18th ed., Vol. 1 (Silver Spring, MD: National Association of Social Workers, 1987), p. 576.

8. Karen Lindsey, *Friends as Family* (Boston, MA: Beacon Press, 1981), p. 13.

9. Rayna Rapp, "Family and Class in Contemporary America: Notes toward an Understanding of Ideology," in B. Thorne (editor) with M. Yalom, *Rethinking the Family: Some Feminist Questions* (New York: Longman, 1982).

10. Gerald R. Leslie, *The Family in Social Context*, 5th ed. (New York: Oxford University Press, 1982), p. 12.

11. Harris, *Family and Industrial Society*, p. 93.

12. Murdock, "Universality of the Nuclear Family," pp. 37–51.

13. Clyde Kluckholm, "Variations in the Human Family," in Bell and Vogel (editors), *The Family*, p. 48.

14. Mark Poster, *Critical Theory of the Family* (New York: Seabury Press, 1978), p. 141.

15. Harris, *Family and Industrial Society*, pp. 30–31.

16. Norman W. Bell and Ezra F. Vogel, *The Family* (Glencoe, IL: Free Press, 1960), p. 32, italics added.

17. E. Kathleen Gough, "Is the Family Universal? The Nayar Case," in Bell and Vogel (editors), *The Family*, p. 90.

18. Harris, *Family and Industrial Society*, p. 40.

19. Michael Mitterauer and Reinhard Sieder, *The European Family* (Chicago: University of Chicago Press, 1982), p. 83.

20. See Lucille Duberman, *Marriage and Other Alternatives*, 2nd ed. (New York: Frederick A. Praeger, 1977), pp. 18–22.

21. Robert K. Merton, *Social Theory and Social Structure*, 3rd ed. (New York: Free Press, 1968).

22. Mary Ellen Goodman, *Race Awareness in Young Children* (New York: Collier, 1964).

23. Phyllis A. Katz, *Toward the Elimination of Racism* (New York: Pergamon Press, 1976).

24. Harry H. L. Kitano, "Passive Discrimination: The Normal Person," *Journal of Social Psychology*, vol. 70 (October 1966), pp. 23–31.

25. Mary Richmond Abbott, *Masculine and Feminine: Sex Roles over the Life Cycle* (New York: Random House, 1983), pp. 89–98.

26. John Scanzoni, *Sexual Bargaining: Power Politics in the American Marriage*, 2nd ed. (Chicago: University of Chicago Press, 1982), p. 48.

27. Robert R. Sears, "Development of Gender Role," in F. A. Beach (editor), *Sex and Behavior* (New York: John Wiley and Sons, 1965), pp. 133–63.

28. Caroline Smith and Barbara Lloyd, "Material Behavior and Perceived Sex of Infant: Revisited," *Child Development*, vol. 49 (December 1978), pp. 1263–65.

29. Duberman, *Marriage and Other Alternatives*, p. 21.

30. Ruth Schwartz Cowan, *More Work for Mother* (New York: Basic Books, 1983).

31. Mitterauer and Sieder, *European Family*, pp. 83–84; Kenneth Kenniston, *All Our Children* (New York: Harcourt Brace Jovanovich, 1977), pp. 13–17.

32. Christopher Lasch, *Haven in a Heartless World: The Family Besieged* (New York: Basic Books, 1977).

33. Talcott Parsons, *The Social System* (New York: Free Press, 1964). pp. 58–67, 151–57. Also see Parsons, "The Normal American Family," in S. M. Farber, P. Mustacchi, and R. H. L. Wilson (editors), *Man and Civilization: The Family's Search for Survival* (New York: McGraw-Hill, 1965), pp. 31–50.

34. Eli Zaretsky, *Capitalism, The Family, and Personal Life* (New York: Harper Colophon, 1973), pp. 56–77.

35. Poster, *Critical Theory of the Family*, pp. 166–205.

36. U.S. Bureau of the Census, *Statistical Abstract: 1992*, Tables 62, 67; also see Sheila Kammerman, "Families, Nuclear," in *Encyclopedia of Social Work*, Vol. 1, pp. 542–43.

37. U.S. Bureau of the Census, *Statistical Abstract: 1992*, Table 620.

38. Nancy Barrett, "Women and the Economy," in S. E. Rix (editor), *The American Woman 1987–88: A Report in Depth* (New York: W. W. Norton, 1987), p. 100.

39. U.S. Bureau of the Census, *Statistical Abstract: 1992*, Table 621.

40. Kammerman, "Families, Nuclear."

41. Philip Blumstein and Pepper Schwartz, *American Couples: Money, Work, Sex* (New York: William Morrow, 1983), p. 144.

42. Arlie Hochschild with Anne Machung, *Second Shift: Working Parents and the Revolution at Home* (New York: Viking Penguin, 1989), p. 4.

43. Ibid., p. 3.

44. Lillian Rubin, *Intimate Strangers* (New York: Harper Colophon Books, 1984).

45. U.S. Bureau of the Census, *Statistical Abstract: 1992*, Table 67.

46. Ibid., Table 69.

47. See U.S. Commission on Civil Rights, *A Growing Crisis: Disadvantaged Women and Their Children*, Clearinghouse Publication 78 (Washington, DC: U.S. Government Printing Office, 1983), and Ruth A. Brandwein, C. A. Brown, and E. M. Fox, "Women and Children Last: The Social Situation of Divorced Mothers and their Families," *Journal of Marriage and the Family*, vol. 36 (August 1974), pp. 498–514.

48. U.S. Bureau of the Census, *Statistical Abstract: 1992*, Table 697.

49. Rix (editor), *American Woman 1987–88*, Figure 11, p. 306.

50. Paul Glick, "How American Families Are Changing," *American Demographics*, vol. 6 (January 1984), pp. 23–24.

51. Andrew Cherlin, "Women and the Family," in Rix (editor), *American Woman 1987–88*, p. 67.

52. Ibid., pp. 74–75.

53. U.S. Bureau of the Census, *Statistical Abstract: 1992*, Tables 131, 63.

54. Blumstein and Schwartz, *American Couples*, pp. 36–38.

55. Eleanor Macklin, "Nonmarital Heterosexual Cohabitation," in A. Skolnick and J. Skolnick (editors), *Family in Transition* (Boston: Little, Brown, 1983).

56. Cherlin, *Marriage, Divorce, Remarriage*, pp. 13–14.

57. Gearge P. Murdock, *Social Structure* (New York: Macmillan, 1949), p. 8.

58. Scanzoni, *Sexual Bargaining*, p. 22.

59. Blumstein and Schwartz, *American Couples*, pp. 44–45.

60. Alan P. Bell and Martin S. Weinberg, *Homosexualities: A Study of Diversity among Men and Women* (New York: Simon and Schuster, 1978).

61. "Counseling for Gay and Lesbian Couples," *Practice Digest*, vol. 7 (Summer 1984), pp. 13–16.

62. See Bell and Weinberg, *Homosexualities*, p. 219.

63. Cherlin, *Marriage, Divorce, Remarriage*, pp. 6–19. Also see Edward L. Kain, "Surprising Singles," *American Demographics*, vol. 6 (August 1984), pp. 16–19, 39.

64. U.S. Bureau of the Census, *Statistical Abstract: 1992*, Tables 51, 130.

65. Peter Stein, "The Lifestyles and Life Chances of the Never-Married," *Marriage and Family Review*, vol. 1 (July–August 1978), pp. 1–11.

66. Margaret Adams, "The Single Woman in Today's Society: A Reappraisal," in H. Wortis and C. Rabinowitz (editors), *The Women's Movement* (New York: John Wiley and Sons, 1972), pp. 89–101. Also see Peter J. Stein, *Single* (Englewood Cliffs, NJ: Prentice-Hall, 1976.)

67. Cynthia Harrison, "A Richer Life: A Reflection on the Women's Movement," in Rix (editor), *The American Woman 1988–89* (New York: W. W. Norton, 1988), p. 56.

68. Naomi Gottlieb, "Sex Discrimination and Inequality," in *Encyclopedia of Social Work*, Vol. 2, pp. 561–69.

69. Thomas M. Kando, *Sexual Behavior and Family Life in Transition* (New York: Elsevier, 1978), pp. 345–54.

70. Harrison, "Richer Life," p. 73.

71. U.S. Bureau of the Census, *Statistical Abstract: 1992*, Tables 706, 709.

72. Associated Press report, December 17, 1992.

73. U.S. Bureau of the Census, *Statistical Abstract: 1992*, Table 654.

74. Ibid., Table 722.

75. Deborah Swiss and Judith Walker, *Women and the Work/Family Dilemma* (New York: John Wiley and Son, 1993).

76. Lloyd DeMause, "The Nightmare of Childhood," in B. Gross and E. Gross (editors), *The Children's Rights Movement* (New York: Anchor Books, 1977), pp. 17–36.

77. Letty Cottin Pogrebin, *Family Politics: Love and Power on an Intimate Frontier* (New York: McGraw-Hill, 1983), p. 42.

78. U.S. Bureau of the Census, *Statistical Abstract: 1992*, Tables 718, 730.

79. Jonathan Kozol, *Rachel and Her Children: Homeless Families in America* (New York: Fawcett Columbine, 1989), p. 181.

80. U.S. Bureau of the Census, *Statistical Abstract: 1992*, Tables 718, 721.

81. Ibid., Tables 105, 19, 20.

82. Robert N. Butler, *Why Survive? Being Old in America* (New York: Harper & Row, 1975), pp. xi–xiii.

83. Robert Butler, "2020 Vision: A Look at the Next Century," *Modern Maturity*, April–May 1984, p. 49.

84. *Los Angeles Times* report in *Chicago Sun-Times*, May 4, 1989, p. 5.

85. P. K. Ragan and J. B. Wales, "Age Stratification and the Life Course," in J. Birren and R. Sloane (editors), *Handbook of Mental Health and Aging* (Englewood Cliffs, NJ: Prentice-Hall, 1980), p. 396.

86. Vern L. Bengtson, "Comparative Perspectives on the Microsociology of Aging: Methodological Problems and Theoretical Issues," in V. Marshall (editor), *Later Life: The Social Psychology of Aging* (Beverly Hills, CA: Sage, 1986), pp. 304–36.

87. See Victor G. Cicirelli, "Adult Children and Their Elderly Parents," in T. H. Brubaker (editor), *Family Relationships in Later Life* (Beverly Hills, CA: Sage, 1983), p. 39.

88. U.S. Bureau of the Census, *Statistical Abstract: 1992*, Table 721.

89. News item, *Chicago Tribune*, December 28, 1988, Sect. 1, p. 4.

90. George P. Murdock and Caterina Provost, "Factors in the Division of Labor by Sex: A Cross Cultural Analysis," *Ethnology*, vol. 12 (April 1973), pp. 203–25; Margaret Mead, *Sex and Temperament in Three Primitive Societies* (New York: Dell, 1963).

91. Mitterauer and Sieder, *European Family*, pp. 86–90.

92. See Philip Lichtenberg, "Men," in *Encyclopedia of Social Work*, p. 97.

93. Hochschild, *Second Shift*, pp. 15–16.

94. Betty Friedan, *The Second Stage* (New York: Summit Books, 1981), pp. 15, 59.

95. Susan Faludi, *Backlash: The Undeclared War Against American Women* (New York: Doubleday Anchor Books, 1991), pp. 54–55, 58, 72.

96. Nancy Gibbs and Jeanne McDowell, "How to Revive a Revolution," *Time*, March 9, 1992, pp. 56–57; Gloria Steinem, *Revolution from Within* (New York: Little, Brown, 1992).

97. Lichtenberg, "Men," pp. 95–102.

98. For a brief discussion of this point see Kammerman, "Family, Nuclear," pp. 544–45. Also see Joseph L. Pleck, "Men's Family Work: Three Perspectives and Some New Data," *The Family Coordinator*, vol. 28 (October 1979), pp. 481–88.

99. Joseph H. Pleck, *The Myth of Masculinity* (Cambridge, MA: MIT Press, 1981).

100. Barbara Ehrenreich, *The Hearts of Men* (New York: Anchor Books, 1983).

101. Lichtenberg, "Men," p. 100.

102. Barbara Ehrenreich, Elizabeth Hess, and Gloria Jacobs, *Remaking Love: The Feminization of Sexuality* (New York: Anchor Doubleday, 1986).

103. Ibid., pp. 74–102, 134–60.

104. DeMause, "Nightmare of Childhood."

105. Phillipe Aries, *Centuries of Childhood*, translated by Robert Baldick (New York: Vintage Books, 1962), pp. 411–15.

106. Valerie Polakow Suransky, *The Erosion of Childhood* (Chicago: University of Chicago Press, 1982), p. 8.

107. Eugene Litwak, "Extended Kin Relations in an Industrial Democratic Society," in E. Shanas and G. Strieb (editors), *Social Structure and the Family: Generational Relations* (Englewood Cliffs, NJ: Prentice-Hall, 1965), pp. 290–323.

108. M. B. Sussman, "Relationship of Adult Children with Their Parents in the United States," in Shanas and Strieb (editors), *Social Structure and the Family*, pp. 62–92.

109. Elaine M. Brody and Stanley J. Brody, "Aged: Services," in *Encyclopedia of Social Work*, vol. 1, pp. 33–34.

110. Ibid., p. 34.

111. Ken Dychtwald with Joe Fowler, *Age Wave: The Challenges and Opportunities of an Aging America* (Los Angeles: J. P. Tarcher, 1989), p. 241.

Diversity in Family Lifestyles

MAJOR THEMES DISCUSSED IN THIS CHAPTER

1. **SOCIAL CLASS AND FAMILY LIFE.** The ways family patterns vary along class lines in the United States are indicated by differences to be found among middle-class, working-class, poverty-class, and affluent families.

2. **FAMILIES IN ETHNIC AND RACIAL COMMUNITIES.** Since American society is composed of many racial and ethnic groups, variations in family life also exist along racial and ethnic lines. Seven generalizations can be made about how family ideals and values in racial- and ethnic-minority communities differ from those of the middle class. The family lifestyles of African-American, Native American, Latino, and Asian-American families are described to illustrate these generalizations.

3. **FAMILY LIFESTYLES OF GAY AND LESBIAN COUPLES.** As permanent relationships are increasing in the gay and lesbian community, new norms, values, and traditions for homosexual coupling are emerging.

4. **IMPLICATIONS FOR PRACTICE.** Social service workers must acknowledge the ideals and aspirations of the individuals and families with whom they work. Assessment should focus on the ways in which family members as well as the external social environment foster or limit family well-being. Plans for intervention should also attempt to work with family members and the environment in order to improve family functioning and support family goals.

IN EXAMINING THE FAMILY LIFESTYLES—THE roles, norms, values, and traditions of family life—which are likely to be found in different communities in American society, we will consider the diversity deriving from social class and race and ethnicity. Lifestyles for long-term relationships by gay and lesbian couples also will be considered as an example of how family lifestyles are developed in a community. Despite the diversity in family lifestyles, however, most Americans seem to be striving for similar ideals: monogamy in long-term sexual relationships, greater equality in spousal roles, more democratic parent-child relations, strong ties with kin, and a nurturing and supportive interpersonal emotional climate. These are the ideals guiding Americans' attempts to redefine the family as a social institution.

∞ SOCIAL CLASS AND FAMILY LIFE

To many social scientists, the nature of family life significantly varies as a consequence of the family's socioeconomic status. In this view, family lifestyle is a function of the status and roles of the head of the household in the economy of the society. The householder's occupation and employment status or, in the two-paycheck family, those of both householders are highly related to the form and dynamics of family life.[1]

As we noted in Chapter 4, social classes can be defined in terms of social roles or positions in the work force, particularly the opportunities provided for a person to exercise self-direction in performing the work. Melvin Kohn maintains that such self-direction is unattainable to the extent that a worker is highly supervised, or the work is highly routinized and provides only limited ways to carry out the routines, or the work is simple and lacks challenge.[2] Higher-class status accompanies occupations that are challenging, varied, and unsupervised; and lower-class status accompanies those that are unchallenging, routinized, and highly supervised. Middle-class occupations are somewhere between these two extremes. Status is lowest in the poverty class, where just getting or keeping a job may be a primary concern.

The division of American society into middle-class, working-class, poverty-class, and the families of the rich in this section follows the definition of social classes as descriptions of the economic opportunities available to people, the goods and resources they can secure, and the occupations they follow. These are not rigid distinctions with upper and lower limits, however. As we have noted, the majority of American families would be placed in the category ranging from upper to lower middle class. Changes in the shares of the total money income of families are an indication of the fluidity of social class distinctions (see "Shares of Money Income of Families, 1969–1990"). If those in the working class lose their middle-class-income jobs, they can easily slip down into the poverty class. For those in the very-rich category, with accumulations of assets and wealth, the changes may be only a matter of how rich they are.

Just as there are no rigid boundaries between social classes, there are no rigid differences in family forms and lifestyles related to social class. Rather, there are tendencies among middle-class, working-class, poverty-class, and upper-class individuals and communities which are reflected in certain family patterns. The general tendencies described here, identified by Rayna Rapp, provide a social scientist's view of family and class in contemporary American society.[3]

Middle-Class Families

Most studies of American family life focus on the middle class on the assumption that not only are these families by far the most numerous but they also personify the ideal of the society as a whole. Rapp defines middle-class families as those headed by men (or women) who "own small amounts of productive resources and have control over their working

---

Shares of Money Income of Families, 1969–1990

Between 1969 and 1990, rich families in the United States got richer and poor families got poorer. The table below gives the percentage of total income earned by families in the five quintiles (20 percent) of the population. Those in the bottom fifth lost a whole percentage point before leveling off at 4.6 percent, while those in the top fifth increased their share by 3.7 points, reaching 44.3 percent of all the income earned in 1990. Family income in the middle class lost even more ground; it dropped by 1.6 percentage points in the second quintile and by 1.1 points in the third, or middle, quintile. According to Kevin Phillips, "the United States in the late twentieth century led all other major industrial countries in the gap dividing the upper fifth of the population from the lower—in the disparity between top and bottom." (p. 8)

Percentage of Total Family Income Earned by Quintiles

Year	First (bottom)	Second	Third (middle)	Fourth	Fifth (top)
1969	5.6	12.4	17.7	23.7	40.6
1974	5.5	12.0	17.5	24.0	41.0
1980	5.1	11.6	17.5	24.3	41.6
1984	4.7	11.0	17.0	24.4	42.9
1986	4.6	10.8	16.8	24.0	43.7
1988	4.6	10.7	16.7	24.0	44.0
1990	4.6	10.8	16.6	23.8	44.3

Source: Data from U.S. Bureau of the Census, *Current Population Reports*, Series P-60, and *Statistical Abstract of the United States*, various editions; see Kevin Phillips, *The Politics of Rich and Poor: Wealth and the American Electorate in the Reagan Aftermath* (New York: Random House, 1990).

---

conditions."[4] Middle-class family heads depend largely on wage labor to maintain the household, but they generally have occupations with a fair amount of prestige and autonomy—professional and managerial occupations in industry or government. In general, these families have a stable economic base which allows for some degree of luxury and discretionary spending.

Many middle-class families aspire to the equal-partner marriage, in which husband and wife share responsibilities and make mutual decisions. As we have seen, however, equality in the family often is more illusion than reality. In the traditional middle-class family, the career of the husband was all-important and women were expected to be knowledgeable so that they could entertain intelligently and instill the proper educational and social values in the children. In the contemporary middle-class family, women are likely to have careers of their own and to regard them as personally satisfying. As the old ideals and role expectations change, family tensions surface.[5] When both partners work outside the home, conflict over whose career is to be considered most important and who is to perform the necessary household chores and child-care functions increases. For women, the conflict lies in balancing the needs of work and family and trying to satisfy the demands of both personhood and motherhood. Men must try to accommodate their desire to increase their participation in family life to the demands of careers that are determined by corporate policies which give lip service to fatherhood but make few concessions to it.

By middle-class ideals, children should be loved and nurtured unconditionally. Physical punishment is avoided, and every effort is made to let children develop and discover their full potential. Lineal and generational ties are very important in providing for the proper education of children, helping them establish careers or professional practices, or financing weddings and the formation of neolocal families. The accumulation of money and resources and the development of strategies for passing them on from one generation to the next is a central concern in middle-class families. In socializing the children, the family attempts to assure that as adults they will have comfortable middle-class living standards and will not move downward into the working or poverty classes.

Friendship networks also serve a utilitarian or status-seeking function, and there is considerable concern that friends are the "right" kind of people as regards their education, work, residential neighborhoods, clothing, and club memberships. Friendships are a badge of status and a connection to be used in getting ahead and assuring proper marriages for children.

Working-Class Families

Working-class families may be getting closer to middle-class families in terms of ideals (see "Emotional Climate in the Working-Class Family" in Chapter 8), but some important differences emerge as a function of their economic position. The most distinctive feature of the stable working class is its dependency for survival on labor for wages. The household sends out its members to work and bring in an income, which provides food and shelter and allows for child rearing and the consumption of goods and services. How many members must be sent out to work depends on how much money each can earn.

Young working-class couples generally marry for love, with the hope that love will last forever. When it is economically feasible they follow the traditional family pattern of their parents, with the husband as head of the family and the wife as homemaker and child-care provider.[6] Most working-class families today require two incomes, however; the wife also works, if only part-time.

The financial problems of working-class families formerly were eased by having many children who eventually could earn wages and contribute to the family's support. Labor laws now prevent children and adolescents from participating in the labor force, and parents generally want their children in school rather than at work.[7] Working-class children, in fact, may be kept ignorant of their parents' economic burdens. This creates tension because peer pressure and advertising encourage children to "need" more things, and they may feel deprived if their parents cannot or will not satisfy these needs.

Working-class husbands and wives have generally judged their marriages not so much in terms of personal fulfillment and happiness as in terms of their ability to fulfill their primary roles in maintaining the household. Ideally, in this class, a good husband works steadily, supports the family, and never harms anyone in it. A good wife is able to run the house without bothering the husband; she prepares good meals, keeps the house clean, and controls the children so the husband can relax and get ready for the next day's work. There is little room for compromise when both must get ready for the next day's work. Rubin points out that working-class women in the labor force do not "want to" work so much as feel they "have to" work to assure the solvency of the family.[8] They continue to do most of the housework in addition to their work outside the home, and their housework contributes to economic survival of the family because it eliminates the need to pay for cooking, cleaning, and caring for children. When the wife has to perform two roles at the same time, family tensions invariably surface.

Poverty-Class Families

Poverty-class families are statistically identified as having incomes below the poverty level, which is determined each year by the federal government on the basis of household money income and the Consumer Price Index. In 1990, the money income of 10.7 percent of all families in the U.S. population was officially below poverty level, which was $12,292 for a family of four.[9] The poverty index does not take into account noncash benefits such as food stamps, Medicaid, and subsidized housing.

The adults in poverty-class families are chronically unemployed, underemployed, dependent on welfare, or working for a subsistence wage. The family structure is altogether different from the one that prevails in the middle class. Both in the majority white community and the minority racial and ethnic communities, lower-class families are typified by high rates of divorce or separation, births to unwed mothers, and female-headed, single-parent families. There are few father figures, and physical punishment is a common child-rearing technique. Family life is centered around networks of two or more households, usually those of relatives but sometimes those of friends. Carol Stack calls this arrangement a **domestic network,** "an extended cluster of kinsmen related chiefly through children but also through marriage and friendship, who align to provide domestic functions." In the black urban neighborhoods she studied in the 1970s, these networks formed around women because of their role in child care, but men played a positive role in them as fathers of the children and contributors to the resources of the network.[10]

Examples of poverty-class families often come from the study of family life in ethnic-minority communities, which will be considered in the following section. The major debate about poverty-class family life is whether the norms and values governing it are inferior to those for families in the middle and upper classes, or whether lower-class family arrangements represent a reasonable adaptation to the economic insecurities confronting poor people. This is an extension of the two explanations for the continued existence of poverty and the urban underclass—as the result of a culture of poverty or the effects of discrimination (see "Explaining the Underclass" in Chapter 7). Studies of lower-class black and Puerto Rican family life have pointed to its positive aspects, such as willingness to take in children of relatives and build resource networks which spread out economic and interpersonal risks.[11] The love and nurturance provided children in such families often is as great as or greater than that provided in more affluent families. According to Stack, "The value placed on children, the love, attention, and affection children receive from women and men, and the web of social relationships spun from the birth of a child are all basic to the high birth rate among the poor."[12]

While networks of families living in poverty survive, it often is at great personal cost. The sharing of resources produces a leveling effect under which no one is expected to aspire to live better than the rest of the network. There is great pressure to keep everyone involved, and this makes marriage and stable family life, as well as upward mobility, difficult. Women in domestic networks may have to try to meet the expectations of their kin and the expectations of a spouse simultaneously.[13] Moreover, in a society which values upward mobility, competition, and individual effort, there is great personal and interpersonal stress for members of the poverty class.

The Families of the Rich

In the class of people to whom the term *rich* can be applied, income and wealth are derived from executive positions in large corporations, ownership of large businesses or professional practices, or sizable blocks of corporate stocks and other investments. This upper class includes the top 5 percent of families by money income who in 1990 had annual incomes of $102,358 or more and controlled 17.4 percent of the income earned in the United States.[14]

The family lives of the very rich have seldom been studied, and little real knowledge about them exists. From the evidence, Rapp suggests that while male dominance is unchallenged, women have a central role in the family and the society. These households usually include domestic help, which frees the wife to socialize the children, take part in civic affairs, and organize social gatherings. According to Rapp, because women in upper-class families represent the idea of family to the rest of society, they profoundly influence perceptions about the wife's role. This is an unfortunate image, since less wealthy women cannot experience the lifestyles of the rich. Another family pattern is found in two-career families where the wife's income, added to the husband's, places the family in the upper-income class. In these families the availability of live-in household and child-care help greatly adds to the woman's ability to advance in her career.

The few studies that have been made of the children of the rich have focused on delinquency. It has been argued that these children are as delinquent as the children of the poor but that they are less likely to be caught or, if caught, more likely to be let off with a warning. In the early 1970s William Chambliss studied two groups of white boys in a small-town high school: "the Saints," from upper-middle-class families, and "the Roughnecks," from lower-class families.[15]

The Saints were popular, good precollege students, active in school affairs; they were also frequently truant, were involved in vandalism and petty theft, drank heavily, and drove at breakneck speed. In the two-year period of the study, none was arrested. They were mobile, having access to cars, and clever in performing delinquent acts out of sight of adults. If caught they acted contrite and respectful and were dismissed. The Roughnecks were boys from the other side of the tracks who received average grades in school and were constantly in trouble with the police, though their rate of delinquency, mostly petty theft and fights, was about equal to that of the Saints. Since they did not have cars or much money, they actually drank less. If they were stopped by an authority, they reacted with hostility and disdain. In the period of observation each member was arrested at least once, and they were regarded by teachers, police, and merchants as delinquents, as "roughnecks."

According to Chambliss, the different treatment of the two equally delinquent gangs was due to their class background, their visibility, and the biased perceptions of their activities by the authorities and the community. He concludes:

> …visible, poor, nonmobile, outspoken, and undiplomatic "tough" kids will be noticed, whether their actions are seriously delinquent or not. Other kids, who have established a reputation for being bright…, disciplined and involved in respectable activities, who are mobile and monied,

will be invisible when they deviate from sanctioned activities. They'll sow their wild oats—perhaps even wider and thicker than their lower-class cohorts—but they won't be noticed.

∞ FAMILY LIFE IN RACIAL AND ETHNIC COMMUNITIES

In a multiethnic society such as that in the United States, variation in family life along racial and ethnic lines is to be expected. As we pointed out in Chapter 8, family lifestyles have few universal features, and the diversity in them reflects historical and cultural relativity. In our consideration of racial and ethnic communities, we will maintain the relativist position that there is no one way by which families are or ought to be organized.

In the United States, differences in family life in various racial and ethnic communities are usually studied in terms of whites, blacks, and Hispanics. Data compiled by the U.S. Bureau of the Census most often are derived from these three groups (see "Characteristics of Households and Families"). Studies of family lifestyles in these groups and others, such as Native Americans and Asian Americans, have contributed to knowledge about the diversity of family life in American society.

Ethnic-minority families often have been studied with an eye toward uncovering presumably inherent pathologies, or abnormalities. With the white, middle-class family taken as the norm, black families, especially, have been seen as "disorganized" because on the surface they do not resemble such mainstream families. Specifically, they appear to be matriarchal rather than patriarchal; often, in fact, the fathers are absent.[16] Native American families have been criticized for their matriarchal patterns and permissiveness in child rearing,[17] and Mexican-American families have been criticized for being too "familistic" and having patriarchal norms that are *too* strong.[18] These conditions have been labeled pathologies and taken as the basis for explaining away the deprived socioeconomic status of many ethnic minorities. Pathological family lifestyles, not discrimination or a lack of legitimate educational and occupational opportunities, are said to be responsible for the persistent poverty and unemployment experienced by such families.

In this section we take a **cultural relativist** position. Family lifestyle patterns develop for a multiplicity of reasons, and no family pattern is inherently better than another. They may develop because they are fervently desired, or because the social and economic conditions confronted in everyday life by members of the community force adaptations that are necessary, if not always desirable. Often both reasons operate simultaneously.

Taking a cultural relativist position does not mean presenting only the strengths of minority family life and disregarding the weaknesses, as some social scientists, reacting against the pathology viewpoint, have done.[19] While social service workers and policy-makers must build on the strengths of minority groups, they cannot avoid examining the negative aspects of family life, in both minority and majority groups.[20] No one family pattern is superior, but some patterns, given the nature of the environment in which they operate, have more liabilities than others.

To help social workers get in touch with the aspirations of minority as well as majority communities, we start our consideration of the family as a social institution in racial- and ethnic-minority communities with some generalizations about the ideals that guide these diverse family lifestyles. In the next section these generalizations are illustrated with descriptions of the rich complexity of family lifestyle patterns found among Native Americans, African Americans, Lations, and Asian Americans.

Characteristics of Households and Families, 1970–1991:
Whites, Blacks, and Hispanics

Data on family characteristics in various racial and ethnic communities are presented in terms of households or families. Using the Census Bureau definitions, a family is a group of persons related by birth, marriage, or adoption who reside together in a household. A household includes the related family members and everyone else who occupies a housing unit. A nonfamily household may be an individual living alone or a group of unrelated persons sharing the same housing unit.

Examination of the data for 1970, 1980, and 1991 provides a statistical portrait of trends in family lifestyles. It can be seen, for example, that the numbers of both families with a female householder and nonfamily households increased for all three communities, whites, blacks, and Hispanics. The percentage increase, however, was highest among Hispanics, 74 percent in both categories. Nevertheless, blacks continued to lead in the percentage of children under 18 living with the mother only or neither parent.

	1970	1980	1991
Household Type (number, 1,000)			
Family Households			
White, total	46,166	52,243	56,803
Married couple	41,029	44,751	47,014
Female householder	4,099	6,052	7,471
Black, total	4,856	6,184	7,471
Married couple	3,317	3,433	3,569
Female householder	1,358	2,495	3,430
Hispanic, total	2,004	3,029	4,981
Married couple	1,615	2,282	3,454
Female householder	307	610	1,186
Nonfamily Households			
White	10,436	18,522	24,166
Black	1,367	2,402	3,200
Hispanic	299	654	1,238
Family Size (average number of members)			
White	3.52	3.23	3.12
Black	4.13	3.67	3.51
Hispanic	4.28	3.90	3.82

Generalizations on Family Ideals and Norms

Generalizations summarize a body of knowledge and serve as an orientation to expected behaviors and attitudes. They have built-in limitations, however, and should not be taken to mean that every person or family in a group fits the description. A good generalization describes as many people in a group as possible, but, by definition, it allows for exceptions. To generalize, after all, is only to speak "in general."

Number of Own Children under 18 (percent distribution)

No Children

White	45%	49%	53%
Black	39	38	41
Hispanic	30	31	36

One Child

White	18	21	19
Black	18	23	25
Hispanic	20	22	22

Three or More Children

White	19	11	10
Black	29	18	15
Hispanic	31	23	19

Children under 18, Living Arrangements (percent distribution)

With Both Parents

White	90%	83%	79%
Black	59	42	36
Hispanic	78	75	66

With Mother Only

White	8	14	17
Black	30	44	54
Hispanic	NA	20	27

With Neither Parent

White	2	2	2
Black	10	12	7
Hispanic	NA	4	4

Source: U.S. Bureau of the Census, *Statistical Abstract of the United States: 1992,* 112th edition (Washington, DC, 1992), Tables 57, 66, and 69.

In making the following generalizations, therefore, we start with the assumption that all minority-group families are not the same. Each group is a distinct, complex entity, and there is likely to be variation within groups as well as between groups. The generalizations in this section should serve to sensitize social service workers to probable differences. They are rules of thumb which provide a starting point for assessing minority families, and they should be quickly discarded when they do not seem to fit.

1. Minority and majority ethnic and racial communities share a common set of basic values. There are more similarities than differences in the family-life ideals of Americans.

This might seem to be a surprising generalization, but the literature appears to support it. While most social scientists and social service workers use the terminology of cultural diversity, they also give considerable attention to cultural similarity. People in minority and majority groups alike espouse the ideals of heterosexuality, monogamy, the two-parent nuclear family, relatively egalitarian roles for husband and wife, involvement in the rearing of children by both parents, and the maintenance of close kinship ties. In terms of the ambience of family life, most people, in both minority and majority communities, aspire to endow family life with the qualities of caring, acceptance, nurturing, warmth, cooperativeness, and openness. There are a few racial- and ethnic-community members who advocate truly alternative family structures; Paula Gunn Allen, for instance, argues for the large matriarchal, matrilocal, extended-kin families among Native Americans.[21] But few minority-group members champion such family forms as cohabitation or single-parent families, and none would suggest that family life should be typified by such qualities as coldness, insensitivity, neglect, or abuse.

Jerold Heiss supports this generalization with data from 1974 and 1979 national surveys on the attitudes of black and white women on a number of family issues. While there were some differences in attitudes, most of them were trivial, and the differences in the history and experiences of blacks and whites did not produce major differences in their attitudes toward the family.[22] A number of studies of family life take the same position. Studies by Walter Allen and John McAdoo, for instance, demonstrate the similarities of black and white fathers.[23] The generalization is supported with respect to other groups as well. John Price notes that today most Native Americans and Alaskan Natives adhere to family lifestyle patterns that are more or less in keeping with middle-class aspirations.[24]

2. When racial- and ethnic-minority families do not aspire to these common ideals, generational differences may be operating.

Differences between minority and majority families most often center around husband-wife and parent-child relations, as well as relations with kin. A major reason for variations in the family lifestyles of racial and ethnic minorities is that these patterns were established in different cultures or native homelands. Their family lifestyles in the United States are carryovers from another social context. As the different groups that make up the mosaic of contemporary American society became incorporated, they brought with them certain values and preferences about the ways family life ought to be organized. In their own eyes, their ways of organizing family life were correct and natural, but in the United States they were confronted with different values and realities. While many immigrants strove to retain their old ways, as each generation came to adulthood it began to adopt the family lifestyle aspirations of mainstream Americans.

The painful changes that were made by southern and eastern European Catholics and Jews as they confronted life in the United States have been described by Michael Novak. Assimilation into the American mainstream for these immigrants meant exchanging the extended-kin family form for more nuclear family forms and discarding patterns of self-help. In the process they had to learn to accept loneliness and the disintegration of family ties; they had to learn that it is all right to put their own interests above those of others, including family members; and they had to learn to rely only on themselves and not to expect family help.[25]

Families whose historical origins are in African, Asian, European, or Latin American societies contain structural and functional elements associated with family life in those societies. These elements will be more visible if a particular family is newly arrived and less visible when the family has been in the United States for several generations. For recent immigrant groups like East Indians, Mexicans, and Haitians and refugee groups like Cubans, Vietnamese, and Central Americans, the ideals of the home country are fresh in their minds. In most of these new groups there is likely to be greater control over family life by members of the older generation, greater emphasis on male dominance, and greater respect for parental authority than in middle-class American families. Joan Jensen reports, for instance, that concerns about male and parental authority are common among East Indian immigrants to the United States:

> The economic independence of some women concerned their husbands; working wives were not able to provide traditional care and services.... Parents were concerned about the erosion of traditional family authority, and the effect it would have on their children as they grew up. They worried about the lack of respect for the elderly.[26]

Similarly, Mary Bowen Wright reports that Vietnamese refugees rebelled against the family attitudes that were being taught their children in the refugee camps: "The program stressed assertiveness and independence...which clashed sharply with the tradition of respect for and submission to parental wishes." In Vietnam they had lived in large extended families dominated by a patriarch, and they were offended by the pressure on family heads to split their extended families into smaller units.[27]

3. When racial- and ethnic-minority families do not aspire to these common ideals, continued contact with a foreign homeland or social isolation from the dominant white majority may be operating.

Families that have been in the United States for many generations may continue to espouse ideals that are somewhat at variance with middle-class ideals. One reason that a culturally different pattern may continue to exist is that the link with the native culture has not been entirely broken, and the pattern continues to be reinforced.[28] Family life in Mexican-American and Puerto Rican communities is a case in point. Because of geographical proximity to the native culture and the relative ease in going to and from the native land, these families can be expected to maintain their Latin American cultural traditions. Many make numerous trips between their homeland and the United States and maintain close ties to relatives remaining behind.

A second reason a culturally different pattern may continue to exist is that the experiences of the minority group in the United States are so hostile that it becomes socially and physically isolated from the dominant group. Under these conditions the group must rely on its own inner strengths, resources, and traditions in order to maintain dignity and cohesion. In African-American and Native American families, family life has a history of existing in a context of hostility.[29] American Indians were forced to live on reservations, and blacks were segregated from whites and their mobility was severely restricted. Systematic efforts were made by the white majority group to eliminate family traditions. In the case of blacks, marriage between slaves was illegal, and couples who considered themselves a family could be broken up at the whim of a slave owner. In the case of Native Americans, Christian missionaries systematically undermined all forms of family life that did not correspond to the patriarchal, nuclear family. Nevertheless, family life continued to be strong in both groups. There is evidence that black family life persisted even under slavery,[30] and the West African heritage has continued to influence the family life of African Americans.[31] Similarly, matriarchal norms have persisted among Native American families, in spite of all attempts to make them patriarchal. In at least one-fourth of the federally recognized tribes, women function as council members and tribal chairs, and many tribes have women as heads of state.[32]

4. When racial- and ethnic-minority families do not conform to these common ideals, social class factors within the group may be operating.

The relevance of social class factors in explaining differences among racial and ethnic groups is a subject of debate. It has been pointed out that comparisons between the white and black middle classes are hazardous because the criteria used to measure white middle-class status are not accurate for the black middle class.[33] Most of the literature on Mexican Americans and other Latinos also has emphasized that cultural traditions are more relevant than class to differences in individual and family behavior. Others, however, have presented data indicating the relevance of social class.[34] The point is not that class is more relevant than culture but rather that, within a culture, social class differences operate to bring about diversity.

The reality of family life for any particular minority family may not conform to middle-class ideals or even to the cultural ideals of the minority group. Thus Robert Hill acknowledges that there are families within the black community that deviate from its norms, even as he quite correctly denies that the black community is by definition deviant.[35] These kinds of within-group differences are better explained by socioeconomic factors than by cultural factors; that is, they do not reflect the values and traditions of a group so much as they reflect adaptations to the improved socioeconomic circumstances of many people in minority groups.

5. When the ideals of racial- and ethnic-minority families differ from these common ideals, a desire for greater involvement in extended-kin networks is likely to be evident.

Both minority- and majority-group families differ in their involvement with extended-kin networks. The traditional extended-kin family included several generations of related individuals living under one roof, headed by a matriarch or patriarch. For the most part, such families do not exist in contemporary American society, except possibly among some Native American tribes.[36] More likely are multigenerational families or modified extended families, networks of independent households living in relative proximity which serve as a source of mutual assistance and maintain strong affiliations.[37] While the basis of the ties among household members is usually common blood (consanguinity), it is also not unusual for **fictive relatives**, that is, close friends, to also achieve status as family members. The literature on minority-group families, much of which is not empirical, suggests that ethnic-minority families are more involved with extended-kin networks than majority families are.

This distinction should be made cautiously, however. Although the nuclear family has replaced the traditional extended-kin family in most industrialized nations, ties to extended kin remain strong.[38] Kinfolk serve many important functions, and a focus on intergenerational ties is the basis of much social work with white middle-class families.[39]

In any case, the literature on minority groups does emphasize kin ties. Certainly, for many Asian Americans, respect for elders and acquiescence to their authority are essential. Among Native Americans, Puerto Ricans, and Mexican Americans, *familism*, a byword meaning strong extended-kin attachments, is frequently used. Puerto Ricans and Mexicans also have strong ties to fictive relatives, giving them such titles as uncle, aunt, godparent (*padrino, madrina*), or co-parent (*compadre, comadre*). Because of their intense family involvement, it is often believed that in these groups family needs supersede individual needs, and the family takes precedence over the individual. Extended-family relationships—those that go beyond the nuclear family—are also highly visible in the African-American community. In the late 1970s, Elmer and Joanne Martin described the black family as a "multigenerational, interdependent kinship system which is welded together by a sense of obligation to relatives." A typical family network could include five or more affiliated households centered around a household with an informally acknowledged, "dominant family figure," often an elderly female or couple. The households might include blood relatives or relatives through marriage, as well as friends.[40]

For many racial and ethnic groups, the ideal of intense involvement with kin may not be evident in reality. While multigenerational families may be necessary to help minorities deal with racism, only mixed support has been found in studies which have attempted to document the existence of strong cooperative, intergenerational ties among minorities. There is little evidence that minorities are exceptionally committed to caring for elderly parents or demonstrating filial responsibility. In these respects, social class and generational differences may be as important as cultural differences.[41] Intense multigenerational involvement thus may be more of an ideal, something to be desired and striven for, than a reality.

6. When the ideals of racial- and ethnic-minority families differ from these common ideals, a greater adherence to paternalistic values is likely to be apparent.

This generalization also must be advanced cautiously. The debate in American society about more egalitarian relations between spouses in marriage applies to minority communities. In certain groups, in particular Asian Americans and Latinos, paternalistic norms are clearly evident. In other groups, such as African Americans and Native Americans, they are not.

Before their unwilling incorporation into American society, both African Americans and Native Americans had strong matriarchal norms. According to certain anthropologists, some Indian tribes or nations were patriarchal and others were matriarchal, but even in the matriarchal tribes women held inferior positions to men. Paula Gunn Allen challenges these assertions, maintaining that the behaviors and thinking of American Indian tribes have been misinterpreted, and "traditional tribal lifestyles are more gynocratic [matriarchal, matrilineal, and matrilocal] than not, and they are never patriarchal."[42] In any case, most writers on Native Americans believe that patriarchal norms now have come into existence as the result of assimilation into the white majority and have been internalized by Indian tribal cultures. It may be that because of the large number of Native American and Alaskan Native peoples, such generalizations should not be made.

Debate on the role of the male in the black family is particularly heated. It has been argued that the black family is matriarchal, and men have only an auxiliary role in it. Increasingly, however, much more variation in black family life is becoming evident in American society. While lower-class black men may have a secondary place in family life, middle-class black men assume roles that are not very different from those of white middle-class men. In general, there is no evidence that black culture values matriarchy higher than patriarchy. Moreover, when black men are absent from home, the reasons are likely to be related to the socioeconomic difficulties they encounter in American society. The argument is that the self-esteem of black men is constantly threatened by racism and economic exploitation, and efforts must be made to call attention to their needs, acknowledge their strengths, and increase their stature.[43] Some writers on the roles of black males clearly assume that they are and should be the rightful head of the family, while others support more egalitarian relationships.[44]

7.   When the ideals of racial- and ethnic-minority families differ from these common ideals, a greater adherence to authoritarian values is likely to be apparent.

In keeping with the multigenerational ideals of many ethnic-minority families, parental obedience and respect for elders are important values. Authoritarian norms are likely to govern parent-child relationships, both between minor children and their parents and between adult children and their elderly parents.

Authoritarian does not necessarily mean that the power structure in minority families is cruel, overbearing, or arbitrary. Parental authority can be expressed in a number of ways: through physical punishment and coercion, social and monetary rewards, or *authoritativeness*, that is, expression of the parents' greater experience and knowledge. In family systems that adhere to authoritarian norms, the vertical hierarchy is specified, and parents or elders are clearly in the role of decision maker. Family life reflects a centralized authority, not a group of peers in which everyone, regardless of age, has more-or-less equal influence.

In the traditional Mexican-American family, a major characteristic is "subordination of the younger to the older."[45] In the Japanese community, *oyakoko* prescribes the respect, awareness of obligation, and dependence that should be reflected in relationships between parents and children.[46] It is considered the cornerstone of morality in the family, requiring children to give their parents unquestioning obedience and loyalty and to be sensitive to their family duties. According to Man Keung Ho, filial piety and dominance and deference based on paternalism are cultural values among all Asian-American groups. Discussion and debate about decisions is precluded in Asian families: "The role of the parent is to define the law; the duty of the child is to listen and obey."[47]

The literature on African Americans and Native Americans is less clear in respect to this generalization, and it may not apply. In relations between parents and minor children, Native Americans are likely to reflect the opposite of authoritarian norms, and permissive child rearing appears to be the ideal. However, as John Red Horse observes, the role of elders in family life and tribal interactions cannot be underestimated: "Elders are important and provide continuity of world view; they also lend wisdom to daily life and bring order to chaos. Elders are reminders of heritage and survival and strength."[48]

With respect to black families, the evidence is also not very clear. In some studies black parents were found to be less permissive than other types of parents.[49] Other studies indicated that while physical punishment of children is likely in black families, it is not likely to be harsh and probably is counterbalanced with a great deal of love. As a result, parent-child relations often are free of the anxiety often found in white middle-class families. After interviewing 160 black mothers and fathers, Karen Bartz and Elaine Levine concluded that black parents typically expect early autonomy in children, do not allow wasted time, are both highly supportive and controlling, value strictness, and encourage egalitarian family roles.[50]

☙ AN OVERVIEW OF RACIAL- AND ETHNIC-MINORITY FAMILIES

To illustrate the generalizations about minority family norms and ideals, we will examine more closely the cultural and family lifestyles of the peoples of color whose attempts to achieve the socioeconomic success of mainstream American society were described in Chapter 5. The following sections on Native Americans, African Americans, Latinos, and

Asian Americans demonstrate how the norms and ideals of racial- and ethnic-minority families differ and the extent to which they have been adapted to the social and economic conditions of life in the United States.

Native Americans and Alaskan Natives

There is no single, definite "American Indian" culture. In colonial times there were hundreds of groups of indigenous peoples, ethnically and even racially distinct, living in the area that is now the United States. The cultural variation that existed among Native Americans and Alaskan Natives was greater than the variation among European groups; that is, the differences between such peoples as the Mohawk, Menominee, Navajo, and Klamath were probably greater than those between the Italians, Germans, Irish, and Polish. These variations were evident in language, in the economy, government, and religion, and in family life patterns and institutions. Price notes that "almost all of the world's major variants of marriage, incest prohibitions, postmarriage residence customs, and in-law relations were practiced by one native North American society or another."[51] In about 20 percent of the native groups, polygamy and homosexual coupling were also practiced.[52]

To demonstrate the diversity that existed among the various groups, Price compared the Eskimo, Hopi, and Kwakiutl tribes in the colonial era of the United States. Eskimos lived in bands in the Arctic region and built their economy around hunting and gathering. They permitted premarital sex; practiced monogamy, although wives were often given to male guests as a token of good manners; had neolocal postmarital residence (the married couple set up their own household); and acknowledged **bilateral descent** (traced through

Extended-family ties are an important part of the Native American culture of this Navaho family living in the Southwest.

both sets of parents). There was a division of labor in the band; men hunted, women gathered, and both fished and built the houses. There was little display of emotion between husband and wife. Sometimes the relationship may have been close, affectionate, and satisfying, but at least from the point of view of outside observers, it appears to have been strained. Eskimo society was patriarchal; men treated their wives as inferiors and avoided deep interpersonal relations with them. The rights of parents over children were not questioned. Infanticide was common; the mother decided whether a newborn was strong and healthy enough to survive the inhospitable climate of the Arctic. Infants who were desired were indulged and nurtured with intense, continuous, warm maternal care.

The Hopi, who continue to live in their ancestral lands in what is now the state of Arizona, subsisted on the fruits of communal agriculture. They permitted premarital sex but insisted on monogamy in marriage. Newly married couples moved to the home of the wife's mother, and descent was traced through the maternal line. However, Hopi men retained ritual, leadership, and disciplinary roles in their family of origin. It was the "social father," that is, the mother's brother, that disciplined the children; the biological father had a passive child-rearing role in his wife's household. The socialization of children was extremely permissive, with little explicit discipline and very gradual weaning and toilet training. The Hopi extended-kin and tribal system allowed for little privacy, and gossip and punishment through ridicule and religious ritual (the *Kiva*) was common. Men hunted and women cultivated; weaving was done by men and house building by both men and women.

The Kwakiutl, who inhabited the Northwest coastal area, were organized into chiefdoms and subsisted largely through fishing. They prohibited premarital sex but allowed for polygamy. The newly married couple moved to the husband's father's residence, and descent was traced through the paternal line. Men hunted and women gathered, but both were involved in fishing. Men did the house building, and women did the weaving.

For many native tribes, co-residence by same-sex partners was also acceptable. The term **berdache** was introduced by Europeans to describe the custom of reversal of the customary gender roles in native cultures. Indian tribes are likely to have their own terms for homosexually inclined people. The Lakota use *koskalaka* to describe a "woman who doesn't want to marry" and *winkte* to describe such a male.[53] In earlier centuries, it was not uncommon for a man or a woman to cross-dress, cross-work, or cross-speak. The man-woman or woman-man was often bisexual, but it is also likely that many were exclusively homosexual. The cross-sex berdache would also live in a sexual relationship with a same-sex partner, and homosexual relations may have existed among others. In any case, sex segregation was common in many tribes, with women and men living in separate structures.

The diverse forms of family life found among the various native groups were looked on with horror by the colonizing Europeans. As they gained superiority, Europeans set out to impose their own concept of "proper" family life on the native populations. They systematically set out to eliminate polygamy, homosexuality, and matrilineal customs and to support patriarchal norms through the activities of Christian missionaries and through legislation. Native groups were forced to give up their hunting and gathering and to turn to agriculture as the major form of subsistence. More recently, they have turned to industrialization and tourism.

Adaptation to Contemporary Life

Research on Native American families has lagged behind research on many other minority communities. As a result, we lack clear understanding of the changes that have been taking place as Native Americans participate fully in contemporary American society. It is reasonable to conclude, however, that most Native Americans and Alaskan Natives have family lifestyles that are more or less in keeping with the norms of the society; monogamous, patrilineal, nuclear families predominate.[54] Although strong and supportive kin networks are still desired, the classical extended-kin family involving multifamily residences and corporate kinship groups is not very common. The ideal of respecting the elderly is still upheld, but it is not uncommon for elders to experience a loss of status and social isolation. One Native American elder put it this way:

> We were put on the sidelines. Left on the bench. There was a time when this was not true. When age and experience was a vital and dynamic part of the Native culture. Traditionally, the elders were held in high regard. They were listened to, honored, and included in the ongoing life of the Indian community. There was no shame in having lived a good and full life. On the contrary, the older Indian was considered wise and knowledgeable. When problems arose, it was our answers, our advice and counsel, to which the people turned. We were the guides, the conscience, of the Indian nation. We were as much a part of tribal life as anyone else. We had our place, our home, among the family of Native people.[55]

Modern Native American families are experiencing many of the same problems confronted by other Americans: high divorce rates; increased cohabitation; more female-headed, single-parent households; greater participation by women in the labor force; and greater numbers of people of all ages who live alone. Robert John concludes that family integration and the strong family networks evident among Native Americans in the past are increasingly less influential in their family life.[56]

The likelihood that an American Indian tribe has adapted its cultural and family life to conform to middle class norms in the United States is related to a number of conditions. One is the historical and geographic isolation of the group from American culture. To the extent that the group continues to live on reservations apart from the white mainstream, the chances of retaining Indian ways are higher. The Hopi and the Inuit have managed to escape most of the destruction and intrusion of European cultures, and in many ways their social patterns and strong tribal identity have prevailed. Yet changes are apparent. The Hopi, for instance, have never been Christianized, and while they have accepted English as the primary language, they retain their native tongue as a second language. They also continue to have strong matriarchal tendencies. But they have accepted free-market economic activities; they work for wages, attend non-Hopi schools, use automobiles and electrical appliances, shop at supermarkets, and wear Western dress.

Changes in family lifestyles occur as Native Americans leave the reservations and establish themselves in urban areas. Relatives function to buffer the move from reservation to city, and urban enclaves of Native Americans serve as temporary reference groups for new arrivals and help them adjust. Red Horse argues that the urban environment has not profoundly influenced family and kin network patterns among North Americans,[57] but high rates of intermarriage across different Indian groups or with non-Native Americans help dissipate the enclaves. Some studies have suggested that Native Americans do not congregate in particular neighborhoods in cities but are integrated, and there are differences among those who live in cities. One study found a wide range in degree of attachment to and involvement in American Indian ways but that, in general, tribal preferences were not strong.[58]

Further changes are likely as Native Americans participate in the national economy and class divisions are created within tribes. Studies on the Menominee of Wisconsin are important in this regard. George and Louise Spindler found five social segments in this tribe, of either acculturated or nonacculturated types. The nonacculturated, those who attempted to adhere to the traditional Menominee culture, include the "native oriented" and the Peotists, who believe that children are reincarnated elders and have supernatural power. The acculturated types include those undergoing transition from the traditional Indian to American culture and the lower-class and elite acculturated. The acculturated derive pride and identity from the native heritage but aspire to imitate the ways of the white American majority.[59]

American Blacks and African Americans

The Africans forcibly introduced into American society through slave trafficking in the early years of the Republic generally were not members of the societies that supplied them to European traders; they were captives. From the beginning, black slaves brought to the United States were cut off from their kinship networks and native cultures. On the journey, the slave masters tried to forestall rebellion by deliberately mixing captives of different societies, thus reinforcing the separation. And after arrival in the United States, the slaves were subjected to restrictive laws which served to prevent the development of community and ethnicity (see Chapter 5). They were forbidden to legally marry and have families, though slave owners sometimes promoted marriage and family ties for their own purposes, with no legal recognition.

The effects of slavery on black family life have been debated. Early in the twentieth century, E. Franklin Frazier argued that because slaveholders often disrespected spousal and parental relationships in selling slaves, they created a hostile environment in which black two-parent family life never had a chance to take hold, and a strong matriarchal pattern emerged.[60] His argument has been used to explain the higher incidence of single-parent families and unwed mothers among lower-class blacks today.

Recent evidence has called this scenario into question. Herbert Gutman and his associates examined census schedules and other documents in the period 1750–1925 and found evidence that most slaves formed stable unions, living together until they died unless one of them was sold away. Most slave children grew up in two-parent families with strong ties to a larger kin group. A high percentage of black families living in New York's Harlem as late as 1925 had two parents.[61] According to Andrew Hacker, the many homes now headed by black single parents "cannot be attributed to a plantation past." Noting that in 1950, only 17 percent of black households were headed by women, the same as the rate for white households in 1990, he concludes that "within living memory, homes with two parents were very much the black norm."[62]

The birth rate for unmarried black women actually declined somewhat between 1970 and 1989, from 95.5 to 93.1 for each 1,000 women; at the same time, it was more than doubling for unmarried white women, from 13.9 to 29.2 births for each 1,000 women.[63] As the data indicate, however, it is still overwhelmingly more likely for black women to bear children out of wedlock. Andrew Cherlin, who observes that "having a first child and getting married appear to have become unrelated events for more and more black women during the postwar period," acknowledges that this is also true for whites, but it is far more pervasive for blacks.[64]

Focusing on such data has encouraged the stereotype of black family life as pathological. Theories of juvenile delinquency among lower-class blacks have pointed to a matriarchal family structure typified by neurotic, ambivalent relationships between mothers and their male offspring in families with absent fathers,[65] or they have blamed "dysfunctional" family life for continued poverty among blacks.[66] While family structure and dy-

---

Social Pressures Producing Single-Parent Families

During the past 20 years, single-parent households, almost all of which are headed by women, have become increasingly common throughout American society. The cause for greatest concern is in the African-American community, where they now represent over half of all households. The loss of male breadwinners in these homes has done much to perpetuate poverty, and the parental controls once exercised by fathers, especially over teenagers, are missing.

In his analysis of the conditions that continue to keep blacks and whites apart, Andrew Hacker points out that since the 1950s the proportion of families with children headed by women has been higher among blacks than among whites by a fairly constant ratio of about 3 to 1. This suggests that the difference is due not so much to racial characteristics as it is to "concurrent adaptations to cultural trends." He identifies two forces at work in the society as a whole that have precipitated the rise in single-parent households: men's liberation and women's right to reproduce.

American men, directed by public opinion, religious beliefs, and a sense of duty, traditionally kept their marriages intact or married and formed families when a child was known to be on the way. Today, with little social censure or economic cost, married men can leave their wives and children and start again with another companion and another family of children. Fathers seldom fully support the children they leave behind, whether or not they had been married to the mothers. If court-ordered payments are made, they do not keep pace with the costs of caring for growing children.

American unmarried women or girls who became pregnant traditionally were forced by public censure to give up their babies for adoption. Today, the decision of a woman (including 15-year-old females) to produce a child, under any conditions, is viewed as a personal right. In over 90 percent of the cases, single mothers now also choose to take the infants home and rear them alone. The choice available to single women to reproduce and start families of their own has exerted great upward pressure on the number of households headed by women.

Hacker concludes that "little will be gained by lecturing only one race on its domestic duties. To ask black Americans to show greater discipline carries the implication that only they have deviated from national norms. In fact, if any strictures are in order, they apply equally to white Americans." (p. 72)

Source: Andrew Hacker, *Two Nations: Black and White, Separate and Unequal* (New York: Charles Scribner's Sons, 1992), pp. 69–72.

---

namics may have some role in causing delinquency and maintaining poverty, family factors cannot be seen as the primary cause, nor can they be separated from the social context which produces them.[67] The reasons for the preponderance of single-parent black families, for example, can be found in developments in American society that are unrelated to race or social class (see "Social Pressures Producing Single-Parent Families").

Diversity in Black Family Lifestyles

Andrew Billingsley argued in the late 1960s that black families must be understood in terms of their variation and complexity, thereby acknowledging that the African-American community is diverse and incorporates a number of family lifestyles.[68] What might appear on the outside to be unusual or pathological may not be so on closer inspection. In the case of single-parent black families, for instance, the idea of a single parent suggests a lone woman in social isolation struggling to rear her children, but this situation is not common in the black community. A single-parent family often includes a number of kin, such as a mother, aunt, or brother, in a number of households making up a domestic network. The network of supportive relatives is the family, rather than the single parent alone.

Hacker, writing in 1992, agrees that "No law of humanity or nature posits a precise format for the family." In his opinion, black Americans are fully aware that households headed by women and births outside of marriage have become basic facts of life within the African-American community. The real problem now is that increasing numbers of black infants are being born to mothers who are immature and poor, and the support systems provided by their extended families that blacks could rely on in the past can no longer take on these obligations as they once did. Relatives have burdens of their own, and the resources of blacks have been depleted by increasing unemployment, greater use of drugs, and a higher proportion of people in prison. The key change in recent years, Hacker says, is in the balance of dependency; instead of being the exception, single parents now outnumber conventional households among blacks as a whole.[69] As we indicate in the table in "Characteristics of Households and Families" in this chapter, the proportion of black children living with both parents declined from 59 percent in 1970 to 36 percent in 1991; in the same period, those living with the mother only increased from 30 percent to 54 percent.

Much of the diversity in family lifestyles in the African-American community is class-based. Black families in which the husband and wife have stable employment are not much different from working-class and middle-class white families. Poverty-class blacks are likely to have a very different family pattern, however. In attempting to describe the complexity of the black community in the late 1960s, Ulf Hannerz devised a classification of four lifestyles: mainstreamers, swingers, street families, and street-corner men. In a similar vein, Charles Willie's classification in the early 1980s distinguished among the family lifestyles of conformists, innovators, and rebels.[70] Social class is the underlying dimension in both of these typologies. In the following sketches of black family lifestyle differences, which incorporate the ideas of both Hannerz and Willie, the terms might seem dated in some parts of the black community but the attributes generally apply to different types of black families in the 1990s.

Affluent blacks, who might be described as *mainstreamers*, aspire to the ideals of American society and approximate them quite well in reality. In their values and beliefs and their organization of family life, they are largely indistinguishable from other middle-class Americans. A Puritanical orientation emphasizes work, success, and self-reliance. Having managed to overcome prejudice and discrimination and achieve material success, they often are sensitive to racism and the way it hinders the well-being of blacks. Generally, they are married, live in nuclear families, and maintain stable family relations. Relatively high incomes are largely attributable to two-parent employment. They attach great value to home ownership, educational achievement, and family-oriented leisure activities. Because both parents work, however, there may be little socializing. As blacks continue to achieve middle-class status, the mainstreamer perspective on family life can be expected to increase.

Swingers is the term Hannerz used to describe black youths who are in many ways like "liberated" white, middle-class, young adults whose lifestyles are built around peer-oriented social, athletic, economic, and political activities. Often the children of mainstreamers, they generally are not family oriented but spend their leisure time exploring personal interests and experimenting with the opportunities available to single people in contemporary society. This lifestyle is related more to young-adult status than to a permanent way of life. Eventually most marry, settle down, and take up lifestyles similar to those of mainstreamers.

Working-class black families might be described as *innovators*. In these families, caught up in a struggle for survival, family cohesiveness is based less on understanding and tenderness than on the need to stave off adversity. Working-class couples may have several children in whom they take great pride; children are considered successful if they can avoid illegal or deviant opportunities in the neighborhood. Working-class blacks generally have a strong sense of morality and are deeply religious, even if they do not participate fully in church activities. The relationship between husband and wife is likely to be egalitarian, since cooperation is essential to survival. Nevertheless, male and female roles are specified clearly; both may work, but husbands make financial and housing decisions and give advice to boys, while wives clean, cook, and give advice to girls. Their values emphasize upward mobility, and they are committed to rearing children as good citizens.

Poor black families are "forced to make a number of necessary, clever, and sometimes foolish arrangements," according to Willie.[71] The term *street families* has most often been applied to the poor, single-parent, female-headed family. This family pattern is associated with poverty-level blacks in the urban underclass; the single mother, lacking in education and employment opportunities, must maintain the family household. Street families are often viewed with contempt, not only by whites, who see in them all the pathology of black community life, but also by middle-class blacks, who object to what they perceive as instability and a lack of concern for sexual and family respectability. Where street families headed by single mothers have been able to attach to a network of households, they can share economic and social resources in the extended family. The fastest-growing black family form, according to Hacker, consists of three generations residing in a single household—a mother, one or more adolescent daughters, and the daughters' children. The mother becomes a grandmother, and the household includes one or more subfamilies headed by the daughters.[72] By expanding the family in this way, economic and social resources can be shared. The flexibility of the network of street families, their willingness to include friends as well as relatives and to share and cooperate, is crucial to the survival of unemployed and underemployed blacks. Willie notes, however, that street families are likely to experience internal conflict. Parents love their children but seldom understand them; the scapegoating of deviant children is common. Men or women who become sexually involved outside the network may be afraid to marry and rely solely on one other person.

Street-corner men represent the other side of the street families headed by women in Hannerz's typology. Street-corner society, consisting of lower-class black men of all ages, has been the subject of a number of studies.[73] With few or no educational and economic opportunities, these men seldom make or maintain domestic attachments and often live among others like themselves, filling the ranks of the homeless. They may survive by making temporary attachments to street families, by working at occasional jobs, or by seizing illegal opportunities. There is a comaraderie among the men which offers economic and emotional support, but there is also animosity and violence. It is a difficult life, made up of monotonous routines.

Latinos

The central role of family life in Latino communities has been described as *familism*. In the Mexican-American community, the term includes immediate family, extended kin (aunts, uncles, grandparents, cousins, and in-laws), and co-parents or godparents.[74] In

Puerto Rican culture, although the nuclear family pattern is increasingly apparent, value is also attached to strong, intimate ties with kin and companion parents, that is, godparents, witnesses at a marriage, or close friends. As with blacks living in poverty, single-parent families and common-law marriages are frequent among impoverished Puerto Ricans, but ties to the households of relatives and companion parents remain strong.[75]

The traditional Latino culture was marked by a strict dichotomy between men and women in the family. Men were supposed to be *macho*, while women were supposed to be bound to the house, caring for children and husband, uninterested in sexual fulfillment yet submitting to the desires of their husbands out of respect for male "needs." This sexual division, which has been labeled *machismo* for men and *marianismo* (after the Blessed Virgin Mary) for women, is seen by many inside the Latino community as a major source of strain in family life. Sonia Ghali draws a particularly negative image of the Puerto Rican male in the traditional marriage: "He advocates a double standard of sexual morality. The Puerto Rican husband may not be home often, preferring the company of his male friends or his mistress. The married woman, usually aware of her husband's extra-marital affairs, is expected to suffer in silence."[76]

There is considerable ambivalence toward these roles within the Latino community, however. Some see the male's role as a positive attribute and maintain that Americans' use of *macho* distorts the true meaning of the word. David Alvirez, Frank Bean, and Dorie Williams, for instance, caution against a narrow, overly sexual interpretation. They do not deny that the *macho* tradition gave the male license to pursue sexual affairs, but they argue that it also imposed important values such as "courage, honor, and respect for others, as well as the notion of providing fully for one's family and maintaining close ties with the extended-kin family." Male authority in the household was never absolute and was always expected to be used in a just and fair manner.[77]

Studies of class differences among Mexican Americans suggest that, compared to lower-class families, middle-class families are less patriarchal and relationships between spouses are more egalitarian. In one study middle-class and lower-class Mexican-American women were asked what they expected from their husbands. Middle-class wives demonstrated a greater desire for expressive qualities (sensitivity to needs and affection), while lower-class wives were more likely to want instrumental qualities (doing house repairs, mowing the lawn, etc.). While middle-class Mexican-American women are more likely than those in the lower class to desire an egalitarian relationship with their husbands, in neither group was this preference cited by even half of the women.[78]

Asian Americans

Family life is strong in Chinese and Japanese communities. The importance of the family in Chinese culture cannot be overemphasized, and the Japanese show great concern for family reputation and strive not to bring shame on the family line. In both groups the effect of an individual's actions on the family governs behavior, and the personal desires of the individual are expected to be subordinated to the needs of the family. The Japanese term *kenshin* expresses the renunciation of selfish desires in favor of common family interests. In both groups, also, the family is multigenerational and includes extended kin, although fictive relatives do not have an important role in Japanese and Chinese family life.[79]

Traditional Japanese and Chinese families were strongly hierarchal, with male authority clearly in control. In Chinese culture the ideal family is multigenerational, marked by patrilineal descent and patrilocal residence. In Japanese culture maintenance of the reputation of the *ie*, the lineage of the father, is of most concern. The head of the family is accorded the respect due his position and expects loyalty and obedience from his family. Males are given prerogatives and status that are generally superior to those accorded women.[80]

The survival of the Japanese family and its traditions was the subject of a recent study by Harry Kitano, who notes that with improvement in the socioeconomic status of Japanese Americans, outgroup marriages have increased greatly. Japanese-American females are more likely to marry out than Japanese-American males, and Japanese in general are more likely to marry into the dominant white community than any other group. Kitano suggests, however, that outmarriages are likely to increase in other Asian groups such as the Chinese and Koreans, even though they include large numbers of first-generation immigrants.[81]

✆ FAMILY LIFESTYLES OF GAYS AND LESBIANS

The members of the gay and lesbian community described in Chapter 4 have developed distinctive family lifestyles, both as couples outside marriage and as partners of heterosexual mates and parents. Lesbian and gay couples seldom are included in definitions of marriage and the family, but their nonfamily households are often built around lasting relationships. Their relationships as spouses of heterosexuals and as parents may pose problems that require special care.

Couples in Lasting Relationships

The number of homosexuals seeking to form lasting relationships apparently is growing, and as they live together they are fashioning family lifestyles with unique roles, norms, and values. The problems gays and lesbians encounter in these attempts are related to the discrimination they face in American society. Legal and social obstacles are erected to obstruct their efforts to achieve a family lifestyle, in the same way the extended-kin, plural-marriage, matriarchal family pattern of Native Americans was considered savage and its eradication was attempted and slaveholders tried to destroy black family life by outlawing marriage and separating families. The implications of two lesbians or two gay men forming a long-term union are threatening to those who see in homosexuality a challenge to family values. There have been concerted efforts, for instance, to block the passage of local ordinances to permit cohabiting couples, both heterosexual and homosexual, to register their relationships in much the same way couples apply for marriage licenses (see Chapter 4). Such "domestic partners" then have the same legal standing as families in specific matters such as medical insurance coverage and residential zoning regulations. Critics maintain that legislation of this type redefines the family by function rather than structure, and it is regarded as a threat to the support of marriage and family life in American society.

Homosexual couples with lifestyles analogous to those of heterosexual couples constitute a relatively new development in Western societies. In ancient Greece and Rome and in Victorian England, homosexuality apparently existed within a heterosexual context. Some married men (such as the tragic Oscar Wilde) lived bisexual lives, compartmentalizing their homosexual and heterosexual interests.[82] Imitation of heterosexual roles, with one partner taking the role of the husband and the other the role of the wife, apparently

A lesbian mother and her partner provide a caring family lifestyle for
rearing their 2-year-old son on a California farm.

was prevalent in the past. For instance, in the berdache custom, many American Indian
tribes allowed for marriages between same-sex partners. Sometimes, as among the Zuni,
this included a ceremony recognized by the whole community. The berdache always involved a man who became a woman or a woman who became a man, each fulfilling the
achieved gender role according to the customs of the tribe.[83] In Western societies it appears that in the recent past it was quite common for these couples to imitate heterosexual role patterns. Two well-known homosexual couples were Gertrude Stein, who is said
to have played husband to Alice B. Toklas, and George Merrill, who apparently assumed
the wife role for Edward Carpenter.

Crafting a Contemporary Lifestyle

The gay and lesbian community in contemporary American society is necessarily creating
its own roles, norms, and values to govern long-term relationships as couples. Homosexual couples must define their roles with few models of same-sex intimacy to guide them.
An article in *Practice Digest* notes that such couples are:

> ...raised by heterosexual parents, lacking marriage manuals and images of conjugal bliss
> on film or television, faced with a situation where gay couples who do develop successful
> relationships are seldom visible, unable to acquire the socially sanctioned same-sex dating
> experiences equivalent to that which non-gay men and women get with each other dur-
> ing adolescence, and lacking structured courtship rituals,...[84]

Like other discriminated-against groups, the gay and lesbian community is extremely diverse. Same-sex couples living together represent only one lifestyle (see "Diversity in Homosexual Lifestyles" in Chapter 4). While the practice of coupling is growing, it has not been institutionalized in the community because the appropriate values to sustain long-lasting relationships have not been developed. According to Philip Blumstein and Pepper Schwartz in their study of American couples:

> There is a general fear in both gay and lesbian circles that relationships are unlikely to last. Long-lasting relationships are seen as quite special. They are unexpected and therefore newly formed couples are not treated as though they will remain together for fifty years. People are less likely to ask, "How's Jerry?" and more likely to say, "Are you still with your lover?"[85]

The ideals for which gays and lesbians are searching as they seek out relatively same-age, long-term partners are more egalitarian than those expressed in the role patterns of heterosexual partners. David McWhirter and Andrew Mattison surveyed 156 male couples and found that only among older couples, those who had been together for over 20 years, was the male-female, husband-wife pattern followed.[86] Lesbian families that include children typically make nonsexist role assignments in which the mother and her partner, as well as the children, take a wide range of family roles.[87] Allen Bell and Martin Weinberg also found relatively little evidence for widespread imitation of heterosexual gender roles or sexual techniques among gay and lesbian couples.[88]

Homosexual liaisons are generally believed to be temporary and promiscuous, and studies have found that it is not uncommon for gay men to experience many sexual encounters in their lives. Among the homosexual males surveyed by Bell and Weinberg for their study published in 1978 (before the first cases of AIDS had been reported), almost half of the whites and one-third of the blacks said they had had at least 500 different sexual patterns.[89] While even long-term sexual relationships among gay men are not likely to emphasize sexual fidelity, they do expect emotional fidelity in the relationship. McWhirter and Mattison conclude that

> ...the majority of couples in our study, and all of the couples together for longer than five years, were not continuously sexually exclusive with each other. Although many had long periods of sexual exclusivity, it was not the ongoing expectation for most. We found that gay men expect mutual emotional dependability with their partners and that relationship fidelity transcends concerns about sexuality and exclusivity.[90]

In contrast, the norm of sexual fidelity is expected in lesbian relationships. Lesbians reported far fewer multiple experiences in the Bell and Weinberg survey; about a quarter said they had had less than 5 liaisons, one-third said they had had between 5 and 6, and another third, between 10 and 50. However, Blumstein and Schwartz note that because the lesbian community is based on tightly knit friendship groups, unlike the more open gay male community, it also tends to undermine sexual fidelity. The closeness of the friendship ties often slips over into love relationships which disrupt the friendship network.[91]

The evidence on number of partners and sexual fidelity suggests that homosexual men have generated norms which are significantly different from those of either heterosexual or lesbian couples. For some writers on the subject, multiple sexual partners and emotional dependability without sexual exclusiveness mean liberation; they do not use the term *promiscuity* in reference to the sexual behavior of gay men. Others do not take a moral stance but explain it in terms of male socialization, both heterosexual and homosexual. Since in American society men have been expected to be more sexually active, more independent, and less intimate than women, it should be expected that exclusivity and faithfulness would not figure very prominently.[92] Still others see these norms as an indication of the oppressive circumstances confronted by gay men, an aberration that will disappear as gays achieve legitimacy and respectability within society.

A development that has encouraged the formation of monogamous, long-term relationships among gay men and lesbians is the continuing spread of AIDS (see "AIDS and the Gay and Lesbian Community"). The first cases of AIDS reported in the United States were found among homosexual men in 1981. By the end of 1992, according to the U.S. surgeon general's report to the American people, 1 million Americans—1 in about every 250—was infected with HIV, more than a quarter of a million had developed AIDS, and more than 170,000 had died. Gay men still accounted for the majority of AIDS cases, but the disease was becoming more prevalent in children and adolescents and in heterosexual men and women. The surgeon general concluded, "AIDS is now becoming a disease of families."[93]

In many ways gay and lesbian couples face the same social situations and problems as heterosexual couples do, though there are unique qualities in their lifestyles. Couples have problems in both kinds of sexual orientation because the partners have different expectations, having grown up in different cultural or socioeconomic settings or having come from different racial, religious, or educational backgrounds. Like heterosexual couples, lesbian and gay couples "go to work, plan vacations, pay bills, and deal with illness, aging parents, and the deaths of family and friends."[94]

Relations with Heterosexual Spouses and as Parents

In two of the earliest contemporary studies on sexual behavior in human females and males, Alfred Kinsey and his colleagues reported that only a small percentage of women and men are exclusively homosexual throughout their lives.[95] Many are bisexual or go through a period of relatively homosexual or heterosexual behavior. Lesbians and gay men, in fact, often are heterosexual spouses and parents.

Gay men and lesbians may marry before they become aware of their sexual orientation or they can adequately accept it. Del Martin and Phyllis Lyon observe that lesbian mothers often are

> ...women who were unaware of their Lesbian tendencies until after they had married and had children. Or they are women who suppressed their Lesbian feelings, convinced, as most heterosexuals are, that these feelings merely represented a natural phase in their lives and would disappear after they experienced marriage and motherhood.[96]

Norman Wyers asked a nonrandom sample of 77 lesbian wives and gay husbands why they had married. Among the lesbian wives, the three primary reasons given were "always expected to" (38 percent), "love of spouse" (24 percent), and "pregnancy" (18 percent). Among the gay husbands, the primary reasons were "love of spouse" (34 percent), "always expected to" (28 percent), and hopes for "conversion to heterosexuality" (19 percent). Most of the lesbians and gay men responding to this survey had divorced or were separated from their heterosexual spouses. Among the lesbian wives, the most important reason given for the divorce was that they and their husbands were "always incompatible." Only secondarily did the women believe they had divorced because of their homosexual orientation. The gay husbands, on the other hand, overwhelmingly indicated that their homosexual orientation was the major reason for the divorce.[97]

AIDS and the Gay and Lesbian Community

Acquired immune deficiency syndrome (AIDS) is an infectious, chronic, and fatal disease caused by a retrovirus known as the human immunodeficiency virus (HIV). HIV is transmitted through unprotected sexual intercourse with an infected person; via contact with infected blood, semen, or vaginal secretions; or by being passed to an infant from an infected mother before, during, or shortly after birth. Once transmitted, the virus attacks and undermines the immune system, making the infected person vulnerable to cancer, nervous system degeneration, and opportunistic infections caused by other viruses, parasites, bacteria, and fungi. When first recognized in the early 1980s, AIDS was considered a crisis event leading inevitably to quick and early death. With advances in treatment, it is now viewed as a chronic illness that can be managed but not cured.

HIV disease has become a pandemic threatening to devastate millions of men, women, and children. Worldwide, heterosexual men and women and their children make up the majority of cases, and 5 to 10 million people are believed to be infected. In the United States, 315,390 cases of AIDS had been reported to the U.S. Department of Health and Human Services by June 1993, and 61 percent of all adult cases reported have involved "men who have sex with men."

Because of the stigma attached to those with AIDS, many gays and lesbians feared the disease would not only destroy the lives of those affected but would also bring down their fledgling human rights movement. It appears, however, that the disease has served to rally the resolve of lesbians and gays, thereby strengthening the community. Although lesbians have generally not fallen victim to HIV, they, along with heterosexual women, have joined gay men in fighting the disease.

In the process the culture of the gay male community in particular and the lesbian community more generally appears to have changed dramatically. Where once it was identified with youth, barhopping, free sexual expression, and abundant drugs, it is now a more serious community rich in social services and political lobbies, in volunteerism and civic spirit, and in a new respect for long-term committed relationships. The AIDS epidemic has also served to familiarize members of the larger heterosexual community with the roles, norms, and values of lesbians and gays. It has brought franker and less judgmental discussion of lesbian and gay issues into the nation's media and college classrooms and opened the doors of charities and foundations and of government officials, even the president. Although lesbians and gays are still not accepted by many conservative religious and political interests, the nation has witnessed a general opening up to their cause. AIDS is clearly a major catastrophe in American society, but gays and lesbians have come to recognize that it has not been without help in their struggle for social and political acceptance.

Sources: Cary A. Lloyd, "AIDS and HIV. The Syndrome and the Virus," in *Encyclopedia of Social Work*, 18th edition, 1990 Supplement (Silver Spring, MD: NASW Press, 1990); U.S. Department of Health and Human Services, *HIV/AIDS: Surveillance Report*, 2nd qtr. ed., vol. 5 (July 1993); William A. Henry III, "An Identity Forged in Flames," *Time*, August 3, 1992, pp. 35–37.

When gay husbands and lesbian wives announce their sexual orientation, the heterosexual spouse is clearly affected. Sandra Auerback and Charles Moser did group work with 50 heterosexual wives of gay and bisexual men. The majority had been married for over ten years, and very few of the wives suspected their husbands' sexual orientation before they married. After learning of it, the wives had to work through some difficult feelings, including anger, hurt, a sense of betrayal, homophobia, fears for their children, and fear of AIDS. The wives were in need of social support and tended to regard themselves as "superwomen" because of the extraordinary effort required to cope with their situation.[98]

Having children presents special difficulties for lesbian wives and gay husbands. In the Wyers survey, gay fathers said they feared that their sexual orientation might damage their children and were more tentative about their willingness to inform their children of it than lesbian mothers were. Gay fathers generally were less likely than lesbian mothers to have custody of their children after divorce and more likely to be dissatisfied with the custody arrangements. Many of the fathers who had informed their children of their sexual orientation believed it had had a negative impact on the relationship. Lesbian mothers were more comfortable about informing their children of their sexual orientation, and many of those who had done so believed it had enhanced their relationship.[99]

Nevertheless, lesbian mothers often live in fear that they will lose custody of their children. This fear has a realistic basis; the harshest discrimination a lesbian mother can encounter is losing custody of her children. In 1993 it was legal in four states—Virginia, Arkansas, Missouri, and North Dakota—for courts to remove custody from lesbian mothers on the grounds that living with a same-sex partner makes them unfit mothers. In others, such as New Jersey, Massachusetts, and California, family courts have allowed lesbians to become adoptive second parents of their partners' children. (In only two states, New Hampshire and Florida, were gays forbidden outright to adopt children.) Studies have generally supported the ability of lesbian mothers to raise emotionally healthy children. Charlotte Patterson of the University of Virginia reviewed 22 studies of the children of gays, ranging from toddlers to adults, and found none presented evidence that the children had suffered or were more than ordinarily inclined to develop homosexual orientations. The basic finding in her own study of the sexual identity, social skills, and self-image of 37 children of lesbians living in San Francisco in 1990 and 1991 was that "children of lesbian families are developing much like children of heterosexual parents."[100] Another study concluded that motherhood, not self-indulgent sexuality, was the central organizing factor in the lives of the lesbian mothers studied.[101]

Nevertheless, children of lesbian mothers and gay fathers do experience difficulties as they grow and develop. When Karen Gail Lewis studied 21 children of eight mothers who were newly declared lesbians, she found that the children were proud of their mothers for the step they had taken. Nevertheless, many of them did not feel free to express their ambivalence about their mothers' behavior, they worried about their own sexuality, and they indicated a lack of support from other family members, from peers, and from society in general.[102] Sensitive counseling, building social support among children of gays and lesbians, and promoting greater social acceptance should go a long way toward assuring that children of gays and lesbians mature and develop in positive ways.

⚭ IMPLICATIONS FOR PRACTICE

In this chapter we have explored diversity in family lifestyles according to social class, racial and ethnic communities, and sexual orientation in contemporary American society. There are differences between and within the various social classes, and between and among racial- and ethnic-minority groups. In all of these, however, movement toward similar ideals is clearly evident. Family dynamics are working toward a redefinition of the family as a social institution. Family relations seem to involve a search for marriage, monogamy, more egalitarian gender-role expectations, more democratic parent-child relations, and close kinship ties in a nurturing and emotionally supportive environment. Similar aspirations are evident in the long-term commitments of lesbian and gay couples. In developing a family lifestyle outside of marriage, these couples are adopting egalitarian roles that do not emulate traditional heterosexual roles and are stressing monogamy or loyalty and mutual respect.

Although Americans seem to be moving toward a consistent set of family-life ideals, communities differ in the extent to which change is taking place. Very close kin ties and paternalistic and authoritarian norms, for instance, are considered more desirable in some communities than in others, The reasons for these differences include such considerations as generation or length of time in the United States, social isolation from a foreign homeland or from the American mainstream, and economic necessity. Social service workers have to respect, understand, and support differences in family ideals, even as they work to help people achieve new ones.

The ability to achieve ideals also varies from family to family. It should not always be assumed that the behaviors exhibited by a family or couple represent their ideals. There is often a large gap between ideals and actual behaviors. In no community, even the white middle class, have the ideals discussed here been totally achieved. Social-environmental, biophysical, and psychological reasons can limit the ability of individuals to achieve the ideals to which they aspire.

To build strong helping relationships with families and couples, social service workers need to understand the connection between the ideals people hold and the services they require. Families and couples often seek service when their lifestyles do not conform to their ideals or those of their community. Many come voluntarily into service—spouses and partners who cannot seem to resolve the inequalities in their relationships, for instance, or adult children whose ties to parents and siblings create severe stress. Involuntary services for families and couples whose behaviors stray too far from the ideals of their communities may be mandated by law, as in the case of violence toward children, spouses, or elderly members.

If social workers are to meet the needs of families or couples, they must begin by tuning in to their ideals and aspirations. Assessment should focus on clarifying the ideals and the ways in which the social environment as well as the biophysical states, perceptions, motives, and behavioral inclinations of family members foster or limit the attainment of ideals and aspirations. Plans for intervention, of course, follow from this assessment. Where the social environment limits the attainment of family ideals, ways must be found to make social systems and the individuals who compose them more supportive. When the failure to achieve ideals resides in the abilities and capacities of individual family members, plans must be made to improve these and thereby promote better family functioning.

☞ DISCUSSION QUESTIONS AND CLASS PROJECTS

1. Determine the social class background of each student (use small groups if the class is large). Have each one discuss the extent to which his or her experiences fit with the research on family life in different social classes. Compare the experiences of students who were raised in the same social class situation. How similar were these experiences?

2. List and discuss the seven generalizations on similarities and differences between the ideals of white middle-class families and racial- and ethnic-minority families. Design a class project to test one or all of these generalizations. For instance, you could decide to talk to Latinos or to Asian Americans about the family ideals and norms they see in their families.

3. Describe the family patterns found in each of the following communities, paying particular attention to the social class, generational, and other differences that are likely to be seen in any one group: African Americans, Native Americans, Latinos, or Asian Americans.

4. Identify a particular subgroup from one ethnic or racial community (such as Jamaican Americans, Haitian Americans, Navajos, urban Indians, Cuban Americans, Dominican Americans, Korean Americans, or Vietnamese) and gather information from your library or from professionals about the family patterns that might

be evident in them. Pay particular attention to the differences between family ideals and family realities.

5. Latino men are often said to be *macho*. How do people in the United States use this term? How is this usage different from the usage among Latino people?

6. How do the roles, norms, and values of gay men and lesbians seeking long-term relationships differ from those of heterosexual couples? To what extent are they the same?

7. Define and identify the importance of the following terms:

mainstreamers
innovators
street families
street-corner men
cultural relativism
multigenerational family
fictive relatives
familism
marianismo
companion parents
berdache
domestic network

☞ NOTES

1. See Mark Poster, *A Critical Theory of the Family* (New York: Seabury Press, 1978), and Eli Zaretsky, *Capitalism, the Family and Personal Life* (New York: Harper Colophon, 1973).

2. Melvin L. Kohn, "The Effects of Social Class on Parental Values and Practices," in P. Voydanoff (editor), *Work and Family* (Palo Alto, CA: Mayfield, 1984).

3. Rayna Rapp, "Family and Class in Contemporary America: Notes toward an Understanding of Ideology," in B. Thorne (editor) with M. Yalom, *Rethinking the Family: Some Feminist Questions* (New York: Longman, 1982), pp. 168–87.

4. Ibid., p. 180.

5. Ibid., pp. 180–81.

6. Lillian Brewslow Rubin, *Worlds of Pain* (New York: Basic Books, Harper Colophon, 1976), pp. 69–92.

7. Joseph Kett, *Rites of Passage* (New York: Basic Books, Harper Colophon, 1977), pp. 168–71.

8. Lillian B. Rubin, *Intimate Strangers: Men and Women Together* (New York: Harper Colophon, 1984).

9. U.S. Bureau of the Census, *Statistical Abstract of the United States: 1992*, 112th edition (Washington, DC, 1992), Tables 724 and 730.

10. Carol B. Stack, "Sex Roles and Survival Strategies in an Urban Black Community," in H. R. Clark and C. Clark, *Social Interaction: Readings in Sociology* (New York: St. Martin's Press, 1983), p. 423. Based on Chapter 7 in Stack, *All Our Kin: Strategies for Survival in a Black Community* (New York: Harper and Row, 1974).

11. See, for example, Stack, *All Our Kin*, and Oscar Lewis, *La Vida* (New York: Random House, 1966).

12. Stack, "Sex Roles and Survival Strategies," p. 434.

13. Stack, *All Our Kin*, pp. 32–45, 105–07.

14. U.S. Bureau of the Census, *Statistical Abstract: 1992*, Table 704.

15. William Chambliss, "The Saints and the Roughnecks," *Society*, vol. 11 (November–December 1973), pp. 24–31.

16. Jualynne Dodson, "Conceptualizations of Black Families," in H. P. McAdoo (editor), *Black Families* (Beverly Hills, CA: Sage, 1981), pp. 23–36.

17. See Howard M. Bahr, Bruce A. Chadwick, and Joseph H. Strauss, *American Ethnicity* (Lexington, MA: D. C. Heath, 1979), pp. 504–08.

18. Miguel Montiel, "The Social Science Myth of the Mexican American Family," *El Grito: A Journal of Contemporary Mexican American Thought*, vol. 3 (Summer 1970), pp. 56–63.

19. See Robert B. Hill, *The Strengths of Black Families* (New York: Emerson Hall, 1971); Robert Staples, "The Black American Family," in C. H. Mindel, R. W. Habenstein, and R. Wright, Jr. (editors), *Ethnic Families in America: Patterns and Variations*, 3rd ed. (New York: Elsevier, 1988), pp. 303–24; and Robert Staples and Alfredo Mirande, "Racial and Cultural Variations among American Families: A Decennial Review of the Literature on Minority Families," *Journal of Marriage and the Family*, vol. 4 (November 1980), pp. 151–73.

20. See William Julius Wilson, "Cycles of Deprivation and the Underclass Debate," *Social Service Review*, vol. 59 (December 1985), pp. 541–59.

21. Paula Gunn Allen, *The Sacred Hoop: Recovering the Feminine in American Indian Traditions* (Boston, MA: Beacon, 1986).

22. Jerold Heiss, "Women's Values Regarding Marriage and the Family," in McAdoo (editor), *Black Families*, p. 197.

23. Walter R. Allen, "Moms, Dads, and Boys: Race and Sex Differences in the Socialization of Male Children," and John L. McAdoo, "Involvement of Fathers in the Socialization of Black Children," both in L. Gary (editor), *Black Men* (Beverly Hills, CA: Sage, 1981), pp. 99–114 and 225–37.

24. John A. Price, "North American Indian Families," in C. H. Mindel and R. W. Habenstein (editors), *Ethnic Families in America: Patterns and Variations*, 2nd ed. (New York: Elsevier, 1981), p. 265.

25. Michael Novak, *The Rise of the Unmeltable Ethnics* (New York: Macmillan, 1973), pp. 103–36.

26. Joan M. Jensen, "East Indians," in S. Thernstrom (editor), *Harvard Encyclopedia of American Ethnic Groups* (Cambridge, MA: Belknap Press, 1980), pp. 299–300.

27. Mary Bowen Wright, "Indochinese," in *Harvard Encyclopedia of American Ethnic Groups*, p. 510.

28. See Leon F. Williams and Carmen Diaz, "Family: Multigenerational," in *Encyclopedia of Social Work*, Vol. 1, p. 532.

29. Leon Chestang, "Character Development in a Hostile Environment," in M. Bloom (editor), *Life Span Development*, 1st ed. (New York: Macmillan, 1980), pp. 40–50.

30. Herbert G. Gutman, *The Black Family in Slavery and Freedom: 1750–1925* (New York: Pantheon, 1976).

31. Niara Sudarkasa, "Interpreting the African Heritage in Afro American Family Organization," in McAdoo (editor), *Black Families*, pp. 37–53.

32. Gunn Allen, *Sacred Hoop*, pp. 1–7, 31.

33. Dodson, "Conceptualization of Black Families," pp. 23–36.

34. See Heiss, "Women's Values Regarding Marriage," pp. 186–98; Allen, "Moms, Dads, and Boys," pp. 99–114; and McAdoo, "Involvement of Fathers in Socialization," pp. 225–37.

35. Hill, *Strengths of Black Families*.

36. John G. Red Horse, "Family Structure and Value Orientation in American Indians," *Social Casework*, vol. 61 (October 1980), pp. 462–67.

37. Williams and Diaz, "Family: Multigenerational," pp. 530–32.

38. See Eugene Litwak, "Extended Kin Relations in an Industrial Democratic Society," and Marvin B. Sussman, "Relationships of Adult Children with Their Parents," both in E. Shanas and G. Streib (editors), *Social Structure and the Family* (Englewood Cliffs, NJ: Prentice-Hall, 1965), pp. 290–323 and 62–92.

39. Elizabeth A. Carter and Monica McGoldrick, *The Family Life Cycle: A Framework for Family Therapy* (New York: Gardner, 1980), pp. 3–20.

40. Elmer P. Martin and Joanne Mitchell Martin, *The Black Extended Family* (Chicago: University of Chicago Press, 1978), p. 1.

41. See Williams and Diaz, "Family: Multigenerational," pp. 534–35.

42. Gunn Allen, *Sacred Hoop*, p. 2.

43. See Thomas J. Hopkins, "The Role of the Agency in Supporting Black Manhood," *Social Work*, vol. 18 (January 1973), pp. 53–58. Also see Gary (editor), *Black Men*.

44. See Allen, "Moms, Dads, and Boys," pp. 99–113, and McAdoo, "Involvement of Fathers in Socialization," pp. 225–37.

45. David Alvirez, Frank D. Bean, and Dorie Williams, "The Mexican American Family," in Mindel and Habenstein (editors), *Ethnic Families in America*, 2nd ed., pp. 269–92.

46. Hideki A. Ishisaka and Calvin Y. Takagi, "Social Work with Asian- and Pacific-Americans," in J. W. Green, *Cultural Awareness in the Human Services* (Englewood Cliffs, NJ: Prentice-Hall, 1982), p. 136.

47. Man Keung Ho, "Social Work with Asian Americans," *Social Casework*, vol. 57 (March 1976), p. 196.

48. Red Horse, "Family Structure and Value Orientation," p. 466.

49. Mary E. Durrett, Shirley L. O'Bryant, and James W. Pennebaker, "Child Rearing Reports of White, Black and Mexican American Families," *Developmental Psychology*, vol. 11 (June 1975), p. 871.

50. Karen W. Bartz and Elaine S. Levine, "Childbearing by Black Parents: A Description and Comparison to Anglo and Chicano Parents," *Journal of Marriage and the Family*, vol. 40 (November 1978), pp. 709–19.

51. Price, "North American Indian Families," p. 246.

52. Jonathan Katz, *Gay American History* (New York: Discus/Avon, 1978).

53. Gunn Allen, *Sacred Hoop*, pp. 258–59.

54. Robert John, "The Native American Family," in Mindel, Habenstein, and Wright (editors), *Ethnic Families in America*, 3rd ed., pp. 325–63.

55. Quoted in *The Continuum of Life: Health Concerns of the Indian Elderly*, final report on the Second National Indian Conference on Aging, Billings, Montana, August 15–18, 1978 (Albuquerque, NM: National Indian Council on Aging, 1979), p. 176.

56. John, "Native American Family," pp. 325–63.

57. Red Horse, "Family Structure and Value Orientation," p. 463.

58. Nancy Brown Miller, "Social Work Services to Urban Indians," in Green (editor), *Cultural Awareness in the Human Services*, pp. 157–83.

59. George Spindler and Louise Spindler, *Dreamers without Power: The Menomini Indians* (New York: Holt, Rinehart, and Winston, 1971), pp. 2–6.

60. Edward Franklin Frazier, *The Negro Family in the United States* (Chicago: University of Chicago Press, 1939).

61. Gutman, *Black Family in Slavery and Freedom*, pp. 455–56.

62. Andrew Hacker, *Two Nations: Separate, Hostile, and Unequal* (New York: Charles Scribner's Sons, 1992), p. 69.

63. U.S. Bureau of the Census, *Statistical Abstract 1992*, Table 89.

64. Andrew Cherlin, *Marriage, Divorce, Remarriage* (Cambridge, MA: Harvard University Press, 1981), pp. 95–97.

65. See, for instance, Walter B. Miller, "Lower-class Culture as a Generating Milieu of Gang Delinquency," *Journal of Social Issues*, vol. 14 (Summer 1958), pp. 5–19.

66. Daniel P. Moynihan, *Maximum Feasible Misunderstanding: Community Action in the War on Poverty* (New York: Free Press, 1969).

67. Ludwig L. Geismar and Katherine M. Wood, *Family and Delinquency: Resocializing the Young Offender* (New York: Human Sciences Press, 1986).

68. Andrew Billingsley, *Black Families in White America* (Englewood Cliffs, NJ: Prentice-Hall, 1968), pp. 3–4.

69. Hacker, *Two Nations*, pp. 45, 78–79.

70. Ulf Hannerz, *Soulside: Inquiries into Ghetto Culture and Community* (New York: Columbia University Press, 1969); Charles Vert Willie, *A New Look at Black Families*, 2nd ed. (New York: General Hall, 1981).

71. Willie, *New Look at Black Families*, p. 55.

72. Hacker, *Two Nations*, p. 72.

73. For a study by a social worker, see Douglas G. Glasgow, *The Black Underclass: Poverty, Unemployment and Entrapment of Ghetto Youth* (New York: Vintage, 1981). Also see Elliott Liebow, *Tally's Corner: A Study of Negro Streetcorner Men* (Boston: Little, Brown, 1967).

74. Jack Rothman, "Spoken But Not Heard: Communication Gaps between Minorities and Social Service Professionals," *UCLA Social Welfare*, vol. 1 (Spring 1986), pp. 13–15.

75. Sonia Badillo Ghali, "Understanding Puerto Rican Traditions," *Social Work*, vol. 21 (January 1982), pp. 98–102.

76. Ibid., p. 99.

77. Alvirez, Bean, and Williams, "Mexican American Family."

78. Ibid., pp. 184–87.

79. Ishisaka and Takagi, "Social Work with Asian- and Pacific-Americans," pp. 129, 135–38.

80. Ibid., p. 135.

81. Harry H. L. Kitano, "Will Your Daughter Marry One?" *UCLA Social Welfare*, vol. 1 (Spring 1986), pp. 5–6.

82. Jeffrey Weeks, *Sex, Politics, and Society: The Regulation of Sexuality since 1800* (New York: Longman, 1981), pp. 97–121.

83. Katz, *Gay American History*, pp. 423–29.

84. "Counseling for Gay and Lesbian Couples," *Practice Digest*, vol. 7 (Summer 1984), p. 14.

85. Philip Blumstein and Pepper Schwartz, *American Couples* (New York: William Morrow, 1983), p. 322.

86. David McWhirter and Andrew M. Mattison, *The Male Couple: How Relationships Develop* (Englewood Cliffs, NJ: Prentice-Hall, 1984), p. 231.

87. D. G. Wolf, *Lesbian Community* (Berkeley: University of California Press, 1979).

88. Allen P. Bell and Martin S. Weinberg, *Homosexualities: A Study of Diversity among Men and Women* (New York: Simon and Schuster, 1978), pp. 106–11, 160–70.

89. Ibid., pp. 85, 93.

90. McWhirter and Mattison, *Male Couple*, p. 285; italics in original.

91. Bell and Weinberg, *Homosexualities*, p. 93; Blumstein and Schwartz, *American Couples*, pp. 322–23.

92. Blumstein and Schwartz, *American Couples*, pp. 319–24.

93. Centers for Disease Control and Prevention, *Surgeon General's Report to the American Public on HIV Infection and AIDS* (Washington, DC, 1993), p. 1.

94. "Counseling for Gay and Lesbian Couples," p. 14.

95. Alfred C. Kinsey et al., *Sexual Behavior in the Human Female* (Philadelphia: W. B. Saunders, 1953), and Kinsey et al., *Sexual Behavior in the Human Male* (Philadelphia: W. B. Saunders, 1948).

96. Quoted in Sandra J. Potter and Trudy E. Darty, "Social Work and the Invisible Minority: An Exploration of Lesbianism," *Social Work*, vol. 26 (May 1981), p. 190.

97. Norman L. Wyers, "Homosexuality in the Family: Lesbian and Gay Spouses," *Social Work*, vol. 32 (March–April 1987), pp. 143–48.

98. Sandra Auerback and Charles Moser, "Groups for the Wives of Gay and Bisexual Men," *Social Work*, vol. 32 (July–August 1987), pp. 321–25.

99. Wyers, "Homosexuality in the Family," pp. 145–46.

100. William A. Henry, III, "Gay Parents: Under Fire and on the Rise," *Time*, September 20, 1993, pp. 66–71.

101. See Potter and Darty, "Social Work and the Invisible Minority," p. 190.

102. Karen Gail Lewis, "Children of Lesbians: Their Point of View," *Social Work*, vol. 25 (May 1980), pp. 198–203.

The Family as a Social Organization
Identifying Well-Being

MAJOR THEMES DISCUSSED IN THIS CHAPTER

1. **IDENTIFYING FAMILY WELL-BEING.** The assessment of family life is both a primary task for social service professionals and a means of studying the family. Research has determined various characteristics of healthy families and happy marriages.

2. **FAMILY FUNCTIONING.** Study of the family as a social organization focuses on determining how families diverge from some optimum level of functioning and identifying directions for change. Our understanding of how the family functions as a holon has been furthered by examination of how well a family can satisfy its needs, both basic survival needs and developmental needs for family well-being. The ways a family functions also have to do with its boundaries and structural and interactional patterns.

3. **FAMILY PROBLEMS: DOMESTIC VIOLENCE.** Family life offers numerous pleasant and rewarding experiences, but it also has a darker side. Violence, neglect, and abuse are problems in many families today. Three forms of domestic violence are of special concern—violence against spouses, against children, and against elderly family members.

4. **FAMILY PROBLEMS: MARRIAGE, DIVORCE, AND OTHER STRESSFUL PATTERNS.** Family lifestyles in contemporary society create a number of stresses. Growing numbers of Americans are likely to have children outside of marriage; to cohabit without marriage; to marry, separate, or divorce; to live for some period as single parents; or to remarry after divorce or the death of a spouse, and stresses are associated with each of these family patterns or lifestyles.

5. **IMPLICATIONS FOR PRACTICE.** This overview of the identification of strengths and problems in families has implications for primary prevention, early intervention, and crisis and long-term treatment of families.

STUDY OF THE FAMILY AS A social institution, the topic of Chapters 8 and 9, forms the basis for social service practice and policy on family life. In providing direct services, however, another dimension of family life must be considered: the family as a social organization, which focuses on the functioning of actual families in their everyday lives. In this dimension the family is viewed from the systems perspective as a holon, simultaneously a whole and a part of a larger system. It is concerned with the interactions within families and between families and the social environment of which they are a part.

While most approaches to social service work with families claim in one way or another to be based on the systems perspective, many of them examine the family only as a whole with subsystems: the spouse subsystem, the parental subsystem, the sibling subsystem, the parent-child subsystem, the adult child-elderly subsystem. These approaches do not conceptualize the family as a part of a larger community and social system.[1] In Chapters 10 and 11 we take a holistic approach to study of the family as a social organization. The goal is to identify and analyze **family well-being**, or the optimum level of family functioning: how well the family satisfies its needs, keeps its boundaries open and flexible, and maintains beneficial structural and interactional patterns. We are concerned with identification of the strengths and problems of families and how they differ in terms of family functioning. Chapter 11 discusses five perspectives on family functioning with different points of view on analyzing family well-being and dealing with the problems experienced by families.

IDENTIFYING FAMILY WELL-BEING: HEALTHY FAMILIES AND HAPPY MARRIAGES

The assessment of family life not only is a primary task of social service professionals, it also is a means of studying what makes for well-being or ill-being in family functioning. Most social service work with families now takes the approach of family therapy, in which treatment is directed not to individuals with problems but to the family systems of which they are a part. Salvador Minuchin has defined the framework of structural family treatment as a body of theory and techniques in which the individual is placed in a social context. Changes in the structure of the family also change the positions of family members, and thus the individuals also change.[2]

When the family is the client—or the patient, in the therapeutic sense—the treatment goal is to achieve a state of health in the family. The characteristics of healthy families and happy marriages in contemporary American society have been variously identified by numerous researchers.

Definitions of the Healthy Family

Definitions of the term *healthy family* usually are stated in terms of their characteristics. In *Traits of a Healthy Family*, Dolores Curran, for instance, presents a list of characteristics based on the opinions of professionals. She consulted "the teachers, doctors, principals, pastoral ministers, directors of religious education, Boy Scout directors, YMCA leaders, Big Brothers, 4-H leaders, family counselors, and other persons of similar positions who work closely with lots of families" and concluded that the healthy family:

A happy middle-class, African-American family registers pride of ownership of their new home in Queens, New York. Happy families exist in all racial and ethnic groups.

1. Communicates and listens.
2. Fosters table time and conversation.
3. Affirms and supports one another.
4. Teaches respect for others.
5. Develops a sense of trust.
6. Has a sense of play and humor.
7. Has a balance of interaction among members.
8. Shares leisure time.
9. Exhibits a sense of shared responsibility.
10. Teaches a sense of right and wrong.
11. Has a strong sense of family in which rituals and traditions abound.
12. Has a shared religious core.
13. Respects one another's privacy.

14. Values service to others.

15. Admits to and seeks help with problems.[3]

Researchers at the University of Wisconsin–Madison have approached the study of healthy family life by attempting to identify the strengths of families. Hamilton McCubbin and Anne Thompson developed a series of typologies of families in which the characteristics of regeneration, resilience, rhythm, and traditionality figure prominently. These characteristics emerge from combinations of eight specific strengths (see "Adaptive Strengths in Families"). McCubbin and Thompson also have designed a series of assessment instruments which can be used by practitioners to determine what strengths exist and then build on these in family practice.[4]

Variations in Happy Marriages

The characteristics considered typical of healthy families all have a quality of goodness about them and reflect the cultural ideals described in Chapter 9. They give the impression that in these families conflict is at a minimum and always under control and that all family members always (or at least most of the time) behave in an exemplary manner.

This view of healthy relationships in the family may not be too realistic, however. John Cuber and Peggy Harroff challenge the rosy picture created by many researchers on family life. They chose to study "normal" couples, those "who had not received clinical help for whatever problems they may have had" or "who were apparently self-directed, not failures in any reasonable sense of the word." Starting from a larger sample, they interviewed 107 men and 104 women who had been married to the same partner for at least 12 years and who had never seriously considered divorce or separation. They concluded that there are at least five types of happy marriages, two of which might qualify as healthy families, but some of which in no way resemble them.[5]

The *total marriage*, which does have qualities similar to those described by other researchers, is very rare but does exist and can endure. Cuber and Harroff describe the total marriage as multifaceted, vital relationships in which there is practically no pretense between the partners, and almost all of the important focuses of life are shared. The various parts of the relationship reinforce one another, and there are few areas of tension. Differences of opinion may exist, but they are settled easily through yielding or compromising.

The *vital marriage* also comes close to the healthy family mode. It is less multifaceted than the total marriage and somewhat more common. In the vital marriage, sharing between the partners and togetherness are genuine, and the relationship is the essence of life for each of them. There is an exciting mutuality in the ways the partners operate, but they do not lose their separate identities, and on occasion they can be rivals and competitive. When there is conflict it is usually over important issues, and it is handled without resorting to name calling or accusation.

In contrast to these two types of happy marriages, which resemble the stereotypical happy family, are three other types: conflict-habituated, devitalized, and passive-congenial. In the *conflict-habituated marriage* there is considerable tension and conflict, although they are mostly controlled. At best the couple is discreet and mannerly in public, though the verbal barbs may start flying. At worst, they indulge in private quarreling, nagging, and "bringing up the past." The conflict-habituated couple seems to need conflict and depends on it to solidify the relationship. Indeed, to stop quarreling would probably end the relationship.

In the *devitalized marriage*, the love and romance that marked the early years

---

Adaptive Strengths in Families

Why is it that some families are able to handle their troubles better than others? Some seem to cope well and even thrive in times of economic hardship or interpersonal conflict, while others, faced with similar troubles, give up and disintegrate. Hamilton McCubbin and Anne Thompson propose that the answer may lie in the existence of eight adaptive strengths. While some families lack some of these strengths, most have them to a greater or lesser degree.

The family's adaptive strengths are:

1. *Family coherence.* The ability of family members to share values and be accepting, loyal, proud, faithful, trusting, respectful, and caring.

2. *Family hardiness.* Internal strengths and durability. Hardiness gives the family a collective sense of control over life events and hardships, a sense of meaningfulness in life, involvements in activities, and a commitment to learn and explore new or challenging experiences.

3. *Family bonding.* The existence of meaningful, integral emotional attachments among family members.

4. *Family flexibility.* The ability of the family to alter its rules, boundaries, and roles to accommodate to changing pressures and stress.

5. *Family intentionality.* The value members give to family routines and spending time together.

6. *Family structurality.* The time allotted by the family to family routines and interacting together.

7. *Family traditions.* Behaviors, practices, and beliefs families adopt and pass on from one generation to the next.

8. *Family celebrations.* Behaviors and practices organized to observe occasions and circumstances that are important to family members.

McCubbin and Thompson have also developed scales to measure these strengths so social workers who wish to build on them can systematically assess a particular family for the extent to which it incorporates each of them.

Source: Hamilton J. McCubbin and Anne I. Thompson (editors), *Family Assessment Inventories for Research and Practice* (Madison: University of Wisconsin–Madison, 1991).

---

of marriage have given way to a sense of duty and obligation. This kind of marriage is exceedingly common. Where the partners were once deeply in love, enjoyed sex, and spent a great deal of time together, they now more or less go their separate ways. Their time together is likely to be structured around activities involving the children, extended kin, or community responsibilities. There is typically very little sharing of important life events beyond acknowledgment of their mutual dependency on each other. There is a gracefulness between partners and even the sense that the marriage has meaning. They do share occasionally, and they have memories of a more vital past. They see themselves as being like most of their friends. Many believe that the marriage is no more and no less than what should be expected in the middle years of life.

The *passive-congenial* marriage usually does not have a loving or romantic past. From the beginning, the passive-congenial marriage has been a passive relationship with little expectation for anything else, so there is little sense that anything has been lost or that there was ever anything special about it. The couple feels comfortable and adequate, and there is little conflict. Some couples become passive-congenial by default, others by intention. The partners have found their real pleasures and interests outside the marriage, in their careers, children, or community activities. But the marriage fits their needs in a utilitarian sense. They are seen as family people. There is peace and quiet in the home. There may even be love and gratitude that the spouse is like she or he is. For people who require considerable independence and freedom, this kind of relationship can be fulfilling.

∞ FAMILY FUNCTIONING

The study of family functioning directs attention to various aspects of the family as a holon, a system made up of its parts and also interacting within the social environment. Family well-being can be determined by studying how well the family satisfies its needs. It also is related to the family's boundaries—the members and their roles, norms, values, and traditions which distinguish the family from other families—and to its structural and interactional patterns.

Needs Satisfaction

A major part of the assessment of family well-being is evaluation of the family's ability to satisfy its needs. According to Kenneth Terkelsen, the ultimate purpose of family life is to provide "the context that supports need attainment for all its individual members."[6] Following Abraham Maslow (see Chapter 2), he outlines two basic kinds of needs, survival and developmental. **Survival needs** are basic requirements for nourishment, shelter, and protection, while **developmental needs** have to do with psychological well-being, sensing that one belongs, experiencing self-esteem, and fulfilling one's developmental potential. Only when survival needs have been met does meeting developmental needs become possible.

Ann Hartman and Joan Laird also focus on family needs, giving attention to both survival and developmental types and the environmental resources that must be available to families if they are to satisfy these needs. The authors' perspective is that the extent to which a particular family can meet its needs is dependent on the resources available to it. Thus a family's needs for nutrition can only be met if an adequate, varied diet, clean air, and pure and plentiful water are available to it; the family's needs for shelter require available, affordable housing that provides living conditions with adequate space, light, warmth, privacy, communality, and safety[7] (see "Family Needs and Environmental Resources").

Survival Needs in Poor and Minority Families

Because most students of the family have focused on developmental rather than survival needs, studies on the internal dynamics of family life generally fail to address how the need for basic survival impinges on interpersonal well-being. One reason is that most studies are based on white, middle-class families, and it is likely that in these families the basic survival needs are being met. Researchers are therefore inclined to gloss over the very real survival needs of families in other racial and ethnic communities and lower social classes.

Studies that have been sensitive to the issue of family survival have focused on poor families, including many racial- and ethnic-minority families and single-parent families headed by women, including whites. In examining the life cycle of multiproblem poor

---

Family Needs and Environmental Resources

In order to help families, social service workers need to know how well particular families can meet their needs for a healthy family life with the resources available to them. From an ecological or environmental perspective, they can do this by making an assessment of the social context of family life in order to determine how it does or does not support the family. Ann Hartman and Joan Laird have developed the following lists of needs and resources to be used in making this assessment:

Need	Resource
Nutrition	Adequate, varied diet Clean air Pure, plentiful water
Shelter	Housing (space, light, warmth, privacy, communality, safety)
Protection	Safe neighborhoods Police, fire fighting, traffic control
Health	Clean environment Preventive, developmental, and rehabilitative health care Adequate, accessible medical system
Belongingness, intimacy, connectedness	Lovers, kin, friends Neighbors, social organizations, interest groups
Communication, mobility	Telephone and postal systems, newspapers Public and private transportation
Education, enrichment	Good schools (for children and adults) Arts, recreation
Spiritual needs	Religious organizations Opportunities to share meaning and values Preservation of cultural, ethnic, racial, and other differences
Autonomy	Gratifying work in or out of home Community participation Opportunities for new experiences
Generativity	Opportunities to contribute to the future

Source: Adapted with permission of The Free Press, a Division of Macmillan, Inc. from *Family Centered Social Work Practice* by Ann Hartman and Joan Laird. Copyright © 1983 by The Free Press.

---

families, Fernando Colon, for instance, suggests that family assessment must address their physical situation (level of food and clothing, condition of housing), employment situation (income, unemployment or under-employment), and social context (isolation, alienation from others).[8] Assessment of the well-being of such families must take into account the likelihood that the environmental resources necessary to meet their survival needs are at the most limited. When family life is constrained by economic insecurity, there undoubtedly will be insufficient resources to sustain the family.

It should not be assumed, however, that all families struggling for economic or social survival will suffer from some form of pathology. Families can be amazingly resilient, even under conditions of severe emotional stress. The strengths of families as well as their deficiencies must be acknowledged, as we noted in Chapter 2. Robert Hill points out that black families have a number of strengths which can help them survive racial discrimination and economic insecurity. He does not doubt that some black families collapse under such stress, but he believes that most of them survive. These families provide adequately for the physical, emotional, and spiritual needs of members; show concern for family unity, loyalty, and cooperation; develop healthy interpersonal relationships; help each other in healthy ways; and perform family roles flexibly. After examining the literature on black families, Hill asserts that in most families there are strong kinship bonds, a strong work ethic, a strong need to achieve, a strong religious orientation, and very adaptive family roles.[9]

Family Boundaries

The family is a bounded system in interaction with its environment. Within the **family boundary** are its members and their roles, norms, values, traditions, and goals, plus other elements that distinguish one family from another and from the social environment. Researchers have looked at family boundaries in terms of their implications for good family functioning. In general, they have found that families whose boundaries are open and flexible are the most healthy.

Families with random, closed, and open types of family boundaries have been described in terms of their ability to meet survival and developmental needs by David Kantor and William Lehr.[10] They consider the most unhealthy families to be *random families*, which typically have boundaries that lack clarity or are constantly shifting and changing. There is no sense of family cohesion, and each member seems to be doing his or her own thing.

Closed families, in contrast, tend to be rigid, with well-defined roles. They are well organized and directed by planned goals and schedules. Family projects and concerns take precedence over individual desires; the family always comes first, and family stability is of great importance. Kantor and Lehr do not consider these families to be necessarily unhealthy. Because of their closed nature, however, they do not deal adequately with the normal crises that arise in family life.

The healthiest families are **open families**, which are well organized in the sense that there is a clear boundary; goals, roles, and membership are well defined and well understood. But there also is flexibility in these families. While the concerns of individual members are responded to, there is genuine concern for the family as a whole.

Structural Patterns and Family Well-Being

Family well-being has also been examined in terms of the operational or transactional patterns evident in families. Following the earlier work of Minuchin, research by Harry Aponte and John Van Deusen which originated in therapeutic work with the families of

12 poor Puerto Rican or black delinquents contributed to the development of structural family therapy.[11] This technique has been used in work with middle-class families as well as those with limited economic resources.

Aponte and Van Deusen argue that families living under poverty are "particularly vulnerable to dysfunction."[12] They clearly state, however, that their work should not be taken to mean that poor Puerto Rican and black families are *always* dysfunctional. They focus on three elements of the family system: the boundaries among members, the power structure of the family, and the alignment that exists among members. Dysfunctions may arise from any of these.

In this perspective *boundary* refers not to relations between the family and its environment but to the boundaries among family members, defined in terms of rules about who may and may not participate in any family activity. In the healthy family, the boundary among members is neither too rigid nor too diffuse. The individuals are independent of one another yet united and focused on the needs of the family as a whole. Unhealthy families are described as either enmeshed or disengaged. In **enmeshed families**, the boundaries between some or all of the family members are undifferentiated, permeable, and fluid. The individuals lack a sense of independence and act as if they were physically and emotionally dependent on one another. In **disengaged families**, the members have little to do with one another, and the independence of each member is rigidly respected.

Family alignment refers to "the joining or opposition of one member to another,"[13] or the coalitions that form among members and the manner in which they compete or cooperate. Coalitions are not necessarily dysfunctional, and neither is a certain amount of competition among them, provided the coalitions are not rigid. As long as family members can move in and out of these coalitions easily, they can be quite useful for decision making. Coalitions are like family party politics; if members of a coalition always follow the party line and never cross it, dysfunction can result. This could take three forms: stable coalitions, triangulation, or detouring coalitions. *Stable coalitions* exist where two or more members have rigidly joined together against the others. *Triangulation* exists when individuals are caught in the middle between two coalitions and are forced to join one or the other. *Detouring coalitions* project their internal conflict onto others outside them.

All families require a power structure, a "force" which makes decisions possible. In the ideal, the power structure operates in a democratic way, with all members participating, up to the level of their developmental capacity, in family decisions, and all members capable of influencing one another. In underorganized families, the force is not distributed in an orderly fashion. It may be concentrated in one person who makes all the decisions, or it may be decentralized, with too many people exerting influence and no one person responsible for making the decisions. In both there is a lack of functional power in the way the family functions.

Interactional Patterns and Family Well-Being

Based on clinical experience as well as on in-depth analyses of small, nonrandom samples of white, middle-class and black working-class, two-parent families, Jerry M. Lewis has developed a guide for identifying the interactional patterns that contribute to family well-being. Lewis and his associates believe that there is "no single thread" in healthy families and that a number of factors can combine to produce the result. These factors have to do with the marriage itself, power relations, closeness, communication, problem-solving abilities, the expression of feelings, dealing with loss, family values, and intimacy and autonomy.[14]

Lewis identifies the good marriage and the healthy family in terms of optimally functioning interactions.[15] In good marriages power is shared between husband and wife. Both parties are competent and have areas of special expertise. They like each other as friends, trust each other, and do not feel vulnerable in the relationship. They maintain their autonomy and are not fused as a couple. They define themselves a being "in love," though many years may have passed. Sexual intercourse might not be frequent, but the relationship is considered good by both partners.

Decision-making power is fully in the hands of the parents in healthy families. Power is expressed as a quality of easy leadership, with a sincere interest in the points of view of the children. These families are closely knit, and each member feels strongly connected. Because there is no effort to have everyone agree on everything, individuality is also evident. Healthy families have good communication patterns, Lewis says. They make things clear between one another, and there is little difficulty knowing what each member thinks or feels. They handle problems well: identify them early, do not deny them, do not try to blame or scapegoat a member for them, and solve them constructively.

These families express feelings freely—sad, angry, loving, hurt, fearful. There is a great sense of openness, and they are able to deal with loss openly. Lewis maintains that healthy families share a value premise that assumes people are mostly good rather than evil. There is little authoritarianism; these families combine intimacy and individual autonomy easily. They also are very much involved with the world around them and rather than being isolated are active participants.

In addition to defining healthy or optimally functioning families, Lewis describes the *faltering family*, which "just misses" being healthy. These are competent families, but considerable pain is evident. The primary difference between healthy and faltering families appears to be in the relationship of the married couple. In the faltering family the parents are somehow unable to meet each other's needs, but this does not reflect on how they raise the children. The children turn out healthy, and problems arising from the outside environment are handled pretty well. According to Lewis, "The failure of the couple to achieve the intimate level of communication is the central flaw in these families."[16]

Lewis suggests that there are three levels of faltering or troubled families. In dominated families, one parent takes control and a level of closed relations results. When the other partner accepts the subordinate position, the family may get along fairly well, but some dominated families are marked by constant conflict and rebellion. In conflicted families, power is not shared or controlled by one of the partners. There is an open struggle between them to control one another, and no stable set of rules and roles is developed. Coalitions are common but often fleeting. Anger and other hostile feelings are expressed; nurturing, loving feelings are not. Blaming others is common. Family values are often intensely competitive. The severely disturbed families are chaotic families. The couple fails miserably in attempts to meet each other's needs and the needs of the children. No one has enough power to structure the family. Communication lacks clarity, and the flow of ideas is confusing and obscure. The family cannot solve problems at all, and individuality, independence, autonomy, and change are discouraged.[17]

Interactional Patterns in Black Families

Charles Willie paints a picture of black family life that he considers healthy but nevertheless does not fit the interactional patterns that have been identified as characterizing healthy families. He notes, for instance, that regardless of socioeconomic level, black families have relatively little togetherness and are relatively isolated from the community. Willie says affluent and middle-class blacks spend much time working and involvement in community affairs is limited. They are concerned with staving off the effects of racism and direct their energies to making sure that family members do not fail or fall behind. Similarly, at the working-class and poverty-class levels, blacks are largely occupied with meeting survival needs; for family heads, socializing, communications, and the like require real effort. His point is not that these families are therefore unhealthy but that the sources of cohesiveness and strength lie elsewhere. Black families' strengths derive from their determination to survive despite heavy odds against them. The ability of a family's members to coalesce around the need to stave off adversity makes a powerful difference in its well-being.[18]

FAMILY PROBLEMS: DOMESTIC VIOLENCE

The identification of healthy families and happy marriages lends credence to the popular idea of family life as being inherently good. A darker side must be recognized, however. Domestic violence in all its forms—spouse abuse, abuse of the elderly, child abuse and neglect—is increasingly evident.

Violence in the family, usually defined as physical injury or sexual abuse, also includes emotional abuse as well as neglect or abandonment. Barbara Star considers the term **domestic violence** to be synonymous with family violence, and she uses it to describe any form of violence in the family, including wife battering, elder abuse, and the physical and sexual abuse of children.[19]

Domestic violence is by no means new. In the traditional family of earlier times, however, men had greater autonomy over women and parents had autonomy over children; abuse in the family seldom became known outside it. It is likely that there was more family violence in the past when infanticide and abandonment, as well as sex with children and child beating, were acceptable practices and wife beating was not only accepted but supported by law. As changes have occurred in the norms and ideals governing family relationships, and patriarchal, authoritarian norms have given way to more egalitarian, more democratic norms, greater attention is being paid to domestic violence. Thus family violence appears to have been "discovered" in recent times.[20]

Social service workers have had a role in making society aware of domestic violence. Direct-service social workers in family and child welfare services not only have provided treatment in instances of domestic violence but have served to identify cases and to advocate for preventive programs and policies. The abuse of elders (parent battering), particularly, was identified through case findings by agency personnel in contact with the elderly.

Spouse Abuse

The true incidence of domestic violence cannot be known since many instances are not reported. **Spouse abuse** is no exception. It has been estimated that one-fourth of all couples have engaged in at least one violent episode during the life of their marriage. A true incidence rate may involve up to 60 percent of all couples.[21]

With the exception of homicide by spouses, in which men and women are equally victimized, women are more likely to suffer serious physical injury as victims of domestic violence. Federal Bureau of Investigation reports indicate that in 1990, 82 percent of the

Every 12 seconds a woman is beaten in the U.S.

25% of the violent crime in America is wife assault.

4 women are killed every day by their husbands or partners.

60% of battered women are beaten while they are pregnant.

DON'T DIE FOR LOVE

STOP

DOMESTIC VIOLENCE

▲ Liz claiborne

Billboard erected on I-55 in Chicago by a corporate sponsor to call
attention to the need for action to stop violence against women, most
of which occurs in the context of family life.

persons arrested in the crime category of offenses against family and children were males
and 64 percent of those arrested were in the age category of 25–44 years.[22] Not only are
husbands in general physically stronger than wives and so less likely to be battered, they
also are far less likely to report it to authorities. Victimization reports are mostly made by
women, and much of the information on spouse abuse derives from clinical populations,
especially women receiving shelter services.[23]

In any case, physical abuse occurs in the context of psychological abuse and exploitation. In the verbal abuse that often accompanies it, wives may be made to feel
worthless, incompetent, unlovable, insignificant, and less than human. But wives can
hold their own in verbal abuse and can inflict similar psychological scars on their husbands. Abuse rarely occurs just once. After the barrier to physical abuse has been broken,
it often becomes an integral part of the husband-wife relationship.

Spouse abuse is evident in all ethnic groups and in all social classes. There has been
evidence, however, of higher incidences among lower-income couples and among African
Americans, Latinos, and other ethnic minorities. Studies from services that offer shelter
to abused women suggest that white women are more likely to seek help than ethnic-
minority women.[24]

Shelters for battered women are a social service provided in most cities and regions of the United States. The literature on battered women has tried to determine why a significant number of women remain with their spouses or partners despite repeated physical abuse. One reason suggested is that many women still are economically dependent on men even if they are abused by them, particularly when the family includes dependent children. One study found that in addition to such external constraints, there are internal constraints that discourage battered women from leaving these relationships. These include "feminine" attributes such as emotional dependence on mates, a poor self-image or low self-esteem, and traditional ideas about the "proper place" of a woman, as well as constraints that follow from the process of victimization, such as the fear of reprisal, so that women find it subjectively difficult to leave.[25] Concern for the maintenance of the family also subjects battered women to a great deal of psychological and emotional turmoil in considering their options (see "Mourning the Loss of an Abusive Husband").

Elder Abuse

Less is known about the incidence of **elder abuse** than that of any other form of domestic violence. It is the most recent form to be identified, and though there have been hearings before congressional committees on aging, no accurate estimates of the number of abused, neglected, or exploited elderly in the United States are available. According to Gloria Cavanaugh, executive director of the American Society on Aging, "Elder abuse is one of the fastest-growing crimes of our times, but it is mostly unreported and almost totally neglected in the budgets of local, state, and national government."[26]

Knowledge about elder abuse has come largely from the victims. They are most likely to report psychological and financial abuse and physical neglect; direct physical abuse is less commonly reported. The elderly may be physically or mentally unable to ask for help. They also may be unwilling to report abuse because they are afraid of retaliation, they are ashamed and do not want to accuse close relatives, or they fear they will be considered unable to care for themselves and so will be sent to a nursing home.[27]

An elder abuser is usually a member of the family, most often a son or daughter. Studies have found variously that middle-aged women related to the older person by blood or marriage and providing primary care or middle-aged men of low socioeconomic status are the most likely abusers.[28] Other studies have indicated that elder abuse is a recurring problem which is aggravated by stress. In many families the elderly are regarded as stressful members because they need extra care and are a financial burden. Providing care is especially difficult when both husband and wife are working; and families faced with poverty, alcoholism, drug abuse, or marital discord find the responsibility an additional source of stress.[29]

Elderly women are more likely to be victims than men, especially widows who live with the abuser. Many of the elderly have physical or mental disabilities which make them dependent on family members to meet their needs. For the frail elderly 75 years and older, the fastest growing portion of the over-65 population, abuse often takes the form of neglect. In a study by the University of Maryland, passive neglect, usually in the form of abusive inattention or isolation, was found to be the most common form of elder abuse, followed by verbal abuse, physical abuse, and financial exploitation.[30]

Mourning the Loss of an Abusive Husband

Susan Turner describes separation from abusive husbands as a series of losses which initiates a mourning process. Since women traditionally have been socialized to need relationships, they may feel inadequate and lonely on their own. Marriage represents an idealized relationship to which women bring very high expectations, and when the marriage proves abusive this relationship is lost. Marriage also represents an expansion of roles and a gain in status; a woman who marries becomes not only a wife and, often, a mother, but a full adult in the community. Separating from an abusive husband is a role loss, and it is often perceived as a sign of personal failure as well. The woman may lose economic security, safety, social support, esteem, and fulfillment.

These potential losses must be mourned. At first the mourning may be expressed through denial—denying the battering, covering up bruises, or being ashamed to admit what has happened. Often when the abuse has been acknowledged, anger sets in, either openly or in the form of a high level of energy or self-punishment. Grief is likely to be present throughout the mourning period. It is often difficult to detect, however, and may take the form of feeling tired or other physical complaints.

The period during which an actual decision is made to stay with or leave the relationship is often typified by bargaining. Husbands may attempt to apologize and may feel dejected or promise to change. Wives may be willing to listen, given the losses they are experiencing. It is not uncommon for battered wives to maintain a good deal of loyalty toward their spouses and to find it difficult to contemplate leaving. They often find themselves torn between wanting to assure their own and their children's safety and wanting to shield and help the abuser.

Source: Susan F. Turner, "Battered Women: Mourning the Death of a Relationship," *Social Work*, vol. 31 (September–October 1986), pp. 372–76.

Child Abuse and Neglect

Attention to child abuse and neglect in recent years has been stimulated by the development of more accurate diagnostic techniques by the medical profession, such as designation of the term *battered child syndrome* to describe evidence of maltreatment. It also reflects changing expectations about the exercise of authority by parents and others in their relations with children, as well as the passage of legislation in most states under which social workers, doctors, and others dealing with children are required to report bruises, burns, or broken bones, other visible signs of abuse or neglect, and behaviors that might indicate fear, shame, or confusion in children's dealings with adults.[31] The rate of reports of child neglect and abuse by state child protective services to the National Study on Child Neglect and Abuse Reporting more than doubled between 1980 and 1987, going from 3.5 per 1,000 population to 8.3 per 1,000. In 1991 1.8 million child abuse and neglect cases involving 2.7 million children were referred for investigation by state child protective services.[32]

Under the Child Abuse Prevention and Treatment Act of 1974 (as amended in 1978), child abuse and neglect are defined as the physical or mental injury, sexual abuse or exploitation, negligent treatment, or maltreatment of a child under the age of 18 by a person who is responsible for the child's welfare, under circumstances that indicate the child's health or welfare is harmed or threatened. Individual states also have defined the terms.

Child abuse usually involves some kind of harmful act perpetrated against a child, while child neglect usually involves abandonment of responsibility for the child. The legal definitions usually includes intention on the part of the perpetrators (see "Intention in Child Abuse"). Both abuse and neglect can have emotional and psychological as well as physical aspects. Reports of abuse or maltreatment by neglect are the most common form, 46 percent of all substantiated cases of child abuse and neglect in 1991, according to the National Center on Child Abuse and Neglect of the U.S. Department of Health and Human Services. That same year, physical abuse accounted for 24 percent of substantiated cases, sexual abuse for 16 percent, emotional maltreatment for 6 percent, and a variety of other offenses for 8 percent of the cases.[33]

The criteria for identifying physical abuse are much clearer than for any other type of abuse or neglect, but the distinction between parents' rights to discipline their children by spanking and beatings that become outright cruelty or life-threatening may be hard for authorities to draw. Given the lack of clarity in the criteria for identifying other kinds of abuse and neglect, social workers and others providing service must be cautious in assessing cases. Child protective services are provided by state agencies in all 50 states as mandated by Title XX of the Social Security Act in 1975, but federal funding was restricted by reorganization of the program under the Title XX Services Block Grant in 1982.

Estimates of the prevalence of child abuse and neglect are derived from varied sources. Official data taken from child welfare services are likely to give very different information than unofficial data taken from direct surveys of children and families. It does appear, however, that the official data underestimate the true incidence of abuse and neglect in the population. A conservative estimate would be that between 10 to 20 out of each 1,000 children experience abuse or neglect at some time.[34]

Knowledge of the demographic characteristics of victims of abuse and neglect derives in large part from official statistics. Thus it may reflect the extent to which people report incidents involving children and how they deal with such problems rather than the true characteristics of victims. In general, the likelihood that a child will experience neglect or abuse in any form increases with age. Adolescent children have the highest incidence, followed by preadolescents, preschool children, and infants. If only the data on physical neglect are examined, however, the youngest children have the greatest likelihood of being victims. Boys and girls have an approximately equal likelihood of experiencing abuse and neglect. While all ethnic, racial, and socioeconomic groups are represented in the statistics, it appears that blacks and other lower socioeconomic groups are overrepresented.[35]

The majority of child abusers are parents, and they often are the natural or biological parents of the abused or neglected children. Mothers are more likely to be implicated than fathers, largely because they spend more time with the children. It has been suggested that child abusers were often abused themselves as children, but more recent data question this conclusion. Kinard reports that "careful examination of the empirical evidence reveals that only a small proportion of abusing parents experienced abuse in childhood. Thus, many abusing parents were not abused as children, and many parents who were abused as children do not abuse their own children."[36]

Child Sexual Abuse

Child sexual abuse, which is distinguished from physical and emotional abuse by the explicitly sexual nature of the act, is particularly troublesome. Criteria for identifying sexual abuse usually specify an age difference between the sexual partners of five or more years, use of force or coercion, and determination of developmentally appropriate

---

Intention in Child Abuse

There is a fine line in Illinois law that separates a child murderer from an unintentional killer. Within a few months in 1986, two men were convicted of getting angry at the toddlers they were taking care of and beating the children to death. One man was convicted of murder and sentenced to 70 years in prison. The other was convicted of involuntary manslaughter and received the maximum possible sentence—10 years' imprisonment.

In an article in the *Chicago Tribune* for March 31, 1986, Linnet Myers analyzed the difference in convictions and sentences:

It isn't the way the child dies: Bruises covered the legs, arms, buttocks, and abdomens of both toddlers, one 22 months old and one 24 months. Both also had severe internal injuries.

It isn't the motive: In both cases, the children were beaten because they had an accident while being toilet trained. They were "disciplined."

It isn't the evidence: Both men admitted they hit the children, but said they didn't mean to kill them.

The difference lies in a few lines of Illinois law. If the killer knew he was creating "a strong probability of great bodily harm" to the baby, he is a murderer. If he killed the baby "recklessly," he is not.

The law, according to the state's attorney, is "crystal clear—it all goes to the state of mind." Deciding a person's state of mind in cases where a child is killed as the result of "discipline" is extremely difficult, however. The crucial difference is the judge assigned to the case and the judge's particular interpretation of the law. Many judges find it hard to believe that anyone would deliberately murder a child.

Source: Linnet Myers, "Technicality Decides When Killing a Baby Isn't Murder," *Chicago Tribune,* March 31, 1986, sect. 1, p. 7.

---

behavior.[37] Especially with regard to the latter criterion, there may be ambiguity as to whether a particular act is abusive. While it is clear that coercive sexual intercourse between a father and a child is abusive, for instance, it may not be considered abusive for a father or mother to walk around the house naked. The National Center on Child Abuse and Neglect defines sexual abuse of children as "Contacts or interactions between a child and an adult when the child is being used for the sexual stimulation of that adult by another person."[38]

As with other domestic violence, there are few reliable and valid statistics on child sexual abuse; many cases are unreported, and trends are difficult to discern. Official data are considered inaccurate measures of the true incidence in the total population, but studies of social populations, such as college students and people in psychotherapy, suggest an incidence too high to be readily accepted (see "The Repression of Memories" in Chapter 15). The methodologically soundest studies suggest that some 20 to 30 percent of all adults were sexually abused before their 18th birthdays. These studies also indicate that in the majority of cases, sexual abuse takes place within the context of family life and is perpetrated by men—fathers, stepfathers, grandfathers, brothers, and friends of the family.[39] Little is known of the ethnic, racial, and socioeconomic correlates of child sexual abuse.

Although all victims do not suffer severe or permanent harm, sexual abuse by family members and friends is extremely difficult for children to handle. John Conte notes that abused children can experience a wide range of negative effects, including "depression, guilt, learning difficulties, sexual acting out, running away, somatic complaints (such as headaches and stomachaches), hysterical seizures, phobias, nightmares, compulsive rituals, self-destructive behaviors, and suicide."[40] These effects can continue to plague the individual well into adulthood, taking such forms as a negative self-image, depression, and sexual problems.

∽ FAMILY PROBLEMS: MARRIAGE, DIVORCE, REMARRIAGE

Family dissolution, or the end of a marriage, has always been a possible outcome in family life. In the past, however, family dissolution was largely a result of the death of a parent or, in some cases, both parents. Today it is much more likely to be a result of divorce.

Marriage and Divorce Rates

In 1860 about 5 percent of all couples who married could be expected to divorce eventually. In the next 100 years, the divorce rate generally increased, but between 1960 and 1980 it more than doubled.[41] In 1981, the number of divorces peaked at 1.21 million and there were twice as many marriages, 2.42 million. The **marriage rate**, 10.6 marriages per 1,000 population, was also double the **divorce rate**, 5.3 divorces per 1,000 population (the same as in 1980).[42] In terms of a ratio of divorces to marriages, there were about 500 divorces for every 1,000 marriages. After 1981, the divorce rate began to decline; it fell to 4.7 per 1,000 in 1990. The marriage rate also declined, falling to 9.8 that year[43] (see "Changes in Marriage and Divorce Rates"). Still, demographers were predicting that about half of all marriages would end in divorce.

While divorce affects all socioeconomic and racial and ethnic groups, it correlates more highly with some sectors than with others. Compared to whites, the likelihood of divorce is higher for blacks but lower for Hispanics. In 1991, divorce was the marital status for 8 percent of whites, 11 percent of blacks, and 7 percent of Hispanics.[44] One study found, for example, that Mexican Americans have less marital instability than whites, and increases for divorce among them have been smaller.[45]

The relationship between divorce and educational level, one indicator of social class, is quite complex. In general, the likelihood of divorce is highest among those with "some college" (even higher than among those with less than high school educations), and it is lowest among college graduates. When education goes beyond a college degree, divorce is significantly more likely for women but not for men.[46] A similar situation is found for another socioeconomic indicator, income. While for men each increase in income brings less likelihood of divorce, just the opposite is true for women. Divorce rates are highest among women earning high incomes and lowest among those earning little or no income.[47]

For some years demographers have stated that over 90 percent of the adult population of the United States will be married at one time or another in their lifetimes. The proportion of the population 18 years and older whose marital status is "married" in a given year is considerably less, however, and it has been falling, from 72 percent in 1970 to 61 percent in 1991. In the same period, the percentage classified as single increased from 16 to 23, the percentage widowed declined from 9 to 7, and the percentage divorced grew from 3 to 9.[48]

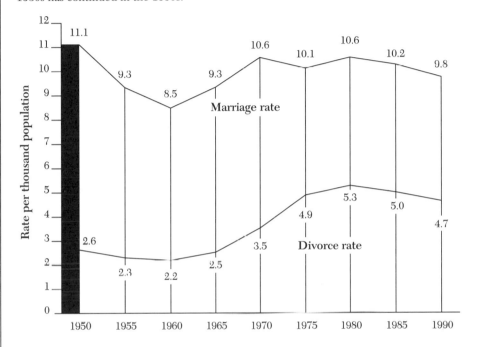

Changes in Marriage and Divorce Rates, 1950–1990

The U.S. Bureau of the Census measures marital status in terms of marriage rates, the number of marriages per 1,000 population in a given period, and divorce rates, the number of divorces per 1,000 population. A decline in both marriage and divorce rates which began in the 1980s has continued in the 1990s.

Source: U.S. Bureau of the Census, *Statistical Abstract of the United States: 1992*, 112th edition (Washington, DC, 1992), Table 127.

The Never-Married and the Remarried

The population of single, never-married people in the United States was almost as high at the turn of the twentieth century as it is now. In 1890, for instance, 27 percent of men and 15 percent of women between the ages of 30 and 34 had never married. But this percentage dropped considerably in the 1950s, after the return of servicemen at the end of World War II, and it did not start to rise again until the 1970s. By 1990 the percentage of never-married men aged 30–34 was the same as it was 100 years ago, and the percentage of women was 3 points higher. In 1991, in the entire population aged 18 and over, 26 percent of the males and 19 percent of the females had never married.[49]

Among women, staying single is related to education and occupation. Those with more education and career potential are less likely to marry. There are no comparable data on never-married men.[50]

Remarriage after divorce is fairly common, but, according to census data, the percentage of people who remarry after a first divorce has steadily declined since 1970. The remarriage rate for divorced women, 123 per 1,000 in 1970, fell to 79 in 1988. For divorced men it was 205 per 1,000 in 1970 and 110 in 1988.[51] The drop in remarriage rates, and the smaller rate for women than for men, is largely attributed by sociologists and demographers to middle-aged women who have gained financial and sexual independence. In a series of interviews with men and women aged 40–54, *The New York Times* found in December 1992 that women said they were not remarrying because they preferred being single to losing their independence. The men interviewed were either ambivalent about remarriage or valued it as a way of securing regular companionship and the amenities of domestic life.[52] The demographer Paul Glick arrived at a related conclusion. He found that the likelihood a divorced woman will remarry is related to education; those with no college education remarry more quickly than those who are college educated.[53]

Few people have experienced divorce twice, but their numbers are growing. Whites are more likely to have multiple divorces than blacks, and second marriages are more likely to end in divorce than first marriages. Glick projected that 61 percent of the men and 54 percent of the women in their thirties in 1980 who married a second time would experience a second divorce.[54]

Interpreting the Data

To some observers, the data on marriage, divorce, and remarriage are overwhelming evidence that family life is diminishing in importance in American society; that is, the data are said to demonstrate the ill-being of family life.[55] Others do not agree. Mary Jo Bane believes that divorce and remarriage rates merely show that the specific marital partner is being rejected, not marriage itself. She demonstrates that Americans continue to be committed to a stable family life and the nurturing of children.[56]

Most of the argument about the meaning of marriage and divorce rates is best understood as an assessment of the traditional two-parent, never-divorced family as a social institution. Under the assumption that anything less than the traditional nuclear family is harmful for society, the single-parent families and even the stepfamilies that follow divorce may be judged to be deviant and therefore troubled. In our view of the family as a changing institution, however, diversity in the structure and organization of family life is simply an indication of ongoing changes. A particular form of family life should not be seen as deviant in itself. Nevertheless, change predictably brings about conflict and stress in the family.

∞ STRESSFUL FAMILY PATTERNS

The stress associated with divorce affects not only the separating couple and their children but the family patterns that follow it. The economic problems of single-parent families are heightened by psychological problems when they are formed as a result of divorce. Remarriage and the formation of blended or reconstituted families with the children of one or both partners have their own stressful circumstances. When marriage is avoided by the formation of single-parent families (especially when the head of the household is a teenaged girl), psychological stress is added to economic burdens. For these families and the family lifestyles of homosexual couples, the particular stress of societal disapproval can be anticipated.

The Stress of Divorce

Tolerance of divorce has increased in American society since the 1950s, along with tolerance for other variations in family life. Lenore Weitzman suggested in 1981 that "the decline in social stigma traditionally attached to divorce is one of the most striking changes in the social climate surrounding divorce."[57] Naomi Gerstel suggests, however, that, depending on the specific conditions of a divorce, some divorced people still experience disapproval. At least one party to a divorce may feel held accountable and blamed, as evidenced in the practice of "splitting friends." Individuals who divorce also suffer informal, relational sanctions. They often are excluded from social contacts with married couples and seek out other divorced persons like themselves, though they may fear that becoming identified with other divorced persons in support groups would reinforce their own devaluation. Thus, she says, "Although a majority of Americans claim they are indifferent in principle to those who make a 'personal decision' to leave a 'bad' marriage, the indifference does not carry over into the social construction of private lives. The divorced believe they are the target of exclusion, blame, and devaluation."[58]

Divorce undoubtedly produces stress, as the life-cycle perspective on study of the family demonstrates (see Chapter 11). It is not clear, however, that the stress is always intense or long-lasting. According to Doris Jacobson, most studies show that divorcing and divorced adults experience depression, loneliness, low work and school efficiency, trouble sleeping, somatic symptoms, feelings of incompetence, and even suicidal or homicidal feelings. Children involved in divorce commonly show increased acting out, antisocial or aggressive behavior, and feelings of anger, sadness, or guilt. Although these findings make intuitive sense, they should be evaluated cautiously. Many of these studies suffer from methodological weaknesses such as nonrandom samples and overreliance on white, middle-class subjects. They also tend to emphasize short-term effects. Among children, for instance, considerable distress is reported during the first two years after separation or divorce, but there is little knowledge of whether this leads to later psychological problems. Similarly, most studies of the effects of divorce on adults focus on the divorce period and its immediate aftermath.[59]

Moreover, all studies do not find evidence of negative emotional effects. Jacobson reports that the least distress has been found among divorced women who do not remarry. It has also been found that children from intact but conflict-ridden households have more psychological troubles than children from divorced or separated households in which there is less conflict (see "Divorce or Stay Together"). Social and psychological factors have been identified as mediating influences which determine the extent to which emotional problems will be experienced. For adults, such factors as preexisting psychiatric disturbances, self-esteem attitudes, and willingness to accept nontraditional gender roles can affect the partners' abilities to mediate the negative effects of divorce. For children, the nature of parent-child interaction, the degree of economic stability, and the existence of social support networks can affect the possibility of psychological disturbances.

Judith Wallerstein, whose California Children of Divorce Study was completed in 1980, followed up in 1989 with a study of how divorced men and women and their children have fared since the divorce. In *Second Chance*, she points to the importance of resolving feelings of anger and betrayal and reclaiming self-esteem in order to cope with the stress of divorce. To help the children of divorce, she suggests that it is vital for both of the parents to maintain their parenting roles by exercising visitation rights or following through on joint custody arrangements. A decade after divorce, the youngest children, girls especially, were doing the best; those who had been preadolescents and adolescents

Divorce or Stay Together: Two Sides of the Question

The following letters contributed by readers to Ann Landers's popular advice column eloquently express the dilemma for children caught in a conflict-ridden family situation. Though they are profoundly affected by the decision to divorce or stay together, they have no real voice in it. Together these letters state the case that while divorce is likely to be stressful, so is maintaining a bad marriage.

Dear Ann Landers:
The worst thing that can happen to children is to have their parents get a divorce.

It makes kids want to fall to the ground and die. When people ask why you changed schools or why your mom and dad aren't at the baseball game, it is agony to try to think of a sensible answer.

Parents always say they would never do anything to hurt their children, but no physical abuse can be as bad as the pain of having parents split. Why can't they understand our feelings? We cry to our friends. We cry to our brothers and sisters. We cry to our pets. We even beg our parents to change their minds. They say we are too young to understand.

We remember all the nights when we heard those terrible arguments. Why would married people say such awful things to each other? We try to block out the fighting but it's impossible. If they hate each other so much why did they get married? Is it possible to go from love to hate? It makes us afraid to get married.

It's not fair for us to have to change schools and lose our friends. Don't they see what they do to our lives when they break up the family? It hurts something awful. I know because it's happening to my brothers and sisters and to me right now. No name, just—

"A Girl Age 12"

Dear Girl:
I'm sad for you, but I hope the next letter will help you understand the other side of the story. Please share it with your brothers and sisters.

Dear Ann Landers:
Every now and then we see an unhappily married couple who stayed together "for the children." I have been wanting to write this letter for a long time. Today I am doing it.

My parents will celebrate their 50th wedding anniversary next year. None of their five children has ever acknowledged their parents' wedding anniversaries because it would have been so phony.

Our mother is a bitter and reclusive woman with a martyr complex. Our father is an unpleasant alcoholic with a mean mouth and a rotten temper. Every one of us kids was messed up because we never learned how to develop positive relationships until we reached our 30's. We have all experienced failed marriages and had other troubles in our lives.

Each of us is engaged in an ongoing struggle to erase the tapes of the destructive and awful behavior of our parents so we will not emulate them. It hasn't been easy. I am writing to tell all parents who are considering staying together for the children's sake to forget it. You will do them no favors.

T.O.

Dear T.O.:
Thanks for the powerful testimony. I am sure your letter was not an easy one to write. I appreciate the effort, as will many readers who are on the fence about this issue. Every effort should be made to save the troubled marriage when children are involved. Counseling should be sought. But if the situation is downright intolerable, it is an injustice to the children to stay together and feed on one another's neurosis and misery.

Source: Ann Landers, syndicated column, *The Oregonian*, August 12, 1986. Reprinted with permission of Ann Landers, Creators, and the Los Angeles Times Syndicates.

at the time of the divorce were having the most trouble. While the evidence bore out the finding that a good divorce is better than a bad marriage, in many postdivorce families the conflict continued. Many children went through a second divorce, and for only one out of seven children were both parents happily remarried. The economic condition of one out of four children dropped severely and stayed that way.[60]

The Stress of Single Parenthood after Divorce

Single-parent families formed by women after divorce are especially likely to experience not only economic problems but psychological disruption. Many of these families must subsist on severely restricted incomes; in 1991, the poverty rate for children in all families headed by single mothers was 59 percent.[61] The economic position of divorced women generally has deteriorated since the passage of "no fault" divorce laws in most states; Weitzman concludes that "the major economic result of the divorce law revolution is the systematic impoverishment of divorced women and their children." She found that, on average, divorced women and the children living with them suffer a 73 percent drop in their standard of living the first year after a divorce. In the same period, the standard of living of divorced men increases 42 percent.[62]

Mothers of young children are also expected to be able to support themselves and their families in short order following divorce. According to Weitzman, since no-fault divorce became the rule some 87 percent of young mothers have received no alimony. Very little child support is awarded—an average of $200 a month for two children—and when it is awarded it is difficult to collect from the father. Moreover, because a couple's property and assets are supposed to be divided equally, women and children often lose the family home when it is sold so the proceeds can be divided. The husband keeps the family's biggest assets—his education and training, his earning capacity, and his pension, health insurance, and other employment benefits.

Women and children experience numerous other consequences of divorce. When they must move from their former neighborhoods, important social networks and support may be lost. Many divorced women enter the full-time labor force for the first time, which may bring changes in their identity. The time mothers can spend with their children is shortened, and the mental health of both the mother and the children may suffer for various reasons. Single mothers report substantially higher rates of anxiety and depression than married women and men do, and service utilization statistics indicate that single-parent families with children headed by mothers consume a large share of community mental health services.[63]

Families of Never-Married Mothers

When single parenthood results from a birth to a never-married woman, rather than divorce, widowhood, or separation, there may be other stressful consequences. Tamar Lewin notes in a 1992 article in *The New York Times* that "As single motherhood becomes an ever more common fact of American life, millions of women raising children by themselves are grappling with practical problems of child care and tight finances, and more elusive concerns about their children's development and their own place in society."[64]

Birth rates of all unmarried women of child-bearing age, but particularly the younger women, multiplied between 1970 and 1990. For those aged 15–19 the rate increased from 22 per 1,000 girls that age to 43; for women aged 20–24 it went up from 38 per 1,000 to 65. Births to unmarried women constituted 27 percent of all births in the United States in 1990 (up from 18 percent in 1980), but they represented 17 percent of all births to whites and 67 percent of births to blacks[65] (see "Social Pressures Producing Single-Parent Families" in Chapter 9).

Never-married mothers are the fastest-growing group of single mothers but they are the minority; two out of three single mothers have been divorced, separated, or abandoned by their husbands, or they are widows. Discussion of single mothers in the media, however, usually centers on older, single career women who decide to have babies without a spouse or on pregnant teen-agers with no means of support. Never-married mothers tend to be younger, poorer, less educated, and more dependent on welfare than those who were married at the time of their children's birth, and they give birth to most of the children now becoming members of single-parent households.[66]

Teenage mothers are on the whole unprepared to be mothers and heads of households. The initial awareness of pregnancy brings difficulties with parents, school authorities, and boyfriends. Many teenagers receive little prenatal care, and often their children are born small, weak, or with birth defects. The mothers have trouble completing high school, despite special programs for them and child care for their children in some schools. They also have trouble providing for themselves and their children and become dependent on public welfare; relatively few receive any support from the father. The mothers often bear additional children with the same or different fathers and add them to the family. Child neglect and abuse are common. The children of young mothers may suffer cognitive development deficits, and some eventually become teenaged parents themselves.[67]

The Stress of Remarriage

Remarriage after divorce carries a high level of motivation to succeed, to avoid past failures in family lifestyles, and to assure the continued growth and development of family members. One obstacle to success lies in the social context of stepfamilies, which often are not accorded the same respect as other families. Legal problems are likely to arise as well. A stepparent does not always have the right to make medical decisions for a stepchild, and stepchildren do not automatically become heirs of the stepparent.[68]

Some of the stress in stepfamilies is likely to be of a psychological nature, as remarried individuals attempt to deal with the tasks involved in setting up another long-term emotional relationship. A. Goetting has described six tasks of remarriage, each of which carries a different kind of stress:

1. Emotional remarriage, the process of establishing a new bond with a chosen partner.
2. Psychic remarriage, the process of changing one's identity from a single individual to a couple.
3. Community remarriage, the process of establishing relationships outside the marriage.
4. Parental remarriage, the process of establishing bonds with the children of a partner.
5. Economic remarriage, the process of becoming interdependent in terms of financial needs and responsibilities.
6. Legal remarriage, the process of settling financial and other responsibilities toward children and former partners.[69]

Seven stages of stepfamily development, each of which poses a potential problem for remarried adults and their children, have been described by Patricia Papernow. First, people planning to remarry are likely to entertain the fantasy that they will be rescuing their new partner or any children from the deficiencies of a previous marriage. These fantasies are likely to be played out in the second stage, assimilation. Awareness is the period in which the fantasy ends and the remarried couple comes to recognize the reality of their situation. Mobilization of energies and resources then takes place, as the new family members attempt to pull together to solve common problems. Action is the process by which the family members begin to work together in an effective way. Contact describes the growing sense of realistic intimacy likely to be experienced by family members working together effectively. Finally, resolution is the stage at which the reconstituted family feels and behaves as a solid unit.[70]

Stresses in Cohabitation

Heterosexual and homosexual cohabitation is susceptible to numerous stresses and difficulties. While the acceptance of heterosexual couples has increased in recent years (see Chapter 8), they, like homosexual couples, still fall outside the norms of marriage and family life, and individuals in such arrangements may have difficulty finding support in the larger society. The relatively clear expectations that govern heterosexual marital relationships and child rearing are absent, and the couple must delineate its own expectations of how the relationship should work. Heterosexual and homosexual cohabitation, therefore, have been described as "experimental forms of marriage."[71]

One reason stress develops in cohabiting couples has been society's disapproval of these arrangements. Parents may have difficulty acknowledging their child's partner as a member of the family or responding to the partner comfortably. For gay male and lesbian couples, the relationship alone often is insufficient to overcome the hostility and pressure toward conformity that derives from family, friends, and civic authorities and from mainstream and fundamentalist religions that forbid them to marry.[72]

Before cohabitation can reliably provide stable, family-life relations, the practice must become institutionalized in the society as a family form, or it must at least develop rules and regulations that are sanctioned by society.[73] Despite their absence, premarital heterosexual coupling is generally recognized as a lifestyle in American society, and in the gay and lesbian community norms, roles, values, and traditions are being developed by couples in long-term relationships. Social resources supporting homosexual couples living together include a guide to legal aspects which covers buying and selling property, relating to former spouses, child custody and visitation rights, estate planning, and living arrangements.[74]

∽ IMPLICATIONS FOR PRACTICE

Study of the family as a social organization is a more concrete guide to assessment and intervention in family problems than study of the family as an institution. Taken together, the two approaches demonstrate how social service workers who take a critical perspective can address public issues through their interactions with clients who have private troubles (see "The Family as Social Institution and Organization" in Chapter 8). When a married couple considering divorce or a legal separation seeks help, for instance, the central issue for the social service worker is whether all marriages should be saved. Those who see in divorce the destruction of American family life would argue that saving marriages is a proper role for social workers. Those who believe that divorce is a rejection of the partner but not necessarily of marriage and parental responsibility would define the social worker's role differently; divorce may be a necessary step in freeing the couple from a negative, dead-end relationship. Thus social workers must help to determine if divorce is truly necessary. If not, they might help revitalize the relationship to make it meet the needs of all the family's members. If divorce is considered necessary, they must try to deal with the stresses generated by the family dissolution.

Primary Prevention, Early Intervention, and Rehabilitation

Family practice and family treatment have become exceedingly popular in social work in recent decades, as well they should. As Ann Hartman has emphasized, the family has been the historical concern of social work and one which distinguishes social workers from other helping professionals.[75] Two practice tasks are served by the assessment of family well-being: determining how families diverge from some optimum level of functioning (the identification of problems and strengths), and determining directions for change in order to improve functioning (intervention objectives). A number of other social work objectives, roles, and tasks also emerge from the consideration of family well-being. These are concerned with primary prevention, early intervention, and rehabilitation.

Primary prevention includes advocacy to assure that economic and other survival needs can be met. It also includes the development of policy and programs in support of such objectives as greater educational opportunities, greater equality in the incomes of male and female workers, greater access to child care, and better enforcement of child support orders. Community and educational services can be promoted to call attention to family problems, including spouse, child, and elderly abuse. Providing information on the conditions that produce such problems and promoting skills that make it possible to overcome them should they arise can contribute to a decline in the number of such incidents.

Early intervention in families likely to experience difficulties also serves to prevent more serious problems. Social workers can set up and facilitate support or mutual-aid groups among people who have recently married or are cohabiting, have been divorced or remarried, or have been victims or perpetrators of family violence. Support groups help people understand that the difficulties they are experiencing are not unique but are often shared by others in similar circumstances. They can be educational, providing information on likely experiences and difficulties, and they can build skills, helping people develop the capacity to handle difficulties when they arise.

Since social workers are most likely to work in the *rehabilitation* of families that are experiencing difficulties, they need to develop skills for crisis intervention and more long-term treatment. Crisis intervention often is needed to provide immediate help or support for families. At the time of a family dispute, divorce or separation, or a violent act, the task of the social worker is to listen and empathize, reinforce strengths, and assist clients in holding their lives together by assuring the satisfaction of their survival needs. More long-term family treatment can explore the whys and wherefores of family problems.

☙ DISCUSSION QUESTIONS AND CLASS PROJECTS

1. Review the characteristics of healthy families presented in this chapter. Do these represent your idea of a healthy family? Would you delete any? Would you add any?

2. Define the following types of marriages: total marriage, vital marriage, conflict-habituated marriage, devitalized marriage, and passive-congenial marriage. Do you think all these types can be "normal" marriages? Do you agree that all can be "happy marriages"?

3. Describe the difference between survival and developmental family needs. Write three sets of themes or questions you might use in an interview to assess whether a family is meeting the survival needs of its members.

4. Family boundaries, both the boundary between families and their environments and the boundary between individual members in a family, have been studied for their implications for family well-being. Review the findings of researchers on both kinds of boundaries.

5. Internal family alignments and power structures have also been studied. What have researchers found about the relationship between these and family well-being?

6. Define and identify the significance of the following terms:

   random families
   closed families
   triangulation
   detouring coalitions
   stable coalitions
   faltering families
   dominated families
   conflicted families
   chaotic families
   disengaged families
   enmeshed families

7. What is meant by domestic violence? What are the three major forms of domestic violence, and what is known of their incidence within families?

8. Those who work in shelters for battered women find that many women choose to remain with husbands who have abused them. Why would this be the case?

9. Define and distinguish among child abuse, child neglect, and child sexual abuse. How clear are definitions of sexual abuse?

10. Do you think that all marriages are worth saving? How would you distinguish between those that are and those that are not?

11. Without forcing anyone to speak, inquire into the experiences of people in class who have gone through a divorce or separation, either as an adult or child. What stresses did they endure? What kinds of help did they ask for or receive? What kind of help would they have liked to have?

12. Goetting has described six tasks of remarriage. List and describe each.

13. Papernow has described seven stages of stepfamily development. List and describe each.

14. Without forcing anyone to speak, inquire into the experience of people in class who have gone through remarriage either as an adult or child. What was the experience like? Do Goetting's tasks and Papernow's stages fit any of their experiences?

◌ NOTES

1. Harriet Johnson, "Emerging Concerns in Family Therapy," *Social Work*, vol. 31 (July–August 1986), pp. 299–306.

2. Salvador Minuchin, *Families and Family Therapy* (Cambridge, MA: Harvard University Press, 1974).

3. Dolores Curran, *Traits of a Healthy Family* (New York: Ballantine Books, 1984), pp. 26–27.

4. Hamilton I. McCubbin and Anne I. Thompson (editors), *Family Assessment Inventories for Research and Practice* (Madison: University of Wisconsin–Madison, 1991).

5. John F. Cuber and Peggy B. Harroff, *Sex and the Significant Americans* (Baltimore, MD: Pelican Books, 1968).

6. Kenneth G. Terkelsen, "Toward a Theory of the Family Life Cycle," in E. A. Carter and M. McGoldrick, *The Family Life Cycle: A Framework for Family Therapy* (New York: Gardner, 1980), pp. 21–52.

7. Ann Hartman and Joan Laird, *Family-Centered Social Work Practice* (New York: Free Press, 1983), p. 165.

8. Fernando Colon, "The Family Life Cycle of the Multi-Problem Poor Family," in Carter and McGoldrick, *Family Life Cycle*, pp. 343–81.

9. Robert B. Hill, *The Strength of Black Families* (New York: Emerson Hall, 1971).

10. David Kantor and William Lehr, *Inside the Family* (San Francisco, CA: Jossey-Bass, 1975), pp. 119–42.

11. Harry J. Aponte and John M. Van Deusen, "Structural Family Therapy," in A. S. Gurman and D. P. Kniskern (editors), *Handbook of Family Therapy* (New York: Brunner Mazel, 1981), pp. 310–60; Aponte, "Underorganization in the Poor Family," in P. J. Guerin, Jr. (editor), *Family Therapy: Theory and Practice* (New York: Gardner, 1976), pp. 432–48. Also see Salvador Minuchin et al., *Families of the Slums: An Exploration of Their Structure and Treatment* (New York: Basic Books, 1967).

12. Aponte, "Underorganization in the Poor Family," p. 433.

13. Ibid.

14. Jerry M. Lewis, W. Robert Beavers, John T. Gossett, and Virginia A. Phillips, *No Single Thread: Psychological Health in Family Systems* (New York: Bruner Mazel, 1976).

15. Jerry M. Lewis, *How's Your Family: A Guide to Identifying Your Family's Strengths and Weaknesses*, rev. ed. (New York: Bruner Mazel, 1989), pp. 85–96.

16. Ibid., pp. 111–20.

17. Ibid., pp. 121–31.

18. Charles Vert Willie, *A New Look at Black Families*, 2nd ed. (New York: General Hall, 1981).

19. Barbara Star, "Domestic Violence," in *Encyclopedia of Social Work*, 18th edition, Vol. 1 (Silver Spring, MD: National Association of Social Workers, 1987), pp. 463–76. The discussion of domestic violence is based in large part on this article.

20. Stephen J. Pfohl, "The Discovery of Child Abuse," *Social Problems*, vol. 24 (February 1977), pp. 310–23.

21. Star, "Domestic Violence."

22. U.S. Bureau of the Census, *Statistical Abstract of the United States: 1992* (Washington, DC, 1992), Table 302.

23. R. L. McNeely and Gloria Robinson-Simpson, "The Truth about Domestic Violence: A Falsely Framed Issue," *Social Work*, vol. 32 (November–December 1987), pp. 485–90.

24. Star, "Domestic Violence."

25. Donileen R. Loseke and Spencer E. Cahill, "The Social Construction of Deviance: Experts on Battered Women," *Social Problems*, vol. 31 (February 1984), pp. 296–310. Reprinted in J. Stimson, A. Stimson, and V. Parillo (editors), *Social Problems: Contemporary Readings*, 2nd ed. (Itasca, IL: F. E. Peacock Publishers, 1991), pp. 250–268.

26. Ken Dychtwald, *Age Wave: The Challenges and Opportunities of an Aging America* (Los Angeles: Jeremy P. Tarcher, 1989), p. 243.

27. Star, "Domestic Violence," pp. 468–69; Jon Nordheimer, "When Security of Old Age Brings Financial Shenanigans and Theft," *The New York Times*, December 16, 1991, pp. A1, B9.

28. Star, "Domestic Violence."

29. Peggy Eastman, "Elders under Seige," *Psychology Today*, January 1984, p. 30. Reprinted in Stimson, Stimson, and Parillo (editors), *Social Problems*, pp. 235–37.

30. Dychtwald, *Age Wave*, p. 243.

31. E. Milling Kinard, "Child Abuse and Neglect," in *Encyclopedia of Social Work*, Vol. 1, pp. 223–31.

32. U.S. Bureau of the Census, *Statistical Abstract: 1992*, Table 300, and *Statistical Abstract: 1993*, 113th edition (Washington, DC, 1993), Table 340.

33. U.S. Bureau of the Census, *Statistical Abstract: 1993*, Table 341.

34. Kinard, "Child Abuse and Neglect," pp. 224–25.

35. Ibid.

36. Ibid., p. 228.

37. John R. Conte, "Child Sexual Abuse," in *Encyclopedia of Social Work*, Vol. 1, pp. 255–60.

38. Renitta L. Goldman and Virginia R. Wheeler, *Silent Shame: The Sexual Abuse of Children* (Danville, IL: Interstate, 1986). Reprinted in Stimson, Stimson, and Parrillo (editors), *Social Problems*, pp. 91–102.

39. Ibid., pp. 225–56.

40. Ibid., p. 257.

41. James A. Weed, "Divorce: Americans' Style," *American Demographics*, vol. 4 (March 1982), pp. 13–17.

42. U.S. Bureau of the Census, *Statistical Abstract of the United States: 1988* (Washington, DC, 1987), Table 126.

43. U.S. Bureau of the Census, *Statistical Abstract: 1992*, Table 134.

44. Ibid., Table 49.

45. W. Parker Frisbie, Wolfgang Opitz, and William R. Kelly, "Marital Instability Trends among Mexican Americans as Compared to Blacks and Anglos: New Evidence," *Social Science Quarterly*, vol. 66 (September 1985), pp. 587–601.

46. Paul C. Glick, "How American Families Are Changing," *American Demographics*, vol. 6 (January 1984), p. 24.

47. Doris S. Jacobson, "Divorce and Separation," in *Encyclopedia of Social Work*, Vol. 1, pp. 450–51.

48. U.S. Bureau of the Census, *Statistical Abstract: 1992*, Table 49.

49. Edward L. Kain, "Surprising Singles," *American Demographics*, vol. 6 (August 1984), pp. 16-19, 39; U.S. Bureau of the Census, *Statistical Abstract: 1992*, Table 51.

50. Kain, "Surprising Singles."

51. U.S. Bureau of the Census, *Statistical Abstract: 1992*, Table 130.

52. Jane Gross, "Divorced, Middle-Aged, and Happy: Women, Especially, Adjust to the 90's," *The New York Times*, December 7, 1992, p. A14.

53. Glick, "How American Families Are Changing."

54. Ibid.

55. Victor R. Fuchs, *How We Live: An Economic Perspective on Americans from Birth to Death* (Cambridge, MA: Harvard University Press, 1983), pp. 220–26.

56. Mary Jo Bane, *Here to Stay: American Families in the 20th Century* (New York: Basic Books, 1976), p. 19.

57. Lenore Weitzman, *The Marriage Contract* (New York: Free Press, 1981), p. 146.

58. Naomi Gerstel, "Divorce and Stigma," *Social Problems*, vol. 34 (1987), pp. 172–183. Reprinted in Stimson, Stimson, and Parrillo (editors), *Social Problems*, pp. 269–77.

59. Jacobson, "Divorce and Separation," pp. 451–57.

60. Judith S. Wallerstein and K. B. Kelly, *Surviving the Breakup: How Children and Parents Cope with Divorce* (New York: Basic Books, 1980); Wallerstein and Sandra Blakeslee, *Second Chances: Men, Women, and Children a Decade after Divorce* (New York: Ticknor and Fields, 1989).

61. U.S. Bureau of the Census, *Statistical Abstract: 1993*, Table 737.

62. Lenore J. Weitzman, *The Divorce Revolution* (New York: Free Press, 1985).

63. Jacobson, "Divorce and Separation."

64. Tamar Lewin, "Rise in Single Motherhood Is Reshaping U.S.," *The New York Times*, October 5, 1992, p. A1.

65. U.S. Bureau of the Census, *Statistical Abstract: 1993*, Tables 101, 98.

66. Lewin, "Rise in Single Motherhood," p. B6.

67. Kristin A. Moore and Martha R. Burt, *Private Crisis, Public Cost: Policy Perspectives on Teenage Childbearing* (Washington, DC: Urban Institute Press, 1982).

68. Esther Wald, "Family: Stepfamilies," in *Encyclopedia of Social Work*, Vol. 1, pp. 558–59.

60. A. Goetting, "The Six Stations of Remarriage: Developmental Tasks of Remarriage and Divorce," in L. Cargan (editor), *Marriage and Family: Coping with Change* (Belmont, CA: Wadsworth, 1985), pp. 323–33.

70. Patricia Papernow, "The Seven Stages of Step-Family Development," *Family Relations*, vol. 33 (July 1984), pp. 355–63.

71. Philip Blumstein and Pepper Schwartz, *American Couples: Money, Work, Sex* (New York: William Morrow, 1983), pp. 355–63.

72. Natalie J. Woodman, "Homosexuality: Lesbian Women," in *Encyclopedia of Social Work*, Vol. 1, pp. 808–09.

73. Blumstein and Schwartz, *American Couples*, pp. 318–19.

74. Hayden Curry and Denis Clifford, *A Legal Guide for Lesbian and Gay Couples* (Reading, MA: Addison-Wesley, 1980).

75. Ann Hartman, "The Family: A Central Concept for Practice," *Social Work*, vol. 26 (January 1981), pp. 7–13.

CHAPTER 11

The Family as a Social Organization
Analyzing Well-Being

MAJOR THEMES DISCUSSED IN THIS CHAPTER

1. **PERSPECTIVES ON FAMILY FUNCTIONING.** The five perspectives for assessing the differences in problems experienced by particular families discussed in this chapter are the ecological model, the psychodynamic model, the developmental model, role theory, and conflict theory.

2. **THE ECOLOGICAL PERSPECTIVE.** In the ecological model, family problems are located in the stresses caused by the interaction between the family and the groups, organizations, and institutions that make up its environment. The degree of economic difficulty experienced by different types of families is closely related to the other problems they face. The eco-map and the genogram are tools created by social service workers to study the dynamics of the social context of families.

3. **THE PSYCHODYNAMIC PERSPECTIVE.** In the psychodynamic model, the origins of family troubles are located in the members' unconscious or neurotic needs and desires. This model is based on Freudian concepts.

4. **THE DEVELOPMENTAL PERSPECTIVE.** In the developmental or family life-cycle approach, the causes of family problems are located in the expected and predictable tasks family members must deal with as they enter into, maintain, and end family relationships. The family is seen as a unique system with developmental processes that operate independently of the individual members' personalities. Diversity in the family life cycle is not adequately accounted for in this perspective.

5. **THE ROLE PERSPECTIVE.** In role theory, the focus is on the strain created when family members try to meet the expectations of themselves and others inside and outside of the family. The assumption is that individuals exist in the family only within the context of the roles and statuses they occupy, and their behavior cannot be understood outside of that context.

6. **THE CONFLICT PERSPECTIVE.** Conflict theory is concerned with how the tensions deriving from the contradictions and inequalities in contemporary Western societies are converted into conflict and coercion. Applied to the family, this perspective has followed Marxian conflict theory, which is based on the assumptions that capitalism has promoted self-interest among family members and conflict is the nature of the system. However, recently the family has been studied as an oasis in capitalism.

7. **IMPLICATIONS FOR PRACTICE.** These five perspectives, taken together, are applicable to social service practice in the assessment and intervention-planning phases.

IN EXAMINING WAYS TO UNDERSTAND THE differences in the strengths and problems faced by families, the question we consider is: Why is it that some families continue to show strength over time, while others become mired in troubles? An understanding of the psychosocial functioning of family life, involving its psychological and social aspects, requires knowledge of both the external social context in which the family is situated and the internal dynamics which operate inside it. Since all systems exist in a state of dynamic change, family processes of interaction and development also must be examined.

No one theory of family life is able to account completely for such differences in family well-being, but many theories offer insightful leads. In the following sections we will examine five perspectives which have been used in analyzing everyday family life. In the **ecological perspective**, family problems are located in the stresses created by the interactions between the family and the groups, organizations, and institutions that make up its environment, while in the **psychodynamic perspective**, the origins are located in the irrational, unconscious, and neurotic needs that govern intimate relationships (see Chapter 15). In the developmental or **family life-cycle perspective**, the causes of family problems can be found in the expected, predictable tasks family members must deal with as they enter into, maintain, and end family relationships. **Role theory** focuses on the strain created for family members when they try to meet the expectations of others as well as the self, and **conflict theory** emphasizes how self-interest motivates family members to put self ahead of others. Each of these perspectives can be incorporated into a systems approach to study of the family as an organization, and each contributes to our understanding of the family.

☞ THE ECOLOGICAL PERSPECTIVE

A major technique of family theorists in examining the relationships between the family and its social context is the ecological model, which attempts to locate families in terms of their interdependence with other social systems in their environment or social context: schools, workplaces, churches, community organizations, welfare agencies, and the other organizations and individuals with which they may interact daily and which exist as both sources of trouble and sources of strength. In one approach taking this perspective, the family's environment is viewed in terms of exosystems and macrosystems and in relation to the economic stresses experienced by some families. Others use tools which have been developed to study the social context of particular families, such as the eco-map and the genogram.

Macrosystems and Ecosystems

As we noted in Chapter 1, transactions between a society and the individuals in it are likely to involve the micro environment of individual beliefs, attitudes, and behaviors as well as the macro environment of social institutions and processes. In the ecological approach to study of the family, private troubles are seen in relation to public issues in the domain of macrosystems. James Garbarino has developed a way of describing the social context of families which orders environmental systems in terms of their size and social distance from the individual.[1]

Garbarino's focal system is the individual, but his ideas also can be applied to the family. The family thus is seen as a **microsystem** surrounded by a mesosystem, exosystem, and macrosystem. The **mesosystem** includes those individuals, groups, and organizations with which the family must deal directly: other families, friends, church, schools, workplaces, and so on. The **exosystem** includes organizations with which the family may never have to deal directly but which nevertheless can influence its well-being, such as local government and voluntary associations like the chamber of commerce. The **macrosystem** reflects the cultural context of family life: the values, traditions, and authority patterns inherent in the social institutions that surround it.

The problems of American social institutions that affect the everyday well-being of families exist primarily in the exosystem and the macrosystem. The effects on families come through the operation of various organizations and institutions and through institutionalized arrangements such as classism, racism, and sexism which are present in the society but are not necessarily identified with specific organizations. In contemporary American society, one of the major sources of stress for families in the macrosystems and exosystems surrounding them is the institution of the national economy.

The Family and Economic Stress

Adults usually marry (or cohabit) in the hope of building an intimate relationship supported by love and respect, but they also create a household which has to be sheltered, fed, clothed, educated, and entertained. Supporting the household is a primary task of families, and difficulties encountered in trying to accomplish it often have adverse effects on their well-being.

The capitalist or free-market economy of the United States has produced a high level of affluence for some families and kept others in poverty or struggling to remain self-sufficient. Problems of inequality in wealth or income, poverty, unemployment, economic cycles, and debt, all of which are related to the national economy, affect certain sectors of American society more than others, but they also affect the well-being of the society as a whole. The Index of Social Health compiled by the Fordham Institute for Innovation in Social Policy expresses statistics on 16 social problems such as child abuse, health care, homicide, and unemployment as a single yearly measure on a scale of 1–100. This index of social well-being stood at 75 in 1970, the first year it was measured; it reached a high of 79 in 1972 and then fell fairly steadily. In 1990 it went down to 42, a decrease of 44 percent over the 21 years. Marc Miringoff, director of the institute and author of the study issued in October 1992, noted that while the economic indicators generally had gone up after the 1982 recession, the social indicators measured by the index had remained at a low point.[2]

Inequality in Wealth or Income

Except for the very rich, the well-being of families ordinarily is to some degree at economic risk. Even in the best of times, when the economy is not in recession and inflation and unemployment are low, goods and resources are inequitably distributed. The ideals of capitalism champion economic opportunity in the form of free competition. In theory, those who have the motivation to "go for it" will achieve; those who are not able to compete or fail in the competition fall behind. Capitalism recognizes neither equality of effort (it's not how well you play the game but whether you win or lose) nor equality of result. Two men with the same education and the same occupational skills may get paid differently simply because one sector of the economy can command more resources than another. Similarly, a woman with less education and less skill and perhaps making less of a contribution to the general welfare than another woman can command greater income and wealth simply because of the operation of the free market.

Income has been defined as the "flow of purchasing power during a fixed time period."[3] As officially measured in government statistics, money income includes wages, pensions, dividends, interest, and rents but excludes such significant sources of income as capital gains and fringe benefits. In 1990, the median money income of families, the point in a distribution of incomes at which 50 percent of the families had higher incomes and 50 percent had lower incomes, was $35,353. Approximately 17 percent of American families had incomes of less than $15,000, and 31 percent earned $50,000 or more. The lowest fifth (20 percent) of families earned just 4.6 percent of all income earned, while the top fifth earned 44.3 percent[4] (see "Shares of Money Income of Families" in Chapter 9).

Inequality in income in the United States is not only great, it is growing. In response to the Great Depression in the 1930s, social welfare services, social security, and income tax policies were designed in part to reduce extremes in inequality. There was a small reduction between 1929 and 1947, but social and economic policies in subsequent years produced even greater inequalities in income distribution.[5] As Kevin Phillips observes, by the end of the 1980s, "if two to three million Americans were in clover—and another thirty to thirty-five million were justifiably pleased with their circumstances—a larger number were facing deteriorating personal or family incomes or a vague but troubling sense of hard times ahead."[6]

Poverty

There are various definitions of poverty. The federal government classifies families and individuals as having incomes above or below a designated poverty level, using the poverty index as revised by the Social Security Administration in 1980. The **poverty index** is based solely on money income and does not include the noncash benefits such as food stamps, Medicaid, and public housing received by many low-income families. The basis for the index is the Department of Agriculture's 1961 economy food plan, but the income thresholds are updated every year to reflect changes in the Consumer Price Index. The different consumption requirements of families, according to their size and composition, are taken into account.[7]

The poverty index is an example of an absolute definition of poverty, in which poverty is regarded as a lack of the necessities of life. By this definition, when all families attain incomes at or higher than the specified level at which family needs presumably can be satisfied, poverty will have been eliminated. A relative definition of poverty would always reflect the bottom of the distribution of wealth or income in the population (such as the bottom fifth), regardless of what the various median incomes are. Poverty is defined in a relative sense by comparing the average income in a society with the income of the poorest people in it. Thus there would always be a portion of the population living in poverty, and greater inequality means greater poverty.[8]

The persistence of poverty   In 1959, the **poverty rate** in the United States was 22.4; that is, 22.4 percent of the population was officially living below the poverty level. The persistence of poverty despite an otherwise affluent society in the United States was brought to public attention in the early 1960s by Michael Harrington in *The Other America*. He describes an "invisible land" in which "tens of millions of Americans are, at this very moment, maimed in body and spirit, existing at levels beneath those necessary for human decency." The main "subcultures of poverty" are identified as the aged, minorities, agricultural workers, and "industrial rejects." Children, families with a female head, and people with little education are also identified as being at a disadvantage.[9]

The governmental response to this problem was a series of social welfare programs and policies which became known as the War on Poverty. As a result, absolute poverty declined between 1965 and 1978. According to the relative measure, however, no decline in poverty was noted during the early part of this period, and there was an increase in the later part.[10] Between 1979 and 1985, according to Census Bureau figures, the percentage of the population living below the poverty level in the United States increased from 11.7 to 14.0. After the data-processing procedures used by the bureau were revised in 1987, the rate officially declined to 12.8 in 1989, but it was back up to 13.5 in 1990.[11] In 1992 the rate was 14.5, representing 36.9 million people living below the poverty level (an income of $14,335 for a family of four). This was the highest number since 1962, when 38.6 million Americans were considered to be living in poverty.

William O'Hare has identified a number of persistent myths about poverty which many people (including social service workers) continue to regard as facts. One myth is that people are poor because they refuse to work. He points out that in more than half of the 7.3 million families living in poverty in 1984, at least one family member was working, and in over one-fifth of them, two or more were working. Poor families headed by men are actually more common than poor families headed by women, since they include both married-couple and single-parent families. Similarly, there are more white families among the poor than black families, because whites are by far the majority in the population, and there are more rural and suburban poor families than poor inner-city families.[12]

The burden of poverty does fall disproportionately on racial and ethnic minorities and on women and children, however. When the poverty rate for all persons was 13.5 in 1990, it was 10.7 for whites, 31.9 for blacks, and 28.1 for Hispanics. The poverty rate in single-parent families with children under 18 and headed by the mother was 54.6. Among all persons 65 years old and over, 12.2 had incomes below the poverty line, but the rate was 10.1 for whites, 33.8 for blacks, and 22.5 for Hispanics. For persons over 65 living in families the rate was just 5.8; for unrelated individuals, it was 24.7.[13]

Unemployment and Underemployment

Official rates of joblessness are derived from monthly household surveys conducted by the U.S. Department of Labor. To be considered unemployed, a person must be 16 years or older, presently out of work, available for work, and have been looking for work during the preceding four weeks. Using this definition, 8.4 million people were unemployed in 1991, up from 6.8 million in 1990. The **unemployment rate** in 1991, or the percentage of the civilian labor force not employed, was 6.7; it was 7.0 for males and 6.3 for females. The rate for whites was 6.0; for blacks, 12.4; and for Hispanics, 9.9. By age, the rate was highest for both males and females 16–19 years old, and the highest rate of all was 36.3 for blacks in this age category. The lowest rate, 3.3, was for persons 65 years and older, most of whom were not considered unemployed because they were not looking for work.[14]

Official rates generally are considered to underestimate the actual extent of unemployment. Among other shortcomings, they do not include **discouraged workers**, those who have been out of work a long time and may have given up looking for employment. In 1991, 31 percent of unemployed males and 23 percent of unemployed females were designated as long-term jobless, having been out of work 15 weeks or more.[15] They also do not include **underemployment**, "a condition in which workers' jobs are incommensurate with their skills, training, expectations, and earning capacity, given the type or amount of work they are equipped to perform."[16] No data are available to measure underemployment adequately. Included are those who work part-time involuntarily, because no full-time work is available, and those who work full time in jobs that do not provide adequate income. In the 1990s large corporations and small businesses alike are increasingly relying on part-time or temporary workers to keep their permanent, full-time labor forces small and avoid the cost of benefits such as health insurance for such workers.

Effects of a Capitalist Economy on Families

A capitalist, free-market economy is subject to cyclical periods of recession and prosperity or inflation. In a recession or depression, jobs and incomes are lost, and families must tighten their belts. In a period of inflation, the price of basic necessities rises faster than incomes. Both make it difficult for families to meet their needs.

The consumer society   The capitalist economy in contemporary American society also places great emphasis on the consumptive function of the family. Until the early twentieth century, the economy was concerned with producing and supplying the basic needs of families for food, shelter, and clothing. Today, technological advances have created an economy capable of producing about as much as it wants to. Consuming everything it produces is another matter.

Lee Rainwater has documented the importance of the function of consumption for the perceived well-being of Americans. He notes that, in general, people assess their well-being not on the basis of how their own lives have improved but on the relative improvement in their lives compared to how much they perceive others' lives have improved. In the early 1970s, national surveys indicated that to "get along," families thought they needed about 106 percent of their take-home pay.[17] When the income earned does not seem to be enough to meet a family's perceived needs, the response in the consumer society is to go into debt.

People learn to desire more and more in the consumer society. The traditional values of thrift and delayed gratification are abandoned and replaced with consumption and immediate gratification. The advertising industry plays a crucial role in this regard, using numerous tactics and enormous advertising budgets to encourage consumption.[18] Advertising aims to make people believe that their happiness, indeed their self-esteem, is dependent on buying the "right" clothes, cars, sunglasses, computers, and so on. A perceived need to consume led to deficit spending in American families as much as in the national economy in the 1980s. Philip Slater calls the emphasis on consumption "wealth addiction"; he compares the need to consume and to accumulate things to a powerful drug which gives a temporary high but eventually weakens and destroys.[19]

Consumer confidence is a necessary condition in the consumer society. The University of Michigan's monthly polls have produced an index of consumer confidence or expectations dating back to 1951. In the nation's oldest measure of public opinion, 500 representative Americans are asked each month whether they believe their own finances, and the national economy, will be better, worse, or the same over the next one to five years. Survey results are calculated for percentages above or below the baseline of 100, the average for all months in 1966. The reading of 76.4 for April 1993, for example, was 23.6 percent below the 1966 average.

In the 1950s and 1960s, the average of the monthly consumer confidence indexes was 94.3 and 95.9, respectively. Louis Ushitelle, writing in *The New York Times* in May 1993, calls this the period of "soaring optimism" in which Americans believed their lives were destined to become ever more prosperous. But the average index dropped to 71.3 in the 1970s and rose only to 78.6 in the 1980s. The early part of the 1980s was a transition period characterized by "fist-banging and frustration as living standards stopped rising for most Americans." In the 1990s, Ushitelle says, the struggle to regain the old prosperity has "dissolved into resignation," and for most Americans optimism about the economy and their own prospects has gradually deteriorated.[20]

Economic conditions and family stress   The economic conditions generated by a consumer-oriented, high-technology, boom-or-bust capitalist economy have produced a great deal of stress for families. Job security has virtually disappeared as corporations have merged or been bought out and have downsized both their white-collar and blue-collar labor forces. A college education no longer guarantees a good job. While the tensions caused by the "need" to consume affect affluent families as well as those of the working and middle classes, economic stress has the greatest impact on lower-income families because survival needs are much more pressing than needs for self-gratification. Industrial and construction workers accustomed to good wages are particularly hard hit if they lose their jobs. As avid consumers, they have little savings; when they can no longer participate in the consumer society, they suffer a loss of social class as well as income.[21] The desire for things creates pressures in even poverty-level families. The social and economic problems confronted by poor and working-class families are very real determinants of their state of well-being.

Lillian Rubin sensitively describes the development of the working-class family of the 1970s, from the time, as newlyweds, their dreams of marital bliss were invaded by the need for economic survival. In the typical working-class family of 20 years ago, the husband ideally was the sole income provider, and the economic hardships worsened with the birth of the first child. Instead of added happiness, quarrels began; the wife felt unappreciated, and the husband felt nagged at. They began to realize that much of their parents' unhappiness was due to economic difficulties like the ones they were facing. The romance of marriage faded by the middle years. Even though the husband might be a steady worker with a rising income, financial security could not be taken for granted; unemployment was a constant threat. The definition of a good husband was, "He's a good worker, he doesn't drink, he doesn't hit me."[22]

Barbara Hochschild describes a different type of family in the 1990s, one in which both partners work.[23] Both the earlier entrance of men into the industrial economy, which gave them the status of breadwinner and ultimate consumer, and the later entrance of women have influenced the relations between men and women within marriage. Most women now work outside the home, and their wages are considered necessary to maintenance of the family. The movement of women into the labor force, however, has not been accompanied by a cultural understanding of marriage and work that would make such arrangements workable. Women still carry the responsibility for care of the children and the home, a "second shift" in addition to their jobs, and men who fully share the second shift are rare. Tensions arise in the two-job couple around who does what at home and what needs to be done; the struggle is to reconcile the demands of two jobs with a happy family life and a good marriage. One reason women feel constrained to do most of the work of the second shift themselves is that men can opt out of the marriage with divorce at little personal cost.

In working-class families, particularly, Hochschild says, the tension may be due to "a clash between a traditional ideal and a thin pocketbook." Some working-class men do their share at home, but they don't feel good about it and count it as a favor. They hate the fact that their wives *have* to work. Some working-class women feel pushed into work and cling to their "right" to stay home. If they have to work, they must manage the conflict between their ideals of male dominance in the family and the reality of their lives as working women.

Social service workers often ignore the economic issues surrounding family life. In a good deal of the literature on family functioning, the implicit assumption is that economic considerations are irrelevant, and only personal and interpersonal dynamics need to be taken into consideration. Thomas Keefe argues eloquently that empathy, a primary relational skill in social work practice, must be based on a sound understanding of economic structures and processes.[24] In order to truly comprehend the frustrations and anger experienced by many clients, the economic realities they confront must be appreciated and shared on an emotional level.

The Eco-Map: Studying the Social Context of the Family

The **eco-map**, developed by Ann Hartman, is a major tool for studying the social context of families. It is primarily offered as a way for practitioners to assess and plan interventions for specific troubles clients bring when they seek service. The eco-map is a paper-and-pencil simulation; the worker and the clients actually draw a map which shows the "major systems that are a part of the family's life and the nature of the family's relationship with the various systems."[25] In the ecological perspective, the term *systems* refers to the particular groups and associations, formal organizations, families, and individuals with which a particular family interacts.

To draw an eco-map, the practitioner first places a circle on a large sheet of paper to represent the family or family system under consideration (see "Eco-Map of the Garcias"). Inside the circle the composition of the family is indicated with small squares to represent males and small circles to represent females, with the symbols for the parents placed above those for the children. A number of other circles are then drawn around the family circle to represent the other systems—the individuals, families, groups, associations, and organizations—with which the family ordinarily interacts. After the nature of the relationships between family and environment is determined by discussion with the client, the practitioner indicates them by different kinds of lines connecting the family circle to each of the other circles representing systems.

A supportive relationship is indicated on the eco-map by a solid, thin line if the system is an ordinary resource for the client or a solid, thick line (or, as in the figure, a dash/dot line) if the relationship is very strong or positive. A broken line (in the figure, a dotted line) indicates a tenuous or uncertain relationship between a system and the family, which may be interpreted as having little or a lot to do with the troubles presented by clients or the solutions to them. Conflicts or stressful relationships related to clients' troubles are indicated by slashed lines (in the figure, broken lines). In a child-abuse case,

Eco-Map of the Garcias

This eco-map indicates the relationships between a hypothetical family, the Garcias, and its environment. The school social worker and the mother of the family work together to develop the eco-map to determine what resources can be used in dealing with the troubles the oldest son is having at school.

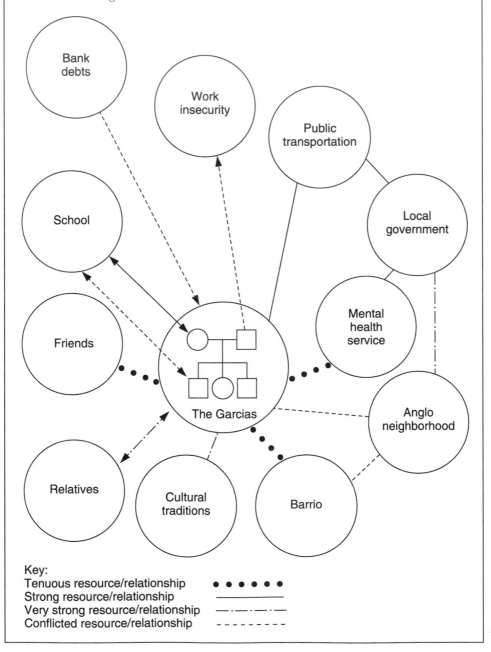

Key:
Tenuous resource/relationship   ● ● ● ● ● ●
Strong resource/relationship   ───────
Very strong resource/relationship   ─ · ─ · ─ · ─
Conflicted resource/relationship   ─ ─ ─ ─ ─ ─

for instance, the parents' unemployment, money problems, fights with relatives, or inability to locate child-care services could be associated with the abuse.

The analysis of family strengths and stresses can be furthered by the use of arrows on the eco-map to identify the direction of the flow of energy. An arrow pointing in the direction of another system means that family energy, in the form of resources, communication, or adaptation, is being directed toward that system. An arrow pointing to the family means that resources and energy are flowing from the other system to the family.

Use of the Eco-Map with a Hypothetical Family

To illustrate how the eco-map of the Garcias might be used to study their social environment, some knowledge of the hypothetical family is necessary. Ricky Garcia, the oldest son, has been truant and is not doing well in his studies, as indicated by the arrows between the symbols for the Garcias and the school. His mother and the school social worker have a positive relationship, and Mrs. Garcia comes in to discuss the problems Ricky is having. She and the social worker consider the various resources available to improve his progress in school. In developing the eco-map the social worker, with Mrs. Garcia's help, is able to identify some of the strengths and weaknesses within the family's social context:

> The Garcias are a fairly traditional family made up of husband and wife and three children. Their social context includes a number of organizations, such as the world of work (Mr. Garcia is employed and Mrs. Garcia, who is disabled, is at home); local government, especially mass transit and mental health services; and the school (the three children are all enrolled in the local elementary school).
>
> The family lives in a *barrio*, or Mexican-American neighborhood, which is adjacent to an Anglo neighborhood, and many of the residents in both areas have strong negative attitudes about the other ethnic group. The Garcias have few close friends, but they depend a great deal on relatives who live close by. Mr. Garcia's job is threatened and he has been forced to take a cut in pay. The family has many debts, so paying for a private tutor is out of the question.
>
> The use of mental health services is a possibility because there is good public transportation, but Mrs. Garcia does not want to use them; she doesn't want her child to be thought of as having mental problems. Besides, because of local politics, the mental health service is located in the Anglo neighborhood, and Mrs. Garcia believes that the service available there will not be suitable for Ricky.
>
> The Garcias are strongly tied to their extended-kin family, however. She has a niece and a nephew who are a few years older than Ricky and who have been excellent students. Mrs. Garcia decides to seek their help, and a plan is set up to ask them to tutor Ricky on a regular basis.

The technique of the eco-map is useful as a means for social service workers to identify the relationships among particular individuals and families and the individuals, groups, and organizations making up their environment. However, its usefulness in developing a more general understanding of how societal and cultural factors impinge on family organization and functioning is limited.

The Genogram: Studying the Individual in the Family System

A technique which can serve as an extension of the eco-map is the **genogram**, developed by a psychiatrist, Murray Bowen. The genogram provides a closer look at the relationships that exist within a family network by displaying family patterns across time and space, which makes it possible to examine how these patterns affect members of the family. This technique is predicated on the assumption that "the family is the primary and, except in rare instances, the most powerful system to which a person ever belongs."[26] Maggie Scarf, who gives an engrossing example of the use of a genogram, says, "A genogram is a road map laying out the important emotional attachments of each of the partners—attachments that lead backward in time, to the parents' and grandparents' generations, and forward to the new one, the children (if any) of the present union."[27]

While the genogram is promoted as a family therapy technique, it does not use the family as the focal system. Instead it identifies an index person, the person with the problem or symptom, and uses the family as part of that person's present and past social context. Thus genograms promote understanding not so much of family problems as of individual problems.

There is no one way to draw a genogram; the method described here was developed by Monica McGoldrick and Randy Gerson[28] (see "Genogram of a Family Member"). As in the eco-map, males are depicted by squares and females by circles. The oldest generation is depicted along the top of the chart, with later generations below. Solid lines connect blood- and marriage-related generations (grandparents, parents, children, aunts, uncles, cousins), and dotted lines (in the figure, dashed lines) indicate a distant relationship.

To determine the relationships between members of the family network, the practitioner records three types of information about them: demographic, functioning, and critical family events. Demographic information includes ages, birth and death dates, locations, occupations, and educational levels, while functioning information includes more-or-less objective descriptions of the physical, emotional, and behavioral functioning of different family members. Family events involve important life changes such as shifts in relationships, losses, failures, gains, and successes. On the basis of this information the practitioner indicates interpersonal relations on the genogram with various kinds of symbols or lines connecting the circles and squares. This involves a good deal of inference, as data are acquired from various family members and from direct observation. Six kinds of relationships can be identified: close, poor or conflictive, very close or fused, fused and conflictive, estranged or cut off, and distant relationships.

Interpreting the Genogram

The genogram offers a number of lines of interpretation to assist in understanding the troubles presented by an individual family member. One area for exploration is the basic family structure. This concerns the composition of the household: single-parent, nuclear, extended-kin, or other family forms. The sibling constellation and birth order might also be considered. From these interpretations hypotheses can be stated about the working agreements or norms that govern family functioning. Through testing these hypotheses, the relationship between family norms and the family's problems may be uncovered.

Other areas for interpretation involve determining the family life cycle (to be discussed later in this chapter) and tracing family history and the repetition of patterns across generations. This makes it possible to determine if a particular problem is recurring and preventive intervention might help the family avoid future repetitions. Interpersonal relationships between and among family members may be examined to determine to what extent they are fused, conflicted, cut off, or distant. Dyadic (two-person) functioning is common, but the genogram also can be used to examine triangles (three-person functioning). This may uncover coalitions of two against one or the connection between one set of antagonisms and another set of loyalties. The functional whole of a family is

Genogram of a Family Member

This genogram of a hypothetical family is drawn from the husband's viewpoint. It portrays his relations with his wife, their three daughters, and the family network of parents and grandparents.

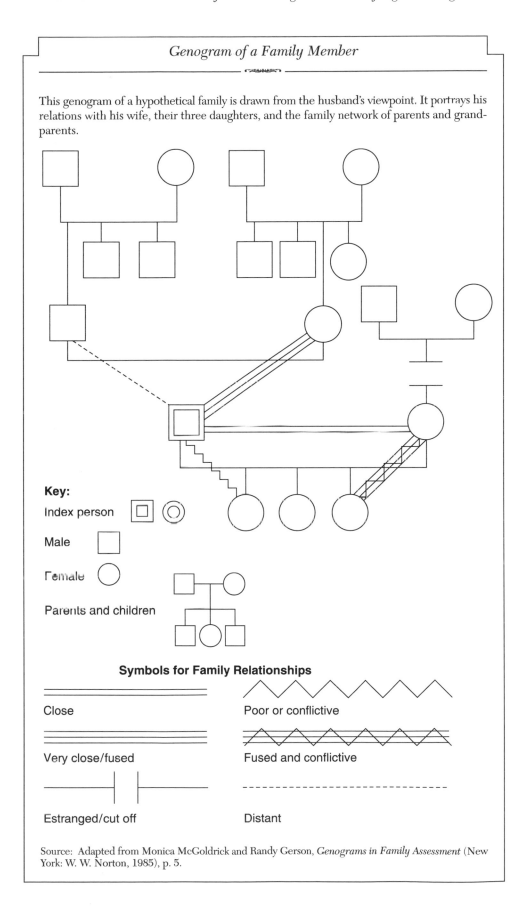

Source: Adapted from Monica McGoldrick and Randy Gerson, *Genograms in Family Assessment* (New York: W. W. Norton, 1985), p. 5.

considered in interpretations of family balance and imbalance. In well-functioning families, there is believed to be a pull toward equilibrium in which family characteristics balance one another. Examining how the whole system functions may identify imbalances and show how they might be corrected.

Taken together, these various lines of interpretation make the genogram an extremely useful tool in examining the social context of the family and the individuals in it. As Scarf says, "Genograms provide a systematic way of looking at each partner's own natural context—the family subculture in which he or she was reared—and discerning those repetitive themes, issues, myths, patterns of behavior, etc., which have been brought forward from the past and resurrected in the marriage of the present."[29]

∞ THE PSYCHODYNAMIC PERSPECTIVE

Psychodynamic perspectives on the family rely heavily on the thinking of Sigmund Freud, which will be discussed further in Chapter 15. Freud advanced the theory that unconscious drives and needs, often connected with the gratification of sensual pleasure, guide human behavior. When parent-child relations go awry, the needs and drives may be converted into neuroses which interfere with interpersonal relations in later life.

The psychodynamic perspective on the family has been examined by Herbert Strean.[30] He maintains that individuals enter marriage with inner scripts, that is, a set of internalized needs. If their psychosexual developmental experiences in early life were gratifying, the chances are high that the marriage will prove successful, because the inner scripts are healthy. If these experiences were frustrating or were dealt with ambivalently or inconsistently, the marriage will be difficult, because the inner scripts are neurotic.

In psychodynamic thinking, falling in love is an irrational process in the sense that unconscious needs and drives dominate conscious attitudes and beliefs. We may think we are getting married because we love someone, or find him or her attractive, warm, and sincere, but the reality is often quite different. We fall in love in an attempt to fulfill deeper inner needs.

Immature love, which is driven by unresolved, frustrating early-life experiences, takes many forms. Strean describes ten of these: clinging love, sadistic love, rescuing love, compulsive love, unrequited love, celibate love, critical love, revengeful love, love of the partner's parents, and homosexual love.[31] These forms of love often underlie marital conflicts and represent the real source of many marital problems.

Clinging love lacks self-confidence. People who love by clinging never feel quite worthy of their partners and are always submissive to them, saying, in effect, "I will do anything for you; just love me in return." In *sadistic love*, a partner is chosen who can be derogated and demeaned as a way of compensating for and defending against one's own sense of weakness. *Rescuing love* is an attraction based on the need to be a savior for unhappy people. This is found more often among men who believe their love will change the lot of their partners and bring them happiness. *Compulsive love* is based on self-doubt. Initially, compulsive lovers must constantly prove themselves, incessantly declaring their love and involving themselves with others who will give them complete attention. As the relationship progresses, however, their real needs are not met, and they begin to resent their partners. Often they drive their partners off with displays of anger.

Unrequited love is the search for the perfect partner. The more unavailable and unattainable the partner appears, the more in love the other person feels. This kind of love is usually based on feelings of guilt; an unattainable partner is chosen as a way of assuring that it will never really be necessary to prove oneself as a lover. *Celibate love* is another attempt to find the perfect partner, so perfect, indeed, that the partner is treated like a parent. Then an incest taboo is applied to the relationship; there can be only tender affection for the partner-parent, and no erotic feelings. Sometimes, indeed, it is not the search for a perfect partner that motivates love but the search for a perfect parent. Individuals who were deprived of loving parents in their childhood may unconsciously long for the love of their partners' parents, in the hope that they will come to be prized as sons or daughters. In *critical love*, externally one partner always seems to be annoyed with the other, while internally there is secret admiration. People who love critically search for partners who enjoy being punished for real or imagined transgressions. Critical lovers complain about all the things that are wrong with the partner as a way of warding off their own childish needs and impulses. *Revengeful love* is based on attempts to overcome feelings of having been scapegoated as a child. People who love in a revengeful way try to get even with their parents through their love relationships.

Strean considers *homosexual love* to be a form of immature love: "Having experienced poor role models who failed to demonstrate that love between members of the opposite sex can be enjoyable and enriching, homosexual men and women are in an acute rage most of the time—even though much of their rage is unconscious."[32] In making this assertion, Strean goes against the view of homosexuals as a discriminated-against minority as well as the position of the American Psychiatric Association, which no longer lists homosexual behavior as a mental disorder.[33]

A common experience in marriage is neurotic complementarity, whereby spouses having difficulties believe they are being victimized by their partners, and if they had another partner all would be well. They fail to realize that their own unconscious needs are at the base of the troubles they are experiencing and that the conflict itself gratifies and protects them; they wouldn't want it any other way. The partners have unconsciously colluded, that is, entered into an agreement which requires them to complement each other's neurosis and thereby maintain a balance in the relationship. According to Strean:

> Married men and women who habitually complain about their spouses' sexual unresponsiveness are those who constantly disparage their spouses' attempts to respond sexually. Those husbands and wives who deride their spouses for their lack of cooperation are also those who frequently frustrate their partners' attempts to cooperate. And those marriage partners who chronically complain that their spouses are poor parents for their children are frequently sabotaging their spouses' efforts to relate to their children.[34]

THE DEVELOPMENTAL OR LIFE-CYCLE PERSPECTIVE

Some researchers have taken a developmental approach in their attempts to understand the processes of family formation, maintenance, and dissolution. In their view, there is a **family life cycle** composed of a natural sequence of stages or periods, and many of the troubles families confront have to do with how transitions are made from one period to the next. The family is seen as "a basic unit of emotional development," and the focus is on psychological well-being as people proceed through the phases of family life.

The idea that the family should be understood as a unique system with its own developmental processes, separate from the personalities of its members, has been around for a number of years.[35] Many theories of family development have been proposed, but no agreement exists on such basic issues as the number of developmental periods or the tasks associated with each of them. In this section, the ideas of Elizabeth Carter and

Monica McGoldrick, which represent a synthesis of much of the literature, are highlighted.[36]

The Normal Troubles of Family Life

The life-cycle approach makes an important contribution to the understanding of why families ordinarily have troubles. Family developmental theorists relate family troubles to normative stress, the normal and expected difficulties of living up to society's expectations. Carter and McGoldrick use the term *horizontal or normative stressors* to explain "the anxiety produced by the stresses of the family as it moves forward through time, coping with the changes and transitions of the family life cycle."[37]

Normative stress, however, is not the only recognized source of difficulties in family life in this approach. **Transgenerational stress** derives from the fact that the family is a three-generational unit which includes the entire kin network of a family. Since individuals are reared in their family of origin and, as they mature, form their own family of procreation, their experiences in the first carry over to the second. According to Carter and McGoldrick, there is a "flow of anxiety" in family life which operates by passing on "family attitudes, taboos, expectations, labels and loaded issues" across generations. As children grow they are socialized into the culture and history of their family and thereby internalize them. When they marry, they bring this history with them into their relationships with their spouses and their children. Carter and McGoldrick also propose the concept of the stress of *living in this place at this time*, which is not very well developed. As examples they cite the public issues of stress created by the women's movement, the sexual revolution, and ecological pollution. The everyday stresses generated by changing social institutions and problems also create troubles for families.

The primary contribution of the life-cycle model, however, is to call attention to normative sources of stress. In this concept, Carter and McGoldrick emphasize that family troubles (perceived stress and anxiety) are normal and to be expected. There is no such thing as a family without troubles, and just because a family has troubles it should not be assumed that it is somehow abnormal. The troubles families confront are predictable because they derive from specific developmental processes through which all family members pass. These processes are related to family life events, such as getting married or having a baby, but also the developmental stage the family member is in, such as young, middle, or later adulthood.

Six Stages of the Family Life Cycle

The six life-cycle developmental stages identified by Carter and McGoldrick are:

1. The unattached young adult.
2. The joining of families through marriage.
3. The family with young children.
4. The family with adolescents.
5. The separation of children from the family and moving on as a couple.
6. The family in later life.

These phases describe the family as a series of membership changes, changes in social roles and statuses, and changes in boundaries, as new members continually enter and old members continually leave.

As this portrait of three generations of women shows, families are multigenerational systems in which children enter and older members leave. Each person moves through the family life cycle attending to different developmental tasks.

Unattached young adults must deal with separating from the family of origin and achieving independence. In this process they must differentiate their own identity, learn how to form intimate adult relationships, and establish an occupational or work identity. When young adults marry, a new emotional process takes place in which the couple learns to commit themselves to a new family, their own family of procreation. Troubles may arise in the tasks of forming a healthy marital relationship, becoming committed to a spouse, and realigning relationships with extended families and friends to include the spouse.

When a child is born to the couple, the task is to incorporate a new member in the family. The marital relationship has to be joined with a parental relationship. Husbands and wives become fathers and mothers; in-laws become aunts and uncles; parents become grandparents. There are normal difficulties in assuming the new set of roles, all of which require personal and interpersonal adjustments. Adolescence brings new kinds of stress to the family. Whereas family boundaries tend to close in as a way of assuring protection with young children, with adolescents the family boundary must open up to allow their search for independence. The couple has to start thinking of themselves less as mother and father and more as husband and wife; they must begin to rediscover themselves in their midlife crisis.

When adolescents become young adults and leave home, new troubles surface. The couple must confront each other and renegotiate their dyadic relation in an "empty nest." They must prepare to take on the role of grandparent, accept their own aging, and deal with the disability and death of their own parents. Major shifts in status take place as the family loses members and takes on new ones.

In later life, the couple must accept their age-related roles. Their physical decline is evident, the death of a partner is inevitable, and their adult children, likely with adolescents at home, assume some responsibility for their care, even as they begin to face their own mortality.

Derailed Families

Many families take the normal troubles of family life in stride. As families confront the tasks presented by the various life phases, however, these troubles may become serious. When a family cannot successfully meet the difficulties presented by a singular developmental phase, Carter and McGoldrick consider them derailed and in need of being placed back on track:

> Family life cycle passages are concerned with shifting membership over time, and the changing family status of family members in relation to each other. Dysfunctional families characteristically confuse shifts in status, exits, and functions.... Parents may pretend that their children are not growing up and leaving, or that their own parents are not dying when they are.... This occurs when the family pretends to have more power over the membership or status of family members than it actually has.[38]

Derailments lead to conflict and occasionally to domestic violence.

Diversity in the Family Life Cycle

While the family life-cycle perspective has made significant contributions to knowledge of family well-being, it is not without its limitations. There is a clear and often acknowledged emphasis on the traditional two-parent, white, middle-class family with a small number of children who are born within a few years of one another and progress through the life stages more or less at the same time. Other forms of family life are not adequately handled, though the principles are applicable to some extent.

There have been efforts, however, to apply the developmental model to nontraditional and alternative family forms, such as divorced couples, single parents, remarriages, and poor and minority families. David McWhirter and Andrew Mattison identify seven developmental stages in the family lifestyles of homosexual male couples which can overlap, go forward or backward, and even go in circles: blending, the first year; nesting, the second and third years; maintaining, the fourth and fifth years; building, the sixth through tenth years; releasing, the 11th through 20th years; and renewing, beyond 20 years.[39]

Divorce, Single Parenthood, and Remarriage

Divorces are sometimes referred to as dislocations in the family life-cycle perspective. Divorcing families often go through additional developmental phases with distinctive sources of stress before the separated partners and the children can get back on the normal developmental track. First, divorcing couples face the task of deciding to divorce. That is, they need to accept that they are unable to resolve the troubles they have confronted as a couple. Second, after the decision is made, they must take on the task of breaking up the family system. Divorce requires cooperation in decisions on custody, visitation, and financial settlements. Extended-family members must be faced and brought into the process. Ties to in-laws must be redefined. Third, the actual divorce brings a number of difficult tasks to be completed. The attachments to the former spouse do not automatically disappear, and mourning for the lost relationship and family is normal. New relationships between the divorced husband and wife must be worked out.

Other stressful family patterns described in Chapter 10 also are related to divorce. For both the custodial and noncustodial parents, there is the emotional task of maintaining personal contact and supporting healthy relationships with the children. There is also a need to rebuild the social network of the new single-parent family. When divorced parents remarry and form stepfamilies, the emotional tasks involve entering a new relationship, joining together in a new marriage, and reconstituting or blending two families. The partner or partners who have been divorced must recover from the loss of the first partner, master fears about entering a new relationship, and be patient as new roles, boundaries, and feelings are confronted. The new family must accept itself as a different, nontraditional family with boundaries that are much more permeable.

Poor and Racial- and Ethnic-Minority Families

Poor and minority families must adapt to the considerable stress that comes from "living in this place at this time." Both the time and the place typically are harsh, with substandard housing, poor-quality food and clothing, and deteriorating neighborhoods. They are likely to be underemployed if not unemployed, and often they are isolated and alienated from other types of individuals and families. As a result, their family life cycles often lack certain elements which usually are present. According to Fernando Colon, the multiproblem poor family has only three developmental phases: unattached young adults, family with children, and family in later life. Colon also says that the effects of a hostile social, economic, and physical context make for considerable underorganization in family life.[40]

Ethnic family life cycles differ, and study of the life cycles of the various ethnic groups making up American society has only begun. C. J. Falicov and B. M. Karrer did clinical practice with Mexican-American families in a large Midwestern city. They note that there is the same number of life-cycle phases as in Anglo families, but the speed with which they are negotiated differs. In the Mexican-American family, marriage is often at an earlier age; children become a part of the family earlier, go to school later, and complete or drop out of school earlier; and later-life family relations may be cut off earlier by death.[41]

Usefulness of the Family Life-Cycle Model

The life-cycle model directs attention to the normal and predictable troubles which both traditional and nontraditional families are likely to experience as they traverse their life course. By normalizing troubles, it helps to reduce victim blaming. When things go wrong in families, it is not necessarily the fault of family members.

Social service workers can apply this model to help derailed or dislocated families get back on track. Through family therapy techniques, they can help enable family members to fulfill the tasks associated with the family life-cycle phase they are in and to anticipate changes and make the transitions from one period to the next.

The family life-cycle model is more descriptive than explanatory, however. It teaches what kinds of troubles to expect, but it does not adequately explain why some families handle troubles effectively and others do not. Some reasons are hinted at: external here-and-now stresses, deficiencies in individual competence, neuroses derived from experiences in the family of origin. But the perspective does little to increase understanding of why such troubles as domestic violence or divorce occur.

∞ ROLE THEORY AND THE FAMILY

Role theory in contemporary sociology and psychology has emerged from diverse sources; as used most frequently, it is heavily influenced by functional theory. With regard to family life, in the role perspective the basic units that make up the family as a system are considered to be social positions which are referred to as roles and statuses (see Chapter 3). Status refers to the position or "office" itself, but often it also implies some rank in a social hierarchy. Role refers to the more dynamic aspects of the position; it has more to do with what the people in various positions do or are expected to do. In family life, roles and statuses include husband, wife, lover, companion, mother, father, son, daughter, sister, brother, grandmother, grandfather, aunt, uncle, and the like. In the family, individuals exist only within the context of the roles and statuses they occupy; for instance, Mary as wife and stepmother, John as husband and father. Role theory maintains that the behaviors of family members cannot be understood outside the context of the roles they occupy.[42]

Dynamics of Role Relationships

Roles can be defined in three ways: the prescribed role, from the point of view of others; the perceived role, from the point of view of the person in the role; and the enacted role, from the point of view of the actual behaviors performed by the person in the role[43] (see "Definitions of Role" in Chapter 3). To understand the roles of members of a particular family, all three definitions have to be taken into account. Family therapists, for instance, have to inquire of all family members what they expect of others and of themselves and then observe what they actually do in their roles.

To illustrate the dynamics of role relationships, we will focus on the role of Martha, the mother in the hypothetical Jones family. This is a reconstituted or stepfamily of three African Americans: Martha; her husband, John; and his son Tom by a previous marriage. The role of mother is defined in terms of the expectations of others, Martha's own expectations, and her actual behaviors.

Expectations of Others and Expectations of Self

Martha receives expectations from her husband and her stepson as to how her role as stepmother is to be enacted. In the form of verbal and nonverbal messages, they instruct her as to how they expect her to function in the mother role. John tells her he would like her to play the role in the same way his mother did, and Tom wants her to play it just like his best friend's mother does. Members of the immediate family are not the only ones who communicate their expectations about how Martha is to perform the role of mother. Jerome, her widowed father; Susan, her sister; and Margaret, her mother-in-law, also have expectations, as do some of the groups and organizations with which she interacts. The school tells her what a mother who is supportive of a sound education should be like. The church she belongs to tells her what a religious mother should be like. The community of which she is a part also has expectations. Because she is a black woman, she receives expectations from the African-American community about how a good mother should act. Because she is an American black woman living today, she receives expectations from the larger society about how she should be an American mother in the latter part of the twentieth century.

When the role of mother is defined in terms of expectations of the person occupying the role, the emphasis is on how Martha—with her own socialization history, her own personality, her own developmental stage, and her own perceptions and values—makes up her mind about what she should be like in the role of mother. It involves sorting through many of the expectations she has been receiving from others, as well as being aware of her own needs and interests.

Family Roles as Actual Behaviors

The mother role may also be seen in terms of Martha's actual feelings, thoughts, and actions as a stepmother. Expectations emanating from self and others are just that: things that are expected. Sometimes we conform to the expectations of others, but we do not always do what others expect of us. Sometimes we do what we ourselves want, but just as often we put aside our own needs and interests. Sometimes the things we do are influenced by a complex decision-making process, sorting through the things others expect of us and the things we expect of ourselves and coming to a conclusion about what we are to do. Sometimes the things we do just seem to happen, a mystery to ourselves and others.

Role Conflict or Strain

The special contribution of role theory to the study of family problems lies in the concept of **role conflict**, or strain. Role theorists point out that many of the troubles individuals experience derive directly from problems which are inherent in social roles. They argue that understanding troubled families in terms of role conflict is more accurate than assuming that personal deficiencies or abnormalities are at the root of family troubles. The concept of role conflict, like the concept of normative stress, emphasizes the normality of conflict and change; conflict is expected to occur because it is inherent in the nature of family roles. In functionalist terms, role conflict and change contribute to the ultimate survival of the system.

Each member of a family takes on not just one role but multiple roles. Some of these roles are defined exclusively as lying within the family system. Martha, in addition to being a stepmother, is also a wife and a lover in this example of a nuclear family. Other roles are related to the groups to which people belong. Martha belongs to the extended family and so is also a daughter-in-law, a daughter, and a sister. She may take on the role of friend to a neighbor. Since Martha is employed she is also in the role of worker (a working stepmother), and since she is actively involved in her stepson's education, she has the role of PTA member. Martha may be functioning in a number of other roles which are not directly connected to but nevertheless influence her role as mother in the Jones family. She may be a member of a religious group, a political party, and a neighborhood association, for example.

Types of Family Role Conflict

In taking all these roles, Martha may be caught up in various kinds of family role conflict. There may be conflicts in other family members' perception of her roles in the family, conflict among her various roles inside and outside the family or in several family systems, conflict that comes from receiving mixed messages from her environment, or conflict between her personality and her role (see "Types of Family Role Conflict").

Types of Family Role Conflict

Intrarole Conflict

Mary, I don't think we should let Marsha go out alone with Tom. She's only 15.

What am I to do?

Mom, All my friends date. Why can't I?

Father

Mother

Daughter

Intrarole conflict   The possibility of **intrarole conflict** arises from the fact that people have different ideas on how any family role should be enacted. If Martha's stepson, husband, father, sister, and mother-in-law, as well as first-grader Tom's teacher, all see eye to eye on how Martha is to be a mother, she is likely to avoid trouble in filling her role. When each of these individuals has different expectations of Martha in the role of mother, the disparity is likely to involve her in intrarole conflict. If the teacher wants her to

Types of Family Role Conflict

Interrole Conflict

insist that her stepson keeps up with the class; if her father reminds her that she is not the boy's natural mother and should not assume the responsibility of making him learn; if her husband wants her to lay off because Tom is "only a kid"; if her mother-in-law tells her she should be strict with the boy, the same way she was strict with her sons—if all these people have different expectations for how Martha should be a stepmother, she will have

Types of Family Role Conflict

Mixed Messages

A woman should marry and have children.

Be anything you want to be.

I get the feeling she really doesn't want me to be what I want.

Mother

Daughter

trouble filling the role. If she goes to a therapist who tells her not to pay attention to others and to do what she thinks is right, the therapist is likely to add to Martha's troubles.

Interrole conflict   The fact that individuals simultaneously function in a number of roles sets up the possibility of **interrole conflict**. There are at least two kinds; interrole conflict may be associated with playing different roles in different family systems or different roles within the same system. In the first kind, when all the different expectations emanating from others outside the family system are in agreement with the expectations of those inside it, a person's social world exists in consensus, and all the person's roles are compatible. When the expectations from inside and outside the family differ, the social world exists in dissensus, and the person may be pulled and pushed and tormented by the competing expectations. For instance, Martha the worker's boss wants her in the office at 9:00 A.M. or he says he can easily find an unemployed person to take her job; Martha the mother has a stepson who wants her to stay home because he has a sore throat; Martha the wife has a husband who wants her to take the family car in for service because he will not be paid unless he works all day; and Martha the relative has a sister who is in a marital crisis and needs desperately to talk to her. When different expectations operate at the same time, interrole conflict produces a good deal of trouble.

The second kind of interrole conflict occurs when individuals play more than one role in complex systems such as the family can be. Martha the wife is also Martha the mother,

and competing expectations from husband and stepson can put her in interrole conflict. When her stepson wants Martha to read him a story and at the same time her husband wants Martha to devote some attention to him alone, Martha is forced to make a decision that causes her stress.

Mixed messages as role conflict Individuals may communicate in such a way that two competing expectations are being promoted at the same time. Often one message exists at the verbal level but another message exists at the nonverbal level. Suppose Martha is trying to decide whether she should take a new job which offers her more money, prestige, and security. She feels that John's approval is essential, so she asks him what he thinks about her role as working mother and wife. John says: "Honey, it's up to you. Do what you want. I only want what's good for you." On the surface he appears very supportive, but Martha is uneasy; he just didn't say it right. He turned his head away from her, and there was something wrong about his tone. Somehow it sounded like: "If you only want to think of yourself, then do it, but if you really loved me you wouldn't." When people trying to fulfill a role hear such **mixed messages**, they may experience them as role conflict. They may become stymied and unable to make decisions; they experience trouble.

Personality-role conflict Sometimes the roles individuals occupy are well suited to them, and they have the proper attitudes, knowledge, and skills to carry them out. Martha really likes being a homemaker, for instance; while it is a lot of work, she likes to keep house, to cook and sew and clean. She recognizes that having children is a lot of responsibility, but she genuinely wants lots of children. She was proud of her family name but willingly gave it up and took on her husband's. She might like to have a career, but she is content to think of her work as a means to a supplemental income. Since Martha's whole being is caught up in the role of homemaker, she would not be overwhelmed by the conflicts that multiple roles and expectations might bring. If she were not really suited for or happy in that role, she would be likely to experience trouble in the form of **personality-role conflict**.

Role Overload

Even though individuals are suited to their roles and the expectations of others are not necessarily incompatible, they can experience conflict in the form of role overload if there do not seem to be enough hours in the day to complete all the tasks required of them. Martha may feel obliged to work eight hours a day, to cook and clean, to spend time with her aging mother-in-law and her energetic father, to be a romantic partner for her husband, to help her stepson learn to read and her sister to deal with her problems. If she wants to do all these things equally as much, she is likely to be troubled by having more things to do than she can handle.

Family Responses to Role Conflict or Strain

All the various forms of role conflict have in common a tension in the working agreements within and between systems in the family and its environment. Whether or not a family experiences role conflict or strain depends on whether or not there is consensus in expectations and they are clearly stated. In regard to role strain in the family, Wesley Burr et al. put forth the following propositions:

1. The more individuals perceive consensus in the expectations about a role they occupy, the less their role strain.
2. The greater the perceived clarity of role expectations, the less the role strain.[44]

The responses of family members to the various role-conflict situations range along a continuum from conformity to nonconformity. A person in a role usually conforms to the expectations of others, as long as the expectations are clear and consensus exists among the various expectations. In functionalist and other consensus approaches to the analysis of social systems on which role theory is based, the assumption is that people in systems share values and function to maintain the system. Indeed, there is considerable evidence that conformity is the usual response to the expectations of others, but not necessarily because people want to conform. Sometimes people conform because they feel they have to.

Clarifying expectations may be necessary in order to achieve conformity. In role theory, it is generally assumed that dissensus in expectations is not real but rather reflects poor communication. On the surface there is a communication breakdown, but underneath there is consensus. Thus when strain is evident, people in roles attempt to communicate better and clarify their expectations. Once clarification occurs, conformity with expectations follows.

Sometimes nonconformity results when people in roles attempt to make innovations in what is expected of them through feedback to other system participants or to other systems. If the innovation is accepted, the system is righted again and in balance; if it is not accepted, the process begins again. When consensus cannot be reached, the family system is likely to break apart (through divorce) or to be trapped in various forms of domestic violence.

⚮ CONFLICT THEORY AND THE FAMILY

Conflict perspectives hold in common the notion that utilitarian self-interest is at the core of human behavior. Unlike the functionalists, who maintain that conflict and change are normal only when they contribute to maintenance of the system, conflict theorists believe that conflict and change are the normal and expected state in any system, and stability can only be achieved if it reflects equality among the elements of the system (see "Conflict or Consensus" in Chapter 3).

When conflict theory is applied to the family, the idea is that conflict develops because each member is expected to look out for his or her own best interests, even at the expense of other members. There is no assumption that the family is some kind of special system in which love and altruism predominate. To conflict theorists, conflict does not represent a breakdown in normal, stable relations; instead it indicates that systems are functioning in the expected way. Indeed, if stability and harmony were present, conflict theorists would get suspicious. They would suspect that some family members are forcing their wills on other family members.

Two Views on Marxian Theory and Family Conflict

Family conflict in contemporary Western, capitalist societies has usually been studied in the context of Marxian conflict theory (see Chapter 13), which starts with the assumption that self-interest among family members is promoted under the influence of capitalism. As the search for rewards and profits became more acceptable in everyday life, it also became more acceptable within the family. The self-interest evident in the family led some theorists to argue that the family is so corrupt it should be abandoned and replaced. For instance, David Cooper denounces the family as a destructive social institution rife with emotional blackmail and terrorism.[45]

Other conflict theorists have argued somewhat more recently that the family represents an oasis in capitalism rather than an expression of its values. In this view, the family is a humane institution besieged by capitalism and in need of protection from it. Capitalism is said to have subverted the human values underlying social relations. As a result, the masses are exploited and have lost control over their creative processes. They are treated and treat themselves like commodities with a specific economic value, packaged like so many bottles of beer to be placed on sale, bought, and consumed. Family life is understood within a context of contradictions and competing values.

Philip Wexler describes negotiations over contradictions in values as *the dialectic of intimate relations.* In advanced capitalist societies, he argues, there are at the same time tendencies toward social fragmentation and excessive individualism, rationalization and routinization, and alienation and exploitation. Competing tendencies exist simultaneously. People yearn for cooperation and communal attachments, for spontaneity and playfulness, for personal autonomy, control, and competence all at once. Family life is the struggle to resolve these competing values: urges to exploit and control versus urges to share and cooperate; urges to treat others as human beings versus urges to make them into objects to be used and consumed; urges to look out for the common good versus urges to look out for self. Wexler believes tradition favors humanist solutions; the family has been institutionalized to foster cooperation, personalism, and collectivism. As capitalist values have become inculcated into everyday life, however, there is less and less support for these values, and this creates continual stress.[46]

Similarly, Ralph LaRossa notes that there are no really acceptable alternatives to family life. From childhood, most people assume they will get married and have children. Thus when people come together to form intimate relations, an ambivalence borne out of not knowing what else is possible sets up tensions. Two people are likely to feel simultaneously pulled toward and away from the relationship. Feelings of attraction and repulsion, of being connected yet wanting to be separate, of unity and individuality exist side by side.[47]

Inequalities in the Family Institution

The way family life has been institutionalized also sets up tensions which must be dealt with. As we noted in Chapter 8, the status of women and children generally remains subordinate in society and in the family. Social norms traditionally have dictated the position of the husband as the head of the household and the authority of parents over children.

Marxian theorists have argued that the source of gender and generational inequality can be traced to free-market economic institutions. In contrast, feminist conflict theorists argue that the source of inequality lies more in gender conflict than in class conflict.[48] In many societies, although not all, men have been able to set up patriarchal norms which create advantage for them and disadvantage for women.

Regardless of their origins and legality, Randall Collins identifies three major sources of potential conflict in the family: conflict over economic property rights, conflict over sexual possession, and conflict over intergenerational control.[49] Family and other intimate relations exist on the razor's edge; the issues surrounding these inequalities can erupt at any moment into conflict. These issues have to do with how much power various family members are to have, how the power is to be used, who is to participate in decisions and to what extent, what rewards members are entitled to, and what privileges and obligations go with the roles they occupy.

In conflict theory, the possibility for conflict is always present because self-interest is inherent in the statuses family members occupy. Most men behave in ways that will protect their power and privilege over women; most parents do the same with children. Women and children's advocates try to improve their statuses and reduce those held by others, encouraged by women's and children's rights movements which have brought into question the authority of males or parents. The successful challenge to male dominance in adult relationships was discussed in Chapter 8, but efforts to make families less patriarchal and more egalitarian and democratic often have inspired family conflict.

In conflict theory, therefore, life in the family is seen as a negotiation in which members attempt to resolve the ambivalence, contradictions, and constraints generated by capitalist and patriarchal institutions. They manipulate whatever resources they have available as a way of holding on to or increasing wealth, power, status, prestige, and other economic and sexual benefits. They also attempt to affirm humanist values such as cooperation, the common good, personal respect, and autonomy.

Conflict between Husbands and Wives

Because Western societies have generally adopted patriarchal norms, men have traditionally held authority over women in the family. This authority is evident in both the economic and sexual spheres. While its extent has been reduced in recent years, male domination nevertheless persists; men and women still do not have equal status, either in the society or in the family. Thus, as women and men attempt to manage the ambivalence and contradictions generated by social institutions, there is a tendency for men to exploit women and a consequent tendency for women to assert their autonomy.

According to Marxian theory, the struggle between men and women in the family is intimately related to control over the economy. Traditionally, men exploited the labor of women by keeping them out of the work force and maintaining them in the home, where they did the work of keeping the house and nurturing the family without pay. In this view, women's economic dependence on men is the key to understanding their subordination in society.

Feminists do not necessarily dispute the economic competition between men and women. They argue, however, that the origins of female-male conflict lie in the exploitation of female sexuality for purposes of male sexual gratification. In taking a feminist position, Collins makes three assumptions:

1. Humans have the strongest sexual drives.

2. Males are, on average, bigger and stronger than females and thus will more often coerce and be aggressive against women.

3. Coercion on the part of males will likely be countered by aggression on the part of females.[50]

From these assumptions, Collins concludes that husbands will claim the right to total sexual possession of wives but will not necessarily grant wives the right to sexual possession over them. Women become the *sexual property* of men through marriage, and it is the control and use of this property that forms the basis of conflict between them.

This view takes into account the historic exchange between the economic and material rewards that men are able to offer and the sexual attractiveness and gratification that women are able to offer. To win his woman, the male attempts to become economically powerful. To win her man, the female attempts to appear attractive and as inaccessible as possible. The posture of women to men is usually defensive and involves a strong degree of sexual repressiveness. Woman cannot appear to like sex. The posture of men to women is aggressive and involves devaluing her intellectual capacities.

Yet women do have certain kinds of power over men. Men fear that women will supplant their authority, and because traditional gender-role norms limit the ability of men to express emotions, they also fear women's expressive powers. Women serve to validate male sexuality, and men fear their power to make them impotent and emasculate them. In this conflict perspective such fears give women leverage over men.

Conflict theorists such as Collins do not disregard the role of the economy in conflict between men and women, however. They point out that in the affluent market economy experienced in the United States in the 1970s, new employment opportunities opened up for women. Their dependence on men was reduced, and they were free to strike their own bargains. Such conditions encouraged the women's movement and the rise in divorce rates that followed as women exercised their options and men reacted; a woman's newfound independence can cause either partner to break off the marriage. As long as women continue to experience occupational segregation and lower average incomes, however, they will not be able to compete economically as equals with men.

Competition among men in the economy also tends to reinforce traditional gender roles. Many working-class and middle-class men experience alienation and exploitation in their jobs. They attempt to exercise power in the only place they have an opportunity to do so, their own homes.

Other forms of social relations also reinforce men's traditional gender roles. Joseph Pleck argues that these roles are maintained both by the ways women and men have responded to each other's self-interest and by the ways men respond to other men. The male-male bond reinforces the male's exploitation of the female. Definitions of masculinity are formulated in the context of the competition among men that is set up by patriarchal norms, not only the acceptable forms of masculinity but the unacceptable forms, such as homosexuality. The worst names men can call each other are "queer," "fag," "sissy," or "girl baby," but other forms of masculinity also are devalued. Traditionally, only aggressive, dominating, competitive, materially oriented men are considered masculine.[51]

Conflict between Parents and Children

Through socialization, adults help children learn to become competent members of society. According to Collins, the traditional literature on socialization considers childhood almost entirely from the point of view of an idealized adult society. It accepts adults' rationalization of their exercise of authority by failing to acknowledge underlying tensions in parent-child relationships. Collins believes that socialization has been regarded as the process which "tames the little barbarians who enter the world as infants and makes it possible for them to associate in the civilized world of adults."[52]

In this respect, Collins and other Marxian-oriented scholars of the family believe that Freudian ideas about early-life socialization patterns are not far off the mark. Freud assumed an inherent conflict between individuals and society. He exposed the basic conflict in parent-child relations by maintaining that newborn children are polymorphous perverse, that is, driven by their need for pleasure, and so can only enter the civilized world of adults by taking on a superego. Freud made an important error, in the view of conflict theorists. He failed to realize that the Victorian family was not a universal type that existed everywhere, at all times, in the same way. He took a nonhistorical approach to the family.

In Collins's conflict approach, socialization processes are seen as a struggle for control over the emotional, behavioral, and cognitive life of the child. Children learn what parents believe are the acceptable ways of feeling, thinking, and behaving. That is, they learn their parents' personal solutions and difficulties with respect to the ambivalence and contradictions generated by society. This is an important point. Whereas the traditional literature on socialization makes it seem as though parents pass on clear and consistent norms and traditions, conflict theory emphasizes that parents pass on a maze of ambivalence and contradictions. Moreover, while children are subordinate to parents, they are not powerless: "The socialization of the child even in infancy, is not simply an imposition of the parent's culture…upon the child, but a negotiated product which can change as the resources available to the parties change."[53]

Resources and Strategies of Control

Parents' ability to use their authority to control children rests, according to Collins, in a time advantage; the parents are older and presumably wiser and smarter. They are also bigger and have more strength. And, perhaps of most consequence, children are attracted to parents and need to be loved and protected. Parents also control the material benefits a child may receive, and parental authority is to a large extent supported and reinforced by society. Children in contemporary society who are labeled incorrigible, or ungovernable, and who habitually disobey or run away from their parents may be declared delinquent.

Parents exercise their advantage primarily through either rewards or punishments such as shaming, love deprivation, or physical violence. The strategies they use are in part controlled by culturally based norms. For instance, the state has increasingly limited the violence and obvious coercion to which parents can subject their children. Society now supports the use of rewards rather than punishments and more subtle ways of manipulating the emotions, behaviors, and perceptions of children. The goal is for children to believe that their parents are not operating out of self-interest.

The ability of children to check the authority of parents depends on their age. Infants have few resources other than their ability to be cute and loving and their capacity for crying and making a nuisance of themselves. Young children are very vulnerable and likely to internalize the ambivalence and contradictions of the parents. The older children are, the more they are able to match brains and brawn with adults. Eventually they can shame parents, withdraw love, run away, or even use physical violence, or they can reward parents with love, affection, good grades, and the like. Children can use their own ambivalence and contradictions to influence parents. Even older children are likely to be economically dependent, however, and thus parents inevitably have the upper hand.

∽ IMPLICATIONS FOR PRACTICE

Each of the five perspectives on family life examined in this chapter—the ecological, psychodynamic, and developmental models and role and conflict theories—makes a unique contribution to understanding the problems confronted by families. They are particularly helpful to social service workers in the first two steps of practice problem solving: assessment and intervention planning.

The ecological model demonstrates that family problems are generated as a result of interaction with other individuals, groups, organizations, and social institutions. This model is useful because it supplies two excellent assessment instruments, the eco-map and the genogram. These tools make it possible to look closely at the relationship between a family and its social environment and to consider the changes that are needed in the environment.

The psychodynamic model looks inside the individuals making up the family to determine their unconscious needs and drives. It proposes that happiness in marriage is largely a function of early-life, family-based experiences. Women and men are attracted to each other based on unconscious needs, but those who bring unresolved, frustrating experiences into their marriages will love in immature ways and will develop ways of protecting against appropriate resolutions of their neuroses. Although most social workers will not be sufficiently trained to assess unconscious motives and drives, some basic understanding of them is necessary in analyzing problems.

The developmental or family life-cycle model shows how to look at the way family members and intimate partners are adapting to expected tasks and stresses as they enter, maintain, and end relationships. It sensitizes workers to the likely troubles people have as they decide to marry or become involved, have children or decide not to, see their children start school, and so on. Role theory focuses on the strain and conflict experienced as family members attempt to meet their own expectations and those of other family members and other people outside the family. Conflict theory emphasizes how contradictions and inequalities supported by the larger society set up tensions that are easily converted into conflict and coercion.

All of the perspectives contribute to good social work assessment; yet, taken independently, each has limitations. For instance, the ecological model is more a general guide than a perspective with substance. It does not provide a very good understanding of the internal dynamics of family life. The psychodynamic model fails to define the societal context of family life adequately and does not promote understanding of the conscious aspects of personality. Although the developmental, role, and conflict perspectives are all social-psychological, the strengths of one seem to be the weaknesses of others. Developmental models and role theory do not call sufficient attention to the harsh realities of industrial societies. Conflict theory pays insufficient attention to the human tendencies for cooperation and harmony.

It would be a mistake, therefore, for social service workers to favor one of these perspectives over the other. The insights provided by each model or theory must be taken into account in the assessment of family well-being.

∞ DISCUSSION QUESTIONS AND CLASS PROJECTS

1. Define and identify the following: eco-map, genogram, microsystem, mesosystem, exosystem, macrosystem.

2. What kinds of economic stress are likely to be experienced by families today? Have you seen any of these stresses operating in the families you have worked with? Has your own family experienced any of these?

3. Form pairs and have one person take the role of social worker and the other the role of client. The social worker interviews the client in an attempt to complete an eco-map of the client. Then reverse roles and begin again. Come together as a class to clarify the use of the eco-map and the difficulties a social worker might have in doing one.

4. Describe the assessment areas a social worker can get into through the use of a genogram.

5. Form pairs and have one person take the role of social worker and the other the role of client. The social worker interviews the client to complete a genogram; then reverse roles and begin again. As a class, clarify the use of the genogram and the difficulties a social worker might have in doing one.

6. Do you think that unconscious motives and drives operate in family troubles?

7. Describe what Strean means by immature love. What are the ways it can be exhibited? Do you agree that these ways are immature? Do you think you see immature love in your clients, your friends, or yourself?

8. Define and identify the following:
   derailed families
   dislocated families
   transgenerational stress
   normative stress
   the stress of living in this place at this time

9. List and describe Carter and McGoldrick's stages of family development.

10. What are some of the tasks and stresses that should be expected when people go through divorce and remarriage?

11. Form groups of four or five students. Each person describes his or her own family life (of origin, of procreation, of partnering) in terms of its present stage of development. What do you see as the normal tasks and problems associated with that phase? Do you

think members of your own family are adapting to these?

12. List and define five major forms of family role conflict. Can you give concrete examples of each? Can you give specific examples by describing situations experienced by your clients, your friends, or yourself?

13. What are the ways by which role conflict can be resolved? In thinking about the examples you have given of

role conflict, how were they, or how are they likely to be, resolved?

14. What is meant by conflict theory? How does it sensitize us to conflict between husbands and wives and conflict between parents and children? Do you ever find yourself dealing with the potential conflict created by status inequalities in the family?

15. Name and define the five perspectives on family functioning discussed in this chapter.

∞ NOTES

1. James Garbarino, *Children and Families in the Social Environment* (New York: Aldine, 1982), pp. 21–61.

2. Marc L. Miringoff, director, Fordham Institute for Innovation in Social Policy, *The Index of Social Health* (Tarrytown, NY, 1991).

3. Robert D. Plotnick, "Income Distribution," in *Encyclopedia of Social Work*, 18th ed., Vol. 1 (Silver Spring, MD: National Association of Social Workers, 1987), p. 881.

4. U.S. Bureau of the Census, *Statistical Abstract of the United States: 1992*, 112th edition (Washington, DC, 1992), Tables 703, 705, 704.

5. Plotnick, "Income Distribution," p. 883.

6. Kevin Phillips, *The Politics of Rich and Poor: Wealth and the American Electorate in the Reagan Aftermath* (New York: Random House, 1990), p. 14.

7. U.S. Bureau of the Census, *Statistical Abstract: 1992*, p. 426.

8. James William Coleman and Donald R. Cressey, *Social Problems* (New York: Harper and Row, 1984), pp. 162–63.

9. Michael Harrington, *The Other America: Poverty in the United States* (Baltimore, MD: Penguin Books, 1973), pp. 1, 195–202. Also see Harrington, *Decade of Decision* (New York: Simon and Schuster, 1980), and *The New American Poverty* (New York: Holt, Rinehart, and Winston, 1984).

10. Sheldon Danziger, "Poverty," in *Encyclopedia of Social Work*, Vol. 2, p. 195.

11. U.S. Bureau of the Census, *Statistical Abstract: 1992*, Table 717.

12. William O'Hare, "The Eight Myths of Poverty," *American Demographics*, vol. 8 (May 1986), pp. 22–25.

13. U.S. Bureau of the Census, *Statistical Abstract: 1992*, Tables 720, 719, 721.

14. Ibid., Table 632.

15. Ibid., Table 636.

16. Katherine Briar, "Unemployment and Underemployment," in *Encyclopedia of Social Work*, Vol. 2, p. 779

17. Lee Rainwater, *What Money Buys: Inequality and the Social Meaning of Income* (New York: Basic Books, 1974), p. 53.

18. Stuart Ewen, *Captains of Consciousness: Advertising and the Social Roots of the Consumer Culture* (New York: McGraw-Hill, 1976).

19. Philip Slater, *Wealth Addiction* (New York: Dutton, 1980).

20. Louis Uchitelle, "Three Decades of Dwindling Hope for Prosperity," *The New York Times*, May 9, 1993, sect. 4, pp. 1, 2.

21. Joan Didion, "Trouble in Lakewood," *The New Yorker*, July 26, 1993, pp. 46–65.

22. Lillian B. Rubin, *Worlds of Pain* (New York: Basic Books, 1976), pp. 70–71.

23. Arlie Hochschild with Anne Machung, *Second Shift: Working Parents and the Revolution at Home* (New York: Viking Penguin, 1989), pp. 12–13, 208, 251–53.

24. Thomas Keefe has written extensively on the theme of empathic understanding of the economic stresses on family life. See "The Economic Context of Empathy," *Social Work*, vol. 23 (November 1978), pp. 460–66 and "The Stresses of Unemployment," *Social Work*, vol. 29 (May–June 1984), pp. 264–69.

25. Ann Hartman, "Diagrammatic Assessment of Family Relationships," *Social Casework*, vol. 59 (October 1978), pp. 465–76.

26. Monica McGoldrick and Randy Gerson, *Genograms in Family Assessment* (New York: Norton, 1985), p. 5.

27. Maggie Scarf, *Intimate Partners: Patterns in Love and Marriage* (New York: Random House, 1987), p. 8. The story of "the Bretts," illustrated with the development of their family genogram, is told in Part I, pp. 27–100.

28. McGoldrick and Gerson, *Genograms in Family Assessment*.

29. Scarf, *Intimate Partners*, p. 40.

30. Herbert S. Strean, *Resolving Marital Conflicts: A Psychodynamic Perspective* (New York: John Wiley and Sons, 1985).

31. Ibid., pp. 10–22.

32. Ibid., pp. 19–20.

33. American Psychiatric Association, *Diagnostic and Statistical Manual of Mental Disorders*, 3rd ed. rev. (Washington, DC, 1987).

34. Strean, *Resolving Marital Conflicts*, p. 43.

35. Evelyn Duvall was one of the first sociologists to describe the family as a unit or system. See her *Marriage and Family Development*, 5th ed. (Philadelphia: J. P. Lippincott, 1971), p. 145.

36. Elizabeth A. Carter and Monica McGoldrick, "The Family Life Cycle and Family Therapy: An Overview," in E. Carter and M. McGoldrick (editors), *The Family Life Cycle: A Framework for Family Therapy* (New York: Gardner, 1980), pp. 3–20.

37. Ibid., p. 10.

38. Ibid., p. 12.

39. David McWhirter and Andrew M. Mattison, *The Male Couple: How Relationships Develop* (Englewood Cliffs, NJ: Prentice-Hall, 1984), pp. 14–18.

40. Fernando Colon, "The Family Life Cycle of the Multiproblem Poor Family," in Carter and McGoldrick (editors), *Family Life Cycle*, pp. 343–81.

41. C. J. Falicov and B. M. Karrer, "Cultural Variations in the Family Life Cycle: The Mexican American Family," in Carter and McGoldrick (editors), *Family Life Cycle*, pp. 383–425.

42. Wesley R. Burr, Geoffrey K. Leigh, Randall D. Day, and John Constantine, "Symbolic Interaction and the Family," in W. R. Burr, R. Hill, F. I. Nye, and I. L. Reiss (editors), *Contemporary Theories about the Family*, vol. 2 (New York: Free Press, 1979), pp. 78–84.

43. Morton Deutsch and Robert M. Krauss, *Theories in Social Psychology* (New York: Basic Books, 1965), pp. 175–77.

44. Burr, Leigh, Day, and Constantine, "Symbolic Interaction and the Family," pp. 78–84.

45. David Cooper, *Death of the Family* (New York: Vintage Books, 1970).

46. Philip Wexler, *Critical Social Psychology* (Boston, MA: Routledge and Kegan Paul, 1983), pp. 141–56.

47. Ralph LaRossa, *Conflict and Power in Marriage: Expecting the First Child* (Beverly Hills, CA: Sage Publications, 1977), pp. 105–14. Also see pp. 103–51.

48. Randall Collins, *Sociology of Marriage and the Family: Gender, Love and Prosperity* (Chicago: Nelson-Hall, 1985), p. 26.

49. Ibid., p. 39.

50. Randall Collins, *Conflict Sociology* (New York: Academic Press, 1975), pp. 221–28.

51. Joseph H. Pleck, "Men's Power with Women, Other Men, and Society: A Men's Movement Analysis," in R. A. Lewis (editor), *Men in Difficult Times* (Englewood Cliffs, NJ: Prentice-Hall, 1981), pp. 234–44.

52. Collins, *Conflict Sociology*, pp. 259–60.

53. Ibid., p. 260.

PART FOUR

Large and Small Groups

Social Interaction in Groups and Organizations

MAJOR THEMES DISCUSSED IN THIS CHAPTER

1. **DEFINING GROUPS.** Groups are human systems in which the members are interdependent and share an identity. All groups have a structure and boundaries that both separate and join them in their environment. They are open and dynamic systems in which change and conflict are ever present. Large, complex, formally structured groups are called bureaucracies. For research purposes, small groups are classified as natural groups or concocted groups.

2. **A CRITICAL APPROACH TO BUREAUCRACY.** *Bureaucracies* are often studied from the point of view of management and as independent entities that exist apart from their environments. A political economy approach to the study of bureaucracies provides an alternative which takes into account the internal and external polity and economy of the group.

3. **SMALL GROUPS: THE NEED FOR A CRITICAL APPROACH.** In small groups, members are interdependent and influence each other through face-to-face interaction. The small group is also believed to be psychologically significant to the members.

4. **POLITICAL ECONOMY AND GROUP DYNAMICS.** The literature on group processes and dynamics can be seen from the perspective of political economy. The remaining sections of this chapter are built around the social processes of recruitment, socialization, interaction, control, and innovation or change through which groups and organizations, as social systems, are maintained or changed.

5. **IMPLICATIONS FOR PRACTICE.** Notions of normalcy as average, health, or utopia can be applied to the study of the functioning of groups. Although conflict is always present in both small and large groups, the role of the social worker involves trying to control the conflict in ways that will enable the group to remain stable and accomplish its tasks in meeting the needs of individual members.

AS A FIELD OF STUDY, THE organization and dynamics of large and small groups has several implications for social service workers. Like communities and families, it is a context for understanding individual behavior and development. Individuals largely live out their lives through participation in groups—families, friendships, schools, work, social life—and their perceptions, motivations, and behaviors are influenced by these interactions. Groups shape individuals' attitudes and values and leave their mark on personality, identity, and self.

Groups also represent focal systems for generalist social work practitioners who deal with them as client systems, those they are intent on helping, and target systems, those they are intent on changing. Direct-service workers are often called upon to lead, coordinate, or facilitate groups or to negotiate, mediate, or arbitrate group conflict. Other levels of practice are also conducted in groups; next to work with individuals and families, group work is the most common area of specialization. In macro practice, social service workers are administrators or managers of agencies, departments, or facilities.

Social workers themselves participate in many groups. Those who are employed by a public or private agency or social service department in a corporation, hospital, or school are participating in a large group. When they meet with others in work groups, task groups, or committees, they are participating in small groups. In private life they participate in the full range of group activities; a worker might be a member of a nuclear family, a community council, a fraternal group, and a major political party, for example.

∞ DEFINING GROUPS

Groups are not simply collections of individuals. People standing on a street corner waiting for a bus are not a group, nor are acquaintances brought together to celebrate a birthday or an audience gathered to watch a concert or movie. These are **aggregates**—collections of people who share a common circumstance or condition; the individuals happen to be in the same place at the same time. Although redheads share a common condition, they are not a group. An entering class of social work graduate students is not a group, either.

Groups are more than aggregates of people; they are systems, "two or more persons who are interacting with one another in such a manner that each person influences and is influenced by each other person."[1] In a **small group**, interaction and influence occur directly through face-to-face contact, while in a **large group**, interaction occurs indirectly through delegates or representatives of different units and subdivisions.

As systems, groups have the following attributes:

1. *Interdependence.* Groups are collections of individuals, each one unique, yet all interdependent.

2. *Structure.* Groups have an internal organization consisting of working agreements or norms and a division of labor marked by roles and statuses. This structure makes groups more than the sum of their individual parts.

3. *Identity.* Groups are self-conscious entities. Group members see themselves as "us" and outsiders as "them"; outsiders reverse these designations.

4. *Boundaries.* A group's boundaries are marked physically by the space it occupies, psychologically by the personalities of its members, and socially by its sense of self and

its special norms and traditions. Those on the inside, the in-group, constitute the "we," while those on the outside, the out-group, constitute the "they."

5. *Organization as a holon.* A group is at the same time a whole in itself and part of another whole; that is, a group is a holon (see Chapter 3). Groups exist within a social environment that impinges on them and can be a source of strength or a source of strain.

6. *Openness.* Groups, like individuals, are open systems that cannot exist independently of their social environment and must interact with it.

7. *Dynamism.* Because of the interdependence among members and openness with the environment, groups are dynamic rather than static. Conflict and change are always present.

Bureaucracies and Small Groups

In the strictest sense, the designations *large* and *small* in reference to groups apply only to the number of people making up a group. The term *group* thus describes every conceivable social system, from the nuclear family to the friendship group, the work group, the business organization, the government agency, the community, the nation, and the international association.

Large-group theory and research, however, are generally limited to the study of organizations or, more properly, **bureaucracy**.[2] The term *bureaucracy* refers to any relatively complex and formal organization. There is no agreed-upon typology of bureaucracies. Yeheskel Hasenfeld distinguishes **human service organizations** from other types of bureaucracy in terms of their technology and resources.[3] By providing services to individuals and families, human service organizations serve the manifest function of protecting, maintaining, or enhancing the personal well-being of citizens. They include hospitals, schools, churches, social services, courts, social groups, law enforcement agencies, and cultural and recreational organizations. Nonhuman service organizations work with things or animals for the purpose of extracting natural resources or making a product. Examples include agriculture, dairy and meat production, mining, forestry, and automobile and other manufacturing industries.

Commonsense typologies usually distinguish between profit and nonprofit organizations or between those in the public and private sectors.[4] Ron Westrum and Khalil Samaha distinguish among government agencies, enterprises or for-profit firms, and nonprofit voluntary associations,[5] for example, and David Stoesz uses these distinctions to describe three different kinds of bureaucracies in the welfare industry: voluntary nonprofit agencies, public welfare agencies, and corporate for-profit agencies.[6]

Research on small groups involves the study of both natural groups, those that exist independent of the researcher's purpose, and **concocted groups**, which have been set up to study group behavior in the laboratory.[7] We are concerned with human behavior in natural groups, but much of our knowledge of natural groups derives from laboratory observations of concocted groups.

Howard Nixon identifies five types of natural groups.[8] **Friendship networks** take shape informally in bureaucratic settings like schools, universities, corporations, agencies, and voluntary associations. Examples include student study groups, faculty research collaboration groups, factory worker cliques, and information networks among business people. **Task groups** are formed by their members or others with authority over them to pursue specific tasks or sets of tasks. These include committees, factory work teams, military details or patrols, debating clubs, and athletic teams. **Resocialization groups** are usually found in social service organizations. They include therapy and rehabilitation groups designed to provide resocialization for people who are troubled or in trouble or what Harry Specht refers to as *developmental socialization*—helping nontroubled people with the tasks of life—and *contextual socialization*—helping people alter their environments.[9] **Friendship groups** and **peer groups** are made up of the friends and social networks with which individuals interact as they go from childhood to adolescence to adulthood. Family groups include families of biological and adoptive origin and families of procreation.

∞ BUREAUCRACY: A CRITICAL APPROACH

Bureaucracies are a major type of social system in an industrial society such as ours in the United States. From an ideal-type perspective, the bureaucratic format is highly rational and formal, but the fact is that organizational processes depend on interpersonal human relations, which can support or undermine the functioning of bureaucracies. Traditional approaches to bureaucracy have been criticized for being too focused on the point of view of management and minimizing the environmental context of large organizations. From the critical perspective, we will take a political economy point of view, which acknowledges that bureaucracies are driven by the political and economic struggles taking place within organizations and between organizations and their social environments.

Weber's Ideal-Type Bureaucracy

The formative work on the concept of bureaucracy was done by Max Weber, a German sociologist, in the earliest twentieth century; his major work, *Economy and Society*, was unfinished at the time of his death in 1920. For Weber, the basis of a bureaucracy is **rational-legal authority**, or the differentiation of members along horizontal and vertical lines based on organizational goals backed up by law or policy.[10] Bureaucracies are seen as social inventions which rely on the power of legitimized leaders to influence actions and behaviors through knowledge, reason, rules, and law. Weber identified the features of a bureaucracy as a type of organization that is marked by specific characteristics.[11]

1. There is horizontal differentiation through a clear *division of labor*; organizational tasks are specified for subunits and for people in particular positions or roles.

2. There is vertical differentiation through a chain of command or *hierarchy of authority*, with superordinates above and subordinates below; authority tends to be centralized, with decision-making responsibilities in the hands of superordinates. The scope of authority is specified according to the limits of each position (see "Organizational Chart for a Social Work Bureaucracy").

3. The horizontal and vertical divisions of labor are linked to *specialization*. Employees are placed in positions on the basis of their technical qualifications (expertise, skills, and experience relevant to the position) and must meet specified standards of work. Duties, obligations, and privileges are connected to the position, not to the person. There is a specialized administrative staff which keeps the bureaucracy functioning.

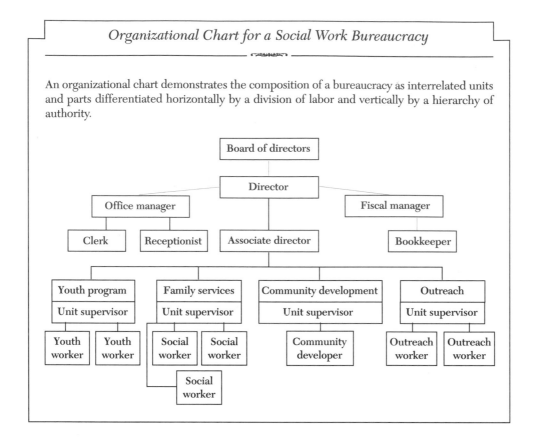

Organizational Chart for a Social Work Bureaucracy

An organizational chart demonstrates the composition of a bureaucracy as interrelated units and parts differentiated horizontally by a division of labor and vertically by a hierarchy of authority.

4. There is an established *system of rules and regulations*, usually specified in writing, which are enforced in the interests of the organization. They let managers and employees know what is expected of them, guide decision making, and govern day-to-day functioning of the bureaucracy.

5. *Universal, impersonal norms* govern the relationships within the bureaucracy and between it and the public. Participants are to treat each other impartially and equitably, within the constraints of their roles and statuses. Employees are to be judged on the merits of performance rather than personal traits, and personal considerations are subordinate to organizational goals.

Weber analyzed bureaucracy in terms of what he called an **ideal type**, an abstract description constructed from observations of a number of cases in order to determine the essential characteristics they have in common. By identifying the principal elements of a bureaucratic organization, Weber prescribed a normative standard for studying actual organizations of this type. The ideal-type bureaucracy is not a prescription about what bureaucracies should be; *ideal type* does not mean *ideal*. Yet there is much in Weber's description of bureaucracy that suggests it can be followed as an organizational design. Weber saw bureaucracy as "attaining the highest degree of efficiency" and "superior to any other form in precision, in stability, in the stringency of its discipline, and in its reliability."[12] He also believed that because of the emphasis in bureaucracy on impartial treatment and selection based on competence, it "greatly favors the leveling of social classes" and

Internal Revenue Service workers in Philadelphia process stacks of federal tax returns. The division of labor, hierarchy of authority, specialization of tasks, rules and regulations, and impersonal relationships are typical of the bureaucratic form of organization.

"inevitably foreshadows the development of mass democracy."[13] Although Weber believed bureaucracy had great potential as a form of organization, he saw a lot in bureaucratic life that was not ideal. He feared it would not prove to be very adaptive, because bureaucracies work best in stable environments, and administrators are inclined to try to prevent change, stifle innovation, and thus limit the growth of democratic organizations. He also called attention to problems such as red tape, or the excessive use of rules and regulations, and the dehumanization that occurs as a result of universal, impersonal norms (see the section on the bureaucratic personality in Chapter 14).

Scientific Management

Weber's emphasis on rationality did give momentum to the **scientific management** theory of bureaucracy, a prescriptive approach designed to help managers optimize production through efficiency. In trying to turn Weber's ideal type of bureaucracy into an ideal, the organization adopts principles of management based on scientific analysis such as time and motion study, experiments, and measurement of production to determine the best ways to improve efficiency and productivity. Hasenfeld points out that adhering to such scientific principles is in the best interest of both workers and managers: "Since workers are primarily motivated by monetary incentives, increased productivity based on scientific management will enable them to earn maximum wages, while at the same time it maximizes the profitability of the organization."[14]

When Weber's ideas about bureaucracy are applied to scientific management, they are usually referred to as the classical or conventional model. The approach has been criticized because in taking the point of view of management, it excludes those of workers and society as a whole, and it fails to recognize the effects of the organization's environment. It is also criticized for its excessively rational and impersonal understanding of large-group behavior.

The Human Relations Approach

An alternative to the scientific management model as a way of understanding how bureaucracies operate is the **human relations approach**. Followers of this approach, such as Elton Mayo and Rensis Likert, argue that because people entering organizations do not leave behind all their individual attributes and needs, they form informal structures in the group, side by side with the formal structures of roles and statuses.[15] Organizations are seen as hierarchical arrangements of overlapping work groups or teams which communicate with one another and with successively higher levels of command, so authority flows upward as well as downward (see "Organizational Chart from the Human Relations Perspective").

In informal organizational structures the emphasis is on the interactions among work-group members and the informal means of communication they develop. Workers are believed to be motivated by job satisfaction as much as by economic incentives. Because the informal structure can either compete with or complement the formal structure, the task of management in the human relations approach is to harness the small-group dynamics of organizations as a resource in improving productivity and efficiency. To do this, managers try to minimize the differences between superordinates and subordinates, use democratic leadership techniques to generate group cohesion and individual attachment, and find ways to allow influence to flow from the bottom to the top of the organization. While there is concern for the alienation of workers and the dehumanizing effects of centralized authority, the goal is not so much to improve the lot as it is to implement the realization of the organization's goals.

Taking the Point of View of Management

The large groups or bureaucracies that have been studied in organizational theory have primarily been business organizations, and the focus has been on interactions between management and workers. Both scientific management and the human relations approach take the point of view of management. Scientific management attempts to put science in the hands of administrators; human relations tries to teach them leadership through group facilitation skills. Although human relations encourages worker participation, it does not start from the point of view of workers. Bureaucracy, as Weber clearly understood, is a tool by which superordinates (owners and executives) control subordinates (lower-level managers and white- and blue-collar workers). On the scale of regions and nations, Charles Perrow describes bureaucracy as a means for "centralizing power in society and legitimating that centralization."[16]

Organizational Chart from the Human Relations Perspective

In the human relations approach bureaucracies are seen as hierarchical arrangements of overlapping work groups or teams. These groups develop informal structures of relationships which allow them to communicate upward throughout the hierarchy.

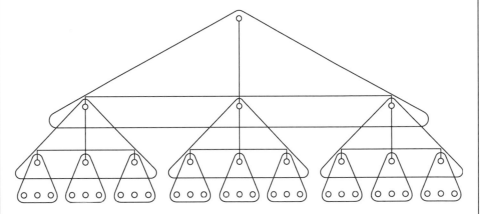

Source: Rensis Likert, *New Patterns of Management* (New York: McGraw-Hill, 1961), p. 105.

To demonstrate this, organizational theorists go no further than the concept of goals. All groups and organizations have goals; that is, the members share objectives they all are aspiring to reach. In fact, the existence of such goals is the justification for the structure of the organization; bureaucracies are organized the way they are in order to achieve their goals.

However, an organization's manifest or official goals are not necessarily its latent or operative goals, the goals that are implicit in everyday tasks and activities.[17] Organizations often engage in activities that seem to have little to do with their official goals. From this perspective, official goals serve more as public relations strategies aimed at rallying internal and external support for the organization. A study by John Meyer and Brian Rowan, for example, concluded that school districts have a largely symbolic function in American society. School officials promote the idea that the goal of public schools is to educate children because the society believes in socializing children through the inculcation of knowledge and skills. While some education does take place in the schools, these researchers contend that the operative goal of schools is to sort, track, and certify students. Schools try to measure their results by counting such things as the number of students processed, the qualifications of teachers, the range of curriculum opportunities, or the number of special programs they offer; they avoid evaluating how much learning takes place. The public is reassured that their taxes are not being wasted, existing social class differences are maintained, and the teaching profession is protected.[18]

Much of the literature on goals and motivation suggests that organizational goals reflect a shared consensus or agreement among the members. Founding members articulate a set of goals, and as new members enter they are socialized to support the existing goals. Goals do change, but as the result of decision-making processes in which everybody participates.

In reality, however, this process of reaching organizational goals is often very different from this consensual model. In proposing the iron law of oligarchy in 1915, Robert Michels recognized that as organizations became more complex and bureaucratized, power eventually comes to reside in the hands of an elite minority at the top of the hierarchy. Increasing size and complexity make it impossible for rank-and-file members to participate, and communications are concentrated in the organizational elite, whose primary goal becomes the preservation of its power and privilege.[19] Organizations develop a culture of their own, a system of informal but binding rules that reflects the power of the dominant elements. The goal of the organization, in this light, is little more than the justification of organizational elites for the division of labor and the distribution of rewards and resources in the organizational structure.

Although the organizational elite often has its way, it rarely goes unchallenged. Organizations also breed an "underlife" of competing groups and groups and coalitions which continually work to subvert the power of the dominant elements and thereby change the organization's goals. Rather than expressing a shared consensus, therefore, group goals often mask ongoing dissensus and conflict.[20]

When organizational theory takes the point of view of management, it gives too little attention to the interests of workers, such as better working conditions, more participation in decision making, and greater access to the resources and rewards emanating from the group.[21] It does not acknowledge the dominance of power and conflict in the organization's goals and structure, and it minimizes the environmental context of organizations. Bureaucracy is presented as a closed system, driven largely by internal needs and energies.

As we have noted, however, organizations—like any social system—are open systems or holons that are at once independent units and interdependent parts of a larger unit. To understand bureaucracy from the critical perspective, we need a point of view that recognizes organizations exist in a world of economic and political realities that shape organizational goals and processes and their interactions with the environment can be either supportive or conflictive.

The Political Economy of Organizations

The political economy framework proposed by Mayer Zald for the study of complex organizations acknowledges the effects of their internal and external environments. In its most general sense, **political economy** is the study of the interplay between political and economic structures and processes. Applied to organizations, the assumption is that organizational goals and attributes ought to be shaped by political and economic processes in the larger environment, as well as by the political and economic processes operating within the organization. The polity and economy components in these processes often overlap, and each has both external and internal aspects.[22]

The External and Internal Polity

Zald defines the *external polity* as the "tangled web of external supporters, competitors, and enemies of an organization, focusing on the alliances, commitments, and structural mechanisms through which organizations relate to the power nodes of their environments."[23] Its components include government regulations, the network of similar organizations of which bureaucracy is a part, and the interest groups competing for influence in American society.

An example is the effects of the external polity on human service organizations. Stoesz describes these organizations as part of the welfare industry, which includes four subdivisions with their own history and ideology. The *voluntary sector*, composed of secular and sectarian nonprofit agencies, stresses the ideal of charity as the basis for community bonds. The *welfare state*, which includes federal, state, and local welfare departments, champions the ideal that services should be offered as a right of citizens. *Corporate welfare* includes for-profit health and other welfare bureaucracies that exploit markets and offer services to those who can afford them. *Private practitioners* are individuals or small associations that also offer treatment on that basis.[24]

These four sectors of the welfare industry may be seen as structured interests competing for the leading role in the provision of social services. At present the welfare state predominates; that is, most welfare policy is formulated by government, and welfare funding is generated through taxes. Because government funding reaches the other sectors through such means as contracts, regulations affect the entire welfare industry. Under the Reagan and Bush administrations, however, the welfare state came under heavy attack from political conservatives, initiating a trend toward the privatization of public services. The voluntary sector was revitalized to some extent, private practice burgeoned, and welfare corporations challenged public welfare. Different philosophies of social service delivery emerged under which the right of all citizens to service is challenged by the concepts of service as charity or service for those who can afford it.

There are indications that the welfare state is holding its position of dominance in the industry, however. While the middle class is unwilling to accept more radical interpretations of welfare, it still supports the basic structure of the welfare state.[25] Marginal groups or special populations that have been neglected, excluded, or oppressed in American society, including African Americans, Native Americans, Latinos, women, and residents of rural areas, depend on it.[26] Almost all parts of the welfare industry are feeling the effects of various movements for civil rights or human rights, and many social service organizations are reshaping their goals, hiring procedures, and services accordingly. Despite the emphasis in bureaucracy on impartial treatment, marginal groups argue that discrimination, in the form of limited opportunities to work or to receive services, nevertheless exists.

The *internal polity*, or the system of control and influence operating inside an organization, concerns the amount and distribution of organizational power. It includes mechanisms for resolving organizational conflicts and for hiring, promoting, or dismissing personnel.[27] The internal polity is readily seen in problem solving and decision making. Rather than seeking rationally optimal solutions, organizational members may try to achieve *satisficing decisions*, which are based on limited knowledge and on negotiation and compromise among the contending individual and group interests in the organization.[28]

The External and Internal Economy

The *external economy* has to do with the functioning of the economic system as a whole, its state of health, the strength of capital and labor, the technology at its disposal, and the supply and demand for products and services.[29] The effects of economic conditions are easy to understand in human service organizations. As noted in Chapter 11, the decline in the manufacturing and the rerouting of workers into jobs in the service industry that offer lower wages and few if any benefits have pushed many workers out of the middle class. Corporate downsizing and the decline of defense industries have forced the layoff of business and professional employees. But lower-class Americans have been especially hurt by the redistribution of the shares of money income of families to the richest Americans. As more people have been forced to seek welfare services, those who are more fortunate have responded by seeking tax cuts and tax breaks. A barrage of cutbacks and downsizing has worked to eliminate or at least limit the kinds and extent of services offered by the welfare state.

The *internal economy* of an organization includes its budgeting and accounting systems and the distribution of incentives, rewards, and resources through its division of labor and its allocation of roles and statuses.[30] In economic processes the emphasis in the organization is on the bottom line, as played out in decision making and problem solving for fiscal management. But when different types of organizations must downsize because profits are unsatisfactory, or government contracts have been reduced, or charitable contributions are less than anticipated, or tax revenues have been curtailed, there are major repercussions for the members. Contending coalitions with their own visions and priorities must negotiate the new shape of the organizations, often in a very hard-nosed way.

✆ SMALL GROUPS AND THE CRITICAL APPROACH

Contemporary definitions of the small group evolved out of the work of Charles Cooley, in which the primary group is described as one of intimacy, face-to-face association, and cooperation. In his terms, groups like the family, peer groups, and neighborhoods are primary because "they give the individual his earliest and completest experience of social unity, and…they do not change in the same degree as more elaborate relations, but form a comparatively permanent source out of which the latter are ever springing."[31]

The qualities of small groups described by Cooley have become the bedrock of definitions of small groups. Donelson Forsythe, for instance, identifies the characteristics of small groups as face-to-face interaction, mutual recognition and influence, interdependence, and psychological significance (the group has meaning for the individual).[32] Thus the small group is treated as an ideal type, as in Weber's approach to the definition of large groups, or bureaucracies. This enables researchers to compare small groups on dimensions that are considered essential to all such groups. But there is a difference in the use of ideal types with bureaucracies and with small groups. Most researchers do not think of bureaucracy as an ideal, even though it can be studied as an ideal type of organization. In the literature on small groups, however, the ideal type of organization is clearly considered ideal.

Because the ideal small group would seem to embody some of the noblest elements of human behavior, such as cooperation, interaction, and mutual recognition, it may appear that there is no need for a critical approach to the study of small groups. The research on small groups, however, suggests that such an approach is quite relevant. The study of small-group dynamics was very popular during the 1950s and 1960s but had diminished considerably by the 1970s, not because researchers had resolved all the issues in the study of small groups but because they had concluded that research on groups often was irrelevant to contemporary realities. With some important exceptions, the research had largely been conducted in laboratories with college students (most often white males), in situations that were only vaguely related to group life in the real world.

One criticism of the research on small groups is the tendency to equate them with goodness in human nature and regard them as oases in contemporary society wherein people naturally share and care and relate in meaningful ways. The family, as noted in Chapter 11, may be seen as an oasis in capitalism. But anyone who has observed the darker side of family life, peer-group relations, or any other type of small-group process can readily see that this is not the case; violence in the family and coercive peer and work-group pressures are commonplace. The destructive tendencies of such types of small-group techniques as group-guided interaction and encounter groups have also been documented.[33] The position we take is that small groups are inherently no better and no worse than the larger organizations and institutions in which they are embedded.

The criticisms of bureaucracy are also valid with respect to small groups. Groups have been studied as if they exist in a vacuum, free of environmental constraints, or as consensual units free of contending elements and competing points of view. Decision making and problem solving have been approached as a rational process in which the central importance of power is obscured and conflict is treated as a stage that groups go through.

In the social services, these criticisms readily apply to the literature on resocialization groups. Treatment groups are described as going through a process of determining their goals, as if the members are free to select any goal they wish. A group of adolescents receiving service for delinquent behavior, for instance, could just as well select the goal of developing greater employment opportunities in their community as one of improving their personal skills and correcting their inadequacies; but the former goal is rare in practice, while the latter is common. Is this because delinquent youth automatically confront their shortcomings? Hardly. The fact is that the group treatment is offered within the context of an agency that has been funded to provide a certain kind of service in a certain way, and social workers are assigned as group leaders to assure that the services are delivered that way. Far from being an independent small-group process, the treatment group is embedded in a political economy that gives it a particular configuration.

A critical approach to the study of small groups would emphasize their external and internal political economy, but such an approach has not yet been taken by researchers. In considering how the study of small groups might incorporate the political economy framework, we can only call attention to the limits of present knowledge and suggest how consideration of these principles could improve the fit between small groups and their members with the political and social environments in American society.

∞ THE POLITICAL ECONOMY OF GROUPS AND THE STUDY OF GROUP DYNAMICS

The political economy approach to the study of groups is based on the assumption that all groups exist within a political and economic context and cannot be treated as independent units. The dynamics taking place in a group, therefore, will always be a function of the transactions between the group or its members and the environment, and group behavior will be influenced by events and conditions existing in the larger environment as well as by those existing within the group itself. The political economy approach to the study of small groups requires special attention to issues of power and conflict. Social roles determined by such ascribed characteristics as race and ethnicity and gender, for example, clearly affect group dynamics (see "Behaviors of Women and Men in Groups").

Behaviors of Women and Men in Groups: A Brief Review of the Literature

The social roles of women today are no different from those of men, aside from their roles as daughters, wives, and mothers. They are taking on roles in formal organizations and groups in politics and public administration, community affairs, the arts, and sports and recreation. In work they fill roles as white- and blue-collar workers, as supervisors, managers, and occasionally as executives, or they fill professional roles like social worker, physician, or attorney.

Despite the increasing similarity of gender roles in group life, research on small groups has suggested that the sex composition of groups has implications for group dynamics and performance. However, the methodology has not always produced valid or reliable findings, and there is considerable disagreement on their interpretation and implications. The findings on the relation of gender to group dynamics, therefore, must be viewed with relation to the political economy, or the environmental context, of the organization. The processes that are bringing women fully into the world of formal organizations and groups are likely to be found to have effects on the group behaviors of females and males. These findings are summarized below.

1. *Group formation.* Men and women do not differ in the likelihood of joining groups, and they are somewhat the same in their willingness to join. When differences are evident, the explanation has more to do with social constraints than with genetic predispositions.

2. *Personal space.* Women appear to require less personal space than men. They let others get physically closer to them, and they approach others more closely. Women also take up less space by holding their arms close to their bodies and crossing their legs, whereas men enlarge their personal space by assuming expansive, open positions.

3. *Performance.* Men and women perform differently in groups but the level of performance has a great deal to do with task content. In studies where males perform well, the task is likely to be consistent with the traditional skills, interests, and abilities of men, such as mathematical expertise and physical strength. Women are likely to outperform men on verbal tasks.

4. *Interactions in mixed-gender groups.* The interactions in mixed groups are different from those in same-sex groups; in general, both males and females interact in less stereotypical ways. Men are more willing to talk about themselves and their feelings, and they exhibit a more personal orientation and less disagreement and conflict. Women are less likely to express their personal views in mixed-gender groups; they exhibit more disagreement and conflict and increased instrumental or task-oriented behavior.

5. *Task versus expressive behaviors.* Gender theory suggests that men's behaviors are instrumental while women's are expressive or interpersonally oriented; men are expected to outperform women in task-completion activities, and women are expected to outperform men in social activities. A possible explanation is offered by the concept of expectation states, which maintains that the expectations of group members about the

The relations of small groups to political economy underlies our discussion of the five basic social processes or interactions between individuals and systems through which small groups are maintained or altered: interaction, recruitment, socialization, innovation, and control. These processes, identified by George McCall and J. L. Simmons, were introduced in Chapter 3 in reference to systems theory.[34] It is through such processes

behaviors of others often are based on external status characteristics such as sex. In this view, males assume greater leadership over tasks than females because they are expected to. As the reliance on external status characteristics diminishes, women can be expected to make more contributions to group tasks.

6. *Competitiveness.* Findings on competitiveness in two-party conflicts of interest vary considerably. Among 48 studies on competitiveness, women were found to be more competitive than men in 21 studies and less competitive in 27.

7. *Coalition formation.* In coalitions situations, women are more likely than men to adopt anticompetitive norms. Women also are more likely to divide up payoffs on the basis of equality rather than equity (fairness) and less likely to exclude powerful persons from a coalition or to take full advantage of the weaknesses of others.

8. *Conformity.* While studies generally find that women conform more than men in group situations, variables other than sex may be accountable for these findings. For instance, women conform more than men in studies that involve face-to-face social pressure or that focus on male-oriented topics. In more anonymous, low-surveillance situations or on less sex-role-typed topics, few differences are apparent.

9. *Leadership.* In studies of the emergence of leaders in small, unstructured discussion groups, men generally are found to outnumber women in leadership roles. This occurs even when women appear to be the more dominant personalities. The task content may have something to do with this, and sexist attitudes also play an important role. When warned about a tendency to favor men, men and women are more likely to share leadership.

10. *Leadership style.* The leadership styles of women and men have been found to differ. Women in laboratory groups performed more relationship-oriented acts than men and described themselves in relationship terms on questionnaires, but women in organizations did not. As managers, women tend to be both task- and relationship-oriented, while men are primarily task-oriented. In organizations, it is more likely for women to use a democratic style and men to use an autocratic style.

11. *Leadership effectiveness.* Men and women are equally effective as organizational and group leaders. Because many people assume that men will make better leaders, however, they express a preference for male leaders. This bias is changing as more women are given leadership opportunities and evaluations demonstrate that males are no more effective as leaders than females.

Sources: Donelson R. Forsythe, *Group Dynamics*, 2nd ed. (Pacific Grove, CA: Brooks/Cole, 1983); B. F. Meeker and P. A. Weitzel-O'Neill, "Sex Roles and Interpersonal Behavior in Task-Oriented Groups," *American Sociological Review*, vol. 42, (February 1977), pp. 91–105; Patricia Yancey Martin, "Transcending the Effects of Sex Composition in Small Groups," *Social Work with Groups*, vol. 6, nos. 3–4 (1983), pp. 19–32.

that groups, defined by Ralph Anderson and Irl Carter as "an arena of social interaction," can provide for such human needs as to belong and be accepted, to be validated through feedback, to share experiences with others, and to work with others on shared tasks.[35]

In the discussion of small-group dynamics we will assume that the immediate context of the group is some kind of a bureaucracy, either a private, for-profit or nonprofit organization or a public, governmental agency. Many of the small groups to which people belong in contemporary society are embedded in bureaucracies. Friendship groups, for example, may derive from or be part of large groups like schools, churches, governmental agencies, or voluntary associations. In the social services, employees such as social workers work together with volunteers in groups that are usually part of larger organizations that also include client groups. The family, discussed in Part Three, is perhaps the only small group not directly embedded in a bureaucratic structure.

∞ RECRUITMENT INTO GROUP MEMBERSHIP

Recruitment describes the processes by which we became members of the many groups and organizations we participate in throughout our lives. It refers both to how groups go about attracting members as well as how individuals become members. From the point of view of a group, recruitment is the process of setting up criteria and selecting members. From the individual's point of view, it covers the ways prospective members experience becoming a part of a group. Large organizations are likely to use formal recruiting procedures, but small groups often recruit in an informal, more casual way.

Recruitment is an important aspect of the external political economy of a group. The emphasis in the literature on how to select or join groups suggests that membership is always voluntary and opportunities to join are distributed equally to all. This, of course, is far from the truth in contemporary American society. Despite laws assuring equal opportunities, bureaucracies and the small groups that comprise them do not always adhere to the bureaucratic principle that competency alone determines opportunity. Race, ethnicity, age, gender, physical appearance, and other requirements figure prominently in informal, if not formal, membership requirements. Even peer groups, households, and families may exclude certain members on the basis of social criteria. The ways members choose other members thus are very much in keeping with how the group fits in the political and economic struggles going on in the larger environment.

Recruitment also figures in the group's internal political economy. Many groups and organizations are divided by factions and conflict, and recruitment of new members can be a part of the internal struggle for dominance and control. Recruits are selected in part for their potential to fit in with existing or new coalitions, and they are evaluated on the basis of their ability to add to or subtract from a particular power block, even though they may not be aware of the group conflicts.

Voluntary and Involuntary Membership

We become members of groups in which we participate in various ways. We may choose to join a group, be more-or-less coerced into it, or join out of some sense of obligation. Researchers have found that individual attachment and performance as a member of a group are in part dependent on whether recruitment was voluntary or involuntary. To the extent that recruitment was coercive or obligatory, it can be expected that participation will be less wholehearted, satisfaction will be lower, and both group and individual performance will suffer. Involuntary members are less likely to use the group as a positive reference point, to trust other group members, or to totally accept the norms, goals, and activities of the group.

Attraction in Voluntary Membership

People in industrialized, free-market societies have a lot of freedom to join groups. The emphasis on volition represents an advance from agricultural societies where to a large extent birth determines social participation. Peasants, for instance, were tied to the land and did not have the freedom to sell their skills to an employer for wages. Affiliation in religious groups, in friendships, and in marriage were largely functions of birth. Marriages were arranged and friendships flowed out of the class divisions in the society.

Today it is taken for granted that we can choose our occupations, places of employment, friends, religious affiliations, marital partners, and the neighborhoods, areas, and sometimes even nations in which we live. These **voluntary membership** choices symbolize the essence of what is meant by democracy. In exercising these freedoms, we usually go through some process of being attracted to a group, aspiring to be a member, preparing for membership by learning about the group, and finally joining it.

Researchers have studied the factors that lead people to join groups voluntarily. One is proximity or *propinquity*, that is, nearness in place or time in the physical environment. It is easiest to get to know people and bring them together in groups that are physically close. Material needs also lead to group membership. An underlying reason for joining a work organization or attending a school or university is the possibility of earning enough money or accumulating enough wealth to live well. Meeting basic physical needs may even be a reason for joining a friendship clique, a household, or a partner in matrimony.

Most research on voluntary group formation, however, has found that people join groups largely to meet social-psychological needs. They believe group membership can either directly meet their needs or can lead indirectly to the same result. The research findings about the sources of need satisfaction that follow from this motivational theory of voluntary group formation have been described by Marvin Shaw.[36]

1. *Interpersonal attraction.* Individuals join up with others when they are physically or socially attracted. This is especially the case with regard to friendship formation, but in becoming a part of any group recruits are likely to take into account the attractiveness of existing members and whether they can expect to get along with them. People can be attracted to others because of the way they look, dress, or act or because of attitudes and values they have in common; similarity in attitudes and personality are particularly important in joining friendship groups.[37] Similarity in socioeconomic position, in race, and in sex also is related to recruitment, although this may be less important than attitudinal and physical similarity.[38] Voluntary members have been found to take race into account in forming hypothetical groups, even though many groups now have political and social mandates to achieve racial and ethnic balance (see "Recruiting African Americans into Groups").

2. *Attraction to the activities and goals of the group.* People often join groups because they enjoy the things the group does. A man takes a job in a social service agency because it offers him the ability to do the kind of social work he wants to do. A woman joins an environmental group because she enjoys the outdoors and working on behalf of clean air and the protection of endangered plants and animals.

3. *Attraction to membership.* Some people are attracted to groups because group life is rewarding. They need the company of others.

4. *Need fulfillment.* A number of studies have shown that people sometimes join groups as a means to an end outside the group. A businessperson may join a civic club be-

Recruiting African Americans into Groups

The political economy of many groups and organizations in the United States today indirectly requires them to find ways to recruit members from racial and ethnic minorities. Civil rights legislation and regulations have established that discrimination barring membership in most groups on the basis of race and ethnicity will not be tolerated. However, Americans generally have a long way to go before they can say that formal groups and organizations are truly integrated.

In the social services, group composition poses a particular problem. Although group workers may wish to be color blind in recruiting members, race is a factor in American society that cannot be ignored. The recruitment of minorities into treatment groups is especially sensitive because members are expected to share their most private thoughts and feelings without fear of prejudice, and the tensions provoked by racism may make this impossible.

Larry E. Davis approached the problem of recruiting black and white members into treatment groups through an experimental study of individual preferences for group membership among 80 black and 80 white undergraduates attending a large university. Told they were part of a study on the formation and leadership of groups, the participants were asked to make up a series of groups they would join from descriptions of hypothetical people which included race as one characteristic. Davis wanted to see if race would be ignored or taken into account when the students made up the groups they wanted to be a part of. Because private feelings can differ from public attitudes, they were assured they could fill out the questionnaire in privacy, with confidence that they could not be identified as individuals. And because the race of the experimenter might influence attitudes, 40 white and 40 black participants were led by a black experimenter, and the other 40 of both races were handled by a white experimenter.

Results of the study can be summarized as follows:

1. Both black and white participants preferred groups with different racial compositions, but in putting together ten-member

cause it is considered good for business. Students may enroll in a particular university because of the prestige bestowed on those who attend. Clients may join an interpersonal skills training group in the hope of learning how to get along with others.

Involuntary Membership and Mixed Motives

Even though we have great opportunities for voluntary membership, we may also be pressed into **involuntary membership** in groups. Involuntary membership may be an accident of birth; as infants we have no control over the household, community, or nation into which we are born, for instance. Where recruitment is concerned, however, the central issue is whether people are coerced to enter a group against their will.

Incarceration in a prison or being drafted into military service during war are the most obvious examples of coercive recruitment. But there are others; as we noted in Part Two, the African-American and Native American communities were forced into membership in American society. There is also involuntary membership in social service organizations; although many clients voluntarily seek service, for a sizable number it is

groups, blacks selected significantly more black members than whites did. On average, blacks selected 4.82 black members, while whites selected 3.45. Blacks also selected more of their own race in putting together five-member groups, 2.78 compared to 1.72 blacks selected by whites.

2. The nature of the group task was a significant factor in determining the racial composition of groups. When told that the group would be very informal and intimate, blacks increased the number of other blacks selected; whites did not.

3. The number of blacks selected for the groups depended both on the size of the group that was to be selected and the number of blacks in the selection pool. Regardless of either factor, blacks selected significantly more blacks than whites did. The difference in the number of blacks chosen by blacks and whites declined, however, as the size of the group and the number in the selection pool increased.

4. Race was only one of eight characteristics used in describing potential group members; some of the others were age, interests, academic major, and personal traits. Yet the only variable on which blacks and whites differed in selecting group members was race. On the whole, blacks placed significantly more importance on race as a requisite for group participation than whites did.

5. The race of the group leader did not significantly influence the selection process.

The findings of this study represent an attempt to make generalizations about the group membership preferences of black and white Americans. The situation was hypothetical, and the sample was drawn from young adult college students. More research is needed to replicate the findings and explore the effects of race on voluntary group membership and the formation of racially balanced groups.

Source: Larry E. Davis, "Racial Composition of Groups," *Social Work*, vol. 24 (May 1979), pp. 208–13.

ordered because they are in some kind of trouble. They may be institutionalized in a mental hospital or correctional facility, or they may be under court order to participate in a counseling group or community service organization. These often are the most resistive clients, and they require special handling.[39]

We also become members of groups for reasons that involve a mix of voluntary and involuntary motives. Some members voluntarily join groups because of underlying involuntary processes, such as the expectations others have of them. Students study medicine or attend religious services because their parents expect them to. They join sororities or fraternities because their best friends do. Workers accept appointments to task groups or committees because their bosses expect them to or it would look good on a resume. Sometimes the underlying process is not attraction to one group but lack of attraction to another. Homeless people take menial service jobs because living on the streets is worse, economically and in terms of self-esteem. In each case, the people do not have to join, but they can't afford not to.

Many social service clients have mixed motives for group participation. They come for service because they have to as much as because they want to. Children are sent to counselors by parents or by teachers. Adults come out of necessity because the problems they are dealing with begin to overwhelm them. Some come because their spouses or partners have cajoled them into it.

∽ SOCIALIZATION INTO GROUP ROLES

We learn how to function as group members through a process of socialization which makes us aware of the expectations of others and helps us develop the abilities, knowledge, and attitudes necessary to comply with those expectations. In the context of the group, socialization refers to the processes through which individual participation is defined and refined. It is not a one-way process, however, but should be seen in terms of a process of negotiation between old and new members, a means through which control is exercised but innovation can also be introduced. Neither is socialization limited to infants and children. It is a much broader phenomenon which takes place throughout the life course whenever an individual participates in social life.

Socialization into adult roles differs from the process in early life. Orville Brim hypothesizes that the content of socialization changes in six basic ways as we move from childhood and family socialization to adulthood and socialization in large and small groups. These changes move the individual:

1. From values and motives to overt behavior.
2. From the acquisition of new material to the synthesis of already-acquired knowledge.
3. From idealism to realism.
4. From expectations to the mediation of conflict.
5. From the general demands of society to role-specific demands.
6. From the egocentric "I-me" to the other centered "I-them" or "they-me."[40]

Some of these shifts in the content of socialization can be seen in the processes that take place when clients become involved in group work in social services. Some socialization takes place formally, perhaps through an open discussion with the group leader and members or the distribution of printed handouts about the group. Some takes place informally, through nonverbal communication, off-the-cuff remarks, open debate, or the exchange of information between new and old members. Most socialization, however, is focused on explaining the role-specific demands and behaviors associated with being a client: the meetings members will be expected to attend, the topics and focus of group discussion, and the need to talk openly, express feelings, be nonjudgmental, and hold group discussions in confidence. Group work teaches clients to be realistic; they learn that discussion will not cure them of all problems but perhaps provide them with some insight or skill for coping with future difficulties. They also learn that in being helped they can be helpful to others, because the group is focused not just on a particular member but on ways the members can help one another.

The internal political economy of the group has a lot to do with the socialization of the members. While the literature on socialization suggests that groups are typified by *consensus*, a set of shared values and purposes they pass on to new members, from a political economy perspective group socialization occurs within the context of conflict over goals, values, and the means to achieve them. Individuals are in effect socialized into the conflicts of the group; they learn not only how to perform a role within a group or organization but how to understand the politics of that role.

Socialization across the Life Cycle of Membership

Our socialization into a group is not a single event in our lives but a continuing process that stretches from our recruitment to our withdrawal. Phases of ongoing socialization have been identified by theorists such as Brim, Stanton Wheeler, and R. L. Moreland and J. M. Levine.[41] The anticipatory, entry, maintenance, resocialization, and exit phases can be considered from a political economy perspective.

1. *Anticipatory socialization.* People being recruited into a group usually are given information about it and may prepare by becoming better acquainted with the group, its members, and the kind of political economy they can expect to find.

2. *Entry socialization.* New members pass through a process of assimilation during which they review their preconceptions about the group and its political economy and change these ideas if necessary. Often they approach the group cautiously, especially if they have mixed motives in joining. They may remain quiet or aloof, or they may misinterpret the information they are being given about the roles they are expected to assume.[42] As new members assimilate the political economy of the group and their place in it, the group begins to accommodate itself to them. Other members come to understand their values, abilities, and capacities and may realign themselves in these terms. If the needs and interests of new members are not accommodated in a positive way, they might become rebellious, quit the group, or make some other kind of adaptation.

3. *Maintenance socialization.* In this period the focus is on the processes of role negotiation and renegotiation. Full membership is achieved when members accept their roles and statuses within the group and begin to participate fully in group activities. Nevertheless, socialization continues, because groups and organizations change according to internal and external demands. In businesses, product lines and production schedules shift; in government agencies, policies and directives change; in social services, programs may be eliminated or added. Members find that what is expected of them can change.

4. *Resocialization of marginal or failing members.* As group change occurs, some members may not assimilate the new expectations, or the group may not continue to accommodate them. Members may fail in their roles or become marginalized and no longer participate fully. Resocialization is an attempt to revitalize role performance and maintain the connection between the individual and the group.

5. *Exit socialization and remembrance.* Some people leave groups because of their inability to resolve problems of role failure or marginalization. Others leave because they find other groups and organizations that are a better match for their interests. And some leave as a matter of course; they die, retire, or reach a built-in limitation where they are expected to leave, as in a treatment group or a university program. When members leave this way, the departure may be marked by a rite or ritual such as a funeral, retirement party, or graduation ceremony. A period of remembrance follows in which former members may try to fit their experiences in the group to a new definition of self and the group may reminisce about them and incorporate experiences with them into its history and traditions.

⊗ INTERACTION IN TASK PERFORMANCE

Our participation in groups is implemented through processes of interaction whereby members influence one another and groups or organizations are shaped, reshaped, or terminated. Rather than being a separate process, interaction refers to any of the day-to-day transactions in which we engage as we are brought into groups and socialized into group roles, and our participation is controlled or changed. We will consider interaction in terms of task performance, which involves the processes of decision making and problem solving.

Task performance, the fulfillment of the official or operative goals of the group, is usually seen as a rational process in which tasks are accomplished in a series of sequential, logical steps. Although the specific nature of these steps or phases varies in theorists' views of group task performance, there is general compatibility among them (see "Three Views on Phases in Group Task Performance").

From the critical perspective, there are a number of problems with using rational change models such as phases in task performance to describe group behavior. One is that conflict is not adequately taken into account. Rational change models reflect a consensus bias; conflict is seen as only a phase sandwiched between normally harmonious group relations, as in B. W. Tuckman's storming phase.[43] Even more problematic, the logical and rational progression of stages hypothesized in such models is rarely observed in natural groups. There are no set phases in group problem solving; some groups avoid particular stages and others move through them in a unique order, or they may develop in ways that are not described by the model.[44]

Nevertheless, stages of group behavior can be a useful device for thinking about group processes, particularly for understanding common kinds of group phenomena. Joseph McGrath uses phases as a way of examining knowledge on such relevant issues as planning and creativity, problem solving, decision making, and conflict resolution.[45] These processes may not always follow in order or be present in every group, but they do represent processes that are common in groups.

Planning and Creativity

Many students of group processes make the assumption that normal group behavior does not lead to very creative planning. This may be the case, since decision making can easily go awry. The term *social loafing*, coined to account for the common finding that individuals in groups are not likely to work up to their maximum potential in terms of physical effort,[46] has also been documented in terms of creativity.[47] To increase the creative capacity of groups, various methods have been devised and tested.

Brainstorming is a technique developed by Alex Osborn to help groups generate ideas or overcome blocks in their thinking. Members are asked to think of as many ideas about a particular problem as they can within a stated time period. There is a sense of openness, because other group members may not interrupt, question, or challenge emerging ideas.[48] Brainstorming is often used as a group technique, but its success in generating creative thinking is not always clear. Status and perceived authority among group members can operate to inhibit their responses. According to McGrath, the research finding that stands out is "individuals working separately generate many more, and more creative (as rated by judges) ideas than do groups." Nevertheless, when the technique is

---

Three Views on Phases in Group Task Performance

The commonalities in the phases or steps in group task performance proposed by various theorists are readily apparent in the lists below. The phases are numbered in sequence for organizational purposes, though they may overlap or take different positions in practice. In task performance, however, the process always starts with planning the task and ends with its completion.

Donelson Forsythe (1983)	B. W. Tuckman (1965)	Joseph E. McGrath (1984)
1. ORIENTATION Define problem, plan process	1. FORMING Exchange information, increase interdependence, explore task, identify commonalities	1. GENERATE Generate ideas, plans
2. DISCUSSION Gather data, identify/ evaluate	2. STORMING Deal with conflict and resistance	2. CHOOSE Solve problems, make choices
3. DECISION MAKING Choose solutions	3. NORMING Develop cohesion, establish roles, standards, relationships	3. NEGOTIATE Resolve conflicts of ideas and interests
4. IMPLEMENTATION Adhere to decision, evaluate decision	4. PERFORMING Goal achievement, perform tasks	4. EXECUTE Perform tasks
	5. ADJOURNING Complete task, terminate role, reduce dependency	

Sources: Donelson R. Forsythe, *Group Dynamics*, 2nd ed. (Pacific Grove, CA: Brooks/Cole, 1983), pp. 285–94; B. W. Tuckman, "Developmental Sequence in Small Groups," *Psychological Bulletin*, vol. 63, no. 6 (1965), pp. 384–99; Joseph E. McGrath, *Groups: Interaction and Performance* (Englewood Cliffs, NJ: Prentice-Hall, 1984), pp. 60–66.

---

used correctly in groups, they will generate more ideas, perhaps even more creative ones, than groups in which no idea-generating techniques is used.[49]

The **nominal group technique** (NGT) differs from brainstorming in that the members of a group work independently and then bring their ideas to the group to participate in a round robin exchange of ideas. Each idea presented is recorded on a flip chart and discussed for clarification, and the group then chooses the best ideas and rank orders them.[50] Research has not established that groups using NGT necessarily improve their results; it has not been adequately tested on natural groups and falls short when used by researchers other than those who have invented or developed it.[51] Nevertheless, the claims made for NGT are impressive. Among other things, it promises to serve the members' social and emotional needs while focusing on task, to foster the generation of ideas, to reduce conformity, to produce greater equality in participation, and to keep conflict from becoming personalized. It appears to be a promising if not completely proven strategy for improving group creativity and planning.

Solving Problems and Making Decisions

Problem solving and decision making are at the heart of the phases of group task performance. Forsythe's four phases—orientation, discussion, decision making, and implementation (see "Three Views on Phases in Group Task Performance")—closely follow the management by objectives (MBO) process that has been applied in social service organizations. The problem-solving process for the basic helping approach, for example, is described in Chapter 2 as a series of four steps: needs assessment, determining the objectives of intervention and formulating an intervention plan, putting the intervention strategies into practice, and evaluation. As a phase of group task performance, problem solving and decision making may be more of a circular process than a linear one, as different alternatives are tried and new objectives and plans are chosen.

Social Decision Schemes

Problem solving and decision making in groups concocted for the purposes of research have been examined through the lens of *social decision schemes*, the implicit rules that govern group decisions. These schemes include: truth wins (the correct answer, once stated, is chosen), truth supported wins (at least two members find the correct answer and the group is swayed), unanimity wins, strong majority wins, and bare majority wins. Groups usually adopt the "truth supported wins" scheme when there is a clearly correct answer or there is a correct answer but it is not easily demonstrated. However, most groups find themselves trying to make decisions or solve problems in situations where there is no compellingly correct answer. This is the reality in most bureaucracies as well as in families and small groups.[52]

To study how groups behave in these situations, a good deal of research has focused on decision making in mock juries. Real juries cannot be studied because of legal and ethical considerations, so groups of participants are put in situations that resemble jury duty. They are given a summary of a case and asked to discuss it and reach a verdict. Examination of the decisions clearly indicates that such groups do not act according to a "truth wins" or a "truth supported wins" scheme. They try to reach a consensus, but they do not seem to strive for unanimity. Rather, a strong majority wins.

Groupthink

There is no assurance that group processes inevitably produce good decisions. Sometimes the decisions made by groups are so bad that the wonder is they were ever arrived at. President J.F. Kennedy remarked, "How could we have been so stupid?" when told of the outcome of the decision he and his advisers reached to intervene in Cuba shortly after the socialist revolution led by Fidel Castro. The Bay of Pigs invasion in 1961 was a humiliating defeat for the troops of Cuban refugees who had been trained by the CIA. Irving L. Janis studied this and other examples of disastrous decisions and concluded that the

The director of a program for children with disabilities leads a team of
teachers and social workers in the problem-solving and decision-
making phases of task performance. The everyday functioning of large
bureaucracies often takes place in the context of such small, more
informal work groups.

errors stemmed from a process he named **groupthink**: "a quick and easy way to refer to
the mode of thinking that persons engage in when *concurrence-seeking* becomes so dominant in a cohesive ingroup that it tends to override realistic appraisal of alternative courses of action" (italics in original).[53]

Some of the symptoms of groupthink, in addition to a powerful, personally experienced pressure to conform, are :

1. Self-censoring of doubts and critical thoughts.
2. Mindguards, or self-appointed vigilantes who act to assure that only certain kinds of
   information and opinions are expressed.
3. An illusion of unanimity within the group.
4. An illusion of invulnerability that leads to overoptimism and risk-taking.
5. Negative stereotypes of out-groups and their leaders.
6. Belief in the morality of the group and avoidance of the ethical consequences of decisions.

Such group characteristics may make rational decision making impossible. Assessment of
diverse opinions and alternatives is limited, and little use is made of available resources for
knowledge and information.

Conflict Resolution

In the context of group task performance, there are two major kinds of group conflict: **cognitive conflicts**, arising from differences among individuals in perceptions, beliefs, and ways of thinking, and **conflicts of interest**, or conflicts arising from motives or the possibility of differential rewards and benefits.

Cognitive Conflict

Cognitive conflict in groups is basically concerned with differences of opinion. One way it has been studied is with **social judgment theory**, which uses laboratory techniques to determine the ways different personal and organizational "judgment policies" affect the decisions. Typically, the research design uses two-person, concocted groups. Participants either are trained to take opposite sides of an issue or are chosen because they think differently about it.[54] In one group of experiments, the two-person groups were asked to predict the future level of democracy in a certain country. One member was trained to believe that democracy was dependent on a government chosen by elections, and the other was trained to believe that it depended on the degree of control by the state over behavior. The situation was designed to produce a high degree of objective disagreement in judgments, rather than a subjective feeling that disagreement existed. When the two members disagreed they were given an opportunity to discuss their differences and try to come to some agreement.

The situation created is a benign form of conflict, since the participants have nothing personally to gain or lose from reaching these agreements. Nevertheless, researchers have found that disagreement remains high even after the groups have had a good many chances to smooth out their differences and learn from each other. They come to think alike in the course of their interaction, but the way they apply their new thinking is inconsistent. They may agree that democracy depends on both the level of individual control and the level of government by elections, for instance, but they do not apply this new way of thinking consistently. Thus they achieve "policy similarity" but not "policy consistency."

Researchers also have found that any change in organizational policy leads to conflict in the application of the new policy. This is evident even when group members start out thinking the same way and there is no basic disagreement. Although the laboratory manipulation simplifies real-life cognitive conflicts, social judgment researchers have found the same results in actual labor-management disputes and in government bureaucracy. Through group discussion cognitive disagreements can be erased, but conflict persists because new ways of thinking are applied inconsistently.

The study of racial- and ethnic-group and gender differences has shown that these conflicts are often cognitive in nature; women are believed to speak from a "different voice,"[55] while ethnic minorities are believed to operate from different cognitive maps.[56] The results of experiments using men and women and people of different nationalities suggest that while such differences in cognitive styles may be resolved and agreements reached on issues, conflict is likely to continue until people learn to apply the new way of thinking consistently.

Conflicts of Interest

Among the studies that have focused on conflicts of interest in group task performance, those that have examined negotiation and bargaining tasks typically focus on how people with competing objectives and goals compromise and reach a common ground. One approach to the study of these processes is based on the level of expectation. Concessions by one bargaining party are said to raise the expectation of the other party, who then takes a get-tough stance; expecting more, more is demanded.[57] The opposite is said to be true when negotiations are deadlocked; then one side must initiate a small concession, which will be reciprocated with a concession by the other.[58] Both of these theories are correct, but they apply to different situations.[59] When there is no bargaining deadlock, getting tough will help to produce further concessions in favor of the demanding party. When there is a deadlock, offering concessions is a necessary step in unlocking it.

∞ INNOVATION AND CONTROL PROCESSES IN GROUP CHANGE

Innovation and control are the processes through which participation in a group or organization is altered or changed. Control and innovation are two sides of the same coin; group control refers to how our participation is constrained by the expectations of others, while group innovation refers to how we respond to the constraints imposed by others and alter our expectations. Innovation and control have been studied by focusing on the related factors of leadership, power, and conformity.

Leaders and Leadership

In our participation in groups we take the roles of leaders or followers to varying degrees. Formal organizational charts such as the one in "Organizational Chart for a Social Work Bureaucracy" readily indicate the positions of the designated leaders; in this one, they are the director, the associate director, and the unit supervisors. Families and other small groups also have leaders, either formal leaders designated by law, religious tradition, or group members, or informal leaders such as opinion leaders and others who emerge through group processes. It is the task of the leader to lead, but this truism raises a number of troublesome questions. Does it mean that if we are not in leadership positions but are followers we cannot lead? How does a leader lead? Is any way of leading more effective than another?

While *leader* is a role people occupy in a status hierarchy, *leadership* is a behavior that influences others to do something. Thus the exercise of leadership is independent of one's role or position in a group. Designated leaders may or may not show leadership, and the same holds for followers. However, the literature on leadership is overwhelmingly focused on the role of the leader. Reflecting political and economic realities, most researchers have set their sights on understanding how leaders lead and subordinates follow.

Leadership Style

A major research topic is whether leaders should allow subordinates to demonstrate leadership, that is, to participate in decision making. The question is: Is leadership more effective when it controls subordinates or when it allows them to innovate? The answer that has been found by researchers is very complex and filled with if, ands, or buts.

Kurt Lewin, one of the early theorists in group dynamics, conducted laboratory experiments to test whether democratic leadership styles are superior to authoritarian and laissez-faire leadership styles.[60] He and his associates set up a simple research situation: groups of boys 10 and 11 years old met after school to work on hobbies in the presence of three types of leaders. **Authoritarian leaders** totally controlled the behaviors of group members by making decisions and assigning tasks with no input from them. **Laissez-faire leaders** allowed group members to do anything they wished; they offered no direction, made no decisions, and simply acted as a source of technical information. Total innovation was allowed for group members. The style of **democratic leaders** fell between the two extremes. They discussed goals and activities with the group members, encouraged the development of an egalitarian atmosphere, and allowed members to make decisions about specific projects and to choose work partners. Democratic leaders controlled the general work situation but allowed innovation within it.

The results showed that the determination of effective leadership depends on the criteria being investigated. Democratic groups were the friendliest, the most group-oriented, the least likely to express discontent, and the least dependent on the actions of the leader. But these groups were neither the most productive nor the most likely to work hard when the leader was absent. Autocratic groups spent the most time working in the presence of the leader and the least time working when the leader was out of the room. Laissez-faire groups did the opposite, spending the least time working in the leader's presence and the most time working in the leader's absence. Democratic groups were a close runner-up in both these situations; they worked fairly hard regardless of whether the leader was present or absent.

Although this study is methodologically primitive, its findings that democratic leadership does not necessarily bring about the highest level of productivity has been supported by many other studies. R. M. Stogdill reviewed some 40 studies and concluded that no one single leadership style is consistently better at encouraging productivity than another.[61] Given the emphasis on productivity in an industrial, free-market society, the finding that democratic leadership does not necessarily generate the highest levels is troublesome. If the primary goal is to create friendly, cooperative groups, a democratic style is great. If the goal is to maximize production, then democracy will not necessarily work.

Many factors have to be taken into account in predicting productivity. Victor Vroom and his associates hypothesize that democratic processes that allow for considerable participation by group members increase the satisfaction and productivity of a group, but only in certain situations. In his *normative model of leadership* he outlines a range of leadership styles, from those that emphasize complete leader control to those that allow for maximum member participation. He argues that no one style will work in every situation; rather, the most effective leadership style depends on such things as how knowledgeable the leader is, whether group members accept organizational goals, how structured the task is, and how much conflict exists in the group.[62]

Fred Fiedler's *contingency model of leadership* also recognizes that no one style of leadership will work in every situation. He posits two basic styles, task-oriented and interpersonally oriented leadership, each of which can be effective in particular situations. Three aspects of the situation need to be taken into account: the relationship between the leader and the members, the structure of the task, and the authority of the leader. A task-oriented style is recommended, for instance, when there is a good relationship between leader and members, the task is highly structured, and the leader enjoys a high level of support in the bureaucracy. In other situations, a more interpersonal style of leadership may be needed.[63]

Power in Groups

In group task performance, power is our ability to influence others and get our way in social interaction. One way power has been studied is in terms of nonzero-sum and zero-sum outcomes. In a nonzero-sum approach, power is seen as a shared resource of groups and organizations; people have "power with" others. Therefore power resides in the total ability of group members working together toward some common effort. The "pie" to be shared is assumed to be always expandable, and there are no conflicts of interest. If the leader can unify members around a common goal, the group or organization will have considerable power. In a **zero-sum approach**, a gain for one person or group means a loss for the other. Power is held at the expense of others; people have "power over" others. Since risks and benefits are not equally distributed among groups or group members, they have different stakes in the outcome. The "pie" is not expandable, and there is debate over how to cut it up. Zero-sum power is present in situations of inequality, and it is used to maintain and increase differences.[64]

Although both these ways of understanding the use of power in groups are valuable, zero-sum power is a more basic approach. Power as a shared attribute of a group comes into play only when no inequalities exist or people are satisfied with their position in a hierarchy, and both of these situations are relatively rare in a free-market, democratic society. Zero-sum differences in power are often evident in family and friendship groups, and status differences between women and men and between children and adults underlie family conflicts. They are even more common in bureaucracies and small groups. Most theories of bureaucracy take as a given an unequal distribution of resources and rewards and attempt to explain how power over others is (or should be) wielded.[65]

Power and Authority

A distinction must be made between power and authority, though both have elements of power. **Authority** is power legitimated by appointment or election or power that accrues to individuals as a function of their position or role in society or the groups and organizations that make it up. **Power** refers to behaviors of individuals that enable them to prevail in interactions with others, regardless of any social position they may hold. Power differs from authority in one other respect. Authority is rooted in a status relationship, that is, relationships between superiors and subordinates, and power is not. Anyone in any position can conceivably exercise power.

In Weber's theoretical work on bureaucracy, he distinguished two other bases of authority in addition to rational-legal: charismatic and traditional. *Charismatic authority* is based on the special characteristics of an individual—a commanding presence, a unique message, or an overwhelming personality—that give him or her social legitimation. Charismatic leaders need not personify values we consider good or worthwhile; they lead by the force of their personalities. *Traditional authority* is based on social norms and values implanted in social institutions. For instance, Judeo-Christian religions support the authority of the patriarch, that is, the supposedly preordained power of men over women. *Rational-legal authority*, as we have noted, is based on the power of laws, rules, and regulations that emerge from democratic processes and are presumably connected with desirable goals and outcomes. It is limited authority in most contemporary bureaucracies that attaches to group members solely as a function of their position.

Types of Power

J. R. P. French and B. Raven, working in the context of small groups, have identified five bases of individual power: legitimate, reward, coercive, referent, and expert.[66] *Legitimate power* is based on the right of one person to require and command compliance from another. This is similar to rational-legal authority, although it does not require an officially recognized status relationship; it may be as simple as the situation of one man who has been done a favor by another who is now cashing in his bargaining chips. Legitimate power exists anytime people have internalized a value that dictates others have a right to influence them.

Reward power and coercive power refer to the "carrot or stick" approach to getting one's way. *Reward power* involves the distribution of monetary, social, and other benefits to gain compliance; *coercive power* derives from the capacity to physically or psychologically punish those who fail to comply. *Referent power* is based on identification, attraction, or respect. This is akin to Weber's charismatic authority; referent power is charisma before it is legitimated by society. *Expert power* derives from the possession of superior ideas, skills, or abilities.

The ideas of French and Raven have been applied in testing power relations in real-life interactions between superordinates and subordinates.[67] In general, these studies conclude that the use of expert power and referent power is positively related to subordinate performance, job satisfaction, and satisfaction with supervisors; reward, coercive, and legitimate power are generally not related or are negatively related to these outcomes. However, caution must be taken in interpreting these findings. Phillip Podsakoff and Chester Schriesheim, in an extensive review of these studies, point out that a majority of these studies have severe methodological shortcomings, and studies in different theoretical frameworks have found that the use of rewards is a very effective mode of influence. Studies based solely on the attitudes of subordinates may be picking up a social desirability effect; that is, subordinates say they are influenced by expertise and respect because these are socially approved ways for accepting influence; a desire for rewards or a fear of punishment are not.[68]

Other studies on the use of power suggest that these five bases of power are often used in combination; and when people are asked to describe the kinds of tactics they use to influence others, there appear to be more than five. Forsythe, in reviewing the literature, found 22 different tactics of power. Some are variations on reward, coercive, and legitimate power: the use of rewards, promises, punishments, threats, bullying, demands, supplication, and pressure. Others are variations on referent and expert power: the use of charm, ingratiation, instruction, discussion, and persuasion. But a number of others are somewhat independent types, including fait accompli (just doing it), negotiation, persistence, manipulation, evasion (power by avoiding issues), and disengagement (power by breaking off the interaction).[69]

Power tactics often depend on the status of the person using them. One study found that managers tend to mix a number of "strong" tactics (threats, demands, fait accompli) and "weak" or indirect tactics (manipulation, ingratiation, dropping hints, and evasion) when dealing with subordinates. In dealing with superiors, they rely on "rational" tactics like persuasion, discussion, and bargaining.[70] Personality also plays a part in the use of power. People who are concerned about acceptance tend to use indirect or rational tactics; those who indicate a manipulative personality also tend to use indirect tactics but use nonrational ones such as emotionality and misinformation as well.[71]

Conformity

The study of conformity is one of the most perplexing topics in group dynamics. As social systems, groups have considerable power over their members, and those who persist in deviating from group norms may be scapegoated or ostracized. Conformity to the expectations of the group often is the rule rather than the exception.

One of the earliest studies on conformity was conducted by Solomon Asch. He concocted groups of supposedly randomly chosen members who were actually in league with the experimenter and were trained to behave in a predetermined way. An innocent or uninformed participant then joined this group and was asked to judge which of three lines was equal in length to a fourth line. While two lines clearly matched, the trained members all stated that other lines that were obviously not equal in length were the match. The innocent member thus was confronted with "two irreconcilable forces: the evidence of his own experience of an utterly clear perceptual fact, and the unanimous evidence of a[n apparent] group of equals." Although most participants trusted their own judgment, fully a third went along with the group. The fact so large a minority would conform in a situation where the group was so obviously wrong was disturbing.[72]

This experiment and others like it set off a debate about the nature of conformity. The results of the Asch experiment suggest that conformity is wrong and people should stand up for the things they believe in. Conformity is seen as a loss of individuality, a restriction of autonomy, and a reduction of all to a level of mediocrity. Others have pointed out that conformity has positive functions: It introduces order into a group and allows for the coordination of activities, and without a certain level of conformity, group life would be chaotic because members would never know what to expect.[73] Both sides, of course, are correct. Conformity is at once necessary and unfortunate, good and bad. The situation in the Asch experiment is clearly one in which conformity is bad, because it shows that group pressure is capable of forcing people to doubt their judgments.

Another experiment by Stanley Milgram also demonstrated the invidious nature of conformity in the face of unjust pressure.[74] His experiment differed from Asch's in two basic ways. Whereas Asch concocted a peer group in which the members were relative equals, in Milgram's research situation there was a clear leader, an experimenter representing Yale University or a fictitious corporation. Milgram's experiment therefore has to do with obedience to authority. And while in Asch's experiment the innocent participants were asked to perform a harmless task, in Milgram's an authority told them to do something harmful to others.

Two people were told they were to take part in an experiment to examine the connection between punishment and learning. One of them was in fact a confederate of the experimenter and was assigned to play the role of the learner, and the other was the real participant, who, as the teacher, was to apply increasing levels of shock whenever the learner made an error. No actual shocks were administered, but the learner acted as if they were. The shock levers were marked from 15 to 450 volts and labeled "slight shock," "extreme shock," "danger: severe shock," and the like. When teachers could not see or hear the learners, all were willing to apply the highest, potentially most lethal levels of shock. Even when the teachers could hear pounding on the wall and screaming, over 60 percent were willing to apply very high levels of shock. Thus in the Milgram experiment, as in the Asch experiment, people in groups appear prone to go against what assuredly must be their better judgment.

To fully understand the functioning of conformity and obedience in groups, the social and psychological processes that mediate them must be taken into account. With regard to social processes, the power and number of individuals making up the group and their physical and social proximity to each other are important considerations. The number of individuals for and against an issue is particularly crucial, because the existence of allies alters the likelihood of conformity. In the Asch experiments, for instance, conformity decreased sharply when there were two innocent targets of group pressure. With regard to psychological processes, cognitive factors mediate conformity. Individuals are likely to define a situation as one in which rebellion or conformity is called for. If they hold personal values that are in opposition to the position taken by the group and realize them through an exchange of information with others, and if those values are triggered by others in the group who model rebellious behavior and it is reinforced by group pressures, they are more likely to disobey authority or refuse to conform to peer pressure.[75]

⌘ IMPLICATIONS FOR PRACTICE

The study of group organizations and dynamics has implications for the issue of normal functioning in social service practice. The three ways of describing normal individuals introduced in Chapter 2—normal as a statistical average, as healthy, and as utopia—can be applied to groups as well. The concept of normality as transactional social systems is also very much related to life in groups and organizations.

The normal functioning of a group or organization from a political economy point of view can be described in terms of the discussion of large and small groups in this chapter. The average group is likely to be a difficult experience for the individuals in it because group dynamics are marked by conflict and the use of power tactics. Recruitment and socialization, as well as task accomplishment through decision making and problem solving, take place in a context of contending political and economic realities and competing forces of control and innovation. The external environment is not always supportive. In the internal environment, also, people in positions of authority have the upper hand, and obedience is demanded even when rational-legal authority oversteps its bounds.

Social service workers should not be surprised by the conflict present in a group but see it as a normal, ongoing process. Group conflict is not something to be eliminated or accepted as a necessary phase in getting to more harmonious relationships. It has positive functions because it is through conflict that power structures can be changed and with them the goals and activities of the group. The idea of a group without conflict is appealing, but it is a fiction. Peaceful and harmonious groups are exceptional or a temporary pause in ongoing conflict.

Nevertheless, while group and organizational conflict is normal in the statistical sense, social workers are committed to moving a group toward a state of normalcy that can be described as healthy. The role of the practitioner, as a leader of a small group, a manager or executive, or a line worker, is to demonstrate leadership in terms of task performance and social and emotional harmony. The goal is to keep conflict at a workable level, one where the group or organization remains stable and accomplishes its tasks. When this goal cannot be achieved, the practitioner is faced with difficult choices: to dissolve the group, to vacate the leadership position, or to simply endure the conflict, especially if alternative employment opportunities are unavailable.

Some group theorists go a step further and propose more utopian visions of groups and organizations. Feminist ideals on how to organize and manage social services, for example, are based on the premise that effective services must meet the immediate needs

---

Feminist Human Service Agencies

A vision of bureaucracy that follows from the human relations approach but is infused with unique feminist goals and values lies behind the proposal of Claudette McShane and John Oliver for the development of distinctively feminist human service agencies. In comparing various dimensions of conventional agencies and alternative agencies that would embody feminist ideals, they juxtapose the normal-as-average agency with a utopian feminist vision of the normal agency.

	Feminist Agency	Conventional Agency
Authority structure	Collegial	Hierarchical
Performance guides	Internalization of feminist ideology	White male ideology, a priori rules
Problem-solving process	Collective decision making	Formalized, standardized, routinized
Relations among staff/clients	Personalized	Impersonal
Client feelings and attitudes	Belonging, solidarity, collective potency	Unwanted, individualistic, impotent
Funding and in-kind support	A. Solicitation from female system B. Formation of feminist coalitions	A. Proposals to conventional sources B. Collateral support from status quo
Funding consequences	Feminist goals maintained	Social-change goals compromised

Source: Adapted from Claudette McShane and John Oliver, "Women's Groups as Alternative Human Service Agencies," *Journal of Sociology and Social Welfare,* vol. 5 (September 1978), pp. 615–25.

---

of women and enhance their political, economic, and social positions in society (see "Feminist Human Service Agencies"). Another utopian vision of the normal group underlies the proposal by Urania Glassman and Len Kates that group workers strive to build a humanistic group (see "Values of the Humanistic Group"). Neither of these alternatives attempts to shut out conflicts; rather, each incorporates it under special principles and rules of operation.

Utopian visions are unrealistic, but they serve a very important purpose in a critical perspective on social service practice. These visions push social service workers to think about the full potential of groups and organizations. The remaining chapters of Part IV examine four theories of social interaction, each one with a particular understanding of social organization and a particular utopian vision of what might be possible in group and organizational life. Focusing on the full human potential takes into consideration both the pragmatic, the probable and likely, and the ideal, the maximum to be striven for. In the real world of social service practice, the pragmatic will likely win out, but highlighting utopian visions may light the torch for progress through interpersonal, group and organizational change and reform.

Values of the Humanistic Group

In the utopian vision of the normal group adopted by Urania Glassman and Len Kates, the values are humanistic, supporting the dignity and worth of the individuals participating in groups and organizations.

People have inherent worth and capacities regardless of race, class, status, age, and gender, as well as physical and psychological condition.

People are responsible for and to one another because social life is a natural and necessary human characteristic.

People have a right to belong and to be included.

Because people have emotional and intellectual voices that are essential to their existence, they have a right to take part and to be heard.

People have the right to freedom of speech and freedom of expression.

Differences among members provide enriching experiences.

People have a right to freedom of choice, to determine their own destinies.

People have the right to question and challenge professionals who have sanction to guide and direct their lives.

Source: Urania Glassman and Len Kates, *Group Work: A Humanistic Approach* (Newbury Park, CA: Sage, 1990), pp. 23–24.

DISCUSSION QUESTIONS AND CLASS PROJECTS

1. Identify the following terms and concepts:

   groups
   aggregates
   large group
   bureaucracy
   rational-legal authority
   specialization
   formalization
   standardization
   routinization
   ideal type
   scientific management
   human relations approach
   internal economy
   external economy
   internal polity
   external polity

2. Name and describe the five types of small groups that have been identified

   in the literature. Have you had experiences in any of these? If so, describe them.

3. Describe the ideal-type features of a bureaucracy as envisioned by Max Weber. Compare and contrast this with the scientific management, human relations, and political economy approaches to bureaucracy. Where does a feminist vision of bureaucracy fit in?

4. Have you had experiences in large groups?

   a. To what extent did the organizations you have been a part of include the features of an ideal type as described by Max Weber?

   b. What was your position in the organization? Were you a client, a line worker, a supervisor or management-level worker, or an executive? To what extent is your analysis of the organization influenced by the position you held in it? If you asked people who were in different positions than you, do you think they would agree with your assessment?

5. Some students of bureaucracy believe that advanced, industrial societies are impossible without bureaucracy. Do you think this is true? Do you think that a contemporary society could be organized without bureaucracies? Do you think that social welfare services can be delivered without bureaucracies?

6. Distinguish between Max Weber's approach to bureaucracy and the scientific management approach.

7. What is the contribution of the human relations approach to the study of bureaucracy?

8. Conventional and human relations approaches to bureaucracy have been criticized on a number of grounds. Describe some of these and indicate how a political economy approach helps to overcome them.

9. Describe what is meant by a political economy approach to the study of bureaucracy. Do you believe that the political economy approach helps you understand your own experiences in bureaucracies better?

10. For an organizational analysis project, students identify an organization they are a part of as a worker, volunteer, or student. The following week, they study the organization using a political economy approach and then present their findings to the class.

11. Define the qualities usually associated with small groups.

12. Reflect on your experiences in small, natural groups. To what extent have they been good experiences? Do you

believe that small groups are inherently any better than large groups?

13. What is meant by a political economy approach to the study of small groups?

14. Describe what is meant by the terms recruitment, socialization, interaction, innovation, and control.

15. Why do people join groups? Is joining a group always a voluntary act? Are groups receptive to everyone who wants to join? Describe the voluntary and involuntary ways by which you have become a member of a group or have felt rejected by a group.

16. Read "Recruiting African Americans into Groups." If you had been part of this experiment, what mix would you have been comfortable with? If you were asked to be part of a mixed-gender or mixed-age or mixed sexual orientation group, what mix would you feel comfortable with?

17. Brim lists six ways in which socialization in later life differs from socialization in early life. Describe these. How accurate do you think these differences are?

18. Some have described socialization as a process that takes place across the life cycle of group membership. What might be the stages of socialization a person passes through in a group? What special insights might a political economy approach give you in understanding these socialization processes?

19. Read "Behaviors of Women and Men in Groups." To what extent do the generalizations presented reflect what you have observed or experienced in groups? Do you believe that the differences between men and women in groups are learned or innate?

20. Researchers have identified various phases in group task performance.

Describe the common features of such approaches. Do you believe groups go through these phases in an orderly fashion? Where does conflict fit in? Is it a phase or something that is evident in all group processes?

21. Distinguish between conflicts of interest and cognitive conflicts in groups. Give examples based on your own experiences in groups.

22. Distinguish between the concepts of leader and leadership. As you prepare for the role of leader, what kind of leadership style do you want to assume? Is there a good or best kind of leadership style? As you prepare for the role of group member, do you think you can demonstrate leadership? Can you trust that the leader will accept it?

23. Distinguish between power and authority. Name and describe five different ways by which power can be exercised and three different ways by which authority can be exercised. Based on your own experiences with people in authority, can you identify the kind of authority they represented and the ways they wielded their power? When you have been willingly influenced by people in authority, has the way they wielded their power been an important consideration? Have you ever exercised power while a member of a group? If so, describe the situation and the kind of power you thought you were using. To what extent have your responses reflected a social desirability effect?

24. Explain the following statement: Conformity is at once necessary and unfortunate, good and bad. What factors are likely to lead to conformity with the demands of a group?

25. Identify the following group-related concepts and issues:

natural groups
concocted groups
brainstorming
nominal group technique
groupthink
social loafing
cognitive conflict
conflicts of interest
normative model of leadership
contingency model of leadership
zero-sum power

⊗ NOTES

1. Marvin E. Shaw, *Group Dynamics: The Psychology of Small Group Behavior*, 3rd ed. (McGraw-Hill Book Co., 1981), p. 8.

2. Charles Perrow, *Complex Organizations: A Critical Essay*, 3rd ed. (New York: Random House, 1986).

3. Yeheskel Hasenfeld, *Human Service Organizations* (Englewood Cliffs, NJ: Prentice-Hall, 1983).

4. Rhoda Lois Blumberg, *Organizations in Contemporary Society* (Englewood Cliffs, NJ: Prentice-Hall, 1987), p. 49.

5. Ron Westrum and Khalil Samaha, *Complex Organizations: Growth, Struggle and Change* (Englewood Cliffs, NJ: Prentice-Hall, 1984).

6. David Stoesz, "A Theory of Social Welfare," *Social Work*, vol. 34 (March 1989), pp. 101–08.

7. Joseph E. McGrath, *Groups: Interaction and Performance* (Englewood Cliffs, NJ: Prentice-Hall, 1984), pp. 41–50.

8. Howard L. Nixon, II, *The Small Group* (Englewood Cliffs, NJ: Prentice-Hall, 1979), pp. 15–18.

9. Harry Specht, *New Direction for Social Work Practice* (Englewood Cliffs, NJ: Prentice-Hall, 1988).

10. Max Weber, "Legitimate Authority and Bureaucracy," in D. S. Pugh (editor), *Organization Theory* (New York: Penguin Books, 1981). See Weber, *The Theory of Social and Economic Organizations*, trans A. Henderson and T. Parsons (New York: Free Press, 1947), originally published 1913–1922, and a representative collection of essays in *From Max Weber: Essays in Sociology*, trans. Hans Gerth and C. Wright Mills (New York: Oxford University Press, 1946).

11. Ibid., pp. 15–29.

12. Ibid., p. 25.

13. Ibid., p. 28.

14. Hasenfeld, *Human Services Organizations*, p. 18.

15. Elton Mayo, *The Social Problem of an Industrial Civilization* (Cambridge, MA: Harvard University Press, 1945); Rensis Likert, "The Principle of Supportive Relationships," in Pugh (editor), *Organization Theory*, pp. 279–304, and *New Patterns of Management* (New York: McGraw-Hill, 1961), pp. 97–118.

16. Charles Perrow, *Complex Organizations: A Critical Essay*, 3rd ed. (New York: Random House, 1986), p. 5.

17. Hasenfeld, *Human Service Organizations*, p. 85.

18. John W. Meyer and Brian Rowan, "The Structure of Educational Organizations," in M. W. Meyer and associates (editors), *Environments and Organizations* (San Francisco: Jossey-Bass, 1978), pp. 78–109.

19. Robert Michels, *Political Parties* (Glencoe, IL: Free Press, 1966).

20. Mary Zey-Ferrel and Michael Aiken (editors), *Complex Organizations: Critical Perspectives* (Glenview, IL: Scott, Foresman, 1981), pp. 6–7, and Petro Georgiou, "The Goal Paradigm and Notes toward a Counter Paradigm," in Zey-Ferrel and Aiken (editors), *Complex Organizations*, pp. 69–87.

21. Graeme Salaman, "Towards a Sociology of Organizational Structure," *The Sociological Review*, vol. 26, no. 3 (1978), pp. 519–54.

22. Mayer N. Zald, "Political Economy: A Framework for Comparative Analysis," in Zey-Ferrel and Aiken (editors), *Complex Organizations*, pp. 237–62.

23. Ibid., p. 245.

24. Stoesz, "Theory of Social Welfare," pp. 101–07.

25. Charles Atherton, "The Welfare State: Still on Solid Ground," *Social Service Review*, vol. 63, no. 2 (1989), pp. 167–79.

26. Stoesz, "Theory of Social Welfare," pp. 104–05.

27. Zald, *Political Economy*, pp. 247–54.

28. The term *satisficing* is reinterpreted in a political economy context. James G. March and Herbert A. Simon, who introduced the term, see satisficing decisions as a problem of bounded rationality or limited knowledge rather than in terms of internal power processes. See J. G. March and H. A. Simon, *Organizations* (New York: John Wiley and Sons, 1958).

29. Zald, *Political Economy*, pp. 254–59.

30. Ibid.

31. Charles Horton Cooley, *Social Organizations: A Study of the Larger Mind* (Glencoe, IL: Free Press, 1956), pp. 26–27.

32. Donelson R. Forsythe, *Group Dynamics*, 2nd ed. (Pacific Grove, CA: Brooks/Cole, 1983), pp. 6–8.

33. See William R. Coulso, *Groups, Gimmicks and Instant Gurus: An Examination of Encounter Groups and Their Distortions* (New York: Harper & Row, 1972); Morton A. Lieberman, Irvin D. Yalom, and Matthew B. Miles, *Encounter Groups: First Facts* (New York: Basic Books, 1973), pp. 167–210.

34. George J. McCall and J. L. Simmons, *Social Psychology: A Sociological Approach* (New York: Free Press, 1982).

35. Ralph E. Anderson and Irl Carter, *Human Behavior in the Social Environment: A Social Systems Approach*, 4th ed. (New York: Aldine de Gruyter, 1990), p. 133.

36. Shaw, *Group Dynamics*, pp. 82–117.

37. Donn Byrne and William Griffitt, "Developmental Investigation of the Law of Attraction," *Journal of Personality and Social Psychology*, vol. 4 (1966), pp. 699–702; W. A. Griffitt, "Interpersonal Attraction as a Function of Self-Concept and Personality Similarity-Dissimilarity," *Journal of Personality and Social Psychology*, vol. 4 (1966), pp. 581–84.

38. Shaw, *Group Dynamics*, p. 90.

39. Judith Cingolani, "Social Conflict Perspective on Work with Involuntary Clients," *Social Work*, vol. 29 (September–October 1984), pp. 442–46.

40. Orville G. Brim, Jr., "Socialization through the Life Cycle," in O. G. Brim, Jr. and S. Wheeler, *Socialization after Childhood: Two Essays* (New York: John Wiley and Sons, 1966), pp. 24–32.

41. Ibid; Stanton Wheeler, "The Structure of Formally Organized Socialization Settings," in Brim and Wheeler, *Socialization after Childhood*, pp. 83–98; R. L. Moreland and J. M. Levine, "Socialization in Small Groups: Temporal Changes in Individual-Group Relations," in L. Berkowitz (editor), *Advances in Experimental Social Psychology*, vol. 15 (New York: Academic Press, 1982), pp. 137–92.

42. Moreland and Levine, "Socialization in Small Groups."

43. B. W. Tuckman, "Developmental Sequence in Small Groups," *Psychology Bulletin*, vol. 6, no. 6 (1965), pp. 384–99.

44. J. A. Seeger, "No Innate Phases in Group Problem Solving," *Academy of Management Review*, vol. 8 (1983), pp. 683–89.

45. McGrath, *Groups*, pp. 60–66.

46. K. B. Williams, S. Harkins, and B. Latane, "Identifiability as a Deterrent to Social Loafing: Two Cheering Experiments," *Journal of Personality and Social Psychology*, vol. 40 (1981), pp. 303–11.

47. Forsythe, *Group Dynamics*, p. 272.

48. Alex Osborn, *Applied Imagination* (New York: Scribner, 1957).

49. McGrath, *Groups*, p. 131.

50. A. L. Delbecq, A. H. Van de Ven, and D. H. Gustafson, *Group Techniques for Program Planning: A Guide to Nominal Groups and Delphi Processes* (Glenview, IL: Scott, Foresman, 1976).

51. McGrath, *Groups*, p. 129.

52. P. R. Laughlin and J. Adamopoulos, "Social Decision Schemes on Intellective Tasks," in H. Brandstatter, J. H. Davis, and C. Stocker-Kriechgauer (editors), *Group Decision Making* (London: Academic Press, 1982).

53. Irving L. Janis, "Groupthink," reprinted from *Psychology Today* in James B. Lau (editor), *Behavior in Organizations: An Experimental Approach*, rev. ed. (Homewood, IL: Richard D. Irwin, 1979), pp. 109–16; also see Janis, *Victims of Group Think* (Boston: Houghton Mifflin, 1972).

54. Berndt Brehmer, "Social Judgement Theory," *Psychological Bulletin*, vol. 83 (November 1976), pp. 985–1003.

55. Carol Gilligan, *In a Different Voice: Psychological Theory and Women's Development* (Cambridge, MA: Harvard University Press, 1982), p. 156.

56. James W. Green, *Cultural Awareness in the Human Service* (Englewood Cliffs, NJ: Prentice-Hall, 1982), pp. 28–86.

57. Sidney Siegal and Lawrence E. Fouracker, *Bargaining and Group Decision Making: Experiments in Bilateral Monopoly* (New York: McGraw-Hill, 1960).

58. C. E. Osgood, *An Alternative to War or Surrender* (Urbana, IL: University of Illinois Press, 1962).

59. McGrath, *Groups*, p. 98.

60. See R. K. White and Ronald Lippitt, "Leader Behavior and Member Reaction in Three Social Climates," in D. Cartwright and A. Zander (editors), *Group Dynamics: Research and Theory*, 3rd ed. (New York: Harper & Row, 1968), pp. 318–35.

61. R. M. Stogdill, *Handbook of Leadership* (New York: Free Press, 1974).

62. Victor H. Vroom and A. G. Jago, "On the Validity of the Vroom/Yetton Model," *Journal of Applied Psychology*, vol. 63 (1978), pp. 151–62; and

V. H. Vroom and P. W. Yetton, *Leadership and Decision Making* (Pittsburgh, PA: University of Pittsburgh Press, 1973).

63. Fred E. Fiedler, "A Contingency Model of Leadership Effectiveness," in L. Berkowitz (editor), *Advances in Experimental Social Psychology*, vol. 1 (New York: Academic Press, 1964), pp. 150–90.

64. See Perrow, *Complex Organizations*, pp. 258–60.

65. Ibid., p. 258–59.

66. J. R. P. French and B. Raven, "The Bases of Social Power," in Cartwright and Zander (editors), *Group Dynamics*, 3rd ed., 1959, pp. 259–69.

67. See, for example, J. G. Bachman, C. D. Smith, and J. A. Slesinger, "Control, Performance, and Satisfaction: An Analysis of Structural and Individual Effects," *Journal of Personality and Social Psychology*, vol. 4 (1966), pp. 127–36.

68. Philip M. Podsakoff and Chester A. Schriesheim, "Field Studies of French and Raven's Bases of Power: Critique, Reanalysis, and Suggestions for Future Research," *Psychological Bulletin*, vol. 97, no. 3 (1985) pp. 387–411.

69. Forsythe, *Group Dynamics*, pp. 187–88.

70. David Kipnis, "The Use of Power in Organizations and in Interpersonal Settings," in S. Oskamp (editor), *Applied Social Psychology Annual*, vol. 5 (Newbury Park, CA: Sage, 1984), pp. 179–210.

71. Toni Falbo and Letitia A. Peplau, "Power Strategies in Intimate Relationships," *Journal of Personality and Social Psychology*, vol. 38 (1980), pp. 618–28.

72. Solomon Asch, "Effects of Group Pressure upon the Modification and Distortion of Judgements," in D. Cartwright and A. Zander (editors), *Group Dynamics: Research and Theory*, 2nd ed. (Evanston, IL: Row, Peterson, 1960), pp. 189–200.

73. See Shaw, *Group Dynamics*, p. 289.

74. Stanley Milgram, *Obedience to Authority* (New York: Harper & Row, 1974).

75. See Roger Brown, *Social Psychology: The Second Edition* (New York: Free Press, 1986), pp. 29–41.

CHAPTER 13

Social Interaction
Social Exchange and Marxian Theories

MAJOR THEMES DISCUSSED IN THIS CHAPTER

1. **THEORIES OF SOCIAL INTERACTION.** Utopian visions of group and organizational life focus on social interaction. In conflict theories, change and conflict are assumed to be the normal state of interaction; in consensus theories, stability is the norm. In this chapter we examine two conflict approaches: social exchange and Marxian theories.

2. **SOCIAL EXCHANGE THEORY: INVESTMENTS AND OUTCOMES.** Social exchange theory applies an analogy of economic exchanges in the marketplace to human social interaction in small and large groups. Individuals are self-interested and attempt to maximize their rewards and minimize their costs in social exchange transactions.

3. **EQUITY THEORY: DISTRIBUTIVE JUSTICE.** When people perceive that there is an inequity between the rewards they are achieving and the costs they are incurring, they seek distributive justice, or norms of fairness and justice for all, in transactions with others. Everyone's outcomes, or rewards minus costs, should be in balance with their inputs, or investments.

4. **IMPLICATIONS OF SOCIAL EXCHANGE FOR PRACTICE.** In applying exchange theory, social workers assess group and organizational behavior in terms of the fairness of the reward structure. Intervention focuses on helping people choose among various ways of bringing about greater fairness in their relationships with others.

5. **MARXIAN THEORY: EXPLOITATION AND ALIENATION.** Marx believed that humans are not by nature self-interested but had become so as a result of the development of capitalism. As a social and economic institution, capitalism produces alienation and exploitation, which Marx believed could only be overcome by giving workers rewards that are equal to those accorded to owners and managers. He called for workers to directly confront them and wrest control over economic organizations.

6. **EXPLOITATION AND ALIENATION IN CONTEMPORARY SOCIETY.** Marxian theorists today generally believe that Marx's conflict theory must be reinterpreted. They suggest that exploitation and alienation can be overcome and more equitable relationships established in social relationships by a number of strategies, but the best way is through collective action against the dominant interests.

7. **IMPLICATIONS OF MARXIAN THEORY FOR PRACTICE.** Marxian theory teaches social service workers to be concerned about equality among the members of groups, organizations, and communities. When social relationships are exploitative or alien-

ating, they can work to organize those who are affected so they can negotiate with the dominant interests.

☙❦❧

THE POLITICAL ECONOMY FRAMEWORK FOR THE study of small and large groups described in Chapter 12, which acknowledges their existence in a world of political and economic realities where goals and dynamics are shaped in an atmosphere of power and conflict, utilizes both of the basic approaches to the study of human behavior in the social environment taken in this book. It takes a systems approach in which groups and organizations are seen as holons or systems open to change interacting with their environments. It also takes a critical perspective which calls for the formulation of group goals and processes that lead to social progress.

In this chapter and the next we will apply a critical approach to the study of individuals' interactions in the context of membership in groups, organizations, and communities. We will consider four theoretical frameworks—social exchange, Marxian theory, functionalism, and symbolic interactionism—which look at individuals' transactions with their environments, as well as their interactions with others as members of groups and organizations. These theories are useful in understanding the social processes described in relation to group dynamics in the preceding chapter: recruitment, socialization, interaction, innovation, and social control. The focus, however, is on interaction as a general social process, that is, the continual, overarching process through which individuals influence one another and social systems are shaped and refined.

☙ THEORIES OF SOCIAL INTERACTION

No one theory is capable of explaining all there is to know about a topic such as social interaction, and each of the theories discussed in Chapters 13 and 14 presents a unique understanding of the reality of this process. These theories are classic in the sense that they are often used by researchers, and by making valuable contributions to the study of human behavior they have enhanced the theoretical background for social service practice.

The theories are at opposite ends of the conflict-consensus continuum for the characterization of systems (see "Conflict or Consensus" in Chapter 3). Social exchange and Marxian theories are conflict theories; both assume that conflicts of interest and motives undergird social interaction and are its normal state. Both are forerunners of the political economy approach to organizations, and both take a zero-sum approach to power. In these theories, social interaction is essentially a process of continual negotiation and bargaining in which each individual, group, or organization aims to fulfill its interests in competition with those of others. Functionalism and symbolic interactionism are con-

---

Theoretical Frameworks for Utopian Visions of Groups and Organizations

The utopian visions of groups and organizations offered in the four theories of social interaction discussed in this and the following chapters are built on different ideas of the ultimate goals to be achieved through group life. A basic difference is their view of the normal state of group dynamics as either conflict or consensus.

Theory	Utopian Vision
Conflict Theories	
Social exchange and equity theories	Equity and distributive justice
Marxian theory	Equality and the absence of alienation and exploitation
Consensus Theories	
Functionalism	Consensus and shared values
Symbolic interactionism	Mutual self-respect and the absence of labeling

---

sensus theories; they postulate that there is a basic, shared understanding that binds people together. Harmony and stability are believed to mark normal-as-average social interactions, and conflict or change result from some kind of breakdown in group norms.

In addition to each theory's unique understanding of social interaction, it presents a unique utopian vision of the goals to be sought in the ideal group or organization (see "Theoretical Frameworks for Utopian Visions of Groups and Organizations"). Social exchange and equity theories focus on problems that arise when the rewards from group interaction are inequitable. The argument is that such problems can only be resolved by developing norms of equity and fairness. Marxian theory points to the problems of exploitation and alienation and calls for working together to build groups and organizations free of them. Functionalism sees the problems that arise when people do not conform to social norms and calls for consensus and shared values to assure equal opportunity in the pursuit of socially desirable goals. Symbolic interactionism locates perfection in relationships that generate self-esteem for all members.

∞ SOCIAL EXCHANGE THEORY: INVESTMENTS AND OUTCOMES

The origins of contemporary theories of social exchange can be found in the work of classical political economists such as Jeremy Bentham and Adam Smith. The basic proposition is very simple: "an individual will act in a certain way if the consequences of doing so are pleasurable and refrain from doing so if the consequences are painful." Behind this simple proposition, however, lie some not so simple and even debatable assumptions about human nature. The proposition assumes that humans are self-interested, rational creatures operating primarily from utilitarian and hedonistic, or pleasure-seeking, motives.[1]

Social exchange theory focuses on interactions between individuals and the other individuals, communities, groups, and organizations in their social environment. In the most basic social exchange transaction, a "person" is in interaction with an "other," and the person and the other form a dyad, that is, they are two individuals who may in turn be interacting within the context of their environment. The concept of social exchange has also been applied to study the interactions between an individual and a group or between organizational elements in a society, and the relationships between organizations, between units of an organization, or between communities. Social exchange offers a clearly utopian vision about what transactions should be like; unless the outcomes are fair, social interaction will falter.

Social exchange theory has been the basis of research on group behavior, and it has been applied to the study of small and large groups and intimate relations, as well as the interactions between social workers and clients.[2] Its impact on social service practice has not been great, but it has considerable potential in this application. Harry Specht backs up his contention that social exchange could form the basis of a theory for practice by identifying four types of exchange transactions in which practitioners commonly engage: exchanges with client systems, with others in the client's environment, with peer professionals, and with decision makers.[3]

The Marketplace Analogy and the Systems Approach

Social exchange theory uses an analogy of the economic marketplace in investigating human social interaction. The basic idea is that individuals approach social interaction with the expectation of maximizing their own rewards while minimizing their own losses. All interactions, therefore, involve self-interested, profit-and-loss calculations, as each individual attempts to gain as much as possible at minimum cost. Thus as people exchange rewards, they try to profit from one another. Upon entering a social interaction, each person calculates her or his possible interpersonal profits, or payoff, for the interaction by subtracting the expected costs from the likely rewards[4] (see "The Calculation of Interpersonal Profit in Interactions"). Something like the following process is believed to take place in the mind of each participant: If I do such and such, I am likely to give up such and such (costs) but I am also likely to obtain such and such (rewards) in return. If I tell you I care about you, for instance, I am likely to feel embarrassed but I am also likely to learn that you care about me. Thus, since your friendship is important to me, the embarrassment I will suffer in making my feelings known is well worth it.

Social exchange is a systems approach because the actual outcomes or payoffs individuals obtain are a result of the bartering and negotiating that take place in the transactions between individuals and others in the social environment. The person and the other (person, group, or community) have behavior control over one another, which can be differentiated from fate control or autonomous control. In *fate control*, the other is totally in control of the outcomes the person receives. Put another way, the person is completely dependent on the other. *Autonomous control* is the opposite of fate control; in this situation, the person is totally in control of his or her own outcomes; the other has no way of influencing the profit. Fate control and autonomous control represent extreme cases of power in interpersonal relations. For this reason, they are unusual in social interaction;

The Calculation of Interpersonal Profit in Interactions

In social exchange transactions, each individual calculates the possible profits to be gained by entering the transaction, taking into account the possible rewards and costs. The calculation can be expressed as follows:

Interpersonal profit = Rewards to be obtained − Costs to be incurred

The rewards in such transactions can be intrinsic or extrinsic to the situation; unilateral or reciprocal, involving just one participant or both; and entering directly into the interaction or deferred. The costs can be direct costs, with an immediate payoff; investment costs, with a long-term return; or opportunity costs, the cost of giving up other alternatives when one is chosen.

Source: Equation from Peter M. Blau, *Exchange and Power in Everyday Life* (New York: John Wiley and Sons, 1964).

---

it is rare for others to be able to completely determine our destiny or for us to be able to do so.

Behavior control, the more usual form of control, is what makes social exchange a systems theory. *Behavior control* refers to interpersonal situations in which each partner is able to alter the behavior of the other. Others may influence the person's outcomes in important ways, but they are also influenced by how the person responds as an individual.[5] The profits of both actually are interdependent. In other words, in most situations when you and I interact, what I do to try to maximize my rewards is as important as what you do to try to minimize my rewards and maximize your own.

Social Exchange in Small and Large Groups

Because of its marketplace analogy, exchange theory is especially helpful in understanding social interaction in organizations and the small groups embedded in them in a free-market society. The following examples of the use of social exchange in research and theoretical study on small and large group processes demonstrate this.

Exchange Theory and Small Groups

The idea of social exchange suggests that **reward power** has a lot to do with the acceptance of social influence in groups. Reward power is one of the five bases of individual power identified by J. R. P. French and B. Raven which were described in the discussion of power in Chapter 12; the others are legitimate, coercive, referent, and expert.[6] In surveys based on their definitions, subordinates often said that the rewards they might receive had nothing to do with their willingness to accept the direction of superiors.

The ability of reward power to influence social exchange transactions was examined by Wendy Jean Harrod in a laboratory experiment in which young women were recruited to work as paid volunteers in a research organization that supposedly employed many people for data collection and processing. They were not told their duties or the position they would hold, only their wage scales. They were to work in groups of two, one of whom was actually a confederate of the researcher. In one experimental condition the real participant was told she would be paid $3.00 but her partner (the confederate) would get $5.00; in another, the participant was to be paid $5.00 and her partner, only $1.00. The groups were then assigned the task of making a decision on a problem with no clearly correct answer. Each partner was to make the decision on her own, but they were to be informed whether or not they had agreed. The experiment was rigged so that on the majority of decisions they would disagree, and they then were asked to discuss their differences, rethink their decisions, and decide whether to change their answers.[7]

While this research situation was similar to those in the studies on conformity by Solomon Asch and Stanley Milgram described in Chapter 12, this was a pure test of the influence of rewards in changing opinions. Only reward power was manipulated; there were no status or authority differences between the partners. Since there was no correct answer, neither the confederate nor the participant had more expertise than the other. Punishment was not an issue, nor was charisma. Harrod found that the participants were more likely to change their minds when they thought they were being paid less than their partners and more likely to hold firm in their opinion when they thought they were being paid more—the hypothesis that exchange theory would make. She concluded that unequal rewards lead to unequal expectations about responsibility and participation in decisions.

Exchange Relations among Organizations

In an analysis of what Yeheskel Hasenfeld describes as "people-producing organizations," he focused on how the exchange relations these groups develop with their environments affect the structure and content of their activities. A people-producing organization is a type of human service organization that identifies people with problems and refers them to appropriate services such as diagnostic centers and employment services. Their environments consist of the other organizations, clients, and constituencies in the welfare industry with which these organizations must deal.[8]

In keeping with the exchange perspective, Hasenfeld refers to these other organizations as market units and posits that all organizations attempt to minimize their own loss and maximize their own rewards. He defines loss as a condition of dependence and rewards as a situation of "countervailing power." A service organization that is unable to exert power over its environment becomes too dependent on or is controlled by it. As evidence of dependence, regulations may be imposed on the service, it may have little control over its intake decisions, it may be unaware of resources or have too few resources to offer clients, or its market units may not support its organizational goals. An organization that has successfully negotiated with its environment and is free of such conditions will have the power to maximize its rewards. According to this theoretical perspective, organizations exist in a situation of behavior control. They must constantly negotiate with other organizations that exert power in their environment, while they seek to minimize the power the environment has over them.

Intimate Relations and Exchange Transactions

Are there limits to how far we can take the analogy of marketplace relationships to social interactions in small and large groups? When we think of people interacting for monetary benefit—buying and selling, owning and working, giving services for fees—it seems to make good sense. But the image is less obvious in other realms of small-group behavior such as intimate relations. Many theorists maintain that deep interpersonal relationships such as love, family life, and friendship cannot be fruitfully understood as market exchanges. Marxists and other humanists believe that family relationships, for instance, are inherently nurturing, supportive, and free of utilitarian value, though a powerful economy continually threatens to force on family life the values of a free-market philosophy. When intimate relations do take on the characteristics of market exchanges, it is because the market philosophy has successfully invaded them (see Chapter 11).

Nevertheless, exchange theorists who have studied friendship and love in contemporary society have concluded that intimate relations make sense in terms of social exchange. To be sure, love and friendship exchanges do not work in exactly the same way as business and market exchanges. For instance, friendship may be rewarding in itself, since having a friend gives pleasure and security. Friends are not always bargaining over the need for rewards and do not expect to be paid back immediately when they give rewards. But eventually friends have to reward one another, or the friendship is likely to deteriorate and the friends will go their separate ways.

Love and family relationships operate on similar principles as friendships do, but it is much more difficult to separate the individual from the family.[9] Peter Blau and Zick Rubin, who have studied heterosexual attraction in terms of social exchange processes, have concluded that attractiveness is often measured in supply-and-demand terms. Individuals seem to be attracted to others depending on how available they are, how attractive they are to other people, how difficult they are to conquer, and the like. In courtship, the participants manipulate their scarcity value as a way of increasing their reward value. Potential love partners are less likely to invest heavily in the beginning so they do not lose too much if the relationship does not work out. People who have many opportunities for partners are less likely to make a commitment to any one partner.[10]

Even after a commitment is made in intimate relations, self-interest is apparent. Exchange theorists generally conclude that selfless devotion depends on one person's interest in maintaining the other's love.[11] When Ivan Nye and his associates applied social exchange theory to family life, they found that behavioral choices made by family members follow a specific rank-order pattern:

1. Family members choose those alternatives from which they expect the most profit.

2. Costs being equal, they choose alternatives from which they anticipate the greatest rewards.

3. Rewards being equal, they choose alternatives from which they anticipate the fewest costs.

4. Immediate outcomes being equal, they choose alternatives that promise better long-term outcomes.

5. Long-term outcomes being perceived as equal, they choose alternatives that provide better immediate outcomes.[12]

The Calculation of Rewards in Exchange Transactions

People in social interaction often exchange rewards, but rewards can mean many things to many people. Money is the most obvious reward used to influence attitudes or behavior; in a work group, for example, piece rates may be paid to tie compensation to production. Gifts and prizes can be rewarding in the same way. Opportunities may also be exchanged; I will give you the opportunity to play if you give me the opportunity to rest. Usually, however, exchange transactions involve social rewards such as approval, liking or loving, or bestowing esteem, respect, or prestige. A wide range of rewards can be bartered or negotiated in interpersonal encounters.

In the marketplace, the value of rewards is more-or-less standardized. A monetary system is used, and the value of a dollar, a pound, a peso, or a yen is standardized not only within a society but in different societies. Units are usually priced: a toaster costs $30; a worker is paid $5 an hour; a house is valued at $110,000. In human social interaction no standardized monetary system, pay scale, or price schedule exists. In an interpersonal marketplace, then, how do people determine how much reward they are getting or are willing to accept or to give? Social exchange theorists explain the procedure in terms of a number of social-psychological structures and processes.

George C. Homans has identified some of the processes and principles underlying the attribution of value to rewards and the effects on exchange transactions. Most of these have a commonsense meaning; the value proposition, for instance, states that "the more valuable to a person is the result of his action, the more likely he is to perform the action." In the process of supply and demand, rewards that are scarcer have more psychological value than rewards that are plentiful. To the extent that individuals or groups have been deprived of a reward in the past, they are likely to value the reward more in the present. Conversely, the more often in the recent past they have received a particular reward, the less value any further unit of that reward becomes for them. This is Homans's principle of deprivation-satiation, which is built around the notion of supply and demand.[13]

A richer understanding of the cognitive and motivational elements in social exchange is provided by **social comparison processes**, by means of which individuals evaluate rewards and punishments on the basis of their experiences. John Thibaut and Harold Kelley describe two such processes. At the *comparison level*, present rewards and costs are evaluated in terms of past experiences; a person accustomed to receiving substantial rewards in the past is not likely to be pleased when lower rewards are offered. At the *comparison level for alternatives*, expected outcomes in one exchange relationship are compared with opportunities to receive potentially better rewards in another exchange relationship. To the extent that people have limited means for obtaining rewards, they become dependent on the relationship and willing to accept the reward, even though it might not be as great as wished.[14]

A social structure used in evaluating rewards is **reference groups**, the groups and individuals whose beliefs, attitudes, and behaviors the individual respects and is influenced by. Reference groups often supply the norms that regulate behaviors and serve as a source of comparison in evaluating rewards. To the extent that an individual's reference groups consider a particular reward valuable, or others in these groups are accepting the same kind of reward, it is likely that the individual will find the reward valuable and will accept it.

Cooperation, Reciprocity, and Fairness in Social Exchange

The marketplace image—the quest for profits—always puts the person and the other in contention. Each person in a dyad, a family, a small group, or a large organization is in pursuit of his or her best interest, as measured in terms of interpersonal profit. In contending with the other, each attempts to maximize her or his power and profit over the other's power and profit. A number of strategies, both negative and positive, can be used toward these ends.[15] A negative strategy is one-upmanship, in which indifference to the relationship and the existence of other alternatives are declared. Another is putting down others by suggesting that what they are offering has minimal value. A person also can attempt to thwart others' attempts to achieve a desired reward by raising the costs involved. On the positive side, individuals can improve their ability to be rewarding or can create a need in others for the rewards they are offering.

With all this competition it might seem that conflict is the only possible outcome in social relationships, but because of the behavior control people have over one another, social exchange theorists predict that the outcome is more likely to be cooperation. In this view, continual negotiation and bartering lead to stabilizing, relatively harmonious norms of cooperation. These norms are likely to be generated by the **norm of reciprocity**, under which we treat others as they have treated us. Norms of fairness or equity are created under the **principle of distributive justice**, which maintains that participants in an interaction expect to receive according to what they have given. As Homans describes this principle, "a man in an exchange relation with another will expect that the rewards of each man be proportional to his costs—the greater the reward, the greater the costs—and the new rewards, or profits, of each man be proportional to his investment—the greater the investments, the greater the profit."[16]

Social exchange theorists suggest at least two reasons why the norms of cooperation and fairness come to dominate in exchange transactions. First, since approval by others is an important human need, cooperation is likely to flow naturally: If I scratch your back, you will probably scratch mine. Second, when real conflicts of interest occur, the competing parties are likely to build formal rules (norms, laws, and institutions) to regulate the conflict and assure the well-being of all. Reciprocity and justice (equity or fairness) are the likely foundations for such rules.

This does not mean that the society or, for that matter, interpersonal relations will be typified by stability and cooperation or that all people and groups in the society will benefit equally from the exchanges being made. According to Blau, the more stable and cooperative some exchange relationships are, the more likely are other relationships involving the same parties to become unstable and unbalanced.[17] Moreover, nineteenth-century economic exchange theorists argued that the good society does not offer equal rewards to everybody; rather, it grants them to the majority, in order to secure the greatest good for the greatest number. That a minority would not do well in such an exchange was not seen as a problem.

∞ EQUITY THEORY: DISTRIBUTIVE JUSTICE

The classical economists, like those in contemporary society who have espoused trickle-down economics, were not concerned with helping people who come away from transactions without profits or rewards. A utopian transactional approach to groups and organizations derives from a different tradition, one that attempts to secure justice and fairness for all. This is the tradition of distributive justice, defined in terms of the concept of equity or perceived fairness in social exchange.

Equity theory proposes that a sense of fairness enters into all the calculations about rewards and costs in social transactions. Equity exists when both parties in an exchange come away believing that they are getting profits out of the relationship which are constant

Mexican migrant farm workers harvest strawberries in California. An
equitable salary for such workers would be based on a norm of reciprocity between them and those who supervise and pay for their labor.

with what they have put into it.[18] Thus an exchange is considered equitable when the
rewards received by each participant in a social interaction are perceived to be in balance
with the investments each makes (see "Equity in Social Interactions").

In equity, social exchange theory provides a key concept for understanding the transactional problems that can emerge in groups and organizations. When human relations are
strong and stable, the norm of reciprocity is likely to be operating, and all participants in
a transaction are likely to believe that the rewards they are receiving are just and fair.
When the norm of reciprocity is not working, inequity will be perceived, and the participants are likely to feel angry and aggrieved. According to Homans's aggressive-approval
propositions:

> ...(a) When a person's action does not receive the reward he expected, or receives punishment
> he did not expect, he will be angry; he becomes more likely to perform aggressive behavior, and
> the results of such behavior become more valuable to him. (b) When a person's action re-
> ceives the reward he expected, especially greater reward than expected, or does not receive
> punishment he expected, he will be pleased; he becomes more likely to perform approving be-
> havior, and the results of such behavior become more valuable to him.[19]

The principles of equity theory, based on interactions between individuals, can be applied to interactions between an individual and a group, between parties or factions in a

---

Equity in Social Interactions

The extent to which equity is achieved in social interactions depends on the participants' investments or contributions, what each puts into a transaction, as well as their profits or outcomes in terms of rewards and costs. Fairness is said to characterize the exchange when the outcomes of both participants match their investments. In a two-person interaction, for example, the transaction would be shown as:

$$\frac{\text{Person's rewards} - \text{person's costs}}{\text{Person's investment}} = \frac{\text{Other's rewards} - \text{other's costs}}{\text{Other's investment}}$$

OR

$$\frac{\text{Person's outcomes}}{\text{Person's inputs}} = \frac{\text{Other's outcomes}}{\text{Other's inputs}}$$

The important measure in this equation is not whether the inputs or outcomes for the person and the other are equal, but whether the *ratios* between these factors match. In an equitable transaction, the outcomes for each participant are related to that individual's inputs, and the outcomes of all participants, their rewards minus their costs, are approximately in balance. Thus those who put more into a transaction equitably receive more from it, and equity is a relative judgment.

Source: Equation from Gerald Leventhal, "Fairness in Social Relationships," in J. Thibaut, J. T. Spence, and R. Carson (editors), *Contemporary Topics in Social Psychology* (Morristown, NJ: General Learning Press, 1976).

group, or between groups. In a political economy approach which takes into account the political and economic environments of groups, equity takes the form of arguments not so much for equal opportunity as for **comparable worth** for various communities or groups in the society (see "Comparable Worth: Inequity Meets Exploitation").

Equity should not be confused with equality. Equality means that the outcomes people receive in social interaction are more or less the same. Equity allows for a good deal of inequality as a result of social transactions in which the participants' outcomes are in keeping with their inputs. This inequality is justified to the extent that the participants accept it as fair and just, in view of the rewards each receives minus the costs each incurs in the transaction.

When people perceive inequities in their transactions with individuals and groups, J. Stacey Adams suggests a number of strategies they can use to convert inequitable exchange outcomes into more equitable ones:

1. They can alter their inputs of investments. If they think they are doing too much, they might reduce their efforts. If they are doing too little, they might increase them.

2. They might alter their outcomes. If they think what they are getting out of the relationship is too little, they might reevaluate their outcomes in a more favorable light.

3. As a way of reevaluating inputs or outcomes, they might alter their reference groups and individuals. Instead of comparing themselves with people who seem to be getting

Comparable Worth: Inequity Meets Exploitation

The issue of comparable worth in contemporary American society is relevant to both the idea of inequity as defined in social exchange theory and the ideas of exploitation and inequality as defined in Marxian theory. The concepts indeed converge and become blurred, especially in eras like the present in which definitions of fairness are being challenged.

The principal application of the concept of comparable worth has been in the area of pay equity, where it has usually been considered a women's issue. On average, women do not earn as much as men even when they have the same qualifications and abilities, largely as a result of occupational segregation which limits women to jobs and positions that do not pay as well as those traditionally held by men. Under Title VII of the Civil Rights Act of 1964, equal employment opportunities were to be provided to women, but they have been able to make only small inroads into many male-dominated, better-paid occupations. Comparable worth, or pay equity, is a more direct approach to occupational equality for women. The idea is that women should be paid the same as men for jobs that are not precisely equal but are comparable in skill, effort, responsibility, and social and economic value. In practice the goal is being achieved by raising pay scales for the jobs traditionally held by women in business and government.

Thus, despite arguments that supply and demand in the free-labor market ought to be allowed to dictate how much a particular job is worth, women are beginning to make their point that being paid according to their skills, qualifications, and contributions is fair and not being paid on that basis is exploitative and inequitable. Comparable worth goes beyond equity for women, however; the same point also applies to many minorities and working-class people. Moreover, even to a casual observer, it is obvious that the principles by which the free-market economy operates have nothing to do with equal pay for equal work. A rock star without a high school education will make more than a senator or even a Supreme Court justice. A medical doctor with seven years of advanced education will make far more than a university professor with a similar seven years of advanced education. People with degrees in social work are unlikely to command the same salaries as people with degrees in business. The idle daughter of a multimillionaire will acquire, simply through the accident of her birth, far more wealth than the hard-working daughter of an equally hard-working truck driver is likely to attain.

While the U.S. Civil Rights Commission has supported the need for equity, defined as "fair pay," "equal pay for equal work," and "equal reward for equal preparation," it stops short of advocating equality of outcome, the idea that everyone should have the same rewards. The principle of comparable worth is not compatible with capitalism because it challenges the norm of negative reciprocity, by which some people derive more profit in a relationship than others do. Conservatives believe that employees should continue to calculate their inputs and outputs on the basis of this norm, and comparable worth is a step in the direction of socialism. In comparable-worth challenges that have been brought to the courts, the capitalist argument that salaries and wage rates should be set according to free-market principles of supply and demand has been upheld. A person who chooses to become a social worker rather than a business administrator or a medical doctor, therefore, has no right to maintain that the salary paid a social worker is unfair. The assumption is that women are as free to choose their occupations as men are.

Those who argue for the principle of comparable worth maintain that the work of women, minorities, and working-class people is often inequitably rewarded. While they do not advocate equality of outcomes, they do propose that comparable skills, effort, responsibility, and contributions should be rewarded comparably.

so much more out of relationships, they might compare themselves to people who are getting less.

4. They might cognitively distort their inputs or outcomes. People can come to misperceive the reality, seeing things not as they are but distorted, so they sense either more or less equity than actually exists.

5. They might abandon the relationship. When people do not get what they want out of a relationship, the option exists to separat and free themselves from it.

6. They might attempt to get the other party to change by increasing its inputs or decreasing its expectations for reward.[20]

IMPLICATIONS OF SOCIAL EXCHANGE FOR PRACTICE

In social exchange and equity theories, perfection in human social interaction in dyads, small groups, families, or organizations is seen as involving norms of reciprocity and the principle of distributive justice. If we accept the assumption that humans are by nature self-interested, the utopian vision can be no less than fairness and justice, that is, equity.

Social service workers must deal with many situations in which interpersonal relationships are perceived as inequitable. In working in organizations such as social service agencies, they often encounter situations in which some individuals are not pulling their weight and are detracting from the effectiveness and productivity of the whole. In working with small groups of clients, they must handle situations in which some are contributing more to a discussion or task than others. In working with dyads such as friends, partners, or married couples, the problem often is that the parties may feel each is putting more into the relationship than the other one is.

Social workers can use social exchange theory to assess any interpersonal relationship in terms of the degree of equity in it. In the assessment process, they can explore the ways individual members calculate their rewards—the value they hold for the relationship or for the group, their past experiences in similar relationships, the alternatives available to them, the experiences of others whose opinions they value. If inequity is indeed found in the interaction, the worker can lay out the possible strategies for resolving it. However, equity theory often is not able to predict how particular individuals or groups are likely to deal with inequity. Adams has suggested a number of solutions: distorting perceptions, reducing or increasing the amount of energy put into the relationship, trying to change the other party, leaving the relationship, even learning to accept and put up with the inequity.[21] Equity theory does not propose that any one solution is inherently better than another; all of them are considered of equal value.

In some respects this may not be of great concern. A social worker who accepts the ethic of client self-determination may simply seek to help clients identify inequities, offer alternative solutions, and suggest how they might achieve the solutions they choose. Many social workers, however, believe that inequity should be resolved, at least to the extent that various groups and communities have rights to be treated in a way they consider equitable. This value judgment is implicit in the work of Nancy Weinberg, who examined the response of physically disabled people to perceived violations of their rights. In this research she examined autobiographies and interviewed a nonrandom sample of the orthopedically disabled. She discovered that people disabled this way believe the able-bodied violate their rights in four common ways: continual staring, intrusive questioning, unsolicited assistance, and public humiliation.[22]

In Weinberg's study, all of these acts provoked the disabled to react with perceptions of inequity and such feelings as dissatisfaction, anger, and hostility. In response, they developed certain strategies of coping, most of which were passive or accommodating strategies which left them still feeling the injustice. Usually they coped with continual staring by ignoring it; with intrusive questions by responding politely and hoping to terminate the interaction; with unsolicited help by letting it pass without comment; and with humiliation by displays of emotion. More assertive, even aggressive strategies were used by some, but with less frequency.

In most cases, therefore, the experienced inequity was left unresolved, unlike the outcome in the strategies proposed by Adams. Weinberg recommends the use of group intervention techniques to allow the disabled to describe their encounters with social inequity and practice ways of resolving it which would force others to respect their rights. She suggests that often people do not resolve inequity so much as they endure it, learn to put up with it, or learn not to let it bother them. When people cope with inequity in this way, the situations continue to be inequitable.

Weinberg's position that the disabled should require the able-bodied to treat them with greater fairness and justice goes beyond exchange theory. It reflects the new social construction of reality concerning disability which led to passage of the Americans with Disabilities Act of 1990 (see Chapter 2). Called the most sweeping antidiscrimination law since passage of the Civil Rights Act of 1964, it bans discrimination on the basis of physical or mental handicap in employment, public accommodations, transportation, or telecommunications. Its provisions for public accommodations to provide nearly universal accessibility for the handicapped, which began to be phased in in 1992, represent real costs for organizations in the public and private sectors. Whether the law will make a difference in how individuals treat disabled persons, however, depends on the extent to which public attitudes toward the disabled change.

∞ MARXIAN THEORY: EXPLOITATION AND ALIENATION

Karl Marx developed his theory of social interaction in large part as a response to the political economic ideas underlying social exchange theory. Marx was an economist schooled in the classical exchange tradition, but he criticized it, dismissed it, and went on to build his own framework for understanding human behavior.

Marxian theory can be understood on a number of levels. It is usually thought of as an attempt to understand situations at the macro or societal level involving conflict between communities of people in different economic positions and social classes. Nevertheless, Marx's theory includes a number of social-psychological principles, and, as an extremely holistic theory of human behavior, it is suited to the study of small and large groups.[23] It is particularly useful to social service workers as an aid in understanding the large formal organizations or bureaucracies in which they (and their clients) often work.

In the utopian vision of social interaction presented in Marxian theory, the overriding goal is to eliminate exploitation and alienation. Marx's own work, however, deals largely with the ways in which social relationships under capitalism are organized to produce these conditions in groups.

Marx's Ideas on Social Interaction

Marx's ideas about human nature are more in keeping with those of contemporary **humanism** than those of social exchange theory. Humanists stress the individual's worth and capacity for self-actualization through reason. Marx saw humans as an inherently social species; humans need one another not just to satisfy their self-interest, because they can profit from one another, but for the nurturing, camaraderie, and stimulation interaction provides. For Marx, the distinguishing feature of human beings is their capacity for creative, purposive activity in the company of others. Together, humans can create things and master their environment. They can take a piece of wood and whittle it into a beautiful figurine, see grass and realize its potential for wheat and bread, and hear words and convert them into poetry.[24]

Marx's position on human nature nevertheless maintains some elements of the social exchange philosophy. In particular, Marx accepts the assumption that humans are rational creatures concerned with their self-interest. For Marx, however, this is a collective self-interest, the interest of others along with oneself, not egocentric, individualistic self-interest seeking to maximize personal profits and minimize personal costs.

People interacting with other people create the groups and organizations that make up society and its institutions. The products of their social creativity do not always turn out to be beneficial, however; sometimes humans create ideas and things that actually do them harm. For instance, Marx believed that gods did not make people in their image and likeness, as religious doctrine holds, but rather that gods were made in the image and likeness of people. Marx also observed that a product created by human creativity often is treated as if it had a life independent of its creators. Thus when gods, incarnated through religious interpreters, can tell people what they should and should not do, people have lost control over the gods they have created.

Marx refers to the process by which social creations come to have an independent life and exert control over their creators as **reification**, or giving material properties to an abstract idea. It was his belief that the economic organizations created through social processes had been reified and so were seen as human nature, and they often exerted a destructive force in social relationships. Nineteenth-century capitalism, created by humans, had dehumanized them and was socially destructive. While capitalism was based on exchange principles, they worked in very different ways than the classical economic theorists believed they did.

In contemporary society, the belief that "looking out for No. 1" is normal, self-evident, and does not need any particular explanation is widely accepted. Individual self-interest, even in love and friendship, is regarded as human nature. To Marx, these ideas were not human nature but evidence of the ways in which capitalism had debased the human spirit. He argues that such a marketplace, or exchange, mentality developed because as humans created capitalism, they internalized its values. These values eventually pervaded all interpersonal relations, not just those related to work and business. Thus utilitarian social exchange is not natural but is a corruption of the true creative and social nature of humans. Contemporary Marxists argue that social exchange theories are doing little more than helping to further reify and thus perpetuate the values of capitalism.[25]

Capitalism as a Social Relationship

Marx defined capitalism as a particular form of social relationship. What made capitalism unique was not its industrial technology but the way it organized interpersonal relations in the work organization. In his view, capitalism consists of the relationship between owners and managers, on the one hand, and workers who have exchanged their labor for a wage, on the other hand, and this relationship forms the basis of social class position (see Chapter 4). The economic and social relationships of feudalism, which preceded capitalism, were different; property consisted of land owned by a lord and worked by serfs or peasants who were tied to the land by birth. With capitalism came two new classes, owners and managers on the one hand and free workers on the other. The change from serfs to free workers was a great advance which should not be discounted. The free workers, no longer tied to the land and completely beholden to a lord, could find their own employment and had the potential to better their position.

Nevertheless, Marx believed that the things that were wrong with capitalism as a social relationship were so wrong that constructive criticism aimed at improving it was not possible. Instead he proposed *ruthless criticism*, which could only destroy the capitalistic system.[26] Today, the difference between liberals and radicals, both on the political left, is akin to the difference between constructive criticism and ruthless criticism. The two things Marx saw as most wrong with capitalism had to do with the political economy of work organizations: social relationships in them are exploitative, and they produce alienation.

Ruthless Criticism 1: Capitalism Exploits Workers

While capitalism was an advance over feudalism, Marx detected some basic contradictions or flaws in the system. One is that it generates and depends on social inequality. Marx starts with the assumption that workers and owners contribute equally to the work process. The owner gets the money to build a canal, buys the tools, and hires the labor; these are important inputs. But the worker actually builds the canal with sweat and muscle, and this too is an important input. According to Marx, since the owner and the worker put in equal efforts and resources, the worker's benefits—income and wealth and prestige and power—ought to equal those of the owner. If the benefits are not equal, the relationship between the owner and the worker is one of **exploitation**, in which the owner benefits at the expense of the worker. Owners get far more out of such a relationship than they put into it, while workers get much less out of it than they put in.

This sounds like equity theory, but there are differences between the concepts of inequity and exploitation. While both are complaints that a situation is unfair or unjust, equity theory accepts the possibility of inequality in outcomes, and Marxian theory aspires to achieve equality.

Unlike most other social scientists, Marx had no illusions about being neutral in his approach. He deliberately tried to see the world from the point of view of working-class people in the nineteenth century, a time of great social and labor unrest. Conservatives at that time (more or less like conservatives today) argued that workers have no right to demand fair treatment. If equity existed and distributive justice and the norm of reciprocity prevailed, workers had no rational basis for complaint. They only had to calculate their inputs and outputs and weigh them against those of the owners and managers to understand that they were getting what they were worth. Marx says that the trouble with this position is that the calculation was rigged against the workers; it was built on the **norm of negative reciprocity**, under which some people are entitled to get more out of a situation or relationship than others, regardless of how much they put into it.[27]

While owners were trying to convince workers they had nothing to complain about, they were trying to influence the government to create laws which would lend credence to the idea that those who take the risks of starting and maintaining a business should receive greater rewards and privileges than those who only do the work. Indeed, they were quite successful. Most workers today have accepted the owners' point of view and have come to believe that owners ought to profit more than workers do. Marx argues that since workers contribute as much as owners, they should be equal in every respect; there should be no difference whatever in the rewards, privileges, and prestige gained by workers and owners. If workers are not treated as equals, they are experiencing not mere inequity, but exploitation.

Ruthless Criticism 2: Capitalism Alienates Workers

Marx also argues that the social interaction between workers and owners in organizations is alienating: Under capitalism, free workers are dehumanized. The concept of **alienation** refers both to the social situation in which people find themselves (an alienating work situation) and to the perceptions of individuals in those situations (a feeling of being less than human). Alienation is therefore a social as well as psychological phenomenon.[28]

Marx describes four types of alienation that are evident in organizations and groups in a capitalist or free-market society. First and most important is *alienation from production*. As serfs became free workers, they could find jobs and work at what they chose, but once having accepted a job they had to do as the owner or manager wished. Thus through capitalism, workers become separated from the means of production. They cannot use their human powers for creativity, because in taking jobs they give up their right to self-determination. Owners and managers tell workers what to do, when to do it, and how to do it. Workers are not supposed to reason why but simply to do as they are told.

Free workers are also alienated in that they do not own the things they produce or the services they give, so these things have no necessary relation to them as individuals. This is what Marx called *alienation from the product*. It is one thing to build a house for one's own pleasure and another to build a house for the pleasure of somebody else. Moreover, many of the things Americans produce and the services they perform seem to be devoid of real value. This is the ultimate criticism of the consumer society (see Chapter 11). Urged on by advertising, Americans buy superfluous consumer goods, trying to satisfy their "needs." Moreover, they earn their living making products and providing services that do not necessarily contribute to any objective social good.

Alienation from others derives from the basis of capitalism in free competition, not only among businesses but among workers. At its best, capitalism offers equal opportunities to all free workers—that is, equal opportunities to compete for unequal rewards. In a world of competition, the inherent social nature of humans is debased. People treat one another not as individuals with common human needs, equally worthy of dignity and respect, but as competitors; accordingly, small-group relationships in large organizations encourage competition rather than cooperation.

Capitalism not only debases social relationships by de-emphasizing love and nurturing while emphasizing competition and self-interest, it debases human nature, the essence of the individual, as well. *Alienation from self* results from marketplace values which lead people to think of themselves less as humans and more as things to be bought and sold (see "Alienation from Self: Executive Packaging"). Thus we become no different from a product, a machine, a cog in a wheel, a paper pusher. We wear the right clothes, say the right things, live in the right places, go to the right schools. We package and sell ourselves in ways we hope will increase our worth to employers and others who matter to us.

Alienation from Self: Executive Packaging

The perceived need for American business executives to present themselves not as they naturally are but in the way they are expected to look is an example of how capitalism has encouraged alienation from self. Both female and male executives wear suits almost as uniforms; the differences usually are skirts instead of trousers, blouses instead of shirts, and pumps instead of wing-tip oxfords. The emergence of an industry of personal image consultants to help executives package themselves in the proper image for success was described in a 1985 article in *Time* magazine:

> Underneath that overweight, stuttering, bumbling, scuffed-shoe exterior there may be someone with intelligence, wit, competence and true competitive ability. But who knows unless the exterior reveals the interior? And so an industry has come along dedicated to making men and women look good on the job so they can perhaps rise to top management posts in their companies.
>
> The operative word of this business is image, and the practitioners call themselves image consultants. First seen a decade ago, they are now multiplying like reflections off a ballroom mirror...
>
> The stylemakers offer to shape, polish and crease almost all aspects of a person to achieve success in the corridors of corporate power...

At fees that can hit $225 an hour, the specialists try to create a complete image—from corporate hairstyle to speech—for the ambitious man or woman who is still a few tantalizing rungs from the top. Self-styled "wardrobe engineers" advise men to discard cheap ties and reject anything in polyester. Women executives are cautioned to button up at the collar and resist the current custom of walking into the office in running shoes.

Honing one's social small-talk skills is also urged...a person's face must be carefully controlled; let positive feelings show, but reveal negative ones selectively. The complete executive commands a "repertoire of effective facial expressions," writes James G. Gray, a consultant in Washington.... The advisers offer "personal public relations" guidance on looking and acting like an expert in a particular field. Clients are even taught how to stand for success. John T. Molloy, one of the most successful image-makers, says that the "power stance" is with arms hanging down, feet apart, almost in a military fashion.

Source: Excerpted from John S. DeMott, "Looking Good: Consultants Polish Images," *Time*, April 8, 1985, p. 56. Copyright 1985 Time Inc. Reprinted by permission.

Marx's Solution for Exploitation and Alienation

Marx's critical analysis of social interaction under capitalism led to a proposal for resolving the problems of exploitation and alienation through socialism. He called his idea *scientific socialism* to distinguish it from the other forms emerging in the nineteenth century; *scientific* indicated that he had arrived at his solution by means of rigorous investigation and analysis.

Scientific socialism is the idea that control over the economy could be wrested from the hands of owners and placed in the hands of workers, who could then begin to set up social relationships based on equality of input and output. Marx proposed that in the beginning phases workers would set up a socialism based on equal rights to goods and resources; norms of equal reciprocity were to prevail, and people were to receive in proportion to what they contribute. In the later phases—indeed, in a distant future—the norms of reciprocity would no longer be needed, and communism based on "from each according to his ability, to each according to his needs" would become the prevailing norm.

The process of change would not be easy, Marx recognized, but he argued that all major changes in society have come about through conflict. Capitalists could not be expected to give up their power and control freely, since they themselves had wrested control through violence in the French Revolution and the American War of Independence. To Marx, the history of the world was a history of conflict, and alienation and exploitation had to be met head on.

His followers have since tempered Marx's support of conflict, even to the point of violence. After Marx's death, Friedrich Engels, his collaborator and friend, suggested that armed rebellion might no longer be necessary. Working-class people had made significant gains such as the right to vote without owning property, and fair-labor practices such as workers' compensation, a minimum wage, and the 40-hour week were being mandated by law.[29] Non-Marxist leaders such as Mahatma Gandhi and Martin Luther King, Jr., also demonstrated that organized, nonviolent confrontation is able to bring about change.[30]

⌛ ALIENATION AND EXPLOITATION IN CONTEMPORARY SOCIETY

Do Marx's criticisms of social relationships under capitalism, written in the nineteenth century, still hold at the end of the twentieth century? He described the situation of factory workers in a production-oriented society, but capitalism has changed. Our political and economic system can now be described as *advanced capitalism*, or, as some refer to it, as the postindustrial state or the information society.[31] The rise of white-collar and professional occupations like social worker suggests that the simple two-class distinction between owners and managers on the one hand and workers on the other is inadequate. Especially in the United States, production-oriented industries have declined and service-oriented industries have proliferated, and consumer confidence is the driving force of the economy. Alvin Toffler suggests that knowledge, wealth, and violence are now the ultimate sources of social power. The three form a single interactive system, and all three can be used at almost every level of social life, from the home to politics. Within this power triad, however, both force and wealth have come to depend on knowledge, which can be used by people either for or against one another and cannot be used up. According to Toffler:

> But a last, even more crucial difference sets violence and wealth apart from knowledge as we race into what has been called an information age. By definition, both force and wealth are the property of the strong and the rich. It is the truly revolutionary characteristic of knowledge that it can be grasped by the weak and the poor as well. Knowledge is the most democratic source of power.[32]

Some who accept the outlines of Marxian theory nevertheless believe that the contemporary world is very different from Marx's world; Eastern European societies have largely rejected communist governments which claimed to follow Marxian principles. They argue that Marx's analysis of class relations must be altered a great deal, and his theory of conflict between worker and owner must be completely reinterpreted.[33] Others believe that although many positive changes have been made in American society—child labor laws, unemployment compensation, collective bargaining by labor organizations, fringe benefits, social security, Aid for Families with Dependent Children—his basic criticisms of the flaws of capitalism remain applicable. Capitalism is still based on exploitative norms of negative reciprocity. It still alienates people from production, from the products of their work, from others, and from themselves.

The Many Faces of Alienation

The powerful theme of alienation has drawn the attention of many contemporary thinkers, Marxians and others.[34] The terms Marx invented to describe alienation are generally not used, and the concept of alienation has been broadened to include situations outside the workplace. Nevertheless, the ideas on alienation generated by Marx continue to have an influence on the thinking of social scientists.

Melvin Seaman has described how Marx's definitions of the four kinds of alienation resulting from capitalism have been adapted to fit contemporary life.[35] The idea of alienation from production has been redefined as *powerlessness*, people's sense that they lack autonomy and somehow have lost control of their destiny. Powerlessness has also been described as the inability to manage emotions, skills, knowledge, or material resources so effective performance of valued social roles will provide personal gratification.[36] Alienation from the product is expressed as *meaninglessness*, people's feeling that they cannot make sense of the situations in which they are involved. Things don't add up; everything is routine and repetitious, without challenge. People work or study because they have to, not because they want to. Powerlessness and meaninglessness contribute to the alienation that affects some social service workers (see "Burnout and Role Conflict in Child Welfare Administrators" in Chapter 14).

Social isolation is the term likely to be used today to describe alienation from others. People feel they are set apart from friends and associates, out of step with the rest of the world; others have left them out and they cannot get back in. There is a sense that what others are interested in is not what they are interested in.

The term *self-estrangement* is used instead of alienation from the self. People have a sense of some ideal human condition they would like to achieve, but they do not believe they measure up to it. They experience themselves as aliens, with no real sense of what makes them tick, only a sense that they are not what they would like to be.

The Alienating Effects of Unequal Status

Marx's ideas are particularly helpful in understanding interpersonal relationships in the workplace such as powerless and meaningless relations with superiors, competitive relationships with peers, and self-debasing behaviors. It is also useful in understanding social interaction that is not based in social class or occupational categories and does not necessarily take place in work organizations.

W. Peter Archibald has developed a Marxian-oriented theory describing the alienating effects of class, status, and power divisions on interactions between people of unequal status in a wide cross section of small- and large-group situations in everyday life.[37] As we have noted, social classes are defined in terms of roles or positions in the economy, such as blue-collar worker, white-collar worker, manager, and owner (see "Social Stratification and Social Classes" in Chapter 4). Status refers to prestige, and power refers to the ability of one person or group to influence the decisions of another.

Along with class, gender and racial stratification systems create differences in status and power. Men enjoy greater power and privilege in society than women do. People from European backgrounds enjoy greater power and privilege than people from African, Asian, Latino, and indigenous Native American backgrounds. Small-group and interpersonal encounters between men and women and between majority and minority individuals therefore also can be studied in the context of alienation. These encounters take place in families, small groups, large organizations, or communities; and in work groups, clubs, friendship networks, and neighborhood activities.

Archibald asserts that all interpersonal encounters between unequals, regardless of the basis of inequality, are threatening. This is true wherever they take place. People are not at ease in many interpersonal relationships, especially if there are inequalities in class, status, and power among the participants. In face-to-face encounters, they may respond to the threat and discomfort of participating in such interactions with one of four different adaptations, defined in terms of the following generalizations.[38]

1. *The detachment generalization.* People with different class, status, and power positions adapt by trying to avoid one another. Executives and workers use different lavatories, elevators, and eating areas. Neighborhoods are segregated on the basis of income, race, and ethnicity. Men and women organize exclusionary leisure and recreational activities.

2. *The means-end generalization.* Interaction between people with different class, status, or power positions tends to be very narrow and role-specific. People try to relate to others within the context of the formal, impersonal roles they occupy and the expectations for these roles, and they avoid getting to know others in a more personal way. If you are a student and I am a professor, we will keep within the bounds of that relationship even if we should meet at a party or in a restaurant. In short, people tend to "use" one another according to their roles.

3. *The control-purposiveness generalization.* People with high class, status, or power positions tend to initiate activity, make attempts to influence others, and actually do influence others more than people in lower-status positions do.

4. *The feelings generalization.* Hostility underlies much of the interaction between unequals, so rebellion occasionally surfaces. Although rapport may be evident, unequals always tend to dislike one another.

Contemporary Views on Resolving Exploitation and Alienation

Marx believed that society could overcome exploitation and alienation by systematically replacing the status hierarchies that had produced them with a form of socialism. It developed, however, that not all these hierarchies were to be abandoned; according to Engels, authority relationships are destructive only to the extent that they are exploitative and alienating.[39] Thus the socialist ideal became to create work organizations that would be free of oppressive hierarchies and replace them with organizational relationships based on equality of input and output.

This is another respect in which Marxian theory differs from exchange theory. The social exchange position is that inequity can be resolved with a number of strategies that would allow both parties in an exchange transaction to believe their outcomes (rewards minus costs) were proportional to their inputs (investments). Marx proposed that the way to resolve exploitation and alienation was to force people in power to amend their ways; therefore, workers should be dedicated to confronting and overthrowing owners and managers. But history has shown that it is not easy for workers, or any others in situations of social domination, to confront their superiors. Resolution of the conflict in any number of ways, as predicted in equity theory, is more likely. Marxian thinkers today recognize a variety of solutions to the problems of exploitation and alienation.

Resolutions for Subordinated Individuals

Recognizing the gap between Marxian theory and practice which resulted from the prediction that subordinate workers would rise up against their superiors, Peter Leonard examined Marx's failure to develop an integrated understanding of the individuals interacting in groups and organizations. Individual personality is constructed through concrete experiences in the economy, the family, and the state or government. Since there are numerous contradictions in these institutional sectors, these individuals' experiences present conflict.

In work organizations, individuals encounter exploitative and alienating social relationships as they seek to fulfill their human, creative potential. Despite the values of sharing, caring, and cooperation in the typical family, individuals must be socialized into the realities of the hierarchies of gender, age, class, ethnicity, and sexual orientation in the society. In government, a local or national goal of cultural pluralism—a shared identity and a spirit of cooperation—is contradicted by the realities of competing social forces and points of view. The state functions to mediate conflict among the competing sectors of the society through the development of laws and institutions and the establishment of traditions. In a capitalistic society, the state favors the dominant interests in defining normality and deviance and protecting the established hierarchies; it even favors the dominant interests in social welfare policy.[40]

Through such conflictful experiences, individuals' personalities are formed and they locate themselves within the hierarchies of various groups, organizations, and communities in the society. A general sense of superordinacy and subordinacy is inculcated into the personality, and individuals come to feel superior or subordinate in their relations with others. Leonard argues that subordinated people—working-class members, people in stigmatized racial and ethnic groups, women, the powerless young and old, the disabled—adopt modes of avoidance, resistance, or dissent as ways of dealing with the contradictions of social institutions which have been internalized in their general sense of self. In Leonard's terms, contradictory consciousness, unconscious resistance, the development of individual capacities, and participation in collective action are the principal ways in which subordinates respond to the demands of the dominant interests.[41]

1. *Contradictory consciousness.* Dominant elements often are successful in inculcating in subordinated individuals values and beliefs that support their own point of view. The subordinated then perceive the contradictions in social relationships as a private trouble, some indication of personal failure or deficiency. They may continue to submit to the dominant order, albeit with reservations. They may also engage in acts of deviance: They may steal, commit industrial sabotage, or engage in other unlawful behavior as an attempt to undermine authority by being deviant; however, they do not attempt to change their situation. As much as conformists who submit, they work against their own interests.

2. *Unconscious resistance.* Subordinated people may make unconscious attempts to repress drives and needs which they perceive as unacceptable to the dominant interests. Women repress their urge to achieve and excel; gays and lesbians repress their urge to fulfill their desires and try desperately to go straight; the disabled repress their anger and try to accept with humility the stigma attached to their status; racial and ethnic minorities repress their urge to speak out, and try to ingratiate themselves. In its milder forms, such repression may produce anxiety and neurosis; in its more severe forms, full-blown mental illnesses may result.

3. *Development of individual capacities.* Subordinated individuals may deal with contradictions by cultivating skills and interests that somehow take them out of the conflict or make them feel an exception to the rule—read literary works, engage in hobbies, or take up body building, for example. They may attempt to locate themselves within the contradictions in a way that reduces the strain—seek more education or a different occupation, or become entrepreneurs and their own bosses.

In these three adaptations, subordinated individuals attempt to conform as best they can to the demands of the dominant interests. They may deviate, go insane, or locate a protective niche, but in each case they never confront the contradiction head on or try to resolve it, as they do in the fourth adaptation, collective action.

4. *Participation in collective action.* Subordinated individuals may come together in an attempt to deal directly with the contradictions they experience through their participation in the economy, the family, and the state. Although collective action generates new contradictions between hope and despair and between optimism and depression, the advantages to individuals far outweigh the disadvantages. Working together, they can exercise the skills necessary for effective struggle in developing an altered sense of the self, one that is freer of the contradictions in social institutions and in the individual's own personality. For contemporary Marxists, this is the most acceptable adaptation; collective action can produce social change and progress; it can even give workers the power and the will to meet owners and managers on their own terms, if not to overthrow them.

Resolutions of Social Workers' Alienation

As an example of the resolution of alienation in work organizations, Wendy Sherman and Stanley Wenocur suggest six ways social service workers can deal with the feeling of powerlessness they often experience as they attempt to help clients.[42] Four of these can be considered forms of conformity. *Capitulation* involves identifying with agency administrators and incorporating values and behaviors that maintain the alienation of clients from the service. *Niche-finding* is an attempt to sidestep the conflict between client needs and administrative needs by searching out a special position that will give the worker an independent base of power. *Withdrawal* essentially refers to leaving the job; to avoid the conflict, the worker wrongly assumes that it is just a problem in a certain agency or service and will not be a problem in another. *Martyrdom* refers to adaptations in which workers come to identify with the alienation of their clients; they see themselves as alienated but cannot bring themselves to do anything about it. They become victims, incorporating a sense of powerlessness, a sense that there is no solution at all.

The fifth adaptation can be considered either deviant or nonconformist. In *noncapitulation*, social service workers reject the alienation and exploitation of agency directors and attempt to challenge or undermine the agency. According to Sherman and Wenocur,

Unionized Los Angeles County social workers rally to demonstrate
against proposed budget cuts in the Chidren's Social Services Department. Collective action to engage administrators in a process of negotiation and compromise is an effective way of resolving alienation in
work.

this is not a good solution to agency conflict because workers who forcefully challenge the
system may be isolated and "identified as mavericks or house radicals. At best they are discounted as unrealistic, immature, unable to cope. More frequently, noncapitulators will be
harassed, counseled out, or simply fired, if they do not first resign."[43]

The sixth adaptation is in keeping with the views of most contemporary Marxists on
positive solutions to exploitation and alienation. **Functional noncapitulation** occurs
when workers organize together in mutual support and attempt to negotiate with agency
administrators about the conditions of their work with clients. This is a form of compromise, but it is a productive adaptation in which workers consciously and actively decide
whether to capitulate or to hold firm. By maintaining a stance of always being willing to
negotiate, "these workers maintain a range of responses from refusal to acceptance, with
a large middle ground wherein to seek workable compromises. They also develop realistic expectations for changing the organization and establish boundaries of acceptability regarding the demands placed on them."[44]

Conformity, Deviance, and Collective Action

Sherman and Wenocur's six ways of resolving social service workers' feelings of alienation reflect Leonard's four individual adaptations to dominant interests in group life.
Together, they suggest certain generalizations about the ways in which people are likely

to deal with conditions of exploitation or alienation. Three basic adjustments can be made:

1. Conformity or functional capitulation, which involves all strategies by individuals and groups that in effect work to maintain existing exploitative and alienating relationships.

2. Deviance or noncapitulation, which involves rebellious acts by individuals and groups which undermine and subvert the system but do not engage it directly in change.

3. Collective action or functional noncapitulation, which involves individual and collective attempts to engage the system in a process of compromise and negotiation.

As we have noted, Marxian theory holds that the third option, functional noncapitulation or collective action, is the only direct way to resolve alienation and exploitation. Some Marxists have used the term *false consciousness* to refer to solutions such as conformity and deviance that further the power of the dominant interests to exploit and alienate.[45] This is not a very useful term because it suggests that there is only one truth, which is self-evident. There are many reasons why people may choose to conform or to deviate when they encounter alienation or exploitation. Not the least is that when they look around and calculate their ability to command higher rewards, reflect on their experiences, examine their alternatives, or compare their situation to those of others, they may very well conclude that theirs is not so bad after all. The Marxian position that there is only one effective solution is challenged by evidence that, in practice, there are other alternatives to direct confrontation of the dominant interests who are the source of alienation and exploitation.

∞ IMPLICATIONS OF MARXIAN THEORY FOR PRACTICE

In social service practice, Marxian theory underlies the efforts of workers to put functional noncapitulation into practice. Influenced by Marxian thought, workers may turn their attention to large-scale social movements and social change.[46] When an organization is the client system, they may articulate the need for group members to unite to produce more humane working conditions for themselves and, in turn, better results for the organization. In social work with individuals in small groups, Marxian theory provides a basis for assessing the degree to which group relationships are exploitative and alienating. With both small groups and large organizations, the theory suggests that intervention plans should offer clients the clear opportunity to confront such situations, and workers should assist in facilitating these opportunities. Social workers themselves may unite together to protect their own interests with agencies or departments, as Sherman and Wenocur suggest.

Leonard emphasizes that services to individuals in groups and organizations should combine reflection, or consciousness of alienation and exploitation, with action, or actually doing things to alter social circumstances. The approaches being developed by Marxist-influenced practitioners, however, are likely to emphasize one or the other of these functions. In *action-oriented practice,* the emphasis is on achieving concrete changes through such interventions as community organization, community development, and social action. Clients of action-oriented services may have experiences which enable them to develop a new and better sense of self, but no deliberate attempt is made to assure this. In *conciousness-oriented practice*, the emphasis is on altering the personality of clients and inculcating in them better ways of responding to exploitation and alienation. Interventions may focus on rap groups, support groups, consciousness-raising groups, or possibly individual psychotherapy. Involvement in direct social action is hoped for, but it is not the principal focus of the intervention.

∽ CHAPTER SUMMARY

In this chapter we have examined two theories that focus on interaction in personal encounters, small groups, and large organizations. While both regard the individual as self-interested, social exchange theory starts with the assumption that humans are by nature self-interested creatures, and in Marxian theory the assumption is that humans are inherently social and creative, but their nature has been debased by capitalistic economic institutions so that self-interest is now the norm. The visions of utopia in social relationships in these two theories therefore differ markedly.

Social exchange theorists see ultimate perfection in fairness and justice; social inequalities may exist, but only insofar as they are based on norms of reciprocity and the principle of distributive justice. Fairness and justice can be achieved in a number of ways which do not necessarily alter any objective ideas about what would be fair and just but which nevertheless can satisfy the participants in the interaction. Marxian theorists see ultimate perfection in equality of outcome; exploitation and alienation must be overcome if social relationships are to fulfill their promise. Although people may deal with exploitative and alienating situations in any number of ways, only one way—direct attempts to do away with inequality—is regarded as effective.

∽ DISCUSSION QUESTIONS AND CLASS PROJECTS

1. Do you believe that social exchange processes are a good way to describe the interaction between two people who are in love? Between members in a small friendship group? Between people working in the same department in an organization?

2. Describe the principles and processes by which rewards are calculated according to social exchange theory.

3. Distinguish among fate control, behavior control, and autonomous control.

4. Identify and define the following:

   comparison level
   comparison level for alternatives
   the principle of distributive justice
   norms of reciprocity
   norms of negative reciprocity
   comparable worth
   scientific socialism
   reification

5. When people experience inequity in social relationships, what is likely to happen?

6. Do you think workers should be paid according to the principle of comparable worth or according to market principles?

7. Give some examples of inequity in social relationships from your clients' experiences or your own life. Were they resolved? If so, was the resolution a good one?

8. What is the vision of human nature that underlies Marxian theory?

9. Describe Marx's two critiques or ruthless criticisms of nineteenth-century capitalism. Do you think they still apply in the twentieth century?

10. What are the four kinds of alienation described by Marx? How have these been redefined in the twentieth century? Are there any situations in which you have experienced alienation?

11. Describe some situations of alienation or exploitation clients might find themselves in. Make up a series of interview questions or issues that would enable you to assess alienation and exploitation in their lives.

12. According to Archibald, what kinds of adaptations do people make in interactions with others of unequal status? Can you recognize any of your own behaviors in these terms? For instance, does an interaction describe your behavior with respect to professors, supervisors, or administrators of services?

13. According to Sherman and Wenocur, in what ways are social workers likely to handle the exploitation and alienation they encounter on the job? Can you see your own behavior or the behavior of people you have worked with in these terms?

14. When social workers feel burned out, do you think they are experiencing alienation? Identify a representative group of social service workers in either the public or private sector and interview them about how their practice is organized and how it may lead to burnout or alienation.

15. Identify and describe how the following terms are used:

unconscious resistance
contradictory consciousness
development of individual capacities
participation in collective action
capitulation
niche-finding
withdrawal
martyrdom
noncapitulation
functional noncapitulation
the detachment generalization
the means-end generalization
the control-purposiveness
    generalization
the feelings generalization

✐ NOTES

1. See W. Peter Archibald, *Social Psychology as Political Economy* (Toronto, Canada: McGraw-Hill, 1978), pp. 16–31.

2. See F. Ivan Nye et al., "Choice, Exchange and the Family," in W. R. Burr et al. (editors), *Contemporary Theories of the Family* (New York: Free Press, 1979), pp. 1–41; Robert Pruger, "Social Policy: Unilateral Transfer or Reciprocal Exchange," *Journal of Social Policy*, vol. 2 (October 1973), pp. 289–302; and John S. Wodarski, "Clinical Practice and the Social Learning Paradigm," *Social Work*, vol. 28 (March–April 1983), pp. 154–60.

3. Harry Specht, *New Directions for Social Work Practice* (Englewood Cliffs, NJ: Prentice-Hall, 1988).

4. Peter M. Blau, *Exchange and Power in Social Life* (New York: John Wiley and Sons, 1964).

5. See Marvin E. Shaw and Philip R. Costanzo, *Theories of Social Psychology*, 2nd ed. (New York: McGraw-Hill, 1982), pp. 96–97.

6. J. R. P. French, Jr., and B. Raven, "The Bases of Social Power," in D. Cartwright and A. Zander (editors), *Group Dynamics: Research and Theory*, 3rd ed. (New York: Harper & Row, 1968), pp. 259–69.

7. Wendy Jean Harrod, "Expectations from Unequal Rewards," *Social Psychological Quarterly*, vol. 43 (1), 1980, pp. 126–30.

8. Yeheskel Hasenfeld, "People Processing Organizations: An Exchange Approach," *American Sociological Review*, vol. 37 (June 1972), pp. 256–63.

9. See Nye et al., "Choice, Exchange and Family," pp. 9–10.

10. See Blau, *Exchange and Power in Social Life*, and Zick Rubin, *Liking and Loving: An Invitation to Social Psychology* (New York: John Wiley and Sons, 1973).

11. Archibald, *Social Psychology as Political Economy*, p. 27.

12. Nye et al., "Choice, Exchange and Family," p. 6.

13. George C. Homans, *Social Behavior: Its Elementary Forms*, 2nd ed. (New York: Harcourt, Brace, Jovanovich, 1974).

14. John W. Thibaut and Harold H. Kelley, *The Social Psychology of Groups* (New York: John Wiley and Sons, 1959), pp. 21–24, 80–99, and 100–103.

15. See Shaw and Costanzo, *Theories of Social Psychology*, p. 100.

16. Homans, *Social Behavior: Its Elementary Forms*, 1st ed. (New York: Harcourt, Brace, Jovanovich, 1961), p. 75.

17. Blau, *Exchange and Power in Social Life.*

18. For a discussion of equity theory, see J. Stacey Adams, "Toward an Understanding of Inequity," *Journal of Abnormal and Social Psychology*, vol. 67 (1963), pp. 422–36; J. Stacey Adams and Sara Freedman, "Equity Theory Revisited," in L. Berkowitz (editor), *Advances in Experimental Social Psychology*, vol. 9 (New York: Academic Press, 1976), pp. 42–90; Elaine E. Walster, Ellen Berscheid, and G. William Walster, "New Directions in Equity Research," *Journal of Personality and Social Psychology*, vol. 25 (February 1973), pp. 151–76; and G. William Walster and Ellen Berscheid, *Equity: Theory and Research* (Boston, MA: Allyn and Bacon, 1978).

19. Homans, *Social Behavior*, 2nd ed., p. 37.

20. J. Stacey Adams, "Inequity in Social Exchange," in Berkowitz (editor), *Advances in Experimental Social Psychology*, vol. 2, 1965, pp. 283–95.

21. Ibid.

22. Nancy Weinberg, "Social Equity and the Physically Disabled," *Social Work*, vol. 28 (September–October 1983), pp. 365–69.

23. George Ritzer, *Toward an Integrated Sociological Paradigm* (Boston, MA: Allyn and Bacon, 1981), pp. 31–69.

24. For relatively easy reading of Karl Marx's writing on human nature, see "The German Ideology, Part I," in E. C. Tucker (editor), *The Marx-Engels Reader* (New York: W. W. Norton, 1972), pp. 113–19.

25. See Archibald, *Social Psychology as Political Economy*, pp. 24–31.

26. Karl Marx, "For a Ruthless Criticism of Everything Existing," in Tucker (editor), *Marx-Engels Reader*, pp. 7–10.

27. This concept comes from the anthropologist Marshall D. Sahlins. See Archibald, *Social Psychology as Political Economy*, pp. 106–14.

28. Karl Marx, "Alienated Labor," Eric and Mary Redman Josephson, in E. and M. Josephson (editors), *Man Alone* (New York: Dell/Laurel, 1962), pp. 93–105.

29. Friedrich Engels, "The Tactics of Social Democracy," in Tucker (editor), *Marx-Engels Reader*, pp. 406–23.

30. See Richard B. Gregg, *The Power of Nonviolence*, 2nd rev. ed. (New York: Shocken Books, 1966).

31. See John Naisbitt, *Megatrends* (New York: Warner Books, 1982), and Naisbitt and Patricia Aburdene, *Megatrends 2000: Ten New Directions for the 1990s* (New York: William Morrow, 1990).

32. Alvin Toffler, *Powershift: Knowledge, Wealth, and Violence at the Edge of the 21st Century* (New York: Bantam Books, 1990), p. 20.

33. See Ralf Dahrendorf, *Class and Class Conflict in Industrial Society* (Palo Alto, CA: Stanford University Press, 1959), pp. 36–72.

34. See Melvin Seeman, "Alienation Motif in Contemporary Theorizing: The Hidden Continuity of the Classic Themes," *Social Psychology Quarterly*, vol. 46 (September 1983), pp. 171–84.

35. Melvin Seeman, "On the Meaning of Alienation," *American Sociological Review*, vol. 24 (December 1959), pp. 784–90.

36. Barbara Bryant Solomon, *Black Empowerment: Social Work in Oppressed Communities* (New York: Columbia University Press, 1976), p. 16.

37. W. Peter Archibald, "Face-to-Face: The Alienating Effects of Class, Status and Power Division," *American Sociological Review*, vol. 41 (October 1976), pp. 819–37.

38. Ibid., pp. 820–21.

39. Friedrich Engels, "On Authority," in Tucker (editor), *Marx-Engels Reader*, pp. 662–65.

40. Peter Leonard, *Personality and Ideology: Towards a Materialist Understanding of the Individual* (London, England: Macmillan, 1984), pp. 5–7.

41. Ibid., pp. 103–15.

42. Wendy Ruth Sherman and Stanley Wenocur, "Empowering Public Welfare Workers through Mutual Support," *Social Work*, vol. 28 (September–October 1983), pp. 375–79.

43. Ibid., p. 367.

44. Ibid., p. 377.

45. Guenter Lawy, *False Consciousness: An Essay on Mystification* (New Brunswick, NJ: Transaction Books, 1987).

46. See, for instance, Robert Knickermeyer, "A Marxist Approach to Social Work," *Social Work*, vol. 17 (July 1972), pp. 58–65, and Paul Adams and Gary Freeman, "On the Political Character of Social Service Work," *Catalyst*, vol. 2, no. 7 (1980), pp. 71–82.

Social Interaction
Anomie and Symbolic Interactionism

MAJOR THEMES DISCUSSED IN THIS CHAPTER

1. **FUNCTIONALISM AND ANOMIE.** The utopian vision of functionalism is that group processes are normal when agreement exists about norms and expectations and opportunities for meeting them are available to all members. Anomie refers to breakdowns in a social system either because expectations are unclear or contradictory, or because opportunities for meeting them are not present.

2. **ANOMIE IN LARGE AND SMALL GROUPS.** The concept of anomie is applicable to the entire range of social interactions in groups and organizations. It has been used to study such phenomena as the bureaucratic personality, problems in the structure of social service agencies, and difficulties in developing treatment groups.

3. **IMPLICATIONS OF FUNCTIONALISM FOR PRACTICE.** Social service workers should think about anomie when trying to understand the organizations and groups in which they work. They also must take it into account when assessing the problems presented by clients. To overcome anomie social service workers should assure that group and organizational expectations are clarified and opportunities for achieving them are made available.

4. **SYMBOLIC INTERACTIONISM.** This theory focuses on the social processes through which individuals attach meaning to the objects, events, and situations that make up their world, particularly the ways they attach meaning to the self, that is, how they come to understand themselves as objects in social situations. Its utopian vision is that group relationships are normal when each party in a transaction is able to derive from it a positive sense of self.

5. **LABELING AS SOCIAL INTERACTIONISM.** The labeling perspective contributes to an understanding of the development of negative self-images and low self-esteem. It has been applied to the study of achieved labels, a result of actions that offend others, and ascribed labels, attributable to the groups and communities people belong to or into which they are born.

6. **IMPLICATIONS OF SOCIAL INTERACTIONISM AND LABELING FOR PRACTICE.** The potential for stigmatizing clients in the assessment process is very real. Workers must avoid the application of negative labels and strive to develop or sustain positive self-images in clients.

THE EXAMINATION OF SOCIAL INTERACTION CONTINUES in this chapter with two other schools of thought: functionalism and symbolic interactionism. Both of these theories shed light on life in groups and organizations, and both present utopian visions which are useful in guiding social service practice. In functionalism, groups and organizations are regarded as normal when agreement exists as to values, goals, roles, and tasks, and opportunities for complying with these agreements are made available to all participants. In symbolic interactionism, group and organizational life is considered normal when mutual self-respect prevails.

∽ FUNCTIONALISM AND ANOMIE

The origins of functionalism, like those of the social exchange and Marxian theories discussed in Chapter 13, are in the nineteenth century: the theory emerged as a response to both classical economic exchange theory and Marxian theory.[1] Functionalist perspectives dominate in contemporary social science, including social work, and most approaches to the study of social systems in the social services have applied the assumptions and concepts of functional theory.[2] To social service workers, systems theory usually means functionalism.

The Utopian Vision

Emile Durkheim, a French sociologist in the late nineteenth and early twentieth centuries, made significant contributions to functionalist thinking. He saw society as a whole, held together by a collective conscience, a normative or moral order, and a social contract. Today the same concepts are likely to be referred to as cultural norms and values. Norms and values, Durkheim believed, are absolutely essential to group life because they set up the goals for which people should strive and inform people of what is expected of them in achieving those goals. In other words, norms and values establish the working agreements governing social transactions, without which transactions could not occur and groups and organizations would disintegrate.[3]

The division of labor in a society is such that the units or parts are integrated into a whole. Each unit or part serves a purpose, and each contributes to the maintenance of the whole. In these ideas lies the meaning of functionalism: Each unit of a system, or structure, serves a positive purpose, or function, for the whole (see Chapter 3). In the ideal form of human social interaction, therefore, there would be a consensus in values and expectations, and everyone would contribute to this consensus by acting to assure the survival and continued development of the system. This is a utopian vision of perfect harmony which is rarely found in reality. Technological and social changes external to groups or organizations are often believed to be a cause of dysfunction or breakdown in them. The chances for achieving harmony are enhanced by limiting conflict, clarifying expectations, generating consensus, and encouraging conformity.

Anomie Theory: Breakdown in Social Systems

Durkheim coined the term **anomie** to describe breakdowns in a social system that threaten the viability of social interactions in groups and organizations. Anomie has two meanings. The first is **normlessness**, a condition in which the social contract, or the norms and values governing social interaction, seem to have broken down and disintegrated. Under conditions of normative breakdown, people no longer know what is expected of them or others. The second meaning of anomie is a condition in which the multiple, complex norms and values that regulate social interactions somehow contradict one another. In these conditions people are simultaneously pulled in different directions, so they become confused or disoriented and are forced to adapt.

Durkheim looked at the nineteenth century and did not see the norms of fair reciprocal exchange that the classical economists saw, nor did he see the exploitation and alienation that Marx saw. Instead he saw a social condition of normlessness in which people were interacting with one another in hesitant, awkward, and confused ways. The feudal system had been replaced with an industrial economic order devoted to materialism and relentless progress. Released from regulation by the church and the state, the economy sought to perpetuate growth by exciting people's appetites for goods. The social norms to constrain their desires also weakened, and the resulting social condition was anomie. As Durkheim notes, "To pursue a goal which is by definition unattainable is to condemn oneself to a state of perpetual unhappiness." He saw the moral state that results when, "From top to bottom of the ladder, greed is aroused without knowing where to find ultimate foothold" as a principal cause of suicide in modern societies.[4]

Durkheim's Study of Anomie and Suicide

As one of the earliest sociologists, Durkheim studied the causes of suicide to demonstrate how such an individualistic act could be explained in terms of social arrangements. His method was to examine the official records in a number of European countries. He found suicide rates increased in a society as anomie, accompanied by despair, increased in times of social upheaval.

Durkheim's study of recorded suicides led him to some interesting and unexpected observations about the relationship between the society and individual behavior. For instance, living in poverty and squalor did not appear to drive people to suicide. In poor countries the rates of suicide were actually lower than in more wealthy countries. Similarly, in predominantly Protestant areas, where individuality and personal responsibility were likely to be valued, suicide rates were higher than in areas where most people followed moral principles laid down and enforced by the Catholic Church. Whenever the economy was stable, however, suicide rates declined; they increased both when economic conditions deteriorated and people lost wealth or income and when conditions improved and people began to increase their wealth and status. Any kind of change, not the condition people normally found themselves in, could create such private troubles. This was interpreted to mean that poverty and authoritarian regimes could produce a comfortable social order, and industrialization and the norms supporting individual rights could produce a dysfunctional social order. Durkheim's finding that industrial nations could be expected to have higher suicide rates than less developed countries is still substantiated in contemporary comparisons of national suicide rates.[5]

Merton's Study of Anomie and Deviance

When Robert Merton considered the idea of anomie in the twentieth century, he emphasized contradictions among norms rather then normlessness. Merton was trying to understand social deviance, why people break the norms of society and act to threaten its survival. He believed that a society is held together when a moral order exists in which its values or goals are stipulated and the ways of achieving them are clear.[6]

Merton examined American society in the 1950s, a time the media often portray as "happy days" in which daily life was optimistic and orderly. Merton saw the fifties differently, as a time of anomie in the sense of contradictions in normative goals and the means of observing them.

On the one hand, Merton observed, Americans were tied together by a common value: the goal of monetary or economic success and material well-being. Merton saw nothing wrong with this goal; it was, after all, the American dream and a basic reason for the emergence of the United States in the postwar era as a strong and wealthy nation. Furthermore, most Americans shared in this dream; on this issue, there were no cultural or class differences. Almost everyone dreamed of a house in the suburbs, a car or two, nice clothes, good food, and everything that goes with material success.

On the other hand, the goal of economic success was contradicted by the fact that everybody did not have the same opportunities to achieve it. The route was not always clear, nor was it universally available, and many Americans who earnestly wanted to participate in the dream found their access to it blocked. For some sectors of American society in the 1950s, especially the poor and the working class, a situation of anomie existed. Merton maintained that due to the contradictions they experienced between society's goals of success and their own lack of means for achieving it, people were turning to deviance in such forms as crime and delinquency, mental illness, drug and alcohol abuse, depression and disillusionment, and violence. Forced to adapt to these contradictions, they did not always do so in functional or positive ways.

Adaptations to Anomie

Merton described five ways in which individuals adapt to this condition of anomie, ways which are still evident today[7] (see "Merton's Individual Adaptations to Anomie"). Most people respond with *conformity*, trying to achieve economic success and exhausting every possible legitimate opportunity to do so. If at first they don't succeed they try, try again. Some, however, turn to deviant adaptations. One of these Merton called *innovation*, referring to success achieved through illegitimate means such as cheating, stealing, embezzling, committing fraud, selling drugs, or prostitution. Through such means the American dream might be achieved, but not in an acceptable way.

Some people adapt by giving up on the goal of economic success altogether. They become satisfied with what they have and do not feel compelled to pursue the material goals of other Americans. They do not upset the system or cause trouble but continue to perform their expected tasks, though with no real purpose. Merton referred to this kind of deviant adaptation as *ritualism*, in which people just go through the motions of getting ahead. On the surface they appear to be conforming, but they do just what is expected of them, no more and no less.

People making the *retreatism* adaptation give up not only on the goal of economic success but also on any legitimate attempt to pursue that goal. They do not even go through the motions. Merton identified retreatist adaptations in those who abuse drugs,

Commuters trudge through South Station, Boston, on their way to work on a summer day, doggedly pursuing the rewards of the American Dream. In Merton's terms, they may be adapting to anomie by conforming or by simply following the daily ritual.

including alcohol. He also saw mental illness as a retreat from reality into hallucination and fantasy. *Rebellion* goes a step further. Not only do people give up on success goals and legitimate attempts to achieve them, they substitute new goals and devise new strategies for achieving them. Merton and other observers in the 1950s and 1960s saw violent youth gangs who rejected the economic success goal and the work ethic in favor of an ethic of violence and excitement as the major example of rebellion. In contemporary American society, gangs are likely to be engaged in the drug trade, pursuing both economic success *and* violence and excitement, as well as social and political power.

Anomie and Anomia

By anomie, Merton meant an objective environmental situation in which people interact, not a subjective, inner state of individuals. Even in his adaptations, Merton is not describing personality traits or types of people; he does not use the terms *conformist, innovator, ritualist, retreatist, or rebel.* Instead he offers types of adaptations that anyone might choose, depending on the circumstances.

Other theorists have coined the term **anomia** (or *anomy*) to refer to the more subjective, psychological aspects of anomie— feelings of normlessness and the conscious experience of contradictions. According to Robert MacIver, "Anomy signifies the state of mind of one who has been pulled up by his moral roots, who has no longer any standards but only disconnected urges, who has no longer any sense of continuity, or form, or obligation."[8] Those who promote use of the concept of anomia believe that anomie must be

---

Merton's Individual Adaptations to Anomie

According to Robert Merton, anomie is the result of contradictions between success goals set by the society and the individual's opportunities for success. Individuals experiencing anomie are said to adapt with conformity or one of four deviant adaptations:

Conformity   Continual pursuit of success goals, using available legitimate opportunities.
Innovation   Continual pursuit of success goals, using available illegitimate opportunities.
Ritualism   Giving up on success goals but continuing to go through the motions of using legitimate opportunities.
Retreatism   Giving up on success goals and dropping out of legitimate opportunities.
Rebellion   Giving up on both success goals and legitimate opportunities and setting up alternative goals and opportunities.

Source: Robert K. Merton, *Social Theory and Social Structure*, 2nd ed. (New York: Free Press, 1951), pp. 193–211.

---

experienced on some level by the individual before it will provoke the need for adaptation.

To Merton, anomia (feelings) is not an irrelevant concept, but it cannot be substituted for anomie (situation). People experiencing the effects of anomie do not have to realize that the situation is anomic to adapt in the various ways he suggests. For instance, burglars ordinarily do not say they are "innovating" because they are experiencing a contradiction between their desire for success and the legal opportunities available to them. Nevertheless, direct-service social workers who use Merton's idea of anomie in examining the fit between person and environment will find themselves working as much in the environment as in the person. Just asking clients about their perceptions of the opportunities available to them and their feelings about any lack of opportunities is not enough. Social workers must learn about the community, the way it is organized and the opportunities that are actually available to clients. They have to examine anomie as well as anomia.

Comparing Merton, Marx, and Social Exchange

Merton, Marx, and social exchange theorists all are concerned with a similar dimension, the achievement of rewards. For Merton and Marx the principal emphasis is on material rewards, but both theories can easily include a broader range of social rewards, as in social exchange. The points of departure in these three theories are quite different, however. In exchange theory, human nature is assumed to be self-interested, so a system like capitalism is inevitable, a natural law, and an ultimate good. In Marxian theory, humans are rational creatures who are concerned with collective self-interest but nevertheless produce a system like capitalism and reify it; capitalism is humankind gone wrong. Merton does not see human nature as necessarily self-interested or question the effects of capitalism, nor does he argue for or against inequitable outcomes or take a stand on competitiveness, exploitation, or alienation. He does not look much deeper than the general goal of monetary success.

Merton does take a stand on how people should respond in situations where opportunities may not be available: They should conform, or keep trying against all odds. Social exchange theory maintains that people should respond to inequity in any way that will reestablish a sense of equity. The Marxian stand on how exploitation and alienation should be resolved is at odds with Merton as well as with social exchange. While Marxians do not espouse deviance—such acts as stealing, cheating, dropping out, martyrdom, or repressing needs—they do not champion conformity, either. Marx in fact championed rebellion, the substitution of new goals and new means for established goals and means. In Marxian theory, as we noted in Chapter 13, rebellious behavior in the form of social action and functional noncapitulation is the proper response to problems in the organization of society.

Obviously Marx and Merton (and Durkheim) held very different views about the normality of capitalism as a social context for groups and organizations. For Marx, capitalism itself was an aberration. For Merton it was basically good and only needed some tinkering. For Durkheim the particular system, and the goals and values guiding it, did not matter. The only social context of value was the stability that comes with clear and concrete social expectations.

The ideas of Merton and Durkheim demonstrate why functionalist analysis ultimately leans in the direction of conservatism. The argument is that everyone wants to and should conform, and only breakdowns or contradictions in norms will prevent conformity. If only people knew what was expected of them, or if they only had the opportunities to fulfill those expectations, they would gladly do what is expected. People who do not do what is expected—even when the expectations are not clear or are contradictory—are deviants, potential threats to the survival of the system.

Nevertheless, the functionalist theory of anomie has had an important, positive impact on society. In pointing to the contradictions between the goal of economic success and the limited opportunities for achieving it that existed in American society, Merton introduced ideas which were incorporated in the social welfare policies of the Great Society and the War on Poverty of the 1970s.[9] Anomie theory forced Americans to put their free-market house in order; it was applied in efforts to mobilize the poor, women, and racial and ethnic minorities and to seek changes in the political and economic orders to provide them with greater opportunities. Since capitalism offers the opportunity to compete with others for economic success, equality of opportunity was adopted as social policy. But the goal was not equality of outcome or even equity of outcome. Anomie theory led to liberal, progressive changes, but it never aspired to bring radical change.

∞ ANOMIE IN LARGE AND SMALL GROUPS

The concept of anomie is applicable to the entire range of social interaction in large and small groups, including social work practice with individuals.

The Bureaucratic Personality

In large organizations, or bureaucracies, anomie may result in the rigid, impersonal style often developed by bureaucrats in the public and private sectors who lose sight of the organization's goals and focus strictly on operational rules and regulations. Bureaucrats seem to follow the letter of the law rather than its spirit; they get hung up on details and define rules in very narrow terms; they seem unable to think for themselves. They defend these behaviors by claiming they are "only doing their job" or "just following orders." Thorstein Veblen referred to this attitude as trained incapacity," while John Dewey saw it as "occupational psychosis." Merton refers to it as the "bureaucratic personality" and suggests it may be seen as a form of ritualism.[10]

Functionalists maintain that in effective bureaucracies, group goals are clearly connected to the means for achieving them. That is, organizational leaders first identify the goals in the form of policies, procedures, guidelines, or, in general, rules and regulations and then establish plans for achieving them. Conformity to these goals and plans develops in functional organizations because managers keep their eyes on the goals and interpret the rules and regulations in light of them. In dysfunctional organizations, however, overconformity or ritualism can be the result when bureaucrats lose sight of organizational goals and substitute the means—rules and regulations— for the ends of organizational action (see "Becoming a Bureaucrat").

Merton argues that four organizational processes encourage the development of ritualism in bureaucratic personalities:

1. The incentives used by organizations to reward and discipline bureaucrats may work too well. Those who are rewarded with seniority, tenure, or careers become invested in doing the things that seem to be related to the rewards they receive. Just performing the tasks of their jobs becomes more important than meeting the goals of the organization.

2. Group cohesion in organizations develops as strong informal or personal ties emerge in departments and work groups. An esprit de corps motivates members to defend their territory. The ways they do things become sanctified, and the pride they develop in their craft leads them to resist change.

3. Because of the emphasis on impersonalization, bureaucrats may go too far in their desire to treat everyone impartially. They lose sight of the unique circumstances and situations people find themselves in.

4. Acting as a representative of the power and prestige of an organization may lead bureaucrats to adopt a domineering or arrogant style. The goals of the organization get lost, and only its rules and regulations are respected.[11]

Adaptations to Anomie in Social Service Organizations

Recognizing the anomie inherent in the organizational context of social work practice— social service agencies and departments—Ann Hartman suggests a worker-in-situation perspective that takes anomie theory into account. Following Merton, she notes that "an anomic situation is one in which cherished and accepted goals cannot be achieved by the institutionalized means or norms available." The goals of direct-service workers are to improve the welfare of clients by enhancing their social functioning and making their environments supportive. The organizations in which they work, however, are so constrained by political, economic, and social conditions that in practice they have limited opportunities to give professional service. This produces a condition of anomie or alienation which can lead to burnout—feelings of being stressed out, tedium, or inability to accomplish anything—among workers, especially in child welfare (see "Burnout and Role Conflict in Child Welfare Administrators"). Hartman suggests four possible ways workers suffering anomie or burnout can adapt to these feelings.[12]

Becoming a Bureaucrat

Steve Carmichael was a project manager for the Neighborhood Youth Crops when he was interviewed by Studs Terkel for *Working*, a series of interviews with workers and managers. His job, to provide young people of poor families with work experiences, was part of the vast bureaucracy established under the Economic Opportunity Act of 1964 to administer the War on Poverty.

Carmichael became a public administrator, even though he had been frustrated in dealing with administrators as a VISTA volunteer and a school employee, because he thought he could change the system: "I was disdainful of bureaucrats in Washington, who set down rules without ever having been to places where those rules take effect. Red Tape. I said I could replace a bureaucrat and conduct a program in relationship to people, not figures."

His approach to the job was to suggest change, going from administrator to administrator, conniving to be heard. He found that "Gradually your effectiveness wears down. Pretty soon you no longer identify as the bright guy with the ideas. You become the fly in the ointment." He was criticized by his superiors, not directly, but indirectly, by being ignored. His suggestions went through channels, and 90 percent was filtered out by his immediate superior. He was told innova-

tion takes time, documentation, signatures; everybody seemed to forget there were people waiting.

Every night he had to sort out a desk full of reports and memos so they could be filed. He tried to ignore the paperwork: "If I did all the paperwork I should, my sanity would go." He liked to make decisions over the phone, but months later he would be caught without a necessary report.

Nevertheless, Carmichael said,

> The most frustrating thing for me is to know that what I'm doing does not have a positive impact on others. I don't see this work as meaning anything. I now treat my job disdainfully. The status of my job is totally internal: Who's your friend?...Success is to be in a position where I can make a decision.

He doubted that he would be in public administration much longer. One reason: "each day I find myself more and more like unto the people I wanted to replace."

Source: "Bureaucracy: Steve Carmichael," in Studs Terkel, *Working: People Talk about What They Do All Day and How They Feel about What They Do* (New York: Pantheon Books, 1974), pp. 341–43.

Some social workers adapt in ritualized ways: they abandon their goals and aimlessly perform prescribed but ineffective tasks. Others innovate by clinging to the goals of good service yet moving outside the norms of the agency to help the client. This can leave them defeated and exhausted because they are investing themselves beyond the call of duty. Still others retreat; they relinquish the goals and norms of the agency by reducing their involvement in services, finding other work situations where anomie might not be so great, or abandoning social work as a career. The escape into private practice, Hartman believes, may be a retreat from the anomie of agency life. Some social workers rebel by challenging the organization's goals, norms, and means or otherwise acting to bring about social change to make the environment more responsive to the needs of clients.

Hartman applies anomie theory in a unique and flexible way. She does not include conformity as a possible adaptation, and her description of rebellion suggests that she

---

Burnout and Role Conflict in Child Welfare Administrators

A number of theoretical perspectives offer ways of understanding burnout, a sense of physical and emotional exhaustion or defeat in one's work. In Marxian theory, burnout is considered a product of the exploitation and alienation workers experience at the hands of management. In functionalism, burnout is considered a consequence of anomie produced by breakdowns or contradictions in the norms and values that regulate social interactions. In role theory, burnout is considered a possible outcome of role conflict which could be evident among both managers and workers.

Martha Jones studied role conflict among a nonrandom sample of child welfare administrators. She distinguishes role conflict from role ambiguity and role stress. Role ambiguity refers to a situation in which the role expectations are unclear, and role stress refers to situations of work overload. Role conflict refers to situations in which incumbents are expected to fulfill two or more roles that are incompatible with one another.

The agency administrators Jones observed over the course of a year were in situations of role conflict, caught between incompatible expectations. On the one hand they are expected to help families by providing social services that would meet their needs, while on the other hand they are expected to police or control clients to assure their conformance with societal expectations about parenting.

Subjectively, the administrators did report experiencing conflict. Their public presentation of self was one of a person in an impossible situation. They emphasized "how it really is" in child welfare. Yet, their more private presentation of self belied this public image. The administrators studied were very experienced and had confident, consistent, and competent patterns of behavior. Jones found that role conflict among them did not lead to burnout; in fact, they coped with and resolved their role conflict in positive ways. It appeared to energize them rather than burn them out.

How was this possible? The outcome had to do with their ability to devise a new role for themselves by using their coping and problem-solving skills. First they reframed

---

does not see it as a deviant adaptation as described by Merton. She tends to see it more in conflict theory terms; people being treated inequitably should not conform to the system but should strive to change it.

Anomie and Small-Group Development

To Aaron Brower, anomie is one of the phases social work treatment groups go through as they attempt to achieve their group and individual goals. All groups develop according to a process of constructed social reality; that is, the perceptions, understandings, and past experiences of individual members influence their participation in the group. The groups begin with a state of anomie, defined as normlessness, and lack structure, that is, clear norms and role expectations, communication networks, and leadership and power relations. Typically, members want to participate in the group but are not sure how to do so.[13]

Group members adapt to anomie by developing initial schemas, or cognitive representations, based on previous learning about what groups, treatment, and group leaders

situations of ambiguity (What should I do?) into situations of conflict (What decision should I make?). Then they encouraged discussion of the conflict, allowing differences to be aired and promoting consensus about how the conflict should be handled. Through this means they came to recognize the benefits of both policing and serving the public. The consensus led to an expansion of the role of administrator, from experiencing incompatible expectations to accepting and integrating the service and the policing functions. They also reached the conclusion that they needed to develop skills for working with a wide variety of people without compromising their values, but they couldn't expect to make everyone happy.

For the child welfare administrators Jones studied, role conflict had a number of positive outcomes. They became more flexible and expanded their sources of information. They spent a great deal of time networking within their agencies and in the larger community. They reached out to understand the people they were working with and in so doing came to appreciate the

conflicts being experienced by others. Role conflict also helped the administrators remain enthusiastic about their position, prevented boredom, and clarified their goals and mission.

Although the findings of this study were that role conflict did not lead to burnout among child welfare administrators, they cannot be extrapolated to all administrators or to social workers in general. The study examined only administrators who were competent in their positions and did not include any who had been unsuccessful or who had left. More important, it did not examine the effects of role conflict among direct-service providers, who are subordinated to the authority of administrators. In fact, Marxian theory would not predict that role conflict among administrators would lead to burnout. It would suggest, however, that it would lead to burnout among workers.

Source. Martha L. Jones, "Role Conflict: Cause of Burnout or Energizer?" *Social Work*, vol. 38 (1993), pp. 136–41.

and members are like. At this point, these schemas, or the reality of the group, may be quite different for each member.

As members interact they obtain a sense of these different realities, and this provokes what Brower calls the first reality crisis. A leader who can provide a clear statement of purpose and goals can reduce the anomie, but if the leader fails to clarify expectations, anomie may be heightened. Members may hold fast to their initial schemas and drop out of the group, on the assumption that it will be of no use to them, or they may give up their personal expectations and become increasingly dependent on the leader. This produces acute anomia and a sense of loss that can spill over into their lives. Or members may make an in-between adaptation by suspending belief in their initial schemas without feeling overwhelmed by ambiguity.

If the members let go of their initial schemas, a second reality crisis is provoked during which each member looks inward and starts to explore how to exert influence or have power in the group. Members attempt to create new schemas with clearer expectations of their own goals and the goals of the group, and their place in the group becomes clearer and more secure. Through feedback a shared reality emerges; normlessness is replaced with norms that represent a consensus among members, and a cohesive group is formed.

⚭ IMPLICATIONS OF FUNCTIONALISM FOR PRACTICE

Functionalism is a major theoretical perspective that has been highly influential in social service work. Its principal contribution is the concept of anomie.

Functionalism has a clear utopian vision of social interaction in groups, organizations, communities, and society as a whole. Harmony and stability, derived from shared values and expectations, should prevail. Everyone should be assured of equal opportunities to achieve the socially acknowledged goals to which they aspire. What these values are is of much less consequence than agreement about them and opportunities to achieve them. When harmony is broken, that is, when social change occurs or contradictions in norms and expectations exist, then anomie and its psychological counterpart anomia may surface. These strains force individuals to adjust their behaviors, positively or negatively. A positive adaptation, from the viewpoint of functionalism, is usually one that reinforces the existing values while assuring improved opportunities to achieve them. A negative adaptation is one that produces deviance in the form of innovation, ritualism, retreat, or rebellion.

The role of the social service worker is to assess the degree to which groups and organizations are anomic or place clients in situations of anomie. Following anomie theory, the worker must identify the norms operating in the group and assess the opportunities provided for members to conform to group norms and the expected means for doing so. Asking clients to describe the various groups they consider themselves a part of, as they perceive them in terms of their norms and the opportunities they provide, can reveal feelings of anomia. A more complete interpretation of anomie, however, requires the worker to directly observe these groups and their environments. When anomie is affecting the behaviors of clients, social workers can plan strategies for altering the situation or the ways members are responding to it. Following anomie theory, they would reinforce attachment to prevailing social norms and increase the available legitimate opportunities for clients to conform to them by developing and maintaining resources in the environment and linking people to them.

Anomie has a special message for administrators of social service organizations. They must work to rid their own organizations of anomie and try to assure that conformity to its goals and practices does not produce workers with ritualistic, bureaucratic personalities. But they must also reflect on their own leadership styles; if their behavior is ritualistic, they can expect the same kind of behavior in their subordinates.

⚭ SYMBOLIC INTERACTIONISM

The origins of the perspective on social interaction known as symbolic interactionism in the United States were in the early twentieth century. In its behaviorist and utilitarian characteristics, it also represents a criticism of classical economic theory. David Karp and William Yoels defined **symbolic interactionism** as "a theoretical perspective in sociology that focuses attention on the processes through which persons interpret and give meanings to the objects, events, and situations that make up their social worlds." Social worlds represent "the totality of the various social locations individuals occupy in a society,"[14] including families, bureaucracies, small groups, friendships, and even communities and whole societies.

George Herbert Mead, a University of Chicago sociologist who made major contributions to both social psychology and symbolic interactionism, took issue with the "empty headedness" of learning theorists' arguments that human behavior is essentially the product of habits developed through social reinforcement or conditioning processes (see Chapter 15). In *Mind, Self, and Society*, he maintains that the mind is an essential consideration in attempts to understand human behavior.[15]

Mind and Self in the Context of Society

Mind is a function of certain unique features of humans as a biological species that allow for three specific abilities. First, mind gives humans the ability to create symbols; that is, through language and other cognitive processes, they can name and designate objects, feelings, and behaviors in their environment and within themselves. Second, mind gives humans the ability to think and to rehearse alternative lines of action. Thinking is a covert or hidden action which goes on inside the head; it is a private conversation we have with ourselves about what is going on, what we feel, and what we want to do. Mead refers to this as *imaginative rehearsal*. Third, mind gives humans the ability to make decisions about their feelings and behaviors and to *give meaning* to their social worlds. In this respect, mind makes active participation in everyday events possible. Humans influence these events by the way they interpret them, express feelings and attitudes about them, and actually behave in them. No other species can do this in the sophisticated and efficient way that humans can.[16]

While mind is inherent in the biological nature of man, it does not exist outside the context of society. Mind not only produces human society but is influenced and shaped by it. Humans symbolize, develop and use language, and communicate with one another through interactions in social processes. Thus they are involved with one another not as mechanical and utilitarian social rewarders or punishers but as participants in a symbolic interaction. Through such interaction, society, the social system composed of norms, values, social institutions, and institutionalized social arrangements (see Chapter 3), is continually shaped and reshaped.

Self is one of the products created from the relation of mind to society. Karp and Yoels define self as "The view of oneself derived from the ability to evaluate one's behaviors from the point of view of others, ultimately from the point of view of the standards of society as a whole."[17] The self is one of those symbols, imaginative rehearsals, or meaningful lines of action people decide to take.

Different aspects of self have been identified. *Identity* establishes who and what we are in social terms: "I am a man, a Hispanic, a social worker."[18] *Self-image* refers to the sense of self as unique and how we attempt to present ourselves in everyday interaction with others: "I am a secure, confident woman." Sometimes self-image exists in contrast to the *ideal self*, the person we wish we were or want to be: "I wish I were more sophisticated and worldly wise."[19] Sometimes this ideal exists in contrast to the *possible self*, which is what we could be if we tried: "I could be less shy and awkward."[20] The self-image, the ideal self, and the possible self are representations of the essence of humans as individuals, statements about how they see themselves most of the time, if not always. More transitory representations of the self are referred to as *self-precepts*; when we fail at a particular task, for example, we may think of ourselves as incompetent, though we do not normally think of ourselves that way. Another aspect of self is **self-esteem**, which refers to how we evaluate ourselves favorably or unfavorably as a result of a particular event: "What a mess I am," or "What a nice person I am."

Since self is only possible because of the symbolic capacities of humans, it is attached to mind. Self is also attached to society, because it is only through interaction with others that the person gives meaning to and makes sense of who she or he is. Mind, self, and society are all processes. Unlike many other perspectives, symbolic interactionism does not consider stable or unstable social structures. In this perspective everything exists in a state of flux, always emerging but never quite arriving. Mind, self, and society are in continual development.

Development of the Self

Perhaps no other human characteristic is more central to symbolic interaction than the development of the self. The basic process in the development of the self involves taking the role of the other, which must be distinguished from role-playing. **Role-taking** is analogous to seeing the world, including the self, from the point of view of others. In particular, it is "the process whereby an individual imaginatively constructs the attitudes of the other, and thus anticipates the behavior of the other."[21] **Role-playing** refers to the behaviors associated with and undertaken in a particular social position. Thus the self emerges out of the ability to step into the role of others and see oneself through their eyes. The ability to symbolize makes it possible to read the minds of others with whom interactions take place.

The Generalized Other, Reference Groups, and Significant Others

All social interaction is not equally influential in the development of the self. Mead developed the concept of the **generalized other** to describe the "organized community or social group which gives to the individual his unity of self."[22] Karp and Yoels' definition of the generalized other is "An abstract configuration of all the relevant rules and roles that we must take into account to function successfully in any social environment. In the most abstract sense, the generalized other is society as a whole."[23] This idea has also been expressed by symbolic interactionists in terms of the reference group or the reference other.[24] The reference group, introduced in Chapter 13, is very much like the generalized other. It has to do with those groups with which people identify and which are therefore capable of influencing them. Family and the friendship groups found in neighborhoods and workplaces are seen as typical reference points. Such reference groups are used in two ways: in a normative way, to provide standards, norms, attitudes, and values that individuals come to identify as their own, and in a comparative way, to allow individuals to evaluate themselves and their positions.[25]

Reference groups and others need not be actual persons or groups; it is not necessary to have contact with them or to belong to them as members. Referents may be actual people we know, parents, friends, religious leaders, or others we have come to know and respect, or they may be people we do not actually know but only know of or aspire to be like or to be connected with. For instance, a lower-class male whose parents never went to college may aspire to become a college-educated professional. In the process, his referent stops being his membership group (his family) and becomes the professional group to which he aspires. Referents may also be imaginary or symbolic. They may simply exist as ideas in our heads; we may want to be sophisticated or quiet and unassuming, traditional or radical, feminine or masculine, and so on.

Sometimes reference groups and others are not positive referents. *Negative reference groups* are those we do not want to imitate and whose influence we want to avoid. Such negative referents can influence both behavior and self-image. Knowing that you do not want to be a narrow-minded conservative, for instance, can shape your behavior and attitudes as much as knowing that you want to be an open-minded liberal.

The concept of **significant others** is also associated with the development of the self. Significant others are usually considered to be actual people with whom individuals interact and who have influence over them. Most often they are members of the primary groups in which intimate, person-to-person transactions take place at the interactional level: family members, friendship groups, or communities based on common identity. But significant others may also be involved in secondary groups in which social transactions are more restricted and impersonal and take place on the sociocultural level (see Chapter 3). Thus a teacher may serve as a significant other for a student, or a boss may do so for a worker.

The Process of Social Interaction

The self first emerges in childhood, but it is subject to continual change and reshaping throughout life as a function of interactions with others. As one of the basic social processes, interaction operates along with recruitment, socialization, innovation, and control to maintain or change social systems such as groups and organizations.

Situations and Social Positions

Social interaction always takes place in **situations** defined objectively as the actual circumstances under which individuals come together or defined subjectively in terms of the meaning of the circumstances for the individuals who are interacting. At the objective level, a situation could involve, for instance, encounters in the family, among friends, at school, or at work, and these encounters could be further identified as a family dinner, an accidental meeting in an elevator, a student study group, or an evaluation of work performance.

People understand themselves and others only through the social positions they occupy in the situation. In role theory, social position is defined in terms of the related concepts of status and role. As we noted in Chapter 3, *status* is equivalent to the position itself—member of the family, stranger, lover or spouse, student or teacher, boss or worker, social worker or client. *Role* refers to the dynamic aspects of the position, the actions of mothers, strangers, lovers and spouses, students and teachers, bosses and workers, and social workers and clients. Social interaction functions in such a way that people are recruited and socialized into positions, in which they may maintain or change the behaviors and attitudes expected of people in that position.

Definition of the Situation

Symbolic interactionists are especially interested in the subjective definition of the situation, the stage of examination and deliberation which precedes action. Defining a situation gives it and the role of the individual in it the meaning necessary for interaction to occur. George McCall and J. L. Simmons outline the process in the following terms:

1. As humans, we are thinkers, planners, schemers.
2. Things take on meaning in relation to our plans.

3. We act toward things in terms of their meaning for our plan of action.

4. Therefore, we must identify every "thing" we encounter and discover its meaning.

5. For social plans of action, things that are done with others, the meanings of "things" must be consensual; that is, there must be agreement among the participants about those meanings.[26]

This definition of the situation gives the concept of role a special interpretation in symbolic interactionism. As we have noted, people's roles are defined in terms of both the expectations others have of them and the expectations they have of themselves. Thus while there are certain cultural and interpersonal expectations about the way a supervisor, a student, or a social worker should behave, how individuals *interpret* these roles is of paramount importance. Mary's definition of *supervisor* is likely to be quite different from Maria's definition of the term. Your definition of *student* may be quite different from the definition the person next to you in class would give. Symbolic interactionists emphasize the subjective aspects of role, how the individual in a role defines or interprets it.

Negotiated Lines of Action: Behaviors and Self-Definitions

Because there are often differences between the expectations others have of us (the objective situation) and the expectations we have of ourselves (the subjective situation), all social interaction involves negotiation and bargaining about how the behaviors associated with roles are to be enacted. A certain amount of agreement has to be reached in the situation in order for the interaction to go smoothly. McCall and Simmons refer to this as "the negotiation of lines of action."[27]

Behaviors and other role-related tasks are not the only things negotiated in social interaction. Individuals also negotiate their own identities within the situation, that is, how they present themselves. Specifically, they negotiate how much of their own selves they can bring to the situation. Two working agreements must be reached, one with the self and one with the others in the situation. For instance, a social worker may need to negotiate how much of her real self and how much of her expected self as a worker she should bring into an encounter with a client in an unwanted pregnancy. The real self may feel very strongly that abortion is wrong or even a sin but nevertheless feel constrained by the ethics of the social work profession to allow the client self-determination. Or the worker may know she should advise the client honestly and openly about all the alternatives available but still feel the urge to promote the alternative that agrees with her personal views.

McCall and Simmons divide the negotiation process into four "moments": imputation of the role of other, improvisation of a role for self, presentation of self, and altercasting. *Imputation of the role of other* involves the moment of role-taking. We try to step into the roles of others in order to understand where they are coming from. We are interested in their qualities as people, but, more important, we need to understand the roles that are being played and interpreted, that is, the identity they are trying to project. We are interested in others' plans and schemes so that we will know what is giving their role-playing direction, coherence, and meaning. We may not be correct in our understanding of others, but we at least attempt to figure them out.

Improvisation of a role for self is the moment when we come to decisions about how we will play our role, taking into account both our assessment of others and our own decisions. *Presentation of self* is the moment when we express ourselves through our behaviors. The term reflects what has been called the **dramaturgical view** of human behavior, which uses theatrical metaphors to describe social interactions; individuals present themselves in the same ways performers present a role to an audience. Erving Goffman, the leading proponent of this view, describes the presentation of self as a process in which the individual "makes an implicit or explicit claim to be a person of a particular kind, and automatically exerts a moral demand upon the others, obliging them to value and treat the individual in the manner that persons of this kind have a right to expect.[28] *Altercasting* is the moment when we project back to others who we think they should be and what we think they should do. We pass on to them our expectations for them.

The Effects of Social Interaction on the Self

The outcomes of all social interactions affect individuals. In the process of negotiating lines of actions and identities, they come either to maintain or change the meanings they have previously attached to themselves. Some situations do not affect individuals deeply; what they do in them or how they present themselves can be disregarded as being basically irrelevant to the real self. Self-precepts may develop in which they think negatively about themselves, but these pass with time. The term *ingratiation* has been used to describe certain positive presentations of self that are more-or-less momentary, utilitarian, and little involved with the real self. With ingratiation techniques, which are extremely important in situations of threat or in relationships with superiors, those who have power over others try to control or conceal it by being agreeable and compliant. They do not necessarily want to act that way but they do anyway, because they sense, often quite rightly, that their survival depends on it.[29]

Other situations affect individuals more deeply. What happens in them somehow gets right to the core of the self-image, so that the real self becomes embedded in and indistinguishable from the situation. When the situations that affect individuals deeply are rewarding and enable them to think positively about themselves, considerable self-esteem can be built. However, when deeply affecting situations are not satisfying and make individuals unhappy about themselves, the result may be a devalued self, a spoiled identity, or a stigma. Such situations involve what symbolic interactionists call *labeling*.

⌒ LABELING AND SOCIAL INTERACTION

The perspective of labeling within the symbolic interaction tradition is particularly relevant to social service practice because it sheds light on a common problem: Why do so many clients lack self-esteem and suffer from a negative self-image? This perspective suggests the answer is that their self-image reflects how others have responded to them; that is, negative self-images reflect negative social situations.

The labeling perspective emerged out of attempts to understand social deviance and abnormal behavior. The focus is not on the person exhibiting the behavior, however, but on those persons and groups in the society that have the power to define it as not normal, or deviant. **Labeling** thus can be defined as an interactive social process in which some people purposefully apply negative labels to others, who then may internalize the labels and come to consider themselves different from the majority.

The initial applications of labeling theory were in the areas of delinquency and mental health, but it is currently used more broadly to study the negative self-images of individuals who are not deviant in these respects. For instance, Barry Adam uses the perspective to explain feelings of self-hate among Jews, blacks, and homosexuals, and Edwin Schur uses it in examining the process by which women are devalued in American society.[30] The concept of labeling also contributes to a critical practice for social service. Practitioners can help clients keep from internalizing negative labels applied to them by others and coming to think of themselves as somehow inferior.

The Social Process of Labeling

According to the labeling perspective, no status, attribute, or act is in itself inherently negative. Negative evaluations derive from the social process of trying to reach consensus or working agreements about how society and social interactions in large and small groups ought to be organized.

This social process takes place on three levels. At the level of *collective decision making* (that is, the society), working agreements in the form of laws, social policies, traditions, and norms which confer rights and obligations, duties and privileges, are reached. As a result, certain statuses, attributes, and acts come to be valued and others become devalued. At the level of *organizational decision making*, bureaucracies, voluntary associations, schools, clubs, families, and the like reach working agreements about the expectations of members. As a result, certain kinds of participation come to be valued and other kinds become devalued. At the *interpersonal or small-group level*, people generate labels that distinguish favorable or acceptable partners from those who are unfavorable or unacceptable as they devise their own definitions of friendship, love, and other interpersonal relationships.

Labeling is a natural process. It is also unavoidable; social life is impossible unless humans can define things and give them meaning—bad or negative things as well as good or positive things. Negative labeling thus is an unfortunate consequence of symbolic interaction which can be extremely destructive to the self. There are two ways in which individuals come to have negative labels: They can do things that offend others and thus acquire **achieved labels**, or they can have the misfortune of being born into a social status that is negatively valued in the society and thus acquire **ascribed labels**.

Achieved Labels: Blemishes to Individual Character

Most of the work on achieved labels has focused on the applications of such labels as *deviant*, *delinquent*, *mentally ill*, or *misfit*. These are stigmatizing labels; Goffman refers to them as "blemishes of individual character" and says they result in a "spoiled identity."[31] The assumption is that no act is deviant or a sign of mental illness in and of itself. Acts only acquire these meanings through collective or organizational decision making or through interpersonal processes. For such a label to be achieved, the individual must do something which offends others and, moreover, must be caught; that is, the act must come to public attention.

Labeling theory thus is concerned only with what Edwin Lemert calls *secondary deviance*.[32] Almost everyone performs acts of **primary deviance** that might be considered deviant if they were noticed and censured—acts like breaking rules or committing "victimless crimes" such as gambling and prostitution. Deviance remains primary as long as those who commit such acts define them as incidental to their real self-identity. In labeling

Los Angeles police officers arrest suspected gang members in an anti-gang operation. Once arrested, they are likely to suffer the "blemishes to individual character" associated with the successive achieved labels of gang member, delinquent, criminal, and ex-con.

theory, an act to which others do not respond negatively is assumed to have no consequence for the identity of the person. **Secondary deviance**, which refers to the labeling of an act as deviant by society, an organization, or a group, is another matter. Once an individual is caught committing an act considered by society to be deviant, a situation is set up where the individual's personal identity can be transformed from law-abiding or normal to deviant or abnormal.

In its original applications in the areas of delinquency and mental health, labeling theory provided a rationale for diversion and deinstitutionalization programs which now provide limited treatment and supervision in the local community whenever possible. It has also sensitized social service workers to the need to avoid further psychological damage to delinquent or disturbed clients by exercising caution in the use of matizing terminology.

Labeling in Juvenile Service Organizations

The term *delinquent* came into use with the development of the juvenile court, a major social invention in the United States. The Illinois legislation under which the first juvenile court was established in Chicago in 1899 officially designated children who break laws as delinquent rather than criminal. It set the age below which a person could not be treated as a criminal and made provisions for governing and evaluating the behavior of delinquents in hearings rather than trials. The work of the court was placed under chancery (or equity) jurisdiction, so delinquent children became wards of the state. All states now have juvenile court laws, most of which apply to persons under age 18. Recently, the proliferation of armed violence by adolescents has led some state legislatures to lower this age to 17 or below.

The objective of juvenile court proceedings is not to establish the guilt or innocence of a person accused of an offense, as in the criminal court, but rather to ensure the well-being of the child. Children's rights to nurturance and rehabilitation are differentiated from adults' rights to due process of the law and punishment if convicted.[33] The juvenile court legislation also established the special category of *status offenses*, under which certain behaviors are violations if committed by a minor but not if committed by an adult. In earlier times status offenses included a very wide and vague range of behaviors, including such things as immoral or indecent conduct, growing up in idleness, patronizing a public poolroom, wandering about railroad yards, or using vile or vulgar language.[34] Today status offenses are limited to such misbehavior as not obeying parents (unmanageable behavior), not living at home (runaways), not attending school (truants), staying out late at night (curfew violations), or purchasing cigarettes, liquor, or the like.

The juvenile justice system was, in many ways still is, considered very progressive. Nevertheless, in the 1960s it came under attack from labeling theorists who charged that instead of nurturing and rehabilitating children, the system was labeling them, that is, turning them into career deviants with spoiled identities. These critics agreed that the juvenile justice system had been institutionalized as collective decision making based on a philosophy of delinquency and specified offenses. It was being operated as organizational decision making about how rehabilitation was to be accomplished. And at the interpersonal level, court counselors, probation officers, and others within the system were fulfilling their tasks by labeling offenders. According to their argument, the self-images of potentially well-adjusted, normal adolescents were being systematically destroyed.

The labeling argument   Labeling theorists have proposed that instead of labeling delinquents, the juvenile justice system should use what Schur calls "radical nonintervention," which would affect those brought before it as little as possible.[35] In various states, diversion programs have been set up to avoid court hearings and incarceration in correctional institutions, and attempts have been made to decriminalize status offenses or at least reduce their number. Deinstitutionalization, especially for status offenders, has been used as a way to avoid locking up youths who commit less serious offenses with more hardened offenders. Court decisions and legislation have revised juvenile court proceedings, requiring them to adopt criminal-trial procedures to determine innocence or guilt beyond a reasonable doubt and to observe many of the due-process protections accorded adults, including notice in writing of specific charges, the right to be represented by counsel, and the right to avoid self-incrimination. The goal of all these procedures is to help juveniles accused of delinquent acts avoid internalizing the negative label *delinquent* or *deviant*.

Opposition to the labeling argument   The attacks of labeling theorists on the juvenile justice system provoked considerable controversy, including opposition from court counselors, many of whom are social workers. A major concern of critics is whether others' responses, especially those from people in authority, do in fact label adolescents as delinquents, causing them to take on spoiled identities as career deviants who make deviance, and eventually crime, a way of life.

Milton Mankoff, one of the first to argue that this is not the case, points out that delinquency is an achieved status, not a status ascribed by birth. The fact that an offense was committed cannot be avoided, and labeling can take place even though the offender is not caught or processed by an authority. Thus an identity as a career delinquent could develop through interaction with peers, whether or not the adolescent is ever brought into custody.[36] Support for this argument comes from Howard Becker, who helped define the labeling perspective. According to Becker, the development of career deviants is facilitated by their involvement in delinquent subcultures.[37] Walter Gove also emphasizes this point, noting that "a pattern of deviant behavior and low self-esteem occurs long before official labeling. Furthermore, it clearly appears that it is the informal reactions of others, or unofficial acts, that is the major deterrent to deviant behavior."[38] In addition, all youths who pass through the justice system do not end up with spoiled identities. Many ex-offenders are in fact rehabilitated and go on to lead healthy and productive lives.

Whether a young person involved in delinquency incorporates a negative self-image therefore depends on numerous factors. The operation of the juvenile justice system, or any other social service that proposes to treat people who deviate from social norms, is only one contributing factor. The self is not the result of a single experience but develops across the life cycle through interaction with innumerable other individuals. There are endless possibilities for acquiring new identities and for changing old ones.

Labeling in Mental Health Service Organizations

Labeling theory has also been used in the study of the causes and maintenance of mental illness. Thomas Szasz argues that the **medical model**, in which mental health problems are regarded as illness and normality is regarded as health, is inappropriate for understanding the emotional troubles and disturbances individuals experience. Although a thermometer and other objective instruments can be used to give a fairly accurate measure of physical health, there are no such instruments available for determining mental health. Mental illness, Szasz and others believe, is a myth. The behaviors designated as pathogenic are no more than labels applied to people who have given other people trouble. The application of the label, through laws, hospitals and clinics, and contact with psychiatrists and other helping professionals, is a political act through which individuals are forced to take on spoiled identities as mentally ill people. Labeling theorists propose that a more appropriate term in reference to emotional troubles is *problems in living*, rather than mental illnesses.[39]

Goffman documents the ways in which the medical model has been applied in institutions to stigmatize patients, thus contributing to the maintenance of the problem. He describes the mental hospital as an example of a *total institution*, "a place of residence and work where a large number of like-situated individuals, cut off from the wider society for an appreciable period of time, together lead an enclosed, formally administered round of life."[40] Residents are completely engulfed in total institutions, and all aspects of life are conducted in the same place, with little privacy; eating, dressing, sleeping, bathing, and so on, are all done in the company of others. Daily life consists of enforced activities, tightly scheduled and controlled. Officially these activities are supposed to follow a rational plan to realize the official aim of the organization, that is, to cure the patients. Goffman argues that in practice mental hospitals are demeaning, and many patients experience "mortification of the self," which causes them to accept a spoiled identity. The community mental health programs initiated in the 1960s as part of the deinstitutionalization movement were a response to public reaction against the cruel and demeaning conditions of mental hospitals and the stigma and deprivation that ordinarily results for individuals committed to them.

Murray Edelman believes that labeling common, everyday activities as though they are medical interventions is a political act whereby superior and subordinate roles are identified. He regards popular use of the term *therapy* as the ultimate metaphor for the medical model. Mental health professionals redefine common, everyday activities in therapeutic terms, so sitting down and talking about problems becomes *psychotherapy*; asking clients to read books becomes *bibliotherapy*; having a dance becomes *dance therapy*; teaching marketable skills becomes *occupational therapy*, and so on. Professional language, or jargon, is used as a tool of communication to create status differences and remind clients of their inferior position.[41]

In fact, labeling is more likely to occur when people with symptoms of mental illness use mental health services than when they do not. According to Bruce Link, labeling is not just a function of direct, face-to-face interaction with professionals. Stereotypes about the mentally ill are inculcated into individual beliefs through socialization. As a result, people who use mental health services expect to be devalued and discriminated against and act accordingly—a self-fulfilling prophecy. Link presents data to show that people who do not use mental health services, even though they have symptoms that would seem to require it, do not suffer a loss in self-esteem because of their symptoms. He concludes that to the extent that people believe they can handle their own problems, the are less likely to think of themselves as mentally ill.[42]

Challenges to labeling mental illness   The conclusions of labeling theory in respect to the mental health system have been attacked in the same way as its conclusions in respect to juvenile delinquency, using similar arguments. Specific challenges to labeling in mental illness have utilized research that establishes some problems in living, such as schizophrenia, are indeed illnesses.

For years schizophrenia has been described as a kind of mental illness, with some consensus that it is caused by internal psychological conflicts created by neurotic parents who send mixed messages to their children. Recently, however, the search for psychological and social causes has all but come to a standstill. Neuropsychiatric studies using advanced biomedical techniques have convincingly defined schizophrenia as a physical illness, and researchers at the National Institute of Mental Health classify it as a group of brain diseases. According to Edward Taylor, "It is known that individuals with the illness may undergo both structural and functional neurological changes. How the abnormalities occur remains largely a mystery."[43] Viral infections, genetic makeup, and chemical or hormonal dysfunctions have been suggested as causes, and in the future the illness may be described as a group of neurobehavioral diseases.

Ascribed Labels: Tribal Stigmas

Labels are not always acquired as a result of actions which offend others. Some people are born with negative labels. Goffman refers to this kind of negative labeling as *tribal stigmas*, which engulf individuals because they happen to be born into a particular race, ethnic group, or religion. Through collective decision making, societies create status hierarchies that bestow advantages, prestige, and privilege on certain groups, while creating disadvantages for other groups.

Self-Esteem in Minority Groups

Labeling theorists and others have maintained that stigmatized people internalize the negative labels ascribed to them by others in large or small groups, communities, or the society as a whole. Adam, for example, contends that minorities frequently develop low levels of self-esteem because they constantly have to cope with domination by others. Internalizing the hateful, hostile messages they receive, they come to think of themselves as inferior. They may try to cope with a hostile environment through such means as escaping from their identity, withdrawing socially or psychologically, performing "guilt expiation" rituals, accepting "magical ideologies" that promise to release them from bondage, or experiencing self-hate.[44] Goffman's study of interaction between normal and stigmatized people certainly supports these ideas; he notes the "pivotal fact" that "The stigmatized individual tends to hold the same beliefs about identity that normals do."[45]

Many years before either Adam or Goffman, Gordon Allport identified traits due to victimization in minority-group members. In his research he found that they reacted to living under constant victimization by trying to deny their membership in the despised group, withdrawing from social relations and becoming passive, or acting clownish and silly; they would actually hate themselves.[46] After World War II, survivors of the Holocaust noted that some Jews had "identified with the aggressor" to obtain medical and other attention.[47] Observing that sexism has given women the status of a minority group, Gloria Donadello notes that "women take on the behaviors and attitudes of minority-group individuals: self-contempt, helplessness, hopelessness, a sense of inferiority and incompetence, to name some of the most common."[48]

Leon Chestang, a social worker, has suggested that the effects of racism in producing a hostile environment can have negative consequences for personality development. He hypothesizes that many blacks have a sense of injustice, inconsistency, and impotence. Like others experiencing a hostile environment, blacks may be left with a depreciated character.[49] Even as children, many blacks develop low self-esteem (see "Dolls and Black Children's Self-Esteem").

While it should not be surprising that people who live continuously with oppression begin to believe the things they hear about themselves, Adam's conclusions on low self-esteem among blacks created quite a stir.[50] A number of studies had found no relationship between self-esteem and societal factors, leading to the conclusion that while racism might exist in a society, it did not have any bearing on the self-esteem of blacks.[51] Roberta Simmons and her associates, for instance, consistently reported no difference in the self-esteem of blacks and whites. In a reply to Adam, she acknowledged that earlier studies did find low self-esteem among blacks but said this had changed. Later studies were comparatively more scientific and objective, and historical processes had produced changes in black's self-esteem. Inspired by the civil rights movement, several decades of "Black is beautiful" had helped them take on a more positive self-image. Simmons also argues that an individual's self-concept may be determined more by family and community than by the larger society. Blacks might still be receiving negative messages from whites, but they were receiving positive messages from the people who really count—their friends and families.[52]

Adam and Simmons disagree on whether minority people always internalize low self-esteem, but they agree on how dominated people ought to respond to their dominators: Minority-group members should challenge their authority. Adam says they should practice the "arts of contraversion," that is, construct alternative, more positive definitions of themselves by building support and information networks, developing positive literary and

Dolls and Black Children's Self-Esteem

Dolls representing whites and blacks were used in an early study by Kenneth and Mamie Clark to investigate the consciousness of self and racial identity of black children. In 1939, they asked black children 3 to 7 years old to choose whether they wanted to play with a black or white doll, which one they considered "nice," which one "looks bad," and which one was a "nice color." Generally, the black children preferred the white doll and rejected the black one. Over two-thirds (67 percent) wanted to play with the white doll, over half (59 percent) said the white doll was nice and the black doll looked bad, and 60 percent said the white doll was a nice color.

These findings, later substantiated in numerous studies using various test methods and settings, have been interpreted to mean that black children lack group pride and suffer from low self-esteem. K. J. Morland, for instance, generalizes that "in a multiracial society in which there is a dominant and subordinate race, young children of the subordinate race tend to prefer and identify with members of the dominant race, while children of the dominant race tend to prefer and identify with members of their own race."

In 1969, when Joseph Hraba and Geoffrey Grant duplicated the doll study in an integrated elementary school setting, they found that black children who had opportunities to associate with white children preferred and identified with the black doll. In this study, 72 percent of the black children chose to play with the black doll, compared to 32 percent in the Clarks' study. Hraba and Grant interpreted this as evidence that the black children had internalized the message that "black is beautiful."

Almost 20 years later, however, at the 1987 meeting of the American Psychological Association, Darlene Powell-Hopson and Sharon McNichol reported on their independent replications of the Clark study in the United States and Trinidad. Using black and white Cabbage Patch dolls, Powell-Hopson got an almost identical result: 65 percent of the black children preferred white dolls. These studies of black children showed that they were still very likely to prefer playing with the white doll. The researchers concluded that blacks' feelings of inferiority had not disappeared, in spite of the civil rights efforts initiated in the 1960s and 1970s.

Powell-Hopson says the results would be the same if the black doll test were repeated today. Even though race relations have improved, as Jack White observed in *Time* in 1993, the progress has been one way: "To be accepted by whites, blacks have to become more like them, while many whites have not changed their attitudes at all." Children as young as two can pick up damaging messages from racial stereotypes applied to the groups and communities in which they are included.

Sources: Kenneth B. Clark and Mamie P. Clark, "The Development of Consciousness of Self and the Emergence of Racial Identification in Negro Preschool Children," *Journal of Social Psychology*, vol. 10 (1939), pp. 591–99; K. J. Morland, "Racial Awareness among American and Hong Kong Chinese Children," *American Journal of Sociology*, vol. 75 (November 1969), p. 360; Joseph Hraba and Geoffrey Grant, "Black Is Beautiful: A Reexamination of Racial Preference and Identification," *Journal of Personality and Social Psychology*, vol. 19 (November 1970), pp. 398–402; Jack E. White, "Growing Up in Black and White," *Time*, May 17, 1993, pp. 48–49.

artistic traditions, and encouraging other members to subvert the authority and power of those in positions of domination.[53]

The evidence is clear that the labels developed and used by those in dominant positions in the small and large groups and communities in a society to refer to minority members do have the potential for creating spoiled identities. However, whether negative labels become internalized into the self-image of the people they are applied to depends on a number of factors. One is history; to the extent that social movements exist which counter oppressive forces and enable stigmatized people to feel proud about themselves, negative labels are not likely to be internalized. Another major factor is the role of friends and family; to the extent that they offer a buffer against the assault of people in dominant positions, negative labels are not likely to be internalized.

∞ IMPLICATIONS OF SYMBOLIC INTERACTIONISM AND LABELING FOR PRACTICE

The symbolic interactionist tradition starts with the premise that the cognitive abilities possessed by humans make them special. Only humans have the full capacity for communication which makes it possible to invent and manipulate symbols. Through this ability human society develops on the communal level and individuals develop a sense of self. The self, like society, is best thought of as a process, always emerging and coming into being. It never just is.

In the continual process of developing a self, the images individuals have of who and what they are take on great significance. To the extent that these images are negative, a spoiled sense of self can evolve. Symbolic interactionists maintain that such spoiled identities ought to be avoided. In their utopian vision of ideal social relations, mutual respect and understanding would constantly produce positive self-images. The message of symbolic interactionism to social service workers is clear: Help clients deal effectively with those who negatively label them, and avoid as much as possible applying labels that stigmatize clients.

From the perspective of labeling, the potential for social service workers to stigmatize clients is very real. A worker may inadvertently become one of the "others" who contribute to the transformation from normal to deviant of clients who somehow offend others, or they may become one of the "others" who continue to reinforce the stigma carried by clients born into groups that have been discriminated against. In both instances, social service workers must be careful to avoid contributing to poor self-images and low self-esteem in their clients.

Assessment in direct-service social work is inherently a labeling process, since identifying the problems of clients entails calling attention to their limitations. Moreover, labeling is a normal process; it is not possible to give meaning to the social world without creating divisions between normal and abnormal, deviant and nondeviant, good and bad. Social service workers therefore cannot avoid labeling, but they can attempt to make assessments in ways that minimize the possibility of leaving clients emotionally scarred. While it is important to be accurate in describing the presenting problem and locating the situational context in which particular troubles occur, they can also redefine labels in a way that reflects the troubles clients are experiencing more positively. For instance, they can redefine *handicapped* as *differently abled*; *frigid* as *preorgasmic*; or *disordered* as *experiencing problems in living*. They can refer to a person with AIDS instead of to a victim of AIDS or to a person with diabetes instead of a diabetic. The use of such more-positive terms has been criticized as being "politically correct," but it reduces the negative impact of labels that may be considered pejorative by those to whom they are applied.

Social service professionals generally should avoid using essentialist labels, which locate the cause of all problems in the character and personality of the client. Examples of essentialist labels include *neurotic, paranoid, delinquent, criminal, retarded*, and the like. Rather than engulfing clients in a one-dimensional identity as a deviant, they should construct a multidimensional identity for them which recognizes their strengths as well as deficiencies. A client who has committed a crime or suffered an emotional collapse, for instance, may also be intelligent, considerate, or motivated to self-improvement. Workers can take the role of helping individuals who have been negatively labeled by others to respond positively and assertively.

∞ DISCUSSION QUESTIONS AND CLASS PROJECTS

1. Identify and distinguish the ways in which Merton and Durkheim approached the study of anomie.

2. According to Merton, in what ways can anomie be adapted to?

3. Keeping in mind the need for confidentiality, discuss the situation of a client you are working with or you know of to whom anomie applies. How do you see it affecting the client? What adaptation to anomie would you say the client is making?

4. Have you ever experienced anomie in your own life? If so, describe the situation. What adaptation to anomie did you make?

5. Describe how Brower has used anomie to explain group dynamics. If you have worked with groups in your field experience, are you able to point to anomie situations or feelings of anomia?

6. When you think about the dynamics taking place from the first day this class met through the present day, are you able to see anomie in operation?

7. What is Hartman's definition of anomie in social service agencies? In your experiences with organizations, have you encountered anomic situations or feelings of anomie? Describe them.

8. Describe organizational experiences in which you have encountered bureaucratic personalities. Have you ever acted like a bureaucrat yourself?

9. Compare Merton's adaptations to anomie with Marx's adaptations to exploitation and alienation. What do you make of the differences in terms of working with clients?

10. Identify and describe the following terms in relation to anomie:

    normlessness
    contradictory norms
    anomie
    anomia
    ritualism
    rebellion
    retreatism
    conformity
    bureaucratic personality

11. Identify and describe the importance of the following concepts from the symbolic interactionist perspective.

    mind
    self-image
    ascribed labels
    achieved labels
    primary deviance
    secondary deviance
    imaginative rehearsal
    spoiled identity
    significant others
    reference groups
    role-taking
    role-playing
    self-precepts

12. What is meant by a negotiated line of action? What four processes are involved in negotiation? Do you think the assessment process in social work practice can be seen as an example of negotiating lines of action?

13. What is the labeling perspective? What contribution does it make to understanding normal human behavior?

14. Do you think members of minority groups are likely to experience low self-esteem and internalize a spoiled identity?

15. Social critics have accused social service organizations and the professionals working in them of spoiling the identities of delinquent and disturbed clients. To what extent do you think this is a valid criticism?

16. Identify friends or acquaintances who have received social services for personal problems and talk to them about their experiences. Did they experience a threat to their self-image as a result of the service? What do

they think helpers ought to do to avoid labeling people?

17. Select a representative sample of social workers working in mental health and juvenile delinquency services and interview them to determine their attitudes toward labeling. Ask them such things as what they think a label is, whether labeling goes on in their service, whether labeling can or should be avoided, and in what ways they have tried to minimize labeling.

18. What specific ways are recommended for social workers to avoid or minimize the potential for labeling? Can you think of other recommendations?

19. Identify and describe the following concepts:

    tribal stigma
    blemishes of individual character
    arts of contraversion
    essentialist labels
    traits due to victimization
    total institutions
    mortification of the self

∞ NOTES

1. See W. Peter Archibald, *Social Psychology as Political Economy* (Toronto, Canada: McGraw-Hill, 1978), pp. 50–57.

2. See Ralph E. Anderson and Irl Carter, *Human Behavior in the Social Environment*, 4th ed. (New York: Aldine de Gruyter, 1990).

3. Emile Durkheim, *The Division of Labor in Society*, trans. George Simpson (Glencoe, IL: Free Press, 1964); originally published 1893.

4. Emile Durkheim, *Suicide*, trans. John Spaulding and George Simpson (New York: Free Press, 1952), pp. 241–76; originally published 1897. Selection reprinted as Durkheim, "Anomic Suicide," in S. H. Traub and C. B. Little (editors), *Theories of Deviance*, 4th ed. (Itasca, IL: F. E. Peacock Publishers, 1994), pp. 102–14.

5. Stuart H. Traub and Craig B. Little, "Anomie," in Traub and Little (editors), *Theories of Deviance*, p. 100.

6. Robert K. Merton, *Social Theory and Social Structure*, 2nd ed. (New York: Free Press, 1968), pp. 185–248. Selection reprinted as Merton,

"Social Structure and Anomie," in Traub and Little (editors), *Theories of Deviance*, pp. 114–48.

7. Ibid., pp. 193–211.

8. Robert M. MacIver, *The Ramparts We Guard* (New York: Macmillan, 1950), pp. 84–85.

9. See Lamar Empey, *American Delinquency: Its Meaning and Construction*, rev. ed. (Homewood, IL: Dorsey Press, 1982), pp. 240–45.

10. Robert Merton, "Bureaucratic Structure and Personality," in *Social Theory and Social Structure*, revised and enlarged ed. (Glencoe, IL: Free Press, 1957), pp. 195–207.

11. Ibid.

12. Ann Hartman, "Social Worker-in-Situation," *Social Work*, vol. 36 (May 1991), pp. 193–272.

13. Aaron M. Brower, "Group Development as Constructed Social Reality: A Social Cognitive Understanding of Group Formation," *Social Work with Groups*, vol. 12, no. 2 (1989), pp. 23–41.

14. David A. Karp and William C. Yoels, *Sociology in Everyday Life*, 2nd ed. (Itasca, IL: F. E. Peacock Publishers, 1993), p. 31.

15. George Herbert Mead, *Mind, Self and Society*, edited by Charles Morris (Chicago: University of Chicago Press, 1934).

16. See Robert H. Lauer and Warren H. Handel, *Social Psychology: The Theory and Application of Symbolic Interactionism*, 2nd ed. (Englewood Cliffs, NJ: Prentice-Hall, 1983), p. 6.

17. Karp and Yoels, *Sociology in Everyday Life*, p. 56.

18. See Ronald Fernandez, *The I, The Me, and You: An Introduction to Social Psychology* (New York: Frederich A. Praeger, 1977), p. 39.

19. See Lauer and Handel, *Social Psychology*, p. 256.

20. See Hazel Markus and Paula Nurius, "Possible Selves," *American Psychologist*, vol. 41 (September 1986), pp. 954–69.

21. Lauer and Handel, *Social Psychology*, p. 104.

22. Lauer and Handel, *Social Psychology*. p. 115.

23. Karp and Yoels, *Sociology in Everyday Life*, pp. 47, 57.

24. Raymond L. Schmitt, *The Reference Other Orientation* (Carbondale: Southern Illinois University Press, 1972).

25. Harold H. Kelley, "Two Functions of Reference Groups," in G. E. Swanson, T. M. Newcomb, and E. L. Hartley (editors), *Readings in Social Psychology* (New York: Henry Holt, 1952), pp. 410–14.

26. George J. McCall and J. L. Simmons, *Social Psychology: A Sociological Approach* (New York: Free Press, 1982), pp. 75–183.

27. Ibid., pp. 39–40.

28. Erving Goffman, *The Presentation of Self in Everyday Life* (New York: Doubleday/Anchor, 1959), p. 13.

29. Edward E. Jones, *Ingratiation* (New York: Appleton, Century, Crofts, 1964).

30. Barry D. Adam, *The Survival of Domination* (New York: Elsevier, 1978); Edwin M. Schur, *Labeling Women Deviant* (New York: Random House, 1984).

31. Erving Goffman, *Stigma: Notes on the Management of Spoiled Identity* (Englewood Cliffs, NJ: Prentice-Hall, 1963), p. 4.

32. Edwin M. Lemert, "Primary and Secondary Deviation," in S. H. Traub and C. B. Little (editors), *Theories of Deviance*, pp. 298–303; reprinted from Lemert, *Social Pathology* (New York: McGraw-Hill, 1951).

33. Empey, *American Delinquency*, pp. 63–64.

34. Gene Kasebaum, *Deliquency and Social Policy* (Englewood Cliffs, NJ: Prentice-Hall, 1974), pp. 11–12.

35. Edwin M. Schur, *Radical Non-Intervention* (Englewood Cliffs, NJ: Prentice-Hall, 1973); see Empey, *American Delinquency*, pp. 481–89.

36. Milton Mankoff, "Societal Reaction and Career Deviance: A Critical Analysis," *The Sociological Quarterly*, vol. 12 (Spring 1971), pp. 204–18; reprinted in Traub and Little (editors), *Theories of Deviance*, pp. 329–48.

37. Howard Becker, "Career Deviance," in Traub and Little (editors), *Theories of Deviance*, pp. 303–10; reprinted from Becker, *The Outsiders* (New York: Free Press, 1963).

38. Walter R. Gove (editor), *The Labeling of Deviance*, 2nd ed. (Beverly Hills, CA: Sage, 1980), p. 407.

39. Thomas Szasz, "The Myth of Mental Illness," in T. S. Szasz, *Ideology and Insanity: Essays on the Psychiatric Dehumanization of Man* (Garden City, NY: Doubleday/Anchor, 1970). Also see Thomas Scheff, *Being Mentally Ill: A Sociological Theory*, 2nd ed. (Chicago: Aldine, 1984).

40. Erving Goffman, *Asylums: Essays on the Social Situation of Mental Patients and Other Inmates* (Garden City, NY: Doubleday/Anchor, 1961), p. xiii.

41. Murray Edelman, *Political Language: Words that Succeed and Policies that Fail* (New York: Academic Press, 1977), pp. 57–75.

42. Bruce G. Link, "Understanding Labeling Effects in the Area of Mental Disorders: An Assessment of the Effects of Expectations of Rejection," *American Sociological Review*, vol. 2 (February 1987), pp. 96–112.

43. Edward H. Taylor, "The Biological Basis of Schizophrenia," *Social Work*, vol. 32 (March–April, 1987), p.115.

44. Adam, *Survival of Domination*.

45. Goffman, *Stigma*, p. 7.

46. Gordon Allport, *The Nature of Prejudice* (Garden City, NY: Doubleday/Anchor, 1958), pp. 142–62.

47. Bruno Bettelheim, "The Dynamism of Anti-Semitism in Gentile and Jew," *Journal of Abnormal and Social Psychology*, vol. 42, 1947, pp. 153–68.

48. Gloria Donadello, "Women and Mental Health," in E. Norman and A. Mancuso (editors), *Women's Issues and Social Work Practice* (Itasca, IL: F. E. Peacock Publishers, 1980), p. 206.

49. Leon Chestang, "Character Development in a Hostile Environment," in M. Bloom (editor), *Life Span Development*, 1st ed. (New York: Macmillan, 1980), pp. 40–51.

50. Barry D. Adam, "Inferiorization and Self-Esteem," *Social Psychology Quarterly*, vol. 41 (March 1978), pp. 47–53.

51. Ruth C. Wylie, *The Self-Concept*, rev. ed. (Lincoln: University of Nebraska Press, 1979), pp. 138–61.

52. Roberta G. Simmons, "Blacks and High Self-Esteem: A Puzzle," *Social Psychology Quarterly*, vol. 41 (March 1978), pp. 54–57.

53. Adam, *Survival of Domination*, pp. 115–18.

PART FIVE

Individual Development across the Life Span

Three Psychological Perspectives
Psychodynamic, Cognitive Development, and Learning

MAJOR THEMES DISCUSSED IN THIS CHAPTER

1. **THE PSYCHODYNAMIC TRADITION.** The origins of psychodynamic thinking lie in the concern of Freud with the inner space or intrapsychic functioning of individuals. Freud's theory, based on the assumption of instinctual drives, is no longer current in social service practice, but his influence is still felt in such concepts as the unconscious, ego strength, and ego defense and coping mechanisms and in such psychological theories as ego psychology, object relations, and self psychology.

2. **COGNITIVE DEVELOPMENT.** The work of Piaget and Kohlberg on cognitive development, particularly the study of moral judgment, complements the study of autonomous functions in ego psychology. Kohlberg's view of female morality is a topic of debate, and different ideas on the roots of moral behavior have been proposed.

3. **LEARNING THEORIES.** Learning theories examine the processes by which behavior is learned, maintained, and unlearned. Three approaches have influenced social work practice: classical conditioning, operant conditioning, and social learning.

4. **IMPLICATIONS FOR PRACTICE.** The three conceptual frameworks discussed in this chapter can help social service workers arrive at a perspective on human behavior and development that will be useful in the assessment and intervention phases of practice with individuals, regardless of their age.

❦

THROUGHOUT THE HISTORY OF SOCIAL WORK, theories of human behavior and development have provided the basis for understanding the problems and strengths presented by clients. Some social service professionals fear that as the various systems and ecological approaches have come into favor, with their emphasis on person in role in environment, study of the individual has been neglected.[1] It is doubtful that this is the case, but the point is well taken. Direct social service work with individuals, families, and groups must be based on a full understanding of the biological, psychological, and social determinants of normal behavior across the life span. To various degrees, community organization and planning, program development and administration, and social policy formulation and analysis also require this understanding.

In this chapter we will describe three theoretical frameworks on psychological functioning: psychodynamic, cognitive development, and learning theories. Our attention in the remaining chapters in Part V will shift from the study of human behavior to the study of human growth and development across the life span.

As we noted in Chapter 2, human behavior is a general term referring to cognitive, motivational, and behavioral states and processes as they are influenced by biophysical, psychological, and social conditions. Human development is the study of human behavior as it is influenced by aging, which itself may be seen as a biological, psychological, and social process. In most approaches to development the biological-aging component—the growth and maturation of species-related physical and mental capacities—is considered the basic influence, and social and psychological conditions are thought to operate largely to speed up or slow down development. The concept of development also carries a connotation of continual progress. Whereas biophysically we may grow and decline, the notion of development suggests that the aging process promotes a steady flowering of human psychological and social capacities. In reality, progress is not inevitable, and in this regard development may be seen not only in terms of average and healthy but also as a utopian vision about the full human potential.

∞ INDIVIDUAL DEVELOPMENT

Each of the theoretical frameworks examined in the chapter is built around a different subsystem of the psychological domain of the individual (see "The Individual as a System" in Chapter 2). **Psychodynamic perspectives** are concerned with the motivational or affective subsystem—how needs, drives, and feelings motivate behavior. In the cognitive subsystem, **cognitive development theory** is concerned with the ways people attend, think, and reason as they age. **Learning theories**, in the behavioral subsystem, focus on observable behaviors, that is, what people say and do, and the rewards and reinforcements that produce these behaviors. Although each perspective primarily focuses on one psychological subsystem, the others are not excluded. As ego psychology and learning theories have evolved, for instance, they have given increasing attention to cognitive processes. Likewise, cognitive development theory incorporates ideas about learning as well as motives.

While these subsystems are in the psychological domain, their origin is in the biophysical domain of the individual. The foundation of psychodynamic perspectives and cognitive development theories, for instance, is biological determinism. Both postulate the existence of certain innate or inborn properties that generate behavior. Psychodynamic thinking posits the existence of innate needs and drives which propel behavior—the need for love, for aggression, for social contact and attachment, for mastery and competence.

Cognitive development proposes the existence of intellectual processes that unfold as individuals go from infancy to childhood, adolescence, and adulthood. Learning theories have a different foundation with social implications—environmental determinism. They posit that behavior is produced largely through social conditioning; that is, it is a function of the effects on individuals of the external associations and contingencies they encounter in social interaction.

All three approaches focus on the individual, but they do so in different ways. Psychodynamic and cognitive development theory are concerned with processes that are internal to individuals, those that take place in the mind. The concept of inner space, for instance, which is central to psychodynamic thinking, has been defined as the "mental representation of experience, the process involved in reviewing and interpreting experience, and the capacity to plan for new experiences."[2] Psychodynamic perspectives and cognitive development theory do take note of the environment, but generally only the subjective environment, that is, the perceptions individuals have of the external world and their motivations in relation to others. The objective reality is less important; it is generally assumed that people live within what Heinz Hartman calls an "average expectable environment," an external world which provides essential support for normal human development.[3]

While some learning theories (especially social learning theory) also give attention to internal cognitive and motivational processes, their emphasis is on the objective environment. Learning theories focus on the actual experiences people have. They are concerned with the ways various stimuli are paired together, social models are attended to, or rewards and punishments are made contingent upon behavior.

These three theoretical frameworks lay the foundation for understanding individual development. Two of the perspectives speak directly to the issue of progressive psychological change. Cognitive development theory is concerned with tracing human thinking and reasoning from their most primitive level in childhood to their most advanced level, which may be achieved in late adolescence or young adulthood. Psychodynamic perspectives integrate general ideas about psychological functioning with specific ideas of how that functioning changes from infancy through old age. Learning theories are not developmental theories in the strict sense; some learning theorists would even deny that development, as described in cognitive and psychodynamic approaches, actually takes place. Yet learning theories have had much to say about socialization processes in childhood and adulthood, and therefore we include them in our discussion of individual development.

These approaches are often presented as competing views on individual behavior and development, but this will not be the case here. It is true that in some particulars they do not blend easily together, but many social service workers have found connections among them and use them as they fit with clients' situations. The point of view we take is that the approaches complement one another. By highlighting different psychological subsystems and giving differential emphasis to the biological and the social or the inner and the outer dimensions of the individual, these approaches take us toward a unified psychological theory of individual behavior and development.

These three psychological approaches also are not the only relevant theories for understanding individual development. Sociological theories of conflict and consensus as they have been played out in the study of community, family, and large and small groups also are applicable. As individuals grow, mature, and decline their lives must always be seen within the context of the statuses and roles they occupy in social systems.

⸂ THE PSYCHODYNAMIC TRADITION

The origins of psychodynamic thinking lie in the work of Sigmund Freud, who must be ranked among the most influential thinkers ever to examine the workings of the human mind. Over the past century, however, it has evolved so that today psychodynamic thinking is no longer strictly Freudian. In addition to describing **Freudian theory** we will discuss three other psychodynamic views current among social service practitioners: ego psychology, object relations, and self psychology.

Working in the late nineteenth and early twentieth centuries, Freud was one of the first to apply the scientific method to the study of individual behavior. He developed the therapy of psychoanalysis by observing patients, encouraging them to talk about what troubled them, and devising techniques such as free association and dream analysis to study their personalities. He wrote up case studies and generated hypotheses about human behavior. As a man of science, he lifted thinking about emotional problems out of the realm of religious mysticism. Before Freud introduced the medical model which regards emotional problems as mental illnesses, people with such problems were believed to be controlled by spirits or demons. Freud also established the existence of the unconscious level of the mind and the innate, often erotic, needs and drives that motivate individual behavior. He was the first to connect traumatic events of childhood with later personality development.

While these ideas do not seem startling now, they were quite revolutionary during Freud's lifetime. His theories of human behavior and psychosexual development have become part of our cultural heritage. Scholars and professionals in the field of psychology may deny his continued influence and ask "Is Freud dead?"[4] They may criticize the particulars of his theories. Nevertheless, they use and therefore validate and promote the ideas and terminology he introduced, such as the unconscious; the id, the ego, and the superego; and neurosis, which have become incorporated into the language.

Freud was a voluminous writer whose thinking changed over time. Furthermore, analysts trained by Freud and his followers are still making changes in Freudian theory. Thus it cannot be thought of as some finished product. The following description must be regarded as a gross oversimplification; it is useful only as a basic introduction to Freud's ideas.[5]

Freud's Theory of Psychosexual Development

Freud was concerned with emotional development, that is, with the development of individuals' drives, needs, motivations, and feelings. For Freud, a **drive** is "a genetically determined, psychic constituent which, when operative, produces a state of psychic excitation or...tension."[6] Along with survival needs (hunger and thirst), there are two basic instincts, *thanatos*, the drive for aggression or destruction, and *eros*, the drive for erotic or sexual gratification. Because most of his work on individual behavior was built around the latter drive, it is referred to as a theory of **psychosexual development**. Freud believed that the need for erotic gratification—a primary, unlearned, instinctual drive—is present at birth and driven by an energy called **libido**. Although sexual gratification is a fundamental driving force, Freud defined it rather broadly as deriving from all pleasurable sensual sensations, not simply genital orgasm and ejaculation. Since from birth all humans exhibit a concern for pleasurable sensations, children as well as adults could be considered sexual.

Personality Structure and Dynamics

The central concern in individual development for Freud was the personality, structured around three parts: the id, the ego, and the superego. He regarded the personality as a psychodynamic system, each part in transaction with the others and the whole in transaction with both the physical apparatus and the external environment.

Freud believed in a basic conflict between individuals and society; instinct drives people to seek their own pleasure, unconcerned about the needs of others. In this respect, Freudian theory can be seen as a conflict theory of human behavior. Because instinct operates unconsciously in that part of the personality known as **the id**, a set of rules to control children's unbridled pleasure seeking is imposed by society, particularly through family life. Socialization and development in early childhood therefore represent the struggle between the needs of individual children and the demands of society, as expressed by their parents. Healthy personality development requires the building of a **superego**, a conscience which both offers ideals to strive for and acts to prohibit undesirable behavior and attitudes. As the internalization of parental standards and moral values, the superego makes it possible for the individual to fulfill personal needs while coping with the demands of society. **The ego** is that part of the personality which mediates between the individual's libidinal or erotic energies and the constraints imposed by the superego. In his early work Freud emphasized the place of the id in child development; only later did he shift the emphasis to the ego.

Early-life experiences are considered central to personality development. For Freud, individual personality—the product of the continual dynamic transactions among the id, ego, and superego—is generally set by the time a person is 5 or 6 years old. It may develop a bit further during puberty, but essentially the adult personality, for better or worse, is a stable playing-out of childhood patterns.

While Freud did not work directly with children, his theory is about early-childhood development. For instance, in the case of Little Hans, a 5-year-old boy with a phobia for horses, Freud obtained all his information and carried out the treatment through the parents.[7] Nevertheless, Freud maintained that most of the psychological difficulties adults experience result from unresolved conflicts in their childhood. Struggles to meet libidinal needs in childhood could leave an adult fixated in a particular developmental period and therefore neurotic, with a distorted perception of reality. Then only psychoanalysis, the long-term, in-depth therapy he developed to uncover and replay childhood memories and fantasies, could alter the adult personality and make it whole. Later Freudians, however, have questioned the lasting effects of early-life experiences on personality development[8] (see "Early-Life Experiences and Personality Development").

Freud's Developmental Stages

Freud describes five psychosexual stages of development: oral, anal, genital, latency, and puberty. Adulthood is not seen as a period in which development takes place. In the **oral phase**, the libido and therefore the search for pleasure is centered in the area of the mouth; in the **anal phase** it moves to the area of the anus; and in the **genital phase** it is centered in the genital area. In each of these phases the child is using the parent, largely the mother, to fulfill his or her needs. Left to their own devices, infants would remain

---

Early-Life Experiences and Personality Development

Most contemporary views on personality development recognize the influence of early-life experiences, but not to the extent that Freud proposed. Ego psychologists have shown that the human personality can develop and change throughout the entire life cycle, and life-span theorists, some of whom are more wedded to ego psychology than others, have demonstrated that cognitive and emotional development across the life span may be marked by either change and variability or consistency.

Research has shown that individuals' early-life conditions do not necessarily predict subsequent developmental levels. Reviewing studies on infants who suffered through premature and physically debilitating births, for instance, Arnold Sameroff concludes that their subsequent physical, cognitive, and emotional development will not necessarily be limited. Similarly, Jerome Kagan presents evidence that extreme cultural differences in the ways adults care for children do not necessarily alter the level of development that can be expected of the children in later life.

Kagan compares the treatment of American children with that of infants in rural Guatemala, who spend their first year confined to a small, dark hut. They are poorly nourished, are not played with, and rarely are even spoken to. Only when they are about 4 or 5 years old does their social world open so they begin to play with other children and participate in the work of their parents. American parents treat their infants very differently. They believe that unless children are stimulated socially, intellectually, and emotionally, developmental retarda-

tion will result. Kagan found that while the cognitive development of Guatemalan children did appear retarded at early ages, by adolescence there was relatively little difference between them and American adolescents on tests of memory and reasoning.

Longitudinal studies which have traced individuals throughout their life course have found that although some personality variables remain more or less stable, others show a good deal of variation. For instance, many children, both male and female, show such personality traits as dependence, passivity, and aggression in infancy and childhood. Then, apparently through gender-role learning, boys are likely to lose the stereotypical feminine traits and retain the stereotypical masculine traits, while girls tend to retain the stereotypical feminine traits and shed the masculine ones. In another study of working-class and middle-class adults who had grown up in intact homes in Ohio, Kagan and H. A. Moss found little relation between such psychological qualities as fearfulness, irritability, or activity during the first three years of life and any aspect of behavior in adulthood.

Sources: Arnold J. Sameroff, "Early Influences on Development: Fact or Fancy?" in M. Bloom (editor), *Life Span Development*, 1st ed. (New York: Macmillan, 1980), pp. 105–19; Jerome Kagan, "The Baby's Elastic Mind," *Human Nature Magazine*, vol. 1 (January 1978), pp. 66–73; Jerome Kagan and H. A. Moss, *Birth to Maturity* (New York: John Wiley and Sons, 1962). Studies on traits are discussed in Richard M. Lerner and David F. Hultsch, *Human Development: A Life Span Perspective* (New York: McGraw-Hill, 1983), p. 517.

---

at their mothers' breasts, biting them as their teeth emerge; they would wallow in the pleasure of their bowel movements; they would try to masturbate and would use their mothers, or anyone, for genital pleasure. Freud believed children are *polymorphous perverse*; that is, they exhibit sexual tendencies even before they can identify the genitals as sexual organs or coitus as the principal sexual activity. During these stages of development, parents struggle to keep children from total immersion in their perversity and teach them to control their sucking, their bowels, and their genital responses.

The Oedipal Conflict

The conflict between the instinctual needs of children and the social demands of parents is particularly evident during the genital phase. Freud postulated that all children pass through an Oedipal period. In the Greek legend, Oedipus, an abandoned child, grows up, becomes king, and unknowingly marries his mother. When he discovers his sin against the gods, he is so overcome by guilt that he blinds himself with a pin taken from his mother's garment and wanders off. He is finally hounded to his death.[9] Freud saw in this myth a symbol of normal development gone awry. All children, in search of genital satisfaction, attempt to use their parents as their first sexual objects. Since this behavior is taboo, it must be warded off; a child who actually achieved it, as Oedipus did, would be destroyed by the enormous guilt. The intense drive can only be prevented by scaring, even threatening, the child.

Freud describes the psychological result of the male child's attachment to his mother and consequent jealousy of and hostility toward his father as the **Oedipus complex**. The boy experiences castration anxiety out of fear that his rival, a bigger and more powerful father, will cut off his penis, thus making it impossible for him to achieve pleasure. As a result, he represses his desires for his mother and, over the following development stages, transfers his desires to more appropriate women. The female child, according to Freud, goes through a similar experience in the genital period which culminates in the **Electra complex**, named after a daughter in Greek legend who conspires with her brother to murder their mother. The female child believes she has already been castrated, since she has a clitoris but no penis. Out of unconscious envy, she is attracted to her father and turns away from her mother, whom she regards as a rival. The girl must also repress her attraction to the opposite-sex parent and transfer her sexual desires to more appropriate men.

As a direct result of the Oedipal struggle, the superego, or morality, develops. Freud postulates that both girls and boys learn to accept authority and to prefer heterosexual genital satisfaction by identifying with their same-sex parent. This identification comes about out of fear of loss of love, a basic motive to ensure a positive relationship. For male children, it also comes through identification with the aggressor; that is, to ward off the fear of castration, boys internalize the values and behaviors of the father, and in the process they learn to repress genital activity during childhood. Freud maintains that because females do not experience castration anxiety, their superego (that is, their moral judgment) does not develop as fully as the male superego.

The Latency and Puberty Phases

Once the genital conflict is resolved, children enter the **latency phase**, a period in which erotic urges apparently are dormant. Then, in the **puberty phase**, they begin the physical transformation into adulthood. With sexual maturation, the Oedipal tensions resurface; they now must be dealt with positively and put to rest. Children in puberty must once again channel their sexual interests away from the parent and toward the outside community of appropriate opposite-sex friends. Thus normal psychosexual development means internalizing the norms and traditions of society, identifying with the same-sex

Fifth-grade girls conduct a science experiment. As they achieve a feeling of competence in typically male skills and overcome any sense of inadequacy, it is unlikely that they will unconsciously come to envy males, as Freud proposed.

parent, and fulfilling sexual gratification through genital/genital contact with a member of the opposite sex.

Freud on Female Development

Freudian theory has been criticized for its apparent sexist bias. Although the great majority of Freud's patients were women, he never was able to put together a coherent theory of female development. One critic speculates that Freud's theory may derive more from self-analysis than from analysis of his female clients.[10] In any case, Freud devoted relatively little attention to women, concentrating most of his scientific energy on the development of the male personality.

This is true not only of Freud but of Freudians in general. For example, Mary Schwartz notes that Erik Erikson's stages of psychosocial development (see Chapter 16) ignore sexual differences, and as a result of such bias students of personality learn almost nothing about female development and get the implied message that it is not important.[11] In fact, the sexism in Freudian theory may go further; the few things that are said about women suggest a negative understanding of female development.

Freud suggests that girls resolve the Electra complex in a peculiarly feminine way which he does not seem to have thought out very clearly. The dilemma of the genital period is similar for boys and girls; both are attached to and desire genital pleasure from the opposite-sex parent, and both are forced to give up this urge. Because the male personality develops out of fear of castration and the female, having no penis, does not have this fear, her moral development not only is weaker, she also feels incomplete. According to Freud, penis envy causes girls to reject their mothers and love their fathers as a means of acquiring control of a penis; it also is translated in "normal" females into a desire to have babies.

Not surprisingly, many feminist psychologists have rejected the idea of penis envy and see in such an assertion the essence of sexism.[12] They argue that women are not inferior beings; they are proud of their genital organs and do not feel castrated or wish to become men. But some feminists have supported Freud's position. Juliet Mitchell, for instance, argues that the notion of penis envy has been misunderstood, and to some extent Freud's ideas make sense. Penis envy may exist in the unconscious, while at the level of consciousness it is experienced only as a wish to love men and bear children. The wish for a penis exists in the unconscious only because of the sexism and patriarchal norms in the society which have coerced women into a devalued social position.[13]

Mitchell's interpretation suggests that Freud may have been correct in his observations of the unconscious drives of the affluent women he treated around the turn of the twentieth century. However, as the status of women in American society has risen, it is unlikely that early-childhood genital urges in females will enter the unconscious as envy of the male. Where nonsexist behaviors and attitudes are valued, it has become easier for female children to develop unconscious feelings of wholeness, equality, and independence.

In a recent work, Erikson seems to agree with Mitchell. Although he also focused on male development, his work is viewed somewhat more positively by feminists than Freud's is. He acknowledges that during the infantile genital stage of development, boys and girls alike have feelings of both intrusion and inclusion, that is, a bisexual propensity. The inability of girls to intrude (meet their masculine needs) and of boys to include (meet their feminine needs) can create difficulties for both. In a patriarchal, exploitative society, girls may develop envy and become dependent and boys may fear castration and become aggressive. Erikson believes, however, that neither outcome necessarily occurs "under enlightened conditions."[14]

Freud's Contributions to the Study of Human Behavior

Although Freud's theories have been debated and are being extended in directions he might not even have considered, it is clear that he made significant contributions to the study of human behavior. No direct-service social worker seriously interested in assessing and intervening in the troubles of clients can overlook the work of Freud and his followers. Freud's contributions include the following ideas:

1. Psychological processes have a central place in human behavior.
2. The personality must be understood as a psychodynamic system.
3. Unconscious mental activity is a motivating force in human behavior.
4. Two primary drives are the drive for sensual pleasure and the drive for aggression.
5. The drive for sensual pleasure can be studied as a function of psychosexual stages of development.
6. A method of treatment for emotionally disturbed adults is long-term, in-depth psychoanalysis in which childhood memories are examined.[15]

The Ideas of Ego Psychology

Eda Goldstein, who has examined the application of ego psychology to social work practice, describes this theory as one in which primary attention is given to "the executive arm of the personality—the ego—and its relationship to other aspects of the personality and to the external environment." She identifies seven ideas that characterize ego psychology:

1. The theory is based on the assumption that people are born with a capacity to function adaptively.

2. The ego is the part of the personality that allows for successful adaptation to the environment.

3. Ego development takes place in the course of meeting needs, identifying with others, learning, mastering tasks, and effectively coping and solving problems.

4. The ego is only one part of the personality and must be understood in relation to the id and superego.

5. The ego mediates between the individual and the environment but also mediates conflict that arises among the various components of the personality.

6. The social environment shapes the personality and provides the conditions that facilitate or hinder coping.

7. Private troubles result from inadequacies in individuals' coping capacities or deficits in the fit among their needs, capacities, and environmental conditions and resources.

Source: Eda G. Goldstein, *Ego Psychology and Social Work Practice* (New York: Free Press, 1984), pp. xiv–xvi.

Freud also made a contribution in his definition of psychosexual development. In psychotherapies, development in terms of internalizing the norms and traditions of society, identifying with the same-sex parent, and achieving sexual gratification through genital/genital contact may be used as an objective in planning interventions.

As Freud developed his theory, he began to recognize that in addition to the unconscious, conscious mental activity also has a role in determining human behavior. However, this work remained incipient, and most of it has been done by Freudians who call themselves ego psychologists.

☞ EGO PSYCHOLOGY

Freud stated in his early work that the ego is not present at birth, but he came to believe that it exerts an influence over the personality from the beginning of life. He coined the term *ego*, but the major work on the concept was done by Anna Freud, his daughter, and by Heinz Hartman and others.[16]

Study of the ego has taken two principal directions in **ego psychology** (see "The Ideas of Ego Psychology"). One, which focuses on the ego in conflict with the id, is more firmly anchored in the Freudian tradition, which sees psychosexual development as an inherent conflict between the individual and society. The other area, which focuses on the conflict-free zone of the ego, concerns the individual's conscious adaptive and coping responses. In some respects they represent two sides of a coin, as in the conflict and consensus (functional) theories of social interaction.

The Ego in Conflict: Ego Defenses

As one of the three parts of the personality, the ego mediates between the individual and the environment as well as between the id and the superego. Since libidinal needs are so strong and surface in ways that may threaten individuals, the personality must find a way to fulfill libidinal demands and at the same time control them so that they are not overwhelming. One way the individual does this is by developing **ego defenses**, "specific intrapsychic processes, operating unconsciously, which are employed to seek relief from anxiety."[17]

Ego-defense mechanisms are used by everyone; that is, they are part of the normal functioning of the individual. Maladaptive use of defenses prevents personality development and adaptive use promotes it, but particular defenses themselves are not adaptive or maladaptive behaviors. Rather, in adaptive use, the defense must simultaneously protect optimal functioning and enable it. The defense is temporary and flexible, and the conflict that provokes it is eventually resolved. In maladaptive use, the defense is rigid, and, while it might protect for a while, it does not enable optimal functioning.

A number of ego defenses have been identified.[18] *Regression* is unconsciously returning to a type of thought, feeling, or behavior associated with an earlier stage of development to avoid present anxieties and fears. Adults who start to behave as if they were children are regressing. *Repression* involves unconsciously keeping unwanted thoughts, feelings, and behaviors out of awareness. Individuals who do not allow themselves to think about certain things are using repression (see "The Repression of Memories"). In *denial*, the individual unconsciously negates or refuses to accept as real something that is in fact real, such as refusing to acknowledge that a loved one has died. *Rationalization* is the unconscious use of convincing reasons to justify unacceptable thoughts, feelings, and behaviors. Students may be rationalizing when they convince themselves that a low grade was due to a tricky exam or the instructor's lack of clarity about expectations, instead of admitting that they were not prepared.

Other ego defenses include *projection*, unconsciously attributing unacceptable thoughts and feelings to others. Instead of admitting to a particular thought, a person may attribute it to others. *Displacement* is unconsciously shifting unacceptable feelings about one person or situation onto another. A woman, for instance, may get angry at her husband instead of getting angry at her boss. *Sublimation* is unconsciously converting a socially objectionable thought, feeling, or behavior into a socially acceptable one. A man, for instance, may channel his aggression to football or boxing as a way of positively expressing hostility, instead of battering his wife. Sublimation is believed to be the most mature, most effective way to deal with anxiety or fear.

Almost any thought, feeling, or behavior may be considered a defense as long as it functions unconsciously and is an attempt to ward off anxiety. For this reason, the labeling of behaviors as ego-defense mechanisms must be done cautiously.

The Ego in Harmony: Autonomous Functions

Hartman was the first to study the conflict-free aspects of the ego, that is, functions that are not tied to instinctual drives. *Autonomous ego functions* are the tools individuals use to deal directly and adaptively with their environments, such as intelligence, perception, motility (inner feelings of action), speech, thinking, language, and memory. Hartman accepted the function of ego defenses in the personality, but he believed that the study of

The Repression of Memories

An area of research that is currently hotly debated concerns repressed memories of sexual abuse in childhood. Although everyone acknowledges the seriousness of the problem of the sexual abuse of children, researchers are at odds with respect to its true incidence and whether it is possible to repress and later recover memories. At the heart of the debate is the Freudian concept of repression, an unconscious ego-defense mechanism in which people who are overwhelmed with anxiety blot out all existing memory of the offending circumstances. Repression is different from the conscious coping process of suppression or deciding not to think about certain traumatic events.

Elizabeth Loftus, a cognitive psychologist, asserts that memories are ephemeral and untouchable, like the wind or steam rising. Her research focuses on the malleability of memory. In hundreds of experiments with thousands of people, she has found that not only do people remember things and events incorrectly, but they can be made to remember events that never actually happened. Not thinking about some terrible event that a person can be reminded of later in life is clearly possible, but there is no support for the phenomenon of total repression and subsequent accurate recovery. Loftus fears that many psychotherapists, in their zeal to fight the psychologically debilitating effects of abuse, may inadvertently succeed in creating memories out of events that never took place.

John Briere, a clinical psychologist agrees that bad therapists can get clients to believe things that aren't true, but he also strongly believes that memories can be repressed and reawakened. Severe trauma associated with severe sexual abuse is said to be the dynamic that causes repression. He contends that because laboratory studies cannot truly capture such traumatic circumstances, they shed little light on the subject. In his practice, he has seen abuse survivors vomit as they recover lost memories, and he has found that reawakened memories are so painful that clients will do almost anything not to remember. Briere maintains that those who help people recover memories of abuse should not be seen as charlatans nor should those who recover lost memories be seen as pathological self-interested liars.

To support his position, J. Briere and Jon Conte studied a nonrandom sample of 450 adults undergoing psychotherapy. About 60 percent of the women and men studied reported some period before age 18 when they had no memory of their abuse. These people were significantly more likely to have greater current psychological symptoms, to have been molested at an earlier age, to have been the victim of extended and violent abuse, to have been abused by more than one person, and to have feared disclosure.

Source: Laurie Denton, "Sex, Love and Psychology: Loftus, Briere Draw a Crowd to Repressed Memory Debate," *The American Psychological Association Monitor*, vol. 24 (November 1993), p. 5; John Briere and Jon Conte, "Self-Reported Amnesia for Abuse in Adults Molested as Children," *Journal of Traumatic Stress*, vol. 6 (January 1993), pp. 21–31.

the ego could be enhanced by looking at its nondefensive, adaptive functions. His work demonstrates the capacity of the ego for neutralizing conflict and fostering adaptations. Thus it forms the basis of much contemporary psychotherapy.[19]

A number of ego functions have been identified in the autonomous sphere. *Reality testing* refers to the ability to perceive the difference between inner, subjective states, such as wishes, fantasies, hopes, and desires, and objective conditions outside the person, or what is actually taking place. Reality testing emphasizes the need to perceive the world accurately and to understand cause-and-effect relations. The ego also functions to enable the development of a sense of *reality of the world* and *reality of the self* as separate entities at the feeling level rather than the perceptual level. A person may be able to test (that is, perceive) reality accurately but still not be able to sense, feel, or experience the difference between inner and outer reality. *Judgment* involves the ability to sort out different possible responses to objective reality, weigh their consequences, and determine the most appropriate response.

The ego also serves to regulate and control drives, emotions, and impulses. It provides for thought processes which are organized, logical, and oriented to objective reality, but it allows a certain amount of regression; when people are confronted by a reality that appears to overwhelm them, they can let go of their organized, goal-directed thinking, relax, and perhaps come up with more creative adaptations. Other autonomous functions, such as attention, concentration, memory, learning, and perception, are facilitated by the ego, even under circumstances of stress or conflict.

Coping Mechanisms

Adaptation includes conscious as well as unconscious strategies. Behavior that is under conscious control and is adaptive is called **coping**, a mechanism used by the ego to deal consciously with actual situations by actively testing reality, making judgments, and regulating and controlling impulses. For instance, repression, an ego defense, involves keeping unwanted feelings out of awareness; suppression, a coping mechanism, involves consciously deciding to control those feelings.

Robert W. White has identified three components of coping: the ability to gain and process new information, the ability to control one's emotional state, and the ability to move freely within one's environment.[20] An endless variety of coping strategies is possible, most of them created by individuals in accordance with their own personalities and needs. For instance, when confronted with a difficult interpersonal relation with a loved one, different people will cope by going to a therapist, talking to friends, consulting self-help books on intimate relations, ignoring the difficulty, or confronting the loved one with their feelings. Each strategy can be understood as a way to gain information, control emotions, and continue to function socially.

Competence

When ego psychologists turned their attention to autonomous ego processes, the existence of an inborn motive for mastery over the environment became apparent.[21] *Competence* has to do with a person's capacity to interact with the environment effectively, beyond merely surviving, muddling through, or coping. The drive for competence leads to learning, interests, skills, and a sense of identity and esteem.[22]

White's work on the concept of competence has been influential. On the assumption that inherent biological energies in the ego motivate individuals to strive for competence, he describes the developmental skills an individual must have for effective interaction with the environment: self-confidence, trust in her or his own judgment, and the ability to make decisions. Mastery of these skills produces a sense of competence, the subjective feeling or perception of acting in a competent manner, and a feeling of efficacy, the experience of satisfaction and positive self-esteem as a result of having done something active and being in control over one's life.[23]

Anthony Maluccio argues that competence is not a set of personal attributes but a product of the transactions between individuals and their environment, that is, the relationship between the person's needs, qualities, and coping patterns and the properties of the impinging environment.[24] In this transactional view, the attributes of a person are only one component of competence. The nature of the macro, meso, and micro environments and the way they support competence are of equal consequence to individual development (see "Levels of Systems within Individuals" in Chapter 2).

Ego Strength

The concept of ego strength summarizes what many ego psychologists mean by development. **Ego strength** expresses a composite of the internal psychological capacities an individual brings to interactions with others and transactions with the social environment. Its opposite is *ego weakness*, the deficiencies a person brings to social relationships.[25]

Individuals who have ego strength use their defenses adequately, cope well, perceive reality correctly, and have a good sense of themselves and others. They make good judgments, regulate their drives, and think in logical, goal-oriented ways but can let go of logic when necessary. They continue to attend, concentrate, and learn even under stress and maintain mature interpersonal relations. In sum, people with ego strength have the qualities that allow for competence in interaction with the social environment. Ego weakness is evident in individuals with deficiencies in internal functioning so that the ego is unable to perceive, experience, and deal adequately with the demands imposed by reality.

∞ THE STUDY OF OBJECT RELATIONS

As psychodynamic thinking continued to emerge, more attention was given to the social environment, especially the family. A major school of thought which resulted concerns **object relations**, the study of the attitudes people hold toward others and how they influence social behavior.[26] Object relations, also called *interpersonal relations*, may refer to the individual's sense of self and sense of other people or to the capacity for mature interpersonal relations.

Within the Freudian tradition, subjective reality, including fantasy and the imagery evoked by it, often is considered more important than actual events or objective reality. Early in his career, Freud believed that traumatic events experienced during infancy accounted for the neurotic symptoms exhibited by his adult patients; many female clients spoke of memories of incestuous events with their fathers. Later Freud came to believe that in fact these seductive events never occurred and existed only in his clients' fantasies. Why Freud changed his mind has been debated. Jeffrey Masson argues that it was more for personal than for scientific reasons; Freud was unwilling to challenge the medical community or to unmask the behaviors of close associates.[27] According to Alvin Rosenfeld, Freud reversed himself because clinical observations and new insights had raised doubts as to the validity of the accounts of seduction by his patients.[28] In any case, analytically oriented practitioners still give most of their attention to the fantasies of the individual. A social and psychological phenomenon of the 1990s is the proliferation of accusations by younger adults, many of them undergoing psychotherapy, who suddenly seem to recall instances of child sexual abuse or satanic rituals that occurred decades ago (see "The Repression of Memories").

The intense emotions of early childhood lead individuals to incorporate into their personalities images of the important people in their lives which they later project onto others. Perception is always selective; we form attitudes about others based on a complex combination of what the other persons objectively are and what we expect them to be.

Transference and Countertransference

One example of this projection can be seen in therapeutic encounters in which clients' fantasies are transferred onto the therapist or therapists countertransfer these fantasies onto clients. **Transference** is the unconscious projection onto the therapist of the client's attitudes toward a powerful figure in early childhood. **Countertransference** refers to the reactions of the therapist to being treated as a father or a mother. It is a reaction to the patient's neurotic displacements.[29]

Transference and countertransference are, strictly speaking, limited to the therapeutic encounter, but analogies with interpersonal behavior in everyday life are readily apparent. As individuals interact and build relationships with others, they are constantly evoking fantasies and images of the people in their past. Such remarks as "He's attracted to her because she reminds him of his mother" or "She married him because he's a father figure" are common. When the images are pleasant, what may be called a positive transference takes place: Individuals attribute to others good things and are drawn to them. When the images are unpleasant, a negative transference takes place: Individuals can see no good in others and spurn them. Most images are ambivalent, reflecting love and hate simultaneously: Individuals are drawn to others, and they are wary of them. In this sense object relations is the study of how internalized childhood patterns, often based in fantasy rather then real-life events, penetrate the psyche and shape interactions with others.

Self Psychology

A prominent area in the study of object relations is self psychology, which proposes the existence of a set of motives that differ from Freud's instinctual, antisocial, libidinal, aggressive drives. In **self psychology**, developed by Heinz Kohut and Margaret Mahler, drives are much more social in nature.[30]

Newborn infants are believed to have an innate ability to inform others of their needs; they are eager learners, mentally active, and able to observe the world in a structured way. If the response infants evoke from those who care for them is empathic, the primary caregiver becomes a self-object. **Self-objects** constitute the empathic environment into which the child is born, and it is through them that the child begins to internalize a *nuclear self*, a central, enduring, and organized sector of the personality. If the child cannot evoke an empathic response, or if the caregiver is emotionally dull, unavailable or otherwise unable to respond, the child will not develop as an individual with a cohesive, vigorous, and harmonious nuclear self. The child's personality could become weak and fragmented.

The self comes into being through two streams of experience, "that of being mirrored, admired, and guided; and that of being permitted to merge with the power and wisdom of an idealized self-object."[31] In this respect, self psychology and symbolic interactionism propose similar processes in the development of the self. While being comforted, held, fed, and changed, the newborn merges or becomes one with the primary caregiver, who then is a self-object for the infant. The process of internalizing the empathic responses of others in a nuclear self is defined as *transmutation*, to indicate that the individual does not simply incorporate the self of others but is transformed into something unique. Thus the mirroring, guiding, and confirming functions of self-objects become self-functions for the infant, such as the capacity to regulate self-esteem, to monitor stress, and to define and pursue realistic goals. Complementary processes of separation and individuation are involved in transmutation. In *separation*, infants move away from the merged state they have achieved with their primary caregivers, and in *individuation* they develop and assert their own unique characteristics.

In keeping with contemporary views, self psychology recognizes the individual's potential for psychological development throughout the entire life cycle. As individuals go from one age status to the next, the self-objects that influence the nuclear self become more diverse. Some are given up and others added as the role of self-object passes from parents and other caregivers to peers, teachers, fellow workers, partners, or lovers. Self-objects are not necessarily actual people, however; they may be preferences or vocational, professional, religious, civic, or cultural ideals that take on values. For development to occur, the nuclear self must be reevaluated and restructured at each stage.

☙ COGNITIVE DEVELOPMENT

Ego psychology and psychodynamic perspectives have their origins in clinical practice, but other traditions in psychology have developed along with them. The cognitive theory of Jean Piaget and the theory of moral development of Lawrence Kohlberg, for instance, enhance understanding of the autonomous, conflict-free functions of the ego by examining the development of such capacities as learning, memory, attention, and reasoning.

Piaget's Theory of Cognitive Development

As in the psychodynamic perspectives, Piaget's interest is in inner-life experiences and development in the psychological domain of the individual. Rather than being concerned with emotional development, however, Piaget is concerned with **cognitive development**, that is, the development of thinking and reasoning processes through a synthesis of biological maturation and environmental experiences.[32]

Piaget was a twentieth-century Swiss naturalist and biologist whose interest in childhood development was aroused when he became a father. The genesis of his theory of cognitive development was his observations of normal children (his own) and simple experimentation with their learning processes.

Adaptation and Orders of Cognition

For Piaget, cognitive development takes place through a process of adaptation in which individuals seek to establish an equilibrium between their selves and their environment through the logical coding and ordering of intellectual experiences and the behaviors associated with them. Piaget's theory of cognitive development takes into account three levels of thought, or orders of cognition. The lowest is the level of **schemas**, sensory and

A boy about 8 years old, in Piaget's concrete operational stage of development, demonstrates the principle of conservation by showing that two pints of liquid equal one quart, regardless of the shape of the containers.

motor patterns which can be codified to make meaningful, repeatable behaviors possible. **Structures** are related to the organization of thinking; they are subprocesses which link thought and action and are generally associated with more complex cognitive processes. In **operations**, schema and structures may be reversed, transformed, or otherwise manipulated by cognitive processes. Operations are complex patterns which approximate some logical model.

Schema, structures, and operations are produced through adaptation, particularly the subprocesses of assimilation and accommodation. *Assimilation* refers to individuals' attempts to adapt the environment to themselves. If new ideas and experiences are to be processed and accepted they must fit into the existing cognitive equilibrium. To make sense of them, therefore, individuals try to accommodate them to already-present ideas or experiences. For instance, children can learn to jump rope by comparing the skill to others they already have, such as jumping up and down, jumping over a rock, or hopping over a line. *Accommodation* refers to the opposite procedure, accepting new experiences, regardless of how different they may be from what is known. The unique aspects of jumping rope are attended to, and no comparisons are made with other forms of jumping.

Individuals who encounter new experiences simultaneously assimilate and accommodate them, trying to fit them into their thinking patterns even as those patterns are altered. The push-pull effect of assimilation and accommodation demonstrates the dynamic nature of cognitive development.

Stages of Cognitive Development

The three levels of thought produced by assimilation and accommodation in Piaget's theory of cognitive development ordinarily are learned from birth to adolescence in four stages, each with a number of substages. The four major stages are sensorimotor, preoperational, concrete operational, and formal operational thought.[33]

The sensorimotor stage   In the stage of **sensorimotor intelligence**, generally from birth to 18 or 24 months of age, infants and children are socially the most dependent and physically the most limited. For infants, reality has no beginning or end; they and their environment are one and the same, and their experience is limited to what they can see, touch, hear, or smell. Objects are real when they are present and cease to exist as soon as they disappear. While infants perceive and act, they do not have internal representations of the environment, so they must work within these confines to create and control their social world in order to meet their needs. Reflexive behaviors such as sucking slowly take on meaning, become repeatable, and thus form schema in the cognitive repertoire, and by the end of this stage children can endow objects in the environment with object permanence. Once they have internalized basic sensorimotor schema and are capable of imagery, they begin to replace the sensorimotor approach to problem solving with elements of conscious thinking.

The preoperational stage   The stage of **preoperational intelligence**, usually between the ages of 2 to 7, allows for a transition between the egocentric, sensorimotor adaptations of infancy and the more socialized structures of later childhood. During this stage children begin to derive concepts from experiences. Learning occurs through first-hand sensorimotor activities. Thinking is very concrete; reality is exactly what is perceived, no more and no less, and there is little ability to consider alternatives. Intuitive thinking and deliberate behaviors emerge, enhanced by the development of language and the ability to play and pretend.

At the preoperational stage, children are still dependent on direct sensorimotor experiences; unable to consider multiple dimensions simultaneously, they focus on a single aspect of an object and neglect others and cannot rearrange or reorganize information in their minds.[34] They also are unable to comprehend *the principle of conservation*. For adults, a quart container holds a specific quantity of liquid which remains the same regardless of how the contents may be distributed or redistributed. If a quart of milk is divided into four glasses, adults can recognize that it is still a quart. Nothing has changed except that the milk has been redistributed. At the preoperational stage children do not recognize this principle. If they are shown a quart of milk and then it is divided into four glasses, they will say that this makes more milk, since what was just one container of milk now is four. If the four glasses are poured back into the quart bottle, they will say there is less milk.

The concrete operational stage   The principle of conservation becomes evident when **concrete operational intelligence** emerges around age 8, continuing into puberty. Children begin to be able to perform logical and mathematical operations, but they cannot deal with abstract ideas, only with concrete or real objects. For instance, they have a sense of what a particular number is and how it can be presented in different ways: $2 + 3 = 5$, but so does $7 - 2$.

With concrete operational thinking, children can solve problems of *classification*. They can divide fruits into apples, oranges, and peaches, for instance, or distinguish animals from humans and divide animals into four-legged animals like dogs and horses and flying animals like birds and ducks. Classification skills are enhanced by the ability to understand the logic of relations. Children can order things by their relative size from small to large and begin to think abstractly about what certain things have or do not have in common.

The formal operational stage   The fourth and highest stage of cognitive development is **formal operational intelligence**, which ordinarily does not emerge until adolescence or later. At this point reasoning becomes less a matter of trial and error and more a process of thinking through a problem. Abstract reasoning, in the form of propositional thinking (i.e., if this, then that) and combinatorial analysis (i.e., all things being equal) is possible, and the person is able to state and test hypotheses. With formal operational thinking, it is possible to solve problems by varying one factor while holding all other factors constant and systematically excluding explanations until the correct one can be abstracted.

An example of the use of formal operational intelligence is in the pendulum task, for which participants are given a series of weights, strings of varying lengths, and a rod from which to suspend the weights. When asked to state the principle which determines how fast a weight can go back and forth within a given period, they are likely to start by proposing that the principle involves either the length of string or the size of the weight, or some combination thereof. They might decide to see what happens if they alter the length of string while holding the weight constant or change the weight while holding the length of the string constant. In any case, they will conclude that it is the length of the string, not the weight, that determines the speed at which a pendulum swings.

Studies have shown that a significant proportion of the population may never attain the ability to think in formal operational terms. Piaget believed that all normal people can reach this level, but cognitive aptitude becomes differentiated in adolescence and adulthood, so some people have cognitive skills in logic, mathematics, or physics, and others' skills are in such fields as literature, linguistics, or art.[35]

Kohlberg's Theory of the Development of Moral Judgments

In his work on problem solving, Piaget prescribes a shift in moral judgment from heteronomous morality, based on fixed, unchangeable rules, to autonomous morality, based on cooperative agreements. The American psychologist Lawrence Kohlberg has adapted and expanded on these ideas and incorporated them in an influential theory on the development of moral judgments in cognitive thinking.[36] Kohlberg tested his theory by presenting verbal or written accounts of problem situations or dilemmas and asking children or adults to state the "right" solution in each instance. The answers given indicate the stage of moral development achieved by the test participant.

The problems Kohlberg presents are built around such issues as:

1. Should a doctor practice "mercy killing" to end the life of a fatally ill woman who requests death because she is in great pain?

2. Is it better to save the life of one important person or many unimportant people?[37]

Kohlberg's descriptions of the situations in such issues pose moral dilemmas. The mercy-killing issue, for instance, is presented as a problem facing Heinz, whose wife is near death from cancer and who cannot afford a new drug which might save her. The druggist who has discovered the drug paid $200 for the radium he uses in it, but he charges $2,000 for a small dose. Heinz can only raise $1,000. The druggist will not lower his price or let Heinz pay later, so Heinz steals the drug. Respondents then must decide whether Heinz rightly took the drug and why they think so. Kohlberg asks them to consider such questions as whether the husband is motivated by love of wife or regard for humanity and whether the pharmacist has a right to property he has created.[38]

Kohlberg is not interested in the actual solution to a problem, that is, the specific attitudes or beliefs expressed, but in the way the child or adult reasons and thinks through the solution. It is inconsequential whether of not the individual believes in mercy killing or that it is or is not better to save one important person. The reason behind the individual's attitude is the only pertinent point. The morality of individuals is related to their decision-making abilities and their ego capacities rather than their moral habits or feelings. Kohlberg identifies five ego capacities which he believes are related to moral behavior:

1. General intelligence.

2. The ability to anticipate future events and to choose a greater future reward over a lesser immediate one.

3. The capacity to maintain stable, focused attention.

4. The capacity to control unsocialized fantasies.

5. Satisfaction with the self and others.[39]

Levels and Stages of Moral Development

In his early work, Kohlberg postulated three basic stages of moral development: preconventional, conventional, and postconventional thinking. These generally correspond to Piaget's preoperational, concrete, and formal organizational stages of cognitive development (see "Relations between Piaget's and Kohlberg's Stages of Development"). Later Kohlberg redefined his three stages, dividing each into two substages to reflect a more social perspective in which moral development is seen as moving from self-centeredness to awareness of the rights and needs of others.[40] Thus Kohlberg proposes an order of progression in moral development which includes three levels and six stages.

Moral thinking is not present in Piaget's sensorimotor stage of development. Kohlberg, like Freud, believes the earliest level begins around 4 years of age with **preconventional moral development**, which is limited to thoughts about punishment first and then reward. In stage 1, the "egocentric stage," moral judgments are based on fear of punishment and unquestioning deference to authority or superior power. In stage 2, the "concrete individualistic stage," the physical consequences of action, regardless of its human meaning or values, determine for the child whether the behavior is right or wrong. Thus, with respect to mercy killing, a 4-year-old is likely to say it is wrong because "you can go to jail." Somewhat later the child begins to understand the role of rewards in motivating behavior. Some behaviors are considered good because they bring satisfaction in the form of rewards. This is often coupled with basic ideas about reciprocity: "If I am good to you, you will be good to me." Then the child is likely to believe that a doctor in a mercy-killing situation should behave in a way that will produce a reward.

Relations between Piaget's and Kohlberg's Stages of Development

The classifications of developmental skills devised by Jean Piaget and Lawrence Kohlberg both view development as occurring at certain ages or with the master of certain skills. Neither theory proposes that development will begin or end at these points, however. In fact, formal operational intelligence and postconventional morality may never be achieved by many individuals. The systems are related in that at each stage or level certain cognitive skills are utilized in making moral judgments.

Piaget's Stages of Cognitive Development	Kohlberg's Stages of Moral Development
Stage 1: Sensorimotor Intelligence Birth to age 18 or 24 months	No moral thinking

Stage 2: Preoperational Intelligence
    Ages 2 to 7
	Level 1: Preconventional Morality
	    Begins about age 4
	    Moral judgments use preoperational
	        intelligence
	        Stage 1: Egocentrism
	        Stage 2: Concrete individualism

Stage 3: Concrete Operational Intelligence
    Ages 8 to puberty (about 11)
	Level 2: Conventional Morality
	    Begins about age 10
	    Moral judgments use concrete operational
	        intelligence
	        Stage 3: Mutual interpersonal expectations
	        Stage 4: The societal point of view

Stage 4: Formal Operational Intelligence
    May begin in adolescence
	Level 3: Postconventional Morality
	    May begin in adolescence
	    Moral judgments use formal operational
	        intelligence
	        Stage 5: The social contract and
	            individual rights
	        Stage 6: Decisions based on conscience
	            and logic

The **conventional moral development** level begins around age 10, when children become aware of social expectations and norms and are motivated to conform to them. Stage 3 is characterized by "mutual interpersonal expectations." According to Ralph Anderson and Irl Carter, "The child now takes the role of the other, and can see the situation (and self) from the other's perspective."[41] This stage of development has a "good boy–nice girl" orientation. Children follow rules; they want to be considered nice and to receive praise and avoid blame. They seem to be motivated by their ideas of majority or "normal," "natural," behavior, and, for the first time, the intentions of their behavior become important. Thus 10-year-olds believe a doctor should strive to do what is right, should be nice, should mean well, and should try not to hurt anyone. In stage 4, characterized by "the societal point of view," the child recognizes the need to obey laws, perform duties, and respect authority. There is a sense that society could not exist if the existing author-ity is not upheld. Thus doctors should follow the rules of their profession and obey the law; the only way for them to earn respect is to satisfy their professional obligations.

For most people, moral development never gets beyond stages 3 and 4; it is esti-mated that only about 5 percent ever get as far as stage 6. Postconventional moral devel-opment is the most controversial of Kohlberg's levels; the first four stages clearly emerged from his research, but stages 5 and 6 seem to be based more on philosophical ideas than on scientific investigation.[42] Nevertheless, they do follow logically from the first four stages with their incorporation of the ideas of the social contract and individual rights.

Stages 5 and 6 do not begin before adolescence and will not be achieved before young adulthood, if ever. In stage 5, personal moral values are recognized as relevant, but so is the need to show concern for the welfare of others. A legalistic point of view emerges in which values are debated in order to reach a consensus acceptable to the majority of the people. But laws are not considered intrinsically right, and those that do not serve the common good can be changed. Kohlberg believes that the official morality of the gov-ernment of the United States reflects this level of thinking. Stage 6 is marked by "orien-tation toward the decisions of conscience and toward self-chosen ethical principles ap-pealing to logical comprehensiveness, universality and consistency."[43] Concrete moral rules such as the Ten Commandments are likely to be rejected in favor of more universal ethical principles such as the Golden Rule which reflect a sense of justice, equal rights, and respect for the dignity of all human beings.

Kohlberg's research is ongoing. On the basis of cross-cultural studies and research on social class factors, he argues that the stages of moral development can be found across all cultures and all classes and thus should be considered universal, unlearned develop-mental processes. He notes, however, that children in the United States are more likely to reach the higher levels of moral development than children in less developed countries, and middle-class children are likely to develop moral thinking and judgment principles faster and further than those in the lower classes. Religious background is not signifi-cant, however; Catholics, Protestants, Jews, Buddhists, Moslems, and atheists go through similar stages of moral development.[44]

Women's Moral Development

Carol Gilligan argues that much of the research literature on both emotional and cogni-tive development is sexist in that the studies almost exclusively have involved groups of males, and female development has largely been ignored. Gilligan, an associate and col-laborator of Kohlberg's at Harvard, has made the point that moral thinking in women progresses differently than it does in men. She proposes that males and females reason in different ways and that even if they reach the same conclusion about a moral dilemma, they use different inductive reasoning processes to do so.

Gilligan bases her argument for the existence of male and female differences in moral development on the goal specified by developmental theorists. In Kohlberg's stage 6, the highest level of moral thinking, the person, by implication a male, is able to listen to his conscience, determine his own ethical principles, and apply them as he sees fit. But Gilligan says that females define themselves in terms of relationships with others rather than personal autonomy, and concern for others develops at stage 3. Women's responses to Kohlberg's moral problems therefore are at a lower level of development than those specified for men, or they do not fit at any stage. As Gilligan puts it, "male and female

voices typically speak of the importance of different truths, the former of the role of separation as it defines and empowers the self, the latter of the ongoing process of attachment
that creates and sustains the human community."[45]

For Gilligan, the central issue in women's moral development is how to reconcile
responsible, caring relationships with the personal autonomy and individual achievement
that are more valued in the society. Their moral judgment differs from men's because
"sensitivity to the needs of others and the assumption of responsibility for taking care of
others lead women to listen to the voices of others and to include in their judgment
points of view other than their own."[46] This difference has been found to extend to the
opinions and attitudes of women and men in child welfare education and practice (see
"Different Voices in Child Welfare").

Gilligan's critique challenges the destructive force of sexism in moral development,
but, as we noted in Chapter 2, other research has demonstrated that innate, psychological male-female differences prove to be nonexistent or exaggerated when examined closely, and reviews of the literature have found little or no evidence of gender differences in
moral development.[47] Lawrence Walker's review of 19 studies that used Kohlberg's moral
reasoning measures indicated that those that found higher development in adult males
had not controlled adequately for education and occupation, and very few sex differences were evident in the findings of any study.[48]

Some feminists have questioned whether Gilligan's work, by making the argument for
women's "difference," isn't actually a part of the backlash against women's advances in the
1970s that has followed since the 1980s (see Chapter 8). Susan Faludi, for instance, says
that Gilligan's ideas have been appropriated by those seeking to establish that "career
women pay 'a psychic price' for professional success" or that "independence was an unnatural and unhealthy state for women." Faludi notes that while Gilligan acknowledges
that gender differences in thinking are a function of learning, she writes as if they were unlearned, gender-specific traits. Moreover, the differences in moral reasoning that have
been found are linked not with sex but with class and education.[49]

Other Dimensions of Moral Development

A theoretical synthesis which takes into account the behavioral and affective as well as the
cognitive dimensions of morality has been proposed by James Rest. His proposal seeks answers to the question, "What do we have to suppose went on in the head of a person
who acts morally in a situation?" All phases of moral decision making require the cognitive ability to understand and judge as well as the emotional ability to feel and empathize.
Thus a person confronted with a situation which calls for moral judgment must first gather information on the situation and the others in it and interpret the situation in terms of
how a proposed action would affect the welfare of others. Then the person must formulate a moral course of action, identifying the competing ideals which might be realized in
response to the situation. The next step is to select one ideal from among those possible
and decide whether to try to achieve it. Finally, in executing and implementing the intended action, the person must call on ego strength and coping skills in order to overcome
any obstacles to the moral behavior.[50]

Thus Rest's ideas on moral behavior are very much in keeping with the thrust of ego
psychology. The emphasis is on coping mechanisms that utilize what ego psychologists
might call reality testing, a sense of reality about the world and the self, and judgment.

Different Voices in Child Welfare

Ann Hartman and Diane Vinokur-Kaplan have examined the differences in the world views of male and female child welfare teachers and workers to determine whether their judgments and decisions in practice are affected by gender; that is, whether they hear "different voices," as Carol Gilligan suggests. They asked 684 men and 1,315 women working or teaching in child welfare to rate the importance of various content areas in education for child welfare practice.

The greatest difference between the replies of women and men was found on the item called "psychological and social processes of separation and loss," which women rated much higher as an area of study than men did. Items concerned with preserving the family and preventing the placement of dependent children, such as working with families toward reunification, treating troubled families, and preventive outreach to families, were considered important by both genders but ranked significantly higher by women. The researchers concluded that these findings bear out Gilligan's view that women value connection while men value separation, and women have a greater investment in the maintenance of attachment while men's investment is in personal autonomy and achievement.

Men ranked four study topics higher than women did: decision making in child placement, working with involuntary clients, family breakdown, and working with troubled adolescents. These findings suggested that male child welfare workers may tend to use separation developmentally, and "their concern may well be to help teens and children going into placement to make use of these experiences for growth and individuation."

A major finding for child welfare practice that emerged from this study was that "women [practitioners] seem to be more concerned about separation and loss, connectedness, and the maintenance of the family." Whether this difference is translated into the decisions on child placement made by female and male workers was suggested as a topic for further study. Three questions suggested by Hartman and Vinokur-Kaplan that might be addressed are:

1. Are programs headed by females likely to put less emphasis on placement and more on preventive services?

2. Are male direct-service workers more likely than female workers to place a child outside the family or to place an adolescent in a group setting?

3. When administrators and staff members are of different sexes, do gender issues escalate strain and conflict between supervisors and workers in child welfare services?

Source: Ann Hartman and Diane Vinokur-Kaplan, "Women and Men Working in Child Welfare: Different Voices," *Child Welfare*, vol. 64 (May–June 1985), pp. 307–14.

The Roots of Moral Behavior in Childhood Development

Freud, Piaget, and Kohlberg all suggest that moral thinking and feeling are not evident in infancy. Research on empathy, however, suggests that the ability to empathize and take the perspective of others makes children receptive to moral teaching. Barbara and Phillip Newman define empathy as "the vicarious experience of an emotional state that is being expressed by another person."[51] By watching facial expressions and gestures and listening to the sounds of others, infants can discern others' feelings. Studies have found that when one infant in a hospital nursery cries, so do the others, and 3-year-olds can recognize emotions such as happy and unhappy, as well as afraid, sad, and angry.[52] These early empathic abilities appear to be the foundation on which moral development rests.

Kohlberg stresses that moral development has to do with an evolving ability to think through ethical problems and dilemmas. For Freud, moral development has to do with the acquisition of a superego as a result of successfully resolving the Oedipal conflict in the genital stage of development. Thus Kohlberg is concerned with thinking morally and Freud with feeling moral. But what of behaving morally? Learning theory and research on parental discipline and moral decision making are useful in integrating Kohlberg's and Freud's ideas into a more complete understanding of how moral development takes place.

Social learning theory, discussed in the next section, presents evidence that children learn prosocial and antisocial behaviors by observing others. To the extent that the prosocial behavior of others is rewarded, children are likely to imitate it, and to the extent that the antisocial behavior of others is punished, they are likely to inhibit that behavior. Moral behavior also is influenced by social situations and the expectations, values, and objectives of the people involved in them.[53] For instance, people who place a high value on academic achievement may feel pressured to cheat on exams when they fear they will not do well, but it may never occur to them to cheat their friends in money matters. Similarly, if people believe antisocial behavior will not be caught or punished, they are more likely to engage in it.

Parental discipline techniques are also important in instilling moral values and encouraging moral behavior. The Newmans conclude that the discipline techniques that instill moral behavior are those that help children control their own behavior, understand the meaning of it for others, and increase their capacity for empathy. They propose a technique for disciplining children which includes four elements:

1. Discipline should interrupt or inhibit the undesirable behavior.

2. Discipline should demonstrate a more acceptable form of behavior; knowing what to do is as important as knowing what not to do.

3. Discipline should include an explanation, at a level the child can understand, of why an action is right or wrong.

4. Discipline should stimulate the child's empathy for the victim of the misdeed; a boy, for instance, should be encouraged to put himself in the place of his victim and see how the victim feels.[54]

∽ LEARNING THEORIES

Because a good deal of learning occurs in the early stages of the life cycle, learning theories have attempted to decipher the principles under which learning takes place in individuals, particularly in childhood and adolescence. These theories are predicated on the idea that most human behavior is learned as a function of transactions between individuals and their social environments. The two major transactional processes by which individuals learn are through their responses to external or environmental stimuli, in classical conditioning, or their responses that operate on the environment, in operant conditioning. Social learning theory attempts to explain behavior and personality characteristics, particularly in childhood, in terms of cognitive processes as well as classical and operant conditioning.

Classical Conditioning

Classical conditioning derives from the work of Ivan Pavlov, a Russian physiologist who worked out its basic principles in the late nineteenth and early twentieth centuries.[55] The idea of respondent or **classical conditioning** is that when a neutral stimulus is repeatedly paired with another stimulus which normally elicits a particular response, the neutral stimulus itself will begin to elicit a similar response; in this way the response becomes learned or conditioned. In Pavlov's famous experiments, when a hungry dog was shown meat, it began to salivate. The meat acted as an *unconditioned stimulus* because it naturally produced salivation, and *unconditioned response*. Then a bell was rung shortly before the meat was shown to the dog. Normally the sound of the bell would not produce salivation, but because it had been paired with the sight of food, the bell alone became sufficient to generate salivation in the dog. The bell became the *conditioned stimulus*, and salivation became the *conditioned response* (see "The Classical Conditioning Process").

The ideas incorporated in classical conditioning have led to the development of psychotherapeutic techniques such as systematic desensitization and aversion therapy. *Systematic desensitization* is used to treat phobias (fears) and anxiety, which are believed to develop through classical conditioning. A neutral experience (getting on a plane, having sexual intercourse, washing one's hands) becomes associated with an experience that previously produced fear or anxiety (having knowledge that a plane had crashed, believing that it will not be possible to arouse a partner or pregnancy could result, being accused of sloppiness or dirtiness). The treatment technique then is to desensitize or *countercondition* the person through the use of relaxation, so that fear and anxiety are no longer associated with the experience.[56]

Aversion therapy is used to eliminate a conditioned but unwanted or undesirable behavior, such as addiction to substances (drugs or alcohol) or to sexual behaviors (homosexuality or transvestitism). The undesirable behavior is believed to be due to association with some positive stimulus, so the treatment involves associating it with a negative stimulus. The usual technique is to pair the behavior with electric shock, nausea-inducing chemicals, or aversive symbols. Despite some claims of success, aversion therapy is not used a great deal today.[57]

Operant Conditioning

Operant conditioning derives from the work of two American psychologists, John B. Watson and B. F. Skinner. Watson, who is credited with being the originator of behavioral theories, proposed that the legitimate subject of psychology is behavior, not mind or consciousness as Freud maintained.[58] Skinner differentiated between learning through classical conditioning and learning through instrumental or operant conditioning.[59] In **operant conditioning** a neutral response is operated upon by a *reinforcing stimulus* to produce a particular response. For instance, if a pigeon receives a food pellet (the reinforcing stimulus) each time it touches a lever (the desired response), in due time the pigeon begins to act as if it knows that by touching the lever it can obtain food. The pigeon has learned that the lever response produces a reward.

Shaping occurs when the subject is reinforced for approximating the desired response. Since it might take months for the pigeon to touch the lever in the first place, the behavior is shaped or encouraged by rewarding *successive approximations*, behavior that comes closer and closer to the desired result. The food pellet is released further each

The Classical Conditioning Process

While director of the physiological laboratory at the Institute of Experimental Medicine in St. Petersburg, Russia, Ivan Pavlov worked on the digestive system. He devised an experimental apparatus with which he could measure the amount of saliva secreted by dogs when food was placed in their mouths. His observation that dogs in the apparatus began to salivate at the sight of the attendant bringing them food, or even at the sound of his footsteps, led to his statement of the principle of classical conditioning. The experiment included the following steps in the conditioning process:

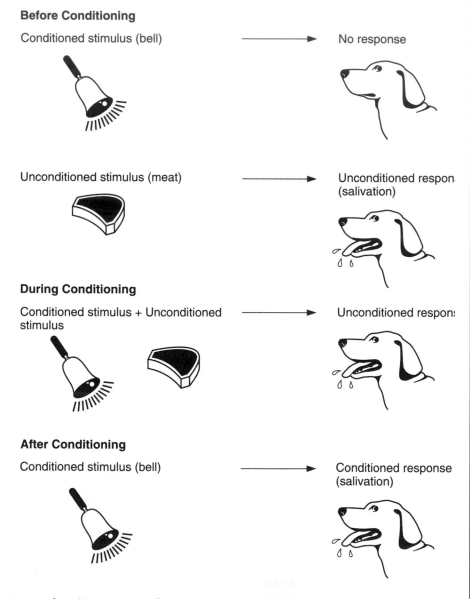

Before Conditioning

Conditioned stimulus (bell) ———————→ No response

Unconditioned stimulus (meat) ———————→ Unconditioned respon (salivation)

During Conditioning

Conditioned stimulus + Unconditioned stimulus ———————→ Unconditioned respon

After Conditioning

Conditioned stimulus (bell) ———————→ Conditioned response (salivation)

Source: Adapted from Dan G. Perkins, "Classical Conditioning: Pavlov," in G. M. Gadza, R. J. Corsini, and contributors, *Theories of Learning* (Itasca, IL: F. E. Peacock Publishers, 1980), pp. 35–36.

time the pigeon gets closer to the lever, but only when the pigeon actually touches the lever does it get the food.

Positive and Negative Reinforcement

Behaviors are increased or learned to the extent that they are reinforced, either positively or negatively. In general, the more a behavior is reinforced, the more it will be repeated. To increase a behavior through **positive reinforcement**, a favorable event or outcome is applied to the behavior, such as giving a reward each time the behavior is exhibited. To increase a behavior through **negative reinforcement**, an undesirable event or outcome is removed, such as taking away a punishment when the behavior is discontinued.

Determining exactly what is reinforcing can be a problem. Certain events are almost always reinforcing, such as giving food or water to a hungry or thirsty person; other events do not work as readily. Practitioners attempting to use reinforcement techniques may be asked to conduct an empirical test to observe clients and determine what normally reinforces their behavior or interview them about their likes and dislikes.[60]

At some point a positive or negative reinforcer is likely to stop being useful in eliciting a behavior. *Satiation* occurs when a reinforcer is provided to such an extent that it no longer affects behavior. If the goal is to increase a response, therefore, a positive reinforcer which will not be tired of easily should be chosen. If the goal is to decrease a response, one strategy is to offer a positive reinforcer so often that it fails to be effective.

Unlearning Undesirable Behaviors

Unlearning can be produced with operant conditioning in a number of ways. In *punishment*, an aversive stimulus is made contingent on a behavioral response; the stimulus will be administered if the undesirable behavior persists. However, certain conditions must be met for punishment to eliminate a behavior:

1. Since the initial reaction is likely to be escape or avoidance, the reinforcing environment must be made escape-proof.

2. Punishment is only effective when it occurs at the same time as the undesirable response; if it is not associated with the response, it will not be of any use.

3. Punishment must be severe enough.

Even if it is possible to meet all these conditions in everyday life, punishment may not work. If a father punishes a child for smoking, for instance, it is likely that the child will not actually stop but will attempt to escape detection by smoking behind the father's back. A form of punishment often used in work with children is time-out, or punishing undesirable behavior by making the child spend a short time alone. In the interval, the child is not receiving any reinforcements and also usually is not able to commit the undesirable behavior.[61]

Many learning theorists prefer extinction as a way of eliminating unwanted behaviors. In *extinction*, reinforcement of a behavior is discontinued; a previously rewarded response is no longer rewarded. If the pigeon has been rewarded with a food pellet for pressing the lever, it no longer receives a pellet when it presses the lever. If the child has been rewarded with parental affection and attention when it has a tantrum, the affection and attention are withdrawn when a tantrum starts. Extinction is not automatic, and, depending on how the rewards were administered in the first place, it may be difficult.

By observing and interacting with his grandfather, this child is being given opportunities to learn not only how to operate a mower but also such abstract concepts as the value of work and responsibility for his actions.

Parents using extinction techniques to eliminate undesirable behaviors must be extremely patient and avoid administering rewards that have reinforced them.

Social Learning Theory

In explaining the development of personality characteristics and social behavior, social learning theory proposes that learning takes place not through conditioning but through humans' ability to observe and imitate the behaviors of others and acquire them vicariously. Such laborious processes as shaping do not seem to capture the way learning takes place. When we learn to drive a car, for instance, we are not shaped or rewarded each time we approach a car, sit in it, touch the steering wheel, put a key in the ignition, and so on. Humans have a capacity for *vicarious acquisition*. From their observation of others (who take the role of models), people can blueprint complex series of behaviors and then think about them and make choices about imitating the models and acquiring those behaviors. We learn to drive cars more or less by observing how others drive and imitating what they do, and children learn prosocial or antisocial behavior by observing and imitating parents, peers, and even televisions shows and computer games.

By allowing for such cognitive processes, social learning theory avoids the principal criticism leveled at classical and operant conditioning theories of learning: They make no room for psychological processes, allowing for no psychological mediating functions or cognitions, motivations, attitudes, identity, or personality beyond a hedonistic, utilitarian need to seek rewards. The learning process in classical conditioning is based on the assumption of a completely passive learner. In operant conditioning the assumption is that rewards and punishments supplied by the environment produce behavior by themselves; they are transactional only in the most minimal sense.

From its origins, social learning theory has established that learning takes place through cognitive processes, regardless of rewards or punishments.[62] Albert Bandura's laboratory experiments on modeling and imitation have provided much of the literature on social learning. A now classic study was designed to determine the extent to which awareness of the reinforcement of a model affects imitation of the model's actions by others. Using three groups of 4-year-old children, Bandura showed each group separately a film in which a male model behaved aggressively toward an inflated "Bobo" doll. One group saw the model being punished for his actions; one saw him being ignored; and the third saw him being rewarded with treats. Later the children were placed in a room with the doll and other toys, and their behaviors were recorded. The group that had seen the model rewarded exhibited the most aggression toward the doll, and the group that saw him punished exhibited the least. Then, without any further training, the children were told they would be rewarded if they could demonstrate the behavior of the model. All of them, regardless of the group they were in, were equally able to imitate his aggressive behavior.[63] This experiment demonstrated that learning involves cognitive processes; it should be distinguished from behavioral responses alone, which are more likely to be controlled by incentives.

Cognitive Processes in Behavioral Responses

Social learning theory considers behavioral responses as a function of the cognitive processes of attention, retention, production, and motivation, though the consequences of being rewarded or punished are also recognized.[64] The process of *attention* is the starting point; learning cannot take place unless the observer is aware of the models and the events being modeled. The level of attention given by the observer is affected not only by the personal and social attributes of the models but by the characteristics of the events; more attention is paid when they are distinct, novel, salient, or complex. Characteristics of the observer such as the capacity to be aroused, personal needs, and perceptual readiness also influence the level of attention.

Retention is the ability to store information observed and remember it when necessary. Organization and such symbolic processes as rehearsal, that is, mentally going over the event and the things learned from it, are included in this process. *Production* refers to the process of converting the retained information, cognitively stored and rehearsed, into action. The observer must have the ability to pull together all the components of the behavior and the physical capacity to actually recreate the behavior. Also necessary is the ability to judge the correctness of recreated behavior and learn from mistakes, through self-evaluation or feedback from others.

Social learning ties in with operant conditioning in the process of *motivation*. This kind of learning does not require reinforcement; people can store much more information than they ever convert into behavior. Nevertheless, reinforcement, either from within or without, supplies the motivation for the actual performance of a behavior. External incentives to behave include tangible rewards such as money and social rewards such as approval and praise. Internal incentives include the tangible rewards individuals give themselves and the positive self evaluation they feel in doing something they want to do.

The role of individuals in regulating their own behaviors has recently been recognized by Bandura, who notes, "People do not behave just to suit the preferences of others. Much of their behavior is motivated and regulated through internal standards and self-evaluative reactions to their own actions."[65] The capacities to observe the self, to judge the self, and to react to the self allow for self-regulation.

Social service practitioners need to examine these four cognitive processes—attention, retention, production, and motivation—to assess why a client who supposedly has learned a particular behavioral response fails to behave that way. The behavior may not have been attended to adequately, retained adequately, carried out adequately, or motivated by reinforcement from others or the client's self-evaluation.

✆ IMPLICATIONS FOR PRACTICE

Psychodynamic Perspectives

The strength of ego psychology and psychodynamic perspectives for social service practitioners is the help they provide in understanding the inner life of clients. Freudian theory sensitizes them to clients' unconscious needs and motives; it provides a theoretical framework for the study of personality structure and dynamics and explains psychosexual development. Those who follow in the Freudian tradition continue to alter his theory and make their own contributions to it. Contemporary psychodynamic perspectives give less attention to the id and more to the ego, examining such processes as ego defenses, ego functions, and object relations. Freud's emphasis on early-life development and his tentative explanation of female development are in a continuing process of revision.

Psychodynamic perspectives also are helpful in providing ways to think about normal individual development. What is considered normal is a function of biological aging; infants and children and adolescents and adults have different needs and different abilities to meet them. For Freud, psychological development is achieved when the adult acquires a superego as a result of successfully dealing with the Oedipal conflict. For ego psychologists, psychological development has to do with the adequate use of defenses and the ability to cope with and master the environment. Individuals who have ego strength can use their defenses, perceive reality accurately, have a good sense of themselves and others, and make good moral judgments. They can regulate their drives; think in logical, goal-oriented ways yet let go of logic when necessary; continue to attend, concentrate, and learn even under stress; and maintain mature interpersonal relations. They have the qualities that allow for competence in interaction with the environment. In contrast, individuals with ego weakness have deficiencies in internal functioning which limit their ability to perceive, experience, and deal with the demands imposed by reality.

In self psychology, psychological development is seen as the achievement of a cohesive nuclear self, that is, a central, enduring, organized sector of the personality which emerges through interaction with others. Development is achieved when people can see themselves and others as separate, three-dimensional individuals. It is aborted for those who seem fragmented, undifferentiated from others, and unable to achieve a positive self-identity.

Psychodynamic perspectives are especially useful in the assessment and intervention phases of practice. For a direct-service social worker, the first decision is whether an ego-oriented assessment should be made of a particular client. Eda Goldstein warns that such assessments are not appropriate in some forms of practice, as in determining clients' needs for entitlement to services such as financial maintenance and homemaker assistance.[66] Ego strength should not be equated with personal worth or goodness, and ego weakness should not be used as a reason to disqualify clients from receiving services. However, when the service being provided has to do with personal and interpersonal problems in living, then the various psychodynamic perspectives can be useful.

In the assessment phase of practice, the various points of view about psychological development can be useful in examining the extent to which a client's problems are related to deficiencies in fulfilling drives or in developing ego strength or a nuclear self. Yet these perspectives are not solely focused on problems or deficiencies; they also provide help in identifying clients' internal strengths and capacities which can be mobilized in helping them. An assessment must take note of the psychic development that the client has achieved, and then three forms of intervention can be tried:

1. To nurture, maintain, enhance, or modify the client's inner capacities.

2. To mobilize, improve, or change environmental conditions that impinge on those capacities.

3. To improve the fit between inner capacities and external circumstances.

Cognitive Development Theories

The work of Jean Piaget and Lawrence Kohlberg can be used as an adjunct to psychodynamic perspectives. It acquaints workers with the client's thinking and reasoning processes, which are essential to the assessment of ego functioning, and provides a way of assessing normal intellectual development in infants, children, and adults. From this perspective, the goal of cognitive development is the ability to use abstract reasoning. In infancy, reasoning is limited to sensorimotor processes. Young children learn to use concrete thinking skills; older children develop operational thinking; adults become capable of formal logic and abstract reasoning. In terms of morality, development progresses from a preconventional emphasis on rewards and punishments through a conventional emphasis on rules and regulations to a concern for social and human rights. Moral development requires the individual to become less centered on the self and more aware of the rights and needs of others.

Cognitive development theories are also useful in assessment and intervention. Social service workers must attend to the ways their clients think and reason and should not make appeals to reasoning processes or moral criteria that are beyond their comprehension. In working with children and adolescents, for instance, information and alternatives must be presented in ways these clients or their parents will understand. Neither should they appeal to processes or criteria that their clients have moved beyond. Rewards, punishments, or rules will not affect adults who can use abstract reasoning or show a concern for social justice.

Learning Theories

Learning theories shed light on the ways by which concrete experiences—associations and contingencies or operations—shape behavior. The have provided social workers with a guide for assessing individual behavior by unraveling the reinforcing contingencies and associations that maintain undesirable behavior. A behavioral assessment instructs workers to be behaviorally specific, that is, to focus not so much on unwanted feelings and thoughts as on unwanted verbal or physical behaviors. By changing their behaviors, learning theorists argue, individuals change their thoughts and feelings as well. The first step in helping clients do this is to determine the conditions that have produced the undesirable behavior.

The greatest contribution of learning theories, however, is the therapeutic techniques derived from them. From classical conditioning came systematic desensitization and aversion therapy to replace unwanted behavior. From operant conditioning came the techniques of punishment and extinction to eliminate unwanted behaviors and positive and negative reinforcement to generate wanted behaviors. From social learning theory came the processes of modeling and vicarious acquisition to teach wanted behaviors.

In the remaining chapters of Part V we turn to development across the life span. The emphasis is that development takes place as a function of biological processes—growth and maturation—in transaction with psychological and social processes. Through the successful negotiation of developmental tasks, crises, and issues, individual development ordinarily progresses across the life course from conception and infancy to adulthood.

∞ DISCUSSION QUESTIONS AND CLASS PROJECTS

1. List the seven ideas associated with ego psychology identified by Goldstein. How are they in keeping with the systems approach described in Chapter 2?

2. Distinguish among the id, the ego, and the superego. To what extent do you believe people have instinctual drives and motives that operate unconsciously? As a social worker, how would you know that unconscious drives are operating in a client?

3. What did Freud mean by penis envy? Do you think the concept captures the unconscious feelings of women in a sexist society? To what extent do you think women are ambivalent toward their sexual identity and men are not ambivalent toward theirs?

4. Identify at least five contributions made by Freud to the study of human behavior.

5. What are ego defenses? How do they differ from coping mechanisms?

6. Describe at least three ego defenses. Can you give examples from your own experience with clients or friends in which defenses were being used? Do you think using ego defenses is a sign of poor psychological development?

7. What is meant by an autonomous ego function? List and describe at least three such functions.

8. What three components are said to comprise coping?

9. What is meant by ego strength and ego weakness? Why are these important concepts for social workers?

10. Describe the following concepts from the study of object relations and self psychology:

    object relations
    self-object
    nuclear self
    separation
    transference
    countertransference
    transmutation
    individuation

11. Describe the following concepts from cognitive development theory:

adaptation
schemas
structures
operations
assimilation
accommodation

12. Describe Piaget's four stages of cognitive development.

13. Describe Kohlberg's six stages of moral development.

14. How is Kohlberg's approach to moral development different from Freud's? What other approaches ought to be considered for a more complete understanding of moral behavior and development?

15. The class chooses one of the two examples given in the text of the type of questions Kohlberg used in the study of moral development and everyone writes complete responses to it (answers can be anonymous). They should remember that Kohlberg is interested not in the yes or no aspect of the question but in the logic and reasoning used in the response. The responses are collected and passed out again, making sure that no one gets her or his own reply. The class tries to determine the stage of moral development represented in each reply.

16. Discuss the difficulties encountered in determining an individual's stage of moral development. How might you revise the procedure? Do you think you would ever use Kohlberg's procedure in working with children, adolescents, or adults?

17. For a variation on Question 15, ask class members to indicate their sex to determine if there are systematic gender-related differences in the responses. Does there appear to be a "male voice" and a "female voice"?

18. For another variation, interview acquaintances or strangers outside the class and ask for their responses to the question being considered. Tell them only that you are studying moral development in class and assure them that their names will not be used. Both sexes and a number of age categories should be included in the sample.

19. Distinguish between classical conditioning, operant conditioning, and social learning theories. Indicate how each has been used in social service practice.

20. Describe the four cognitive processes that produce behavioral responses, according to social learning theory.

21. Identify and describe the following:

    aversion therapy
    systematic desensitization
    positive reinforcement
    negative reinforcement
    successive approximations
    shaping
    satiation
    punishment
    extinction
    models

22. Distinguish between the methods of successive approximation and vicarious acquisition. Which do you think is the more normal form of learning among humans?

∽ NOTES

1. See Judith Marks Mishne, "The Missing System in Social Work's Application of Systems Theory," *Social Casework*, vol. 63 (November 1982), pp. 547–53.

2. Barbara M. Newman and Philip R. Newman, *Development through Life: A Psychosocial Approach*, 4th ed. (Chicago: Dorsey Press, 1987), p. 616.

3.   Heinz Hartman, *Ego Psychology and the Problem of Adaptation* (New York: International Universities Press, 1939); also see Erik H. Erikson, *The Life Cycle Completed: A Review* (New York: W. W. Norton, 1982), p 28.

4.   See Paul Gray, "The Assault on Freud," *Time*, November 29, 1993, pp. 47–51.

5.   The account of Freudian theory is drawn from a wide range of Freud's work and the work of several of his followers. For a good introduction to Freud, see Charles Brenner, *An Elementary Textbook of Psychoanalysis* (New York: Doubleday/Anchor, 1957); Harry Guntrip, *Psychoanalytic Theory, Therapy, and the Self* (New York: Basic Books, 1973); Eunice F. Allen "Psychoanalytic Theory" in F. J. Turner (editor), *Social Work Treatment: Interlocking Theoretical Approaches*, 2nd ed. (New York: Free Press, 1979); and Katherine M. Wood, "The Contributions of Psychoanalysis and Ego Psychology to Social Casework," in H. Strean (editor), *Social Casework: Theories in Action* (Metuchen, NJ: Scarecrow Press, 1971).

6.   See Brenner, *Elementary Textbook of Psychoanalysis*, p. 18.

7.   Eric Fromm, *The Crisis of Psychoanalysis: Essays on Freud, Marx, and Social Psychology* (New York: Holt, Rinehart, and Winston, 1970), pp. 69–78.

8.   See Ann M. Clarke and A. D. B. Clarke, *Early Experience: Myth and Evidence* (London: Open Books, 1976); Jerome Kagan, Richard B. Kearsley, and Philip R. Zelazo, *Infancy: Its Place in Human Development* (Cambridge, MA: Harvard University Press, 1978); and Hans Thomas, "The Concept of Development and Life-Span Developmental Psychology," in P. B. Baltes and O. G. Brim, Jr. (editors), *Life-Span Development and Behavior*, vol. 1 (New York: Academic Press, 1979), pp. 282–312.

9.   Robert Graves, *The Greek Myths*, vol. 2 (New York: George Braziller, 1959), pp. 9–15.

10.   Roger Brown, *Social Psychology* (New York: Free Press, 1965), pp. 374–81.

11.   Mary C. Schwartz, "Sexism in the Social Work Curriculum," *Journal of Education for Social Work*, vol. 9 (Fall 1973), p. 66.

12.   See, for instance, the discussion of Freud in Marie Richmond-Abbott, *Masculine and Feminine: Sex Roles over the Life Cycle* (New York: Random House, 1983), pp. 26–27.

13.   Juliet Mitchell, *Psychoanalysis and Feminism* (New York: Vintage, 1975), pp. 5–15, 95–104.

14.   Erikson, *Life Cycle Completed*, pp. 38–39.

15.   See Morton Deutsch and Robert M. Krauss, *Theories in Social Psychology* (New York: Basic Books, 1965), pp. 126–30.

16.   Anna Freud, *The Ego and the Mechanisms of Defense* (New York: International Universities Press, 1936).

17.   This definition is from the Psychiatric Glossary in Norman A. Polansky, *Integrated Ego Psychology* (New York: Aldine, 1982), p. 47.

18.   Descriptions of ego defenses and autonomous functions, as well as other terms in this section, are based on Eda G. Goldstein, *Ego Psychology and Social Work Practice* (New York: Free Press, 1984).

19.   Hartman, *Ego Psychology*; Carel Germain, "General Systems Theory and Ego Psychology: An Ecological Perspective," *Social Service Review*, vol. 52 (December 1978), p. 541.

20.   Robert W. White, "Strategies of Adaptation: An Attempt at Systematic Description," in G. V. Coelho, D. A. Hamburg, and J. E. Adams (editors), *Coping and Adaptation* (New York: Basic Books, 1974).

21.   See Goldstein, *Ego Psychology and Social Work Practice*, pp. 60–61.

22.   See Germain, "General Systems Theory and Ego Psychology," p. 545.

23.   Robert W. White, "Competence and the Psychosexual Stages of Development," in M. R. Jones (editor), *Nebraska Symposium on Motivation* (Lincoln: University of Nebraska Press, 1960), pp. 97–124.

24.   Anthony N. Maluccio, "Competence-Oriented Social Work Practice: An Ecological Approach," in A. N. Maluccio (editor), *Promoting Competence in Clients* (New York: Free Press, 1981), pp. 6–9.

25.   Goldstein, *Ego Psychology*, p. 62.

26.   Polansky, *Integrated Ego Psychology*, p. 17.

27.   Jeffrey M. Masson, *The Assault on Truth: Freud's Suppression of the Seduction Theory* (New York: Farrar, Straus, and Giroux, 1984).

28.   Alvin Rosenfeld, "Freud, Psychodynamics and Incest," *Child Welfare*, vol. 66 (November/December 1987), p. 488.

29.   Polansky, *Integrated Ego Psychology*, pp. 189–91.

30.   The description of self psychology is largely derived from Miriam Elson, *Self Psychology in Clinical Social Work* (New York: W. W. Norton, 1986). See especially pp. 8–22.

31.   Ibid., p. 4.

32.   Jean Piaget and Barbel Inhelder, *The Psychology of the Child* (New York: Basic Books, 1969).

33.   See Henry W. Maier, *Three Theories of Child Development* (New York: Harper and Row, 1969), pp. 81–157.

34.   Rolf E. Muus, "Jean Piaget's Cognitive Theory of Adolescence," in R. E. Muus (editor), *Theories of Adolescence*, 4th ed. (New York: Random House, 1982), pp. 176–208.

35.   Jean Piaget, "Intellectual Evolution from Adolescence to Adulthood," in R. E. Muus (editor),

Adolescent Behavior and Society: A Book of Readings, 3rd ed. (New York: Random House, 1980), pp. 70–78.

36. Lawrence Kohlberg, *The Psychology of Moral Development* (New York: Harper & Row, 1984), and *Child Psychology and Childhood Education: A Cognitive-Developmental View* (New York: Longman, 1987).

37. Lawrence Kohlberg, "The Child as a Moral Philosopher," *Psychology Today*, vol. 1 (September 1968), p. 28.

38. Lawrence Kohlberg, "The Development of Children's Orientations toward a Moral Order: II. Social Experience, Social Conduct, and the Development of Moral Thought," *Vita Humana* (1963), pp. 18–19.

39. Lawrence Kohlberg, "Development of Moral Character and Moral Ideology," in M. Hoffman and L. Hoffman (editors), *Review of Child Development Research* (New York: Russell Sage Foundation, 1964), pp. 389–91. Also see John W. Lorton and Eveleen L. Lorton, *Human Development through the Lifespan* (Monterey, CA: Brooks/Cole, 1984), p. 248.

40. Kohlberg, "Child as Moral Philosopher," pp. 25–30, and Lawrence Kohlberg, "Revisions in the Theory and Practice of Moral Directions for Child Development," No. 2 (San Francisco: Jossey-Bass, 1978), pp. 83–87.

41. Ralph E. Anderson and Irl Carter, *Human Behavior in the Social Environment: A Social Systems Approach*, 4th ed. (New York: Aldine de Gruyter, 199), p. 198.

42. Ibid., p. 199.

43. Kohlberg, "Child as Moral Philosopher," p. 26.

44. Ibid., p. 30.

45. Carol Gilligan, *In a Different Voice: Psychological Theory and Women's Development* (Cambridge, MA: Harvard University Press, 1982), p. 156.

46. Carol Gilligan, "Why Should a Woman Be More Like a Man?" *Psychology Today*, vol. 16 (June 1982), p. 68.

47. Lawrence J. Walker, "Sex Differences in the Development of Moral Reasoning: A Critical Review," *Child Development*, vol. 55 (June 1984), pp. 677–91; John C. Gibbs, Kevin D. Arnold, and Jennifer Buck Hardt, "Sex Differences in the Expression of Moral Judgment," *Child Development*, vol. 55 (August 1984), pp. 1040–43.

48. Walker, "Sex Differences in Development of Moral Reasoning," p. 688.

49. Susan Faludi, *Backlash: The Undeclared War against American Women* (New York: Crown Publishers, Inc., 1991), pp. 327–32.

50. James Rest, "The Major Components of Morality," in W. M. Kurtines and J. L. Gewirtz (editors), *Morality, Moral Behavior, and Moral Development* (New York: John Wiley and Sons, 1984), pp. 24–38.

51. Newman and Newman, *Development through Life*, p. 250.

52. Ibid., pp. 251–52.

53. Walter Mischel, "Toward a Cognitive Social Learning Reconceptualization of Personality," *Psychological Review*, vol. 80 (July 1973), pp. 252–83.

54. Newman and Newman, *Development through Life*, p. 253.

55. Ivan P. Pavlov, *Conditioned Reflexes* (London, England: Clarendon Press, 1927).

56. See G. Terence Wilson and K. Daniel O'Leary, *Principles of Behavior Therapy* (Englewood Cliffs, NJ: Prentice-Hall, 1980), pp. 152–64.

57. Ibid., pp. 176–82.

58. John B. Watson, *Behaviorism* (New York: W. W. Norton, 1925).

59. B. F. Skinner, *The Behavior of Organisms: An Experimental Analysis* (New York: Appleton-Century-Crofts, 1938).

60. See G. Terence Wilson and K. Daniel O'Leary, *Principles of Behavior Therapy* (Englewood Cliffs, NJ: Prentice-Hall, 1980), pp. 98–101.

61. Robert M. Liebert, Rita Wicks-Nelson, and Robert V. Kail, *Developmental Psychology*, 4th ed. (Englewood Cliffs, NJ: Prentice-Hall, 1986), p. 298.

62. See Ted L. Rosenthal and Barry J. Zimmerman, *Social Learning and Cognition* (New York: Academic Press, 1978), pp. 71–74.

63. Albert Bandura, "Influence of Models' Reinforcement Contingencies on the Acquisition of Imitative Responses," *Journal of Personality and Social Psychology*, vol. 1 (June 1965), pp. 589–95.

64. Albert Bandura, *Social Learning Theory* (Englewood Cliffs, NJ: Prentice-Hall, 1977), pp. 22–29. Also see Bandura, "Model of Causality in Social Learning Theory," in S. Sukemune (editor), *Advances in Social Learning Theory* (Tokyo: Kaneko Shobo, 1983).

65. Bandura, "Model of Causality," p. 92.

66. Goldstein, *Ego Psychology*, p. 127.

CHAPTER 16

Life-Span Development
Prenatal Influences and Early Life

MAJOR THEMES DISCUSSED IN THIS CHAPTER

1. **DEVELOPMENT ACROSS THE LIFE SPAN.** The study of psychosocial development involves examination of the cognitive, emotional, and behavioral changes in individuals as they go from birth to death. Development is regarded as progressive change. Growth, differentiation, maturation, and decline are biophysical conditions that may influence development, and societal, community, and family conditions may also influence it. Progressive psychosocial change, therefore, is a vision of what can happen in the course of life, and, from the critical perspective on social work practice, what should happen.

2. **STAGES OF DEVELOPMENT.** Theorists have conceived of the life course as consisting of a series of stages from birth to death. Biological, social, and psychological clocks are taken into consideration in determining a person's developmental stage.

3. **DEVELOPMENTAL TASKS AND CRISES.** The life course may be regarded as a series of age-related tasks or crises which must be dealt with successfully if development is to occur. Havighurst's concept of developmental tasks and Erikson's idea of eight stages of development, each with a psychosocial crisis, have been influential in life-span or developmental psychology.

4. **THE PERIOD OF PRENATAL GROWTH AND BIRTH.** The possibility for psychosocial development begins at conception; birth follows the embryonic and fetal periods of pregnancy, setting the stage for development across life. The well-being of the unborn child and the newborn infant is inseparable from the physical, social, and psychological well-being of the parents. The mother and father pass on a genetic inheritance of physical characteristics and behavioral dispositions through the mechanism of heredity, which operates through chromosomes and genes; genetics is the study of this mechanism.

5. **EARLY-LIFE STAGES OF DEVELOPMENT.** Physical growth is rapid in the first two years of the child's life, the period of infancy and early childhood. Most children rapidly master the motor skills needed to function independently and the social skills of relating to family members and other, and they learn to negotiate the psychosocial cries of early life. The process of attachment, by which children and parent figures bond with one another, is a central issue at these stages.

6. **IMPLICATIONS FOR PRACTICE.** Genetic counseling and programs to facilitate attachment are two ways social service workers attempt to facilitate development in early life.

THE CONCEPT OF INDIVIDUAL DEVELOPMENT ACROSS the life span was introduced in the preceding chapter with three psychological perspectives. In this chapter development is considered more systematically in terms of the biophysical, psychological, and social factors that make it possible. For life-span researchers, individuals have the potential to develop continually throughout the course of their lives, from birth to death. Development is regarded not as the presence of certain traits or abilities but as the outcome of transactional processes through which individuals strive to master age-related tasks and crises; that is, it is the effects of complex, continual interactions among biological, social, and psychological factors. In keeping with a critical approach to social work practice, we will focus on development as progressive psychosocial change in the cognitive, emotional, and behavioral dimensions.

∞ DEVELOPMENT ACROSS THE LIFE SPAN

The study of human development across life involves examination of the cognitive, emotional, and behavioral changes in individuals as they go from birth to death. The concept of **psychosocial development**, which we use to describe these changes, carries the connotation of progress. The idea is that for individuals in various phases of biological growth and maturity, the goal is continual improvement in their psychological and social functioning. Psychosocial development thus carries the connotations of unidirectionality and irreversibility; as Paul Baltes observes, a person goes in one direction from less developed to more developed, and once there, cannot go back.[1] Although psychosocial development may be looked at in terms of statistical averages and the presence or absence of pathology, at its heart it is the utopian attempt to describe optimum states of human behavior throughout life.

Development, Growth, and Change

A problem in understanding psychosocial development across the life course is a lack of preciseness about the definitions of development, growth, differentiation, maturation, and change. Henry Maier's definitions make these distinctions clear. In his terms, **change** refers to alterations from one condition to another, and it carries no connotation of progress: "Change implies a transition from one state to another, while development focuses upon the dynamic, one-directional elements of change."[2] Change can be physical or biological as well as psychological and social. Change may be for better or worse; no direction or irreversibility is implied.

Growth, differentiation, and maturation all describe progressive physical change. *Growth* refers to physical changes by way of cell or tissue enlargement. In the simplest terms, the body and its organs get bigger. *Differentiation* refers to structural changes through which the interrelations among cells, tissues, and organs or their parts become more specialized and complex. *Maturation* is used to describe the point at which growth and differentiation reach their peak. The term also connotes the ability to procreate; a physically mature person is capable of reproducing life. The opposite of growth, differentiation, and maturation is *decline*. As humans mature, their physical capacities stabilize and then begin to decline toward inevitable death.

In the early theories of Freud and Piaget, growth and development followed similar trajectories. As individuals matured, they also developed. Once they stopped maturing in their late teens or early twenties they also stopped developing. Neither Piaget nor Freud believed development takes place across the life course. In the work of Erik Erikson and other life-span theorists, the concepts of growth and development are more clearly distinguished. The belief now is that psychosocial development can occur even as growth stabilizes and declines.

The concept of development as progressive psychosocial change cannot be taken as a fact of life. Studies have shown that individuals continually change but they do not automatically progress cognitively, emotionally, and behaviorally as they age. There are large intraindividual and interindividual differences in human behavior, and change can be multidirectional or reversible. Individuals may show different rates and directions of psychosocial change at various periods in their lives, changing quickly or changing slowly, going forward, going upward, going backward, going downward, walking in place, or even going in loops. Two people of the same chronological age may show very different psychosocial patterns; one may give evidence of continuous progress and the other may appear static. Change across the life course, therefore, is believed to take place in multidirectional and reversible ways[3] (see "Behavioral Change across a 50-Year Life Span").

By their attention to the conditions that promote continuous forward and upward psychosocial change, life-span theorists have helped social service workers understand the internal struggles individuals encounter and the tasks they must accomplish in order to make development a reality. Their message to policymakers, program developers, and direct-service social workers alike is: Provide services that will help people continually improve their psychosocial functioning.

Society and Individual Development

From the critical perspective on social service practice, with its emphasis on the integral relationship between person and environment, between individual and society, the impact of social, economic, and political conditions on the likelihood of achieving normal human development is substantial. In life-span theory it is often assumed that society is supportive of all the classes, communities, and groups in it, and it thrives when everyone is given equal opportunities to develop. This is the idea behind Heinz Hartman's "average expectable environment" as one that supports the development of human potential.[4] In today's social, political, and economic environment, however, this may not be a viable alternative.

Katayun Gould, taking a feminist perspective, offers a conflict model of development in which society is seen as a struggle between groups with opposing interests and aims. She argues that life-span models overestimate the ability of individual motivation to overcome the effects of unequal power and authority because they focus on intrapsychic and interpersonal conflict but give little attention to conflict engendered by intergroup tensions. Since men control power in society, they also control the resources and opportunities necessary for individual development, and they tend to try to keep those re-

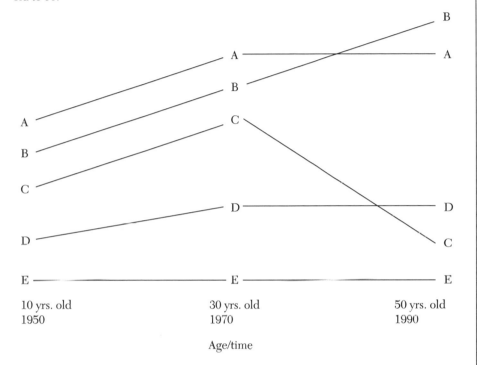

Behavioral Change across a 50-Year Life Span

Changes may occur in different directions over a life span, both within a person and between people. The figure shows how the behavior of five hypothetical individuals (A–E) might progress, remain static, or decline at 20-year intervals, as they grow from 10 years old to 50.

Source: Adapted from M. M. Lerner and D. F. Hultsch, *Human Development: A Life Span Perspective* (New York: McGraw-Hill, 1983), p. 9. Reproduced with permission.

sources for themselves. In effect, gender inequality in society gives men an "above" average environment and women a "below" average environment.[5]

Gould acknowledges that interracial, interethnic, and other forms of societal conflict also affect the likelihood of normal development. Anyone who experiences subordinate status in society—regardless of its basis—may be expected to have more difficulty achieving mastery over developmental tasks and crises at various life stages. This does not mean, however, that members of subordinated groups will necessarily fail to develop, and members of dominant groups are assured progressive improvement. Society provides individuals with only one (admittedly important) level of social support; communities, families, and groups also provide support which can compensate for a subordinated position. Nevertheless, inequality does put people at greater risk for problems in psychosocial development.

∞ STAGES OF DEVELOPMENT

In theories of individual development, the life course is segmented into sequential stages associated with physical growth, maturity, and decline. At each stage, a unique set of tasks and crises is proposed which determines the possibilities for development.[6] As a result, growth and development are expressed as the presence of different traits, characteristics, or abilities in the individual at each stage of life.

There is no agreement as to the number of stages in the life course. Sigmund Freud's five stages of psychosexual development and Jean Piaget's four stages of cognitive development, discussed in Chapter 15, are examples. Erik Erikson, whose work is discussed in this chapter, describes eight stages of psychosocial development, but most contemporary writers add three or four more. Barbara and Philip Newman, for instance, include a prenatal period and divide adolescence and old age into two stages each, for a total of eleven stages of development.[7]

Although a person's chronological age is associated with her or his stage of development, no one-to-one relationship between age and stage has been established. Stages of development are as much cultural invention as biological fact; for instance, childhood and adolescence were not recognized as periods of development prior to industrialization.[8] Adolescence, long believed to be a natural outgrowth of the pronounced biological changes that occur at puberty, is now considered a more arbitrary cultural phenomenon. Young people are classified as adolescents from preteens through college enrollment, and the term *adolescence* is no longer used as equivalent to puberty.[9] There is also no agreement on the definition of adulthood, its span, or its subdivisions.[10] Aging itself has little to do with proposed stages of development.[11] A longitudinal study of two samples of men, for instance, found adult life stages to be more-or-less independent of chronological age.[12]

Differences in response to the life cycle make it impossible to categorize individuals' stages of development solely on the basis of biological age. The age at which children sit up, walk, talk, and control their bowels varies, as does the age at which puberty sets in or young people gain independence. Adults today are flexible about when and if they will marry, have children, or begin a career. The diversity is particularly evident in women. At age 21, for instance, one may decide to concentrate on beginning a career, put off marriage and a family, and not be ready to bear and rear a child until age 35. Another may marry at 21, begin having children, and then, at 35, return to school for a degree or start a new career. From the viewpoint of psychosocial development, these two women of the same age would not be considered in the same stage of development.

Biological, Social, and Psychological Clocks

An individual's stage of development in the life cycle can be thought of as a function of three independent, internal clocks—biological, social, and psychological—ticking away. The biological clock measures chronological age as each person advances in years. Since the state of physical development is important to human behavior, chronological age must always be taken into account in trying to understand the tasks and crises individuals are facing, but by itself age is an insufficient basis for identifying the cognitive, emotional, and social changes taking place in them.

The social clock operates in terms of the roles and statuses individuals occupy across the life course, which are closely related to the tasks and crises confronting them.[13] The social clock measures states of development as a series of structured social roles which individuals move in and out of and which are more-or-less connected with chronological age.[14] Martin Kohli suggests that in industrial societies, four age strata are derived from roles in the economy. Infants play; that is, they have no tasks with respect to the economy. Children and adolescents are given tasks in school to prepare them for participation in economic activities. Adults have the principal roles in economic and household production and services, and older people generally have been retired or released from these roles.[15] Age strata can also be defined in terms of sexual rights and obligations. Children are preparing for participation in procreative roles and are not expected to engage in sexual activity; adults are expected to take on procreative roles within the family but also have the right to seek sexual fulfillment. The cultural norm that older people have no interest in sex and so make up a third age stratum in this respect is increasingly being rejected.

The psychological clock measures how individuals feel about themselves, what their abilities are, what they perceive their expectations to be, and how they behave. Some people feel old when they are 35 years of age, while others feel young at 70. Some adolescents are quite mature, independent, and able to form intimate relations, and some adults are not.

DEVELOPMENTAL TASKS AND CRISES

The developmental tasks and crises that make up the stages in the life course have been identified in various ways by life-span theorists. Our discussion will center on the developmental tasks identified by Robert Havighurst and the psychosocial crises that, according to Erik Erikson, occur at each stage of development.

Havighurst on Developmental Tasks

Robert J. Havighurst, an educational psychologist, has proposed a theory of development based on the concept of **developmental tasks**. He believes that development is achieved as the person, while physically growing and then declining, learns and successfully completes a series of specific age-related tasks. For Havighurst, "The human individual learns his way through life." In this sense he departs from the Freudian emphasis on inherent, instinctual drives, maintaining that while lower animals rely on instinct, humans rely on learning. Nature offers wide possibilities for development, and which skills will be mastered depends on individual learning through socialization.

Havighurst describes a **developmental task** as "a task which arises at or about a certain period in the life of the individual, successful achievement of which leads to his happiness and to success with later tasks, while failure leads to unhappiness in the individual, disapproval by the society, and difficulty with later tasks."[16] Barbara and Philip Newman define the term as an outcome of particular stages in the life cycle: "Developmental tasks consist of a set of skills and competencies that contribute to increased mastery over the environment." These tasks may represent a gain in motor skills, intellectual skills, social skills, or emotional skills.[17] Perhaps the best way to think of the concept of task is as an assigned or expected physical, behavioral, emotional, or cognitive chore to be performed or learned by a person.

According to Havighurst, developmental tasks have three interrelated sources or domains; he adds a cultural or social domain to the biophysical and psychological. They may originate in the biophysical domain and express maturational urges and needs or in the cultural or social domain and reflect expectations about age roles and statuses such as daughter, student, or civic leader. The third source is in the psychological domain, which emerges from the interaction between the biophysical and cultural domains. These tasks reflect values and aspirations that are internalized by the individual. Havighurst believes that by the age of 3 or 4, "the individual's self is effective in the defining and accomplishing of his developmental tasks."[18]

Because these tasks derive from biological needs, from society, and from the self, there is always the potential for conflict. In this respect the idea of developmental tasks is similar to the notion of roles; in fact, one way of thinking about stages is in terms of age status and role. The major divisions in the life span propel individuals into age-related roles: infant, child, adolescent, adult, or elderly. The expectations for these roles derive from both the individual and society (see "Definitions of Role" in Chapter 3), and when expectations for roles and tasks are unclear, mixed, or in other ways poorly communicated, conflict is likely to occur. Successful development, therefore, depends not only on the abilities of the individual to master the tasks but also on the support that is available in the society.

Havighurst's Classification of Tasks

Havighurst differentiates between unique and recurrent developmental tasks. *Unique tasks* are associated with a particular age or stage of development. For these tasks, there is a teachable moment when a person is ready to learn them; toilet training is an example. *Recurring tasks* are never completely or finally learned. A good example is learning to be a man or a woman, roles which cannot be mastered at one moment in the life cycle but require continual attention. Havighurst describes the recurring sex-role task in these terms: It begins in earnest for most people about the time they start school, and in its first phase it is pretty well mastered by the age of nine or ten. But the coming of puberty changes the nature of the task and it has to be carried on into a new phase, that of learning to get along with age-mates of the opposite sex. Soon another phase of the task develops—that of learning to get along with age-mates of both sexes in a socially mature way, cooperating with others not for friendship alone but for some impersonal purpose. And even then the task is not completed. The elderly face it in a new guise when they accept the fact of their aging and learn to associate happily with the "elders" of the society.[19]

Havighurst's unique and recurring tasks can be classified in six general categories. They include tasks associated with physical growth and maturation, sexuality and sex roles, family life, friendships, cognitive development, and moral and civic responsibility (see "Havighurst's Developmental Tasks across the Life Course"). Development occurs as individuals meet these unique and recurring biological, cognitive, psychological, and social expectations and learn the appropriate tasks. Biological tasks occur as a direct result of physical maturation and decline. Cognitive tasks indicate Havighurst's interest in cognitive development theory, and sexual and sex-role tasks show the influence of Freud. Other tasks, which include social behavior, seem to represent Havighurst's own thinking about human development. In short, Havighurst provides a perspective which makes it possible to think about human development in a very broad way.

Rather than attempting to uncover universal laws of human development, Havighurst maintains that each society has distinctive developmental tasks. He explains that the tasks he has identified are to be interpreted only within the context of white, middle-class, American society in the middle of the twentieth century.

Havighurst's Developmental Tasks across the Life Course

In his classification of developmental tasks confronting the individual negotiating the life course, Robert J. Havighurst identifies six categories of tasks and the specific tasks of each type to be learned in infancy, middle childhood, adolescence, middle adulthood, and later maturity.

I. Tasks Related to Growth and Maturation
   A. Infancy
      1. Walking
      2. Taking solid foods
      3. Controlling body wastes
      4. Achieving physiological stability
   B. Middle childhood
      1. Learning physical skills necessary for games
      2. Building wholesome attitudes toward self as a growing organism
   C. Adolescence
      1. Accepting one's physique and effectively using the body
   D. Middle adulthood
      1. Accepting the physiological changes of middle age
   E. Later maturity
      2. Adjusting to decreasing physical strength and health
II. Tasks Related to Sexuality and Sex Roles
   A. Infancy
      1. Learning sex differences and sexual modesty
   B. Middle childhood
      1. Learning appropriate masculine or feminine roles
   C. Adolescence
      1. Achieving a socially approved masculine or feminine role
III. Tasks Related to Family Life
   A. Infancy
      1. Learning to relate to parents, siblings, and others

   B. Adolescence
      1. Achieving independence from parents and other adults
      2. Preparing for marriage and family life
   C. Early adulthood
      1. Selecting a mate
      2. Learning to live with a marriage partner
      3. Starting a family
      4. Rearing children
      5. Managing a home
   D. Middle adulthood
      1. Assisting teenagers to become responsible and happy adults
      2. Relating oneself to one's spouse as a person
      3. Adjusting to aging parents
   E. Later maturity
      1. Adjusting to death of a spouse
IV. Tasks Related to Social Friendships
   A. Middle childhood
      1. Learning to get along with age-mates
      2. Achieving personal independence
   B. Adolescence
      1. Achieving mature relations with age-mates of both sexes
      2. Achieving emotional independence from parents and others
   C. Early adulthood
      1. Finding a congenial small group
      2. Developing adult leisure-time activities
   D. Later maturity
      1. Establishing an explicit affiliation with one's age group
V. Tasks Related to Cognitive Development
   A. Infancy
      1. Forming simple concepts of social and physical reality

continued

---

continued

B. Middle childhood
1. Developing fundamental skills in reading, writing, and calculating
2. Developing intellectual skills and concepts for civic competence

VI. Tasks Related to Moral and Civic Responsibility

A. Infancy
1. Learning to distinguish right from wrong and developing a conscience

B. Middle childhood
1. Developing concepts necessary for everyday living
2. Developing a conscience, morality, and a scale of values
3. Developing attitudes toward social groups and institutions.

C. Adolescence
1. Achieving assurance of economic independence
2. Selecting and preparing for an occupation

3. Desiring and achieving socially responsible behavior
4. Acquiring a set of values to guide behavior

D. Young adulthood
1. Getting started in an occupation
2. Taking on civic responsibility

E. Middle adulthood
1. Achieving adult civic and social responsibility
2. Establishing and maintaining an economic standard of living

F. Later maturity
1. Adjusting to retirement and reduced income
2. Meeting social and civic obligations
3. Establishing satisfactory physical living arrangements

Source: Adapted from R. J. Havighurst, *Developmental Tasks and Education* (New York: David McKay, 1952).

Most social scientists have incorporated the notion of developmental tasks into their ideas on the life course, and there have been few systematic attempts to improve on the work of Havighurst. Thus while his ideas about developmental tasks have been very influential, the specific tasks he has identified have not been systematically utilized or tested. They do have an ad hoc validity which makes them useful in social service practice, but they cannot be applied unthinkingly to individuals outside the mainstream of American society, such as the poor and racial and ethnic minorities. More research is needed on the concept of developmental tasks and specific unique and recurrent tasks throughout the life course.

Erikson's Psychosocial Crises

Psychologists who take a psychodynamic perspective maintain that development occurs in individuals not simply as a function of completing specific age-related tasks, as Havighurst proposes, but as a function of negotiating various inner crises or struggles. Erik Erikson's conceptualization of the psychosocial crises confronting each person throughout the life course has been the most influential theory built around this idea.[20]

By identifying the psychosocial processes that occur as individuals live out their lives, Erikson's work has been of enormous significance to social service practice. It is considered to constitute a theory of psychosocial development that is deeply indebted to Freudian ideas but goes beyond them. As an ego psychologist, Erikson maintains all the contours of the Freudian model, including the emphasis on biology, unconscious instinctual needs, the id, ego, and superego, and the centrality of sexuality. In addition, he recognizes the conflict inherent in transactions between the person and the society and acknowledges the roles of ego processes, social needs, and social expectations in human development. Erikson also breaks with Freud in viewing development as occurring across the entire life course. For Freud and Piaget, human development is largely completed by the end of adolescence. The early childhood years also are the most important in Erikson's formulation, but it takes into account the stages in which physically and sexually mature adults rework the crises of their earlier years and confront new crises as they age.

Stages of Psychosocial Development

Erikson postulates the existence of eight stages, each of which occurs within a "radius of significant relationships" and in a particular social context or environment. In the first three stages, infancy, early childhood, and the play age, the child's social relationships are confined to the family and the role of son or daughter. The school-age and adolescence stages accompany puberty, when sexually maturing girls and boys are still very much involved in the family of origin but also are interacting in the world of the school, the neighborhood, and their peers. In the next two stages, young adulthood and adulthood, the person may take up the roles of spouse, parent, worker, and citizen. The last period, old age, involves the years of retirement when the roles of worker and householder have been released and the individual must confront the inevitability of death (see "Erikson's Stages of Psychosocial Development").

Erikson's developmental stages are defined in terms of a **psychosocial crisis** that typifies each stage. In this term *crisis* does not mean some kind of extreme or traumatic experience but a set of *critical tasks* which require coping or adaptation. Each crisis poses a struggle from which a *basic strength* can emerge. Together, these strengths or ego qualities represent the ultimate possible psychosocial development. If the crisis is not overcome, an ego weakness or *core pathology* can develop.

For resolution of the psychosocial crisis at each stage, the individual relies on the ego strengths built up from past experiences. These strengths involve the proper use of defense mechanisms as well as the conscious use of coping skills, the drive toward competence, and all the other autonomous ego functions. Resolution is also helped along by society or, more particularly, by others in the radius of significant relationships. Erikson's focus on the individual's inner life does not provide a systematic understanding of the ways in which society can provoke or exacerbate crises or can support and help people through them.

Borrowing Hartman's concept of an average expectable environment, Erikson makes the assumption that all societies provide the support necessary for development. This is a useful concept, but, as conflict models of development such as Gould's discussed above point out, everyone does not receive equal support in American society. Social conditions such as alienation, anomie, inequity, and attacks on self-esteem (see Chapters 13 and 14) can have negative effects on the individual's efforts to resolve psychosocial crises. Access to the necessary resources and opportunities remains out of reach for some women,

---

Erikson's Stages of Psychosocial Development

Erik Erikson's theory of psychosocial development covers the life course from infancy to old age. In each stage a particular psychosocial crisis must be resolved within a radius of significant relationships with others. Successful resolution endows the personality with a basic strength; the result of unsuccessful resolution is a core pathology.

Stage	Psychosocial Crisis	Radius of Significant Relationships	Basic Strength	Core Pathology
Infancy	Trust vs. mistrust	Maternal person	Hope	Withdrawal
Early childhood	Autonomy vs. shame, doubt	Parental persons	Will	Compulsion
Play age	Initiative vs. guilt	Basic family	Purpose	Inhibition
School age	Industry vs. inferiority	Neighborhood, school	Competence	Inertia
Adolescence	Identity vs. confusion	Peers, outgroups, models of leadership	Fidelity	Repudiation
Young adulthood	Intimacy vs. isolation	Partners in friendship, sex, competition, cooperation	Love	Exclusivity
Middle adulthood	Generativity vs. stagnation	Divided labor and shared household	Care	Rejectivity
Later Adulthood	Integrity vs. despair	Mankind, my kind	Wisdom	Disdain

Source: Adapted from THE LIFE CYCLE COMPLETED, A Review, by Erik H. Erikson, pp. 32–33, by permission of W. W. Norton & Company, Inc. Copyright © 1982 by Rikan Enterprises Ltd.

---

racial and ethnic minorities, disabled persons, and homosexuals, as well as for members of the working and poverty classes.

Erikson's stages are epigenetic in nature; that is, one follows from another in a sequential order. According to the **epigenetic principle**, "proper developmental progress requires the meeting and surmounting of the distinctive critical tasks of each developmental phase at the proper time in the proper sequence."[21] Although the stages follow one after the other, however, the crisis of each stage is believed to exist in an embryonic form before that stage begins. Moreover, all the crises are believed to be systematically related to all the others, so that as people work through any one crisis, they simultaneously work through past crises and lay the groundwork for the resolution of future crises. Erikson believes individuals have endless possibilities to rework their inner experiences and reach maximum development. The idea that it is always possible to get people back on course, confronting new, past, and future crises in their development, is Erikson's major contribution to social service practice.

∞ THE PERIOD OF PRENATAL GROWTH AND BIRTH

Development across the life span begins with conception and the prenatal period. Although this is usually not included as a period of development with specific tasks and crises, it is clear that conditions in the period before birth set the stage for development of the fetus (the organism from the third through ninth month) and the birth of the infant.

The Parents' Influence

The well-being of the unborn child is inseparable from the physical, social, and psychological well-being of the adults responsible for its existence. There is clear evidence of the effects of the socioeconomic position and the physical and psychosocial condition of the parents on the prenatal and postnatal development of children.[22] While the focus has been on the mother's health, nutrition, and behavior, fathers share equal responsibility. The production of healthy sperm, the endowment of a good genetic inheritance, and the provision of dependable economic support to assure satisfaction of the basic needs for food and shelter are responsibilities of the male partner. Nevertheless, in society's eyes, the mother bears the burden of providing a safe, nurturing environment for development of the fetus. Marilyn French notes, for instance, that:

> Judges and medical experts persecute mothers who use drugs or alcohol, even though it has never been proven that moderate use of alcohol harms a fetus, and even though no one would think of punishing male alcoholics for damaging their sperm. In the campaign to force mothers to uphold standards of behavior not demanded of men, the judicial and medical establishments have the eager cooperation of the press. *The New York Times* made much of the "fact" that a single drink during pregnancy can cause intellectual and physical defects in a fetus, although the research on which the report was based asserted fetal damage could not be shown under *three drinks a day*, and that poverty and lack of education were more serious and widespread causes of birth defects.[23]

This conclusion is echoed on a global scale in *The Progress of Nations*, the 1993 report of the United Nations Children Fund, which states that "Empowering women with at least basic education and literacy is therefore one of the most important single elements in the developmental process." The education of women has been shown to be associated not only with their ability to earn higher incomes but with such trends as greater use of social services, better child care and nutrition, and the reduction of deaths in children, according to the report.[24]

The Mother's Physical Condition

Although the optimal age for women to conceive and bear healthy infants is between 18 and 35,[25] advances in prenatal care and tests for potential difficulties have made it safer for women to begin their families later. According to the National Center for Health Statistics, in the past 15 years the number of first births to women between 30 and 39 has

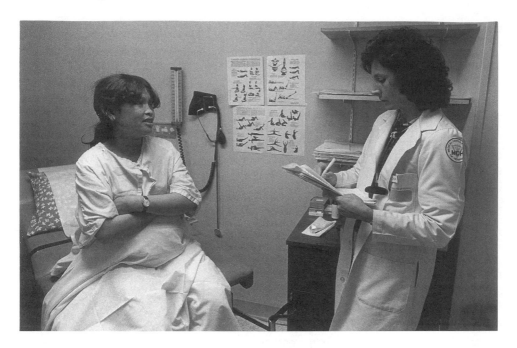

A Cambodian refugee in Vermont receives care for herself and her unborn child from a medical center doctor. The well-being of the fetus is
inseparable from the physical, social, and psychological well-being of
the adults responsible for its existence.

more than doubled, and there has been a 50 percent increase in first births to women over
40. New technology has produced a variety of treatments for infertility, which tends to increase in women over 35, and with advances in the new field of maternal-fetal medicine
women with chronic illnesses and those who develop medical problems during pregnancies can deliver normal, healthy babies and survive pregnancy themselves.[26]

A study by Gertrud Berkowitz of 3,917 women who had babies at Mount Sinai Hospital in New York City found that for a woman over 35 who is physically healthy and has
no history of infertility, miscarriage, or stillbirth, the chances of having a normal, healthy
baby are not significantly different from those of a 20-year-old. This finding contradicts
previous studies that found older women could be expected to have babies who are premature, smaller, or more likely to die or to have health problems. While it has also been
found that chances of having a Down's syndrome baby are nine times greater for a 40-
year-old woman than for a 30-year-old, on average older women have less than a 1 percent
chance of having a child with this disability.[27]

A number of correlational studies have indicated a relationship between deficiencies
in maternal diet and stillbirths, prematurity, low birth weight, and growth retardation
and poor mental functioning in infants.[28] Particular physical conditions in the mother
also put the fetus at risk; for instance, if the mother contracts rubella, or German measles,
in the first three months of pregnancy, the fetus is likely to be harmed. Rh blood-factor
incompatibility in the mother and the fetus (an Rh-negative mother and Rh-positive
fetus) is a major cause of a serious condition in infants, hemolytic disease of the newborn (anemia).

Women infected with the HIV virus that causes AIDS can infect their newborn infants. According to the U.S. surgeon general, about one of every four babies born to infected women will have HIV infection. Most often, the mother passes HIV to her baby before it is born or during birth, but a baby can also become infected by breastfeeding from an infected woman. The time from birth to the development of AIDS for children who are infected varies from weeks to years.[29]

All babies born to HIV-infected mothers test positive for HIV at birth, whether or not they are actually infected, since the positive antibody is transferred from the mother. For babies who are not infected, their HIV tests will become negative within about one and one-half years. While the majority of babies born to HIV-infected mothers will escape HIV infection, they may well be orphaned; their mothers—and often their fathers—are infected and likely to die before the children are grown.

The Mother's Behaviors and Emotional States

The behaviors and mental or emotional states of pregnant women can adversely affect development of the fetus in other ways. Excessive consumption of alcohol can lead to fetal alcohol syndrome in the child, an irreversible condition characterized by growth deficiency, abnormally small heads, joint defects, and abnormalities in heart development and facial characteristics. Expectant mothers who smoke cigarettes have been found to have more unsuccessful pregnancies and premature babies than those who do not. Even the excessive consumption of caffeine in coffee and other beverages is being discouraged. In the environment, toxins and other health hazards such as radiation and pollution can lead to miscarriages, sterility, or birth defects.[30]

Prenatal and postnatal development are negatively affected when expectant mothers regularly use addictive drugs. Heroin, morphine, or methadone used during pregnancy may produce addicted infants who display withdrawal symptoms at birth, and cocaine is responsible for many babies born with birth defects. Cocaine is absorbed through the mother's placenta, cutting off the flow of oxygen to the baby and causing permanent brain damage. Other likely consequences are retarded growth, seizures, abnormalities of the genital and urinary organs, and incomplete intestines. The babies are irritable, upset by the slightest stimulus, and unable to focus on sights or sounds. They often withdraw into a deep protective sleep.[31]

The mother's emotional state also can be a profound influence on prenatal development. Pregnancy is a time of stress for almost every woman.[32] It reshapes the body and can cause physical discomfort, irritability, or nausea. The woman is projected into new roles and statuses in preparation for motherhood. An expectant mother's peers and parents and the father-to-be all are likely to treat her differently and expect different things of her than they did before she became pregnant. Such changes require considerable adaptation.

The stresses of pregnancy are particularly harmful if the expectant mother has little understanding of the process of conception, how the fetus grows, and the needs of newborns. If these stresses are not handled well or they are worsened by a lack of social support or conflict with parents, peers, or the father, the development of the fetus or the newborn child may be threatened. Women suffering from postpartum (after-birth) depression may even subject their infants to neglect or abuse.

A few upsetting experiences during pregnancy are not likely to harm the fetus, but prolonged emotional distress is. Tense and anxious mothers are more likely to have colicky babies. Women with a positive attitude toward pregnancy and motherhood will spend more time in face-to-face contact with their newborn children and interact more with them during infancy.[33]

Support of the Father

There are significant differences between the birth weight and health of infants born to single women and those born to married couples. Even in the latter case, an infant who is unplanned for or unwanted is at a disadvantage.[34]

Fathers are becoming more involved in the pregnancy and the birth process. Both are enhanced if the father is present, supportive, interested in learning, and capable of sharing the mother's feelings about the coming child. Fathers who participate actively in the delivery and care of the infant are more likely to become engrossed with the child. Such fathers are visually and tactilely aware of the infant and its distinctive characteristics and tend to perceive it as perfect.[35]

Genetic Inheritance

The child's physical characteristics, including external features such as eye color and stature and internal features such as metabolism and blood type, as well as the child's behavioral dispositions, are passed on from the parents through the mechanism of heredity. **Genetics** is the study of this mechanism, which operates through the elements of chromosomes and genes. **Chromosomes** are the beadlike strings of genes present in every cell, generally occurring in pairs that reproduce and split during cell formation. **Genes** are the microscopic elements carried by the chromosomes which contain the codes that produce inherited traits and dispositions.

The parental genes are carried in the chromosomes of the female ovum (egg) and the male sperm, which unite in an act of conception when the sperm fertilizes the egg. A gene thus may be considered a chromosomal unit of inheritance; specifically, it is a segment of a DNA (deoxyribonucleic acid) molecule which contains a complex chemical code that provides all the biochemical information needed to enable cells to make the many kinds of molecules that determine physical characteristics.[36]

An example of the important bits of information carried in the chromosomes is information on sex. The 46 chromosomes in each cell are made up of 23 pairs, each with one chromosome from the sperm and one from the ovum. In 22 of these pairs, the two chromosomes are similar in size; in the other pair, which distinguishes sex, the sizes differ, X denoting big and Y denoting small. The sex chromosome is an XX pair in females and an XY pair in males, and the sex of the child is highly influenced by the chromosomal information carried in the sperm of the father. If the sperm that fertilizes an ovum carries an XY chromosome, a male child is likely to be produced. If the sperm carries an XX chromosome, the child will probably be female.

Genetic inheritance is not a simple addition of the traits of the father and the mother. The genetic pattern inherited by an individual at conception is called the **genotype**. The visible expression of the individual's overall genetic makeup, that is, the physical appearance, is called the **phenotype**. Only dominant inherited genes are incorporated in the phenotype; the recessive genes remain in the genotype, where they may affect the development of an individual in a future generation. The meeting of the dominant and recessive genes is the process through which many characteristics of physical appearance are passed on from parents to their children, each of whom may look like one parent or the other, like a combination of the two, or different from either one.

Almost all complex human characteristics, such as intelligence, behavioral and emotional patterns, and physical abilities, are acquired through genetic inheritance, a process in which many genes operate simultaneously. Nevertheless, very few human characteristics are purely genetic in origin. For instance, Americans are much taller than they would be if height were determined simply on the basis of genetic inheritance. Due to the effects of environmental factors such as changes in nutrition and health care, between 1860 and 1960 American adults became, on average, six inches taller. These effects are less visible today, which seems to imply that height has reached a plateau or possibly its outer human limit.[37]

Genetic Disorders

Genetic disorders transmitted from the parents to the fetus constitute a major category of birth disabilities. The National Center for Health Statistics cites congenital anomalies as the leading cause of infant mortality in the United States, accounting for 20.5 percent of the deaths to infants under 1 year old in 1989.[38] Genetic disorders also produce severely disabling or chronic conditions that may not become apparent until years later in the child's life cycle. The genetic disorders passed on by parents have a number of sources: a single abnormal gene, multifactorial inheritance, chromosomal aberrations, or exposure to harmful agents in the environment[39] (see "Categories of Genetic Disorders").

All humans carry abnormal, potentially harmful recessive genes of which they are not aware. If two people who carry the same abnormal gene reproduce, the chances are one in four that the gene will be inherited by their offspring. Examples of conditions associated with a single gene are cystic fibrosis, sickle-cell anemia, Huntington's disease, and hemophilia. Other common genetic disorders are the product of a multifactorial inheritance which includes polygenic factors, (several genes with an equal effect in producing a characteristic) and environmental factors. An infant may inherit all or none of the harmful genes that exist within its immediate or extended family. Examples include cleft lip, cleft palate, club foot, diabetes mellitus, spina bifida, and some forms of mental retardation.

Some genetic disorders are not passed on from one generation to the next but result from accidents as chromosomes are replicated and cell division produces sperm and eggs. Often these accidents result in spontaneous abortion, but sometimes the embryo or fetus survives. Conditions resulting from such chromosomal aberrations include Down's syndrome, certain learning disabilities, and some sex chromosome anomalies. Exposure to destructive environmental agents can damage chromosomes and disrupt normal genetic processes, producing such disorders in newborns as fetal alcohol syndrome and Rubella syndrome.

Effects on Psychosocial Development

The individual's cognitive, emotional, and behavioral development also is affected by both genetic and environmental conditions. Temperament, for instance, apparently is influenced by genetic endowments. In an often-cited series of studies, Alexander Thomas, Stella Chess, and Herbert Birch found nine basic personality dimensions on which children were likely to vary at birth. On the basis of interviews asking parents to describe the characteristics of their children, babies were found to differ in level of activity, rhythm,

Categories of Genetic Disorders

Category	Subcategory	Examples
Single-gene disorders	Autosomal recessive	Cystic fibrosis
	Autosomal dominant	Huntington's disease
	x-linked recessive	Hemophilia
	X-linked dominant	Vitamin D–resistant rickets
Multifactorial disorders	Polygenic plus environmental factors	Spina bifida
		Cleft lip/palate
		Arteriosclerotic heart disease
Chromosomal disorders	Abnormality in number of chromosomes	Klinefelter syndrome
		Down's syndrome
	Structural defects of chromosomes	Translocation Down's syndrome
Environmental disorders	Teratogen	Rubella syndrome
		Fetal alcohol syndrome
	Carcinogen	X-ray microcephaly
	Mutagen	Benzene liver cancer

Source: "Resource Guide on Peer Support Training," prepared by the Planning Committee for the National Conference on Peer Support Training for Genetic Support Groups, Washington, DC, March–April, 1990.

willingness to approach new things, adaptability, intensity of reactions, responsiveness, moods, distractibility, and attention span.[40]

Using these dimensions, the researchers were able to categorize most of the children they studied into three basic personality types. The *easy child* is biologically regular and rhythmical, eats and sleeps more or less on schedule, accepts new food and new people with relative ease, and is not easily frustrated. Forty percent of the children studied were of this type. The *slow-to-warm-up child* (15 percent) tends to withdraw quietly but shows interest in new things when not forced and given time to adapt. The *difficult child* (10 percent) is negative, withdraws noisily, and is very slow to adapt. Approximately 35 percent of the children studied were not easily classified into one of these three categories. The temperaments evident at birth do not always survive infancy. Thomas and Chess found that while a number of characteristics identified were maintained, others changed as children grew older, and by adolescence many of them evidenced different personality traits than they had at birth.[41]

Infants' temperaments have been found to affect their early interactions with parents and other adults. Rather than being passive creatures unable to influence their environments, even very young infants are quite active and can influence their caregivers. The physical appearance of an infant, for instance, can elicit positive or negative reactions from adults. The emotional treatment of babies born prematurely often suffers because of their unattractive appearance; indeed, there is evidence of a link between prematurity and the probability of child abuse.[42] The actions of an infant also can affect the giving or withdrawing of care. Crying behavior takes on a cyclical rhythm which becomes predictable to the caregiver, who responds with the necessary attention.[43] Excessive crying, however, can lead to the withdrawal of attention or even to punishment. In a study of 54 mothers, it was found that the attachment of mother to child builds during the first months after birth but decreases when the child will not stop crying.[44]

The Embryonic and Fetal Periods and Birth

Human development becomes possible at the moment of conception when a single male sperm joins with a single female ovum or egg cell to form a **zygote**. Usually this occurs through normal heterosexual intercourse; in a single emission of semen, as many as 250 million sperm may be released, but only a few reach the egg in the woman's fallopian tube, and only one can enter the egg. For a substantial number of couples, conception does not take place. The two major reasons for infertility are low sperm count in the male and failure to ovulate in the female. The use of artificial insemination, fertility drugs, microsurgery to unblock the fallopian tubes, and test-tube methods of impregnation have increased the likelihood of conceiving and having children.

If impregnation does take place, the pregnancy or gestation period, normally nine months, begins. Within 24 hours, the single-celled zygote divides into two, which soon becomes four, eight, sixteen, and so on. As the zygote divides it travels down the fallopian tube to the uterus, and at the end of this journey, which takes about a week, the fertilized ovum has developed into a ball of 32 or 64 cells. When the **embryo**, or the growing human organism, attaches itself to the lining of the uterus, it contains more than 100 external and internal cells. Through the external cells nourishment is passed from the placenta; thus the embryo has an independent blood supply and also makes use of the mother's. The internal cells are attached to the placenta through the umbilical cord, which contains veins and arteries to carry nutrients in and waste products out.

The embryo grows rapidly and in an orderly fashion in the *embryonic period,* which lasts about seven weeks. Crucial structural differentiation occurs with the appearance of an *ectoderm,* which becomes the skin; an *endoderm,* which becomes the digestive system and lungs; and a *mesoderm,* which becomes the musculature, skeleton, and other circulatory, excretionary, and reproductive organs. Often even before the woman knows she is pregnant, the embryo develops rudimental hands, arms, fingers, legs, feet, and toes, and a heartbeat can be distinguished. Miscarriages and spontaneous abortions are most likely to occur in the embryonic stage.

The third through ninth months of prenatal growth is referred to as the *fetal period.* The embryo becomes a *fetus,* and the organs, limbs, and muscles and other systems developed in the embryonic period become functional. Sex differentiation occurs around the third month of pregnancy. By the fifth month the fetus has sleeping and waking periods and mothers can feel it moving about. By the end of the sixth month the fetus is considered viable; that is, capable of surviving outside the womb if it is given special attention and placed in an incubator. During the ninth month growth begins to slow and the fetus stops changing position, turns head down, and moves into the woman's pelvic cavity in preparation for birth.

The Process of Birth

In a normal or vaginal birth, the muscles of the uterus begin to alternately contract and relax, and the cervix dilates or widens a centimeter or two. Labor begins as the contractions become more regular and closer together. By the end of the first stage of labor the cervix is wide enough to allow the baby's head to move from the uterus to the vaginal opening. This is a very difficult transition; for a successful normal birth, the woman must control her breathing and relaxation. In the second stage of labor the baby's head and body move through the vagina; the baby is delivered. In the third stage, contractions of the uterus expel the placenta.

If a vaginal birth would threaten the life of the mother or baby or the labor process becomes too difficult, a surgical incision may be made in the wall of the woman's abdomen and uterus for removal of the baby. Surgical methods for such a cesarean section have been improved to the point that the operation is almost as safe as a vaginal delivery. It is often recommended when the mother has physical characteristics or conditions such as hypertension or diabetes that might complicate delivery. It may be used for the delivery of breech babies, who exit the womb feet first; babies lying in a transverse presentation, crossway in the womb; twins and other multiple births; large babies carried by small women; and babies who show distress during their last weeks of pregnancy. Use of the procedure has become so widespread, however, that medical providers and insurers question its routine application in nonemergency situations.

The Newborn Baby

Newborns normally breathe and cry as soon as they are born. An assessment instrument developed by Virginia Apgar, the Apgar Scale, is used to check their physical condition by evaluating their heart rate, effort in breathing, muscle tone, color and reflexes. By detecting significant difficulties, this scale has helped save many new lives since its development in the 1950s.[45]

Birth complications include premature birth, low birth weight, difficulties in breathing or respiratory distress, and the genetic disorders discussed above. Birth conditions such as the use of forceps during delivery or the administration of medication or drugs to the mother during labor may also be harmful. Most children overcome birth complications and develop normally, however, provided there has been no brain damage. The ability of the family to provide adequate care and the parents' attitudes about the difficulties also are factors.[46]

Children who are born with disabilities or who experience stressful conditions at birth or in their early years may suffer lasting psychological harm (see "Children of the Garden Island"). Severe birth disabilities such as blindness, deafness, mental retardation, orthopedic disabilities, and neurological impairments, many of which are organic in origin, are not only physical disabilities but can be detrimental to the child's cognitive and emotional development. A gross disability evident at birth also can affect the development of attachment between the parents and the child. Parents generally are more successful in dealing with the disability if it develops after the attachment has been formed.[47]

∽ EARLY-LIFE STAGES OF DEVELOPMENT

Infancy (from birth to 2 years of age) and early childhood (from about 3 to 6 years old) is a period of profound physiological growth and differentiation. Growth is exceptionally rapid in the first two years after birth, as children take on such tasks as walking, talking,

Children of the Garden Island

To test the proposition that children born with disabilities or experiencing stressful early lives will suffer irrevocable psychological harm, a group of researchers followed all 698 infants born in 1955 on Kauai, the Garden Island, which lies at the northwest end of the Hawaiian chain. Of these infants, 422 were born without complications, following uneventful pregnancies, and raised in supportive environments. The other 276 children were born "at risk" because they had suffered prenatal or perinatal stress or their infancy was marked by a discordant or impoverished home or uneducated, alcoholic, or mentally disturbed parents. All the children were followed at ages 1, 2, 10, 18, and 31 or 32 years of age.

Reproductive stress did have an effect for the 23 infants who suffered severe prenatal or birth complications. Only 14 lived until age 2, and by the age of 18, two trends became apparent among the surviving children. The impact of moderate and severe reproductive stress diminished with time, and the developmental outcome of virtually every biological risk condition was dependent on the quality of the rearing environment. The better the quality of the home environment, the more competence the children displayed. Infants who were raised in middle-class families or in a stable family setting did almost as well developmentally as infants who had experienced no reproductive stress.

A troubled environment also negatively affected the children's psychosocial development. Some 30 percent were classified as "vulnerable" because they had experienced moderate to severe perinatal stress, were reared in chronic poverty, had parents with no more than eight years of formal education, or lived in a family environment torn by discord, divorce, parental alcoholism, or mental illness. Two-thirds of these children did develop serious learning or behavior problems by the age of 10 or had delinquency records, mental health problems, or pregnancies by age 18. Yet fully one-third of the vulnerable children grew into competent, psychologically healthy young adults. Against all odds, these children succeeded in school, managed home and social life well, and set realistic educational and vocational goals. By the time they were 18, they were confident, sensitive people with high self-esteem who were ready to take advantage of the opportunities available to improve themselves.

The researchers identified a number of factors in and outside of family circles and within the children themselves that distinguished between those who overcame their vulnerability and those who did not. Children who succeeded seemed to be constitutionally predisposed. From early on they were active and had a low level of excitability and distress and a high degree of sociability. They were often described by their parents as affectionate, cuddly, easygoing, or even-tempered. Environmental factors were also important. Resilient youngsters tended to come from families having four or fewer children, with a space of two years or more between siblings. In spite of poverty and other problems, they had the opportunity to establish a nurturing bond with at least one caregiver, most often a family member other than the parent—a grandparent, older sibling, aunt, or uncle. Sometimes the bonding took place with a baby-sitter, classmates, or a supportive adult in the community. Resilient children were very good at recruiting people from whom they could receive nurturing.

Source: Emmy E. Warner, "Children of the Garden Island," *Scientific American*, vol. 260 (April 1989), pp. 106–11.

and controlling bodily wastes, and generally growth continues into puberty. Cognitive development proceeds from sensorimotor to preoperational abilities. Children learn how to form simple concepts of social and psychological reality, including the first sense of self.

Erik Erikson's eight stages of psychosocial development and the crises at each stage provide a framework for the discussion of cognitive, emotional, and social development at the various life stages (see "Erikson's Stages of Psychosocial Development" in the section on developmental tasks and crises). He identifies three stages of development during the years of significant growth from birth through age 6; after infancy, he includes both early childhood and the play age.

For infants the radius of significant relationships is what Erikson refers to as the *maternal person,* that is, the person who assumes the mother role in caring for the child. In early childhood the significant relations open up to include other parental persons, and in the play age the entire family becomes the significant social context for development. It is up to these persons to supply the direct support necessary for the psychosocial development of the child.[48]

Physical Growth

Normality as average is the focus of much research on child growth and development; it is important to know when children can be expected to cut their first teeth, walk, talk, control their bladders, and so on. The number of such tasks normally accomplished in the first two years of life is remarkable (see "Growth and Behavioral Development from Birth through 6 Years Old)."

At birth, American infants on average weigh about 7.5 pounds and are about 20 inches long. By the end of the second year they have grown a great deal. Most girls have achieved 52.8 percent of their final adult height and most boys have achieved 49.5 percent of theirs by the time they are 2 years of age.[49]

Many infants lose weight immediately after birth but soon begin to take it on rapidly; some double their birth weight in the first four months. Most of the initial weight gain is in the form of fat, which provides insulation and calories for nourishment. After about nine months, the weight gained goes more to bone and muscle. Once children start walking the proportion of body fat decreases, and by the time they are ready for school they have lost most of their "baby fat."

The heads of newborn infants comprise about one-fourth of their total length, and with age this proportion decreases. By age 2 the brain weighs about 75 percent of what the adult brain does. The primary motor and sensory areas of the cortex, which control the senses and simple motor skills, increase most rapidly during the first months. Areas that coordinate more complex skills begin growth later.

Infants can lift their heads before they can sit up, and they sit up before they can stand. They first learn to move by pulling themselves along with their arms and usually progress to crawling on their hands and knees. At about a year they begin to walk tentatively. By age 2 most children can walk forward and backward, run, and climb stairs. There is continued maturation in motor abilities through the preschool years. Three-years-olds pay less attention to what their feet are doing; four-year-olds can run fast or slowly; and five-year-olds can skip, balance on one foot, and move to the cadence of music.

Newborns can wave their arms when they see dangling objects, but they cannot aim

---

Growth and Behavioral Development from Birth through 6 Years Old

The following chart illustrates the relationship between early life physical changes and the development of motor skills in young children. It also illustrates the concept of normal-as-average development.

Age	Physical Changes	Motor Development
1st Year (birth to 12 months)	**Weight and height:** The average child weighs about 7 pounds at birth and is about 20 inches in length. By the end of the first year, an average child weighs between 21 and 24 pounds and is about 29 inches in height.	Development of control over various portions of the body; turning head, lifting head, turning body, purposive grasping, apposition of thumb and forefingers, sitting up, crawling, climbing up low furniture, cruising (walking with support). Black children are a little larger than whites, and they tend to mature somewhat sooner.
	Feeding: From 5 to 8 times a day to 3 regular meals plus snacks; teeth begin to erupt.	
	Sleeping: From 20 hours a day to about 12 hours, plus naps.	
	Sensory: From learning to use oral and visual modes of exploration to greater differentiation and control of these modes. It takes about a year to develop normal vision.	
	Mortality: Males have higher mortality rates than females during the first year. Lower-class black infants have about twice the mortality rate of white infants.	

continued

well enough to grab them. By six months they can reach, grab, and hold on to a dangling object but have difficulty letting go. Then they develop the ability to pick up small objects and become more dexterous in manipulating the fingers. At birth there is involuntary release of waste products, but by four months more-or-less predictable intervals between feeding and bowel movements have been established.

Until recently it was believed that infants are born blind. Now it is known that they have blurred vision but can focus reasonably well on objects between seven and ten inches away. They often prefer to focus on faces, perhaps out of a social instinct but more likely because faces have interesting patterns. Babies seem to be curious about colorful, moving objects. Depth perception develops in the first months of life. Hearing also is well developed early in life. Sudden noises easily startle newborns and make them cry; rhythmic sounds such as lullabies are soothing and help put them to sleep. At one month many infants are able to distinguish their mothers' voice, and by the seventh month they can locate other sounds.

continued

Age	Physical Changes	Motor Development
2nd Year (12 to 24 months)	Feeding: Able to grasp objects (finger-thumb apposition), to feed self. Sleeping: About 13 hours at night, 1 long daytime nap. Sensory: More hand-eye coordination, as in drawing on paper.	High level of activity: walks, creeps upstairs and down; jumps, both feet; seats self in chair; turns pages, several at a time; runs; other gross motor skills in play. Basic control of body is complete: bladder control—dry during day; capable of bowel control. Feeds self.
3rd Year (25 to 36 months)	Sleeping: About 12 hours at night, some short naps.	Continued high-level activity; jumps; is able to ride a tricycle. Helps to dress him/herself.
4th Year (37 to 48 months)	No significant differences in height and weight between the sexes.	Dresses him- or herself. Increasing large muscle control and some small muscle control. Eye-hand coordination developing. Brushes teeth.
5th Year (49 to 60 months)	Muscles growing more rapidly than rest of body. Appetite is usually good.	Mature motor control, with increasing developments in small muscle movements.
6th Year (61 to 72 months)	Eruption of first permanent teeth. General growth continues. Appetite good. Sensory: About one fifth of all children have some visual problems; another 3 percent have hearing impairments.	Very active physically, but still clumsy; apt to have accidents. Works hard in sports but tires easily.

Source: Reprinted with permission of Macmillan Publishing Company from *Life Span Development* by Martin Bloom. Copyright © 1985 by Martin Bloom.

Psychosocial Crises in Early Life

Erikson describes the psychosocial crisis of infancy as basic *trust vs. mistrust*. Infants are born relatively helpless and must learn to depend on, that is, to trust, adults. Since the mother usually is most responsible for the welfare of the infant, infants must trust that their mothers will not abandon them and will be there to nourish them and satisfy their needs. In gaining this basic trust, infants incorporate a larger sense of trust in the world and the adults who control it. The gaining of trust is an interactive process; it involves the things that mothers do and the things that infants do. Infants must learn not only to trust mother but also to trust their own ability to control their urges to bite and swallow and not injure mother. Mothers must learn to trust the child and to encourage trust from the child. Erikson notes that "babies control and bring up their families as much as they are controlled by them; in fact, we may say that the family brings up a baby by being brought up by him."[50]

The quality of the mother-child relationship is more important than the quantity of nourishment or love given. If the relationship goes well, *hope*, "an enduring belief that one can attain one's deep and essential wishes,"[51] will be incorporated into the child's personality. If the relationship falters, a basic mistrust may be incorporated which will make it difficult for the person to form attachments throughout life. *Withdrawal* occurs as the person becomes socially and emotionally detached. Later stages of development may provide opportunities to rework the mother-child relationship and establish trust and hope, but failure to do so leaves a residue of mistrust and withdrawal.

In Erikson's early childhood period (ages 2–4), the psychosocial crisis is *autonomy vs. shame and doubt*. As the child's musculature matures and libidinal impulses center around the anus, new social needs and expectations are experienced. Parents motivate their children to control their bowels in particular and to control themselves in general, starting with arm and leg movements. Thus children begin to experiment with "holding on and letting go." If during this period they can learn to control themselves, they establish a sense of autonomy and develop the ego strength of a *will*, "a determination to exercise free choice and self-control."[52] If self-control is thwarted by the interaction of child and parents, a sense of shame and doubt comes to pervade the personality. *Shame* is the sense of being completely exposed, so everyone can see failures. It is demonstrated in self-consciousness and often exhibited by children as hiding their faces or sinking to the ground. *Doubt* is the sense of having a hidden side which others may expose. A sense of paranoia about being threatened or found out is experienced. If shame and doubt are not resolved, the result can be *compulsion*, "repetitive behaviors motivated by impulse or restrictions against the expression of impulse."[53] Compulsive people are excessively disciplined, orderly, neat, and organized and are easily shaken when their routines are interrupted.

Initiative vs. guilt is the psychosocial crisis of the play or early school arc (ages 5 and 6). As children grow physically stronger and get greater control of themselves, their behavior becomes more deliberate, taking on the quality of undertaking, planning, and attacking that Erikson calls *initiative*. Since libidinal impulses are now focused in the genital area, the initiative is in part directed at genital pleasure with parents, usually the mother. But it need not be thought of only in terms of sexual development. Psychosocially this is a period in which more general ambitions and interests appear in the child's interactions with the entire family.

The play age is a particularly important phase in the life course because it marks the emergence of "the slow process of becoming a parent, a carrier of tradition."[54] In developing a superego, a sense of what is right and wrong about their needs and desires, children accept adult authority and lay the foundation for taking the role of adult themselves.

Mutual regulation of the behaviors of the child, parents, and siblings is essential. In this way children gain a sense that their plans and behaviors are good and proper and their initiative is being channeled correctly. They develop the ego strength of *purpose,* "the courage to imagine and pursue valued goals."[55] Without mutual regulation, children may experience deep guilt about their interests and goals. Then *inhibition* sets in, "a psychological restraint that prevents freedom of thought, expression and activity."[56]

Family Life

Infants are extremely vulnerable and unable to perform the most basic tasks of life. They are usually sheltered in the protective environment of the family, where the mother's early importance soon is matched by that of the father, siblings, and other relatives. Infants are dependent, but because they can enter into interactions with caregivers and can influence them, socialization is not a process whereby parents simply introduce completely malleable children to the tasks expected of them.

Since family roles and relations are central in the early years, infants and young children assume a number of family tasks. They learn to relate to parents, siblings, and other relatives as a son, daughter, brother, sister, niece, nephew, or cousin. They learn sex differences and sexual modesty. They also learn about society and social institutions indirectly, through the adults and older children caring for them. Their social class and political, social, ethnic, and racial status are completely ascribed, an accident of their birth. Their parents' advantages and disadvantages become their own. The struggles of disadvantaged parents against poverty, unemployment, low wages, prejudice, and discrimination, as well as the struggles of advantaged parents to sustain the privileges associated with their social class, race, and ethnicity, permeate the relationship between parent and child. The struggles of fathers and mothers to resolve issues related to gender-role status also affect their relations with their young children. Thus children are not so much socialized into society as they are socialized into the conflicts and changes taking place in it and their families' points of view or ambivalence in those conflicts.

∞ ATTACHMENT: A CRITICAL ISSUE IN EARLY-LIFE DEVELOPMENT

A tenet of psychodynamic thinking is that the bond between parent (generally the mother) and child holds the key to understanding personality development. In Erikson's view, the first crisis of life takes place within the context of the mother-infant relationship, which should encourage the child to acquire a sense of trust or confidence in the mother. Other psychodynamic thinkers have approached the crisis between trust and mistrust in terms of the concept of **attachment**, the process whereby parent and child attach or bond themselves to each other.

Attachment Theory and Research

In early Freudian theory, infants were thought to be narcissistic, turning to others only to meet their egocentric needs. Attachment behaviors—crying, clinging, cooing, smiling, or otherwise trying to hold the attention of others—were believed to be motivated by the excess energy generated by unsatisfied drives, in particular the needs for food and for sensual pleasure. The drive was to be satisfied by feeding, stroking, rocking, or some other warm and sensitive behavior on the part of the mother so that attachment behavior could be terminated.

As object relations became a central focus in psychodynamic thinking, a quite different understanding evolved. It was proposed that children are born with a social need, an instinct to seek out and attach themselves to others. This newer understanding was promoted by John Bowlby, Mary Ainsworth, and others who followed their thinking.

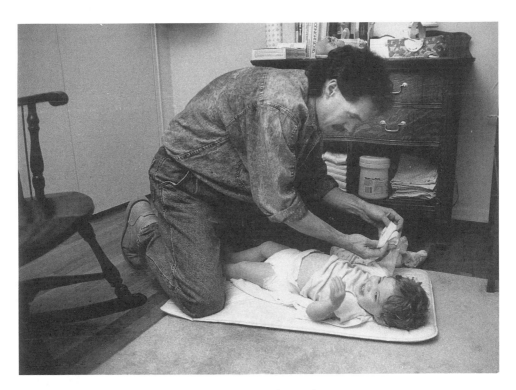

A father dressing his child is forming a bond of attachment by intimately interacting and providing care in the early-life stages of development. While the first attachment figure is usually the mother, if both parents are nurturing, the child will learn to trust them equally.

Bowlby's Control Theory: Attachment Figures

In his early studies in the 1950s, John Bowlby observed that delinquent boys had suffered early maternal separation and concluded that a strong mother-child bond is essential to psychological well-being. He warned against separating children from their mothers; even well-run and well-meaning institutions, he argued, were likely to cause irreversible psychological damage in children. From these observations he began to piece together a theory of attachment.[57]

On the basis of his practice with children, Bowlby hypothesized that infants begin life with unlearned, fixed action patterns that are primitive but allow for survival. Included is an innate tendency to "goal correct," that is, to monitor goal-seeking performance through information and feedback. As children mature they take in information which they integrate into their genetically determined capacities. One of the goals infants seek is attachment to other humans, generally to the primary caregiver, that is, the person who takes charge of caring for the child. Since mothers are often the first to have a long-term association with the child, the first and perhaps most important attachment figure is the child's mother.[58]

There are some innate tendencies that lead to attachment. Newborn infants are attracted to moving objects and have a tendency to look toward anything resembling the human face and voice. According to Bowlby, infants are not passive blobs but actually take the lead in promoting attachment. They show distinct forms of attachment as they pass through four periods. Initially, infants behave toward others in an undiscriminating way; they are attracted to all human faces and voices. By the third month, a noticeable preference for a particular attachment figure is evident. At around the ninth month, and lasting till about age 2, children exhibit the ability to seek and maintain physical closeness with the attachment figure. Thereafter they generally are able to maintain a partnership with their attachment figure, thinking of their partner as an independent person with personal goals and behaviors. Children also are able to adjust their own goals and behaviors in order to change, influence, or correspond to those of the attachment figure.

The instinctual ability of infants is the primary motivating force, according to Bowlby, but the behavior of mothers or other primary attachment figures also applies. Adults have innate tendencies that make them desirable objects of attachment; for instance, mothers encourage attachment by holding children close to their breasts or in face-to-face contact. Furthermore, some maternal behaviors work against the development of attachment. The most common obstacle is neglect or physical and emotional inaccessibility of the caregiver. Compulsive or overprotective behaviors can also interfere with the development of attachment, although Bowlby sees this as much less of a problem.[59]

Ainsworth and the "Strange Situation"

Mary Ainsworth's most important contribution to the study of attachment may be her origination of a laboratory method of observing parenting styles, maternal separation, and attachment behaviors in the laboratory. She and her team of researchers observed the interaction between mothers and babies in their own homes, paying particular attention to the unique ways the mothers responded to their children, how they fed them, cuddled them, and handled crying and similar behaviors.

When the babies were about 12 months old they were taken to the laboratory, a strange situation for them where unexpected things happened. The mother brought the child into the observation room and left. During some intervals a person unknown to the child was present in the room; during others, the child was left alone.

These children reacted to the separation in three basic ways. The majority appeared *securely attached.* While the mother was in the room the child used her as an anchor, moving away from her to explore and gravitating to her when feeling unsure. When the mother left the room the child cried and protested, but when she returned the child greeted her with pleasure and occasionally wanted to be picked up and held. Some children were *anxiously resistant;* they tended to cling and were afraid to explore on their own. When their mothers returned these children sought contact with them but were clearly angry and inconsolable. Other children were *anxiously avoidant;* they gave the impression of independence, moving about and exploring the room without using their mothers as a base. When their mothers left the children seemed unaffected, and when they returned the children seemed indifferent.[60]

Ainsworth considers the securely attached child a normal child, in the sense that not only is this the most common type of attachment, but it is an ideal. Like Bowlby she sees attachment as a transaction between mother and child, but her message is mostly directed at mothers. Mothers who are nurturing, dependable, and consistent are most likely to have securely attached children. Resistant children are seen as desperately trying to influence mothers who can only occasionally be depended upon; they cling and cry and express anger as a way of seeking more dependable nurturing behavior. Avoidant children, whose mothers are also inconsistent, seem to reach the conclusion that they do not need their mothers and can only depend on themselves. Mothers play into this by coming to believe that the child indeed does not need them.

Attachment across Cultures

Ainsworth, Bowlby and others view attachment as a universal phenomenon, an evolutionary or sociobiological principle of human behavior. Since Ainsworth's studies on American children found that most of them showed secure attachment, this form of attachment came to be seen as normal (average, healthy, and ideal).

Cross-cultural studies suggest that attachment is a universal phenomenon, but average attachment behavior changes from culture to culture. A survey of attachment research found that it does not develop in a uniform way across all cultures. In Japan and Israeli kibbutzim a higher percentage of anxious-resistant children were found than in the United States, but in West Germany, a very high percentage of anxious-avoidant behavior was reported.[61] Given such differences, to assert that one kind of attachment behavior is best amounts to judging other cultural patterns as inferior. Nevertheless, secure attachment is generally considered the most desirable form in American society.

The Maternal-Sensitive Period

Some researchers have proposed the existence of a *maternal-sensitive period* during which a bond between mother and child is first forged.[62] It is usually thought to occur between the end of pregnancy and the first few weeks after birth, during which time mothers are advised to encourage attachment by making skin-to-skin contact with their infants as soon as possible. According to Marshal Klaus and J. H. Kennel, however, this is not the period in which attachment does or does not occur. Rather, it is the first stage in the attachment process, and if dealt with successfully it makes a secure lifelong attachment more likely. They also say it is not clear that such a period exists or that it has an enduring effect on the mother or the child. They believe, in fact, that the emphasis on a sensitive period has had a negative impact on mothers and has caused them emotional stress about their response to the birth of their children.[63]

The Effects of Poor Attachment

Attachment theory corroborates that problems in the relationships between mothers and children can hinder psychosocial development. When children are neglected they may become unable to trust or attach themselves to others, and if they are overprotected they may become dependent and unable to detach themselves from others. Studies conducted by Ainsworth's followers have determined that at age 2, insecurely attached children often lack confidence and have difficulty with problem solving. In day care or kindergarten they have trouble getting along with teachers and/or their peers. At age 6, imagined separations from parents often produce feelings of hopelessness. Kathleen Pullan Watkins suggests that a number of behaviors in childhood and adolescence, such as problems in sex-role identity and intergenerational conflict, may be related to a lack of attachment.[64]

Gender and Attachment Theory

Many psychologists and sociologists regard attachment theory as a conservative argument. As the percentage of women with children who are participating in the labor force has grown, demands have increased for reliable, affordable day care for infants and children. Attachment theory goes against this trend with its implication that mothers ought to remain in the home and devote their energies to assuring a secure attachment with their children.

Not all attachment theorists support this conservative position, however. Reviewing the literature on the father's role, Pullan Watkins finds clear evidence that infants can attach to fathers as easily to mothers, and fathers can be as influential in their early care. Fathers who commit themselves to child rearing exhibit the same kind of nurturing behaviors as mothers: vocalizing, kissing, exploring, touching, imitating, feeding, holding, and other tender behaviors. Fathers can also have an indirect impact on attachment. To the extent that the father is emotionally, physically, and financially supportive of the mother, attachment to both parents is facilitated.[65]

∽ IMPLICATIONS FOR PRACTICE

The life-span approach to development is increasingly being used as the basis for the provision of social services to individuals and families. In this approach services are organized around biological periods in the life cycle—preinfancy, infancy, childhood, adolescence, adulthood, and old age—and social service workers help individuals deal with the tasks and crises connected with the appropriate period. For social service workers, the purpose is to ensure that clients are given opportunities to achieve maximum psychosocial functioning. Genetic counseling has emerged as an important area for work with women and couples planning to have children or going through pregnancy. Concern for attachment, the bond between parent figures and children, is another central area in practice.

Genetic Counseling

The revolution presently taking place in knowledge about genetics and genetic disorders has opened new opportunities for practitioners as genetic counselors. People are becoming more aware of the connection between genetics and individual development, and more clients are concerned with the possibility of genetic disabilities in themselves, their children, or other family members.

Julia Rauch identifies two basic uses of genetic analysis. The first is for the prevention, diagnosis, and treatment of genetic disorders, which may be inherited (passed on from one generation to the next), congenital (present at birth because of accidents of chromosome replication), or acquired (contracted through prenatal or postnatal environmental exposure). The second is for determining the genetic contribution to individual behavior, including temperament, intelligence, and problems in living.[66]

Social workers may be involved in four types of screening in genetic counseling. *Carrier screening* is provided before pregnancy to determine the presence of genes or abnormal chromosomes that may be harmful to offspring. *Prenatal screening* detects the presence of genetic disorders in a fetus. Shortly after birth, *neonatal screening* can determine the presence of serious genetic disorders. *Presymptomatic screening* determines if a person carries a genetic disorder that may be harmful in the future.[67]

Genetic counselors provide information to clients undergoing all four types of screening. They are concerned with the ways heredity contributes to growth and development, the risks of genetic disorders, and the various reproductive and treatment options open to women or families who are having babies or are dealing with genetic disabilities. They may assess service needs, make referrals, and serve as case managers to assure that treatment is received. With regard to clinical concerns, social workers can help clients cope with the demands posed by genetic disabilities or deal with physical or psychosocial crises when a disability is particularly troubling.

There may also be a social change component in work with children or adults who have genetic disabilities. Social service workers can develop new services, improve existing services, or work to educate the public to avoid negative labeling and discrimination directed at the disabled.

Facilitating Attachment

Because poor attachment has negative consequences for psychosocial development, social service workers are increasingly interested in ways of preventing it. Frank Bolton has formulated a strategy for assessing the likelihood of the attachment problems of child abuse and neglect that builds on many of the ideas of Ainsworth and Bowlby. He recognizes that a secure attachment is a reciprocal process in which parent and child participate equally and that a balance must be reached between competition and cooperation in the parent-child partnership. While the physical and emotional resources necessary for a secure attachment are often limited, he assumes that parents are able to use intelligent decision making to compensate. Bolton refers to his approach as *family resource theory* because the assessment focuses on the resources available for both the parents and the child.[68]

Both the capacity for attachment and the resources for attachment are assessed. To assess the attachment capacity of parent and child, the worker asks questions about the reasons for pregnancy, circumstances of the pregnancy and delivery, and the feelings, attitudes, and behaviors of both of them in infancy and as the parent-child relationship developed in the early years of life. To determine the resources available to parent and child, the worker first evaluates the physical abilities and capacities of each as well as basic environmental supports such as income and the capacity to meet basic needs. Then the social support systems available, the emotional resources present in the parent and the child, and their knowledge and intelligence are assessed to determine their ability to learn different ways of relating to each other.

☙ DISCUSSION QUESTIONS AND CLASS PROJECTS

1. Identify the following terms: zygote, embryo, fetus, gene, genotype, phenotype, rubella, fetal alcohol syndrome, cesarean section, Apgar scale, placenta, polygenic inheritance, multifactorial genetic disorders, chromosomal aberrations, single gene disorders, sensitive period, strange situation, average expectable environment.

2. Do you believe American society provides an average expectable environment for all infants?

3. Why is development better thought of as a value rather than an inevitable fact of life?

4. Describe three considerations that have to be taken into account in determining a person's stage in life.

5. In the period of conception through birth, the physical well-being of the unborn child is inseparable from the physical, psychological, and social well-being of the parents. Why is this the case?

6. How is the sex of the child determined by the father?

7. What is meant by genetic inheritance, and how may it affect early life growth? For a social worker interested in becoming a genetic counselor, what might be involved in working with clients?

8. Describe the four major types of genetic disorders that can affect individual growth and development. Give some examples of each. If you are not knowledgeable about any of the examples you give, look them up in a medical dictionary.

9. Describe three types of temperaments often seen at birth. Will these temperaments remain the same as the child grows into adulthood?

10. Ask students in the class who have given birth to or fathered a child and wish to talk about it to describe their experiences, using the chapter section on the prenatal period as a stimulus. They can either illustrate some of the issues discussed or introduce other issues.

11. Distinguish between Havighurst's unique and recurrent tasks. Can you give examples of each?

12. According to Havighurst, what are the sources of developmental tasks?

13. Describe the life course in terms of the physical growth or decline that can be expected in early childhood, later childhood, adulthood, and old age.

14. Describe the social relationships that are likely to influence growth in the prenatal and early life periods.

15. What does Erikson mean by the epigenetic principle? Why is it important for social work?

16. What does Erikson mean by the term *psychosocial crisis*?

17. List and describe the developmental crises Erikson associates with early childhood. Reflecting on your own experiences with very young children, have you observed behaviors that might indicate such crises?

18. Describe Bowlby's control theory. How does it differ from Freudian and early psychodynamic theory?

19. What are the three common patterns Ainsworth has observed by which infants attach to their mothers?

20. Ask women and men in the class who have been closely involved in parenting an infant to describe their observations about their own and the babies' attachment behavior. Do they think there is a maternal-sensitive period? Is only the mother important in bonding with an infant?

21. In what ways would a social worker be expected to work with parents on attachment issues?

∞ NOTES

1. Paul B. Baltes, "Life-Span Developmental Psychology: Some Converging Observations on History and Theory," in P. B. Baltes and O.G. Brim, Jr. (editors), *Life-Span Development and Behavior*, vol. 2 (New York: Academic Press, 1979), p. 262.

2. Henry W. Maier, *Three Theories of Child Development* (New York: Harper & Row, 1969), pp. 4–5.

3. Baltes, "Life-Span Developmental Psychology," p. 263.

4. Heinz Hartman, *Ego Psychology and the Problem of Adaptation* (New York: International Universities Press, 1939).

5. Katayun H. Gould, "Life Model versus Con-

flict Model: A Feminist Perspective," *Social Work*, vol. 32 (July–August 1987), pp. 346–51.

6. All psychologists do not posit stages of life, and some critics argue that the emphasis on stages creates many more differences among people than actually exist. See Carel B. Germain's recent review of the developmental perspective, "Human Development in Contemporary Environments," *Social Service Review*, vol. 61 (December 1987), pp. 565-80; and Victoria Fries Rader, "The Social Construction of Ages and the Ideology of Stages," *Journal of Sociology and Social Welfare*, vol. 7 (September 1979), pp. 643–56.

7. Barbara M. Newman and Philip R. Newman, *Development through Life: A Psychosocial Approach*, 4th ed. (Belmont, CA: Dorsey Press, 1987), p. 381.

8. For social histories of childhood and adolescence, see Phillipe Aries, *Centuries of Childhood: A Social History of Family Life*, translated by Robert Baldwick (New York: Vintage Books, 1962), and Joseph Kett, *Rites of Passage: Adolescence in America 1790 to the Present* (New York: Basic Books/ Harper Colophon, 1977). Also see William Kessen, "The Child and Other Cultural Inventions," in F. Kessel and A. W. Sieger (editors), *Houston Symposium #4: The Child and Other Cultural Inventions* (New York: Frederick A. Praeger, 1983), pp. 26–39.

9. Daniel Offer and Melvin Sabshin, "Adolescence: Empirical Perspective," in D. Offer and M. Sabshin (editors), *Normality and the Life Cycle: A Critical Integration* (New York: Basic Books, 1984), p. 77.

10. Robert L. Arnstein, "Young Adulthood: Stages of Maturity," in Offer and Sabshin (editors), *Normality and the Life Cycle*, p. 108.

11. K. Warner Schaie, "Psychological Changes from Midlife to Early Old Age: Implications for the Maintenance of Mental Health," in C. H. Meyer (editor), *Social Work with the Aging* (Silver Spring, MD: National Association of Social Workers, 1986), pp. 44–63.

12. George E. Vaillant and Eva Milofsky, "Natural History of Male Psychological Health: IX. Empirical Evidence for Erikson's Model of the Life Cycle," *American Journal of Psychiatry*, vol. 137, no. 11 (November 1980), pp. 1348–59.

13. Bernice Neugarten coined the term *social clock* to mean subjective or "socially defined" time. We are using it in a somewhat different way; her use is more akin to what we call the psychological clock. She emphasizes personal expectations about when and how life events are to be experienced. See Neugarten, "Time, Age, and the Life Cycle," in M. Bloom (editor), *Life Span Development*, 2nd ed. (New York: Macmillan, 1985), pp. 360–69.

14. Linda K. George, *Role Transitions in Later Life* (Monterey, CA: Brooks/Cole, 1980), pp. 1–12.

15. Martin Kohli, "The World We Forgot: A Historical Review of the Life Course," in V. W. Marshal (editor), *Later Life: The Social Psychology of Aging* (Beverly Hills, CA: Sage, 1986), p. 272; also see Fries Rader, "Social Construction of Ages."

16. Robert J. Havighurst, *Developmental Tasks and Education* (New York: David McKay, 1952), p. 1.

17. Newman and Newman, *Development through Life*, p. 32.

18. Havighurst, *Developmental Tasks and Education*, p. 4.

19. Ibid., p. 31.

20. Erik H. Erikson, *Childhood and Society*, 2nd ed. (New York: W. W. Norton, 1963); *Identity: Youth and Crisis* (New York, W. W. Norton, 1968); *The Life Cycle Completed: A Review* (New York: W. W. Norton, 1982).

21. Theodore Lidz, *The Person* (New York: Basic Books, 1968), p. 79.

22. Arnold J. Sameroff, "Early Influences on Development: Fact or Fancy?" in M. Bloom (editor), *Life Span Development*, 1st ed. (New York: Macmillan, 1980), pp. 107.

23. Marilyn French, *The War against Women* (New York: Summit Books, 1992), pp. 143–44.

24. Linda Lehrer, "Inch by Inch," *Chicago Tribune*, December 26, 1993, sect. 6, pp. 1, 9.

25. M. D. Jensen, R. C. Benson, and I. M. Bobak, *Maternity Care: The Nurse and the Family*, 2nd ed. (St. Louis, MO: Mosby, 1981).

26. See "Pregnancy after 35," in Denise Foley and Eileen Nechas, *Women's Encyclopedia of Health and Emotional Healing* (Emaus, PA: Rodale Press, 1993), pp. 368–77.

27. Ibid.

28. Hilda Knobloch and Benjamin Pasamanick, *Gessell and Amatruda's Developmental Diagnosis* (New York: Harper and Row, 1974).

29. Centers for Disease Control and Prevention, *Surgeon General's Report to the American Public on HIV Infection and AIDS* (Rockville, MD, 1993), p. 7.

30. See Newman and Newman, *Development through Life*, pp. 137–38.

31. John W. Lorton and Eveleen L. Lorton, *Human Development through the Life Span* (Monterey, CA: Brooks/Cole, 1984), pp. 65–69.

32. Elaine R. Grimm, "Psychological and Social Factors in Pregnancy, Delivery and Outcome," in S. A. Richardson and A. F. Guttmacher (editors), *Childbearing: Its Social and Psychological Aspects* (Baltimore, MD: Williams and Wilkins, 1967), pp. 1–52.

33. Lorton and Lorton, *Human Development through the Life Span*, pp. 69–70.

34. Kathleen Stassen Berger, *The Developing Person* (New York: Worth, 1980), pp. 118–31.

35. Martin Greenberg and Normal Morris, "Engrossment: The Newborn's Impact upon Father," *American Journal of Orthopsychiatry*, vol. 44 (July 1974), pp. 520–31.

36. Stassen Berger, *Developing Person*, p. 76.

37. Ibid., p. 86.

38. U.S. Department of Commerce, *Statistical Abstract of the United States: 1992*, 112th edition (Washington, DC, 1992), Table 111.

39. Julia B. Rauch, "Social Work and the Genetics Revolution: Genetic Services," *Social Work*, vol. 33 (September–October 1988), pp. 389–95.

40. Alexander Thomas, Stella Chess, and Herbert B. Birch, *Temperament and Behavior Disorders in Children* (New York: New York University Press, 1963); Stella Chess, "Temperament in the Normal Infant," in J. Hellmuth (editor), *The Exceptional Infant*, vol. 1 (Seattle, WA: Special Child Publications, 1967); Alexander Thomas and Stella Chess, *Temperament and Development* (New York: Brunner/Mazel, 1977).

41. Thomas and Chess, *Temperament and Development*, pp. 21–23.

42. Michael E. Lamb (editor), *Social and Personality Development* (New York: Holt, Rinehart, and Winston, 1978).

43. Peter H. Wolff, *The Cause, Controls, and Organization of Behavior in the Neonate* (New York: International University Press, 1966).

44. Kenneth S. Robson and Howard A. Moss, "Patterns and Determinants of Maternal Attachment," *Journal of Pediatrics*, vol. 77 (December 1970), pp. 976–85.

45. Virginia Apgar, "Proposal for a New Method of Evaluating the Newborn Infant," *Anesthesia and Analgesia*, vol. 32 (1953), pp. 260–67.

46. See Sameroff, "Early Influences on Development"; Bruce Balow, Rosalyn Rubin, and Martha J. Rosen, "Perinatal Events as Precursors of Reading Disabilities," *Reading Research Quarterly*, vol. 11 (1975–1976), pp. 36–71; and Michael J. Chandler and Arnold Sameroff, "Reproductive Risk and the Continuum of Caretaking Casualty," in F. D. Horowitz and F. Degen (editors), *Review of Child Development Research*, vol. 4 (Chicago: University of Chicago Press, 1975), pp. 187–244.

47. Harriet Johnson, "Human Development: Biological Perspective," in *Encyclopedia of Social Work*, 18th ed., Vol. 1 (Silver Spring, MD: National Association of Social Workers, 1987), pp. 839–40.

48. Erikson, *Life Cycle Completed*, p. 31. Also see Erikson, *Childhood and Society*.

49. Richard M. Lerner and David F. Hultsch, *Human Development: A Life Span Perspective* (New York: McGraw Hill, 1983), p. 144.

50. Erikson, *Childhood and Society*, p. 69.

51. Newman and Newman, *Development through Life*, p. 45.

52. Ibid., p. 45.

53. Ibid., p. 46.

54. Erikson, *Childhood and Society*, p. 225.

55. Newman and Newman, *Development through Life*, p. 45.

56. Ibid., p. 46.

57. John Bowlby, *Maternal Care and Mental Health* (Geneva, Switzerland: World Health Organization, 1952).

58. John Bowlby, *Attachment* (New York: Basic Books, 1969).

59. L. W. C. Tavecchio and M. H. Van IJzendoorn, "Perceived Security and Extension of the Child's Rearing Context: A Parent-Report Approach," in *Advances in Psychology*, vol. 44 (1987), p. 39.

60. M. D. Salter Ainsworth et. al., *Patterns of Attachment: A Psychological Study of the Strange Situation* (New York: John Wiley and Sons, 1978).

61. Abraham Sagi and Kathleen S. Lewkowicz, "A Cross-Cultural Evaluation of Attachment Research," in *Advances in Psychology*, vol. 44 (1987), 427–59.

62. Kathleen Pullan Watkins, *Parent Child Attachment: A Guide to Research* (New York: Garland Publishing, 1987), pp. 25–35.

63. Marshal H. Klaus and J. H. Kennel, *Parent Infant Bonding*, 2nd ed. (St. Louis, MO: C. V. Mosby, 1982), p. xiii.

64. Pullan Watkins, *Parent Child Attachment*, pp. 104–09.

65. Ibid.

66. Rauch, "Social Work and Genetics Revolution."

67. Ibid.

68. Frank B. Bolton, Jr., *When Bonding Fails: Clinical Assessment of High-Risk Families* (Beverly Hills, CA: Sage, 1983).

CHAPTER 17

Life-Span Development
Childhood and Adolescence

MAJOR THEMES DISCUSSED IN THIS CHAPTER

1. **SCHOOL-AGE CHILDREN AND ADOLESCENTS.** The startling growth of infancy and early childhood slows as the child enters school, and growth speeds up again during adolescence with sexual maturity. Older children play out their status of minors in society in roles within family life as sons or daughters; in schools as students; and in peer groups as friends. Psychosocial crises and tasks at this stage are generated both by physical and sexual maturation and by status and role expectations.

2. **ADOLESCENCE AS A TIME OF STRESS AND CRISIS.** Adolescence is often described as a particularly troublesome period in life. Research has found that all adolescents do not experience crises and conflict, but the period is marked by struggles to achieve self-esteem and identity. The identity-achieved adolescent experiences the crisis and resolves it.

3. **ACHIEVING IDENTITY.** Among the types of identity adolescents must achieve, the most compelling include gender role, sexual orientation, and identification with others in a racial or ethnic group. Resolution of these recurring tasks in the life cycle is initiated as the child experiences the biological, cognitive, social, and psychological changes of puberty.

4. **PHYSICAL DISABILITY AND SELF-IMAGE IN ADOLESCENTS.** Illness or disability might be expected to put adolescents caught up in the search for identity at risk for psychological difficulties. However, research has found little support for the idea that ill or disabled adolescents have a poor self-image or lose self-esteem.

5. **IMPLICATIONS FOR PRACTICE.** Social service work with children and adolescents provides opportunities to give immediate assistance to clients, as well as to work toward the solution of public issues.

∞ GROWTH AND DEVELOPMENT IN SCHOOL-AGE CHILDREN AND ADOLESCENTS

Erik Erikson defines the stages of psychosocial development in later childhood as school age (ages 7–12) and adolescence (ages 13–22). These stages are marked by psychosocial crises involving the acquisition of industry and identity, within the context of continued physical growth and the significant biological changes of puberty. The resolution of these crises is reasoned through the cognitive capacities for concrete operational thought and, in later adolescence, formal operational reasoning, and it takes place in a wider radius of significant relationships which include not only the family but the school, the neighborhood, peer groups, and models of leadership in the society. The ego strengths that can emerge from a successful resolution of these crises are competence and fidelity; the pathologies that can emerge from a poor resolution are inertia and repudiation.

Physical Growth and Maturation

While school-age children do not grow at the same startling rate as preschool children, they ordinarily continue to grow. They learn the skills necessary for complex physical maneuvers such as those needed in games and begin to acquire a positive sense of themselves as physical beings. With the arrival of the teen years and puberty, adolescents accept their changing physiques and begin to deal with sex-role expectations. Cognitively, most school-age children master fundamental skills in reading, writing, and calculating and learn to follow rules. In adolescence they begin to acquire the intellectual skills necessary for eventual civic competence.

The most important biological experience during these years is **puberty**, defined by James McCary as "the time when the sexual organs become capable of reproduction and the influence of sex hormones first becomes prominent." The period is sometimes divided into two, with *pubescence* referring to the years just prior to puberty.[1] Although males and females both undergo changes during puberty, the substance of the changes and the rate of change vary. Girls tend to develop earlier than boys and often are physically mature by age 16.[2] Boys begin pubescence later, and maturation proceeds at a slower pace and over a longer period.

Sexual Maturation in Girls

Pubescence in females, which begins at approximately ages 8–11, is marked by distinct physical changes. The breasts enlarge, the nipples project, the body contours round out, the pelvic area broadens, and fatty pads develop around the hips. The vaginal lining thickens and pubic and auxiliary hair appears. About two years after the first signs of pubescence comes **menarche**, the beginning of menstruation, the monthly discharge of blood and other material from the uterus through the vagina. **Ovulation**, the release of a mature egg from the ovary, begins about a year after the first menstrual period. With these developments, the girl is able to procreate; she has entered puberty.

There is great variation in the age at which females begin to menstruate and ovulate. For approximately half of all American girls, the age of ovulation is between 12.5 and 14.5 years. Nutrition, the physical environment, and physiological factors such as body weight all influence the onset of menstruation and ovulation.

During puberty the sex glands or gonads begin to produce and emit hormones which influence sexual desire. In females the gonads are the *ovaries*, which produce *estrogen*. This hormone controls body structure, is important in the development and functioning of the genital organs, and influences the menstrual cycle as well as the development of secondary sexual characteristics. The ovaries also produce *progesterone*, which is of primary importance in preparing the lining of the uterus for implantation of fertilized eggs and maintaining pregnancy. Progesterone also enlarges the breasts of pregnant females and inhibits premature uterine contractions as birth approaches.

Sexual Maturation in Boys

Pubescence in males is also marked by physical changes. A "fat period" usually begins around age 11. At the same time erections of the penis begin to occur, and as the penis and scrotum enlarge, erections are more frequent. **Ejaculation**, the expulsion of semen from the urethra, is usually possible by this time. The secretion of sperm follows, although mature sperm may not be present yet. Spontaneous nocturnal emissions of sperm, or "wet dreams," are common. Secondary sex characteristics such as the growth of pubic and auxiliary facial and body hair, changes in muscular and skeletal structures, and changes in the male voice, which drops about an octave, appear as puberty progresses.

The male gonads (*testes*) produce and emit *testosterone*. This hormone is responsible for the development and preservation of masculine secondary characteristics. Testosterone used to be considered responsible for the greater height of males, but this belief was discarded when it was learned that estrogen also controls height.[3] Each sex possesses hormones associated with the opposite sex, and excessive amounts can have implications for sexual functioning and secondary sexual characteristics.

Psychosocial Crises

Erikson describes the psychosocial crisis faced by school-age children as *industry vs. inferiority*. Going off to school full time produces a new set of needs and demands. The egocentricity of earlier stages is loosened as children begin to learn about their society and find they can win approval and recognition by their industry in producing things. Parents, friends, and especially the school focus on the ability to complete intellectual and physical tasks.

School-age children who learn to produce, that is, are successful academically, gain assurance that they are capable and can expect to participate effectively in society. They acquire the basic strength of *competence*, which in this sense means "the free exercise of skill and intelligence in the completion of tasks."[4] Competent children feel at one with the school and the society. They gain the sense that they can learn and do what is expected of them. Children whose school experiences are not productive may develop a sense of inferiority. They experience *inertia*, "a paralysis of action and thought that prevents productive work."[5] In other words, they doubt their abilities and become afraid of the tasks that are presented to them. They prefer to complete nothing rather than risk failure.

In adolescence, the crisis is *identity vs. identity confusion*. Puberty is a time of turmoil in which adolescents seem to feel the need to question all their earlier adaptations to the demands of parents and teachers. Adulthood lies just ahead, and needs become centered on locating the self within the society. Adolescents often are caught up in the issue of "what they appear to be in the eyes of others as compared with what they feel they are."[6]

In their search for identity, adolescents must make many decisions: who their real friends are and what kind of adult they want to be; what their sexual identities are and how to relate sexually to others; what their interests are and how to prepare for their chosen occupations. They may develop a political allegiance, question adult authority, and challenge traditional ideology. Adolescents who can manage the search for identity develop a clear sense of who they are and acquire the strength of *fidelity*, "the ability to freely pledge and sustain loyalties to others."[7] Thus they become able to commit themselves to friends and leaders whose values and way of life have meaning for them. When the crisis

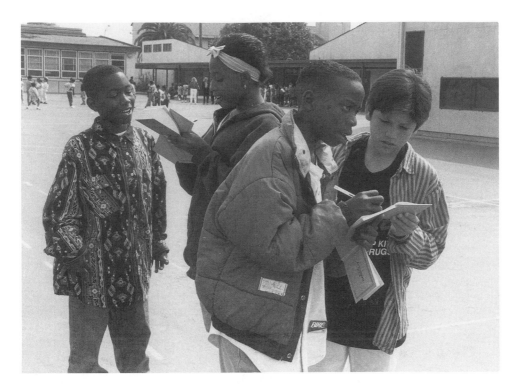

Sixth-grade graduates of a school in Oakland, California, seek out friends for their autographs. As children approach the teen years, peers, neighborhood, and school become significant influences on their development.

of adolescence is unresolved, adolescents suffer identity confusion, which can follow them throughout life. This may be expressed in *repudiation*, the "rejection of roles and values that are viewed as alien to oneself."[8] Those who are not able to give fidelity to any one person tend to reject all loyalties. They approach life with indifference and sarcasm; nothing seems to have meaning for them.

Family, School, and Peer-Group Relations

School-age children learn to get along with age-mates and acquire a sense of personal independence. In later childhood they try to achieve mature social relationships with friends of both sexes. Adolescents are deeply involved in attempts to achieve emotional independence from parents and, as they approach adulthood, in relationships with peers. Adolescence ends when young adults prepare to leave their family of origin and set up their own independent households.

While schools and peers are strong sources of influence on school-age children and adolescents, the family remains equally important. School-age children devote much time and attention to relationships with teachers and with peers but generally remain closely attached to and influenced by their families of origin.[9] Both the family and the school are instrumental in encouraging them to build self-esteem and a sense of responsibility, which can help them deal with the social problems affecting them in American society (see "Building Self-Esteem in Children and Youths").

Building Self-Esteem in Children and Youths

In 1990 the California Task Force to Promote Self-Esteem and Personal and Social Responsibility was set up by the state department of education as a bipartisan effort to develop a strategy for dealing with the major social issues affecting youth: education and academic failure, drug and alcohol abuse, crime and violence, poverty and chronic welfare dependency, and lack of employment. The task force concluded that self-esteem is a unifying concept for understanding such problems and developing primary intervention strategies.

The basic argument developed by the task force is that central to most of the personal and social ills plaguing California in particular and American society as a whole is a lack of self-esteem, and children and young people can be helped to enhance their feelings of their own worth. Self-esteem is defined as "Appreciating my own worth and importance and having the character to be accountable for myself and to act responsibly toward others." Four key principles are highlighted in this definition:

1. Appreciating our own worth and importance involves accepting ourselves, setting realistic expectations, forgiving ourselves, taking risks, trusting, and expressing feelings.

2. Appreciating the worth and importance of others means affirming the unique worth of others and giving them respect, acceptance, and support.

3. Affirming accountability for ourselves requires assuming responsibility for our decisions and actions.

4. Affirming our responsibility toward others means respecting the dignity of being human, encouraging independence, and creating a sense of belonging.

According to the task force, the family is the most important social institution affecting the self-esteem of children. Parents who do not have high self-esteem themselves cannot pass it on to their children. The task group recommended educational and social services in the form of workshops and classes in parenting and family life to prepare adolescents, particularly young parents, for the task of inculcating self-esteem in children.

The task force pointed to the schools as the second most important institution. Because they are central to the development of competence and industry, the schools have a role in nurturing self-esteem and personal and social responsibility. Educators can do this by educating teachers, altering the curriculum, providing opportunities to young people for community service, developing programs to counteract bigotry and prejudice, and expanding counseling and peer assistance for students.

The workplace and the community were also designated as sources of self-esteem and responsibility. The task force recommended programs to deal with each of the social problems associated with childhood and adolescence. It affirmed that a positive environment in the home, school, workplace, and community is crucial to the development of self-esteem, and it must be accepted as a personal and public responsibility.

Source: *Toward a State of Esteem: The Final Report of the California Task Force to Promote Self-esteem and Personal and Social Responsibility* (Sacramento, CA: California State Department of Education, 1990).

Girls are more likely than boys to lose self-esteem as they enter adolescence, according to a survey of 3,000 children (2,400 girls and 600 boys) in grades 4 through 10 at 36 public schools throughout the country in the fall of 1990. The survey, commissioned by the American Association of University Women, found that at the age of 9 a majority of girls are confident, assertive, and feel positive about themselves, but by the time they reach high school fewer than a third feel that way. Boys also lose some sense of self-worth, but they retain more self-esteem on entering high school. For example, when elementary school children were asked whether they were happy the way they were, 67 percent of the boys and 60 percent of the girls answered "always." In high school, this answer was given by 46 percent of the boys but only 29 percent of the girls.[10]

Among the girls race was apparently a factor in the retention of self-esteem. Far more black girls surveyed remained self-confident in high school compared to white and Hispanic girls, and whites lost self-esteem sooner than Hispanics. Black girls did not have good relationships with teachers, however, and the researchers concluded that they drew their self-confidence from their families and communities rather than the schools.

Functions of the Schools

Education is the social institution which, along with the family, most directly affects children during the school-age years and adolescence. In an extension of the parent role, teachers assist children to develop the basic intellectual, moral, and behavioral tools necessary for entry into the adult world. Before public schools were common, the education of children was often through apprenticeships, a kind of on-the-job training in direct contact with experts in a particular task or craft. In the early schools, academies, and universities, students of very different ages often were taught together.[11] Education today is age-graded and much more formal, especially in the elementary, middle, and high school years.

As in the family, today's schools have both manifest and latent functions. At the manifest level, the purpose of schools is to prepare children for successful participation in society.[12] Students are introduced to concepts, theories, and relationships to enable them to organize their everyday experiences. They are taught and evaluated on knowledge in a range of disciplines, including arithmetic, language, art, music, science, and social science, and become acquainted with methods of investigating and solving problems. Contacts with teachers and exposure to the various disciplines help children discover their interests and channel their commitment to personal and career goals and standards.

In the 1990s there has been a call for values education to deal with such proliferating problems as racism, teen-age pregnancy, and violence in the schools. The problem is to determine the agreed-on values of the society and avoid imposing the values of special-interest groups. Programs are being tried that include curriculum materials and student participation in mediation and conflict resolution interactions with their peers. A program to teach basic emotional skills in the first three grades at John Muir Elementary School in Seattle, for instance, shows children how to resolve disagreements without fighting, build friendships with other children and ties to teachers, and handle such feelings as anger, jealousy, fear, and grief. According to Dr. Mark Greenberg, a psychologist at the University of Washington who is one of the designers of the program, "The point is to get kids used to trying out many solutions until they find one that works for them."[13]

At the latent level, the school's functions are similar to the family's —the socialization of children into the inequities associated with classism, racism, and sexism in the society. Christopher Jencks maintains that problems in education cannot be resolved without dealing with such social inequities.[14] It is often through the schools that children first receive messages about what they can and cannot expect to accomplish as adults. Sex-role stereotypes, by which girls' interests are channeled to motherhood and traditional women's careers such as secretary or social worker[15] and boys' interests are directed to such careers as businessman, doctor, or lawyer, are no longer the rule, but they persist in some school districts. Because of the diverse ways in which schools are financed, teachers are moti-vated, and parents participate in the work of the school, children from lower-class and ethnic-minority groups are less likely to have educational experiences which will develop their interests and talents and encourage them to succeed. As a result they are likely to perceive the curriculum and being in school as irrelevant, and they may follow peers who feel that way and drop out.

Peer-Group Influences

Peer-group relations become more influential as children reach puberty and the teen years. Friends are important during the early school years, but being a member of a de-finable group becomes essential for adolescents, who may feel pressured to be part of a particular group by their families, schools, or friends. Friendship cliques go by such names as "the leading crowd, populars, socialites, preppies, rah-rahs, jocks, eggheads, nerds, ginks, eraserheads, dirtballs, potheads, greasers, and hoods." Similar labels for so-cial groups may be found in all schools, regardless of neighborhood.[16]

Peer groups exert pressure on adolescents to own material possessions they value, such as cars, stereos, and clothes, and to secure them many take part-time jobs while still in school. However, the effects of such employment may not be positive for their academic careers or psychosocial development (see "Part-Time Work and Adolescent Development").

Peer groups also may exert pressure on adolescents to become involved in delin-quency and violence. Although delinquent behavior (usually defined as acts considered il-legal when committed by youths under 17 or 18) is supported by gangs or cliques at all levels of society, the police focus largely on members of black and Latino gangs in inner cities. A small but apparently increasing part of the nation's gang problem in the 1990s is represented by affluent white youths in some sections of the country who join estab-lished gangs like the Crips and Bloods or form what are sometimes called copycat or mutant yuppie gangs. Looking for excitement or a sense of group identity, they adopt the basic street philosophy of gang solidarity and may engage in vandalism, graffiti, drug dealing, and violence.[17]

Peer-group relations also influence adolescents who can't achieve status in school in an acceptable way—through scholarship or social standing—to drop out in order to save face with their peers.[18] Nevertheless, peer groups generally have positive functions. Through relations with their peers, adolescents learn the value of collective action, the in-creased influence of an individual which comes from participation with others. Peer groups support feelings of self-worth and offer protection from loneliness. When troubles exist between parents and children, peers can give comfort and nurture.[19]

Learning about Sexuality

At the end of the twentieth century in American society, older children and adolescents are increasingly faced with problems of sexuality—sexual abuse, sex education, and sex-ual experimentation and its consequences, HIV infection and teenage pregnancy. Sexual behavior is engaged in at an increasingly younger age. On the basis of a study by the U.S. Center for Disease Control in 1990, it is estimated that more than half (54 percent) of the high school students in the United States have had sexual intercourse. The proportion of students who said they had ever had sex increased from 40 percent in the ninth grade to

Part-Time Work and Adolescent Development

Because of social policies designed to provide low-wage jobs and the growth of service industries, there are many opportunities in American society for teenagers to earn wages while still attending school. Studies have found, however, that such part-time work may be harmful.

When Ellen Greenberger and Laurence Steinberg surveyed a sample of 530 youths from largely middle-class backgrounds, 82 percent white, 10 percent Hispanic, and 8 percent black or Asian (chiefly the latter), they found some disconcerting results. When teenagers work, academic grades are likely to decline, money earned is rarely saved but is spent on consumer goods, and students internalize many negative values associated with the competitiveness of the economic order. Greenberger and Steinberg conclude that "excessive commitment to a job may pose an impediment to development, by causing adolescents to spend too much time and energy in a role that is too constraining and involves tasks that are too simple, not very challenging, and irrelevant to their future to promote development." (p. 7)

Delbert Elliott and Sharon Wofford present preliminary evidence that adolescent employment might actually stimulate involvement in delinquent behavior. These researchers used a national probability sample of 1,725 adolescents aged 11 to 17. The students were interviewed about their involvement in delinquent activities each year from 1976 to 1980 and thereafter at three-year intervals. Adolescents who worked while in school were found to be slightly more likely than those who did not to engage in minor delinquency and considerably more likely to engage in serious delinquency. For adolescents working full time or no longer in school, the rates were even higher.

The problem may be not that adolescents lack economic resources but that too many are available to them, and they have been caught up in the pursuit of immediate material rewards. A study of lower-class adolescents, however, found that meaningful work activities for pay can be a way of opening opportunities. Terry Williams and William Kornblum developed a program based on paying students for completing difficult writing assignments. They were concerned with deterring adolescents in a neighborhood that had been abandoned by industry, leaving a scarcity of jobs, from turning to crime or prostitution in order to achieve material gains. Eighty-six disadvantaged youths between the ages of 14 and 20 were trained to participate in the world of work by offering pay for writing assignments on such topics as "life histories of themselves and their peers, interviews with their peers and parents, descriptions of their experience in other employment situations, field notes about events in their neighborhoods, and evaluations of their experience in the demonstration." The results indicated that success is possible, given close supervision, support, and demanding assignments. Nevertheless, the researchers refer to the lack of legitimate opportunities to achieve the goal of economic success in American society as "social dynamite." Lower-class teens will take the illegitimate opportunities available to them in the absence of legitimate opportunities. Drug dealing in the inner cities relies on this proposition.

While on the surface these studies point in different directions, in many ways they are not at odds. They indicate that work experiences for youth should assure positive personal and interpersonal development. They also affirm that work will be of developmental value only if it is challenging, meaningful, well supervised, and leads to increased opportunities in the future. Work simply for conspicuous consumption has no value.

Sources: Ellen Greenberger and Laurence Steinberg, *When Teen-Agers Work: The Psychological and Social Costs of Adolescent Employment* (New York: Basic Books, 1986); Delbert Elliott and Sharon Wofford, "Adolescent Employment," unpublished report, 1992, University of Colorado at Boulder, Institute of Behavior Science; Terry Williams and William Kornblum, *Growing up Poor* (Lexington, MA: Lexington Books, 1985).

48 percent in the tenth grade, 57 percent in the eleventh grade, and 72 percent in the final year of high school.[20]

The Youth Risk Behavior Surveillance System of the CDC interviewed 11,631 students in grades 9–12 in all 50 states, the District of Columbia, Puerto Rico, and the Virgin Islands. They found that male high school students are more likely than female students to say they had ever had sex, 61 percent to 48 percent. Black students are more likely than Hispanic or white students to report having had sex, 72 percent to about 52 percent. Most of the students who said they'd had sex also said they'd done so within the preceding three months—39 percent of students in grades 9–12.

Among the sexually active students, about 78 percent said they used some form of contraception during their last experience. Hispanic females used contraception less than either black or white females, and whites were more likely to use it than blacks. Condoms were used by 49 percent of male students and 40 percent of female students' partners.

The distribution of condoms in school health clinics has become an issue in the controversy over what should be taught about sex to children in school. Just making condoms available may not have much effect in reducing either teen pregnancies or sexually transmitted diseases unless the programs include counseling and social support. Follow-up services to provide counseling or guidance to teens who might face such problems also are not provided in the abstinence-only programs to teach "sex respect" which conservatives favor as a means of teaching young people to "just say no."

Fear of the spread of AIDS is the most powerful force behind the call for more effective sex education. It is now required or recommended in 47 states, up from only three in 1980, and all 50 support AIDS education. Lacking a public consensus about what to teach, however, most secondary schools provide only between 6 and 20 hours a year. The curriculum may consist of one or two days in fifth grade dealing with puberty; two weeks of an eighth-grade unit on anatomy, reproduction, and AIDS prevention, and a 12th-grade elective course on sexuality.[21]

The schools may also be called on to help students understand the implications of changing gender roles. Parents' expectations of chaste sexual behavior usually apply to their daughters but not their sons. Encouraged by the greater equality developing in gender roles, however, today's teenage girls may adopt the more aggressive sexual approach or response expected of males. The confusing message may be interpreted by adolescents coming to terms with their sexuality as an excuse for undisciplined behavior. Violence in interactions as teens enter into romantic relationships with the opposite sex is a new topic of research (see "Teen Dating Violence").

∽ ADOLESCENCE AS A TIME OF STRESS AND CRISIS

Many of the issues in adolescent development have to do with the nature of the developmental period, which is seen by some as a tumultuous time. The issues discussed in this section concern how the hassles and uplifts experienced by sixth-grade boys and girls in their everyday lives act as stressors, and whether or not crises and conflict are the normal state of adolescence.

Stress and Early Adolescence

Stress theory has a prominent place in the study of development across the life course. While it is usually applied to adult development, it has also been used to examine the be-

Teenagers answering the phones for the Teen Line at a Los Angeles hospital are guided by adult supervision and information files on help-providing resources. Teen hotlines throughout the country offer a helping hand to adolescents with everything from ordinary hassles to suicidal feelings.

havior of children and adolescents. Stress is a major cause of private troubles, and social service interventions known as stress management have been devised to help clients troubled by it.[22]

Hans Selye introduced the term *general adaptation syndrome* in 1936 as "a nonspecific response of the body to readjust itself following any demand made upon it." This response produces **stress**, defined as "the physiological changes in the body that prepare it for fight or flight."[23] The changes are elicited by the direct influence on body tissues of neural impulses from the hypothalamus in the brain and by the secondary influence on these tissues of the release of epinephrine or adrenaline.

Stressors and Perceived Stress

The origin of stress in individuals is most often found in conditions that arise in the physical or social environment. Some events or conditions act as **stressors**, situations that provoke the physiological response of stress. In his pioneering studies, Selye discovered that if rats were injected with a variety of foreign substances, the same physiological response was always produced: The intrusion of any foreign matter produced stress.[24] In the study of human stress, the events or stressors are generally believed to be social rather than biological intrusions. In addition to physiological changes, stressors can cause negative psychological outcomes such as depression and low self-esteem.

Teen Dating Violence

Although the teen years are popularly associated with such pleasant experiences as puppy love, going steady, and attending the prom, there is evidence that for girls, especially, they can be a time of traumatic experiences, even sexual assault and rape. Researchers have studied the extent and implications of teen dating violence, and social service workers are beginning to deal with this negative consequence of gender-role expectations.

For one study conducted in three high schools in Sacramento, California, 135 girls and 121 boys filled out questionnaires about their experiences with violence in sexual encounters. The sample was drawn from randomly selected general education classes required of all students. Most of them (about 90 percent) were juniors or seniors, and a scant majority were from middle-class, intact families. The racial composition was 65 percent white and 35 percent black, Asian, or other. Although the sample adequately estimates teen dating violence in the high schools sampled, care should be taken in generalizing the results to other schools in other parts of the country.

Dating violence was measured using a scale of "conflict tactics" that differed in severity. The measurement instrument also distinguished between threats and actual violence. Students were asked to indicate whether they had experienced each form, and most reported that they had never done so, as victims or perpetrators. Only 27 percent reported actual violence, and the most common forms of violence reported were "threatened to hit but did not" and slapping. Other forms reported were pushing and shoving, punching, and throwing an object.

The researchers found no difference between males and females in the likelihood of experiencing violence or in being a victim or a perpetrator. They point out that they did not take into account the physical size and strength of the students and have no way of determining whether boys engaged in more severe violence than girls. Violence was also not statistically associated with race, economic status, or marital status of the parents, nor was it associated with abuse as a child. Those who reported violence between their parents, however, were more likely to experience violence in their dating relationships. The effect of the violence for 46 percent of the respondents was to damage or end the relationship. About one-third said it had no effect, and one-fifth said it had improved the relationship.

Source: Nona K. O'Keeffe, Karen Brockopp, and Esther Chew, "Teen Dating Violence," *Social Work*, vol. 31 (November–December 1986), pp. 465–68.

Initially, stressors were measured in terms of major life changes or events. For children and adolescents, these could be disruptions such as the death of a parent, but they could also be happy changes such as academic success or a new romance.[25] Major life events do create stress, but such an approach often failed to predict the amount of stress experienced. Recently the study of stress has shifted from major life events to the more mundane **hassles and uplifts** of everyday life. *Hassles* are "the irritating, frustrating, distressing demands that to some degree characterize everyday transactions with the environment, and *uplifts* refer to "positive experiences such as the joy derived from manifestations of love, relief at hearing good news, the pleasure of a good night's rest, and so on."[26] Ordinary hassles and uplifts appear to be better predictors of stress than major changes in life events.

Environmental stressors do not automatically lead to negative psychological outcomes. Of central importance is how the individual perceives the stressor; what may be stressful for one person may not be stressful for another, and some people are affected more or less than others by the same level of stress. In short, the individual's definition of the situation, or *perceived stress*, must be taken into account. Stress only exists if people think it does.

Hassles and Uplifts in Early Adolescents

Comparatively little attention has been given to the study of stress in childhood and adolescence. One attempt to do so is a study by A. D. Kanner and associates using a sample of 91 boys and 141 girls in the sixth grade in two school districts in the San Francisco Bay area. The majority were white, though there were substantial numbers of Asian and Latino children, and most were from intact families, though single-parent and step families were represented.[27]

Stressors were measured using the Children's Hassles Scale and the Children's Uplifts Scale. Perceived stress was measured by taking into account whether the existence of a hassle or uplift made the child feel bad or good. The potency of a stressor was also measured by determining the stressors that often made children feel good or bad when they occurred. Scores on these scales were then correlated with self-reported measures of negative outcomes, such as depression and anxiety, and positive outcomes, such as peer friendship support, competence, and self-worth. In stress theory the assumption is that children who experience numerous hassles will also experience a number of negative psychological outcomes. The theory is not clear as to the effects of uplifts, however. Females and males seem to respond to them differently; females said they increased depression, while males said they were not related to negative outcomes.

Hassles were common in the lives of these sixth-graders (see "Hassles in the Lives of Sixth-Grade Children"). The most common hassles reported were having to clean their rooms, feeling bored, feeling that others were better than they were, losing something, being bugged by siblings, being punished, and not liking the way they looked. Yet these events were not always experienced as negative, nor were they always likely to make children feel bad. Some hassles that occurred less frequently actually were more likely to do this. For instance, under 50 percent of the children reported that they were punished for something they didn't do, or that their parents fought, or that their pet had died, but they said they felt bad over 80 percent of the times these things happened.

Uplifts were more common than hassles, and most often an uplift made the child feel good. The most common uplifts for these sixth-graders were getting a good mark at school, playing with friends, having a teacher they liked, going out to eat, having a school holiday, spending time with parents, getting a phone call or a letter, learning something new, and getting new clothes. Getting good grades and playing with friends were especially likely to make the children feel good.

Boys and girls did not differ in the number of hassles and uplifts they reported or the ways they perceived uplifts, but, they did differ in the ways they perceived hassles. Girls were significantly more likely than boys to feel bad about hassles, in particular being teased, losing something, losing a best friend, not liking their looks, hearing or seeing parents fight, being bugged by siblings, and not having enough privacy. Children who experienced hassles in a negative way were also highly likely to experience depression, anxiety, and distress and moderately likely to experience poor peer support and poor self-worth. Uplifts were consistently linked to more-positive psychological outcomes such

Hassles in the Lives of Sixth-Grade Children

In the study of stress, stressors, which produce the physiological response of stress, are being viewed less in terms of life events and more as the hassles and uplifts encountered in everyday life. A study of sixth-graders' reactions to hassles and uplifts produced the following list of most commonly reported hassles. However, these were not necessarily the most likely to be perceived as negative or to always make the children feel bad

	Percent of Children		
Hassle	Reporting Occurrence	Perceiving Occurrence as Negative	Feeling Bad about Occurrence
Had to clean room	83%	21%	25%
Felt bored	81	48	59
Others could do things better than you	75	30	41
Lost something	73	30	41
Siblings bugged you	73	37	51
Were punished	66	52	79
Don't like way you look	66	45	69
Parent got sick	59	47	80
Punished for something you didn't do	50	44	88
Parents fighting	43	35	81
Pet died	36	32	89
Parents upset about bad school report	35	28	80

Source: Adapted from A. D. Kanner, S. S. Feldman, D. A. Weinberger, and M. E. Ford, "Uplifts, Hassles, and Adaptational Outcomes in Early Adolescents," in A. Monet and R. S. Lazarus (editors), *Stress and Coping: An Anthology*, 3rd ed. (New York: Columbia University Press, 1991), pp. 158–79.

as feeling supported by friends, competent, and worthy. According to gender, however, some interesting differences appeared. The correlations between perceived stress and psychological outcomes were stronger among boys than girls (a pattern that differs for adults); that is, hassles and uplifts were less powerful predictors of psychological outcomes for girls than for boys. There was also a small but significant tendency for uplifts to produce anxiety among girls.

The authors suggest that the differences found between boys and girls are best explained in developmental terms. They argue that since in general sixth-grade girls are more physically mature than sixth-grade boys, the reactions of girls and boys to hassles and uplifts are likely to differ. Another possible interpretation is that male and female childhood socialization sets up clearer expectations for boys than girls. Girls at this age are starting to realize the implications of their gender for their eventual adult status. In a psychodynamic interpretation, this budding realization may make girls more ambivalent about themselves, more easily hassled, and less sure of how to react to hassles and uplifts.[28]

Is Crisis Normal in Adolescence?

The teen years have traditionally been seen as particularly beset by conflict. G. Stanley Hall, the first psychologist to study this stage of development, defined adolescence in the United States at the turn of the twentieth century as a period of *Sturm und Drang*, storm and stress.[29] Others have followed suit. Anna Freud, for instance, characterized normal (or average) adolescence as a period in which:

> ...aggressive impulses are intensified to the point of complete unruliness, hunger becomes voracity and the naughtiness of the latency period turns into the criminal behavior of adolescence.... Habits of cleanliness...give place to pleasure in dirt and disorder, and instead of modesty and sympathy we find exhibitionistic tendencies, brutality and cruelty to animals.[30]

As recently as 1983, Carl Tischler stated that "crisis, stormy emotions, and psychic instability are characteristic of adolescence."[31]

Study of the Normal Adolescent

In a ten-year longitudinal study of "normal" adolescents, those who have not been adjudicated as delinquent or institutionalized for mental disorders, Daniel Offer found that a significant proportion do not experience turmoil. Only 21 percent of those he studied were classified as exhibiting severe turmoil, or *tumultuous growth*. They were troubled by self-doubt and escalating conflict with their parents, had debilitating inhibitions, and often responded inconsistently in social and academic environments. In contrast, *continuous growth* was demonstrated by 23 percent of the adolescents. They were purposeful and self-assured, accepting social norms and feeling comfortable in them. When they experienced trouble, they coped, using adaptive ego processes. Another 35 percent demonstrated *surgent growth*. These adolescents were not as confident, and their self-esteem wavered. Some were afraid of their emerging sexual feelings and were awkward in relationships with members of the opposite sex. All in all, however, they coped with troubles and did not suffer from severe breakdown. The remaining 21 percent of the adolescents studied could not be classified in any category.[32]

Offer believes his findings demonstrate that crises and conflict are not normal to adolescence, or, by extension, to any period in the life course. Using Offer's findings, David Oldham suggests that the stereotype of storm and stress should be discarded. Thus, rather than seeing adolescent conflict as normal, social service workers should take any such conflict seriously, as an indication of possible pathology.[33]

Offer's findings are suspect, however. Most of the adolescents studied experienced at least some turmoil, and 21 percent experienced tumultuous growth. It might be assumed that some of the 21 percent who could not be classified did experience something akin to surgent or tumultuous growth. He did not include delinquent or emotionally disturbed adolescents in his study, all of whom could be said to have experienced tumultuous growth. He studied only white, middle-class youth, and even with this group there were differences in economic status; lower-middle-class boys were significantly more likely to evidence tumultuous growth than upper-middle-class boys. One clinician who refers to the work of Offer and recognizes that every adolescent will not be disturbed nevertheless concludes:

> It seems safe to assert that all adolescents are probably shaken by emotional storms and troublesome floods of impulse; for many, these experiences are transient and readily mastered, whereas

for a minority, the same issues lead to far more serious reactions.... Anna Freud's observation about the normalcy of adolescent turmoil is probably as accurate a statement as one can make.[34]

Thus Offer's study can be used to support the view that turmoil is normal in adolescents, the same view he attempts to disprove.

James Marcia on Identity and Role Confusion

Using empirical methods, James Marcia identified four **adolescent** *identity statuses* representing the ways youths adapt during these years. Following Erikson, he proposes that all youths must experience and resolve crises before they can establish a true identity. Abnormality consists in not experiencing the crisis, or in experiencing it and not being able to find a solution. His point of view is also supported by empirical studies, but it conflicts directly with Offer's.[35]

Marcia describes two kinds of identity status among normal youths. One is a *moratorium*, a state of crisis marked by active searching for the identity that will give form and coherence to their being. The second is *identity-achieved*, for those who experience the crisis and resolve it successfully. They truly understand who and what they are. He also describes two kinds of status among troubled youths. The *identity-confused* youth has not yet experienced an identity crisis or made any commitment to a vocation or to a set of beliefs about the self and the social world. The *identity-foreclosed* youth also has not experienced an identity crisis but nevertheless appears to have made a commitment to a particular identity. From Marcia's point of view, it is necessary to distinguish between youths in turmoil because they are actively dealing with their identity and youths who have not allowed themselves to experience conflict. Both may need help.

Conclusions about Adolescent Crises

Although the evidence is not conclusive, a fair amount of crisis apparently is endemic to adolescence. Some adolescents may experience no conflict; others experience severe conflict; and most seem to experience at least some crises. The crises, in both amount and intensity, are undoubtedly a function of biological changes, cognitive capacities, psychological needs, motives, and abilities, as well as environmental considerations such as the effects of inequalities on family, school, and peer-group life. Young people who experience inequity, alienation, anomie, or labeling are likely to have a tumultuous adolescence.

There is a difference between the experience of conflict and the inability to resolve conflict, however. Experiencing conflict is undoubtedly normal in the statistical sense. Not being able to experience it or not being able to resolve it when it is experienced may be a sign of abnormal development. Normal (as healthy) adolescents do not avoid conflict in their transactions with others; when they experience it, they are able to deal with it effectively. The developed adolescent is one who meets the crises successfully.

⌒ GENDER-ROLE DEVELOPMENT AND SEXUAL ORIENTATION

Gender-role development and the achievement of a sexual identity are recurring developmental tasks. From early childhood, males and females begin to complete tasks that ultimately define them within a gender-role or sex-role context.

Eight Definitions of Gender

Sex-role or gender-role development is a complicated process involving eight different ways of differentiating males from females. Theories of sex-role development must examine the relationship between the genotypical (internal and not visible) and phenotypical (external and visible) aspects of gender.

Types of Definition	Males	Females
Genotypical		
Chromosomal gender	XY	XX
Gonadal gender	Testes	Ovaries
Hormonal gender	Mostly androgens	Mostly estrogens
Organal gender	Prostate glands, ejaculatory ducts, vas deferens, and seminal vesicles	Uterus and fallopian tubes
Phenotypical		
Genital gender	Penis and scrotal sacs	Clitoris, labia, and vagina
Gender of rearing	"It's a boy"	"It's a girl"
Gender identity	_X_ Male __ Female	__ Male _X_ Female
Gender role	Masculine behavior	Feminine behavior

Source: Adapted from Katherine B. Hoyenga and Kermit Hoyenga, *The Question of Sex Differences* (Boston: Little, Brown, 1979), p. 5. Used with permission of the authors.

According to Freudian theory, girls learn to be women and boys learn to be men as a result of emotional conflicts. Early-life experiences continually narrow the range of satisfactions that are permitted the child and that the child permits itself. These experiences reach their culmination in the genital or Oedipal period discussed in Chapter 15. The Freudian model of sex-role learning suggests that a set of complex emotional responses and counterresponses results in identification with the same-sex parent and the internalization of heterosexual mores.

The Biology of Sex

A major difficulty in unraveling the processes by which men and women take on a sexual identity is that sex or gender itself is not easily identified. We cannot therefore assume that boys just become boys and girls just become girls.

Katherine and Kermit Hoyenga point out that there are at least eight different aspects of **gender**, not necessarily related to one another. Some aspects are *genotypical*, that is, internal to the organism and not visible to the naked eye. These include chromosomal, gonadal, hormonal, and organal gender. Other gender categories are *phenotypical*, that is, external to the organism and therefore visible. These include genital gender, the gender of rearing, gender identity, and gender role[36] (see "Eight Definitions of Gender").

The most basic way of defining gender is genotypical, in terms of differences in *chromosomal gender*. As we noted in Chapter 16, females normally inherit an XX pair of chromosomes and males normally inherit an XY pair; if this does not occur, the embryo is often aborted. Other pairings of chromosomes are possible, however. In Turner's syndrome only one chromosome, an X, is present in the fetus. A person with this syndrome will look female but will almost always be infertile. In Klinefelter's syndrome, a person is born with a Y chromosome coupled with two or more X chromosomes. The person is male, yet the multiple X chromosomes often overwhelm the Y chromosome, and complete masculinization does not take place. The person has a male chromosome but often has a small penis, low levels of testosterone (the male hormone), breast enlargement, and little body hair. Other persons are born with one X chromosome and two Y chromosomes. There is some speculation that such double-Y chromosome males are particularly aggressive, but the data are not clear; many such men appear to live normal lives.

Other genotypical definitions are gonadal and hormonal gender and the gender of the internal accessory organs. *Gonadal gender* refers to testes in males and ovaries in females. Gonads produce hormones, which enter the brain and affect behavior. Although males and females share all hormones, *hormonal gender* is determined in males by the testes, which mostly produce androgens (as testosterone), and in females by the ovaries, which mostly produce estrogen and progesterone. *Organal gender* refers to the internal accessory organs. In males, these include prostate glands, ejaculatory ducts, the vas deferens, and seminal vesicles. In women, they consist of the uterus and the fallopian tubes.

Some XX fetuses (females) emit high amounts of androgen (male hormones), while some XY fetuses (males) appear to be insensitive to androgen. When this occurs the XX fetus can become masculinized, and the XY fetus becomes feminized in the external organs. Thus while the internal apparatus may be of one gender, the external appearance may be of another. Sometimes these processes can reverse themselves. For instance, enzyme deficiencies were found in males born in rural villages in the Dominican Republic. At birth, these boys looked like females and were dressed and treated accordingly, but upon puberty they began to produce testosterone, their testes descended, their penises emerged, their voices deepened, and their muscles developed in conformity with the male body.[37]

Among the phenotypical definitions, *genital gender*, the physical external appearance of the genitals at birth, most often determines how a child will be raised (the *gender of rearing*). **Gender identity** is self-identification as male or female, and **gender role** is the taking on and preference for culturally appropriate male and female behaviors.

Theories of gender-role development must examine the relationship between genotypical and phenotypical gender. Studies of individuals whose genotypes differ from their phenotypes demonstrate that biology and socialization are equally important, although very few such studies exist. For instance, the enzyme-deficient boys in the Dominican Republic who were reared as girls took on all the expected demeanor of girls, suggesting the importance of socialization. Nevertheless, all but two of them easily assumed male identities once their genotypic gender became apparent, suggesting the importance of biology. Most theories of gender-role identity are limited to explaining the relationships among the gender of external genitals, gender role, and gender identity.

Gender-Role Identification

In Barbara and Philip Newman's concept of sex-role identification, which incorporates a psychodynamic perspective, there are four dimensions: applying the correct gender label, differentiating sex-role standards, developing a preference for one's own sex, and identifying with the parent of the same sex.[38] They believe that heterosexual gender-role identification is largely a cognitive process in which the child comes to terms with his or her changing physical and genital appearance.

First, children come to *understand their gender*, that is, they correctly use the gender label others are applying to them. They reply "I'm a boy" or "I'm a girl" when asked, "Are you a girl or a boy?" They also come to understand that gender is stable and lasts a lifetime—boys become men and girls become women; that gender is constant—a child is a girl or boy regardless of clothing, hairstyle, toys, and the like; and that gender has a genital basis, and sexual identity has to do with the appearance of the genitals.

The second dimension of sex-role identification concerns *sex-role standards*, the cultural expectations about appropriate behavior for boys and girls, men and women. Although these expectations are often unclear or undergoing change, they are the bases on which parents socialize children. Because they reward and punish behavior in accordance with their own understanding of cultural expectations, parents have much to do with the sexual identity of their children. There is evidence that by age 5 children have internalized their parents' expectations and are applying them to themselves and to other children. During the early school years they seem to have clearly fixed sex-role stereotypes and are strict with regard to proper sex-role behavior.

The third dimension is *preference for one's own sex*. Children who understand the genital origins of their sex and are taught culturally approved sex-role standards ordinarily come to prefer for themselves those identities and roles. The more the child's innate competencies approximate sex-role standards, and the more the child likes the parent of the same sex, the more will that child prefer being a member of her or his sex. Cultural values about the status of the child's own sex also influence preference. The Newmans say that where the society gives more status to the male, males are more likely to prefer being male, but females are likely to experience some ambivalence toward their sex group, if not rejection of it.[39]

The fourth dimension is *identification with the same-sex parent*. Following Freud, the Newmans refer to fear of loss of love and identification with the aggressor as two primary motivations for sex-role identification, but they take into account at least two others. One is the need for status and power, an idea which derives from social-learning theory. When children are confronted with two models, one controlling rewards and the other receiving them, they will imitate the behavior of the person who controls, that is, the more powerful person. Because rewards affect the behaviors of children, however, they must be rewarded for imitating their parents.[40] The other motive is perceived similarity. Children behave like their same-sex parents in order to increase the similarity that they perceive exists between them, which they accomplish by observing physical and psychological similarities themselves, adopting their parents' behaviors, and being told by others that they are similar to their parents.[41] But the Newmans accept the idea that children are bisexual by nature and see no strong evidence to indicate that boys inherently identify with their fathers and girls with their mothers. They suggest that it is the warmth and dominance of the parent rather than the actual sex-role behaviors of the parents that promote identification.

Sexual Orientations

The Newmans's ideas on sex-role (or gender-role) identification are concerned only with heterosexual development, the process by which female and male infants come to take on heterosexual behaviors and fantasies. All other forms of sexual orientation, in their view, indicate some problem in the socialization of sexuality. But the expression of a person's sexual orientation is complex. While two major categories are recognized, heterosexual and homosexual, a range of orientations has been found to exist.

The pioneering studies of Alfred Kinsey were among the first to call attention to the complexity of sexual orientation. Kinsey was interested in sexual conduct, which he defined as sexual behavior to the point of orgasm. He believed sexual conduct could be measured on a scale, with total involvement in heterosexual or homosexual conduct at the extremes and a wide range of bisexual conduct in between. In his interviews in the 1940s and 1950s, less than 5 percent of men and women said they were exclusively homosexual throughout their physically mature lives, but 37 percent of men and 13 percent of women reported some experience of sex to orgasm with a member of their same sex.[42]

The more recent work of Michael Storms has led to a rethinking of these categories. Storms's interest is in "erotic orientation," by which he means the type, extent, and frequency of sexual fantasies. He argues that homosexuality and heterosexuality are separate erotic dimensions rather than opposite extremes on a continuum, and homoerotic fantasies can vary independently of heteroerotic fantasies. Thus there are four types of sexuality: asexuality, heterosexuality, homosexuality, and bisexuality. Heterosexual people are sexually aroused by members of the opposite sex but not by members of their same sex. Homosexual people are sexually aroused by members of their same sex but not by members of their opposite sex. Bisexual people are aroused both by members of their opposite sex and their same sex. Asexual people are aroused by neither members of their same sex nor those of the opposite sex.[43]

Homosexual Identification

In Freudian theory, a homosexual identity and preference develop because certain things go wrong in early-childhood development. Homosexuality is believed to come about as a result of traumas in pre-Oedipal and Oedipal periods, and thus it represents neurosis. Erikson includes the capacity for heterosexual, procreative sex in his definition of a normal adult. For the Newmans, it is clear that a homosexual identification and preference results only if children do not understand sex, cultural standards are not taken into account, motivations break down, or the person's competencies do not fit the expected mold. For older children and adolescents, confusion or ambiguity over their sexual identity is a source of stress. The reactions of peers, parents, and others if they express a preference other than the heterosexual orientation can produce feelings of despair in them that can lead to suicide (see "Adolescent Suicide and Homosexuality").

The American Psychiatric Association voted in 1973 not to include homosexuality as a mental illness or disorder in their *Diagnostic and Statistical Manual*, and the World Health Organization has eliminated it from its categories of diseases. The revised third edition of the *DSM* does include an entry for "persistent and marked distress about one's sexual orientation" in the category of "sexual disorders not otherwise specified." This "ego-dystonic homosexuality" pertains only to those who are disturbed by their homosexual behavior and wish to alter it.[44] There are those, both in and outside of the psychiatric community, who propose that homosexuality ought to be reintroduced as psychopathology. They often cite the work of Freudians to defend their point of view, in which homosexuality is seen as an illness.[45]

Adolescent Suicide and Homosexuality

After accidents and homicides, the leading cause of death for Americans 15 through 24 years old is suicide. Suicides and suicidal tendencies have been increasing in this age group; the rate of suicide was 9.0 per 100,000 in 1970, 12.3 in 1980, and 13.2 in 1990. Although suicide rates are higher for all age categories over age 24, the increasing rates coupled with the feeling that suicide is particularly senseless with regard to the young has made adolescent suicide a major social problem.

A number of causal factors are associated with adolescent suicide: depression, stress associated with education and achievement, family problems, and peer problems. Recent evidence suggests that problems related to sexual orientation are often embedded in these problems, and youths who come to realize that they may not be heterosexual are particularly at risk for suicide.

Paul Gibson asserts that suicide is the leading cause of death among gay, lesbian, bisexual, and transsexual youth. As evidence, he presents statistics from social services for these youths in New York, Minnesota, Seattle, Los Angeles, and San Francisco indicating that 20 to 35 percent of them have attempted suicide and 50 percent experience suicidal feelings. Among homeless gay and lesbian youths, as many as 65 percent report feeling suicidal.

The pressure for suicide appears directly related to negative family and peer-group attitudes. James Price studied attitudes toward homosexuality among students in a white, middle-class school in a small midwestern town. He found that male and female adolescents were very likely to hold negative attitudes and stereotypes regarding homosexuality, males more than females, although the differences were not always statistically significant. He concludes that one of the loneliest persons in any high school in America is the rejected and isolated gay adolescent.

The relationship between gay and lesbian youth and their parents is also important in understanding the likelihood of suicidal tendencies. Ritch Savin-Williams tested an idea from symbolic interactionism, namely, that the self-esteem of gay and lesbian youths is related to the kinds of appraisal they believe they are receiving from their parents. He predicted that those who believe their parents still value them would be more comfortable about their sexuality than those who thought their parents do not. Using a sample of 214 gay and 103 lesbian youths, he found some support for this hypothesis. This was particularly true for lesbians and was also important for gay males when the parents were perceived to be "important" for the boy.

In a study of 329 adolescent youths using a social service for gays and lesbians, E. S. Hetrick and A. D. Martin found that these youths often felt separated emotionally from all social networks, especially their family. One-third had suffered violence because of their orientation, very often at the hands of their families. It is not surprising, therefore, that 20 percent of the adolescents studied had attempted suicide or thought about it.

Sources: J. S. Wodarski and P. Harris, "Adolescent Suicide: A Review of Influences and the Means for Prevention," *Social Work*, vol. 32 (November–December 1987), p. 477; Paul Gibson, "Gay Male and Lesbian Youth Suicide," in M. R. Feinleib (editor), *Report of the Secretary's Task Force on Youth Suicide* (Washington, DC: U.S. Department of Health and Human Services, January 1989), pp. 3–110; James H. Price, "High School Students' Attitudes toward Homosexuality," *Journal of School Health*, vol. 52 (October 1982), pp. 469–74; Ritch C. Savin-Williams, "Parental Influences on the Self-Esteem of Gay and Lesbian Youths: A Reflected Appraisals Model," *Journal of Homosexuality*, vol. 17 (1989), pp. 93–109; and E. S. Hetrick and A. D. Martin, "Developmental Issues and Their Resolution for Gay and Lesbian Adolescents," *Journal of Homosexuality*, vol. 14 (1987), pp. 25–43. Data from U.S. Bureau of the Census, *Statistical Abstract of the United States: 1993*, 113th edition (Washington, DC, 1993), Tables 128 and 137.

Juliet Mitchell argues forcefully that the justification for considering homosexuality a disorder is not to be found in Freud, since he always recognized the bisexual nature of human behavior. She quotes a letter from Freud to a distraught mother in which his opinion on homosexuality was quite enlightened:

> …Homosexuality is assuredly no advantage, but it is nothing to be ashamed of, no vice, no degradation; it cannot be classified as an illness; we consider it to be a variation of the sexual function….It is a great injustice to persecute homosexuality as a crime—and a cruelty too….
>
> By asking me if I can help you, you mean, I suppose, if I can abolish homosexuality and make normal heterosexuality take its place…. What [psycho] analysis can do for your son runs in a different line. If he is unhappy, neurotic, torn by conflicts, inhibited in his social life, analysis may bring him harmony, peace of mind, full efficiency whether he remains homosexual or gets changed….[46]

Hormones, Genetics, and Homosexuality

More recent thinking on the origin of homosexuality in individuals is that it may be biological. Researchers have examined the possibility that hormonal differences between homosexual and heterosexual women and men may account for differences in sexual identity. The hypothesis is that women with high levels of androgens and low levels of estrogen are more likely to be masculine and to adopt homosexual behaviors; for men, the opposite is likely. In studies on adults, alterations in the level of masculine and feminine hormones have had no effect on sexual orientation, but there is some evidence that hormonal alterations before birth may lead to homosexual conduct. Female monkey fetuses that are artificially androgenized by being bathed in masculinizing hormones do not become exactly like male monkeys after birth, but they do behave in more masculine ways. They engage in rougher activities and are more threatening and more likely to mount other monkeys than ordinary female monkeys.[47]

With humans, studies on women born with the andrenogenital syndrome have proved instructive. Something goes wrong with the adrenocortical glands in the fetal period, and an androgenized female is born. The newborn has ambiguous external organs and a male-differentiated brain, and at puberty male secondary sexual characteristics appear. This syndrome is correctable through surgery and cortisone injections, but the initial androgenization that occurred in the womb cannot be undone.

Among 30 fetally androgenized women studied, all reported being "tomboys" in childhood. Five reported they were homosexual as adults and six said they were bisexual. This suggests that fetal hormonal imbalances may be related to adult homosexuality. However, 19 of the 30 androgenized women reported exclusive heterosexuality as adults.[48]

A recent study by Simon LeVay suggests that genetic differences in brain structure may be related to homosexual conduct in adults. He examined the brains of a small sample of men who died of AIDS, most of whom had contracted the disease through unsafe sexual behavior with other men, but for some it was through intravenous drug use. He examined a part of the hypothalamus located on the floor of the brain which is believed to influence sexual behavior, and found it to be significantly smaller in homosexual men than in heterosexual men. Furthermore, this region of the hypothalamus is roughly equal in women and homosexual men. Although he does not rule out the contributing effects of environment, LeVay believes that this hypothalamic segment induces males to seek females and its relative absence in men could be one predisposing element toward homosexuality.[49]

LeVay's study is couched in terms that favor gays and lesbians. Many homosexuals believe that it confirms what they have experienced—their sexual orientation is deeply rooted in their personality and is not the result of poor socialization and learned or arbitrary preferences. Yet there are a number of problems with the study. It says nothing about homosexuality among women, and it was done on a small, nonrandom sample of men. It also perpetuates the idea that homosexual men are less normal than heterosexual men. Marcia Baranaga notes that homophobes could point to brain "defects" in homosexuals as a reason to practice prenatal screening for homosexuality.[50]

∞ RACIAL AND ETHNIC IDENTITY

Achieving an **ethnic identity** is another recurring life-cycle task which gains prominence at this stage of the life course. Children start to become aware of their racial or ethnic heritage during early childhood, and in later childhood and adolescence they begin to put together a vision of what this means for them as individuals. Developing a healthy identity can be particularly problematic for children and adolescents who are members of racial and ethnic groups that experience institutional discrimination in American society, because they might internalize the hostility and come to see themselves as inferior. This does not usually happen, however, because there are social and psychological processes that work to avoid it.[51]

Prior to the civil rights struggles of the 1960s, psychologists and sociologists believed that minority racial and ethnic group members would make one of four types of adaptation. They might conform, that is, identify with the dominant majority and internalize a negative self-image. They might develop a feeling of anomia and never understand who they are and where they fit in the society. They might make a liberal adaptation, basically accepting the negative self-image promoted by the dominant group but also seeing possibilities for social change. Or they might become militant and organize with other group members to produce social changes that would help achieve equality.[52]

The current approach is to think of ethnic and racial identity in terms of psychosocial development. Researchers now believe that rather than adapting in only one way, minority youths may go through stages in which identity shifts in predictable ways. In order to acquire a healthy racial and ethnic identity, they must successfully complete the task of dealing with the negative images of themselves being projected by the dominant group, until they experience a healthy adaptation. Then, being at ease with themselves and with the dominant group, they can join with others to change the status of their group.

Jean Phinney reviewed the literature on ethnic identity formation and synthesized the ideas of several researchers with James Marcia's theory of adolescent identity.[53] She identifies three periods in the formation of an ethnic identity, from early adolescence to young adulthood. Early adolescence is likely to be marked by a period of *unexamined ethnic identity*. These youths experience either identity diffusion, a lack of interest in or concern for ethnicity, or identity foreclosure, in which they hold views about themselves that are based on the opinions of others. A foreclosed adolescent may hold a very negative identity and prefer to be known as a member of the dominant group, especially if that is her or his reference group.

Next, according to Phinney, is the period of *ethnic identity search*, during which the youths try to understand the meaning of ethnicity for their personal identity. This may be exhibited in a crisis, where they challenge everything associated with the dominant group, or in a moratorium, where they become totally immersed in their cultural heritage. After a successful period of search, the young adult emerges with an *achieved ethnic identity*. At this point members of ethnic and racial minorities have a clear and confident sense of self which includes being able to evaluate critically their own culture and that of the dominant group. For William Cross, this last stage also involves joining in political activity to improve the status of one's group in society.[54]

Ethnic Identity and Social Service Work

Donald Atkinson, George Morten, and Derald Sue draw some important conclusions about ethnic identity for social service workers counseling American minorities. They suggest that as these individuals pass through the stages of ethnic identity, there are changes in their mental health needs, the service personnel they are willing to work with, and their attitudes toward other minority groups. These authors make the following projections for various stages of the search for identity.[55]

To the extent that minority youths are identity diffused or have a preference for the dominant culture, they will express self-deprecating attitudes toward the self and their group of origin. They are likely to direct prejudice and discrimination toward people from other minority groups. When they seek help they are likely to behave in white middle-class ways, to deny the existence of minority problems, and to be uninterested in working on identity problems.

When minority youths are in an identity crisis, or dissonance, they will be ambivalent about themselves and their group, at once deprecating and appreciating. They will also be in conflict about the dominant group and about other minorities. When they seek help they are likely to be preoccupied with concerns about their identity. Self-exploration will be the focus of counseling.

If they are immersed in their racial or ethnic group and show active resistance toward members of the dominant group, they will believe that all their problems result from the oppressive conditions experienced by their group. They will deprecate the dominant group and be ambivalent toward other minority groups, at once feeling empathy toward them but negative about them. Immersed youths often insist on working only with social service workers from their own group.

As minority group members begin to achieve a clear and confident identity, they are likely to become introspective. They will reflect upon their attitudes and take on a more critical view of themselves, their group, the dominant group, and other minorities. Introspective young adults will feel constricted by the role of minority and will search for freedom to be themselves. They may at this point be willing to work with culturally competent counselors from other groups.

Once an identity is fully achieved, minority individuals will appreciate their own group but be able to evaluate it critically. They will have a selective appreciation of the dominant group and other subordinated groups. Attitude and value similarity, rather than group membership, will determine their willingness to seek help from social service workers.

∞ DISABILITY AND ADOLESCENTS' SELF-IMAGE

Illness or disability can have serious consequences for the individual's psychosocial development. Those who are physically incapacitated—from the time of birth, temporarily, or over the long term—often become cut off from social relationships or are treated differently from others, which can make them feel inadequate or inferior. It might seem that adolescents caught up in a search for identity would be put at risk for psychological difficulties by chronic illness or disability.

Self-image—the ways people think and feel about themselves—is a central factor in the development of normal adolescent functioning. It has an evaluative component; young people can feel relatively good or bad about themselves. It also incorporates a number of different dimensions. The Offer Adolescent Self-Image Questionnaire is designed to evaluate five different aspects of the self:

1. The *psychological self* involves mood, body image, and impulse control.

2. The *social self* has to do with feelings about social relationships, morality, and vocational and educational goals.

3. The *sexual self* involves sexual attitudes and behaviors.

4. The *familial self* involves feelings about relationships with parents and family members.

5. The *coping self* involves feelings about efforts to deal with struggles in everyday life.[56]

A number of researchers have examined the question of whether the self-image of adolescents suffers when they experience a serious illness or disability. In general, they have found little support for the idea that these adolescents inevitably have a poor self-image, lose self-esteem, or exhibit psychopathology or other indicators of inadequate coping.

Daniel Offer, Eric Ostrov, and Kenneth Howard compared the self-images of over a thousand physically healthy youths throughout the United States with nonrandom samples of adolescents challenged by asthma, cancer, or cystic fibrosis. On the assumption that illness in the family of an adolescent might affect psychological functioning, they also studied children of parents with multiple sclerosis. They compared male and female adolescents and ranked the illnesses in terms of seriousness.[57]

The adolescents suffering from asthma were not very impaired; the disease did not affect their lives appreciably, and only two ever needed hospitalization. Those with cancer were rated as being moderately disabled; most were diagnosed with leukemia, and all were outpatients who had been ill for less than a year and were undergoing chemotherapy or radiation treatment. Adolescents with cystic fibrosis were the most severely incapacitated; the disease is a congenital condition which causes chronic respiratory and digestive problems, and they had experienced multiple hospitalizations and serious medical problems throughout their lives. The parents with multiple sclerosis were considered mildly to moderately impaired. They had had the condition for at least five years but none had been hospitalized for at least a year.

Results of this study indicated that among young people with disabilities caused by illness, girls generally adjusted better than boys. Whether the self-image of these adolescents was high or low compared to those of healthy adolescents depended on the seriousness of their illness. The self-images of youths with asthma were comparatively more positive than those of healthy youths, those of youths with cancer were about the same, and those of youths with cystic fibrosis were more negative. Adolescents whose parents had multiple sclerosis generally had a poorer self-image than others whose parents were not affected.

Such studies demonstrate that there is no one-to-one correspondence between disability and psychological disturbance. Adolescents with asthma and cancer can and do cope in positive ways. However, severe or stigmatizing disabilities such as cystic fibrosis are likely to lead to negative feelings about the self on a number of psychosocial dimensions.

∞ IMPLICATIONS FOR PRACTICE

In the social work literature, it is often assumed that practitioners whose job is to provide direct or clinical services have no opportunities to promote large-scale, progressive social change. The material reviewed in this chapter suggests otherwise.

Childhood and adolescence are periods in the life span when the individual begins to enter into the larger world. Although the family still dominates, as children go to school they become exposed to a wide range of adults from their own and other neighborhoods, and they begin to enter into peer-group relations. The norms embedded in family, community, school, and peer-group relations are expected to influence the self-esteem and identity acquired by young people. To the extent that they are hostile or promote an image of inferiority or inadequacy, young people are at risk of psychological difficulties. This is particularly the case with regard to girls, children from ethnic and racial minority groups, and children with disabilities. Although we have not discussed the issue here, it is true of children from lower-class and poor families as well. Working with these children therefore provides social service workers with opportunities to be of immediate assistance to clients, as well as to work toward the solution of social problems.

In the past, social service workers were criticized for taking the point of view of the dominant elements of society. In working with young women, they often aimed to reinforce women's traditional roles as homemaker, dependent wife, and mother. Counselors channeled girls into educational and occupational paths in keeping with these roles, and young women who questioned these roles or sought others were deemed not normal. In working with homosexual adolescents, mental health providers often reinforced heterosexual norms: they saw homosexual behavior as a passing phase or deliberately tried to alter the youth's sexual orientation. In regard to racial and ethnic identity, they were inclined to reinforce assimilation rather than a bicultural identification among children and adolescents.

Today social workers are more likely to take the point of view of women, ethnic and racial minorities, lesbians and gays, and people with disabilities. They define their role not solely as social control agents but as agents of progressive social change. Thus in working directly with older children and adolescents, they help to expand the norms of society.

∞ DISCUSSION QUESTIONS AND CLASS PROJECTS

1. Describe the life course in terms of the physical growth or decline that can be expected in childhood and adolescence.

2. Describe the social relationships that are likely to influence development as people pass through childhood and adolescence.

3. Identify the following concepts: puberty, gonads, progesterone, testosterone, estrogen, stress, stressors, perceived stress, hassles, uplifts, tumultuous growth, surgent growth, continuous growth, identity confused, moratorium, identity achieved, identify foreclosed.

4. Compare Offer's view on adolescent development with Marcia's. Do you believe that turmoil is normal in ado-

lescence? Does that mean social workers should not take crises in adolescent clients seriously?

5. In groups of five, describe the psychosocial crises Erikson associates with childhood and adolescence. By reflecting on your own experiences and those of others in the class, discuss whether such crises are common experiences. In your discussion, determine whether gender, race and ethnicity, and ability status make for different crises.

6. What do we know of the stresses of early adolescence? What kinds of hassles and uplifts are they likely to experience? Do boys and girls have different experiences? What is likely to account for different experiences? Do you think it is related to biological maturational issues or to social issues?

7. In groups of no more than six, discuss your own adolescence in terms of the amount of turmoil you experienced. Describe Marcia's theory and whether it is helpful to you in understanding your adolescence.

8. Describe the theory of heterosexual gender-role identification formulated by the Newmans. Does it make sense as you think about your own gender-role identification? Do you think it satisfactorily explains homosexual identification? How would you describe the process of homosexual identification?

9. Describe the processes that are likely to occur in developing a positive ethnic or racial minority identity. Do members of ethnic and racial majority groups go through an identity process? What might that process be like?

10. Are adolescents with disabilities likely to have special difficulties in achieving positive self-esteem?

11. The following role play can be done in front of the class or more privately as a three-person discussion group, after students have read the chapter. One person plays the role of the social worker, another the role of an adolescent client, and the third (or the class) the role of observer.

    The person playing the role of the adolescent client assumes one of the following identities: a girl, a lesbian or gay adolescent, an ethnic or racial minority adolescent, or a disabled adolescent. In playing the role, the client should (without saying so) project a type of identity issue—a particular level of turmoil or a particular type of identity crisis or problem, based on his or her understanding of the identity issues raised in the chapter. The social worker engages the client and, avoiding jargon, makes an assessment. When the interview is completed (about ten minutes), the social worker announces to the class the level of turmoil and type of identity problem being played out. The observer then comments on the assessment, indicating whether the social worker is correct. The observer may ask the client additional questions, but the client must stay in role.

    The client then describes to the class the identity issues she or he was trying to play out. The class can use the exercise as a way of discussing identity issues and problems in doing assessments.

12. What is meant by the epigenetic principle? Why is it important for social work?

∽ NOTES

1. James Leslie McCary, *Human Sexuality: A Brief Edition* (New York: D. Van Nostrand, 1973).

2. Daniel Offer and Melvin Sabshin, "Adolescence: Empirical Perspectives," in D. Offer and M. Sabshin (editors), *Normality and the Life Cycle: A Critical Integration* (New York: Basic Books, 1984), p. 84.

3. Ibid.

4. Barbara M. Newman and Philip R. Newman, *Development through Life: A Psychosocial Approach*, 4th ed. (Belmont, CA: Dorsey Press, 1987), p. 45.

5. Ibid., p. 46.

6. Erik Erikson, *Childhood and Society*, 2nd ed. (New York: W. W. Norton, 1963), p. 261.

7. Newman and Newman, *Development through Life*, p. 45.

8. Ibid., p. 46.

9. Fumiyo T. Hunter and James Youniss, "Changes in Functions of Three Relations during Adolescence," *Developmental Psychology*, vol. 18 (November 1982), pp. 806–11; Martin Gold and Denise S. Yanof, "Mothers, Daughters, and Girlfriends," *Journal of Personality and Social Psychology*, vol. 49 (September 1985), pp. 654–59.

10. Suzanne Daly, "Little Girls Lose Their Self-Esteem on Way to Adolescence, Study Finds," *The New York Times*, January 9, 1991, p. B6.

11. Phillipe Aries, *Centuries of Childhood: A Social History of Family Life*, translated by Robert Baldwick (New York: Vintage Books, 1962), Joseph Kett, *Rites of Passage: Adolescence in America, 1790 to the Present* (New York: Basic Books/Harper Colophon, 1977).

12. Manifest functions are stressed in the discussion of the importance of education in the lives of school-age children by Newman and Newman, *Development through Life*, pp. 306–08.

13. Daniel Goleman, "Schools Try to Tame Violent Pupils, One Punch and One Taunt at a Time," *The New York Times*, August 19, 1993, p. B11.

14. Christopher Jencks et al., *Inequality: A Reassessment of the Effect of Family and School in America* (New York: Harper & Row, 1972). For other critiques of school life, see Ralph W. Larking, *Suburban Youth in Cultural Crisis* (New York: Oxford University Press, 1979), and Miriam Wasserman (editor), *Demystifying School: Writings and Experiences* (New York: Frederick A. Praeger, 1974).

15. See Betty Levey, "The School's Role in the Sex-Role Stereotyping of Girls: A Feminist Review of the Literature," and Phyllis Taube MacEwan, "Girls Don't Play with Cars, Linda," in Wasserman (editor), *Demystifying School*, pp. 111–14, 327–29.

16. Herman Schwendinger and Julia Siegel Schwendinger, *Adolescent Subcultures and Delinquency* (New York: Frederick A. Praeger, 1985), pp. 3–58.

17. Seth Mydans, "Not Just the Inner City: Well-to-Do Join Gangs," *The New York Times*, April 10, 1990, p. A10.

18. Newman and Newman, *Development through Life*, p. 359.

19. Ibid., p. 357.

20. U.S. Department of Health and Human Services, Center for Disease Control, *Morbidity and Mortality Weekly*, vol. 40, nos. 51 and 52 (January 3, 1992).

21. Nancy Gibbs, "How Should We Teach Our Children about Sex?" *Time*, May 14, 1993, pp. 60–65.

22. Richard Toman and Sheldon D. Rose, "Coping with Stress: A Multimodal Approach," *Social Work*, vol. 30 (March–April 1985), pp. 151–52.

23. Kent M. Van DeGraaff and Stuart Ira Fox, *Concepts of Human Anatomy and Physiology* (Dubuque, IA: William C. Brown Publishers, 1986), p. 600. See Hans Selye, *The Stress of Life* (New York: McGraw-Hill, 1956) and *Stress without Distress* (Philadelphia: J. B. Lippincott, 1974).

24. DeGraaff and Fox, *Concepts of Human Anatomy and Physiology*, p. 600.

25. James H. Johnson, *Life Events as Stressors in Childhood and Adolescence* (Beverly Hills, CA: Sage, 1986), pp. 23–26.

26. A. D. Kanner, J. C. Coyne, C. Schaefer, and R. S. Lazarus, "Comparison of Two Modes of Stress Measurement: Daily Hassles and Uplifts versus Major Life Events," *Journal of Behavioral Medicine*, vol. 4 (1981), pp. 3, 6.

27. A. D. Kanner, S. S. Feldman, D. A. Weinberger, and M. E. Ford. "Uplifts, Hassles, and Adaptational Outcomes in Early Adolescents," in A. Monat and R. S. Lazarus (editors), *Stress and Coping: An Anthology*, 3rd ed. (New York: Columbia University Press, 1991), pp. 158–79.

28. Ibid., pp. 176–79.

29. See John and Virginia Demos, "Adolescence in Historical Perspective," *Journal of Marriage and the Family*, vol. 31 (November 1969), pp. 635–36.

30. Cited in Erikson, *Childhood and Society*, pp. 306–07.

31. Carl Tischler, "Detection and Prevention of Suicidal Behavior in Adolescents," in L. E. Arnold (editor), *Preventing Adolescent Alienation* (Lexington, MA: Lexington Books, 1983), p. 98.

32. Daniel Offer, "Adolescent Development: A Normative Perspective," in S. I. Greenspan and

G. H. Pollock (editors), *The Course of Life*, vol. II: *Latency, Adolescence, and Youth*, U.S. Department of Health and Human Services Publication No. (ADM) 80–999 (Washington, DC, 1980), pp. 357–72.

33. David G. Oldham, "Adolescence Turmoil: A Myth Revisited," *Journal of Continuing Education in Psychiatry*, vol. 39 (March 1978), pp. 23–32.

34. Joseph D. Noshphitz, "Disturbances in Early Adolescent Development," in Greenspan and Pollock (editors), *Course of Life*, vol. II, pp. 316–17.

35. James E. Marcia, "Identity in Adolescence," in J. Adelson (editor), *Handbook of Adolescent Psychology* (New York: John Wiley and Sons, 1980), pp. 159–87.

36. Katherine B. Hoyenga and Kermit Hoyenga, *The Question of Sex Difference* (Boston, MA: Little, Brown, 1979), p. 5.

37. Marie Richmond-Abbott, *Masculine and Feminine: Sex Roles over the Life Cycle* (New York: Random House, 1983), pp. 26–27.

38. Newman and Newman, *Development through Life*, pp. 236–45.

39. Ibid., p. 243.

40. Walter Mishel, "A Social-Learning View of Sex Differences in Behavior," in E. Maccoby and C. Jacklin (editors), *The Psychology of Sex Differences* (Stanford, CA: Stanford University Press, 1974), pp. 56–81.

41. Paul B. Mussen, J. J. Conger, and Jerome Kagan, *Child Development and Personality* (New York: Harper & Row, 1974).

42. Alfred Kinsey et al., *Sexual Behavior in the Human Male* (Philadelphia: Saunders, 1948), and *Sexual Behavior in the Human Female* (Philadelphia: Saunders, 1953).

43. Michael D. Storms, "Theories of Sexual Orientation," *Journal of Personality and Social Psychology*, vol. 38, no. 5 (1980), pp. 783–92.

44. American Psychiatric Association, *Diagnostic and Statistical Manual*, 3rd ed., rev. (Washington, DC, 1987), pp. 296–560.

45. For a strong statement on homosexuality as a pathology, see Robert Endleman, *Psyche and Society: Exploration in Psychoanalytic Sociology* (New York: Columbia University Press, 1981), pp. 235–330.

46. Juliet Mitchell, *Psychoanalysis and Feminism* (New York: Vintage, 1975), p. 11.

47. John Money, *Gay, Straight, and In-Between: The Sexology of Erotic Orientation* (New York: Oxford University Press, 1988), pp. 9–50.

48. Roger Brown, *Social Psychology: The Second Edition* (New York: Free Press, 1986), pp. 359–60.

49. Simon LeVay, "A Difference in Hypothalamic Structure Between Heterosexual and Homosexual Men," *Science*, vol. 253 (5023), August 30, 1991, pp. 1034–37.

50. Marcia Baranaga, "Is Homosexuality Biological?" *Science*, August 31, 1991, vol. 253 (5023), p. 956.

51. Joseph A. Baldwin, "Theory and Research Concerning the Notion of Black Self-Hatred: A Review and Reinterpretation," *The Journal of Black Psychology*, vol. 5 (February 1979), pp. 51–77.

52. M. K. Mayovich, "Political Activation of Japanese American Youth," *Journal of Social Issues*, vol. 29, no. 2 (1973), pp. 167–85.

53. Jean S. Phinney, "Ethnic Identity in Adolescents and Adults: A Review of Research," *Psychological Bulletin*, vol. 108, no. 3 (1990), pp. 502–03. Besides her own theory and that of James Marcia, she incorporates ideas from William E. Cross, Jr., "The Thomas and Cross Models of Psychological Nigrescence: A review," *Journal of Black Psychology*, vol. 5 (August 1978), pp. 13–31, and Donald R. Atkinson, George Morten, and Derald Wing Sue, *Counseling American Minorities: A Cross-Cultural Perspective* (Dubuque, IA: William C. Brown, 1979), pp. 191–201.

54. Cross, "Thomas and Cross Models."

55. Atkinson, Morten, and Sue, *Counseling American Minorities*.

56. Daniel Offer, Eric Ostrov, and Kenneth I. Howard, "The Self-Image of a Group of Physically Ill Adolescents," in R. W. Blum (editor), *The Disabled and Chronically Ill Adolescent* (New York: Grune and Stratton, 1984).

57. Ibid.

CHAPTER 18

Life-Span Development
Early, Middle, and Later Adulthood

MAJOR THEMES DISCUSSED IN THIS CHAPTER

1. **EARLY AND MIDDLE ADULTHOOD.** The adult years are marked by physical and biological changes, by occupational roles, by intimate relationships, and by spousal and parental roles in families. With successful resolution of the psychosocial crises associated with these periods, the individual can achieve intimacy and generativity.

2. **PSYCHOLOGICAL DEVELOPMENT IN ADULT LIFE: CRISIS, STRESS, AND MENTAL HEALTH.** Adults may experience psychological problems that are directly related to their age or to the status and roles they occupy in society. These include a possible midlife crisis, stress, and mental health. Since gender is central to the adult experience, differences between men and women in these areas are highlighted.

3. **SEXUAL HARASSMENT.** For women and men in early and middle adulthood, an issue related to their involvement in work is sexual harassment. As women have entered men's occupations and taken traditionally male roles, the pursuit of equal opportunities has come to include freedom from unwanted sexual attention.

4. **GROWTH OR DECLINE AND DEVELOPMENT IN LATER ADULTHOOD.** Physically, this period is marked by eventual decline, as well as cognitive changes. Psychologically and socially, it may be seen as a period of disengagement initiated by retirement or as a period of continued involvement and psycholsocial growth in which the older person finds ways to remain productive and actively engaged with others. The psychosocial crisis is resolved by achieving ego integrity as the elderly come to grips with the meaning of their lives and their place in society and the spiritual world.

5. **DEPRESSION AND AGING.** Research findings on the relation between depression and aging have not established that depression is likely to be experienced by persons in one stage of adulthood more than those in another stage. The strategies used to study this connection must be improved.

6. **IMPLICATIONS FOR PRACTICE.** Social service workers who work with adults must anticipate and understand the problems such clients are likely to present. Helping them involves individual help with problems as well as work in the political, social, and economic environments to secure the resources necessary to solve these problems.

∞ GROWTH AND DEVELOPMENT IN EARLY AND MIDDLE ADULTHOOD

Erik Erikson proposes three stages of adult development, early, middle, and later adulthood. Early adulthood (about ages 23–30) provokes a crisis of intimacy that has to do with the ability to form deep interpersonal attachments in love and work. In middle adulthood (ages 31–50), the crisis of **generativity** involves the desire and the ability to contribute creatively and productively to society. If the personal and social resources available to adults in these stages enable them to resolve these crises, development occurs, and love and care emerge as basic ego strengths. If not, the pathologies of exclusivity and rejectivity mark the personality.

Physical and Biological Changes

In early adulthood most individuals are at the peak of their biological and physiological capacities. Physical strength and the ability to procreate are fully developed. Depending on the individual, cognitive development at the level of formal operations, which allows for abstract reasoning in the solution of problems, may have been achieved in late adolescence, may appear at this stage, or may never be achieved.

A period of physical stability can be expected until middle adulthood, but susceptibility to disease and decline increase throughout the adult years. The rate of heart conditions per 1,000 persons in 1990, for instance, was 27 for males under 45 years of age but 137 for males 45–64 years old; for females, the rate was 34 among those under 45 and 102 for those 45–64.[1] Eventually skin and muscle start to lose elasticity and tone, and the ability to see, hear, taste, smell, and even feel pain begins to diminish. Motor skills and reaction time decrease, and there is usually some loss of energy.

Accidents are the leading cause of death for persons age 25–44. In 1990, the rate of death from accidents was 34 per 100,000 persons this age, but it was 54 for males and 15 for females. Cancer ranked second as a cause of death in this age group, 27 per 100,000, and HIV infection ranked third, with a rate of 23 deaths per 100,000 persons, 42 for males and 5 for females. For persons aged 45–64, cancer and cardiovascular disease are the leading causes of death. In 1990 the rate of deaths from cancer was 292 per 100,000 persons in that age category, and for deaths from heart disease it was 233, 342 for males and 133 for females.[2]

Although sexual pleasure can be enjoyed throughout the adult years, reproductive abilities decline in the **climacteric period**, and for women, they end. In men, the hormonal changes in testosterone and other androgens which limit reproduction take place gradually, over a long period. In women, the decrease in production of estrogen which accompanies the cessation of menstruation, referred to as the **menopause**, is more abrupt and takes place in their late 40s and early 50s. The climacteric may produce other physical symptoms such as impotence and difficulties in becoming aroused, and it may be accompanied by such psychological states as depression, a loss in self-esteem, and diminished interest in sexual relations. These physical and psychological troubles are related to the social context of aging, including sexism, and are not an inherent part of the aging process.[3]

Psychosocial Crises in Early and Middle Adulthood

Early adulthood is marked by the psychosocial crisis of *intimacy vs. isolation*. A new set of needs and demands emerge as older adolescents complete their education and become ready to enter the adult world. Young adults are ready for intimacy; that is, they have the capacity to commit themselves to concrete affiliations and partnerships and to abide by such commitments, even though doing so may require significant sacrifices and compromises. In large part intimacy is of a sexual nature and is legitimated through marriage, but it can also involve meaningful relationships with friends, teachers, family members, and fellow workers. In committing themselves to one another, young adults give up a part of themselves. Thus the fear is ego loss; if they cannot achieve intimacy, they may develop a deep sense of isolation and self-absorption.

It is in early adulthood that sexual gratification is finally fulfilled. To Erikson, the "utopia" of developed sexuality means:

1. mutuality of orgasm
2. with a loved partner
3. of the other sex
4. with whom one is able and willing to share a mutual trust
5. with whom one is able and willing to regulate the cycles of
   a. work
   b. procreation
   c. recreation
6. so as to secure to the offspring, too, all the stages of a satisfactory development.[4]

Other theorists do not limit normal adult sexuality to heterosexual, procreative functions, as we noted in Chapter 8. Mutuality of orgasm and procreation are not always seen as values or as indications of competent development by contemporary sexologists, and homosexuality is no longer officially recognized as indicative of unhealthy development or mental disorder.

If the young adult does develop the ability to be intimate with others, love emerges as a strength. From a psychosocial point of view, *love* is defined as "the capacity for mutuality that transcends childhood dependency."[5] Thus adult love is different from the love of parent for child; it involves the ability to take care of as well as to be taken care of, being able to depend on another but also being dependable. Adults who become intimate must be able to meet each other's needs and accept each other's weaknesses. If a sense of isolation develops instead, the pathology of *exclusivity*, or shutting out others, takes over the personality. Adults may become excessively possessive and jealous and try to control the ones they love or unable to include and therefore to commit themselves to others. They may never in their lifetimes experience love for others.

Generativity vs. stagnation is the psychosocial crisis of middle adulthood. Adults assume roles such as parent by which they become responsible for establishing and guiding the next generation. Generativity, the drive to contribute to the continuance of the society, includes the creation of objects, services, and ideas of any nature, but Erikson emphasizes its procreative aspects. He believes having children is essential to human development, although he acknowledges that "there are individuals who, through misfortune or because of special and genuine gifts in other directions, do not apply this drive to their own offspring. And indeed, the concept of generativity is meant to include such more popular synonyms as productivity and creativity, which, however, cannot replace it."[6]

Merely having children is not sufficient to establish generativity. The parent role must be taken seriously; parents who are not themselves cognitively, emotionally, and socially developed cannot guide the younger generation effectively. The crisis of middle adulthood thus involves the productive and creative capacities that emanate from maturity. The struggle is against stagnation, that is, not being able to accomplish anything. Stagnation occurs when adults do nothing or are thwarted in the use of their mature abilities. A sense of stagnation is often evident in people who are having difficulties in their roles as parent or worker. Resolving this adult crisis produces the strength of *care*, "the commitment to be concerned for what has been generated,"[7] in order to assure the next generation's life and strength. Life's decisions are weighed against the interests of others, and attachment becomes complete, as much a commitment to others' needs and interests as one's own. When the crisis overwhelms a person, the pathology of *rejectivity*, "the unwillingness to include certain others or groups of others in one's generative concern,"[8] marks the personality. These adults reject the feeling of caring about others and about society.

Social Relationships

The crises of intimacy and generativity are played out within a wide radius of significant relationships with associates in the world of work, acquaintances, friends, and lovers. Most younger adults aspire to form deep, enduring sexual and emotional commitments to other persons, and intimate relationships are central to their individual development.[9] They devote considerable time to dating and selecting a partner, and most eventually marry and have or adopt children. In middle adulthood they get involved in the tasks of learning to live with another person and managing a household; even if they divorce most parents participate in the rearing of their children. They help their adolescent children become independent and at the same time may be called on to help care for their own parents (see the section on the family life cycle in Chapter 11).

A basic way in which creative capacities are applied in the pursuit of generativity is in the realm of occupational success and economic security. While these goals formerly occupied men more than women, most women now pursue them at some time during their adult years, and a growing number support their families. Adults also join political, religious, and other voluntary associations which help them achieve generativity by contributing to their development or serving civic functions.

As adults interact within their radius of significant relationships, they experience the conflicts and contradictions in the society. The class, ethnic, racial, and gender statuses occupied by adults can affect their ability to perform the tasks and negotiate the crises of these periods. As the critical perspective on social service practice recognizes, American society is hostile to the development of some individuals. Economic insecurity, limited opportunities, prejudice, and discrimination impose disproportionate difficulties on members of lower-status groups, and they are more likely to experience the destructive effects of alienation, anomie, and inequity. That many in these groups do manage to achieve psychosocial development is testimony to their own strengths and to the support they receive from family, friends, and others, including social service workers.

∞ PSYCHOLOGICAL DEVELOPMENT IN ADULT LIFE: CRISIS, STRESS, AND MENTAL HEALTH

Erikson was among the first developmental theorists to call attention to periods of psychosocial development beyond adolescence, which he saw as extending through about age 22. Thus five of his eight stages are in the first 22 years of life, and only three are in the remaining 50 or more years in the average life course. In a concept of adulthood that takes into account the total life cycle, however, the personality is not essentially formed by the time adolescence is over but continues to develop throughout life.

Levinson's Seasons of Life

Daniel Levinson developed a psychological theory which focuses on additional periods of adult development, particularly in males, in *The Seasons of a Man's Life*, published in 1978. It is based on empirical research using biographical interviews with 40 North American men between the ages of 35 and 45. This sample was considered to represent diverse backgrounds and circumstances. One-fourth of the men were hourly workers in industry; one-fourth were top- and middle-management executives; one-fourth were university biologists; and one-fourth were novelists. Only 5 percent were black, and all had been heterosexually married at least once.[10]

Levinson did not include women in this study, but he applies his ideas to women as well as men (see "Life Patterns for Women and Men"). While the study used a relatively homogeneous sample of American males in the middle of the twentieth century, the periods and transitions described are considered to be universal. Levinson maintains that life structures evolve through an orderly sequence during the adult years, and "the essential character of the sequence is the same for all the men in our study and for the other men whose biographies we examined."[11]

Levinson's thesis is that there are seasons in the lives of men and women, a series of periods or stages within the life cycle. His seasons, or eras, are based on chronological age, more-or-less unaffected by social or cultural considerations. The seasons he is interested in are early and middle adulthood, which he considers to be the chronological years between ages 17 and 65. (There are two other overlapping eras, childhood and adolescence, 0–22 years, and late adulthood, 60 years and older.) Within each era he articulates stable periods of development lasting about six to eight years. These periods are joined by transitional periods of up to five years in which men evaluate their position in life and explore new options. In the transitional periods individuals acquire their *life structure*, the set of internal values, ideals, and aspirations which are played out through participation in the external world of family and occupation.[12]

Transitional periods are extremely important because they are the times when established life structures are discarded or revised and new life structures are created. To Levinson, a developmental transition marks the termination of a time in a person's life. In these periods, the tasks are to accept the losses of the end of a period, review and evaluate the past, decide what to keep of the past and what to reject, and consider the possibilities for the future. In Levinson's words:

> One is suspended between past and future, and struggling to overcome the gap that separates them. Much from the past must be given up—separated from, cut out of one's life,

---

Life Patterns for Women and Men

Research for the life-cycle study reported in *The Seasons of a Man's Life*, by Daniel J. Levinson and his colleagues, was limited to men because the differences between the genders were considered to be so great that separate analysis was needed. They concluded that women and men go through the same adult developmental periods, but they do so in partially different ways which reflect their biological inheritance and social circumstances.

While there have been no major studies on age-related sequences in female development which are comparable to that done by Levinson et al., Gail Sheehy built on their work in her 1970s best-seller *Passages: Predictable Crises of Adult Life*. Rather than concentrating on a single gender, she set out to compare the "developmental rhythms" of men and women. In her opinion, "The fundamental steps of expansion that will open a person, over time, to the full flowering of his or her individuality are the same for both genders. But men and women are rarely in the same place struggling with the same question at the same age." (p. 22)

To substantiate her ideas, Sheehy collected 115 life stories of Americans in the "pacesetter group"—healthy, motivated members of the middle class from 18 to 55 years old. The men were students, professionals, or businessmen; the women were top achievers or in traditional, nurturing roles. Sheehy found quite different "life patterns" for men and women, determined by the choices they made in their twenties.

Sheehy classified the men as the *transients*, unwilling or unable to make firm commitments; the *locked in*, or committed; and the *wunderkind*, who create risks and play to win. Less common patterns were *never-married men*; *paranurturers*, such as clergymen or husbands who nurture their wives; and *latency boys*, who avoid the process of adolescence and remain bound to their mothers. A seventh category, the *integrators*, was created to describe those men who try to balance their ambitions with a commitment to their families, consciously working to be ethical and of benefit to society while they ensure their own economic success.

She identifies fewer life patterns for the women, who "must improvise a timetable around the needs of others." (p. 157) Traditionally the most common have been the *caregivers*, who have no desire to go beyond the domestic role when they marry in their twenties. *Either-or* women feel required to choose between love and children or work and accomplishment. This category includes both nurturers who defer achievement and achievers who defer nurturing. *Integrators* try to do it all, integrating marriage, career, and children. There are also *never-married women*, as well as *transients* who wander sexually, occupationally, and geographically in their twenties and most of their lives.

Source: Gail Sheehy, *Passages: Predictable Crises of Adult Life* (New York: Bantam Books, 1977).

---

rejected in anger, renounced in sadness or grief. And there is much that can be used as a basis for the future. Changes must be attempted in both self and world.[13]

The changes in the transitional periods leading to mature adult life are described by Judith Viorst this way:

> Breaking away from the pre-adult world—the Early Adult Transition—between ages seventeen and twenty-two. Making, during our twenties, our first commitments to a job, a life-style, a marriage. Revising our selections in our late twenties and early thirties—the Age Thirty

Transition—to add what is missing, to modify and exclude. Settling down and investing ourselves, during most of our thirties, in work, friends, family, community, whatever. And reaching, at about forty, those bridging years which take us from early to middle adulthood. Levinson calls this time the Mid-Life Transition. For most of us it's a crisis—a mid-life crisis.[14]

Transitions to the Midlife Crisis

The Levinson study could be used as a basis for delineating the periods and transitions throughout the life course, but the major aim was to study men as they resolve the crisis of the midlife transition, from about age 40 to 45. Levinson proposes that men form their dream, their vision of what adulthood will hold for them in occupational and familial terms, in the early adult transition, ages 17–22. In developing the dream and learning how to reach it, they benefit from a **mentor relationship** with another man, generally someone eight to ten years older, with experience and seniority in the world they wish to enter. The mentor is a transitory figure, someone extremely important only at that moment in the young man's life. The dream is played out in the stable novice period, marked by the choice of an occupation and the start of a career. The other key relationship for the man in this period is with a woman he loves; this dream is played out by marrying and having a family. The special quality of the loved woman in the man's life at this stage is her connection to his dream, her ability to make him feel capable of achieving it.

Before settling down in early adulthood, the novice undergoes another transition between about ages 28 and 32 during which he works on the flaws and limitations of his dream. He is concerned about advancement, social rank, income, power, fame, creativity, and quality of family life and attacks the dream of life in earnest. He tries to become his own man and to establish his niche in life, to feel self-assured and confident. Sometimes he succeeds and sometimes he does not. By age 40, however, the settled man's quest for advancement, his early adult life structure, no longer is sufficient, and he enters the midlife transition.

The dream is different for women, though Levinson found in a study of 45 women in their middle years that women go through the same sequence of periods at the same ages as men do, and even the most traditional women wrestle with a crisis in midlife.[15] For men, the dream that motivates young adulthood is essentially centered on occupations; while they also have family dreams most believe they are taking care of their families through the economic support they provide. Women have more difficulty forming their dream of adulthood, since they are conflicted between yearnings for a career and yearnings for a family, and the two roles do not mesh as they do for men. Men are the heroes of their own dreams; women participate both in their own heroic dreams and the dreams of their husbands. As a result, many women with careers do not have long-term career goals, and some traditional women consciously marry men who will create a dream in which they can have a significant part. Moreover, few women have either of the relationships on which men can rely in their twenties, the mentor to help them get established in a career or a loving helpmate to provide domestic support.

For the increasingly smaller proportion of women who only participate in their husbands' dreams and devote themselves to family concerns, the midlife crisis can take the form of the **empty-nest syndrome**, a feeling of loss when the youngest child leaves home. Most women today nurture their own occupational goals, however. Midlife may represent the time when, having fulfilled their child-care obligations, they can resume their careers or prepare for and take on new ones. Thus at the same time the husband may be resolving his midlife crisis by reconsidering his career and making firmer attachments to his family, the wife may be devoting less attention to family and more to career. Psychologists call this problem being out of phase, or *the career trajectory problem*.[16]

During the **midlife crisis**, both women and men must find themselves again by participating in a new search for identity. They may become confused about what their actual desires, values, talents, and aspirations really are, and in clarifying them seek to define and understand themselves. According to Levinson, the midlife crisis involves struggles at integration, or unifying opposing tendencies, in four polarities, each a statement about the nature of human development. The *young/old polarity* poses the questions, "What does it mean to no longer be young?" and "What does it mean to be old?" The *destruction/creation polarity* presents the problem of attempting to find a balance between aggressive needs and expressive, creative needs. The *masculine/feminine polarity* confronts individuals anew with their masculine and feminine sides and suggests the need to incorporate them in gender-role behavior. And in the *attachment/separation polarity*, the task is to reconcile the masculine desire for autonomy and independence with the feminine desire for affiliation, affection, and approval.[17]

By age 45, these struggles must be resolved if adult development is to take place. The search for meaning in life requires building a new life structure and putting it into practice. Life goes on.

Is There Really a Crisis in Midlife?

Levinson argues that a midlife crisis is normal, particularly in men, from about age 40 to age 45. He believes this crisis is a function of age per se and not of the social roles and situations that people find themselves in. He recognizes that some men do not experience a midlife crisis, and some experience only a very minor crisis. For a great majority of men, however, Levinson says, "this is a period of great struggle within the self and with the external world."[18]

The idea of an age-40 crisis is suspect to many researchers; conflict in adulthood appears to be very common, but it is not necessarily associated with any particular chronological age. While crisis is often evident in the middle-adult years, it is not singularly noticeable between the ages of 40 and 45; some experience crisis then, and others thrive.[19]

George Vaillant analyzed the results of the Grant Study of Adult Development, which traces the long-range psychological health of 268 men who were Harvard students in the classes of 1942 and 1944. In 1972 he and Charles McArthur published findings that these men worked hard at their careers between the ages of 25 and 35, and by age 30 their potential for excellence had been "lost to conformity." The years from 35 to 49 were much more tumultuous, marked by depression and doubts, but the men who faced up to the reappraisal of midlife looked back at that period as the happiest in their lives.[20] Later research by Vaillant has borne out Erikson's proposal that generativity is the hallmark of midlife development (see "Caring, Not Crisis, at Midlife").

Stress and Adult Roles

Another way of examining adult psychosocial development is by looking at the stresses associated with adult roles as they are affected by aging. Adulthood is not simply a time when individuals act out the feelings and dispositions they acquired in childhood; it offers new experiences which contribute to personality and behavioral change. Two new role experiences dominate the lives of most adults: They enter the workforce, and they form

Caring, Not Crisis, at Midlife

New research that goes beyond the midlife crisis in examining psychological development in the middle years of adulthood has supported Erik Erikson's contention that for a person who has mastered the psychosocial crises from infancy to early adulthood, midlife will be a time of caring for others and contributing to society. Successful resolution of the generativity vs. stagnation crisis requires the individual to find a way to help assure continuance of the society. Daniel Goleman, writing in *The New York Times*, notes that "Researchers are finding that for many, middle age is the most fruitful phase of life, a time when intense preoccupations with marriage and career have faded and the inevitable deterioration of the body is yet to come."

The researchers do not agree on what constitutes middle age. Most go beyond Erikson's ages 31–50 to include the years between 50 and 65 in the period. A survey of attitudes toward middle age in 1989 found that most of the 1,200 respondents defined middle age in terms of events in the life course rather than years. They saw the middle years as a time of concern and caring; 84 percent agreed that "at middle age, a person becomes more compassionate to the needs of others," and 89 percent said middle age is a time of becoming closer to friends and family.

A survey of 12,600 persons age 51–61 for an ongoing study of Americans nearing retirement conducted by the University of Michigan for the National Institute on Aging reported in 1993 that despite their concerns for job security and uncertainty over the future, they are generous to their families. More than one-third gave at least $500 to a child in 1992, two out of five of the grand-mothers averaged 20 hours a week caring for grandchildren, and one-fourth of the single women provided care for their parents.

George E. Vaillant examined the psychological defenses of 204 men from the Harvard classes of 1940 to 1942 whose psychological growth is being studied at regular intervals. His analysis included data from the men's college years to their 60s. He found that as adolescents, they were twice as likely to use immature defenses such as fantasy; as young adults, the results were reversed, and they were twice as likely to use mature defenses such as humor, creativity, and altruism. By midlife, however, they were four times more likely to use mature defenses.

According to Vaillant, the caring and deepening of relationships evident in midlife takes a wide variety of forms: "It can be getting more involved with your grown children or delighting in your adolescents and encouraging them to flourish, coaching Little League, getting a church group off the ground, being the spirit behind a growth company, or a dynamic headmistress of a school." He found that the most giving among the men at middle age had been the most intense about developing their careers earlier in life, and those who had consolidated their careers and formed stable marriages were most caring and compassionate in midlife.

Sources: Daniel Goleman, "Compassion and Comfort in Middle Age," *The New York Times*, February 6, 1990, p. C1; "Midlife Americans Glum about Prospects," *AARP Bulletin*, vol. 34 (September 1993), p. 16; George Vaillant in J. Oldham and R. Liebert (editors), *The Middle Years: New Psychoanalytic Perspectives* (New Haven, CT: Yale University Press, 1989).

lasting sexual relationships. The latter role provides many with still a third new role experience—parenthood.

Leonard Pearlin and his associates have conducted a number of studies on the life strains and psychological distresses experienced by adults as they enter these new roles and the coping mechanisms they use to adapt to them. This research program is based on ideas that fit well with a critical perspective on social service practice. As Pearlin says, "adult emotional development does not represent the gradual surfacing of conditions that happen to reside within individuals. Instead, we see it as a continuing process of adjustment to external circumstances, many of them rooted in the organizations of the larger society and therefore distributed unequally across the population."[21]

Pearlin identifies the stressors associated with the life events associated with the three new adult roles. With regard to occupation, stressors are most likely to derive from the work environment (dirt, noise, or danger) and the social environment (work pressures and overload). In intimate relations, they are likely to be associated with inequalities in give and take, lack of reciprocity, or failure to fulfill expectations. Stressors associated with parenting include children's disobedience, deviations from their parents' expectations, lack of respect for parents, and failure to accept their parents' definitions of morality.[22]

Life events must be seen within the context of biological aging; the stressors experienced by younger and older adults are likely to be different. Life events that are either scheduled or unexpected also are likely to affect adults differently. Pearlin examined stressors with regard to the time of expected events such as entry into and retirement from occupations, marriage and widowhood, and the birth of children and unexpected crises such as being dismissed from a job, having an illness, or getting divorced.

Pearlin concluded that younger adults are more likely to experience work-related stress than older ones; they are more apt to feel job pressures and depersonalization, to have conflict with fellow workers and superiors, and to experience unexperienced events such as being laid off. Younger workers, particularly women, may leave occupations temporarily to care for the family. The only predictable event experienced more by older people is retirement from work, and Pearlin found that this event is not likely to create a great deal of emotional distress. Though it is marked by major changes in lifestyle, many older people look forward to them as offering opportunities to continue learning and developing.

Pearlin found that the stressors of marriage and parenthood are more evenly distributed across the adult life span. The two expected events, marriage and widowhood, usually occur at opposite ends. Younger adults are likely to experience stress related to their ability to fulfill expectations for spousal and parental roles, but the stressors related to parenting also affect older adults. For younger adults the stress comes from taking on the role of parent, rearing children, and seeing them off to school. For older adults, it comes from dealing with adolescents as they come of age and preparing the children for departure from the household.

An indication of the extent of stress-related problems in American society is the estimate by the National Institute of Mental Health's Epidemiologic Catchment Area Program of the number of mentally healthy people at risk of some mental disorder. The survey, described in the following section, found that some 30 to 50 million people in a given period could be expected to "experience a stressful life event that immobilizes their capacity to cope."[23]

Gender Roles and Mental Health

Because men are accorded greater status and privilege than women in American society, it might be expected that women would be more likely to have mental health problems.

The results of a study supported by the National Institute of Mental Health, however, suggest that gender roles place strains on both men and women, and each gender makes a different kind of adaptation.

In a survey conducted over several years in the 1980s, researchers from the National Institute of Mental Health (NIMH) interviewed 18,571 randomly selected, noninstitutionalized women and men 18 years of age or older in five urban or rural epidemiological catchment areas: New Haven, Connecticut; Baltimore, Maryland; St. Louis, Missouri; Durham, North Carolina; and Los Angeles, California. The purpose of the interviews was to determine whether the respondents had experienced a mental disorder during the preceding month, using the NIMH Diagnostic Interview Schedule (DIS), which is based on the *Diagnostic and Statistical Manual of the American Psychiatric Association* (see Chapter 3). The DIS covers cognitive impairment and a range of disorders, including drug and alcohol, schizophrenic, affective, anxiety, somatization (a disorder formerly known as hysteria), and antisocial disorders. The procedure was as follows:

> The DIS questions start with a lifetime frame of reference, such as "Have you ever had a period of time in your life, when you had a particular symptom?" Following this initial question, it is then determined whether the symptom caused sufficient change in a person's life or behavior to be clinically significant, and whether it was always due to drugs, alcohol, or physical disorders. All clinically significant symptoms of a particular diagnosis that were not entirely explained by physical causes were then listed, and the respondent was asked to date the last occurrence of the most recent one. If at least one symptom had occurred in the last month, the disorder was considered to have been present within the current one-month time frame.[24]

The researchers found that 15.4 percent of those interviewed had experienced at least one type of the covered disorders during the month prior to the interview. For the preceding six-month period, the percentage increased to 19.1, and for the lifetime of the individual it was 32.2. When the responses of these Americans were compared with studies in London, England; Edinburgh, Scotland; Australia; Athens, Greece; and Uganda, the results were about the same. The conclusion was that mental disorders are far more common than previously thought.[25]

With respect to gender, the researchers found that for women the one-month prevalence rate for disorders as a whole was only slightly higher than the overall rate, 16.6 percent of the respondents rather than 15.4. Some important differences were evident when individual disorders were compared by gender, however. Men had significantly higher rates of substance use and antisocial personality disorders, while for women, the rates for affective, anxiety, and somatization disorders were significantly higher. When reports of cognitive impairment were controlled by age, the rate was higher for men than for women between the ages of 65 and 84, and it was higher for women than for men at age 85 and over. Rates for schizophrenia and manic episode indicated no significant differences for women or men.

It can be concluded from these results that men and women are more or less equally likely to experience mental disorders, but the type of disorder and when they will experience it are related to gender. While there are significant differences, there is considerable overlap in the disorders experienced by men and by women. Many women do experience substance abuse and antisocial disorders, and many men suffer from depression, anxiety, and somatization.

In any case, gender role and status are important considerations in any explanation of adult mental disorders. Biological and genetic predispositions, stress related to life events, and intrapsychic or personality factors must be taken into account, but other factors related to the position of men and women in the society cannot be ignored. The potential for such disorders weighs heavily on both genders, and psychosocial factors associated with gender-role expectations also affect both. Just as the traditional emphasis on assertiveness and aggressiveness in males encourages substance abuse and antisocial behaviors, the traditional emphasis on passivity and emotionality in females encourages anxiety, depression, and psychosomatic complaints.

Depression in Women

The higher rates of depression among women found in the NIMH research and other studies may be due to the fact that women report relatively mild, clinically trivial symptoms more readily than men do. Joy Perkins Newmann argues that measurement error—mistakes in the way psychological tests are administered and scored—account for the finding that women are more likely to experience depression than men.[26]

A defining characteristic of depression is feeling sad, blue, discouraged, or depressed, but these common feelings do not by themselves justify a diagnosis of clinical depression. To be declared clinically depressed, a person would have to be troubled by chronic, persistent feelings that interfere with normal functioning as a husband, wife, parent, worker, or in some other adult role. Such feelings should not be transient or produced by unexpected events or crises.

In measuring depression, psychologists often compose scales, generally including items on sadness as well as self-deprecation, suicidal impulses, and feelings of hopelessness or worthlessness, on which they ask respondents to indicate their emotions. Newmann finds that if in scoring the responses the psychologist simply adds up a total depression score, women probably will be found to have higher rates of depression. If the scores on items measuring sadness are omitted, however, no significant differences in the depression scores by gender are likely. The difference between men and women in regard to depression is largely in their willingness to express sadness, not in their reports of other, more serious symptoms.

∞ SEXUAL HARASSMENT

Because early and middle adulthood are the years in which men and, increasingly, women, devote a good deal of their attention to their life's work, much of their psychosocial development occurs in this framework. An issue which has emerged in regard to employment in recent years is sexual harassment. Although it has a long history, there is no agreement as to precisely what it means. As a form of sexual discrimination it is covered in regard to equal opportunities for employment under Title VII of the Civil Rights Act of 1964. Lin Farley defines it as "unsolicited nonreciprocal male behavior that asserts a woman's sex role over her function as a worker. It can be any or all of the following: staring at, commenting upon, or touching a woman's body; requests for acquiescence in sexual behavior; repeated nonreciprocal propositions for dates; demands for sexual intercourse; and rape."[27]

Basically two types of sexual harassment are forbidden under Title VII, as specified in guidelines of the Equal Employment Opportunity Commission issued in 1980 and confirmed by the U.S. Supreme Court in 1986. **Quid pro quo harassment** is defined as "unwelcome sexual advances, requests for sexual favors, and other verbal or physical conduct of a sexual nature." Such conduct cannot be made a condition of employment, and a worker's submission to or rejection of it cannot be used as a basis for employment decisions affecting the worker. The guidelines also define in broad terms the second type of sexual harassment, a **hostile or offensive working environment**, which is created when the harassing conduct has the purpose of interfering with a person's work performance or creating intimidating working conditions. Exactly what is included in this category is being more specifically defined in the courts.[28]

In November 1993, the Supreme Court unanimously rejected a lower court's decision that a worker charging sexual harassment by the creation of a hostile working environment must prove psychological injury as well as harassing conduct in order to win the case. The lower court had ruled in *Harris* vs. *Forklift Systems* that even though Patricia Harris had suffered years of sexually derogatory remarks and suggestions from her boss at Forklift Systems, she was not entitled to compensation unless she could prove the conduct was "so severe as to be expected to seriously affect her psychological well-being." For Anita Hill, a law professor at the University of Oklahoma who had forcefully brought the problem of sexual harassment to public attention in the confirmation hearings for Supreme Court Justice Clarence Thomas two years earlier, news that the decision had been overthrown was welcome. In her words, "The harasser does not have the right to harass to the point at which the woman is at her wit's end."[29]

Working women have always had to deal with sexual harassment to some extent, but the problem has worsened as women have entered men's occupations and undertaken traditionally male work roles. Sexual harassment is not limited to the attitudes and behaviors of men toward women, however; cases of sexual harassment of men by women have been reported and some have reached the courts, and gay men and lesbians may be victimized by either or both sexes. Between 1991 and 1993 harassment cases filed in federal and state agencies nearly doubled, from 6,892 to 12,537, and total compensation awarded in these cases rose from $7.1 million to $25.7 million. In 1992 only about 1 in 4 cases was resolved in favor of the person bringing the complaint with the payment of compensation or some other settlement. Investigators could not find enough evidence to prove about one-third of the charges, and the claimants withdrew another fourth of them.[30]

According to a government study of female federal employees which reported in 1988 that 42 percent had experienced some form of sexual harassment during the preceding two years, young women and single or divorced women were more likely to report it than older, married women, and highly educated women were more likely to do so than less educated women.[31] Women have developed several options for dealing with sexual harassment which might also be used by men who find themselves in the position of victim (see "Coping with Sexual Harassment").

Feminist Positions on Sexual Harassment

Sexual harassment may be regarded as a natural result of differences between the sexes or as a consequence of male socialization gone wrong. From a feminist perspective, harassment is the "use of power derived from the economic or occupational sphere to gain benefits or to impose punishments in the sexual sphere."[32] This view emphasizes both the economic and the sexual inequalities underlying harassment; the control of employers over workers intersects with the control of men over women. As we have noted in earlier

---

Coping with Sexual Harassment

Women who experience sexual harassment may need help in coping with it in a functional way. Susan Ehrlich Martin suggests four options they might consider:

1. They may use informal methods of coping; that is, ignore the harasser or ask him to stop. This appears to be the most common method used, but it is not always successful. Some men do stop harassing when they're discouraged or asked to stop, but a sizable number do not.

2. They may quit their jobs or seek transfers. High turnover and absentee rates for female employees suggest that many do resort to this method, even though it may have negative implications for their careers.

3. They may seek formal grievances or bring legal suits. This can have favorable outcomes, but it can also result in reprisals such as being denied a promotion or being labeled a troublemaker.

4. They may acquiesce. The consequences range from having to put up with harassing behaviors such as stares, jokes, or teasing to being subjected to rape, assault, or other forms of force or exploitation.

All four options therefore have drawbacks, and a woman must carefully consider the pros and cons of each one. Martin advises that the best ways to cope with sexual harassment are to use formal procedures to report it and to seek the emotional support of friends and family. Women should learn the work organization's grievance procedures and line of responsibility with regard to harassment and should discuss incidents with trusted confidants to avoid such emotions as self-blame.

Source: Susan Ehrlich Martin, "Sexual Harassment: The Link Joining Gender Stratification, Sexuality, and Women's Economic Status," in J. Freeman (editor), *Women: A Feminist Perspective*, 4th ed. (Mountain View, CA: Mayfield, 1989), pp. 66–67.

---

chapters, despite recent advances women's place in the world of work is still characterized by lower average pay than men's, subordination to male supervisors, and concentration in sex-typed occupations with limited opportunities for advancement. In such circumstances men are likely to try to exercise their power, and women are likely to find it difficult to deal with unwanted sexual advances and innuendoes from males in a position of authority.

Carole Sheffield takes a more radical feminist position, arguing that women in most societies endure sexual terrorism at the hands of men. Sexual terrorism is "a system by which males frighten and, by frightening, control and dominate females," and harassment is one way male terrorism is exercised.[33]

One of the difficulties with a feminist approach is that it assumes only women are the object of sexual harassment. A conflict approach takes into account that men may also be harassed by women. It acknowledges the economic and sexual inequalities experienced by women, but it argues that these inequalities set up tensions which produce conflict between men and women as a natural outcome. Harassment therefore can be seen as a mode of conflict under which men attempt to dominate women and women attempt to challenge their domination. Since the power differential favors men, men are more likely to harass women, but women may also harass men.

☙ GROWTH OR DECLINE AND DEVELOPMENT IN LATER ADULTHOOD

In developmental theory, later adulthood, or maturity, is the last stage. Faced with inevitable physical decline and possible social isolation, individuals think through their lives introspectively, calling on their inner resources as they search for wisdom. The psychosocial crisis involves the conflict between ego integrity, leading to wisdom, and despair, leading to disdain.

The final stage in the life cycle has traditionally been defined as beginning at 65, the time when workers are expected to retire and give up their role of worker. However, this definition no longer holds. Some people retire much earlier, though many take up a second career. Others continue to work well into their 70s; the age at which social security benefits will be paid is scheduled to rise to 66 by the year 2009 and to 67 by 2027. Physically and socially, too, the period that can be called old age is beginning later as life expectancy lengthens. The U.S. Census Bureau reports some data in the categories of 65–74, 75–84, and 85 years of age and older, rather than just 65 and over.

In any case, later adulthood is a distinct stage of the life course. The family's children are grown, often married and with children of their own, and may live far away. Retirement brings changes in the person's identity as a productive member of the community and restrictions on social relationships at work as well as on income. Eventually spouses and friends die, leaving the elderly, women in particular, alone and grieving. Not only do women live longer than men, on average, but as they age they are more likely than men to be poor and living alone. They also shoulder most of the physical burden of caring for elderly members of their families[34] (see the sections on the elderly in the family in Chapter 8).

For these reasons, later adulthood has been described as a time of role loss or a period of disengagement in which the elderly turn inward and are motivated to withdraw from society.[35] However, such pessimistic views of this stage of life are not in keeping with the theory of psychosocial development. While it is certainly a time of role exit, all phases of life can be thought of in terms of role entrances and exits that bring changes in associations and self-concepts.[36] Cross-cultural studies of retired people have failed to demonstrate universal patterns of disengagement, even in similar environments,[37] and the amount of activity or involvement with the environment varies considerably in any society. In some theories of aging, the final stage is seen not as a period of loss but as a period of continued development in which adults take on different roles as learners, doers, and participants in relationships with others.[38] In the spirit of generativity, many older people contribute their knowledge, energy, and resources to their friends, families, and communities as volunteers rather than paid workers.

Life Expectancy and Physical Decline

For most people in the United States, the life cycle includes some period of aging. Life expectancy at birth, the average length of life for an individual, has increased steadily since 1920, when it was 54 years. The average life expectancy in 1991 was 75.7 years. Males born that year could expect to live 72.7 years, and females could expect to live almost seven years longer, to 79.4 years. Projections are that by the year 2010, the average life expectancy will be 77.6 years, 74.2 for males and 81.1 for females.[39]

These women are winners not only in the Senior Olympics but in remaining healthy, active, achieving, and engaged with others in the later
stages of adulthood.

At some point in later adulthood, most individuals begin to experience some degree
of physical and intellectual decline and eventual deterioration. Nevertheless, many older
people are healthy and function physically, sexually, and cognitively as well as they ever
did. As in all life stages, there are wide individual differences.

Studies of cognitive functioning among older people have found differences in the
two types of intelligence identified in human beings in the 1960s by Raymond Cattell and
John Horn: **fluid intelligence**, the ability to use new information, and **crystallized intelligence**, the ability to use old information—the knowledge accumulated from past
experience. While fluid intelligence has been found to decline with age, crystallized intelligence remains stable and may even increase, at least up to the eighth decade of life.
Crystallized intelligence has to do with verbal comprehension, including vocabulary, the
evaluation of experiences, and the association of words and phrases, such as the ability to
connect authors and titles. Fluid intelligence has to do with general reasoning skills, including the abilities to organize information, develop and test hypotheses, and approach
problems logically and systematically.[40]

Sexuality may also decline with age; older people may be slower to arouse due to
changes in hormonal levels in both males and females, and the opportunities for sexual intercourse may not be present. Diminished interest in sex is not a natural consequence of
aging, however; when it occurs the cause is likely to be psychological or social, such as
poor interpersonal relations between husband and wife.[41] With respect to physical capacities, attention to exercise and good nutrition allows many older people to remain
hearty, productive, independent, and active. Nevertheless, the decline in vision, hear-

ing, taste, and other senses that begins to be noticed in middle adulthood becomes very evident at this stage, and by age 70 almost two-thirds of the tastebuds and many of the sense receptors in the nose have died.[42] The rate of blindness and severe hearing loss goes up appreciably. Shrinking muscles, calcification of ligaments, and decreases in flexibility become obvious.

As the immune system produces fewer antibodies, the older person is left with less protection against disease and microorganisms, and acute and chronic illnesses are more likely.[43] About 80 percent of older people have at least one chronic condition, and as they age they develop multiple conditions.[44] The most common chronic conditions for Americans aged 65–74 and 75 and older are arthritis, heart conditions, and hypertension. Women suffer more from arthritis than men; in 1990 the rate per 1,000 persons age 65–74 was 472 for females and 373 for males, and for ages 75 and over, it was 629 for females and 377 for males. The hypertension rate was also higher for women, but men had higher rates for heart conditions, 275 per 1,000 compared to 242 for women at ages 65–74, and 405 compared to 292 for women at age 75 and over.[45] In many cases chronic conditions are not so debilitating that the person is disabled. Major limitations in functioning, to the extent that long-term care in or out of the home becomes necessary, occur in only about 15 percent of the cases.[46]

The elderly are also vulnerable to organic mental disorders, which may involve temporary or permanent brain damage and cause impaired memory, poor judgment, intellectual decline, or disorientation. Chronic brain syndrome, or senile dementia, occurs in about 15 to 30 percent of the population 85 years old and over.[47] Premature senile mental deterioration is now recognized as **Alzheimer's disease**, a degenerative disease of the central nervous system which results in progressive deterioration of brain cells. This life-shortening illness can strike adults of all ages, but only a small minority are under 50 years of age; most are over 65. It produces such effects as memory loss, confusion, speech impairment, and personality changes. Recognition of the disease is helping to destroy the perception of senility as a normal condition of aging. Only about 5 percent of older people are afflicted by Alzheimer's.[48]

The principal cause of death for Americans 65 years and older are heart disease and cancer, in reverse order to the causes for death among those 45–64 years old. At this stage the death rate from heart disease in women approaches that for men, though it is still smaller; in 1990 it was 1,735 per 100,000 population for women 65 and older, and 2,180 for men. The death rate from cancer was much higher for men, however, 1,468 compared to 871 for women. Next in order as the cause of death for people age 65 and older were strokes, pulmonary disease, pneumonia and influenza, and diabetes; accidents came last in the list of principal causes.[49]

The Psychosocial Crisis

According to Erikson, *ego integrity vs. despair* is the psychosocial crisis in later adulthood, as individuals come to grips with the meaning of their lives and their place in the social world and the spiritual order. *Ego integrity* means coming to accept "one's one and only life cycle as something that had to be and that, by necessity, permitted of no other substitutions."[50] The person comes to love and respect not the self so much as all humanity. Those who are not able to accept their lives may fear death, be disgusted with self and humanity, and experience remorse and despair. While old age is marked by physical decline and deterioration, it nevertheless presents additional possibilities for development.

If the crisis of old age is resolved, the strength of *wisdom*, "the detached yet active concern with life itself in the face of death"[51] pervades the personality. Wisdom requires a vision of humankind, that is, an idea of how all the past, present, and future generations fit together. If despair takes over, old age can generate the pathology of *disdain*; the frail elderly may feel scorn for their own and others' weakness and become bitter.

Peck's Crises in Aging

Robert Peck developed a stage theory of aging with three crises rather than one. Two of these, *ego differentiation vs. work-role preoccupation* and *body transcendence vs. body preoccupation*, represent innovations; the third, *ego transcendence vs. ego preoccupation*, is essentially a restatement of Erikson's ego integrity vs. despair. Although Peck, like so many developmental theorists, focuses on men, his ideas have been used as a framework for understanding older women as well.[52]

Peck acknowledges that later adulthood is a time of role loss, when people retire from paid work, become widowed, lose friends, and no longer have direct responsibility for children. But he also sees it as a time of transition in which these losses must be compensated for psychologically, and new positive, useful definitions of the self must be acquired. He defines *ego differentiation* as the capacity to pursue and enjoy activities and to value oneself as a person, without relation to the roles of adulthood.

It is also a time of physical decline. To remain emotionally healthy, older people must be able to overcome their physical concerns and preoccupation with the deterioration of their bodies. *Body transcendence* is the capacity to feel whole, worthwhile, and happy because of one's social and mental powers and activities, regardless of physical health. It also involves the ability to be satisfied with one's body and to continue to have sexual interests.

As the inevitability of death becomes unavoidable, individuals tend to become preoccupied with their private, self-centered desires. *Ego transcendence* is the capacity to engage others in a direct, active, and emotionally gratifying manner. It involves the ability to remain concerned about others and find satisfaction in fulfilling the needs of others.

As a test of his theory, Peck studied personal adaptability and flexibility in a sample of men from ages 45 to 65 living in the Midwest during the 1950s. He was interested in whether aging brings a decline in adaptive capacities, that is, whether older people are preoccupied with their work roles, bodies, and egos. On the basis of cultural stereotypes, he hypothesized that a decline in adaptability would be evident, and as people age they would be vulnerable to emotional turmoil. However, he concluded that this is not the case. Aging did not appear to produce any decline in emotional flexibility or ability to adapt. His data did show a positive correlation with social class; the higher the class, the greater the emotional stability and effectiveness.[53]

∞ EFFECTS OF AGING ON DEPRESSION

One issue in the literature on aging is whether or not increased risk of depression is associated with later stages in the life span. G. L. Klerman, for instance, says that mental illnesses generally are more prevalent among the elderly than among younger adults. He finds the incidence of depression particularly significant in persons 65 and older, for transient symptoms of depression as well as depressive disorders.[54] Depression can appear at any age, and more than half of those who have had one episode of major depression will have another at some point in their lives. When it appears later in life, symptoms such as slowed speech and movement and memory loss may be mistaken for signs of senility or stroke.[55]

However, the research literature does not provide consistent support for the hypothesis that the likelihood of depression will increase with age. Joy Perkins Newmann assessed the relationship between age and depression by reviewing studies that used representative community samples in the United States. Her conclusion was that because of conceptual and methodological problems in the study of depression, relatively little is known about the relationship between it and aging.[56]

In the studies Newmann reviewed, depression was usually measured in one of two ways, by using standardized psychological tests and scales or by making clinically based observations. Both techniques share a common conception of depression, but their purposes and goals differ. Standardized tests attempt to measure a common syndrome in the population, while the clinical diagnostic approach attempts to make further conceptual distinctions, such as those between feeling normal distress and suffering from clinical depression. Studies using standardized scales vary a great deal in the kind of sample, measurement instrument, and statistical procedures used. The findings reported also vary; some find no significant relation between age and depression, and those that do find relationships may conclude that depression is positively related, negatively related, or nonlinearly related to aging. In these studies, depression seems most associated with young adulthood and older adulthood but not with the middle years of adulthood. Studies using clinical diagnostic criteria to assess depression generate a very different generalization. In these studies, younger and older adults are less likely to show abnormal depression than people in the middle years of adulthood.[57]

Newmann argues that for better knowledge of the relation between depression and aging, the research strategies used to study the problem must be improved.[58] While she does not point out the implications for practitioners, her analysis suggests that social service and mental health workers should not just assume that elderly clients can be expected to experience severe depression. The rule of avoiding quick judgments based on stereotypes should be followed, and each client should be assessed independently.

❧ IMPLICATIONS FOR PRACTICE

In this chapter we have examined perspectives and issues on development in adulthood—for young adults, middle-aged adults, and the elderly. Especially with regard to adulthood, social service workers must avoid pigeonholing clients into stages of development based solely on their chronological age. The social roles and positions they occupy as well as their psychological states and processes must be taken into account. Then the concepts of life stages and developmental tasks and crises can be very useful in understanding the dynamics of individual behavior.

Social service workers must be able to anticipate the kinds of psychosocial struggles people in different periods of adulthood are likely to experience. Adults must learn to cope with problems of intimate relationships and with issues related to the meaning and importance of their lives, what they have accomplished, and what they will leave behind. As they age they come to terms with their physical capabilities and their productivity and usefulness. At any point in the life cycle, people may be confronted with death and struggle with its meaning.

The particular stresses and difficulties adults experience depend on a number of factors, especially their age and gender. Adults are affected by workplace-induced stress and the changes in lifestyle and self-concept attendant on retirement. Different kinds of stress are related to marriage and family. For younger adults it is related to starting or building intimate relationships and having and rearing children. For older adults stress follows from maintaining relationships and losing partners to parting, divorce, or death and from severing household bonds to children but maintaining emotional ties. Biological aging creates stress related to declining or changing physical and cognitive capacities as well as changes in environment.

Gender is a major consideration in the kinds of troubles adults experience. Women are much more likely than men to experience sexual harassment at work. They are not more likely than men to experience mental disorders, but the degree to which certain disorders affect the genders varies. Men have higher rates of substance abuse and antisocial personality disorders, and women's rates of affective, anxiety, and somatization disorders are higher. Women's higher rates of reported depression may be accounted for by feelings of sadness more than serious forms of depression.

Gender issues are particularly a factor in later adulthood, since on average women live longer than men. Older women especially may be poor and living alone, and stresses related to caring for the frail elderly fall much more heavily on women.

Being aware of the kinds of problems to be expected in adulthood can help social service workers develop empathy for clients in these stages of life. Compassion and understanding are essential qualities in workers who engage clients in problem solving and treatment. If they are also sensitive to the ways social environments can create difficulties for adults, workers can help them avoid the feeling that they are experiencing unique troubles and are totally to blame. With this kind of background, workers can develop intervention policies, programs, and services to enable adults to face the stresses and crises they encounter. Counseling and therapeutic services should reinforce clients' existing strengths while helping them build additional coping and adaptive capacities. Workers who take a critical social work perspective will also locate and develop the environmental resources necessary to deal with the stresses, troubles, and crises associated with the adult years.

∞ DISCUSSION QUESTIONS AND CLASS PROJECTS

1. Identify the following terms:

   menarche
   menopause
   gonads
   progesterone
   climacteric
   crystallized intelligence
   fluid intelligence
   quid pro quo harassment
   hostile working environment harassment
   Alzheimer's disease
   seasons of life
   mentor relationship

2. Describe the physical growth, change, and decline that can be expected in the adult stages of the life cycle.

3. Describe the social roles and relationships that are likely to form the context of developmental tasks, stresses, and crises in early, middle, and late adulthood.

4. Describe the psychosocial crises Erikson hypothesizes for these stages. To what extent do you believe these are the major crises of adulthood?

5. According to Levinson, midlife transitions for men and women are likely to produce an inner crisis or conflict. What does he see as the origins of the crisis, and what are the polarities around which it takes shape?

6. Robert Peck describes three crises of aging. What are they? What is the likelihood that older people will not be able to deal with these crises?

7. Are adult men more likely than adult women to experience mental disorders and depression?

8. How would you define sexual harassment? Based on your observations or experience, do you believe it is a serious problem for women at work or in school? Do men ever experience harassment? Why do you think sexual harassment takes place? How might you advise people to cope with it?

9. Are the elderly more likely to experience depression than younger adults?

10. To what extent do you believe the negative aspects of aging fall more heavily on women than on men? Is aging more of a women's issue or a men's issue?

11. The following role play can be done in front of the class or more privately as a three-person discussion group. One person plays the role of the social worker and the other the role of a young adult, middle-aged adult, or older adult client. The third person (or the class) plays the role of observer.

   In preparing for the role play the client should decide on his or her age and on the kind of trouble—real or made up—to present. The social worker should interview the client to determine the developmental stresses and crises the client is dealing with, using everyday, jargon-free language. The observer then comments on the interview, calling attention to what the social worker did and didn't do well.

   The next two study questions may be used to review ideas and concepts from Chapters 16, 17, and 18.

12. In groups of no more than six students, discuss the following: Do you believe you are in a particular stage of life? What stage is it? What do you see as the developmental tasks you are dealing with in the present? Do they resemble the tasks identified by Havighurst for someone of your general age category? What do you see as the developmental crises you are dealing with? Do they resemble the crisis Erikson discusses for someone in your age category?

13. How might you use the terms *development*, *tasks*, *crises*, *radius of significant relationships*, *basic strengths*, and *core pathologies* in an interview with a client? Would you use these terms or try to find a jargon-free way of expressing them? Can you think of different ways of saying the same things? For instance, how could you ask clients what their stage of development is or what tasks and crises they are dealing with? How would you inquire into their basic strengths and possible pathologies?

∞ NOTES

1. U.S. Bureau of the Census, *Statistical Abstract of the United States: 1993*, 113th edition (Washington, DC, 1993), Table 206.

2. Ibid., Table 128.

3. Cleo S. Berkun, "In Behalf of Women over 40: Understanding the Importance of Menopause," *Social Work*, vol. 31 (September–October 1986), pp. 378–84.

4. Erik Erikson, *Childhood and Society*, 2nd ed. (New York: W. W. Norton, 1963), p. 266.

5. Barbara M. Newman and Philip R. Newman, *Development through Life: A Psychosocial Approach*, 4th ed. (Chicago: Dorsey Press, 1987), p. 45.

6. Erikson, *Childhood and Society*, p. 267.

7. Newman and Newman, *Development through Life*, p. 45.

8. Ibid., p. 46.

9. Joseph Veroff, Elizabeth Douvan, and Richard A. Kulka, *The Inner American: Life, Work, and Mental Health from 1957–1967* (New York: Basic Books, 1981).

10. Daniel J. Levinson with C. N. Darrow, E. B. Klein, M. H. Levinson, and B. McGee, *The Seasons of a Man's Life* (New York: Alfred A. Knopf, 1978). For his application to both genders see Levinson, "A Conception of Adult Development," *American Psychologist*, vol. 41 (January 1986), pp. 3–13.

11. Ibid., p. 49.

12. See Vimala Pillari, *Human Behavior in the Social Environment* (Pacific Grove, CA: Brooks/Cole, 1988), p. 275.

13. Levinson, *Seasons of a Man's Life*, p. 51.

14. Judith Viorst, *Necessary Losses: The Loves, Illusions, Dependencies and Impossible Expectations That All of Us Have to Give Up in Order to Grow* (New York: Simon and Schuster, 1986), p. 266.

15. This study has yet to be published. Preliminary results were described in a news item by Patricia Leigh Brown, "Studying Seasons of a Woman's Life," *The New York Times*, September 14, 1987, p. 23.

16. Viorst, *Necessary Losses*, pp. 277–78.

17. Levinson, *Seasons of a Man's Life*.

18. Ibid., p. 60.

19. Anne Rosenfeld and Elizabeth Stark, "The Prime of Our Lives," *Psychology Today*, vol. 21 (May 1987), pp. 62–72.

20. George E. Vaillant and Charles C. McArthur, "Natural History of Male Psychological Health: I. The Adult Life Cycle from 18–50," *Seminars in Psychiatry*, vol. 4 (November 1972), pp. 415–27.

21. Leonard I. Pearlin, "Life Strains and Psychological Distress among Adults," in A. Monat and R. Lazarus (editors), *Stress and Coping: An Anthology*, 3rd ed. (New York: Columbia University Press, 1991), p. 325.

22. Ibid., pp. 313–36.

23. Gerald L. Klerman and Myrna M. Weissman, "An Epidemiologic View of Mental Illness, Mental Health, and Normality," in Daniel Offer and Melvin Sabshin (editors), *Normality and the Life Cycle: A Critical Integration* (New York: Basic Books, 1984), pp. 328, 331, 333.

24. Darrel A. Regier et al., "One-Month Prevalence of Mental Disorders in the United States," *Archives of General Psychiatry*, vol. 45 (November 1988), p. 978.

25. Ibid., pp. 977–86.

26. Joy Perkins Newmann, "Sex Differences in Symptoms of Depression: Clinical Disorder or Normal Distress?" *Journal of Health and Social Behavior*, vol. 25 (June 1984), pp. 136–59.

27. Lin Farley, *Sexual Shakedown: The Sexual Harassment of Women on the Job* (New York: McGraw-Hill, 1978), pp. 14–15.

28. Lloyd G. Nigro and Felix A. Nigro, *The New Public Administration*, 4th ed. (Itasca, IL: F. E. Peacock Publishers, 1994), Chapter 12, "Sexual Harassment."

29. Andrea Sachs, "A Dramatic Decision Produces New Guidelines for Judging Sexual Harassment," *Time*, November 22, 1993, pp. 44–45; Nancy Gibbs, "Office Crimes," *Time*, October 7, 1991, pp. 52–64, and "An Ugly Circus" in the same edition, pp. 35–40.

30. "The Supreme Court's Quick Turn," *U.S. News & World Report*, November 22, 1993, p. 11.

31. U.S. Merit Systems Protection Board, *Sexual Harassment in the Federal Workplace: Is It a Problem?* (Washington, DC, 1988).

32. Susan Ehrlich Martin, "Sexual Harassment: The Link Joining Gender Stratification, Sexuality, and Women's Economic Status," in J. Freeman (editor), *Women: A Feminist Perspective*, 4th ed. (Mountain View, CA: Mayfield, 1989), p. 63.

33. Carole J. Sheffield, "Sexual Terrorism," in J. Freeman (editor), *Women*, p. 3.

34. Ann Hartman, "Aging as a Feminist Issue," *Social Work*, vol. 35 (September 1990), pp. 387–88.

35. Bernice L. Neugarten, "Time, Age, and the Life Cycle," in M. Bloom (editor), *Life Span Development*, 2nd ed. (New York: Macmillan, 1985), p. 366; Elaine Cummings and William E. Henry, *Growing Old: The Process of Disengagement* (New York: Basic Books, 1961).

36. Zena Smith Blau, *Old Age in a Changing Society* (New York: New Viewpoints, 1973), pp. 243–44.

37. Vern L. Bengston, "Comparative Perspectives on the Microsociology of Aging: Methodological Problems and Theoretical Issues," in V. W. Marshal (editor), *Later Life: The Social Psychology of Aging* (Beverly Hills, CA: Sage, 1986), pp. 304–36.

38. Ibid., pp. 312–36; Linda George, *Role Transitions in Later Life* (Monterey, CA: Sage, 1980).

39. U.S. Bureau of the Census, *Statistical Abstract: 1993*, Tables 117, 115.

40. John L. Horn, "The Rise and Fall of Human Abilities," *Journal of Research and Development in Education*, vol. 12 (Winter 1979), pp. 59–78.

41. William H. Masters and Virginia E. Johnson, *Human Sexual Response* (Boston, MA: Little Brown, 1966); The American Medical Association, *Guide to Health and Well-Being after 50* (New York: Random House, 1984), Chapter 10, "Sexual Functioning at Mid-Life."

42. Newman and Newman, *Development through Life*, p. 573.

43. Asenath La Rue and Lissy F. Javick, "Old Age and Behavioral Changes," in B. Wolman (editor), *Handbook of Developmental Psychology* (Englewood Cliffs, NJ: Prentice-Hall, 1982), 791–806.

44. Newman and Newman, *Development through Life*, p. 573.

45. U.S. Bureau of the Census, *Statistical Abstract: 1993*, Table 206.

46. Riva Specht and Grace J. Craig, *Human Development: A Social Work Perspective*, 2nd ed. (Englewood Cliffs, NJ: Prentice-Hall, 1987), p. 241.

47. Ibid., p. 243.

48. "Alzheimer's Disease," in Simeon Margolis and Hamilton Moses, III (editors), *The Johns Hopkins Medical Handbook: The 100 Major Medical Disorders of People Over the Age of 50* (New York: Rebus, 1992), pp. 101–07.

49. U.S. Bureau of the Census, *Statistical Abstract: 1993*, Table 128.

50. Erikson, *Childhood and Society*, p. 232.

51. Newman and Newman, *Development through Life*, p. 45.

52. Robert F. Peck and Howard Berkowitz, "Personality and Adjustment in Middle Age," in B. Neugarten (editor), *Personality in Middle and Late Life* (New York: Atherton Press, 1964), pp.15–43.

53. Ibid., p. 42.

54. G. L. Klerman, "Problems in the Definition and Diagnosis of Depression in the Elderly," in L. Breslau and M. Haug (editors), *Depression and Aging: Causes, Care, and Consequences* (New York: Springer, 1983), p. 3.

55. "Depression," in *Johns Hopkins Medical Handbook*, pp. 430–35.

56. Joy Perkins Newmann,"Aging and Depression," in *Psychology and Aging*, vol. 4, no. 2 (1989), pp. 150–65.

57. Ibid.

58. Ibid., pp. 162–63.

Glossary

Acculturation the process whereby minority groups and individuals come to adopt the norms, values, customs, and traditions of majority groups.

Achieved labels negative labels applied by others in response to the actual behaviors of individuals or groups.

Achievement the social process in which group membership is determined by merit; individuals must meet standards for membership.

Adaptation the ways in which individuals change in accordance with biological, psychological, and social influences. In Freudian theory, may take place through conscious and unconscious mechanisms and may be positive (adaptive) or negative (maladaptive).

Affirmative action government mandates to amend the effects of past discrimination in educational and employment opportunities by making special efforts to recruit or promote women and members of ethnic and racial minorities.

Ageism individually held beliefs and attitudes or socially maintained norms and values which promote or justify the subordination of one age group to another. Used to describe the subordination of adolescents to adults or of older adults to younger adults.

Aggregate in sociology, a collection of individuals who share a common condition or characteristic but no sense of unity or coherence. Examples include all first-year students at a large university or all those who earn between $50,000 and $60,000 a year. Aggregates are not social systems.

Alienation a feeling or actual situation of separation or withdrawal from the social environment or from oneself. Marx defines four types of alienation generated by capitalism: alienation from production, from the product, from others, and from self.

Alzheimer's disease a degenerative disease of the central nervous system which results in a progressive deterioration in brain cells and consequent memory loss, confusion, speech impairment, and personality changes.

Anal phase in Freudian theory, the second stage of psychosexual development in which the search for sensual pleasure is centered in the anus.

Anomia the subjective dimension of anomie produced by breakdowns or contradictions in norms which leave people with feelings of uncertainty or confusion.

Anomie a breakdown or contradiction in norms that threatens stable social interaction. See *anomia*.

Ascribed labels negative labels applied by others to individuals or groups because of their inborn characteristics or family background and other statuses over which they have little or no control.

Ascription the social process in which group membership is determined by inborn characteristics such as sex, race, ethnicity, or age.

Assessment that part of the problem-solving model commonly used in social work practice that is concerned with identifying the problems presented by clients, analyzing the factors associated with their existence, and planning interventions that might lead to their amelioration. Commonly involves identifying the strengths of clients and using them in the intervention process.

Assimilation the process or processes whereby distinguishing signs of group differences disappear and are merged with majority groups.

532

Takes place at a number of levels, including cultural assimilation or acculturation, marital assimilation or intermarriage, and identificational assimilation.

Asylum seekers   foreign nationals who enter the United States without visas and then request refugee status.

Attachment   the process whereby parent and child bond or attach themselves to each other. More broadly, any intimate bonding between individuals.

Attribution theory   an area of cognitive study which deals with how people gather, combine, and use information to arrive at causal explanations for their own behavior and that of others.

Authoritarian leaders   persons in leadership positions who attempt to achieve total control over the behaviors of subordinates by limiting their ability to make decisions or to innovate.

Authority   power that is legitimated by appointment or election or that accrues to individuals as a function of their position or role in society or the groups and organizations that make it up.

Behavioral subsystem   a subsystem of the psychological domain of the individual composed of behaviors and processes concerned with the ways individuals express themselves in action. Includes verbal behavior such as expressing an opinion as well as physical behavior or actions.

Bicultural socialization   the process by which members of an ethnic or racial minority learn both their own culture and the heritage of the dominant ethnic and racial group in the society.

Biculturalism   a perspective that espouses the idea that minority-group members should be able to meet the expectations of their own ethnic, racial, or religious communities as well as those of the larger society or dominant group.

Bigots   individuals who act on their prejudices toward out-group members.

Bilateral descent   the custom of tracing lineage or descent of offspring in a family through both sets of parents. Distinguished from patrilineal and matrilineal forms in which descent is traced through either the father or the mother.

Biological determinism   a philosophy with the assumption that all human behavior is genetically programmed.

Biophysical domain   one of two fundamental components of the individual as a system. In addition to inborn capacities, includes all those elements necessary for the functioning of the organism, such as the skeletal, respiratory, endocrine, and central nervous systems.

Blaming the victim   an approach to practice theory which suggests that the causes of private troubles are completely in the person. Ignores the role of the social environment in causing or exacerbating private troubles.

Brainstorming   a group technique used to help members generate ideas or overcome blocks in their thinking.

Bureaucracy   any large, complex, formal social system.

Change   any alteration in a social or human system from one state to another. Carries no connotation of progress.

Child abuse   physical, sexual, and other forms of violence perpetrated by adults against children. Often but not exclusively a form of domestic violence.

Child neglect   abandonment by adult caretakers of their responsibility for the welfare of a child.

Chromosomes   the beadlike strings of genes present in every cell, generally occurring in pairs that reproduce and spit during cell formation.

Class conflict   in Marxian theory, the tension believed to be inherent in social class and stratification arrangements. Levels of conflict change in a social hierarchy as relationships among those making it up change.

Classical colonialism   a system in which a colonizing nation extracts the wealth of a society without necessarily settling in it, altering its language and customs, or granting citizenship to its people.

Classical conditioning   in learning theory, the principle that when a neutral stimulus is paired with another stimulus which normally elicits a particular response, the neutral stimulus itself will begin to elicit a similar response and thereby become learned or conditioned.

Climacteric   the critical turning point when natural reproductive abilities decline for males and eventually cease for females.

Closed families   those that are turned inward, whose boundaries are rigid, and who aim to shut themselves off from contact with their environment. They often find it difficult to cope and adapt to change and crises.

Closed systems   systems that are not interdependent with their environment and do not interact with it.

Cognitive conflict   conflict that derives from differences in perceptions, beliefs, ideas, and ways of thinking in individuals and social systems of any size. Distinguished from conflicts of interest in groups.

Cognitive development   the evolution of such capacities as learning, memory, attention, thinking, and reasoning through biological maturation and environmental experiences.

Cognitive development theory   theoretical perspectives concerned with the development of such capacities as learning, memory, attention, thinking, and reasoning.

Cognitive subsystem   a subsystem of the psychological domain of the individual composed of cognitive states and processes. Includes perception, sensation, memory, imagination, judgment, language, intelligence, and other aspects of intellectual functioning such as knowledge, beliefs, and opinions.

Colonialist analogy   an understanding of the history of ethnic and race relations in the United States in terms of the forced inclusion of groups into American society. The analogy is to the forcible colonization of people of color by European powers.

Community   a large social system distinguished by personal intimacy, emotional depth, moral commitment, social cohesion, and continuity in time. Best understood as a variable; a large social system may more-or-less be a community.

Comparable worth   the principle that different classes of people in a society should receive comparable pay for jobs that are not precisely equal but are comparable in skill, effort, responsibility, and social and economic value. Women have invoked the principle to seek pay in traditionally female occupations that is comparable to pay in traditionally male occupations.

Competence   the capacity of individuals for mastery over the environment; the free exercise of skill and intelligence to go beyond survival to master social reality.

Concocted groups   research groups devised as a way of experimentally studying small-group behavior and dynamics. Distinguished from natural groups such as families, peer groups, or work teams.

Concrete operational intelligence   the stage of cognitive development during later childhood when children begin to be able to perform logical and mathematical operations but cannot deal with abstract matters.

Conflict of interest   conflict between individuals or social systems of any size that derives from differences in motives or in opportunity for rewards and benefits. Distinguished from cognitive conflict.

Conflict theory   theoretical perspectives which posit that change and conflict are the normal-as-average state in which social systems exist.

Conscription   the social process in which group membership is determined by law or regulations requiring participation.

Conservative humanism   a philosophy with the assumption that society and the human condition cannot be changed in any significant way without making things worse.

Conventional moral development   the second level of moral development in which thinking begins with ideas of what it is to be good or nice and evolves into the need to uncritically obey laws, perform duties, and respect order and authority.

Coping   conscious attempts to adapt to stress. In ego psychology, the mechanism used to consciously deal with actual situations by actively testing reality, making judgments, and regulating and controlling impulses.

Countertransference   the unconscious reactions of a psychotherapist to being treated by a client as a powerful childhood figure.

Critical perspective   in social service practice, a point of view formed by the merger of a theory for practice and a theory of caring. Searches out the ways society causes or exacerbates private troubles through its social norms, institutions, and institutionalized arrangements. Social workers using a critical perspective participate in debates on public issues and take sides in the hope of building a better society through social reform.

Crystallized intelligence   the ability to use knowledge that has been accumulated through past experience, including verbal comprehension and vocabulary, the evaluation of experiences, and the association of words and phrases.

Cultural determinism   a philosophy with the assumption that all human behavior is learned. Humans are believed to be born in a blank state.

Cultural pluralism   the simultaneous existence in a society of two or more groups of different racial, ethnic, or religious backgrounds. Also, the idea that a society should accommodate, promote, and appreciate diversity.

Cultural relativism   the view in social science that approved forms of family and social life vary across time and place; no one form is believed to be intrinsically superior to other forms, although some may be better adapted to certain conditions.

Culture as commonly used in social work, the evolving beliefs, values, norms, and traditions that govern social interaction among members of a community or society or between members and outsiders.

Culture of poverty a social science perspective in which the hypothesis is that societies with a cash economy, high rates of unemployment, low wage scales, and values that stress the accumulation of wealth will produce individuals and families who adapt to poverty by developing norms and beliefs that over the long run make their exit from poverty unlikely.

Cycle of race relations a theory of minority-majority interaction which posits that ethnic and racial minorities go through a process of contact, competition, and conflict, accommodation, and eventually assimilation in the majority.

Definition of the situation the subjective understanding of a situation reached in the stage of examination which precedes action.

Democratic leaders persons in leadership positions who fulfill the responsibilities of their positions but also encourage the participation of subordinates and create an egalitarian atmosphere.

Development disability any mental or physical impairment which is manifested by age 22 and is likely to continue indefinitely. Individuals with such impairments are referred to as developmentally disabled.

Developmental needs advanced human needs such as a sense of well-being, feelings of belonging and self-esteem, and self-actualization.

Developmental tasks chores associated with a particular age, period, stage, or phase of the life cycle of an individual or a social system. Tasks may derive from biological and psychological needs or from social influences. Successful completion is believed to bring about a positive, progressive change in the system.

Deviant group a group or individual members whose behaviors, attitudes, or appearance are deemed outside the acceptable norms of the society. The status of deviant may be imposed as a label by one group on another or officially applied to those who reject or violate legal norms.

Differentiation biophysical structural changes through which the interrelations among cells, tissues, and organs or their parts become more specialized and complex. Also used more generally to describe changes in specialization and complexity in any social system.

Discouraged workers long-term unemployed workers who want to work but have given up the search for employment. Not included in the unemployment rate.

Discrimination acts of differential treatment directed at groups or individual members with the effect of creating a disadvantage.

Disengaged families those whose members have little to do with one another and rigidly respect the independence of each other. Disengagement is considered a family dysfunction.

Dispositional causes those causes of individual behavior that are rooted in the relatively permanent and unchanging attributes of individuals, including their genetics, personality, or identity.

Divorce rate the rate of divorces in a society or segment of a society, often expressed as the number of divorces per 1,000 population in a specific period.

Domestic network a pattern of family life centering on two or more households, usually relatives but sometimes friends, who cooperate to perform domestic functions. Associated with lower class, inner-city, African-American families.

Domestic violence physical, sexual, and other forms of abuse among family and household members, including violence between spouses or partners or against children and elderly members.

Dramaturgical view the perspective on human behavior taken by symbolic interactionists who maintain that individuals present themselves to others in a manner analogous to a stage actor's presentation of a role to an audience.

Drive an innately determined need, motivation, or impulse that propels behavior. A concept used in many psychological theories of human behavior and development.

Dual perspective a social work perspective which recognizes that individuals in a multicultural society are simultaneously part of the larger society and a particular ethnic, racial, religious, or other subcommunity.

Dyad a social system consisting of only two individuals.

Ecological perspective a social science perspective which focuses on the social and physical context of individual or family behavior, locating it in the context of interdependence with other social systems.

Eco-map a tool used in assessment to graphically depict the environmental sources of support and conflict operating on individuals or families.

Ego in Freudian theory, that part of the personality which mediates between individual and environment and between id and superego.

Ego defenses in Freudian theory, any number of specific intrapsychic processes, operating unconsciously, which are employed to seek relief from anxiety. Ego defenses may be functional or nonfunctional and used adaptively or maladaptively.

Ego psychology a perspective within Freudian theory which gives special attention to that part of the personality known as the ego. It includes the study of unconscious ego defense mechanisms and conscious autonomous ego functions.

Ego strength in ego psychology, a summary of healthy or utopian individual development; those who have ego strength appropriately use conscious (autonomous) coping mechanisms and unconscious ego defenses.

Ejaculation the expulsion of semen from the urethra in males.

Elder abuse physical, sexual, and other forms of violence perpetrated against the elderly. Often but not exclusively a form of domestic violence.

Electra complex in Freudian theory, the hypothesized internal conflict said to occur in girls during the genital stage of psychosexual development which has to do with sexual identification and the resolution of erotic yearnings.

Embryo an animal or human organism in the early stages of growth and differentiation. In humans, the zygote becomes an embryo when it attaches itself to the lining of the uterus.

Employment-based immigrants a legal designation under recent immigration laws that allots visas to those with occupations and skills deemed necessary in the United States. Included are extraordinary scientists, researchers, educators, businesspeople, athletes, professionals with advanced degrees, and certain unskilled workers.

Empowerment a social work process for increasing clients' personal, interpersonal, or political power so those individuals who are in situations of limited power can take action to improve their life situations.

Empty next syndrome a feeling of loss experienced by some parents when the youngest child leaves home; particularly affects wives in traditional families.

Enacted role the actual behaviors of a person in a status/role.

Enmeshed families those whose members do not maintain clear boundaries among themselves, lack a sense of independence, and are excessively physically and emotionally dependent on one another. Enmeshment is considered a family dysfunction.

Environmentalists in the controversy over the IQ scores of people from different races, scientists who attribute intelligence more to environment than to genetic inheritance.

Epigenetic principle the idea that crises follow in a sequential order but those associated with a particular period of the life cycle are present in embryonic form and are interrelated with crises in other periods. As a result individuals are said to have endless possibilities to rework their inner experiences and reach maximum development.

Equity theory a framework for understanding social interaction in terms of the operation of norms of reciprocity and fairness.

Ethclass the correspondence between social class and ethnic and racial minority status.

Ethnic group a group of people in a national state who share a sense of common ancestry and identity based on perceived similarities in culture, language, or physical type.

Ethnic identity self-identification in terms of racial and ethnic groups.

Ethnic majorities ethnic and racial groups that are advantaged in terms of power, prestige, and wealth and that create the stigmas associated with minority status.

Ethnic minorities ethnic and racial groups that are more-or-less negatively valued and treated with hostility in a society; may be stigmatized and disadvantaged with regard to power, prestige, and wealth.

Ethnocentrism the glorification of one's own ethnic or racial group over all others; one's own group is seen as central or the best, and all other groups or individuals are evaluated in reference to it.

Exosystem the organizations with which microsystems may never have to deal directly but which nevertheless influence their well-being. Includes governmental bodies and agencies, educational systems and boards, and industries and firms.

Exploitation the use of power by a dominant sector of the society to take advantage of a less-privileged sector. In Marxian theory, the differential outcomes of the owner-worker relationship; owners get more out of it than they put into it, and workers get less then they put in.

Expressive roles the role-related expectations associated with creating and maintaining affectional ties among members of a social system. In family life, responsibilities associated with maintaining emotional well-being.

Extended-kin family a family form in which the parent-child relationship includes adult children who continue to be members of, and subject to the authority of, the group into which they were born. More common in industrial societies is the *modified extended-kin family*, in which adult children and their children live near their blood, legal, or fictive relatives and are strongly attached and to some extent dependent upon them.

Family a group of two or more individuals who are related through blood, marriage, or adoption and who share a common residence or household. Also may refer to intimate, affectionate, or long-lasting relationships among individuals who share a common residence but are not married or related by blood.

Family alignment the systematic and recurrent coalitions that form among members in family conflicts.

Family-based immigrants a legal designation under U.S. immigration law that allots visas to those who have immediate relatives, spouses, or children living in the United States.

Family boundaries the biophysical, psychological, and social points where family meets environment, usually defined in terms of family name, members, the status and roles members occupy, or the norms and values that bind members together.

Family life cycle the idea that families, like individuals and societies, have a beginning and an end and must deal with more-or-less predictable tasks as they go through various stages. Also called the developmental perspective.

Family of origin the family a child is born or adopted into and is considered a member of throughout life.

Family of procreation the family created by an adult woman and man for purposes of conceiving and rearing children.

Family well-being positive family functioning operationalized in terms of the ability to achieve needs and goals and to maintain harmony, stability, and cohesiveness. As with normalcy, family well-being may be defined as functioning at an average, healthy, or utopian level.

Feminists women and men who are committed to improving the status of women in society.

Fetus an unborn human in the stages of growth and differentiation beginning about the third month in the uterus.

Fictive relatives close friends who achieve the status of family members.

Fluid intelligence reasoning skills, including the ability to organize information, develop and test hypotheses, and approach problems logically and systematically.

Formal operational intelligence the highest level of cognitive development, when reasoning is based on prepositional thinking (i.e., if this, then that) and combinatorial analysis (i.e., all things being equal). The abilities to state and test hypotheses and to reason abstractly are also evident.

Formal racism racism that is written into the laws and policies of a society or its institutions, organizations, and communities.

Freudian theory the ideas about human behavior and psychosexual development first presented by Sigmund Freud. Also, the ideas of theorists and researchers who have taken psychodynamic perspectives.

Friendship group a collection of people who consider themselves friends.

Friendship network a small group that takes shape informally in the context of community and organizational environments.

Functional noncapitulation collective action. In work organizations, fighting against powerlessness by joining together in mutual support with coworkers and attempting to renegotiate work expectations with executives and administrators.

Functional theory an approach which posits that harmony, integration, shared values, and a concern for the maintenance of the whole are the normal-as-average state in which social systems exist.

Fundamental attributional error the tendency to attribute the behaviors of others to personal dispositional causes such as personality, attitudes, and values while minimizing contextual or situational causes.

Future orientation   norms and values which promote the idea that group members ought to sacrifice present comfort and enjoyment in favor of long-range social and economic advancement.

Gender   all the different components of sex, including chromosomal, gonadal, hormonal, organal, genital, rearing, identity, and role. *Sex* is a more specific term that refers to a presumed simple dichotomy between male and female. The term *gender* was introduced as a way of referring to all possible sex-related differences.

Gender differences   the extent to which women and men think, feel, and behave differently. Whether such differences are related to biophysical or sociocultural factors is questioned.

Gender identity   self-identification as male or female.

Gender (sex) role   culturally appropriate male and female behaviors.

Gene pools   reproductive breeding populations that evolve as a function of geographical or social proximity or isolation.

Generalized other   in symbolic interactionism, the organized community or social group which gives the individual a unified sense of self.

Generativity   the will and ability to contribute procreatively, productively, and creatively to ensure the continuance of the society.

Genes   the microscopic elements, segments of DNA molecules, which are carried by the chromosomes containing the codes that produce inherited traits and dispositions.

Genetic disorders   biophysical disorders passed on from the parents to the fetus. May be inherited (passed on from one generation to the next), congenital (present at birth), or acquired through prenatal or postnatal environmental exposure.

Genetics   a field of biology which deals with the heredity and variations of organisms accomplished through transmission of genes and chromosomes.

Genital phase   in Freudian theory, the third stage of psychosexual development in which the search for sensual pleasure is centered in the genitals.

Genogram   a tool used in family assessment to graphically depict various dimensions of support and conflict across generations for a particular family member.

Genotype   all or part of the genetic pattern or constitution of an organism that is inherited at birth and is not visible to the naked eye.

Gonads   the sex glands which produce and emit hormones. In females the ovaries produce estrogen and progesterone; in males the testes produce testosterone.

Group cohesiveness   the degree to which group members identify with and support collective aims and projects.

Groupthink   the process in group decision making whereby an overriding need to achieve consensus precludes a more open and more realistic discussion of alternatives.

Growth   biophysical changes by way of cell or tissue enlargement. Involves progressive changes in size as well as in specialization and complexity (differentiation), and in maturation.

Hassles   negative everyday experiences that produce stress.

Hereditarians   in the controversy over the IQ scores of people from different races, scientists who attribute intelligence more to genetic inheritance than to environment.

Heritability   a term used in the study of IQ and other human behaviors which expresses the proportion of variation in a behavior that is attributable to genetic variation within a specific population. Heritability measures population, not individual differences.

Hierarchy of needs   the idea that human motives are organized in a hierarchy that goes from those that are basic to physical survival at the lowest level to those that allow for the expression of the self at the highest level.

Holon   a concept in general systems theory that every system is at the same time a whole—a unit unto itself—and a part of a whole.

Homeostasis   a state of balance or equilibrium in a system. The existence of a built-in, self-regulating mechanism that assures balance or equilibrium in systems has been proposed.

Homophobia   an irrational fear of homosexuality, homosexual individuals, or homosexual values and conduct.

Hostile working environment harassment a form of sexual harassment consisting of verbal or physical conduct that interferes with work performance or creates intimidating working conditions and may cause psychological harm.

Household   a group of people who share a common residence or housing unit. Household members may be related through blood or marriage or unrelated.

Human behavior   the dynamics of how behavior in individuals and groups is acquired, maintained, or changed as a function of biological, psychological, and social influences. With regard to individuals, includes cognitions and emotions as well as verbal and physical behaviors.

Human development the process of going from a state considered less advanced to one considered more advanced. Applicable to individuals as well as to groups. With regard to individuals, refers to how cognitive, motivational, and behavioral states and processes are acquired, maintained, and changed as a function of the biological process of aging.

Human genetics organic qualities that distinguish human beings from other species or that differentiate among individuals, families, and human populations.

Human relations approach a conceptual framework for the study of organizations or bureaucracies based on recognition of the importance of interpersonal relations and informal friendship networks in organizational design and operation.

Human service organization a bureaucracy which provides services to individuals and families with the aim of protecting, maintaining, or enhancing their well-being.

Human system a system comprised of one or more human beings which serves as a vehicle through which transactions between individuals and society takes place.

Humanism a philosophy which asserts the dignity and worth of individuals and their capacity for self-realization through reason. Often rejects the idea of a supernatural presence that can affect human outcomes.

Id in Freudian theory, that part of the personality that operates unconsciously and is rooted in instinctive erotic (eros) and aggressive (thanatos) drives.

Ideal type an abstract description developed by identifying the essential components of a particular form of group life, which is then used as a way of comparing actual groups, organizations, or institutions.

Identificational communities communities based on a common sense of identity regardless of place of residence or territory. Examples include the Japanese-American community or the gay and lesbian communities.

Immigrant a person who voluntarily enters a nation to become a permanent resident. In U.S. policy, an alien admitted with a visa and allowed to take up permanent residence and seek employment.

Immigrant analogy an understanding of the history of ethnic and race relations in the United States in terms of the entrance of European immigrants through voluntary migration.

Immigration quotas restrictions in past and present immigration laws limiting permanent residency in the United States to a predetermined number of entrants from specific national groups.

Individual racism racism that is rooted in the beliefs, feelings, and behavioral intentions of individuals.

Informal racism an enduring form of racism that is unwritten but nevertheless evident in the norms, mores, and traditions of a society or its institutions, organizations, and communities.

In-groups the racial, ethnic, religious, or other groups to which an individual belongs and identifies with.

Innovation the social process through which members attempt to alter the structure or organization of a social system or their participation in it.

Institutional arrangements systems of social norms usually found in large, complex societies that impact all the social institutions in a society. An example is language; in the United States, American English is the language of transaction usually used across the economy, the polity, the military, and other social institutions.

Institutional discrimination discrimination that is rooted in the laws, policies, norms, mores, or traditions of the society or the institutions, organizations, and communities that compose it.

Institutional racism racism that is rooted in the laws, policies, norms, mores, or traditions of a society or the institutions, organizations, and communities that compose it.

Instrumental roles the role-related expectations associated with defining and performing the concrete tasks and achieving the goals of a social system. Examples in family life include responsibilities associated with bringing in income, budgeting, cleaning, and cooking.

Intentional racism any deliberate or purposeful form of racism.

Interaction the general or overarching social process through which members of a social system influence one another and their participation in the system is implemented.

Interest communities communities based on common goals and objectives. Examples include professional associations and academic disciplines.

Internal colonialism   a system in which a colonizing nation or dominant ethnic-majority group extracts the wealth of a subordinated group or society by settling it, altering its language and customs, and usually making the colonized people citizens.

Interrole conflict   role conflict that arises when a person holds different roles in different systems, and the expectations of one role make it harder to satisfy the expectations of another role. For instance, fulfilling the role of mother or father may interfere with fulfilling the role of career professional.

Intrarole conflict   role conflict that derives from the competing expectations of others, making it hard for a person in a role to please all system members at the same time. For instance, fulfilling the role of social worker may be difficult if administrators and clients have different expectations of what a worker ought to do.

Involuntary membership   group membership in a social system determined by the actions of others, often involving an element of coercion or force.

Jim Crow laws   a series of laws that evolved largely in the former Confederate states after the Civil Way which sought to keep white and black Americans separate as much as possible by restricting the physical movement and social advancement of black Americans.

Labeling   an interactive social process in which some people apply stigmatizing names to others, who may internalize the names and come to consider themselves deviant or abnormal.

Laissez-faire leaders   persons in leadership positions who allow subordinates to do anything they wish and to innovate without direction.

Large group   a social system with many members, often typified by impersonal relations and limited face-to-face contact. Examples include schools, organizations, voluntary associations, neighborhoods, and whole societies.

Latency phase   in Freudian theory, the fourth stage of psychosexual development, in which the search for sensual pleasure is thought to lie dormant.

Latent functions   the operative or implicit functions of a social system such as a family or organization.

Learning theories   theoretical perspectives—including operant conditioning, classical conditioning, and social learning—that describe the ways behaviors are learned. Also referred to as behavioral theories because they focus on measurable, observable behaviors rather than on inner processes that cannot be directly measured or that must be intuited.

Libido   in Freudian theory, the energy underlying eros, the drive for sensual pleasure.

Locational communities   communities based on common residence or territory that may lack connotations of personal intimacy, emotional depth, moral commitment, social cohesion, or continuity in time. Examples include neighborhoods and small towns.

Locus of control   an area of motivational study concerned with whether individuals believe their behavior is motivated by intrinsic incentives that propel them forward from the inside or extrinsic incentives that pull them forward from the outside.

Macro environment   the external environment that is most distant from a particular human or social system. Society and its social norms, institutions, and institutionalized social arrangements constitute the macro environment of an individual as a system.

Macrosystem   the most distant social context with which a microsystem must deal in the social environment. The macrosystem of a family, for example, consists of its cultural context, that is, the norms, values, traditions, and sanctions that flow from the institutions and institutionalized arrangements of the society.

Manifest functions   the official, readily perceived functions of a social system such as a family or organization.

Marriage rate   the rate of legal marriages in a society or segment of a society, often expressed as the number of marriages per 1,000 population in a specific period.

Marxian theory   a theoretical framework which systematically attempts to apply the ideas of Karl Marx to the study of social interaction. Focuses on the influence of economic institutions and arrangements on human behavior, particularly conflict between people in different social classes and economic conditions.

Master roles and status   roles and statuses that may last throughout life and which serve to define individuals both for themselves and for the society. Examples are gender, ethnicity, and race.

Matriarchy   institutionalized social arrangements in families and other institutions in which power and authority are vested in females.

Matrilocal families   family forms in which married persons are expected to reside near or in the home of the matriarch.

Maturation   the point at which biophysical growth and differentiation have reached their peak. Also connotes the ability to procreate.

Medical model   the belief that mental illness and other mental disorders are diagnosable diseases rooted in biophysical conditions and treatable through medication.

Menarche   the beginning of menstruation, the monthly discharge of blood and other material from the uterus through the vagina in females.

Menopause   the period of natural cessation of menstruation in women; the production of estrogen decreases, inhibiting their ability to reproduce.

Mentor relationship   a relationship with an older, experienced adult that facilitates entry into an organization or career.

Meso environment   the external environment that is neither distant from nor immediate to a social system. Communities and organizations or bureaucracies constitute the meso environment of an individual.

Mesosystem   from the point of view of an individual as a system, the immediate social context with which a surrounding microsystem must deal. The mesosystem of an individual, for example, consists of those individuals, groups, or organizations with which his or her family deals directly.

Micro environment   the external environment that is most intimate to a particular human or social system. Family and peers constitute the micro environment of an individual as a system.

Microsystem   a small social system such as a family or group which is understood within the context of meso, macro, and exosystems. In social service practice usually the client system.

Middleman minorities   ethnic and racial minorities that have achieved relative economic success, often by situating themselves in an economic niche between majority groups and more-disadvantaged minority groups, and whose progress may be blocked at the upper levels of a society. Examples are Jewish Americans and Japanese Americans.

Midlife crisis   a hypothesized period in which adults question and rethink their identity and the choices they have made in life.

Mind   a function of humans which gives them the ability to create symbols, to think and to rehearse alternative actions, and to make decisions about their feelings and behaviors.

Mixed messages   role conflict that occurs when others are not clear or change their expectations. For instance, a parent says one thing to a child but means something else, or a supervisor expects a social worker to do one thing one time but something contradictory another time.

Monogamous marriage   a marriage in which the husband-wife relationship is limited to only one spouse at a time.

Motivational or affective subsystem   a subsystem of the psychological domain of the individual composed of motivational states and processes. Includes motives, needs, drives, feelings, sentiments, interests, and other mechanisms propelling behavior.

Multicentered approach   an approach to practice that avoids blaming the victim by assessing and intervening independently in both the client system (individual, group, family, community, or organization) and its external environment.

Multiculturalism   a perspective akin to cultural pluralism which espouses the idea that multigroup societies should accommodate, promote, and appreciate diversity.

Multigenerational family   a modified extended-kin family.

Negative reinforcement   increasing the likelihood of a response by removing an undesirable event, i.e., taking away punishment as an inducement for a desired behavior.

Neolocal families   family forms in which married persons are expected to set up their own households apart from either set of parents in a place of their choice.

Nominal group technique   a group technique used to help members independently generate ideas and participate in an exchange of ideas with other members.

Non-zero sum approach   the assumption in the study of power that an endless supply of power is available to be shared by all members of a social system. Distinguished from zero-sum approach.

Norm of negative reciprocity   the agreed-on position or working agreement in social interaction that some people are entitled to receive more than they contribute.

Norm of reciprocity   the agreed-on position or working agreement that is believed by many to be basic to human social interaction: We treat others as they treat us.

Normal as average   normal in the statistical sense. Individuals may be considered normal when their behavior or development follows the statistical average, median, or mode for similar individuals or is not too far off them.

Normal as healthy   normal in the sense of not demonstrating any obvious disorder in behavior or development.

Normal as transactions   a concept that asserts that normality is characteristic not of an individual but of the interaction between individuals and their environment.

Normal as utopia   normal in the sense of some ideal behavior or development. Utopian normality may be defined in terms of a particular theory or in accordance with a value or philosophical position.

Normative stress   stress that derives from ordinary, expectable changes in social events. For instance, older adults may experience stress as their spouses, siblings, or friends precede them in death.

Normlessness   a breakdown in the norms governing social interaction, so people no longer know what is expected of them.

Nuclear family   a family form composed of two adults of the opposite sex living in a socially approved sex relationship, together with their own or adopted children.

Object relations   a psychodynamic perspective that focuses on the attitudes people hold toward others and the self and how these attitudes influence human behavior and development. Also referred to as interpersonal relations.

Oedipus complex   in Freudian theory, the internal conflict said to occur in boys during the genital stage of psychosexual development which has to do with sexual identification and the resolution of erotic yearnings.

Open door period   a time in American history (1776–1881) when there were no or very few immigration laws, and all those who wanted to enter the United States could do so.

Open families   those whose boundaries are clear but flexible and whose members interact comfortably among themselves and with their environments. Considered healthy families.

Open systems   systems that are interdependent with their environment. Although human and social systems vary in the extent of openness, survival requires at least some degree of openness.

Operant conditioning   in learning theory, the principle that a neutral response operated on by

a reinforcing stimulus will produce a particular conditioned response, which is then said to be learned.

Operations   the highest order of cognition, complex cognitive processes by which schema and structures are manipulated according to some logical model.

Oral phase   in Freudian theory, the first stage of psychosexual development in which the search for sensual pleasure is centered in the mouth or oral cavity.

Out-groups   the racial, ethnic, religious, or other groups to which others belong but an individual does not identify with. Often an object of hostility or disdain.

Ovaries   female sex glands.

Ovulation   the discharge of mature eggs from the ovaries in females.

Patriarchy   an institutionalized social arrangement in families and other institutions in which power and authority are vested in males.

Patrilocal families   family forms in which married persons are expected to reside near or in the home of the patriarch.

Peer group   a group of friends, usually within the same age and status categories.

People of color   a term applied loosely to describe Americans who are not of European descent. Does not correspond to the U.S. Census categorization of white and nonwhite Americans in that Latinos, who may be of any race, are often included in the designation.

Perceived role   the expectations of self with regard to a social position.

Perceived stress   the cognitive awareness of stress.

Person-centered approach   any social work process that ignores the environment and focuses only on assessing or intervening with individual clients.

Person in environment   an approach to practice which recognizes that the problems and strengths of individuals, and by extension all client systems, must be understood within the context of their external physical and social environments.

Personality-role conflict   role conflict that occurs when the expectations of a person in a role are in conflict with the expectations of the other system members. For instance, others may expect a shy, quiet person to be talkative in a particular interaction.

Phenotype the visible characteristics of the genetic pattern of an organism that are produced by the transactions between genes and environment. Skin color, hair texture, and temperament are examples.

Physical disability any kind of physical impairment brought about in any way. Individuals with a serious or chronic impairment are often referred to as physically disabled.

Physical environment the geographic or spatial context of a human or social system.

Plural marriage a marriage in which the husband-wife relationship is extended to include multiple spouses living together. May be polygamous or polyandrous.

Political economy a perspective for the study of complex social systems from the point of view of the interaction between political and economic processes in their internal and external environments.

Polyandrous marriage a marriage in which there is one wife with multiple husbands.

Polygamous marriage a marriage in which there is one husband with multiple wives.

Positive reinforcement increasing the likelihood of a response by making it contingent upon a favorable event, i.e., giving social or monetary rewards as an inducement to performing a desired behavior.

Postconventional moral development the third and highest level of moral development, in which moral thinking progresses from making decisions based on a concern for the welfare of the group to an orientation based on personal decisions of conscience and ethical principles.

Poverty index a guide developed by the Social Security Administration to measure poverty which calculates the amount of money required annually by individuals and families of various sizes to meet basic needs like food, clothing, housing, transportation, and entertainment. Individuals and families with money income below the required level are considered to be living in poverty.

Poverty rate the proportion of individuals or families in a population with incomes below the poverty index at a specified time.

Power the ability to get one's way in interactions with others.

Practice theory a system of principles which attempts to explain how client and target systems think, feel, and act toward the purpose of enabling practitioners to control and change human behavior and development.

Preconventional moral development the first or early-childhood level of moral development, in which moral thinking begins with considerations of reward and punishment and evolves into basic notions of reciprocity.

Prejudice beliefs and attitudes that prejudge groups or individual members negatively on the basis of group traits or characteristics.

Preoparational intelligence the stage of cognitive development, generally between the ages of 2 and 7, in which thinking is very concrete and children begin to derive concepts from experience.

Prescribed role the expectations of others with regard to a social position. May be formal or informal and explicit or implicit.

Primary deviance deviant acts that go unnoticed and uncensured by society or an organization or group. Nearly everyone performs acts of primary deviance.

Primary groups intimate social systems that are believed to be basic to an individual's identity and personality. Examples are friendship cliques, family, and kin.

Principle of distributive justice the proposition that people expect to receive in accordance to what they contribute to a social transaction.

Principle of equifinality a principle in systems theory that similar results may be achieved from different initial conditions if similar inputs are received. Thus systems may achieve steady state through a variety of ways.

Principle of nondiscrimination a set of beliefs that rejects prejudice and discrimination and supports equal treatment and equal opportunities in employment, education, housing, and family or affectional life for all individuals, regardless of racial or ethnic background.

Priority workers a legal designation under U.S. immigration law that allots visas to those with extraordinary ability or acclaim in the sciences, arts, education, business, and athletics; senior-level professors and researchers with national or international recognition; and executives and managers of multinational corporations.

Private troubles the problems experienced by individuals, regardless of cause.

Problems in living a concept that would replace the notion of normality as average, health, or utopia with the recognition that all people have troubles and what is considered abnormal may simply be a stigmatizing label that more powerful individuals (and professions) apply to the behavior of less powerful people.

Psychodynamic perspective   a perspective in the study of individual and family behavior which focuses on conscious and unconscious intrapsychic states and processes. Often associated with Freudian thought.

Psychological domain   one of two fundamental components of the individual as a system. Includes subsystems made up of cognitive, motivational, and behavioral states and processes which are interrelated and not completely distinguishable.

Psychosexual development   in Freudian theory, the normal-as-healthy evolution of eros, the drive for sensual pleasure from birth to adulthood.

Psychosocial crisis   tensions or conflicts that emerge when individual, instinctive needs come face to face with social expectations. Successful resolution of age-related crises throughout the life cycle is believed to assure normal development.

Psychosocial development   the potential for progressive cognitive, emotional, and behavioral changes in individuals across the life course. Normal development is believed to occur as a function of biological, psychological, and social processes.

Psychosocial functioning   the state of psychological and social well-being of an individual.

Puberty   the period, often in early adolescence, when the genital organs become capable of reproduction. Marked by the influence of sex hormones, the appearance of secondary sex characteristics, and the onset of menstruation in females.

Puberty phase   in Freudian theory, the fifth stage of psychosexual development, in which the search for sensual pleasure is reawakened after remaining dormant during latency, and sexual identity and erotic yearnings are finally resolved.

Public issues   the problems experienced by society that are caused by difficulties in its norms, institutions, or institutionalized social arrangements. Private troubles are often caused or exacerbated by public issues.

Quid pro quo harassment   a form of sexual harassment consisting of verbal or physical conduct of a sexual nature, including sexual advances or requests for sexual favors. Failure to comply usually leads to forfeiture of employment or good grades.

Race   biological differences among people that emerge in groups or communities as a result of normal breeding processes. As commonly used, a construction of reality based on social and political processes.

Racism   beliefs, attitudes, norms, and values which attribute inferiority to others because of their presumed biophysical characteristics. Used colloquially to refer to any form of prejudice or discrimination directed against a racial or ethnic group by individuals or other social systems.

Racist society   a society which encourages racism through its laws, policies, norms, mores, or traditions.

Rationalism   a philosophy with the assumption that society and the human condition can be changed in progressive or positive ways through the use of technological inventions, including the technology of social service practice and policy. Rationalism is the underlying philosophy of the social services.

Rational-legal authority   power that derives from written laws or policies; in bureaucracy, justification for the differentiation of members along horizontal and vertical lines on the basis of organizational goals backed up by law or policy.

Recruitment   the social process by which the participation of an individual in a social system is initiated. May be on the basis of ascription, determined by birth; conscription, determined by law or regulation; or achievement, determined by merit.

Reference groups   the groups or individuals people refer to in formulating their beliefs, motives, and behaviors. Reference may include positive or negative identification.

Refugee   a person who seeks asylum in a country after being forced to flee another because of political, religious, or other forms of persecution. Formerly referred to as *displaced person.*

Reification   giving material properties to abstract or socially constructed ideas. For instance, Marxians argue that economic institutions are socially constructed, but they are defended as if they reflect a natural order.

Resocialization group   a group set up in human service organizations composed of individual clients in need of rehabilitation. Most common examples are treatment or therapy groups.

Reward power   power based on the ability to control monetary, social, and other benefits in a social transaction.

Role the dynamic aspects of a social position which establish the expectations of others and the self with regard to the rights, responsibilities, and duties associated with it. May also refer to the actual behaviors of incumbents in the position.

Role conflict conflict within the context of the positions individuals occupy in social systems. Evolves out of normal social interactional processes of stating, clarifying, and negotiating expectations and may take a variety of forms.

Role-playing assuming and performing a social role or position.

Role-taking seeing situations and persons, including the self, from the point of view of others and adapting one's behavior accordingly.

Role theory a social-psychological framework for the study of small and large groups which uses social position (role and status) as the focus of understanding human behavior.

Schemas the lowest order of cognition, sensory and motor patterns which make meaningful, repeatable behaviors possible. In social psychology, any cognitive representation that gives rise to behaviors and attitudes.

Scientific management a conceptual framework for the study of organizations or bureaucracies based on the premise that productivity and efficiency will be maximized if management principles incorporate scientific analysis of procedures.

Scientific socialism the form of socialism envisioned by Karl Marx under which workers would wrest control of the economy and set up equitable work relationships free of alienation. Said to be scientific because it was derived directly from critical analysis of capitalism.

Secondary deviance deviant acts that are noticed and censured by society or an organization or group which sets up the condition for labeling.

Secondary groups relatively complex and impersonal social systems and institutions that are believed to serve utilitarian functions in the lives of individuals. Examples are large bureaucracies, including work organizations, schools, political parties, and religious organizations.

Self an individual's awareness of having a distinct identity separate from others, derived from social interactions.

Self-object in self psychology, a primary caregiver whose empathic response to an infant enables the development of a nuclear self, the central, enduring sector of the personality.

Self psychology a contemporary school of psychodynamic thought that gives special attention to the emergence and formation of the self across the life span. Diverges from Freudian perspectives in that it posits a set of social drives.

Sensorimotor intelligence the stage of cognitive development, usually during the first 18 to 24 months after birth, which begins with egocentricity and little sense of reality and ends with the ability to endow permanency to objects, including self and others.

Separate but equal doctrine the principle stated by the Supreme Court in *Plessy* v. *Ferguson* (1896) that separate public accommodations could be maintained for blacks and whites as long as the accommodations were equal. Overturned by *Brown* v. *Board of Education* (1954).

Serial monogamy repeated marriages to one person at a time after divorce or widowhood. Also, a series of intimate, nonmarried relations to one person at a time.

Sexism individually held beliefs and attitudes or socially maintained norms and values which promote or justify the subordination of one sex to the other.

Sexual exploitation the unequal treatment of women in sexual relationships. Includes sexual harassment, sexual assault, and the existence of the double standard which allows men more latitude in sexual behaviors.

Significant others others to whom an individual is strongly attached and who are capable of influencing the individual's beliefs, feelings, and behaviors.

Situational causes those causes of individual behavior that are rooted in social circumstances, including history, events, sociocultural norms, and interpersonal influence.

Situations the objective circumstances in which social interactions take place, or the subjective understanding of them by those in the interaction.

Small group a social system with relatively few members, often typified by face-to-face interactions and personal feelings and attachments. Examples include families, friendship cliques, and work groups.

Social class a ranking of statuses in a society based on income, wealth, occupation, and educational differences among individuals and families. May be studied as a form of social stratification or as a dynamic relationship among those in different ranks.

Social comparison processes   the processes by which individuals determine the appropriateness of their rewards or punishments on the basis of their experiences with social transactions. May be a comparison with past rewards in similar situations or with the rewards likely to be received in alternative situations.

Social control   the social process through which individual participation in a system is limited or constrained. May be implemented by positive means (rewards) or negative means (punishments).

Social distance   a concept used by many sociologists to measure a person's willingness to work with, live in the same neighborhood as, befriend, or marry members of different ethnic and racial communities. Also referred to as *racial distance*.

Social environment   the individuals, families, communities, groups, organizations, social norms, institutions, and institutionalized arrangements that impinge on a particular social system and form the situation in which the system is embedded. Also the personal and impersonal relations surrounding individuals and social systems.

Social exchange theory   a framework for understanding social interaction based on the proposition that individuals, as well as groups and organizations, seek to maximize their profit and minimize their cost in transactions with others.

Social functioning   social well-being, especially with regard to the ability of an individual to meet the expectations associated with a particular status or role.

Social institutions   systems or orders of social norms usually found in large, complex societies which are clustered around similar functions or needs and specify the ways they ought to be completed or fulfilled. A capitalist or free-market economy, for instance, establishes certain norms about how the material needs of people ought to be met that differ from those established by a socialist or planned economy.

Social judgment theory   a social-psychological perspective in which group decisions are examined from the point of view of the rules used in making decisions.

Social learning theory   a theoretical perspective that focuses on processes of imitation and learning through observation of others.

Social networks   the interpersonal links between individuals and their social environment.

Social norms   agreements, formal or informal, explicit or implicit, which regulate and give order and purpose to a social system. Includes cultural traditions, mores, folkways, laws, and social policies.

Social positions   the positions or offices in a social system, its micro elements, usually arranged both vertically (dominant and subordinate positions) and horizontally (peer positions). May be referred to as a status or a role; individuals participate in systems through the social positions they occupy in them.

Social stratification   social hierarchies across a range of social institutions, organizations, and communities which often result in the unequal distribution of rewards. May be built around wealth, prestige, or power. Examples include social class, gender, and racial and ethnic hierarchies.

Social support   the comfort, assistance, or information individuals receive through their formal or informal contacts with others.

Social system   a more-or-less conscious collection of interacting and interdependent individuals. Examples include families, friendship groups, communities, organizations, and nations.

Socialization   the social process by which individuals come to know the expectations associated with participation in a social system.

Socioeconomic well-being   the relative success or failure of individuals, families, communities, or subpopulations in regard to such indicators as education, income, wealth, and employment status.

Sojourners   emigrants to another nation who do not plan to become permanent residents.

Spouse abuse   physical, sexual, and other forms of violence perpetrated by one married or cohabiting heterosexual or homosexual partner against the other.

Status   the location of a position within the vertical and horizontal arrangements of positions in a system.

Steady state   a state of approximate balance and equilibrium in a system, both internally and externally, which allows for change.

Stereotypes   evaluative opinions which are uncritically attributed to out-group members. Stereotypes may be either positive or negative.

Strengths approach   an approach to practice that avoids blaming the victim by focusing exclusively on the positive strengths and abilities of client systems.

Stress physiological changes elicited by neural impulses that prepare the body for fight or flight.

Stressors situations that provoke the physiological response of stress.

Structures the intermediate order of cognition, the complex cognitive processes by which thinking is organized and linked to action.

Superego in Freudian theory, the conscience or that part of the personality which represents the internalization of ideals to strive for or inhibits socially unacceptable behaviors and attitudes.

Survival needs basic human needs such as food, shelter, and protection.

Symbolic interactionism a social-psychological framework which focuses on the processes through which persons interpret and give meaning to the objects, events, and situations that make up their social worlds.

Symbolic racism a form of racism in which beliefs in biophysical inferiority are replaced with more general, subjective negative attitudes about racial and ethnic minorities.

System-centered approach any social work process that ignores the environmental context and focuses only on the internal functioning of a family, group, community, or organization during assessment or intervention.

Systems approach an orienting framework for an analysis of human behavior in which individuals, families, communities, and groups are seen as systems of interacting parts and processes. In this book two substantive assumptions are made about the behavior of human systems: the state or condition of a system is a function of the interaction between it and the environment in which it operates, and change and conflict are always evident in a system.

Task group a group set up to complete a specific, often time-limited chore or goal.

Task performance activities undertaken by members to fulfill the official or operative goals of a social system.

Theory for practice a system of principles which attempts to explain the form and structure of practice in the social services. Practice models and principles can be derived from it to maintain or alter future practice.

Theory of caring a system of principles based on the values that dominate practice and inform social service workers about the desired ways for relating to and working with client systems.

Theory of practice a system of ideas or statements about practice derived from observing the way practice occurs in the social services.

Transactional approach an approach to practice that avoids blaming the victim by assessing and intervening simultaneously in both the client system (individual, group, family, community, or organization) and its environment.

Transactional processes social processes through which individuals and social systems interact. Includes recruitment, socialization, interaction, innovation, and control.

Transactions social contacts, exchanges, and influences among individuals or between individuals and social systems. At the interactional level, take place face to face and usually involve relatively deep personal commitments and attachments. At the sociocultural level, are more impersonal and usually take place within the larger, more complex social systems and institutions making up the social environment.

Transference the unconscious projection onto a psychotherapist of the client's attitudes toward a powerful figure in early childhood.

Transgenerational stress in family development, stress that arises when expectations and conflict originating in relationships with one generation are carried to relationships with another. For instance, problems adults had with their own parents can become problems in relationships with their children.

Underclass a social class of individuals or families who appear to live more-or-less permanently in poverty. The incidence and causes of an underclass are debated in the social sciences.

Underemployed workers individuals who cannot find employment which matches their skills, training, expectations, or earning capacity and settle for jobs that provide inadequate income or part-time positions when they want to work full time. No satisfactory measures of underemployment have been developed.

Undocumented aliens foreign nationals who enter the United States without visas and take up residence. Also referred to as *illegal aliens* or *illegal immigrants*.

Unemployment rate the proportion of the civilian population 16 years or older who were out of work, available for work, and actively seeking work in the preceding four weeks of a specified period.

Uplifts positive everyday experiences. Distinguished from hassles.

Values   statements of beliefs, feelings, and behavior intentions that infuse all human behavior, including social service practice.

Voluntary membership   group membership in a social system determined by personal choice.

Zero-sum approach   the assumption in the study of power that there is a finite supply of power so a gain for one person is a loss for another, and some members will always have more than others.

Zygote   a cell formed by the union of a single male sperm and a single female ovum or egg cell. Human and other organisms begin their journey to life as zygotes.

Name Index

Subject Index

HUMAN BEHAVIOR IN THE SOCIAL ENVIRONMENT
Edited by Gloria Reardon
Production supervision by Kim Vander Steen
Designed by Jeanne Calabrese Design, Berwyn, Illinois
Composition by Point West, Inc., Carol Stream, Illinois
Paper, Finch Opaque
Printed and bound by Braun-Brumfield, Inc., Ann Arbor, Michigan